W9-CUH-553

Mathematics Around Us skills and applications

L. Carey Bolster
Gloria Felix Cox
E. Glenadine Gibb
Viggo P. Hansen
Joan E. Kirkpatrick
David F. Robitaille
Harold C. Trimble
Irvin E. Vance
Ray Walch
Robert J. Wisner

Scott, Foresman and Company

Glenview, Illinois; Dallas, Texas;
Oakland, New Jersey; Tucker, Georgia;
Palo Alto, California; and Brighton, England

Authors

L. Carey Bolster
Supervisor of Mathematics
Baltimore County Public Schools
Towson, Maryland

Gloria Felix Cox
Principal
Los Angeles Unified School District
Los Angeles, California

E. Glenadine Gibb
Professor of Mathematics Education
The University of Texas at Austin
Austin, Texas

Viggo P. Hansen
Professor, Mathematics Education
California State University
Northridge, California

Joan E. Kirkpatrick
Associate Professor, Elementary Education
University of Alberta
Edmonton, Alberta, Canada

David F. Robitaille
Assistant Professor
of Mathematics Education
University of British Columbia
Vancouver, British Columbia, Canada

Harold C. Trimble
Professor of Education
Ohio State University
Columbus, Ohio

Irvin E. Vance
Associate Professor
of Mathematics
New Mexico State University
Las Cruces, New Mexico

Ray Walch
Former Teacher of Mathematics
Public Schools
Westport, Connecticut

Robert J. Wisner
Professor of Mathematics
New Mexico State University
Las Cruces, New Mexico

Consultants and Critical Readers

Sidney Sharron
Coordinator, Educational Communications
and Media Branch
Los Angeles Unified School District
Los Angeles, California

Eleanor B. Walters
Head, Department of Mathematics
Delta State College
Cleveland, Mississippi

Emma M. Lewis
Executive Assistant
to the Associate Superintendent
Division of Instructional Services
Public Schools of the District of Columbia
Washington, D.C.

David C. Johnson
Professor of Mathematics Education
University of Minnesota
Minneapolis, Minnesota

Larry L. Hatfield
Associate Professor
of Mathematics Education
University of Georgia
Athens, Georgia

Acknowledgments

Cover: SPORTS ILLUSTRATED photo by Rich Clarkson © Time Inc. Photos courtesy of Anita Douthat, pages 54, 73, 119, 231, 283; NOAA, page 158; Top left: Wide World Photos Inc., page 160; Middle left: UPI, page 160; Bottom left: Wide World Photos Inc., page 160; Top right: Wide World Photos Inc., page 160; Middle right: Automotive History Collection, Detroit Public Library; Photo by Joseph Klima, Jr., page 160; Bottom right: Museum of Science and Industry, Chicago, Illinois, page 160; Mickey Palmer, DPI, pages 248–249; Ken Regan, CAMERA 5, page 273; NASA, page 309

ISBN: 0-673-11726-X

Printed in the United States of America.

Regional offices of Scott, Foresman and Company are located in Glenview, Illinois; Dallas, Texas; Oakland, New Jersey; Palo Alto, California; and Tucker, Georgia.

5 6 7 8 9 10 -RMI- 85 84 83 82 81 80

Level 25

Adding and Subtracting Whole Numbers, Pages 2–29

Multiplying Whole Numbers, Pages 30–51

Polygons, Perimeter, and Area, Pages 52–60

End-of-level Materials

Level 26

Level 27

Level 28

Meaning of Fractions, Pages 178 - 203

Adding and Subtracting Fractions, Pages 204 - 221

Graphing, Pages 222 - 236

End-of-level Materials

Level 29

Meaning of Mixed Numbers, Pages 242–257

Adding and Subtracting Mixed Numbers, Pages 258–281

Measuring Angles, Pages 282–300

End-of-level Materials

Level 30

Multiplying Fractions and Mixed Numbers, Pages 306–327

Multiplying Decimals, Pages 328–347

Congruence, Symmetry, and Similarity, Pages 348–362

End-of-level Materials

Level 25

Addition and Subtraction Basic Facts

You can add on a nomograph by finding numbers in a straight line.

Look at the edge of the card on the nomograph below. The card is placed to show these addition facts.

$$7 + 5 = 12$$
$$5 + 7 = 12$$

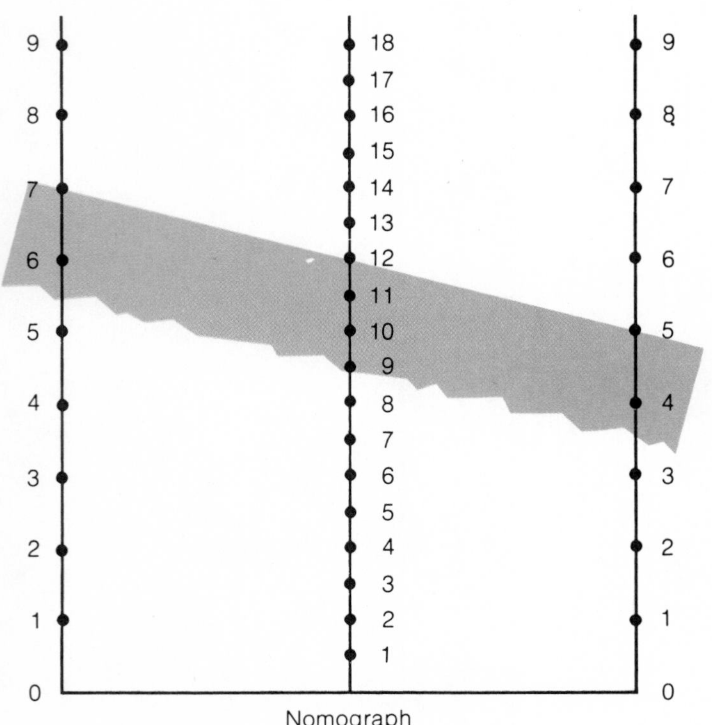

Nomograph

Add. Check your answers by using the nomograph.

1. 8 + 6
2. 7 + 4
3. 9 + 5
4. 8 + 8
5. 7 + 6
6. 9 + 8
7. 8 + 7
8. 7 + 9
9. 6 + 9
10. 9 + 4
11. 7 + 8
12. 5 + 8

The edge of the card also shows these subtraction facts.

$$12 - 5 = 7$$
$$12 - 7 = 5$$

Subtract. Check your answers by using the nomograph.

13. 15 − 8
14. 16 − 9
15. 11 − 3
16. 15 − 9
17. 13 − 4
18. 17 − 8
19. 12 − 6
20. 15 − 7
21. 16 − 8
22. 11 − 6
23. 12 − 3
24. 14 − 6
25. 17 − 9
26. 16 − 9

Addend Addend Sum

$$7 + 5 = 12$$

Use two addends.
Write an equation in which

1. one addend is 8.
2. the addends are equal.
3. both addends are greater than 5.
4. the sum is 10, and one addend is greater than 6.
5. the sum is 12, and both addends are less than 9.

Use two addends. Write as many equations as you can in which

6. the sum is 2.
7. the sum is 3.
8. the sum is 4.
9. the sum is 5.
10. the sum is 6.

★ 11. Guess how many equations you can write when the sum is 7. Write the equations to check your guess.

Complete the following table.

	Addition equations		Subtraction equations	
12.	$6 + 5 = 11$	$5 + 6 = 11$	$11 - 6 = 5$	$11 - 5 = \square$
13.	$7 + 5 = 12$	$5 + \square = 12$	$12 - 7 = 5$	$12 - \square = 7$
14.	$6 + 8 = 14$		$14 - 8 = 6$	
15.		$9 + 7 = 16$	$16 - \square = 7$	
16.			$15 - 8 = 7$	
17.	$4 + 8 = 12$			
18.			$17 - 8 = 9$	
19.		$8 + 5 = 13$		
20.				$15 - 6 = 9$

Place Value

Blocks can be arranged in different groups to show large numbers.

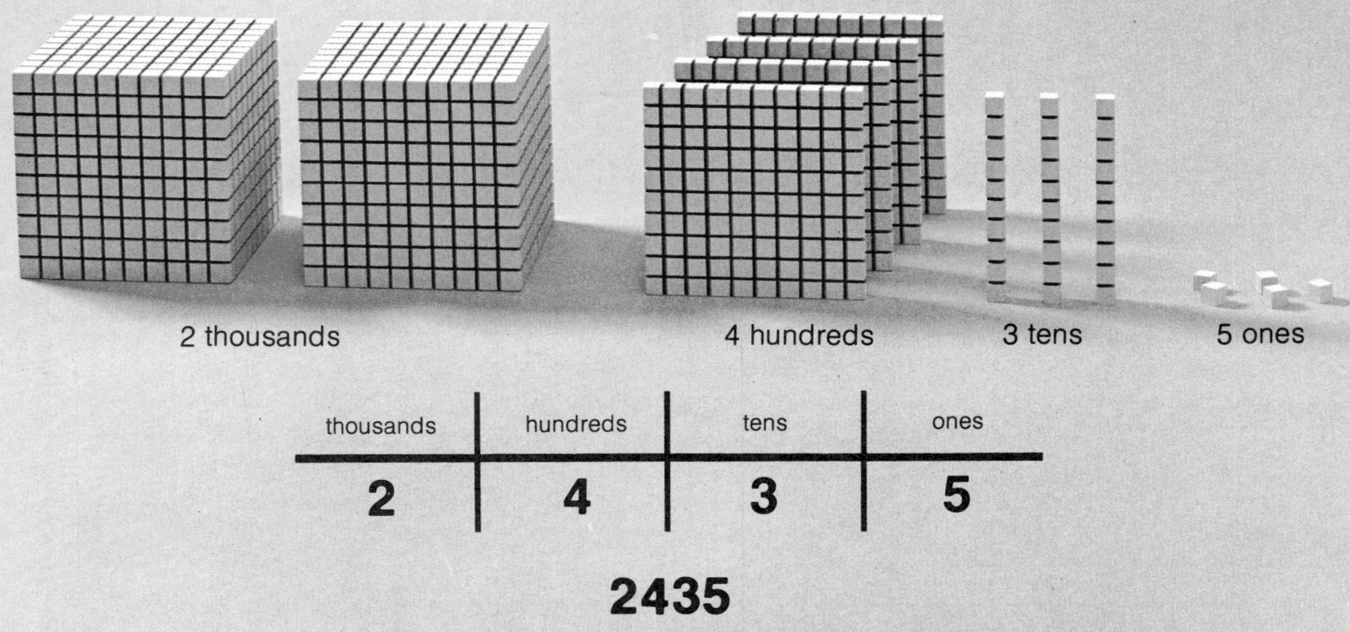

thousands	hundreds	tens	ones
2	**4**	**3**	**5**

2435

two thousand four hundred thirty-five

1. How many ones in 1 ten?

2. How many tens in 1 hundred?

3. How many hundreds in 1 thousand?

• **Discuss** How do you know that the 4 in 2435 means 4 hundreds?

Write the number of thousands, hundreds, tens, and ones.

Here's how

865 *8 hundreds 6 tens 5 ones*

4. 53

5. 967

6. 7142

7. 3333

8. 602

Which numbers have

9. 4 in the tens place?

784 875 46 904

10. 3 in the hundreds place?

893 46 3 398 9035

11. 9 in the ones place?

899 5987 4678 4592

12. 8 in the thousands place?

8945 7834 894 9820

Give the standard numeral.

Here's how

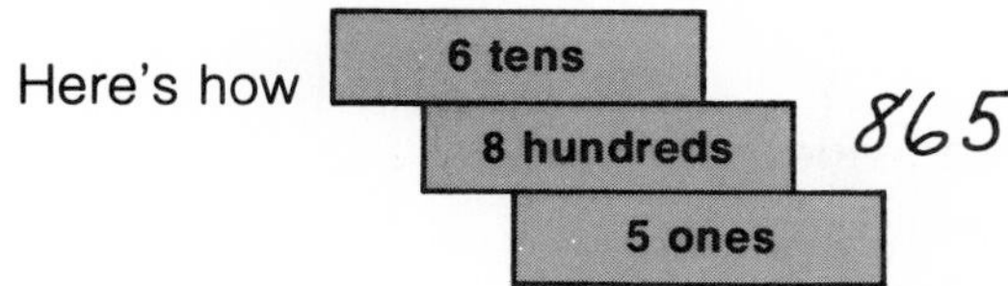

865

13. **14.**

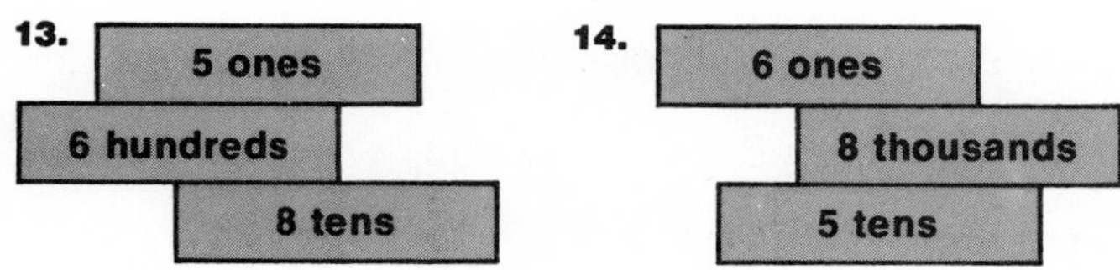

15. **16.**

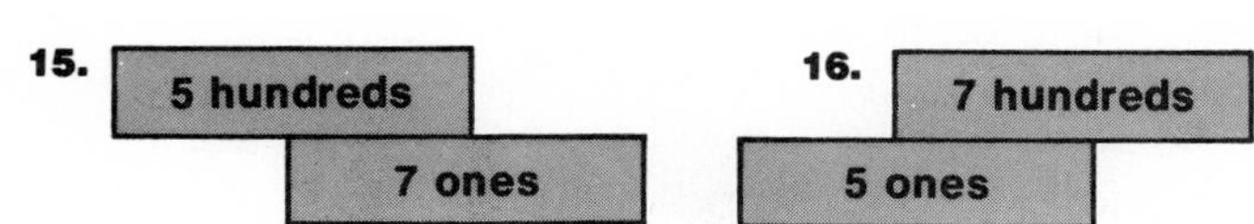

17. Use the three cards below to make as many three-digit numerals as you can.

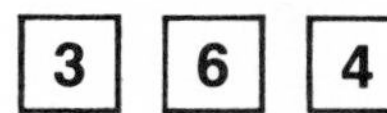

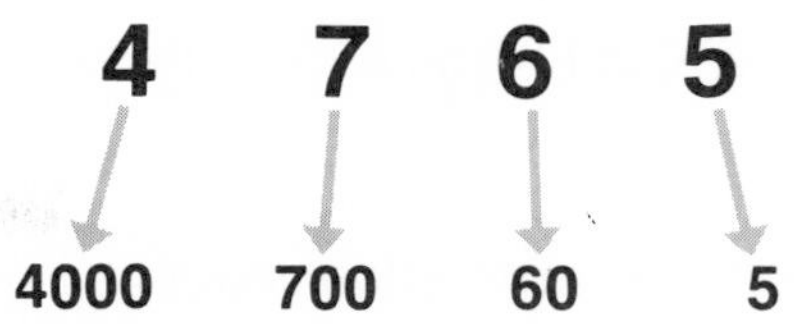

4765 = 4000 + 700 + 60 + 5

Expanded numeral

Give the expanded numeral.

Here's how

354 300+50+4

7042 7000+40+2

18. 19

19. 8947

20. 1960

21. 4444

Give the standard numeral.

Here's how

700 + 50 + 8 758

22. 100 + 4

23. 7000 + 400 + 30 + 2

24. 100 + 90

25. 6000 + 40 + 3

26. 5000 + 500 + 5

Large Numbers

There are about 60,450,800 sensory cells in your skin.

The commas in 60,450,800
separate the number into *periods.*

millions period			thousands period			units period		
hundred millions	ten millions	millions	hundred thousands	ten thousands	thousands	hundreds	tens	ones
	6	0	4	5	0	8	0	0

60 million **450** thousand **800**

sixty million, four hundred fifty thousand, eight hundred

Your skin also contains these tissues.
Read each number.
Then tell what each 4 means.

Here's how

241,000 yards of nerves

4 ten thousands

1. 64,000 yards of blood vessels
2. 243,800 nerve endings for heat
3. 514,500 nerve endings for pressure
4. 40,400 nerve endings for cold
5. 201,400 hairs
6. 4,030,000 nerve endings for pain
7. 2,015,400 sweat glands

Give the standard numeral.

8. 75 thousand 674
9. 9 million 703 thousand 67
10. 42 million 6 thousand 588
11. forty million, seven hundred fifty-six thousand, nine hundred forty
12. seventy-five million, forty-two thousand, fifteen
13. two hundred four million, eighty-five thousand, three hundred
14. two hundred million, forty-eight thousand, five hundred three
15. two hundred eighty-five million, three hundred thousand, eight hundred fifty-three

Ordering Numbers

$>$ means "is greater than."

$<$ means "is less than."

Heartbeats per hour	
Cat	7200
Elephant	2100
Mouse	36,000
Squirrel	8100
Human baby	8400
10-year-old	5400
Adult	4500

Compare these numbers from the table. Use $>$ or $<$.

1. 7200 ◯ 4500
2. 2100 ◯ 36,000
3. 8400 ◯ 8100
4. 5400 ◯ 4500
5. List the numbers in the table in order from the least to the greatest.

Give the number that is 10 greater.

6. 87
7. 452
8. 10,833
9. 5302
10. 735,921
11. 500,000

Give the number that is 1000 greater.

12. 8352
13. 45,673
14. 40,020
15. 534
16. 653,772
17. 48

What is the greatest number you can make

18. using four different digits?
19. using six different digits?
20. using six digits that are all the same?

Explore

Draw 1000 dots on a sheet of paper.

Suppose you made copies of your paper.

How many dots would there be on 10 sheets? On 100 sheets? On 1000 sheets?

There would be one billion dots on one million sheets.

One million sheets of paper would form 65 stacks about as tall as you are.

Adding with Renamings

Tom Sawyer and Huck Finn sailed on the Mississippi River on a raft.

How many miles is a trip down the river from Hannibal to New Orleans?

Find 979 + 265.

hundreds tens ones

```
  1
  979
+ 265
    4
```

Add the ones.

14 ones = 1 ten 4 ones

```
 11
  979
+ 265
   44
```

Add the tens.

14 tens = 1 hundred 4 tens

```
 11
  979
+ 265
 1244
```

Add the hundreds.

12 hundreds = 1 thousand 2 hundreds

The trip is 1244 miles.

Add.

1. 67 + 49

2. 228 + 142

3. 76 + 87 + 95

4. 627 + 905 + 1056

5. 182 + 307

6. 63 + 75

7. 248 + 986

8. 919 + 191

More practice
Set A, page 62

Add across. Add down.

9.

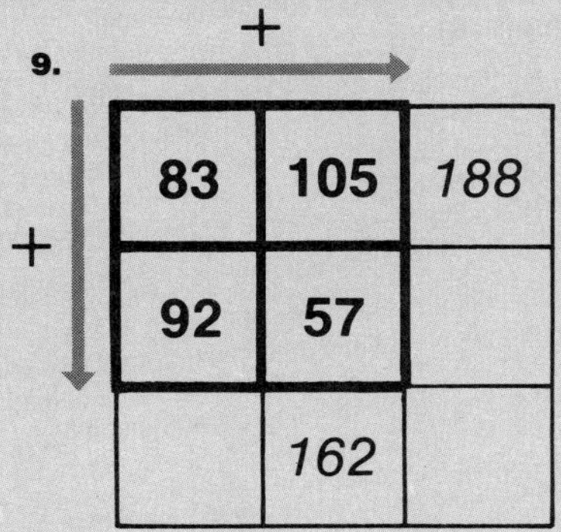

10.

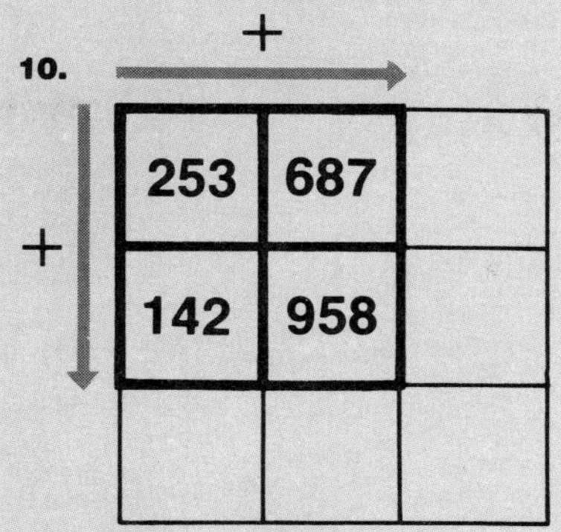

11.

945	69	
624	2478	

Find the missing digits.
Complete the exercises.

12. $\begin{array}{r} 45 \\ +\ 16 \\ \hline ▒1 \end{array}$

13. $\begin{array}{r} 98 \\ +\ 36 \\ \hline 1▒4 \end{array}$

14. $\begin{array}{r} 68 \\ +\ 4▒ \\ \hline 110 \end{array}$

15. $\begin{array}{r} 7▒ \\ +\ 56 \\ \hline 1▒6 \end{array}$

16. $\begin{array}{r} 67 \\ +\ 2▒ \\ \hline ▒1 \end{array}$

17. $\begin{array}{r} ▒7 \\ +\ 3▒ \\ \hline 134 \end{array}$

18. Help Tom Sawyer find the correct path through the woods. The sum of the numbers along the path must be 684.

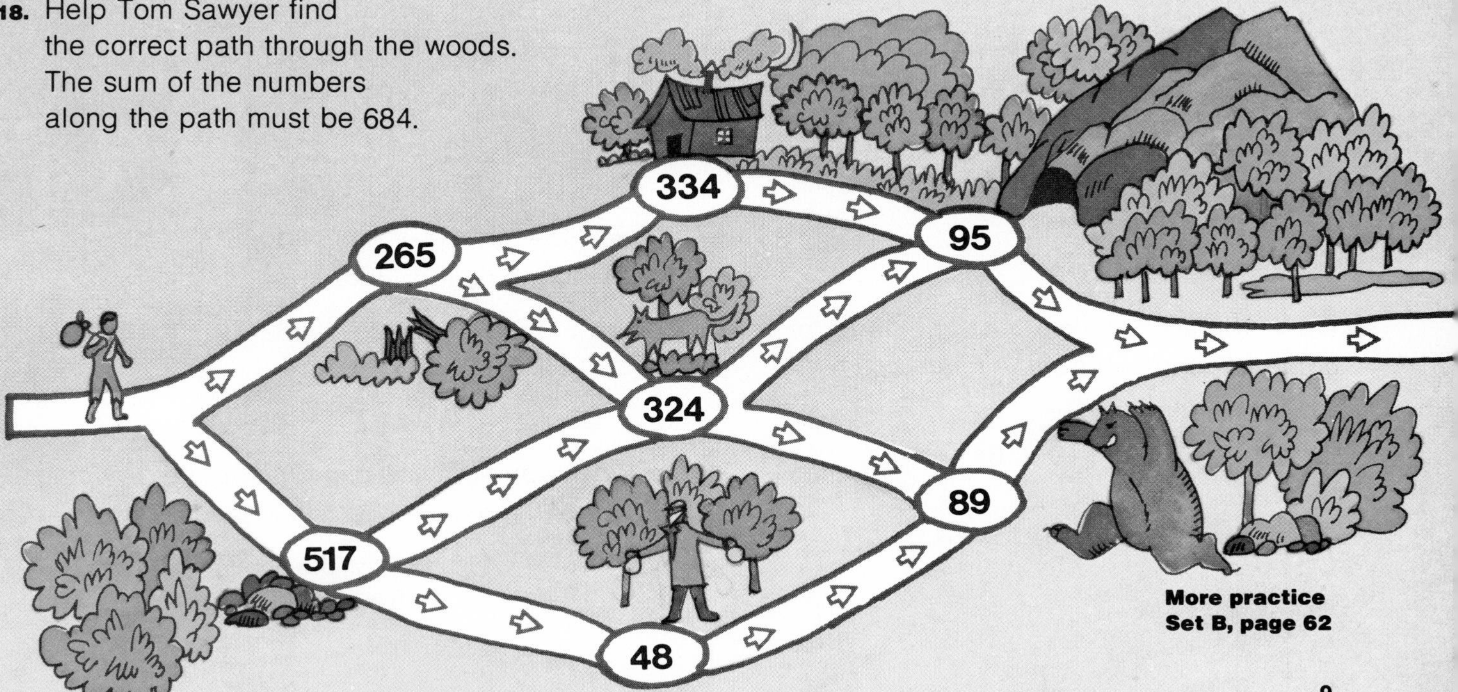

More practice
Set B, page 62

Order and Grouping in Addition

Find each sum.

1. 95 + 36 = ▒
36 + 95 = ▒

2. 153 + 247 = ▒
247 + 153 = ▒

3. 642 + 70 = ▒
70 + 642 = ▒

4. Is the sum 432 + 928 the same as the sum 928 + 432?

Look for an easy way to find each missing sum.

5. 53,666 + 1985 = 55,651
1985 + 53,666 = ▒

6. 496 + 285 = 781
285 + 496 = ▒

7. 5739 + 4865 = 10,604
4865 + 5739 = ▒

8. 3048 + 7692 = 10,740
7692 + 3048 = ▒

■ *When you add, you can change the order of the addends and get the same sum.*

19 + 45 = 64
45 + 19 = 64

Find each sum. Add the numbers inside the parentheses first.

Here's how

(40 + 50) + 70 90+70
160

9. (42 + 9) + 11 = ▒
42 + (9 + 11) = ▒

10. (348 + 5) + 90 = ▒
348 + (5 + 90) = ▒

11. (75 + 80) + 27 = ▒
75 + (80 + 27) = ▒

12. Is the sum (16 + 88) + 12 the same as the sum 16 + (88 + 12)?

Look for an easy way to find each missing sum.

13. (555 + 128) + 94 = 777
555 + (128 + 94) = ▒

14. (116 + 88) + 12 = 216
116 + (88 + 12) = ▒

15. (459 + 241) + 368 = 1068
459 + (241 + 368) = ▒

16. (375 + 48) + 139 = 562
375 + (48 + 139) = ▒

■ *When you add, you can change the grouping of the addends and get the same sum.*

(18 + 6) + 35 = 59
18 + (6 + 35) = 59

Finding Sums of 10

You can add numbers in any order.
Study how Linda, Tony, and Gloria found this sum.

Linda added down.

$$\begin{array}{r} 6 \\ 4 \\ 8 \\ 3 \\ +7 \\ \hline 28 \end{array}$$

6 + 4 = 10
10 + 8 = 18
18 + 3 = 21
21 + 7 = 28

Tony added up.

$$\begin{array}{r} 6 \\ 4 \\ 8 \\ 3 \\ +7 \\ \hline 28 \end{array}$$

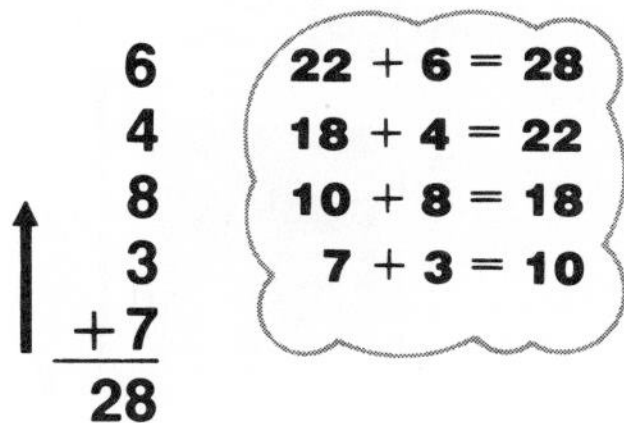

Gloria looked for sums of 10.

$$\begin{array}{r} 6 \\ 4 \\ 8 \\ 3 \\ +7 \\ \hline 28 \end{array}$$

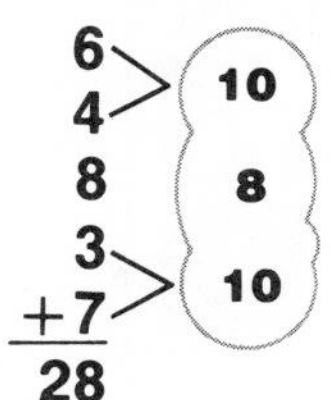

Pam, David, and Ron made scorecards for the game of Yahtzee.® Help them add their scores.
Look for sums of 10.

1.

NAME *Pam*

	Game 1	Game 2	Game 3
ones	4	2	1
twos	6	8	4
threes	15	12	9
fours	16	8	12
fives	15	20	25
sixes	24	24	18
SUBTOTAL			
Add 35 if 63 or more.			
TOTAL of upper half of scorecard			

2.

Game Scores

Players	*Pam*	*David*	*Ron*
Game 1	168	142	123
Game 2	142	173	175
Game 3	135	182	84
Game 4	194	119	123
Game 5	116	87	54
Add 100 for each bonus chip.	100	0	0
TOTAL			

More practice
Set C, page 62

Rounding Numbers

Three magazines reported the 1973 sales of the same record album.

Notice that the magazines reported different numbers.
The *Rock News* and the *Record Scoop* reported the sales in ***rounded numbers.***

A. Round to the nearest ten.

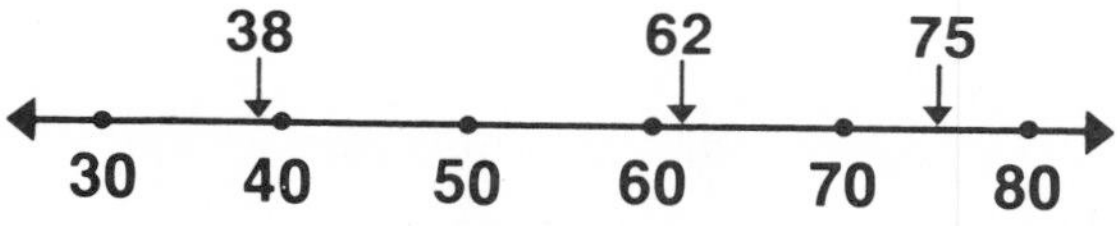

	Rounded number	
38	40	Is 38 nearer 30 or 40? Round up to 40.
62	60	Is 62 nearer 60 or 70? Round down to 60.
75	80	75 is halfway between 70 and 80. Round up to 80.

Round to the nearest ten.

1. 28
2. 387
3. 4321
4. 35
5. 74

B. Round to the nearest hundred.

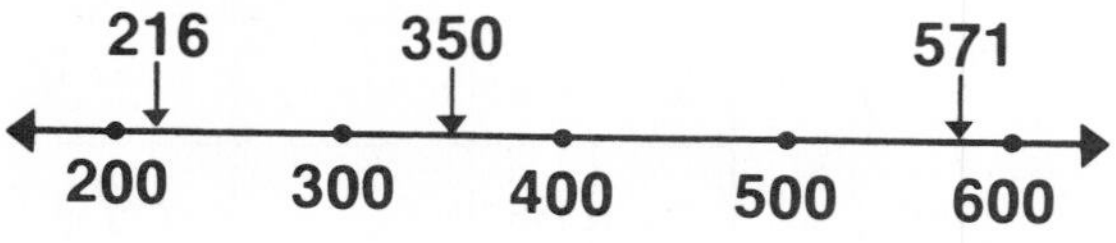

	Rounded number	
571	600	Is 571 nearer 500 or 600? Round up to 600.
216		Is 216 nearer 200 or 300? Round down to 200.
350		350 is halfway between 300 and 400. Round up to ____.

Round to the nearest hundred.

6. 476
7. 2329
8. 34,693
9. 715
10. 8250

Estimating Sums

You can use rounded numbers to estimate sums.

To estimate the sum: Round. Add the rounded numbers mentally.

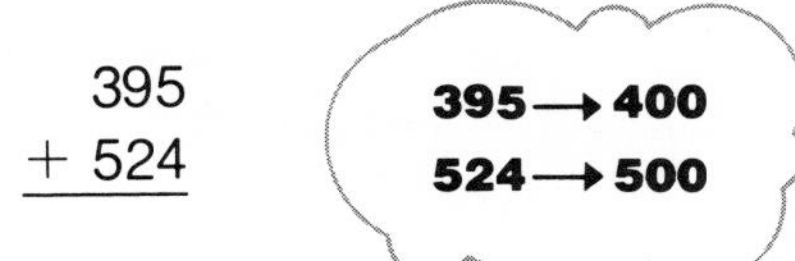

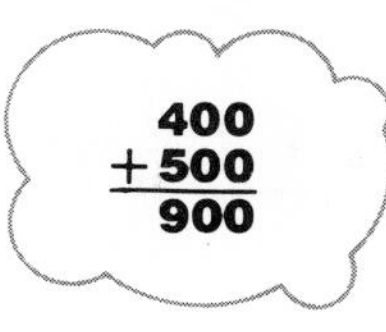

The sum is about 900.

■ *You can estimate sums to see if your answers are sensible.*

Give an estimate of the sum.
Then give the actual sum.

1. 29 + 52

2. 726 + 889

3. 492 + 415

4. 97 + 62 + 71

5. 89 + 18 + 52

■ *You can estimate sums when you do not need an exact answer.*

Estimate the number of miles between these towns.
Use the shortest route.

6. Cherokee and Pawnee

7. Comanche and The Village

8. Cheyenne and Cherokee

9. Comanche and Shawnee

10. Cheyenne and Shawnee

OKLAHOMA

76 Cherokee 52 68 Pawnee 83 72 79 49 39 Cheyenne The Village Shawnee 81 106 78 Comanche

Using Addition to Find Distances

In 1860, mail was carried across the West by pony express. The trip took 8 to 10 days.

Find the total distance for the riders on each section. Estimate to see if your answers are sensible.

	TRAIL SECTION	RIDERS	MILES
1.	Sacramento to Fort Churchill	*Sam Hamilton* *Boston Upson* *Bob Haslam*	63 58 74
2.	Fort Churchill to Ruby Valley	*Bart Riles* *Jay Kelley*	119 118
3.	Ruby Valley to Camp Floyd	*Wash Perkins* *Jim Gentry* *Let Harrington* *Billy Fisher*	64 62 91 37
4.	Camp Floyd to Green River	*Major Egan* *Ras Egan* *Tom King* *Dan Westcott*	78 54 76 77
5.	Green River to Horseshoe	*Deadwood Dick* *Tommy Ranahan* *Bill Cates*	78 144 92
6.	Horseshoe to Julesburg	*Hank Avis* *Jack Keetley*	109 105
7.	Julesburg to Fort Kearney	*Little Yank* *Billie Campbell*	98 106
8.	Fort Kearney to St. Joseph	*Mel Vaughn* *Doc Brink* *Jim Beatley* *Johnny Frey*	63 48 68 84

Territory
Unattached Territory
Minnesota
Iowa
Julesburg
St. Joseph
Fort Kearney
Territory
Missouri
Unorganized Territory
Texas

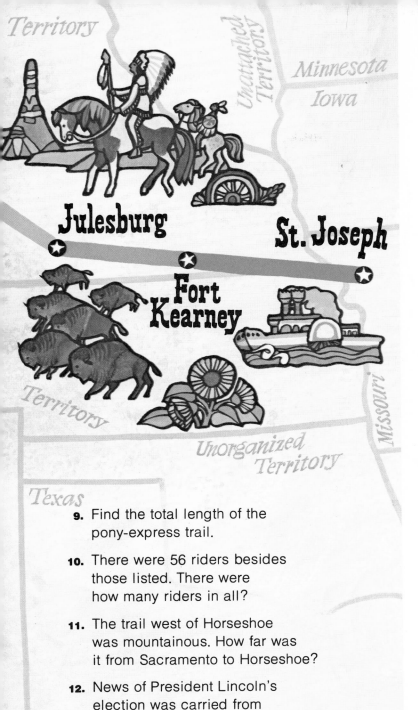

9. Find the total length of the pony-express trail.

10. There were 56 riders besides those listed. There were how many riders in all?

11. The trail west of Horseshoe was mountainous. How far was it from Sacramento to Horseshoe?

12. News of President Lincoln's election was carried from Fort Kearney to Fort Churchill in a record six days. Find the distance between these two towns.

Time Out!

Draw four squares side by side on the lines of a grid.

Here is one shape you can make.

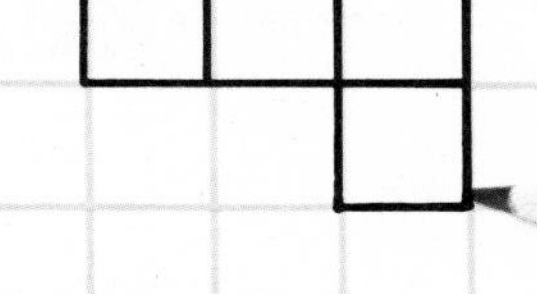

Make four other shapes, using four squares.

Careful!

These are the same shape in different positions.

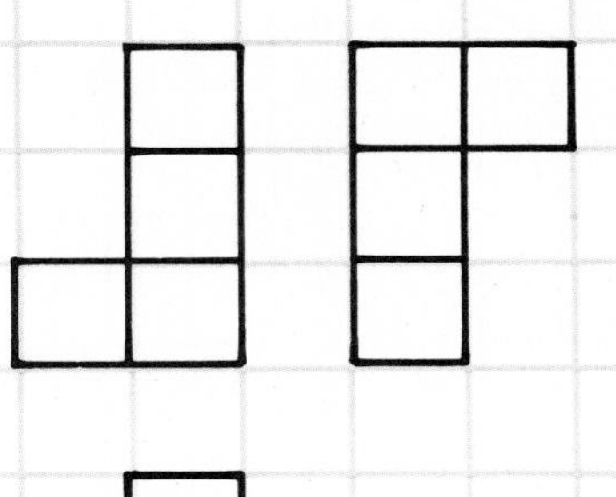

Subtracting: One Renaming

How long is the crocodile's tail?

Find 94 − 56.

tens	ones	
9	4	You need more ones.
− 5	6	Rename to get 10 more ones.

8	14
~~9~~	~~4~~
− 5	6
	8

9 tens 4 ones = 8 tens 14 ones

Subtract the ones.

8	14
~~9~~	~~4~~
− 5	6
3	8

Subtract the tens.

The crocodile's tail is 38 inches long.

Rename to get 10 more ones.

	thousands	hundreds	tens	ones
		3	~~8~~ 7	~~6~~ 16
1.		8	2	5
2.			7	0
3.			5	7
4.		3	4	5
5.			5	0
6.		4	6	3

Rename to get 10 more tens.

	thousands	hundreds	tens	ones
	7	~~3~~ 2	~~5~~ 15	8
7.		7	5	4
8.		5	4	3
9.	9	2	4	7
10.		3	0	6
11.	6	8	0	1
12.	1	2	0	0

Subtract.

13. 75 − 39

14. 34 − 27

15. 63 − 48

16. 98 − 79

17. 42 − 17

18. 35 − 19

19. 40 − 26

20. 70 − 48

21. 305 − 245

22. 609 − 397

More practice
Set D, page 62

World's Tallest Mammal
Giraffe
World's Tallest Bird
Ostrich

How much taller is the giraffe than the ostrich?

Find 213 − 95.

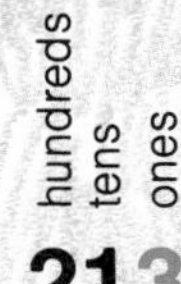


```
  213
−  95
```
You need more ones.

```
   0 13
  2 1 3
−   9 5
      8
```
Rename to get 10 more ones.
Subtract the ones.

```
 1 10
   0 13
  2 1 3
−   9 5
    1 8
```
Rename to get 10 more tens.
Subtract the tens.

```
 1 10
   0 13
  2 1 3
−   9 5
  1 1 8
```
Subtract the hundreds.

The giraffe is 118 inches taller than the ostrich.

Subtract.

```
1.   2 13
       3 12
     3 4 2
   − 2 6 8
```

2. 673 − 484

3. 567 − 79

4. 932 − 56

5. 471 − 287

6. 845 − 478

7. 531 − 259

8. 626 − 438

9. 532 − 384

10. 375 − 186

11. 582 − 95

12. 766 − 689

More practice
Set E, page 62

Subtracting: Two Renamings with Zero

```
  6 10
  7 0 4    You need more ones.
− 2 3 9    First rename to get more tens.
```

```
    9 14
  6 10     Then rename to get more ones.
  7 0 4
− 2 3 9    Subtract the ones.
      5
```

```
    9 14
  6 10
  7 0 4
− 2 3 9    Subtract the tens.
  4 6 5    Subtract the hundreds.
```

Subtract.

1. 703 − 394
2. 804 − 267
3. 205 − 97
4. 907 − 628
5. 603 − 289
6. 504 − 378
7. 608 − 379
8. 704 − 426
9. 305 − 178
10. 705 − 569
11. 603 − 567
12. 3902 − 1627

More practice
Set F, page 62

Using Subtraction

An odometer tells how many miles a car has traveled.
Subtract the odometer readings to find the length of each trip.

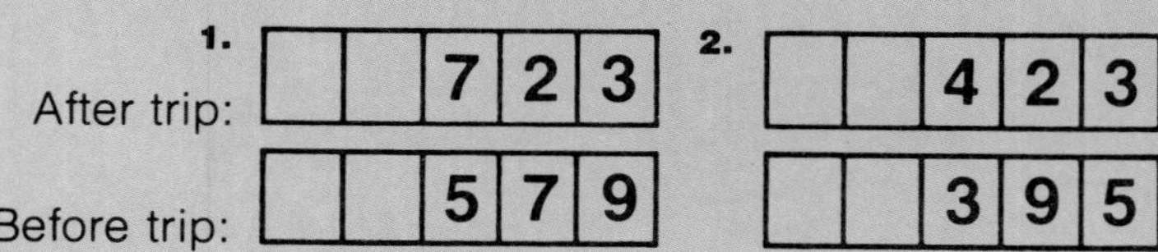

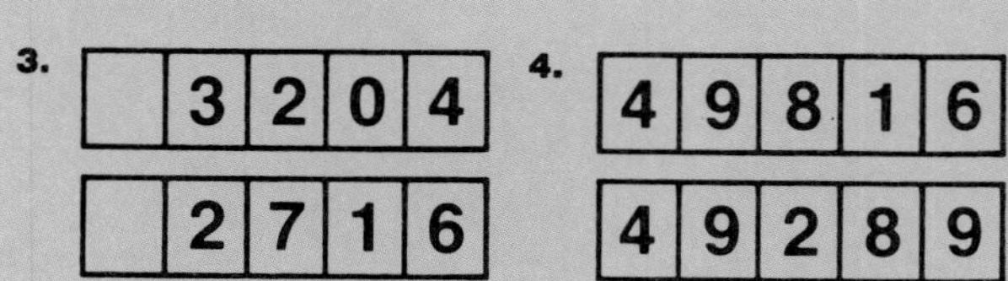

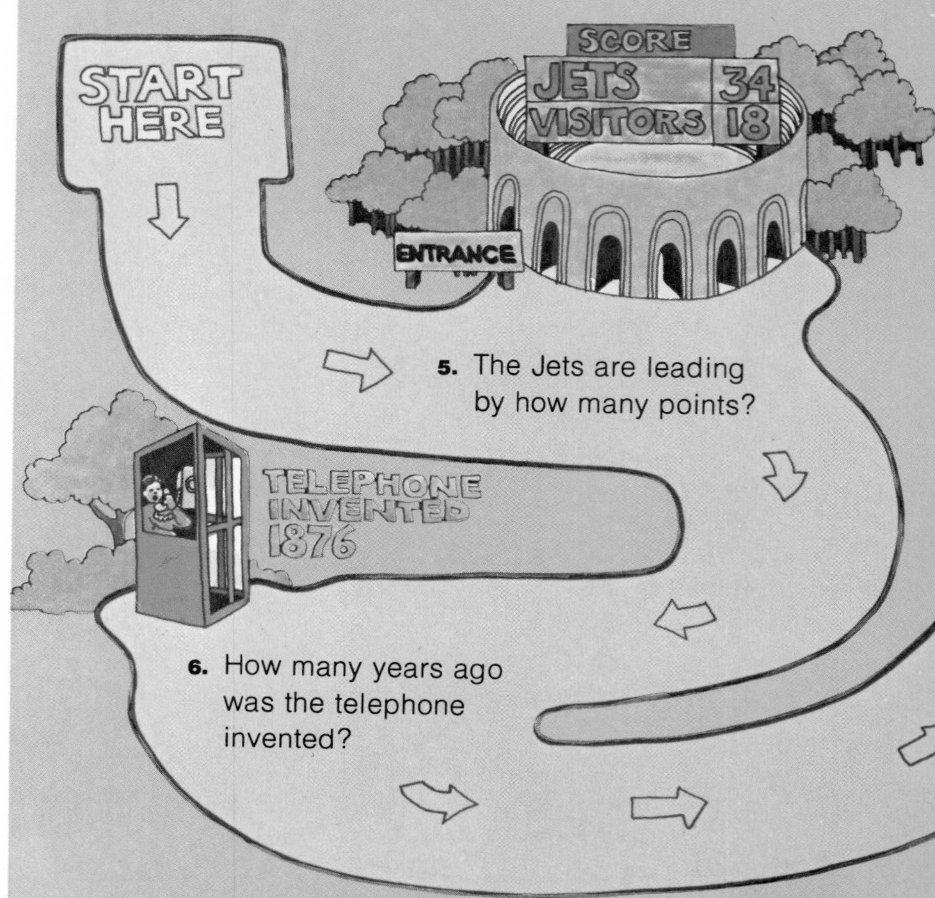

5. The Jets are leading by how many points?

6. How many years ago was the telephone invented?

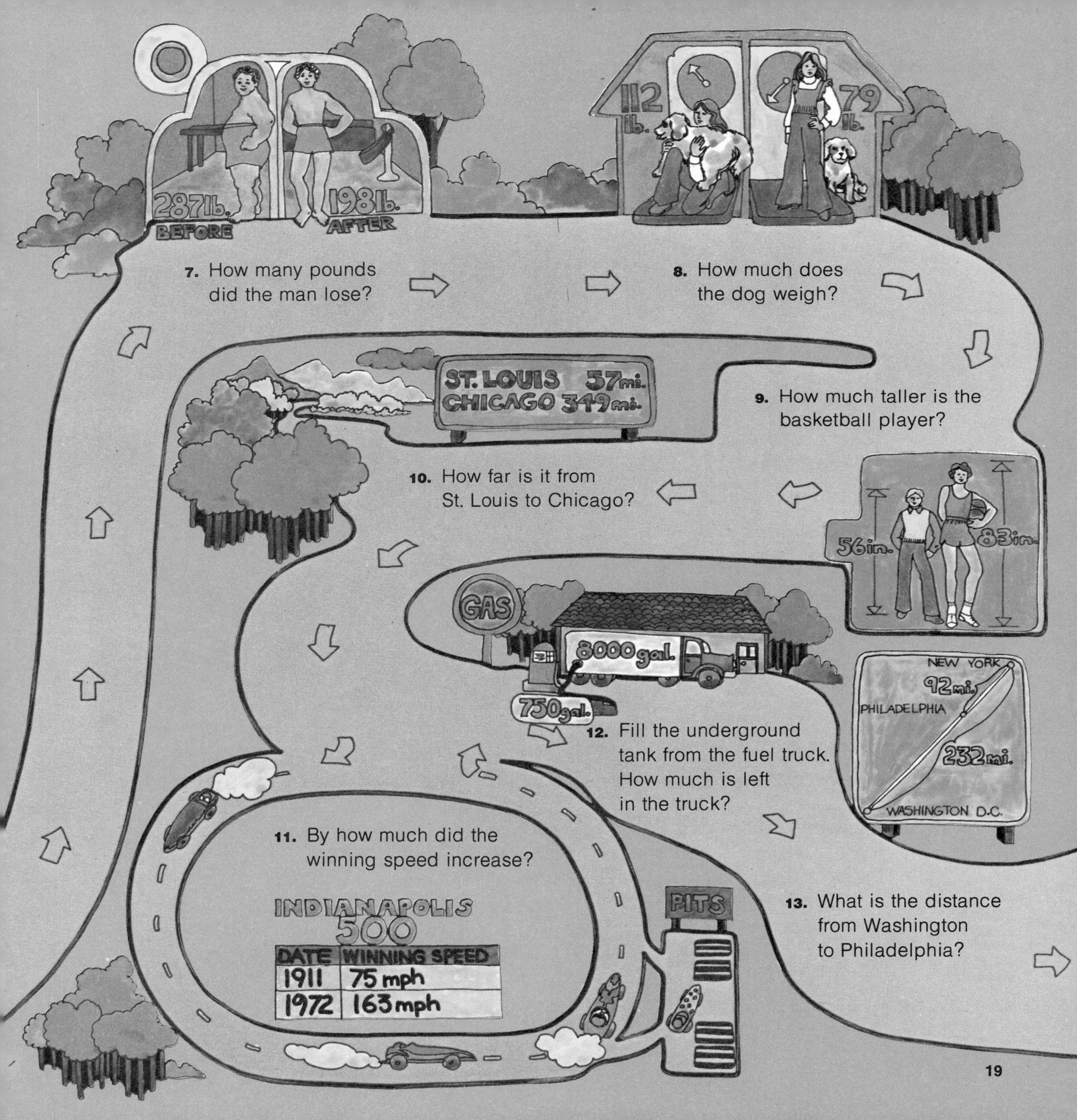

7. How many pounds did the man lose?

8. How much does the dog weigh?

9. How much taller is the basketball player?

10. How far is it from St. Louis to Chicago?

11. By how much did the winning speed increase?

DATE	WINNING SPEED
1911	75 mph
1972	163 mph

12. Fill the underground tank from the fuel truck. How much is left in the truck?

13. What is the distance from Washington to Philadelphia?

Checking Subtraction

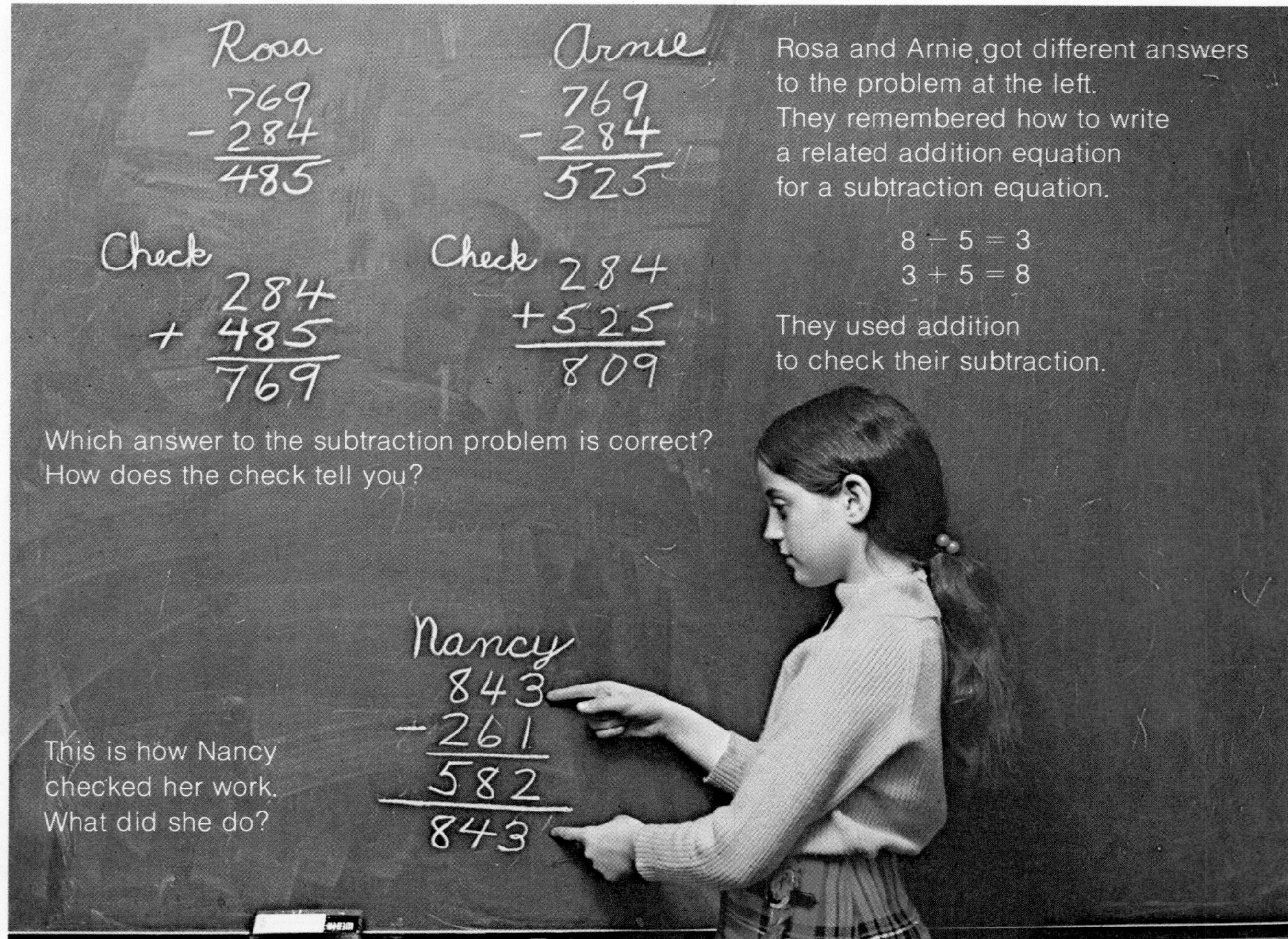

Rosa
769
− 284
485
Check
284
+ 485
769
Arnie
769
− 284
525
Check
284
+ 525
809
Rosa and Arnie got different answers to the problem at the left.
They remembered how to write a related addition equation for a subtraction equation.
8 − 5 = 3
3 + 5 = 8
They used addition to check their subtraction.
Which answer to the subtraction problem is correct? How does the check tell you?
Nancy
843
− 261
582
843
This is how Nancy checked her work. What did she do?

Subtract. Use addition to check your work.

1. 417 − 111 **2.** 982 − 773 **3.** 809 − 235 **4.** 657 − 344 **5.** 910 − 528 **6.** 600 − 283

7. 594 − 219 **8.** 432 − 364 **9.** 796 − 127 **10.** 193 − 167 **11.** 704 − 605 **12.** 972 − 357

More practice
Set G, page 63

Subtraction Patterns: The Good Number 9

Pedro wrote down what his age will be in 10 years. **18**

He reversed the digits **18 → 81**

and subtracted.

$$\begin{array}{r} 81 \\ -\ 18 \\ \hline 63 \end{array}$$

He continued reversing digits and subtracting. **63 → 36**

$$\begin{array}{r} 63 \\ -\ 36 \\ \hline 27 \end{array}$$

27 → 72

$$\begin{array}{r} 72 \\ -\ 27 \\ \hline 45 \end{array}$$

45 → 54

$$\begin{array}{r} 54 \\ -\ 45 \\ \hline 9 \end{array}$$

Follow the same steps using these numbers.

1. Your age 10 years from now
2. Your age 20 years from now
3. Your age 30 years from now
4. Any two-digit number with different digits
5. Is 9 always the final answer?

Write any number. **1776**

Put a zero at the end. **17760**

Subtract the original number.

$$\begin{array}{r} 17760 \\ -\ 1776 \\ \hline 15984 \end{array}$$

Add the digits of this last number. $1 + 5 + 9 + 8 + 4 = 27$

If the sum has more than one digit, add again. $2 + 7 = 9$

Marie followed the above steps using her house number.

374

$$\begin{array}{r} 3740 \\ -\ 374 \\ \hline 3366 \end{array}$$

$3 + 3 + 6 + 6 = 18$

$1 + 8 = 9$

Follow the same steps using these numbers.

6. The number 12
7. The number 333
8. The number 61,852
9. The year you were born
10. Is 9 always the final answer?

Using Addition and Subtraction in Magic Squares

You can use addition and subtraction in interesting patterns, such as magic squares.

1. Find the sum for each row.

15	1	11
5	9	13
7	17	3

2. Find the sum for each column.

15	1	11
5	9	13
7	17	3

3. Find the sum for each diagonal.

15	1	11
5	9	13
7	17	3

4. Are all the sums equal?

You have a magic square if all the sums are equal.

This square is a magic square.

5. What is the magic sum?

15	1	11
5	9	13
7	17	3

Which of the squares below are magic squares? Give the magic sum for each magic square.

6.

24	3	18
9	15	21
12	27	6

7.

41	21	25
13	29	45
33	37	17

8.

25	60	11
18	32	46
51	4	39

Find numbers that make this a magic square.

17	3	13
7	11	
		5

9. What is the magic sum?

10. Find the missing number in the first column.

    17 + 7 + ▒ = magic sum

11. Complete the magic square.

Complete each magic square.

12.

43	34	79
88	52	
25		61

13.

30		75
	49	4
23		

14.

8		16
	17	
18		

★ 15.

21	28	30	35
32			
	22		29
34	31	25	24

★ 16. Make a magic square. Use the numbers 2, 4, 6, 8, 10, 12, 14, 16, 18.

Adding and Subtracting: "Try for 500" Game

Lynn and Angie played a game with ten cards.

They put the cards in an envelope and took turns drawing cards.

Each player started with a score of 100.

On each draw, the player drew two cards to form a two-digit number. Then she added the number to her score.

But when one of the digits she drew was 3, she had to subtract the number from her score.

0 1 2 3 4 5 6 7 8 9

Number added	Number subtracted	Score
		100
54		154
	35	119

After each draw, the two cards were put back into the envelope.

After ten draws apiece, the girl with the score nearer 500 was the winner.

Make ten cards and play this game.

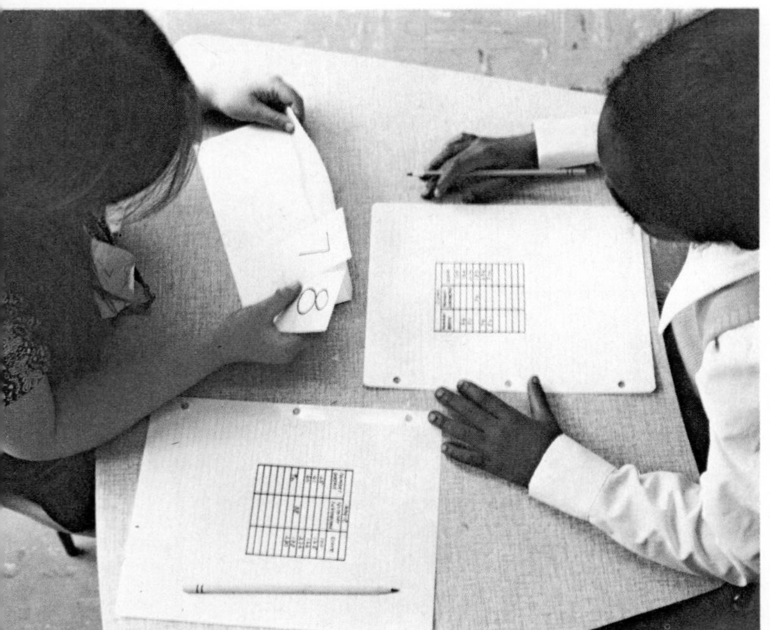

Complete the scorecards. Who won?

Lynn		
Number added	Number subtracted	Score
		100
64		164
50		214
	34	
74		
82		
	32	
87		
42		
52		
	13	

Angie		
Number added	Number subtracted	Score
		100
25		
41		
60		
	38	
92		
40		
	31	
51		
	38	
29		

Solving Equations with Missing Addends

A. You can use an equation to describe the picture.

42 marbles altogether

Number of red marbles		Number of blue marbles		Total number
25	+	**17**	=	**42**
Addend		Addend		Sum

B. This equation uses n for a missing addend.

How many red marbles?

86 marbles altogether

$$\mathbf{n + 34 = 86}$$

$$\mathbf{n = 52}$$

There are 52 red marbles.

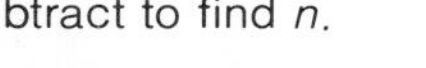
Subtract to find n.

$$\begin{array}{r} 86 \\ -34 \\ \hline 52 \end{array}$$

C. This equation also has a missing addend.

How many green marbles?

63 marbles altogether

$$\mathbf{26 + n = 63}$$

$$\mathbf{n = 37}$$

There are 37 green marbles.

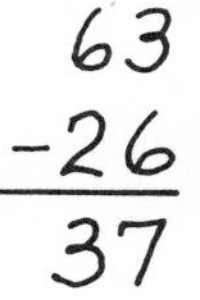
$$\begin{array}{r} 63 \\ -26 \\ \hline 37 \end{array}$$

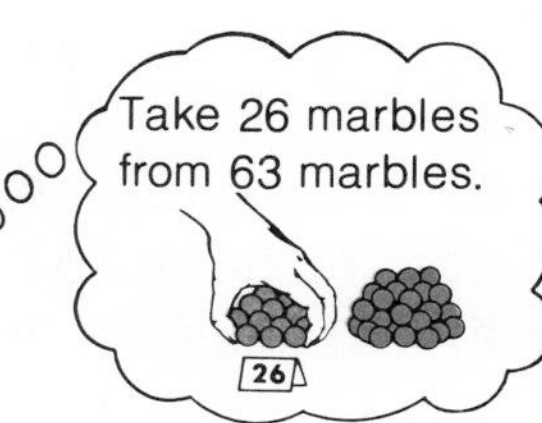

■ *You can subtract to find a missing addend.*

$n + 62 = 85$ $\quad\begin{array}{r} 85 \\ -62 \\ \hline 23 \end{array}$

$n = 23$

$19 + n = 43$ $\quad\begin{array}{r} 43 \\ -19 \\ \hline 24 \end{array}$

$n = 24$

Find the number for n.

1. $27 + n = 82$

2. $n + 53 = 94$

3. $46 + n = 85$

4. $97 = n + 62$

5. $425 = 326 + n$

6. $n + 25 = 92$

7. $325 + n = 726$

8. $n + 72 = 128$

9. $234 = 126 + n$

10. $n + 62 = 521$

Using Equations to Solve Problems

You can use equations to help you solve problems.

93 people live on the first two floors of an apartment building. There are 48 people on the second floor. How many people live on the first floor?

	Number on first floor		Number on second floor		Total number
Write an equation.	n	$+$	48	$=$	93
Find the number for *n*.			n	$=$	45
Answer the question.	45 people live on the first floor.				

$$\begin{array}{r} 93 \\ -48 \\ \hline 45 \end{array}$$

Use the steps above to help you solve these problems.

1. Joe threw a basketball 86 times. He missed the basket 53 times. How many baskets did he make?

Baskets made		Baskets missed		Total number
n	$+$	53	$=$	86

2. There were 58 children living in the apartment building. More children moved in. Then there were 72 children. How many children moved in?

Number to begin with		Number moved in		Total number
58	$+$	n	$=$	72

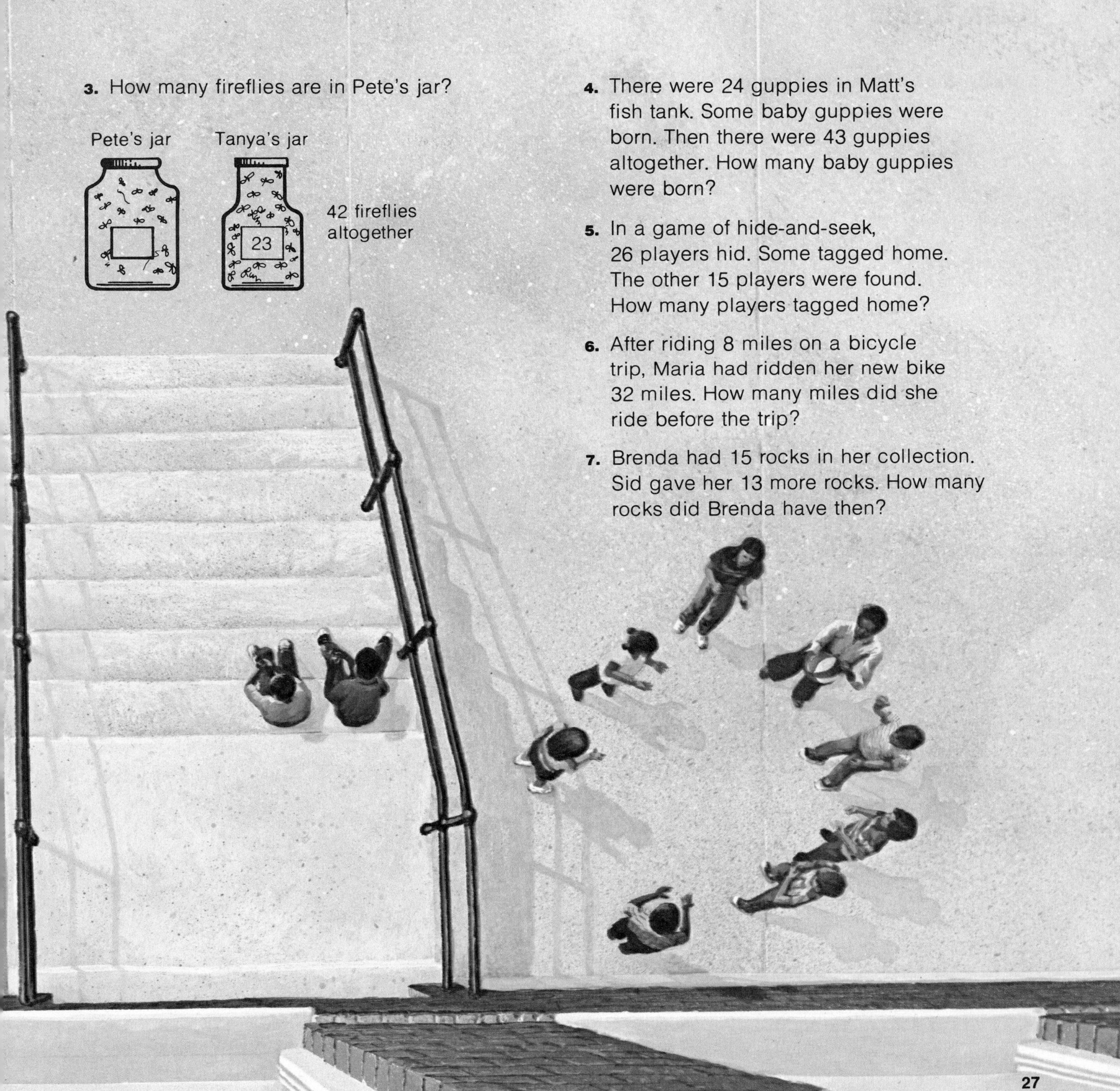

3. How many fireflies are in Pete's jar?

Pete's jar | Tanya's jar

23

42 fireflies altogether

4. There were 24 guppies in Matt's fish tank. Some baby guppies were born. Then there were 43 guppies altogether. How many baby guppies were born?

5. In a game of hide-and-seek, 26 players hid. Some tagged home. The other 15 players were found. How many players tagged home?

6. After riding 8 miles on a bicycle trip, Maria had ridden her new bike 32 miles. How many miles did she ride before the trip?

7. Brenda had 15 rocks in her collection. Sid gave her 13 more rocks. How many rocks did Brenda have then?

SIDE TRIP

A Pattern of Adding and Multiplying

1. Add each number to itself.

   $0 + 0$

   $1 + 1$

   $2 + 2$

   $3 + 3$

   $4 + 4$

   $5 + 5$

   $6 + 6$

   $7 + 7$

   $8 + 8$

   $9 + 9$

   You get even numbers.

2. Multiply each number by itself.

   1×1

   2×2

   3×3

   4×4

   5×5

   6×6

   7×7

   8×8

   9×9

   You get square numbers.

The first even number is 0.
The first square number is 1.

Give these numbers.

3. Fifth even number
4. Sixth square number
5. Ninth even number
6. Ninth square number
7. Which even numbers are also square numbers?

8. What pattern do you see in these sums?

Add 5 and the first 5 even numbers.

$$\begin{array}{r} 5 \\ 0 \\ 2 \\ 4 \\ 6 \\ +8 \\ \hline 25 \end{array}$$

25 is the square of 5.

Add 4 and the first 4 even numbers.

$$\begin{array}{r} 4 \\ 0 \\ 2 \\ 4 \\ +6 \\ \hline 16 \end{array}$$

16 is the square of 4.

9. Use the pattern. Give the sum of 7 and the first 7 even numbers.
10. Give the sum of 9 and the first 9 even numbers.
11. Give the sum of 10 and the first 10 even numbers.

Check Yourself
Adding and Subtracting Whole Numbers, Pages 2–28

Basic facts, pages 2–3

1. $9 + 5 = \square$
2. $15 - 8 = \square$
3. $13 - 6 = \square$

Numeration, pages 4–7

4. Which number has 3 in the hundreds place?

   433 365 730 3832

5. Give the standard numeral.

   25 million 578 thousand 296

6. List in order from least to greatest.

   2279 1102 1098 2287

Adding, pages 8–15

Add.

7. $\begin{array}{r} 57 \\ + 29 \\ \hline \end{array}$

8. $\begin{array}{r} 768 \\ + 439 \\ \hline \end{array}$

9. $56 + 409 + 87$

10. $3 + 7 + 9 + 4 + 6$

11. Write the problem below that has the same sum as

    $254 + 736 = 990.$

    $245 + 763$ $252 + 748$
    $736 + 254$ $745 + 263$

12. Write the problems below that have the same sum as

    $(56 + 23) + 14 = 93.$

    $(56 + 32) + 41$ $(23 + 56) + 14$
    $56 + (23 + 14)$ $14 + (23 + 56)$

13. Round 681 to the nearest hundred.

14. Estimate the sum.

    $58 + 21$

Subtracting, pages 16–24

Subtract.

15. $\begin{array}{r} 71 \\ - 25 \\ \hline \end{array}$

16. $\begin{array}{r} 965 \\ - 487 \\ \hline \end{array}$

17. $\begin{array}{r} 702 \\ - 345 \\ \hline \end{array}$

18. $95 - 28$

19. $827 - 59$

20. $604 - 257$

Problem solving, pages 14, 15, 19, 25–27

21. How far is it from Marlow to Benton?

22. The car is how much longer than the bicycle?

23. Find n.

    $28 + n = 74$

24. Fred had 65 stamps in his collection. He got more stamps for his birthday. Then he had 126 stamps. How many stamps did Fred get for his birthday?

Multiples

Give each product.

1. 6×5
2. 7×5
3. 8×5
4. 9×5
5. 7×6
6. 8×6
7. 9×6
8. 4×9
9. 5×9
10. 6×9
11. 4×4
12. 5×4
13. 6×4
14. 5×7
15. 6×7
16. 7×7
17. 8×7
18. 9×7
19. 8×8
20. 9×8

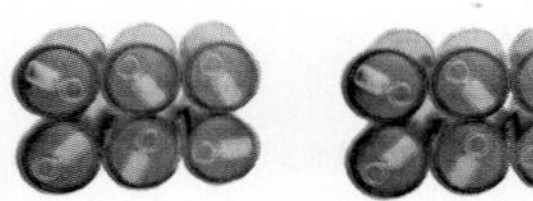

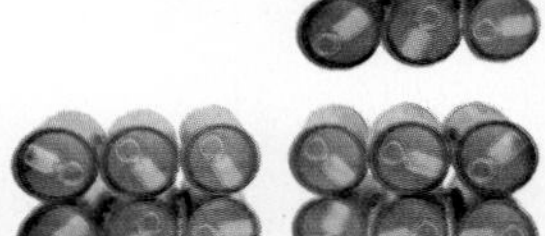

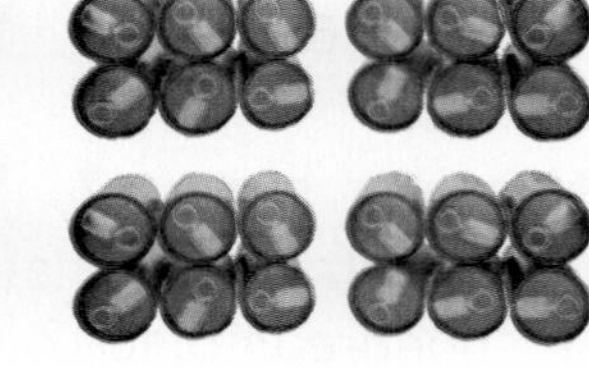

$1 \times 6 = 6$ $2 \times 6 = 12$ $3 \times 6 = 18$ $4 \times 6 = 24$

The numbers 6, 12, 18, and 24 are ***multiples*** of 6.

21. Give the next three multiples of 3.

(1×3)	(2×3)	(3×3)	(4×3)
↓	↓	↓	↓
3			

Complete the table.

	Number	Multiples less than 33
	4	*4 8 12 16 20 24 28 32*
22.	5	
23.	6	
24.	7	
25.	8	
26.	9	

Use your table to give the following numbers.

27. A multiple of both 4 and 7

28. A multiple of both 6 and 8

29. A multiple of both 6 and 9

30. Two multiples of both 4 and 6

Common Multiples and Least Common Multiple

A. Multiples of 3: 3, 6, 9, 12, 15, 18, 21, 24, . . .

Multiples of 4: 4, 8, 12, 16, 20, 24, . . .

Both 12 and 24 are ***common multiples*** of 3 and 4.
12 is the ***least common multiple*** of 3 and 4.

B. Find the least common multiple of 6 and 8.

Multiples of 8: 8, 16, 24, 32, . . .

What is the smallest multiple of 8 that is also a multiple of 6?
The least common multiple of 6 and 8 is 24.

1. List the first five multiples of 4.

2. List the first four multiples of 5.

3. What is the least common multiple of 4 and 5?

4. List the first three multiples of 10.

5. List the first five multiples of 6.

6. What is the least common multiple of 10 and 6?

7. List the first four multiples of 2.

8. What is the least common multiple of 2 and 8?

Give the least common multiple for each pair of numbers.

9. 2 and 3

10. 5 and 2

11. 2 and 6

12. 4 and 6

13. 6 and 5

14. 7 and 5

15. 9 and 6

16. 5 and 8

17. 8 and 3

18. 4 and 7

19. 4 and 8

20. 7 and 3

Multiples of 10, 100, and 1000

A. The school collected 6 truckloads of newspaper, with 1000 pounds of paper in each load. How many pounds of paper were collected?

Sally added to find 6×1000.

$$\begin{array}{r} 1000 \\ 1000 \\ 1000 \\ 1000 \\ 1000 \\ +\ 1000 \\ \hline 6000 \end{array}$$

$6 \times 1000 = 6000$

6000 pounds of paper were collected.

Complete each product.

1. $2 \times 10 = 2\square$
2. $2 \times 100 = 2\square$
3. $2 \times 1000 = 2\square$
4. $5 \times 10 = 5\square$
5. $5 \times 100 = 5\square$
6. $5 \times 1000 = 5\square$
7. $9 \times 10 = 9\square$
8. $9 \times 100 = 9\square$
9. $9 \times 1000 = 9\square$

Give each product.

10. 12×10
11. 35×10
12. 73×10
13. 18×100
14. 62×100
15. 321×100
16. 23×1000
17. 99×1000
18. 742×1000

● **Discuss** How can you find the number of zeros in each product?

Complete this multiplication table.

	×	10	100	1000
19.	7			*7000*
20.	11	*110*		
21.	23		*2300*	
22.	398	*3980*		
23.	4976		*497,600*	

B. For Halloween, Mrs. Lopez bought 10 sacks of candy, with 100 pieces in each sack. How many pieces of candy were there in all?

Steve added to find 10 × 100.

```
  100
  100
  100
  100
  100
  100
  100
  100
  100
+ 100
 1000
```

10 × 100 = 1000

There were 1000 pieces of candy.

Complete each product.

1. 1 × 10 = 1▒

2. 1 × 100 = 1▒

3. 1 × 1000 = 1▒

4. 10 × 10 = 1▒

5. 10 × 100 = 1▒

6. 10 × 1000 = 1▒

● **Discuss** How can you find the number of zeros in each product?

Give each product.

7. 10 × 10

8. 100 × 10

9. 10,000 × 10

10. 10 × 100

11. 100 × 100

12. 1000 × 100

13. 10 × 1000

14. 100 × 1000

15. 10,000 × 1000

Complete this multiplication table.

	×	10	100	1000
16.	10	*100*		
17.	100			*100,000*
18.	1000	*10,000*		
19.	10,000		*1,000,000*	

Multiplying: Multiples of 10

Give the number of zeros in each product.

1. $2 \times 30 = 6$ ▒
2. $4 \times 90 = 36$ ▒
3. $7 \times 300 = 21$ ▒
4. $5 \times 5000 = 25$ ▒
5. $30 \times 60 = 18$ ▒
6. $50 \times 300 = 15$ ▒
7. $20 \times 700 = 14$ ▒
8. $90 \times 6000 = 54$ ▒
9. $400 \times 700 = 28$ ▒
10. $900 \times 300 = 27$ ▒
11. $600 \times 4000 = 24$ ▒
12. $800 \times 9000 = 72$ ▒

• **Discuss** How can you find the number of zeros in 50×700?

Give each product.

13. 40×90
14. 20×400
15. 70×300
16. 30×80
17. 600×30
18. 800×60
19. 6000×30
20. 8000×900
21. 5000×90
22. 2000×9000
★ 23. 400×50
★ 24. 60×500

25. 6 cars pass through a tollgate every minute. How many cars pass through in
    - a. 10 minutes?
    - b. 30 minutes?
    - c. 60 minutes?
    - d. 90 minutes?
    - e. 200 minutes?
    - f. 300 minutes?

26. At another tollgate, 400 cars pass through each hour. How many cars pass through in
    - a. 4 hours?
    - b. 10 hours?
    - c. 30 hours?
    - d. 60 hours?
    - e. 500 hours?
    - f. 1000 hours?

More practice Set H, page 63

Using Multiplication: Ecology

1. In the United States, each person uses about 60 gallons of water per day in the home. About how many gallons does a person use in
   a. 7 days?
   b. 30 days?
   c. 90 days?
   d. 300 days?

2. Each American empties and throws away about 10 bottles each month. About how many bottles are thrown away each month by a community of
   a. 9000 people?
   b. 50,000 people?
   c. 300,000 people?
   d. 4,000,000 people?

3. Each American family empties and throws away about 600 aluminum cans per year. About how many cans are thrown away per year by
   a. 50 families?
   b. 100 families?
   c. 700 families?

4. Oil refineries use about 500 gallons of water to produce 1 gallon of gasoline. About how many gallons of water are needed to produce
   a. 10 gallons of gasoline?
   b. 40 gallons of gasoline?
   c. 200 gallons of gasoline?
   d. 3000 gallons of gasoline?

5. Paper companies use about 50 gallons of water to produce 1 pound of paperboard. About how many gallons of water are needed to produce
   a. 30 pounds of paperboard?
   b. 100 pounds of paperboard?
   c. 2000 pounds of paperboard?

6. It takes 90 pounds of air to burn 1 gallon of fuel oil. About how many pounds of air does it take to burn
   a. 40 gallons?
   b. 500 gallons?
   c. 2000 gallons?

Multiplying: One-digit Multipliers

A. There are 7 rows of dots with 25 dots in each row. How many dots are there in all?

Find 7 × 25.

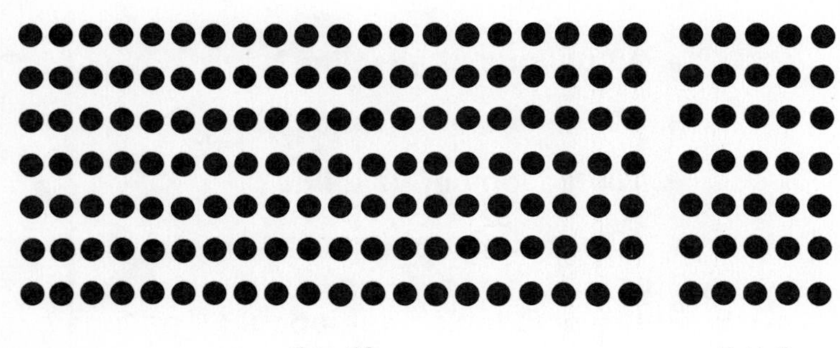

$$\begin{array}{r} 25 \\ \times \quad 7 \\ \hline 35 \\ 140 \\ \hline 175 \end{array}$$

25 (20 + 5)
35: 7 × 5
140: 7 × 20
175: 35 + 140

B. Here is a shorter way to find 7 × 25.

$$\begin{array}{r} {}^{3} \\ 25 \\ \times \quad 7 \\ \hline 5 \end{array}$$

7 × 5 = 35

Show 3 tens 5 ones.

$$\begin{array}{r} {}^{3} \\ 25 \\ \times \quad 7 \\ \hline 175 \end{array}$$

7 × 2 tens = 14 tens
14 tens + 3 tens = 17 tens

17 tens = 1 hundred 7 tens

Give each product.

1. $\begin{array}{r} 24 \\ \times \ 8 \\ \hline \end{array}$

2. $\begin{array}{r} 61 \\ \times \ 5 \\ \hline \end{array}$

3. $\begin{array}{r} 83 \\ \times \ 4 \\ \hline \end{array}$

4. $\begin{array}{r} 17 \\ \times \ 8 \\ \hline \end{array}$

5. $\begin{array}{r} 45 \\ \times \ 6 \\ \hline \end{array}$

6. $\begin{array}{r} 41 \\ \times \ 6 \\ \hline \end{array}$

7. $\begin{array}{r} 52 \\ \times \ 7 \\ \hline \end{array}$

8. $\begin{array}{r} 46 \\ \times \ 6 \\ \hline \end{array}$

9. $\begin{array}{r} 48 \\ \times \ 8 \\ \hline \end{array}$

10. $\begin{array}{r} 89 \\ \times \ 4 \\ \hline \end{array}$

11. $\begin{array}{r} 67 \\ \times \ 5 \\ \hline \end{array}$

12. $\begin{array}{r} 77 \\ \times \ 9 \\ \hline \end{array}$

13. 9 × 45

14. 5 × 67

15. 8 × 67

16. 9 × 43

17. 5 × 81

18. 3 × 62

19. 7 × 99

20. 4 × 57

c. Find 8 × 413.

$$\begin{array}{r} {\scriptstyle 2} \\ 413 \\ \times \quad 8 \\ \hline 4 \end{array}$$

8 × 3 = 24
24 = 2 tens 4 ones

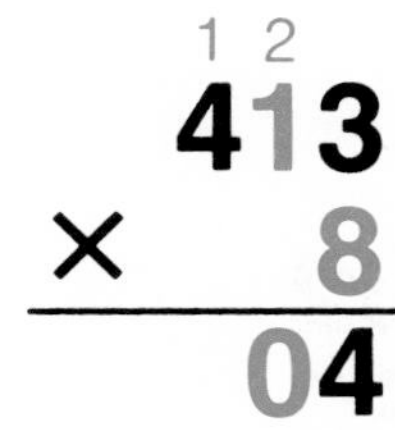

8 × 1 ten = 8 tens
8 tens + 2 tens = 10 tens
10 tens = 1 hundred 0 tens

$$\begin{array}{r} {\scriptstyle 1\,2} \\ 413 \\ \times \quad 8 \\ \hline 3304 \end{array}$$

8 × 4 hundreds = 32 hundreds
32 hundreds + 1 hundred = 33 hundreds
33 hundreds = 3 thousands 3 hundreds

Give each product.

1. 23 × 6

2. 723 × 6

3. 82 × 5

4. 382 × 5

5. 275 × 8

6. 369 × 4

7. 683 × 7

8. 542 × 9

9. 6 × 482

10. 3 × 546

11. 8 × 951

12. 7 × 384

13. 5 × 110

14. 4 × 608

15. 9 × 953

16. Dan bought 19 packages of baseball cards. There were 5 cards in each package. How many cards did he buy?

17. Tim bought 16 packages of football cards. There were 6 cards in each package. How many cards did he buy?

18. Wilma bought 17 packages of basketball cards. There were 4 cards in each package. How many cards did she buy?

More practice
Set I, page 63

Multiplying by Multiples of 10

Compare these two multiplication problems.

$$\begin{array}{r} 62 \\ \times\ 8 \\ \hline 496 \end{array} \qquad \begin{array}{r} 62 \\ \times\ 80 \\ \hline 4960 \end{array}$$

8 × 10

Write 0 to show that you multiply by 10.

8 × 62

Give each product.

1. 32 × 6 = 192; 32 × 60 = 192▒
2. 76 × 3; 76 × 30
3. 27 × 9; 27 × 90
4. 53 × 4; 53 × 40
5. 72 × 50
6. 34 × 80
7. 42 × 70
8. 58 × 60
9. 63 × 90
10. 35 × 40
11. 89 × 20
12. 43 × 70
13. 30 × 26
14. 40 × 75
15. 20 × 49
16. 90 × 38
17. 60 × 45
18. 50 × 56
19. 70 × 39
20. 60 × 92
21. 589 × 2
22. 589 × 20
23. 362 × 8
24. 362 × 80
25. 5 × 407
26. 50 × 407
27. 50 × 127
28. 30 × 804
29. 70 × 692
30. 80 × 975

More practice
Set J, page 63

Time Out!

Build three straight fences across each corral.

Each horse must be in his own section.

No section can be empty.

Multiplying: Two-digit Numbers

There are 38 cases of canned tomatoes,
with 24 cans in each case.
How many cans are there in all?

You can find 24 × 38 in two steps.

$$\begin{array}{rl} 38 & \\ \times\ 24 & (20 + 4) \\ \hline 152 & 4 \times 38 \\ 760 & 20 \times 38 \\ \hline 912 & 152 + 760 \end{array}$$

Complete each exercise.

1. $\begin{array}{rl} 23 & \\ \times\ 16 & \\ \hline 138 & 6 \times 23 \\ \blacksquare & 10 \times 23 \\ \hline 368 & \end{array}$

2. $\begin{array}{rl} 81 & \\ \times\ 42 & \\ \hline \blacksquare & 2 \times 81 \\ 3240 & 40 \times 81 \\ \hline 3402 & \end{array}$

3. $\begin{array}{rl} 79 & \\ \times\ 21 & \\ \hline 79 & 1 \times 79 \\ \blacksquare & 20 \times 79 \\ \hline \blacksquare & \end{array}$

4. $\begin{array}{rl} 46 & \\ \times\ 15 & \\ \hline \blacksquare & 5 \times 46 \\ \blacksquare & 10 \times 46 \\ \hline 690 & \end{array}$

5. $\begin{array}{r} 37 \\ \times\ 12 \\ \hline \end{array}$

6. $\begin{array}{r} 75 \\ \times\ 53 \\ \hline \end{array}$

7. $\begin{array}{r} 57 \\ \times\ 34 \\ \hline \end{array}$

8. $\begin{array}{r} 89 \\ \times\ 52 \\ \hline \end{array}$

9. $\begin{array}{r} 65 \\ \times\ 48 \\ \hline \end{array}$

10. 36 × 67

11. 44 × 92

12. 70 × 38

13. 21 × 43

14. 60 × 46

15. 25 × 34

16. 57 × 96

17. 46 × 19

18. 15 × 35

19. 13 × 98

20. 29 × 68

Denise made a list of items in the storeroom.
Help her find the totals.

	Store Inventory		
	Item		Total number
1.	Eggs	63 cartons 12 eggs per carton	
2.	Cola	78 cases 64 bottles per case	
3.	Tomato soup	42 cases 24 cans per case	
4.	Candy bars	9 boxes 48 bars per box	
5.	Pickles	21 cases 18 jars per case	

Multiply.

6. 96×21

7. 35×7

8. 42×34

9. 81×75

10. 67×70

11. 93×5

12. 472×8

13. 59×46

14. 3×37

15. 6×37

16. 9×37

17. 12×37

18. 15×37

19. 18×37

20. 21×37

21. 24×37

22. 27×37

23. 12×99

24. 23×99

25. 34×99

26. 45×99

27. 56×99

28. 67×99

29. 78×99

30. 89×99

More practice
Set K, page 63

The square at the right is a multiplication magic square. The product of the numbers in each row, each column, and each diagonal is the same number.

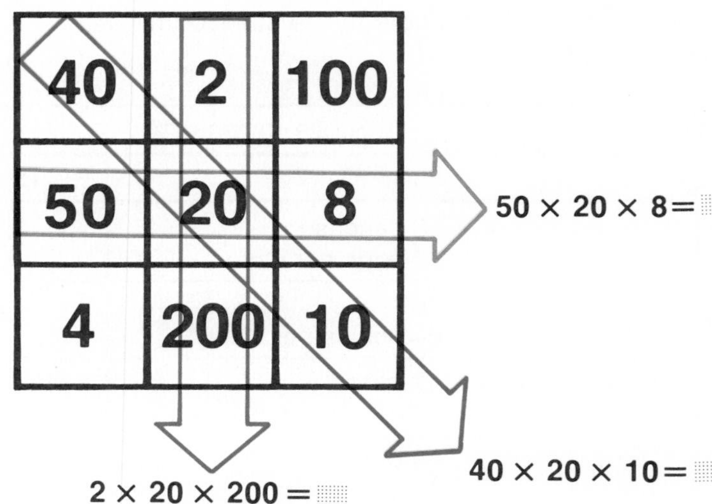

1. What is the "magic product" for this magic square?

Tell whether each square is a multiplication magic square. If it is, give the magic product.

2.

2	36	3
9	6	4
12	1	18

3.

24	18	4
2	12	72
36	8	3

4.

2	25	20
100	10	1
5	4	50

Multiply to find the number for each box.

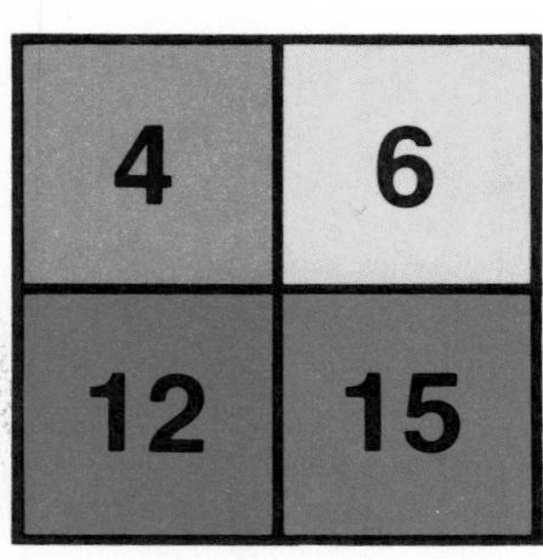

Here's how

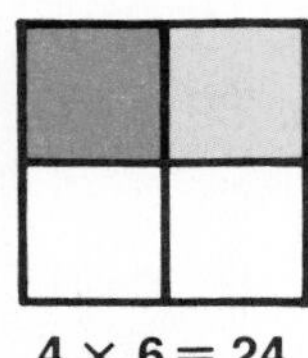

4 × 6 = 24

4 × 6 × 15 = 360

5. 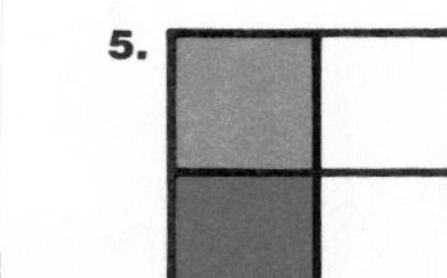

6. 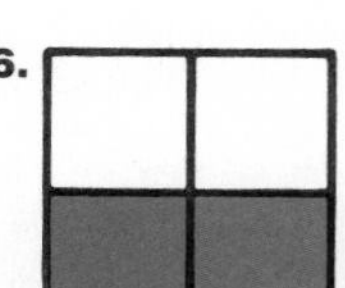

7. 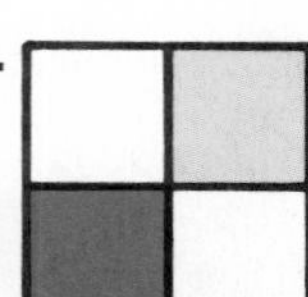

8. 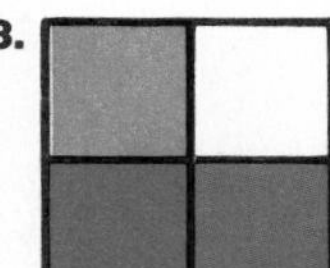

9. 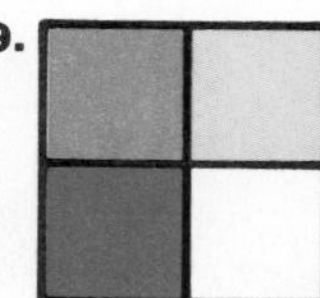

10. 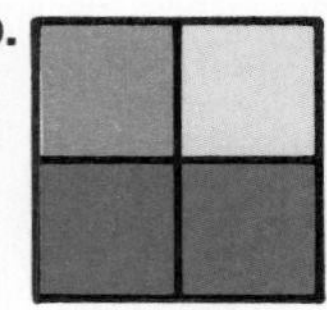

Using Multiplication: Food Consumption

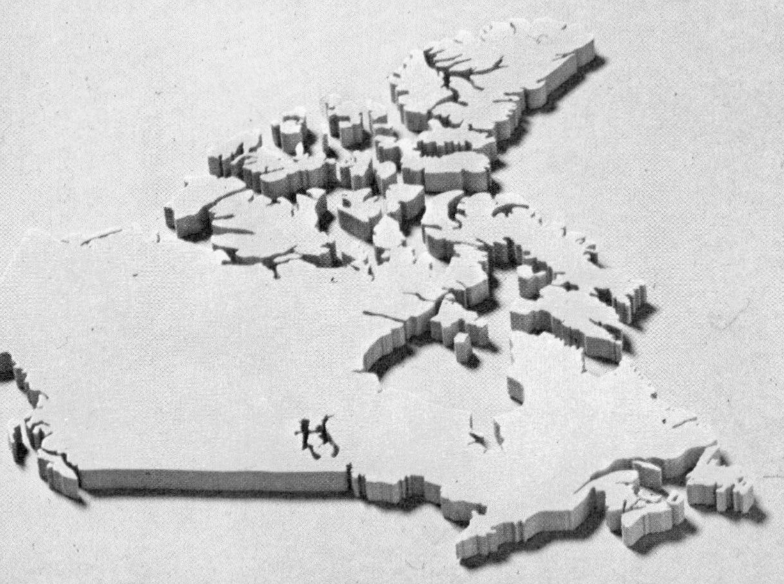

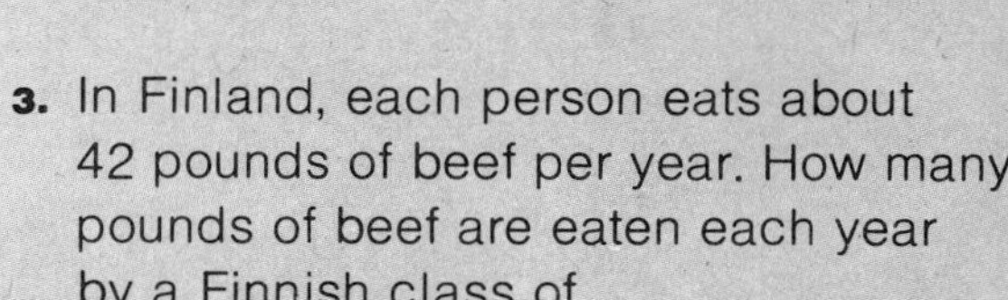

3. In Finland, each person eats about 42 pounds of beef per year. How many pounds of beef are eaten each year by a Finnish class of

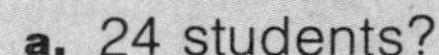

   a. 24 students? c. 33 students?
   b. 35 students? d. 28 students?

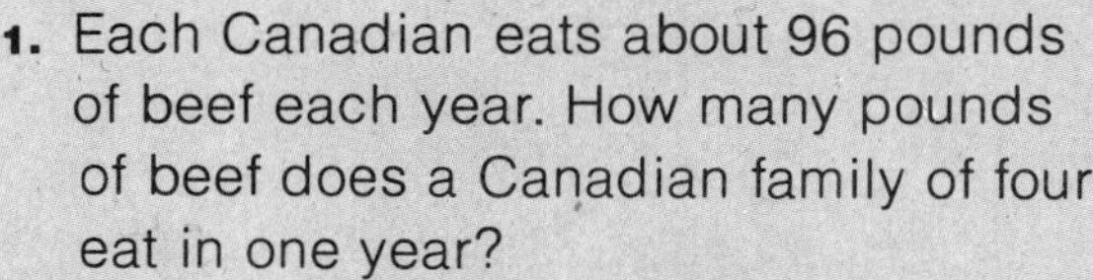

1. Each Canadian eats about 96 pounds of beef each year. How many pounds of beef does a Canadian family of four eat in one year?

4. Each Australian eats about 89 pounds of lamb and goat per year. How many pounds of lamb and goat does an Australian eat in

   a. 11 years? d. 50 years?
   b. 18 years? e. 72 years?
   c. 25 years?

2. In the United States, a family of four eats about 260 pounds of pork each year. How many pounds of pork are eaten each year by

   a. 20 families of four? c. 78 families of four?
   b. 35 families of four?

Multiplying a Three-digit Number by a Two-digit Number

You can find 37 × 526 in two steps.

$$\begin{array}{r l} 526 & \\ \times\ 37 & (30 + 7) \\ \hline 3682 & 7 \times 526 \\ 15780 & 30 \times 526 \\ \hline 19462 & 3682 + 15780 \end{array}$$

Give each product.

1. $\begin{array}{r} 427 \\ \times\ 8 \\ \hline \end{array}$

2. $\begin{array}{r} 427 \\ \times\ 30 \\ \hline \end{array}$

3. $\begin{array}{r} 427 \\ \times\ 38 \\ \hline \end{array}$

4. $\begin{array}{r} 249 \\ \times\ 3 \\ \hline \end{array}$

5. $\begin{array}{r} 249 \\ \times\ 50 \\ \hline \end{array}$

6. $\begin{array}{r} 249 \\ \times\ 53 \\ \hline \end{array}$

7. $\begin{array}{r} 191 \\ \times\ 43 \\ \hline \end{array}$

8. $\begin{array}{r} 628 \\ \times\ 45 \\ \hline \end{array}$

9. $\begin{array}{r} 193 \\ \times\ 75 \\ \hline \end{array}$

10. $\begin{array}{r} 403 \\ \times\ 68 \\ \hline \end{array}$

11. $\begin{array}{r} 374 \\ \times\ 87 \\ \hline \end{array}$

12. $\begin{array}{r} 395 \\ \times\ 64 \\ \hline \end{array}$

13. 17 × 125
14. 35 × 111
15. 64 × 523
16. 63 × 307
17. 42 × 758
18. 38 × 926
19. 49 × 470
20. 62 × 990

21. Justin has filled 40 pages of his stamp book.
Each page has 32 stamps.
How many stamps does he have?

22. Andrea has filled 37 pages of her stamp book.
Each page has 34 stamps.
How many stamps does she have?

23. Who has more stamps, Justin or Andrea?
How many more?

More practice
Set L, page 63
Set M, page 63

Multiplying a Three-digit Number by a Three-digit Number

A. Find 236 × 412.

```
   412   (200 + 30 + 6)
 × 236
  2472   6 × 412
 12360   30 × 412
 82400   200 × 412
 97232
```

B. Find 207 × 436.

```
   436   (200 + 7)
 × 207
  3052   7 × 436
 87200   200 × 436
 90252
```

C. Find 730 × 612.

```
    612   (700 + 30)
  × 730
  18360   30 × 612
 428400   700 × 612
 446760
```

Multiply.

1. 763 × 5
2. 763 × 40
3. 763 × 200
4. 763 × 245
5. 271 × 9
6. 271 × 800
7. 271 × 809
8. 444 × 152
9. 461 × 123
10. 842 × 530
11. 675 × 285
12. 919 × 304
13. 281 × 456
14. 164 × 993
15. 352 × 461
16. 455 × 732
17. 203 × 275
18. 608 × 777
19. 250 × 823
20. 470 × 987

Multiply.

21.
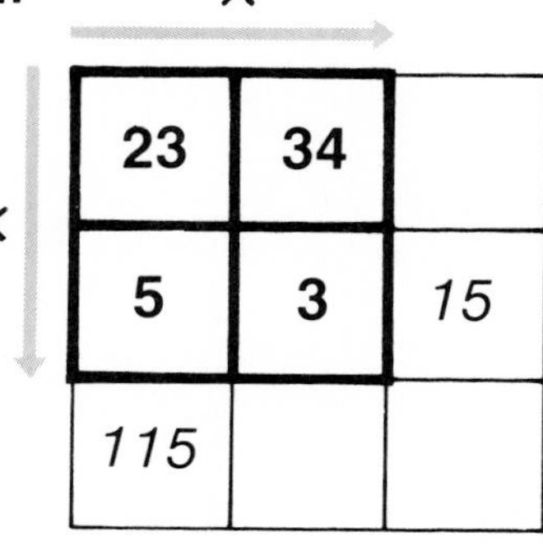

22.
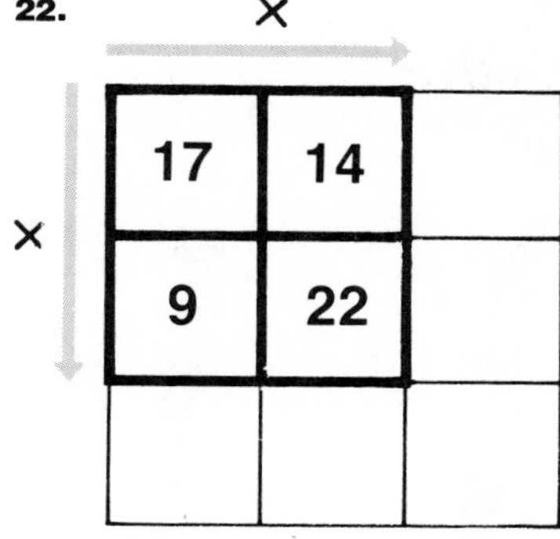

23.
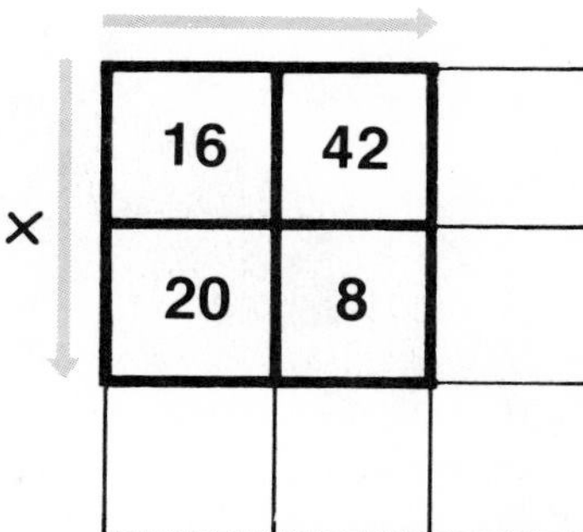

More practice
Set N, page 63

Estimating Products

Jack wonders about how many people are sitting in section A of the hockey stadium.

About the same number of people are sitting in each row. Jack counts 33 people in one row, and 18 rows of seats. Then he estimates the product 18 × 33.

$$18 \times 33$$

He rounds each number. ↓ ↓

$$20 \times 30$$

He multiplies the rounded numbers.

$$20 \times 30 = 600$$

There are about 600 people in section A.

■ *You can estimate products when you don't need an exact answer.*

Estimate how many people are in each section.

1. Section B:
   18 rows
   23 people
   in one row

2. Section C:
   24 rows
   27 people
   in one row

3. Section D:
   21 rows
   12 people
   in one row

4. Section E:
   17 rows
   32 people
   in one row

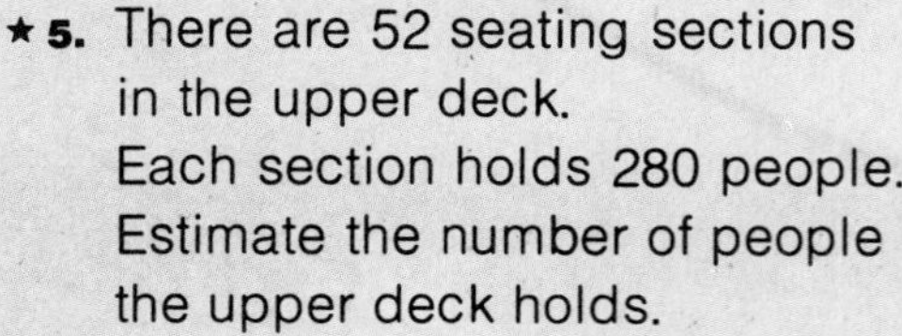

★5. There are 52 seating sections in the upper deck.
Each section holds 280 people.
Estimate the number of people the upper deck holds.

Estimate each product.

6. One hot-dog vendor sold 18 trays of hot dogs. There were 32 hot dogs on each tray. About how many hot dogs did he sell?

7. An usherette sold 34 packages of programs. Each package contained 45 programs. About how many programs did she sell?

8. An ice-cream vendor sold 33 boxes of ice-cream bars. Each box held 25 bars. About how many ice-cream bars did he sell?

9. A vendor sold 47 boxes of hockey buttons. There were 50 buttons in each box. About how many buttons did she sell?

10. Another vendor sold 51 batches of pennants. Each batch consisted of 36 pennants. About how many pennants did she sell?

■ *You can estimate products to see if your answers are sensible.*

	Estimate.	Compute.
88 × 31	**90** **× 30** **2700**	88 × 31 88 2640 2728

Give an estimate of the product. Then give the actual product.

11.	62 × 35	**16.**	78 × 22
12.	76 × 49	**17.**	971 × 770
13.	92 × 83	**18.**	649 × 350
14.	99 × 88	**19.**	932 × 765
15.	98 × 57	**20.**	673 × 428

Order and Grouping in Multiplication

Give each product.

1. $40 \times 90 =$ ▒
   $90 \times 40 =$ ▒
2. $30 \times 47 =$ ▒
   $47 \times 30 =$ ▒
3. $76 \times 94 =$ ▒
   $94 \times 76 =$ ▒
4. Is the product 32×65
   the same as
   the product 65×32?

Look for an easy way to
find each missing product.

5. $676 \times 423 = 285{,}948$
   $423 \times 676 =$ ▒
6. $28 \times 63 = 1764$
   $63 \times 28 =$ ▒
7. $391 \times 45 = 17{,}595$
   $45 \times 391 =$ ▒
8. $78 \times 536 = 41{,}808$
   $536 \times 78 =$ ▒

■ *When you multiply, you can change the order of the numbers and get the same product.*

$$6 \times 12 = 72$$
$$12 \times 6 = 72$$

Give each product. Multiply the numbers in parentheses first.

Here's how $(3 \times 4) \times 5$

9. $(4 \times 5) \times 17 =$ ▒
   $4 \times (5 \times 17) =$ ▒
10. $12 \times (5 \times 30) =$ ▒
    $(12 \times 5) \times 30 =$ ▒
11. $(36 \times 15) \times 4 =$ ▒
    $36 \times (15 \times 4) =$ ▒
12. Is the product $(5 \times 27) \times 18$
    the same as
    the product $5 \times (27 \times 18)$?

Look for an easy way to
find each missing product.

13. $(13 \times 7) \times 90 = 8190$
    $13 \times (7 \times 90) =$ ▒
14. $2 \times (3 \times 178) = 1068$
    $(2 \times 3) \times 178 =$ ▒
15. $(16 \times 5) \times 170 = 13{,}600$
    $16 \times (5 \times 170) =$ ▒

■ *When you multiply, you can change the grouping and get the same product.*

$$(17 \times 4) \times 9 = 612$$
$$17 \times (4 \times 9) = 612$$

Find the products below in an easy way.

16. $2 \times 426 \times 5$
$(2 \times 5) \times 426$
10×426

17. $25 \times 4 \times 328$
$(25 \times 4) \times 328$
100×328

18. $5 \times 84 \times 20$
$84 \times (5 \times 20)$
84×100

19. $247 \times 50 \times 2$
$247 \times (50 \times 2)$

20. $8 \times 173 \times 125$
$(8 \times 125) \times 173$

21. $10 \times 396 \times 10$
$396 \times (10 \times 10)$

22. $5 \times 97 \times 2$

23. $4 \times 81 \times 25$

24. $736 \times 2 \times 5$

25. $20 \times 425 \times 5$

26. $50 \times 984 \times 2$

27. $50 \times 20 \times 73$

28. $20 \times 67 \times 30$

29. $5 \times 40 \times 436$

30. $40 \times 896 \times 25$

Explore

Fill a glass jar with beans.

Ask several people to guess how many beans are in the jar.

Make your own guess. (Do not count the beans one by one.)

How can you use these methods to get the answer?

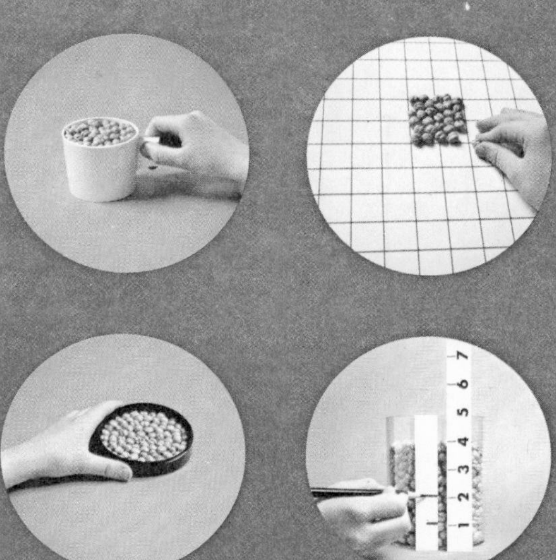

SIDE TRIP

Using Multiplication to Find Sums

Add these numbers: $1 + 2 + 3 + 4 + 5 + 6 + 7 + 8 + 9 + 10$

Here is a quicker way to find the answer.
Pair the numbers so that all pairs have the same sum.

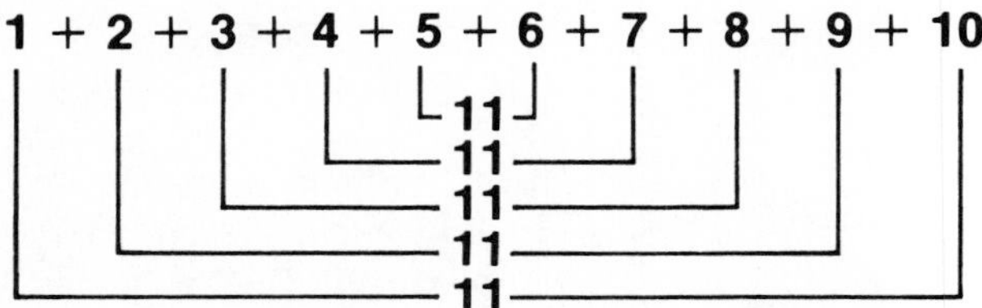

Now you can add: $11 + 11 + 11 + 11 + 11 = 55$

Or you can multiply: $5 \times 11 = 55$

Was 55 your answer when you added the numbers 1 through 10?

Find each sum.
Look for a pattern that will help you.

1. **1 + 3 + 5 + 7 + 9 + 11 + 13 + 15**

   16
   16
   16
   16

   $4 \times 16 =$ ____

2. $2 + 4 + 6 + 8 + 10 + 12 + 14 + 16 + 18 + 20$

3. $8 + 12 + 16 + 20 + 24 + 28$

4. $3 + 6 + 9 + 12 + 15 + 18 + 21 + 24 + 27 + 30 + 33 + 36 + 39 + 42$

★ 5. $20 + 28 + 36 + 44 + 52 + 60 + 68$

Check Yourself
Multiplying Whole Numbers, Pages 30-50

Multiplication basic facts, pages 30-31

1. $7 \times 9 = \square$

2. $6 \times 8 = \square$

3. Give the least common multiple of 9 and 6.

Multiplying, pages 32-49

Give each product.

4. 6×100

5. 37×1000

6. 100×1000

7. 60×700

8. 78×6

9. 94×3

10. 743×5

11. 362×8

12. 64×30

13. 87×36

14. 53×84

15. 26×374

16. 45×806

17. 458×317

18. 302×679

19. Write the problem below that has the same product as

$498 \times 64 = 31{,}872.$

498×46 64×498
64×489 68×496

20. Write the problems below that have the same product as

$47 \times (23 \times 19) = 20{,}539.$

$(47 \times 23) \times 19$ $23 \times (47 \times 19)$
$47 \times (19 \times 23)$ $(23 \times 49) \times 17$

Problem solving, pages 35, 43, 46-47

21. There are 40 nickels in one roll. How many nickels are in 300 rolls?

22. There are 24 hours in a day. How many hours in 7 days?

23. There are 60 minutes in one hour. How many minutes in 24 hours?

24. Estimate the total number of seats.

58 rows
71 seats in each row

Polygons, Perimeter, and Area, Pages 52–60

Meters and Kilometers

This string is about one ***meter*** long.
You can write "1 m" to mean one meter.

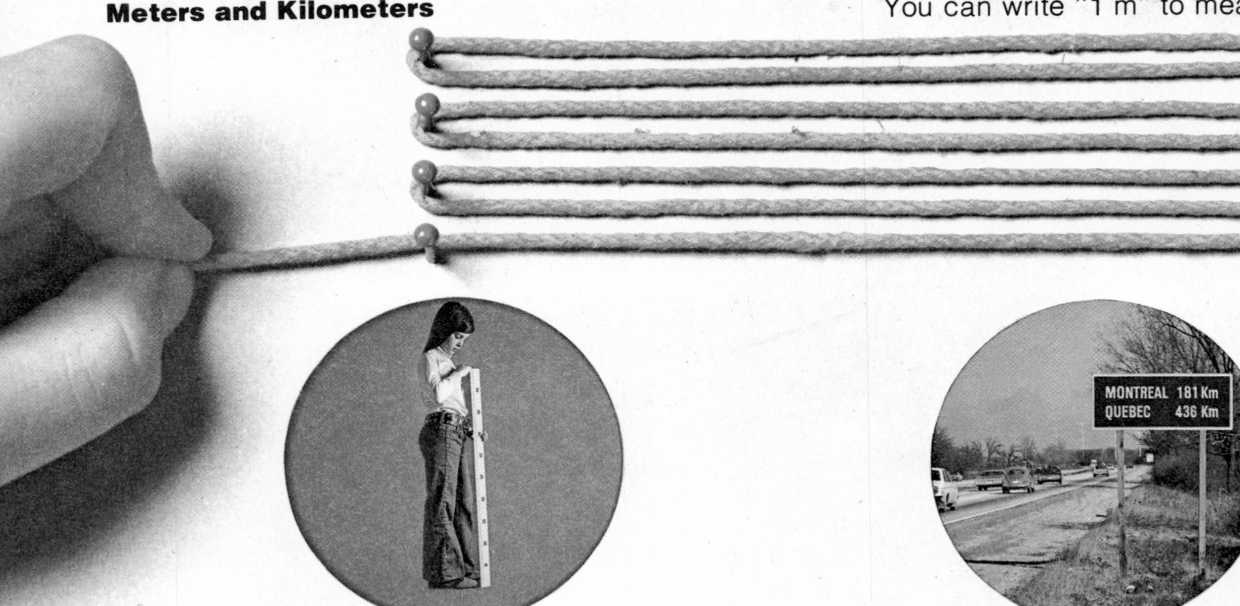

Most students are between one and two meters tall.

Name some things that measure about one meter.

A ***kilometer*** is 1000 meters.
You can write "1 km" to mean one kilometer.

It takes about twelve minutes to walk a distance of one kilometer.

About how many meters is

1. the length of your teacher's desk?

2. the height of the windows?

3. the length of the chalkboard?

4. the height of the door?

5. the width of the classroom?

Which would you use,
meters or kilometers, to measure

6. the distance from your home to school?

7. the length of a bus?

8. the height of the school building?

9. the distance from New York to Chicago?

10. the width of the street?

Centimeters

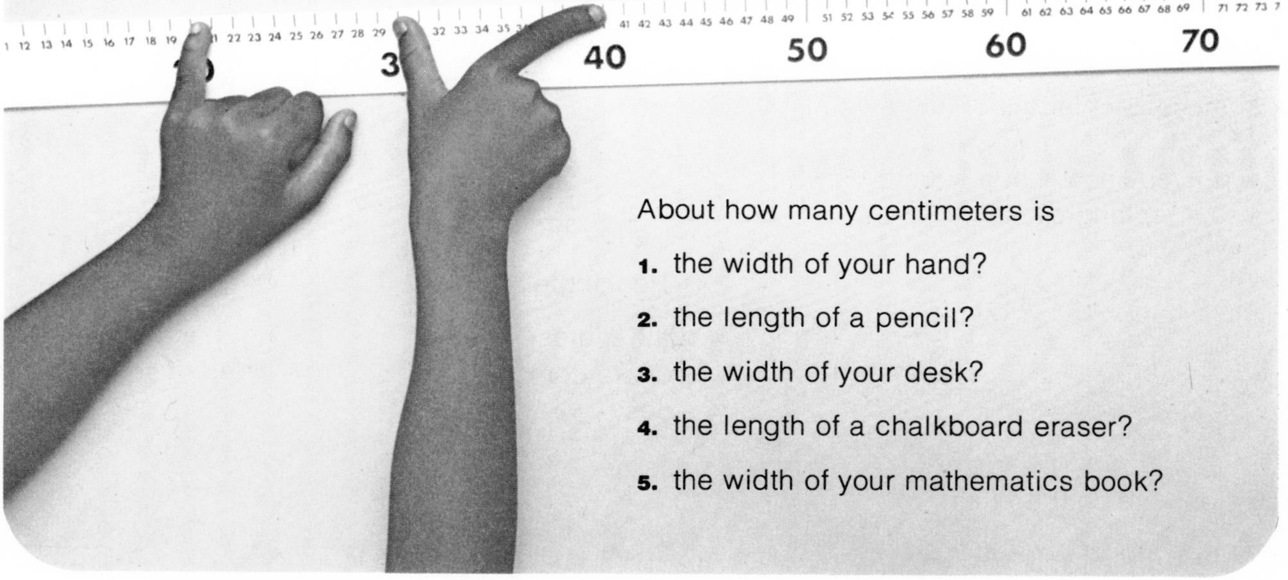

A meter is divided into 100 ***centimeters.***
You can write "1 cm" to mean one centimeter.

Your little finger is about one centimeter wide.

Your thumb and forefinger in this position are about 10 centimeters apart.

About how many centimeters is

1. the width of your hand?
2. the length of a pencil?
3. the width of your desk?
4. the length of a chalkboard eraser?
5. the width of your mathematics book?

Give the length of each object to the nearest centimeter.

6.

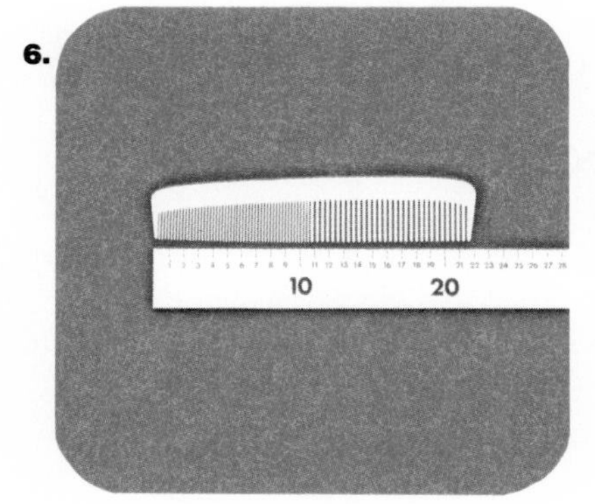

7.

8.

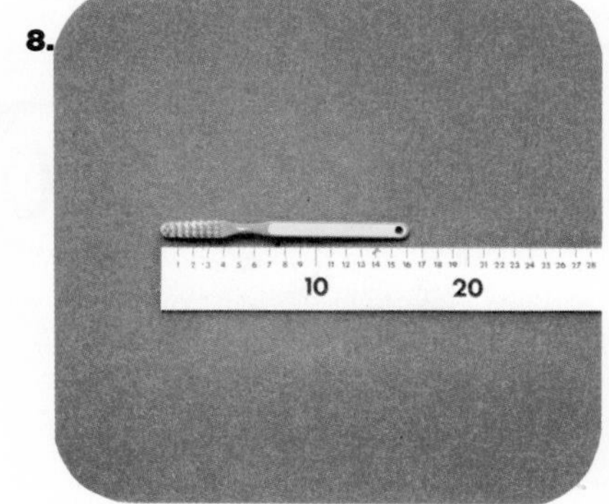

centimeters
ACTUAL SIZE

Polygons

1. ***Polygons*** are made up of straight sides. Count the sides.

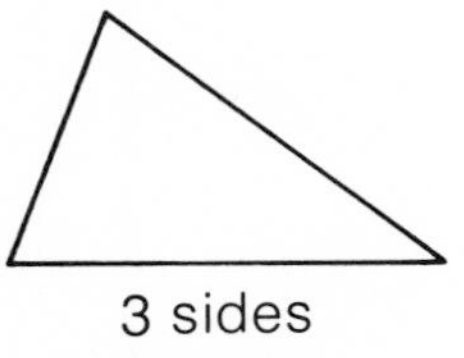

3 sides
Triangle

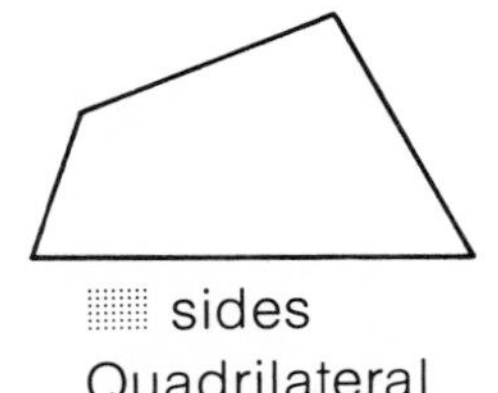

___ sides
Quadrilateral

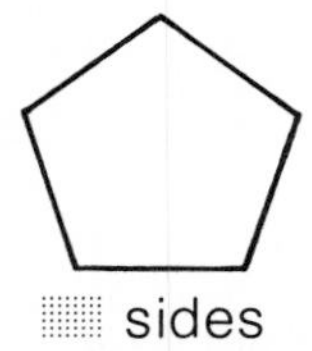

___ sides
Pentagon

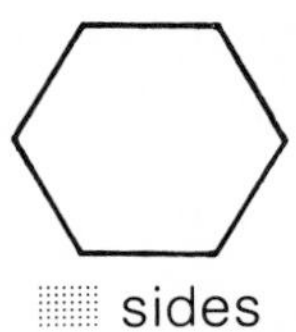

___ sides
Hexagon

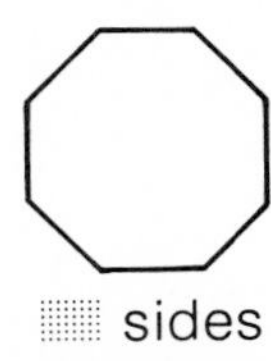

___ sides
Octagon

Look at these special quadrilaterals.

2. How do you know that a square is also a rectangle?

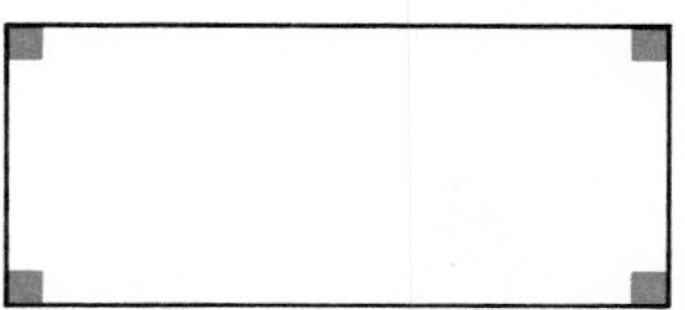

Rectangle

4 right angles
(square corners)
4 sides

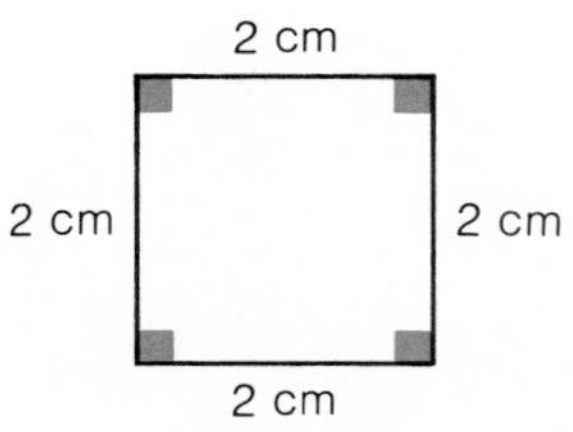

Square

4 right angles
4 sides of equal length

Which signs are shaped like

3. triangles?

4. rectangles?

5. squares?

6. pentagons?

7. hexagons?

8. octagons?

A
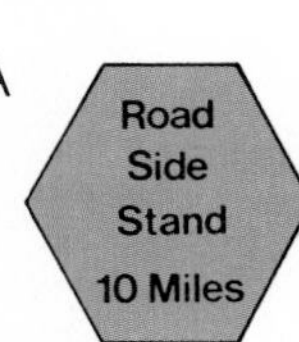

B
STOP

C

D

E

F

G
YIELD

H

I
END
CONSTRUCTION

Perimeter of a Polygon

When you add the lengths of the sides of a polygon, you find the distance around the polygon.

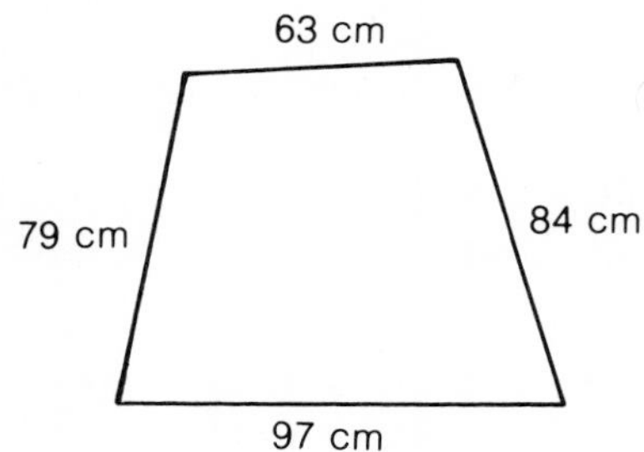

79 + 63 + 84 + 97 = ▒

The distance around is ▒ centimeters.

The distance around a polygon is called the ***perimeter***.

Find the perimeters.

1.

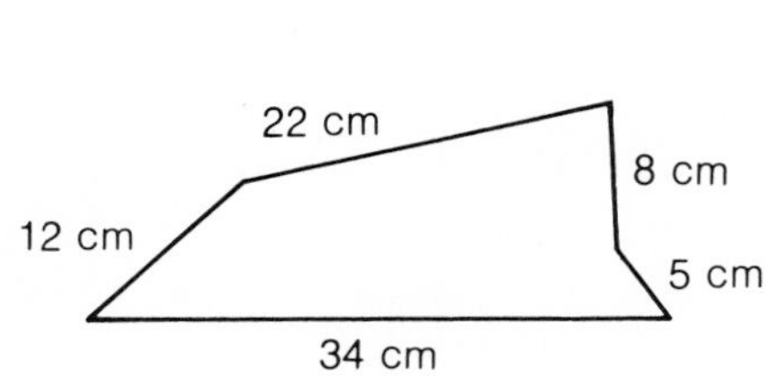

2.

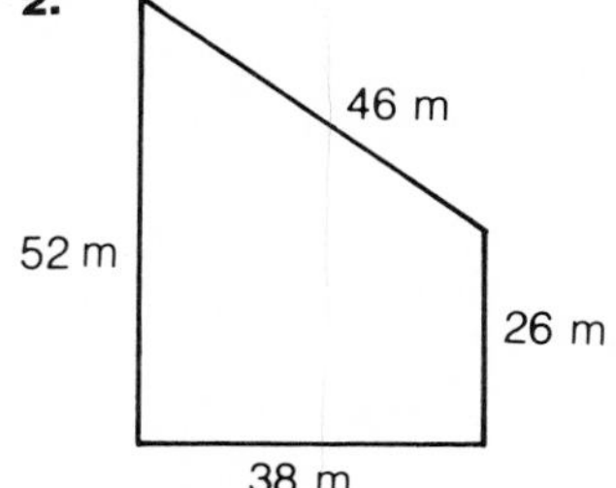

3.

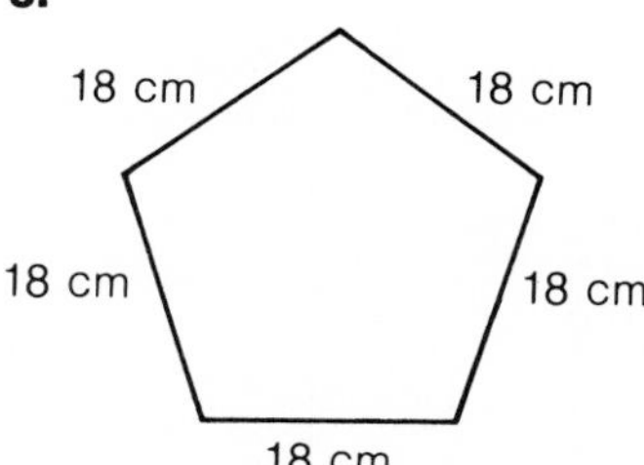

The perimeter of each polygon is given.
Find the missing length.

4. Perimeter: 96 centimeters

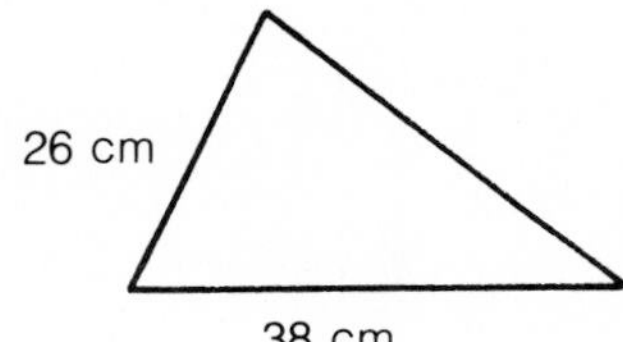

5. Perimeter: 112 meters

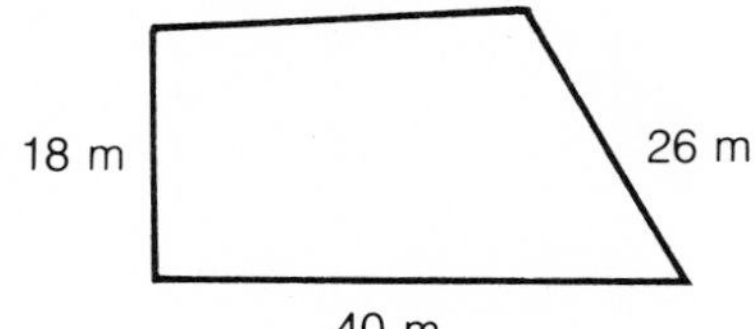

6. Perimeter: 36 kilometers

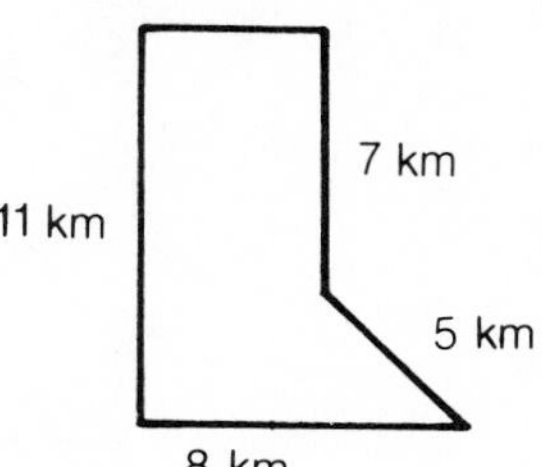

Counting Squares to Find Area

Each square on the grid is 1 ***square centimeter.***

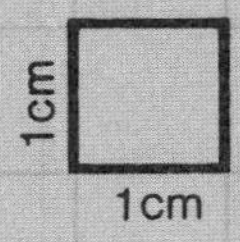

1 square centimeter
1 cm²

1cm

1cm

How many squares in the rectangle?

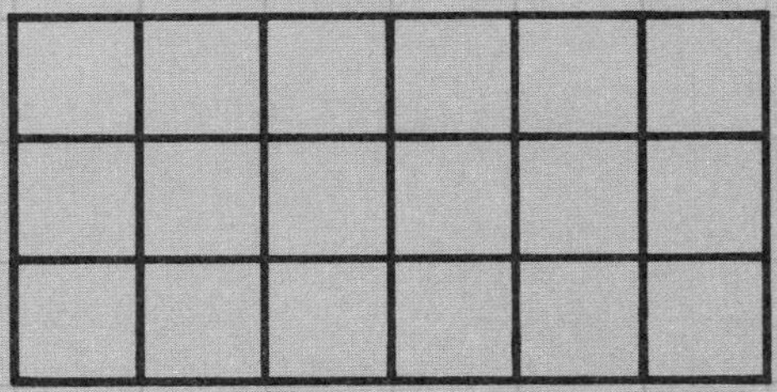

The ***area*** of the rectangle is 18 square centimeters (18 cm²).

Count the squares in these figures. Give each area in square centimeters.

1.

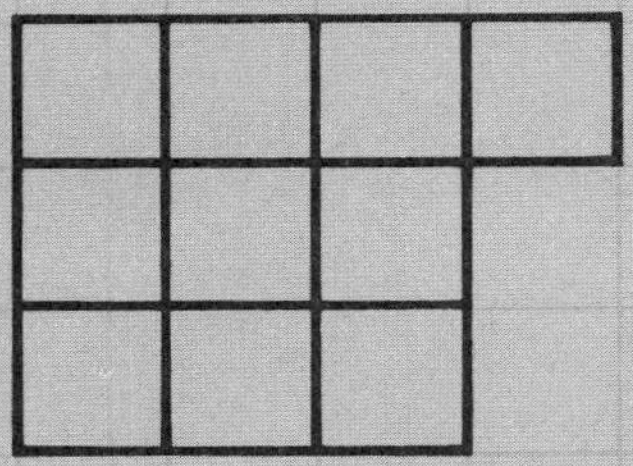

2.

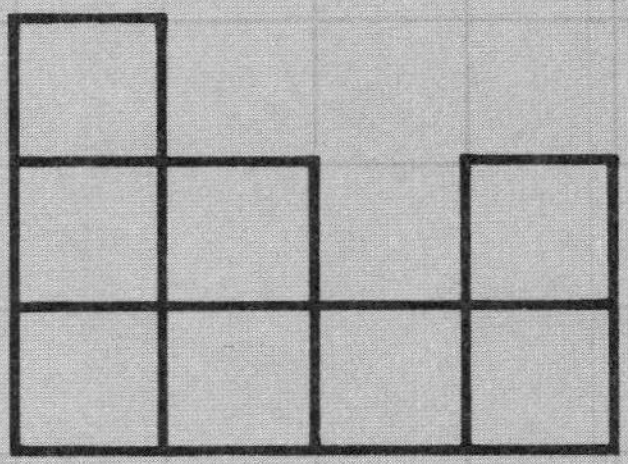

3.

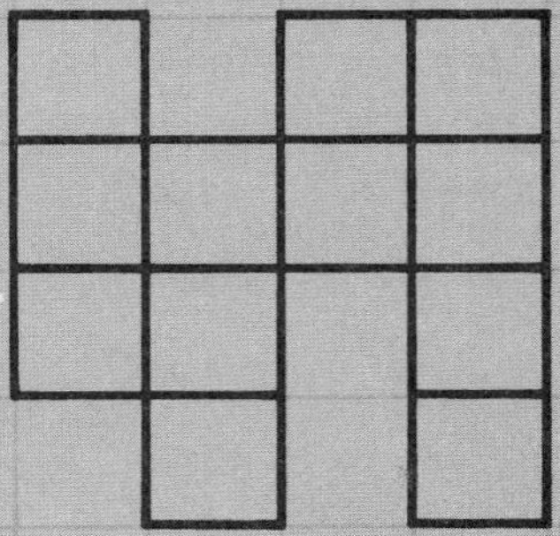

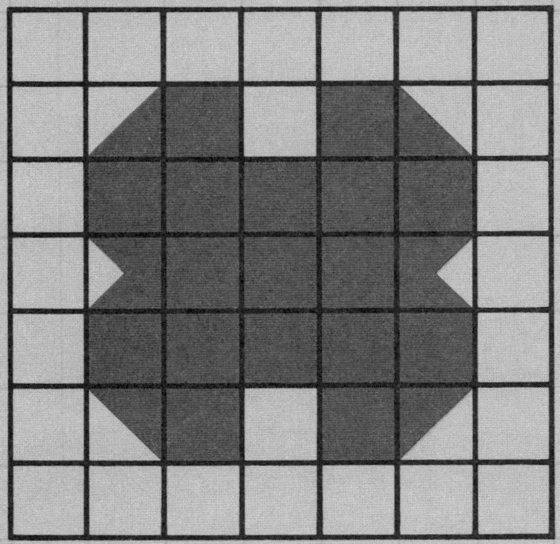

4. How many completely shaded squares?

5. How many partly shaded squares?

6. Add these numbers to get the total.

The shaded design covers more than 17 squares, but fewer than 23 squares.

7. The area of this design is more than ▒ cm² but less than ▒ cm².

Here are some designs that students drew on grid paper.
Each square represents 1 square centimeter.

Describe the area of each shaded design.

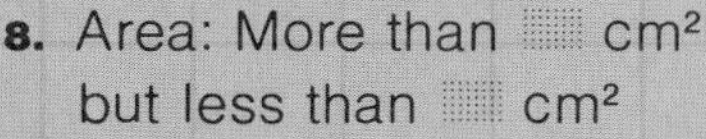

8. Area: More than ▒ cm^2
but less than ▒ cm^2

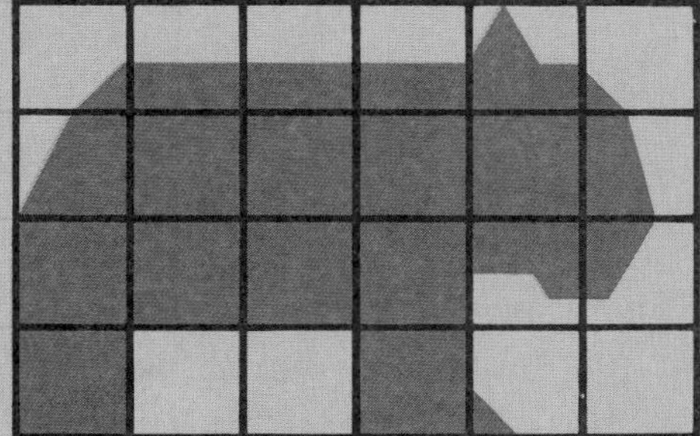

9. Area: More than ▒ cm^2
but less than ▒ cm^2

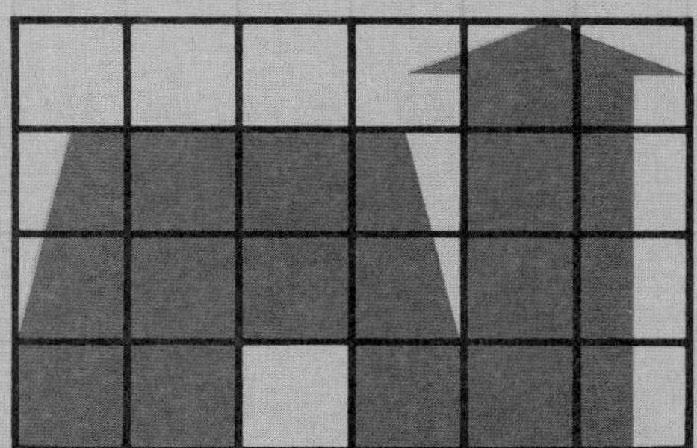

10. Count the square inches to find the area of the palm side of the hand.
The area is more than ▒ sq. in.
and less than ▒ sq. in.

11. Make a grid like this.
Trace around your hand and find its area.
The area is more than ▒ sq. in.
and less than ▒ sq. in.

12. Multiply the area of the bottom surface of your hand by 100. This gives you an estimate of the total area of your skin.
The area of your skin is more than ▒ sq. in.
and less than ▒ sq. in.

Area of a Rectangle

1. 4 rows of squares

7 squares in each row
Area: ____

2. ____ rows

____ squares in each row
Area: ____

3. ____ rows

____ squares in each row
Area: ____

4. ____ rows

____ squares in each row
Area: ____

5. How could you find these areas without counting every square?

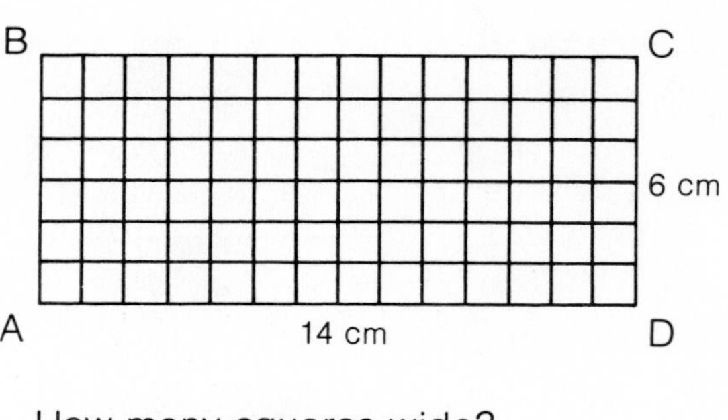

How many squares wide?

How many squares long?

The width tells you:
6 rows of squares

The length tells you:
____ squares in each row

Multiply $6 \times$ ____ to find the area of rectangle ABCD.

Area: ____ cm^2

Find these areas by multiplying.

6. A rectangle that is 15 centimeters long and 5 centimeters wide

7. A square whose sides each measure 7 meters

8. A rectangle that is 26 meters wide and 43 meters long

Find the area of each rectangle.
Multiply.

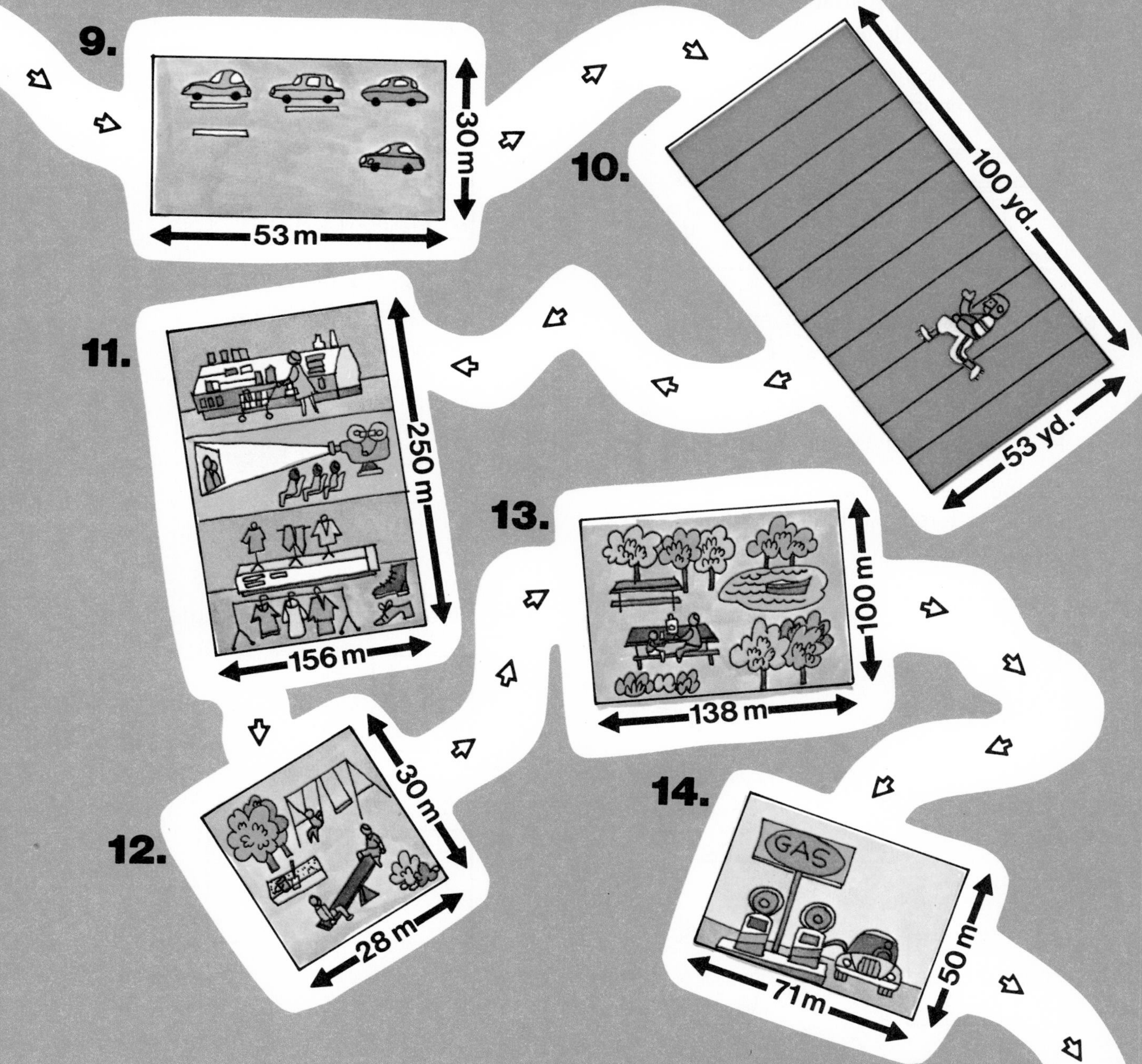

Check Yourself
Polygons, Perimeter, and Area, Pages 52–59

Metric units, pages 52–53

1. Which would you use, meters or kilometers, to give the length of an automobile?

2. Give the length to the nearest centimeter.

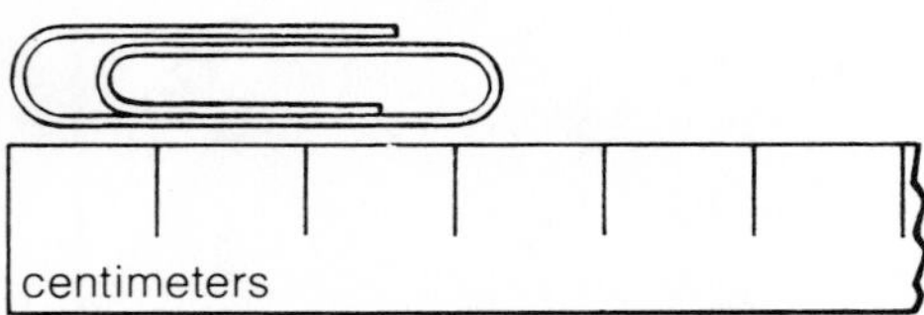

Polygons and perimeter, pages 54–55

3. Which figure below is a square?

4. Which figure is a pentagon?

5. Find the perimeter of figure B.

6. The perimeter of triangle C is 101 meters. Find the missing length.

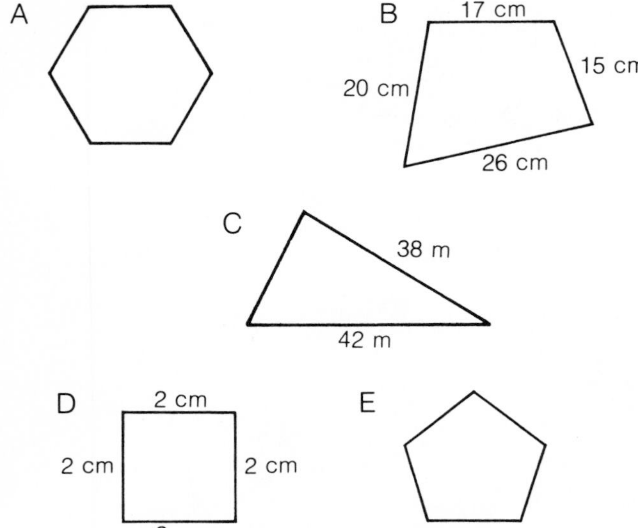

Area, pages 56–59

7. Find the area of this figure. Each square represents 1 square centimeter.

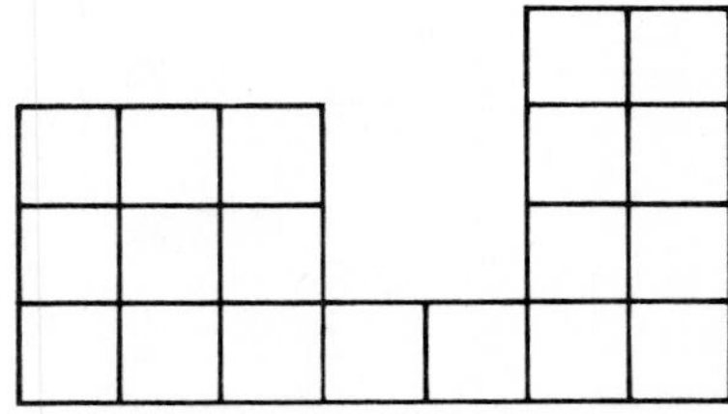

8. The area of this shaded design is more than ____ cm² but less than ____ cm².

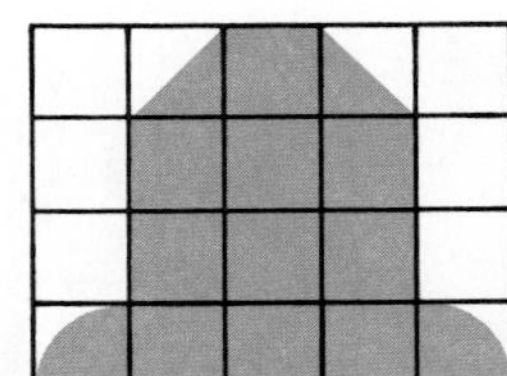

Find the area of each rectangle below.

9.

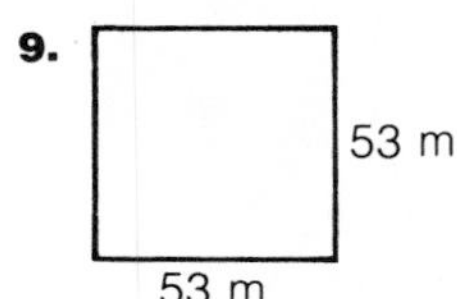

10.

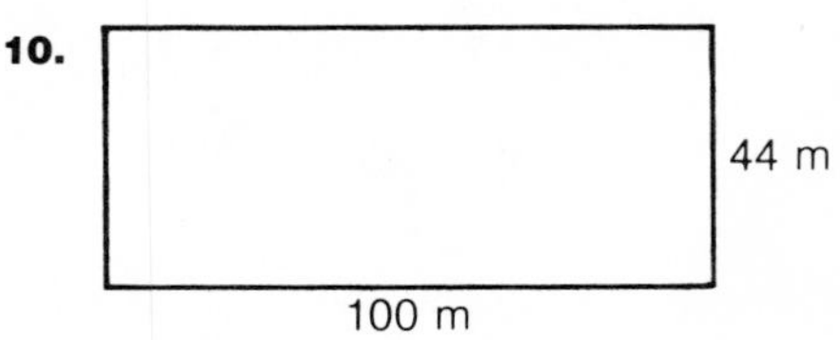

Check Yourself: Level 25

Numeration, pages 4–7

1. Which number has 5 in the thousands place?

   53,400 45,300 50,529

2. Give the standard numeral.

   225 million 463 thousand 129

Adding, pages 8–15

Add.

3. $\begin{array}{r} 87 \\ +\ 36 \\ \hline \end{array}$

4. 759 + 584

5. 65 + 317 + 49

6. Round 496 to the nearest hundred.

7. Estimate the sum 69 + 22.

8. How far is it from Park City to Dover?

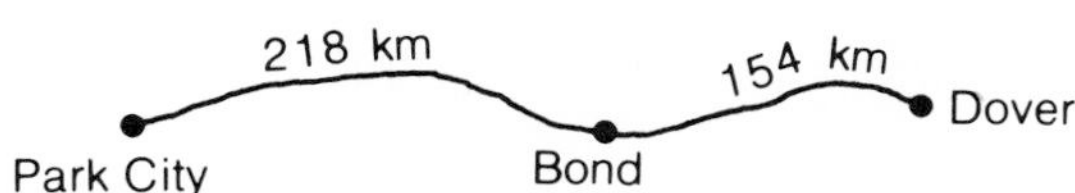

Subtracting, pages 16–27

Subtract.

9. $\begin{array}{r} 62 \\ -\ 18 \\ \hline \end{array}$

10. $\begin{array}{r} 854 \\ -\ 379 \\ \hline \end{array}$

11. $\begin{array}{r} 603 \\ -\ 375 \\ \hline \end{array}$

12. 635 − 79

13. 7003 − 564

14. The elephant is how much taller than the lion?

15. Find the number for *n*.

    $37 + n = 63$

16. Joe had 29 old coins. He bought more coins and now he has 54 in all. How many coins did he buy?

Multiplying, pages 30–47

17. Estimate the product 38 × 72.

Multiply.

18. $\begin{array}{r} 65 \\ \times\ 7 \\ \hline \end{array}$

19. 6 × 78

20. $\begin{array}{r} 549 \\ \times\ 5 \\ \hline \end{array}$

21. $\begin{array}{r} 68 \\ \times\ 47 \\ \hline \end{array}$

22. $\begin{array}{r} 716 \\ \times\ 58 \\ \hline \end{array}$

23. 45 × 849

24. 504 × 367

25. 14 girls made candy.
    Each girl made 24 pieces.
    How many pieces did they make in all?

Polygons, perimeter, area, pages 52–59

26. Give the length to the nearest centimeter.

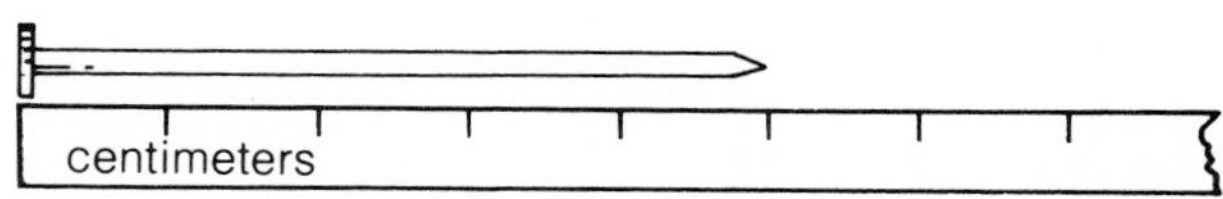

27. Give the perimeter.

28. Give the area.

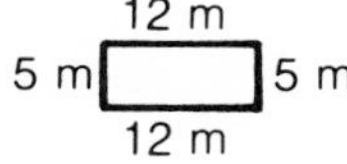

More Practice

Set A

1. $\begin{array}{r} 55 \\ +\ 45 \\ \hline \end{array}$

2. $\begin{array}{r} 66 \\ +\ 45 \\ \hline \end{array}$

3. $\begin{array}{r} 78 \\ +\ 55 \\ \hline \end{array}$

4. $\begin{array}{r} 78 \\ +\ 66 \\ \hline \end{array}$

5. $\begin{array}{r} 87 \\ +\ 13 \\ \hline \end{array}$

6. $\begin{array}{r} 68 \\ +\ 32 \\ \hline \end{array}$

7. $\begin{array}{r} 128 \\ +\ 16 \\ \hline \end{array}$

8. $\begin{array}{r} 130 \\ +\ 14 \\ \hline \end{array}$

9. $\begin{array}{r} 25 \\ 93 \\ +\ 15 \\ \hline \end{array}$

10. $\begin{array}{r} 65 \\ 42 \\ +\ 48 \\ \hline \end{array}$

Set B

1. 122 + 78
2. 120 + 80
3. 75 + 46 + 83
4. 83 + 46 + 75
5. 98 + 98 + 98
6. 55 + 66 + 77
7. 43 + 23 + 89
8. 43 + 24 + 90
9. 67 + 45 + 33
10. 67 + 86 + 14

Set C

1. $\begin{array}{r} 256 \\ +\ 128 \\ \hline \end{array}$

2. $\begin{array}{r} 253 \\ +\ 271 \\ \hline \end{array}$

3. $\begin{array}{r} 885 \\ +\ 377 \\ \hline \end{array}$

4. $\begin{array}{r} 864 \\ +\ 469 \\ \hline \end{array}$

5. $\begin{array}{r} 875 \\ +\ 125 \\ \hline \end{array}$

6. $\begin{array}{r} 898 \\ 781 \\ +\ 298 \\ \hline \end{array}$

7. $\begin{array}{r} 888 \\ 702 \\ 399 \\ +\ 11 \\ \hline \end{array}$

8. 744 + 256
9. 618 + 284
10. 620 + 282
11. 858 + 647
12. 855 + 650
13. 424 + 166 + 333 + 77
14. 782 + 472 + 678 + 438 + 630

Set D

1. $\begin{array}{r} 64 \\ -\ 43 \\ \hline \end{array}$

2. $\begin{array}{r} 75 \\ -\ 57 \\ \hline \end{array}$

3. $\begin{array}{r} 70 \\ -\ 28 \\ \hline \end{array}$

4. $\begin{array}{r} 72 \\ -\ 30 \\ \hline \end{array}$

5. 60 − 27
6. 63 − 30
7. 81 − 45
8. 64 − 36
9. 50 − 18
10. 70 − 27
11. 61 − 16

Set E

1. $\begin{array}{r} 193 \\ -\ 76 \\ \hline \end{array}$

2. $\begin{array}{r} 437 \\ -\ 92 \\ \hline \end{array}$

3. $\begin{array}{r} 144 \\ -\ 66 \\ \hline \end{array}$

4. $\begin{array}{r} 150 \\ -\ 78 \\ \hline \end{array}$

5. 121 − 55
6. 144 − 66
7. 169 − 78
8. 196 − 91
9. 785 − 87
10. 788 − 90

Set F

1. $\begin{array}{r} 537 \\ -\ 219 \\ \hline \end{array}$

2. $\begin{array}{r} 209 \\ -\ 85 \\ \hline \end{array}$

3. $\begin{array}{r} 100 \\ -\ 65 \\ \hline \end{array}$

4. $\begin{array}{r} 707 \\ -\ 585 \\ \hline \end{array}$

5. $\begin{array}{r} 1300 \\ -\ 469 \\ \hline \end{array}$

6. $\begin{array}{r} 1000 \\ -\ 256 \\ \hline \end{array}$

More Practice

Set G

1. 537 − 219
2. 324 − 169
3. 225 − 144
4. 512 − 256
5. 100 − 71
6. 100 − 86
7. 506 − 28
8. 400 − 24
9. 1000 − 667
10. 1000 − 478

Set H

1. 10 × 100
2. 10 × 1000
3. 100 × 100
4. 100 × 1000
5. 6 × 70
6. 6 × 700
7. 6 × 7000
8. 50 × 30
9. 50 × 300
10. 50 × 3000

Set I

1. 25 × 5
2. 78 × 3
3. 64 × 8
4. 81 × 9
5. 256 × 6
6. 289 × 7
7. 512 × 8
8. 666 × 5

Set J

1. 25 × 50
2. 33 × 60
3. 49 × 70
4. 78 × 80
5. 91 × 30
6. 66 × 40
7. 75 × 50
8. 86 × 70
9. 27 × 90
10. 55 × 80

Set K

1. 23 × 15
2. 18 × 18
3. 66 × 44
4. 25 × 25
5. 72 × 16
6. 83 × 16
7. 35 × 55
8. 25 × 65
9. 38 × 74
10. 67 × 66

Set L

1. 169 × 13
2. 225 × 15
3. 256 × 16
4. 289 × 17
5. 324 × 18
6. 361 × 19
7. 512 × 32
8. 256 × 64
9. 144 × 48
10. 667 × 67

Set M

1. 324 × 36
2. 225 × 45
3. 518 × 48
4. 460 × 53
5. 707 × 47
6. 808 × 85
7. 684 × 92
8. 659 × 77
9. 987 × 65
10. 983 × 48

Set N

1. 512 × 333
2. 484 × 484
3. 506 × 267
4. 503 × 305
5. 640 × 512
6. 604 × 512
7. 700 × 370
8. 820 × 404
9. 250 × 400
10. 666 × 303

Check Yourself Answers: Level 25

Check Yourself, page 29

1. 14
2. 7
3. 7
4. 365
5. 25,578,296
6. 1098, 1102, 2279, 2287
7. 86
8. 1207
9. 552
10. 29
11. 736 + 254
12. 56 + (23 + 14)
    (23 + 56) + 14
    14 + (23 + 56)
13. 700
14. 80
15. 46
16. 478
17. 357
18. 67
19. 768
20. 347
21. 279 km
22. 56 in.
23. 46
24. 61 stamps

Check Yourself, page 51

1. 63
2. 48
3. 18
4. 600
5. 37,000
6. 100,000
7. 42,000
8. 468
9. 282
10. 3715
11. 2896
12. 1920
13. 3132
14. 4452
15. 9724
16. 36,270
17. 145,186
18. 205,058
19. 64×498
20. $(47 \times 23) \times 19$
    $47 \times (19 \times 23)$
    $23 \times (47 \times 19)$
21. 12,000 nickels
22. 168 hr.
23. 1440 min.
24. 4200 seats

Check Yourself, page 60

1. Meters
2. 3 cm
3. Figure D
4. Figure E
5. 78 cm
6. 21 m
7. 19 cm^2
8. More than 10 cm^2 but
   less than 14 cm^2
9. 2809 m^2
10. 4400 m^2

Check Yourself: Level 25, page 61

1. 45,300
2. 225,463,129
3. 123
4. 1343
5. 431
6. 500
7. 90
8. 372 km
9. 44
10. 475
11. 228
12. 556
13. 6439
14. 143 cm
15. 26
16. 25 coins
17. 2800
18. 455
19. 468
20. 2745
21. 3196
22. 41,528
23. 38,205
24. 184,968
25. 336 pieces
26. 5 cm
27. 34 m
28. 60 m^2

Level 26

Division Basic Facts

To solve the riddles, answer the exercises.
Then use your answers and the code keys to find the letters.

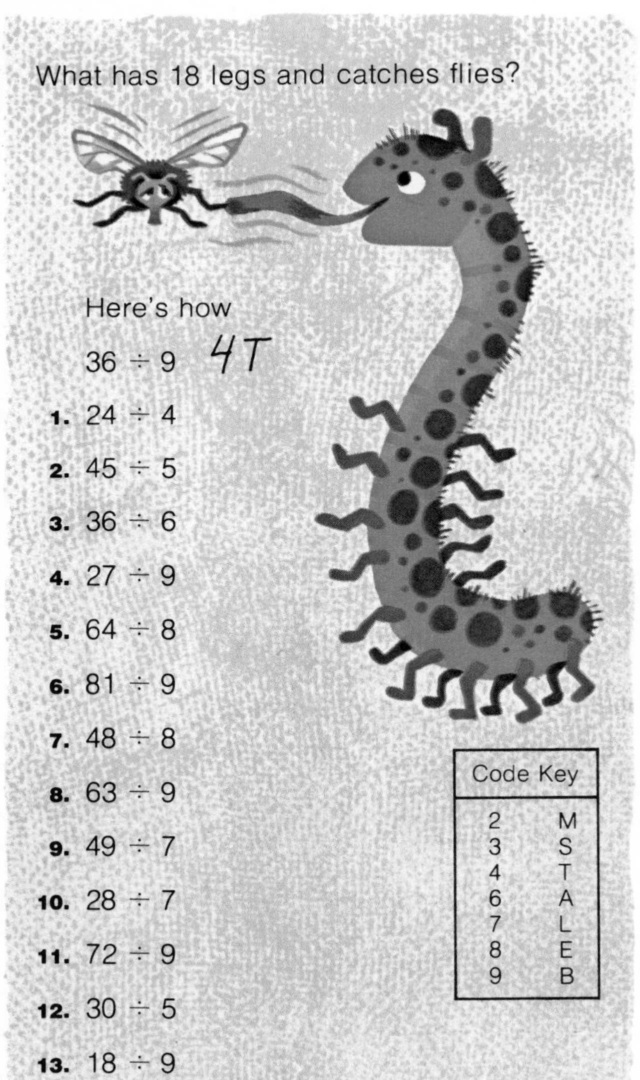

What has 18 legs and catches flies?

Here's how

36 ÷ 9   4T

1. 24 ÷ 4
2. 45 ÷ 5
3. 36 ÷ 6
4. 27 ÷ 9
5. 64 ÷ 8
6. 81 ÷ 9
7. 48 ÷ 8
8. 63 ÷ 9
9. 49 ÷ 7
10. 28 ÷ 7
11. 72 ÷ 9
12. 30 ÷ 5
13. 18 ÷ 9

Code Key	
2	M
3	S
4	T
6	A
7	L
8	E
9	B

If you saw a kidnapping in the park, what would you do?

1. 32 ÷ 4
2. 18 ÷ 2
3. 35 ÷ 7
4. 54 ÷ 9
5. 6 ÷ 6
6. 20 ÷ 5
7. 40 ÷ 5
8. 56 ÷ 8
9. 54 ÷ 6
10. 30 ÷ 6
11. 42 ÷ 7
12. 14 ÷ 7
13. 24 ÷ 8

Code Key	
1	H
2	U
3	P
4	I
5	K
6	E
7	W
8	M
9	A

Multiplication and division are related.

If you know: $6 \times 4 = 24$

you can write: $4 \times 6 = 24$
$24 \div 4 = 6$
$24 \div 6 = 4$

Complete the table.

	Multiplication equations		Division equations	
	$5 \times 7 = 35$	$7 \times 5 = \square$	$35 \div 5 = 7$	$35 \div 7 = \square$
1.	$3 \times 6 = 18$		$18 \div 3 = 6$	
2.		$3 \times 4 = 12$		
3.			$21 \div 7 = 3$	
4.	$7 \times 8 = 56$			
5.				$45 \div 9 = 5$
6.		$6 \times 8 = 48$		
7.			$16 \div 8 = 2$	
8.	$4 \times 7 = 28$			

Here is another way to write $35 \div 7 = 5$. $7\overline{)35}$ with quotient **5**

Give the missing numbers.

9. $6\overline{)12}$ **20.** $5\overline{)20}$

10. $4\overline{)16}$ **21.** $4\overline{)36}$

11. $2\overline{)10}$ **22.** $5\overline{)30}$

12. $9\overline{)27}$ **23.** $8\overline{)72}$

13. $8\overline{)40}$ **24.** $6\overline{)42}$

14. $4\overline{)24}$ **25.** $9\overline{)54}$

15. $3\overline{)27}$ **26.** $7\overline{)63}$

16. $5\overline{)15}$ **27.** $6\overline{)36}$

17. $4\overline{)32}$ **28.** $9\overline{)81}$

18. $3\overline{)15}$ **29.** $7\overline{)49}$

19. $3\overline{)24}$ **30.** $8\overline{)64}$

Division with Remainders

How many 4-inch frogs can sit on a 33-inch log?

Will there be any space left on the log?

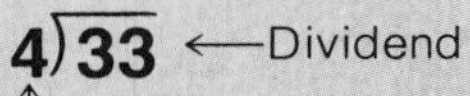

How many 4's in 33?

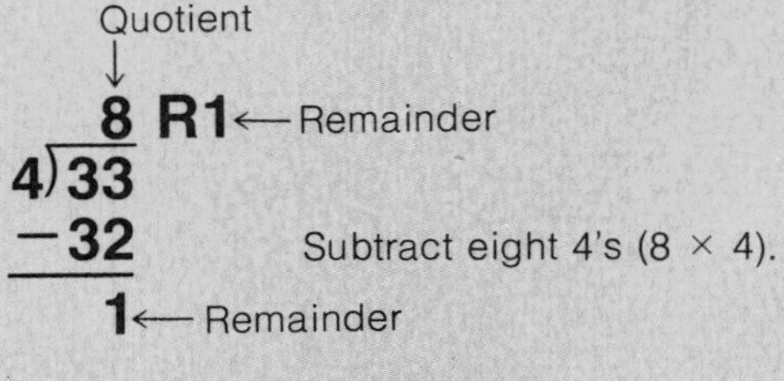

Subtract eight 4's (8 × 4).

There are eight 4's in 33.
The ***remainder*** is 1.

Eight frogs can sit on the log.
One inch of space is left over.

Divide. Give the quotient and the remainder.

1. 8)27 **5.** 3)29 **9.** 8)67

2. 3)22 **6.** 5)39 **10.** 7)43

3. 5)42 **7.** 9)57 **11.** 7)46

4. 6)33 **8.** 7)41 **12.** 9)65

Give only the remainder.

13. 4)25 **17.** 4)29

14. 4)26 **18.** 4)30

15. 4)27 **19.** 4)31

16. 4)28 **20.** 4)32

More practice
Set A, page 126

The frog starts at 0 and hops around the circle.
After 3 hops, he is on lily pad 3.
After 7 hops, he is back on lily pad 0.

Complete the table.
The frog starts at 0 each time.

	Number of hops	Number where frog stops
	7	*0*
	9	*2*
1.	10	
2.	12	
3.	14	
4.	16	
5.	25	

6. How many hops in each complete trip around the circle?

● **Discuss** How does dividing by 7 tell you where the frog stops after 25 hops?

$$\begin{array}{r} 3 \text{ R4} \\ 7\overline{)25} \\ -21 \\ \hline 4 \end{array}$$

● **Discuss** How does dividing by 7 tell you where the frog stops after 37 hops?

$$\begin{array}{r} 5 \text{ R2} \\ 7\overline{)37} \\ -35 \\ \hline 2 \end{array}$$

Without counting, tell where the frog stops each time.

7. After 30 hops　**9.** After 47 hops　**11.** After 57 hops

8. After 38 hops　**10.** After 54 hops　**12.** After 65 hops

Keeping Skillful

Subtract.

1. $\begin{array}{r} 495 \\ -\ 381 \\ \hline \end{array}$

2. $\begin{array}{r} 94 \\ -\ 28 \\ \hline \end{array}$

3. $\begin{array}{r} 847 \\ -\ 253 \\ \hline \end{array}$

4. $\begin{array}{r} 757 \\ -\ 688 \\ \hline \end{array}$

Multiply.

5. $\begin{array}{r} 67 \\ \times\ 5 \\ \hline \end{array}$

6. $\begin{array}{r} 43 \\ \times\ 7 \\ \hline \end{array}$

7. 20×3

8. 20×2

9. 20×4

10. 40×3

11. 30×5

12. 80×7

13. 70×6

14. 50×8

15. 40×4

A.

$2\overline{)95}$ How many 2's in 95?

Are there 10? $10 \times 2 = 20$
Are there 100? $100 \times 2 = 200$

The answer is between 10 and 100.
Try a multiple of 10.

$$\begin{array}{r|r} \overline{47}\ \text{R1} & \\ 2\overline{)95} & \\ -40 & 20 \\ \hline 55 & \\ -20 & 10 \\ \hline 35 & \\ -20 & 10 \\ \hline 15 & \\ -14 & 7 \\ \hline 1 & 47 \end{array}$$

Fred first tried 20.
Notice that he subtracted four times.

Here is a method that helps you keep your work short.

To find the best multiple of 10, think: How many 2's in 9? (4)

$$\begin{array}{r} 40 \\ 2\overline{)95} \\ -80 \\ \hline 15 \end{array}$$

Use 40. Write it on top.

40×2

$$\begin{array}{r} 7 \\ 40 \\ 2\overline{)95} \\ -80 \\ \hline 15 \\ -14 \\ \hline 1 \end{array}$$

How many 2's in 15? (7)

$$\begin{array}{r} \underline{47}\ \textbf{R1} \\ \overline{7} \\ 40 \\ 2\overline{)95} \\ -80 \\ \hline 15 \\ -14 \\ \hline 1 \end{array}$$

Add to find the total number of 2's in 95.

1 Remainder

B. Here is a problem Jean did using the short method.

How did she decide to use 20?

$$\begin{array}{r} \underline{24}\ \text{R2} \\ 4 \\ 20 \\ 3\overline{)74} \\ -60 \\ \hline 14 \\ -12 \\ \hline 2 \end{array}$$

Find the quotient and the remainder.

1. $3\overline{)64}$	**5.** $7\overline{)94}$	**9.** $7\overline{)91}$	**13.** $2\overline{)55}$
2. $4\overline{)92}$	**6.** $8\overline{)89}$	**10.** $2\overline{)74}$	**14.** $4\overline{)67}$
3. $2\overline{)43}$	**7.** $3\overline{)76}$	**11.** $6\overline{)97}$	
4. $5\overline{)88}$	**8.** $6\overline{)90}$	**12.** $3\overline{)84}$	

More practice
Set B, page 126

1. How wide is each town house?

   Find 56 ÷ 4.

2. How many grams in each chocolate?

   Find 90 ÷ 6.

3. Each person is carrying about ▒ pounds.

   Find 74 ÷ 2.

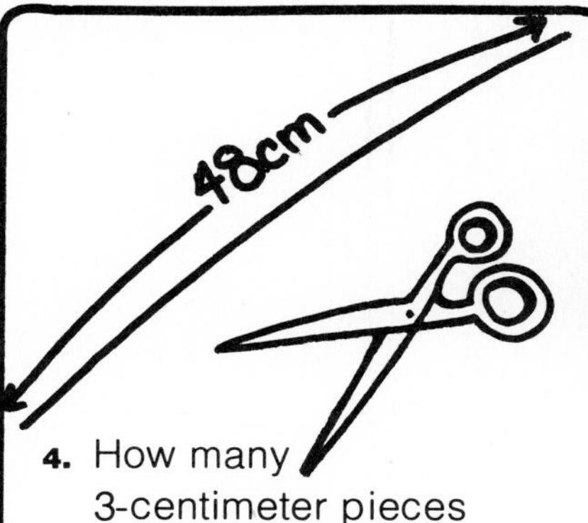

4. How many 3-centimeter pieces of string can be cut?

5. How many rows of 5 chairs are needed to seat 65 people?

6. It will take ▒ complete turns for the wheel to roll 98 feet.

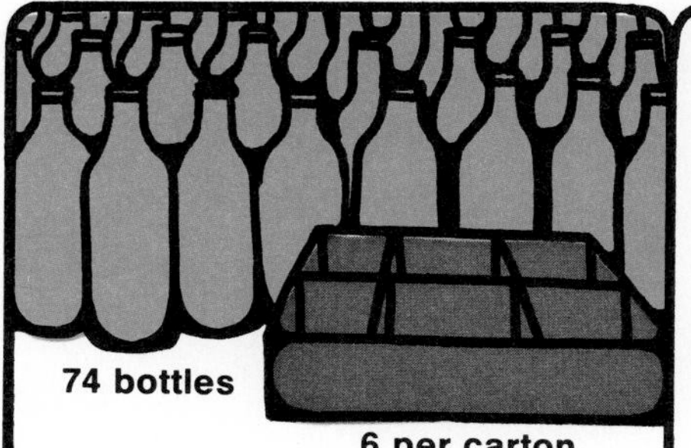

7. ▒ cartons can be filled. ▒ bottles will be left over.

8. How many stamps can you buy? How much money will be left?

9. You can fill ▒ 4-ounce cups. Then ▒ ounces will be left in the can.

Dividing: One-digit Divisors, Three-digit Dividends

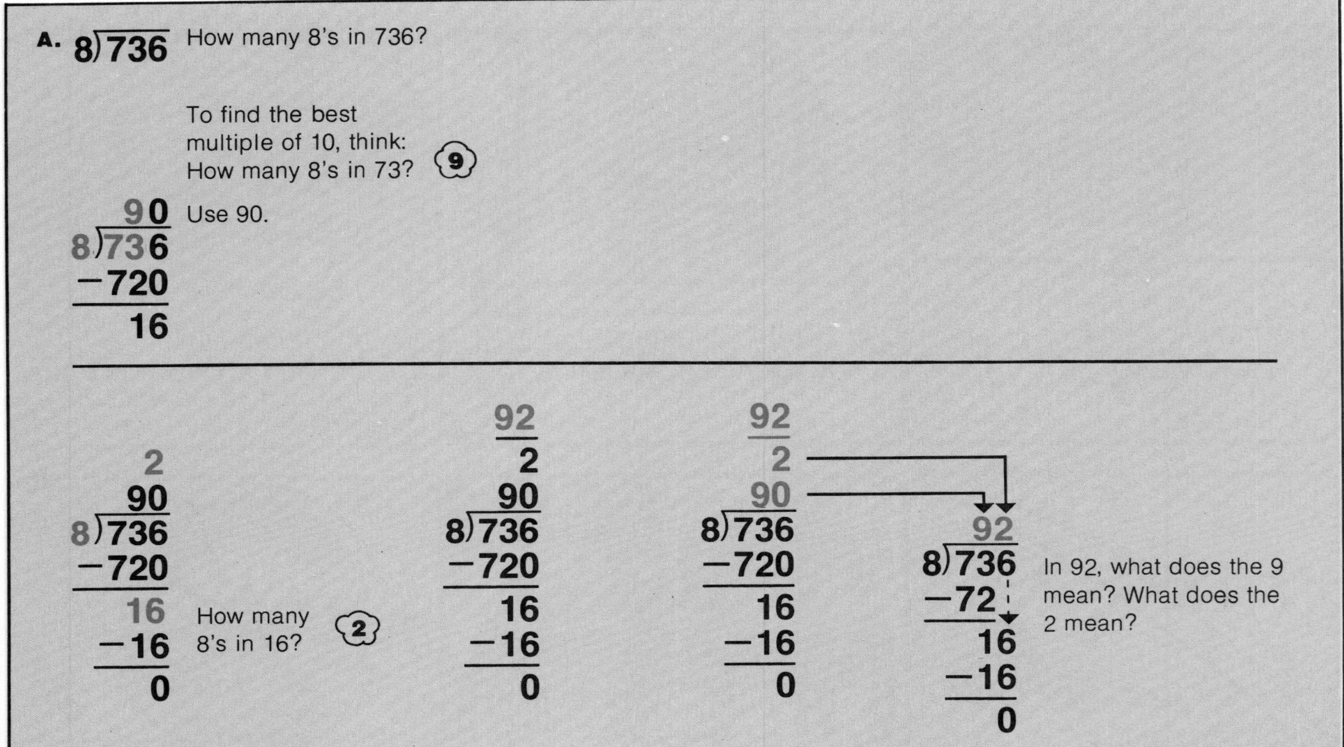

A. 8)736 How many 8's in 736?
To find the best multiple of 10, think: How many 8's in 73? 9
Use 90.
90
8)736
−720
16
2
90
8)736
−720
16
−16
0
How many 8's in 16? 2
92
2
90
8)736
−720
16
−16
0
92
8)736
−72
16
−16
0
In 92, what does the 9 mean? What does the 2 mean?

B. Here is a problem that Carl and Rosa worked. How did each student show the work?

Carl	Rosa
41 R6 1 40 7)293 −280 13 −7 6	41 R6 7)293 −28 13 −7 6

Find the quotient and the remainder.

1. $5\overline{)421}$	**6.** $4\overline{)330}$	**11.** $5\overline{)83}$
2. $7\overline{)614}$	**7.** $8\overline{)525}$	**12.** $3\overline{)92}$
3. $2\overline{)124}$	**8.** $2\overline{)85}$	**13.** $6\overline{)238}$
4. $5\overline{)95}$	**9.** $3\overline{)211}$	**14.** $4\overline{)125}$
5. $9\overline{)729}$	**10.** $6\overline{)395}$	**15.** $8\overline{)391}$

More practice
Set C, page 126

Using Division in Magic Squares

Remember, in a magic square, the sum of the numbers in each row, each column, and each diagonal is the same. This sum is called the magic sum.

1. The first square is a magic square. What is the magic sum? Divide each number by 6 to get a new square.

360	72	324
216	252	288
180	432	144

÷6

	12	
36	42	48
		24

What is the magic sum of the new magic square?

2. What is the magic sum in this magic square? Divide each number by 9.

378	81	351
243	270	297
189	459	162

÷9

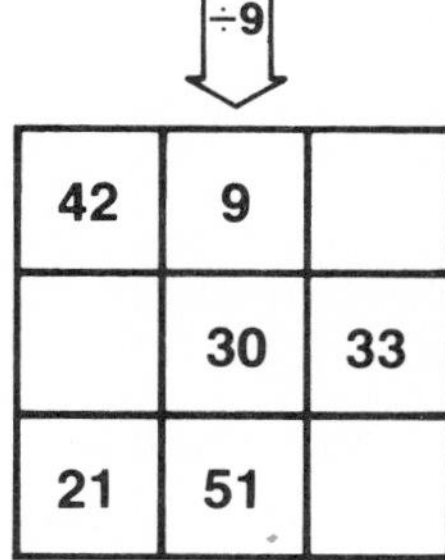

42	9	
	30	33
21	51	

Is this a magic square? If so, what is the magic sum?

Explore

How many cans of garbage does your family throw away in one week?

How many cans in one year (52 weeks)?

How many people are in your family?

About how many cans of garbage does each person in your family throw out in a year? Divide to find out.

Dividing: One-digit Divisors, Three-digit Quotients

When you divide, it is sometimes best to start by using a multiple of 100.

A.

4)955 How many 4's in 955?

Are there 10? 10 × 4 = 40
Are there 100? 100 × 4 = 400
Are there 1000? 1000 × 4 = 4000

The answer is between 100 and 1000.
Try a multiple of 100.

```
  200
4)955
 -800
  155
```

To find the best multiple of 100, think: How many 4's in 9? (2)

Use 200.

```
   30
  200
4)955
 -800
  155
 -120
   35
```

Now try a multiple of 10.

How many 4's in 15? (3)

Use 30.

```
  238 R3
    8
   30
  200
4)955
 -800
  155
 -120
   35
  -32
    3
```

```
  238 R3
    8
   30
  200
4)955
 -800
  155
 -120
   35
  -32
    3
```

```
  238 R3
4)955
 -8
  15
 -12
   35
  -32
    3
```

In 238, what does the 2 mean? What does the 3 mean? What does the 8 mean?

B. How did each show the work?

Esther

```
   567 R3
     7
    60
   500
7)3972
 -3500
   472
  -420
    52
   -49
     3
```

Herlinda

```
   567 R3
7)3972
 -35
   47
  -42
    52
   -49
     3
```

Divide. First decide whether to start with a multiple of 10 or a multiple of 100.

1. 4)83	**4.** 7)1436	**7.** 5)81	**10.** 7)2755
2. 6)372	**5.** 2)1387	**8.** 4)137	**11.** 9)8147
3. 3)825	**6.** 8)805	**9.** 3)681	**12.** 7)820

More practice
Set D, page 126

Checking Division

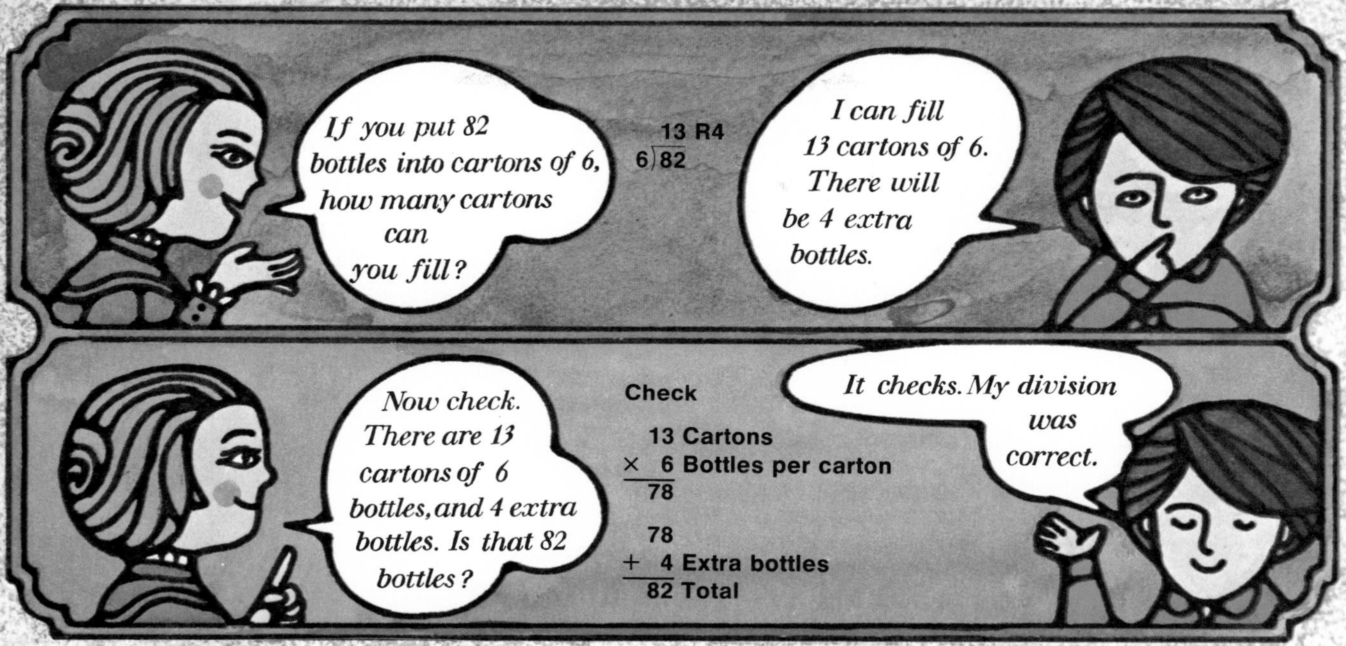

This equation shows what you do when you use multiplication and addition to check division.

$$82 = (13 \times 6) + 4$$

(13: Quotient; 4: Remainder)

Multiply and add to check which answer is correct.

1. $4\overline{)273}$ 67 R2; 68 R1
2. $3\overline{)773}$ 245 R1; 257 R2
3. $6\overline{)1846}$ 307 R4; 300 R4
4. $5\overline{)743}$ 148 R3; 147 R4
5. $7\overline{)901}$ 143; 128 R5
6. $9\overline{)1492}$ 165 R7; 210 R7

Divide. Check your work by multiplying and adding.

7. $4\overline{)754}$
8. $8\overline{)2573}$
9. $5\overline{)1326}$
10. $4\overline{)207}$
11. $3\overline{)1385}$

Finding Averages

At the right are six basketball scores.

To find the *average* score:

a. Add the scores to get the total (426).

b. Divide the total by the number of scores (6).

Scores
74
59
66
79
68
80
426

Total points		Number of games		Average score
426	÷	6	=	71

If the team had scored 71 points in each of the six games, they would have had the same total score of 426.

Miss Jensen's students play a game called Toss a Clip.

They attach a paper clip to a folded tissue.
Each player tries to toss the clip
so that it lands exactly 80 inches away.

The players record each distance to the nearest inch.

The winner is the team whose average is closest to 80.

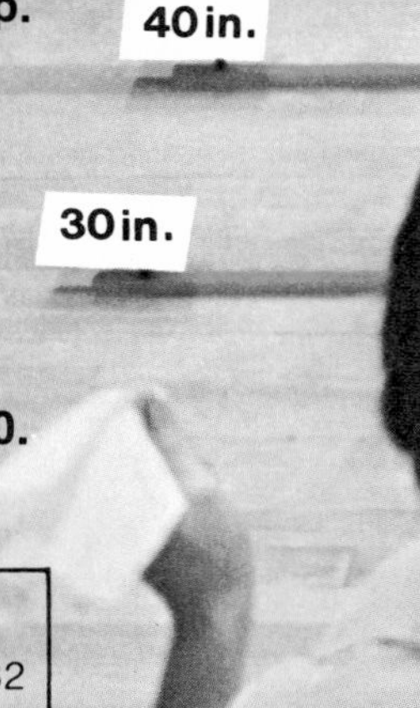

1. Find the average for each team. (Hint: Add the results. Divide by the number of tosses for the team.)
2. Which team won?

Length of tosses (inches)

Team A	89	91	90	78	74	82
Team B	100	88	65	77	80	
Team C	89	73	77	81	90	88
Team D	73	87	61	80	84	

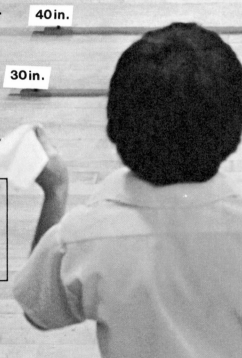

Five students collected information about themselves.
Find the average of the numbers in each row of the table.

		Mike	Joan	Luis	Pete	Anna	Average
3.	Weight (kilograms)	47	34	43	35	41	
4.	Height (centimeters)	150	139	143	139	144	
5.	Arm length (centimeters)	60	58	59	59	59	
6.	Distance of softball throw (meters)	28	21	27	26	28	
7.	Money in pocket or purse (cents)	28	25	40	31	36	
8.	Score on Friday's quiz	15	20	18	11	16	
9.	Number of blocks from home to school	3	12	7	4	4	
10.	Guess for length of teacher's desk (centimeters)	80	150	100	200	170	

Dividing: Two-digit Divisors

A.

$30\overline{)168}$ How many 30's in 168?

Are there 10? $10 \times 30 = 300$

The answer is less than 10.

$$\begin{array}{r} 5 \text{ R18} \\ 30\overline{)168} \\ -150 \\ \hline 18 \end{array}$$

To find the number, think:
How many 3's in 16? (5)

B.

$42\overline{)296}$ How many 42's in 296?

Are there 10? $10 \times 42 = 420$

The answer is less than 10.

$$\begin{array}{r} 7 \text{ R2} \\ 42\overline{)296} \\ -294 \\ \hline 2 \end{array}$$

To find the number, think:
How many 4's in 29? (7)

Divide.

1. $20\overline{)93}$ **4.** $60\overline{)315}$ **7.** $39\overline{)85}$ **10.** $87\overline{)452}$ **13.** $47\overline{)239}$

2. $40\overline{)95}$ **5.** $30\overline{)184}$ **8.** $51\overline{)274}$ **11.** $54\overline{)333}$ **14.** $84\overline{)603}$

3. $40\overline{)127}$ **6.** $23\overline{)97}$ **9.** $75\overline{)468}$ **12.** $61\overline{)368}$ **15.** $53\overline{)284}$

	Dividend	Divisor	Quotient	Remainder
16.	98	12		
17.	98	24		
18.	98	48		
19.	98	96		

	Dividend	Divisor	Quotient	Remainder
20.	35	32		
21.	70	32		
22.	140	32		
23.	280	32		

More practice
Set E, page 126
Set F, page 127

Using Division: Counting Calories

Food	Calories
Milk	21 per ounce
Bacon	50 per strip
Sausage	83 per slice
Toast	67 per slice
Eggs	82 each
Orange juice	14 per ounce

Terry's activities	Calories used in 15 minutes
Sleeping	22
Standing	28
Walking	105
Bicycling	165
Running	201
Swimming	300

Use the information in the tables to help you solve these problems.

1. Julie uses 246 calories riding her bicycle to school. How many eggs would supply these calories?

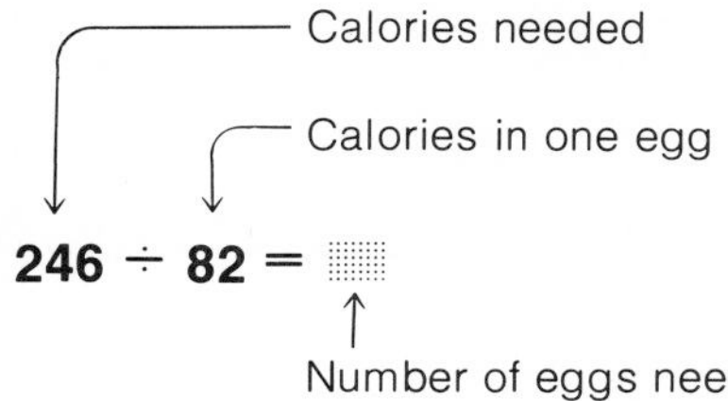

2. Isabel uses 168 calories walking to school. How many ounces of milk would supply these calories?

3. David uses 581 calories paddling a canoe. How many slices of sausage would supply these calories?

4. Ed uses 335 calories practicing the piano. How many slices of toast would supply these calories?

5. How many ounces of milk would supply the calories Terry uses in 15 minutes of walking?

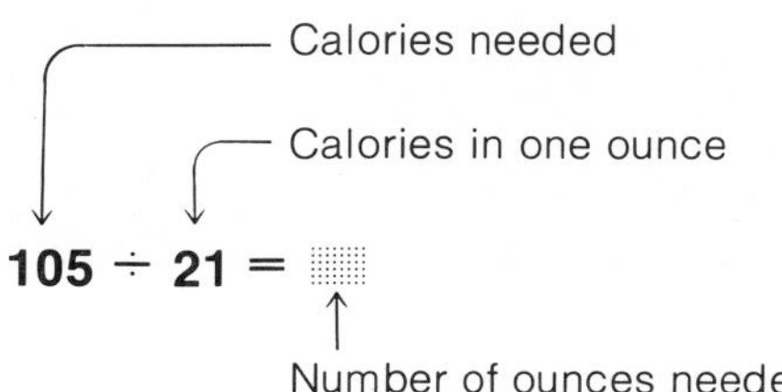

6. How many ounces of orange juice would supply the calories Terry uses in 15 minutes of standing?

7. How many strips of bacon would supply the calories Terry uses in 15 minutes of swimming?

8. How many slices of toast would supply the calories Terry uses in 15 minutes of running?

Dividing: Two-digit Divisors, Two-digit Quotients

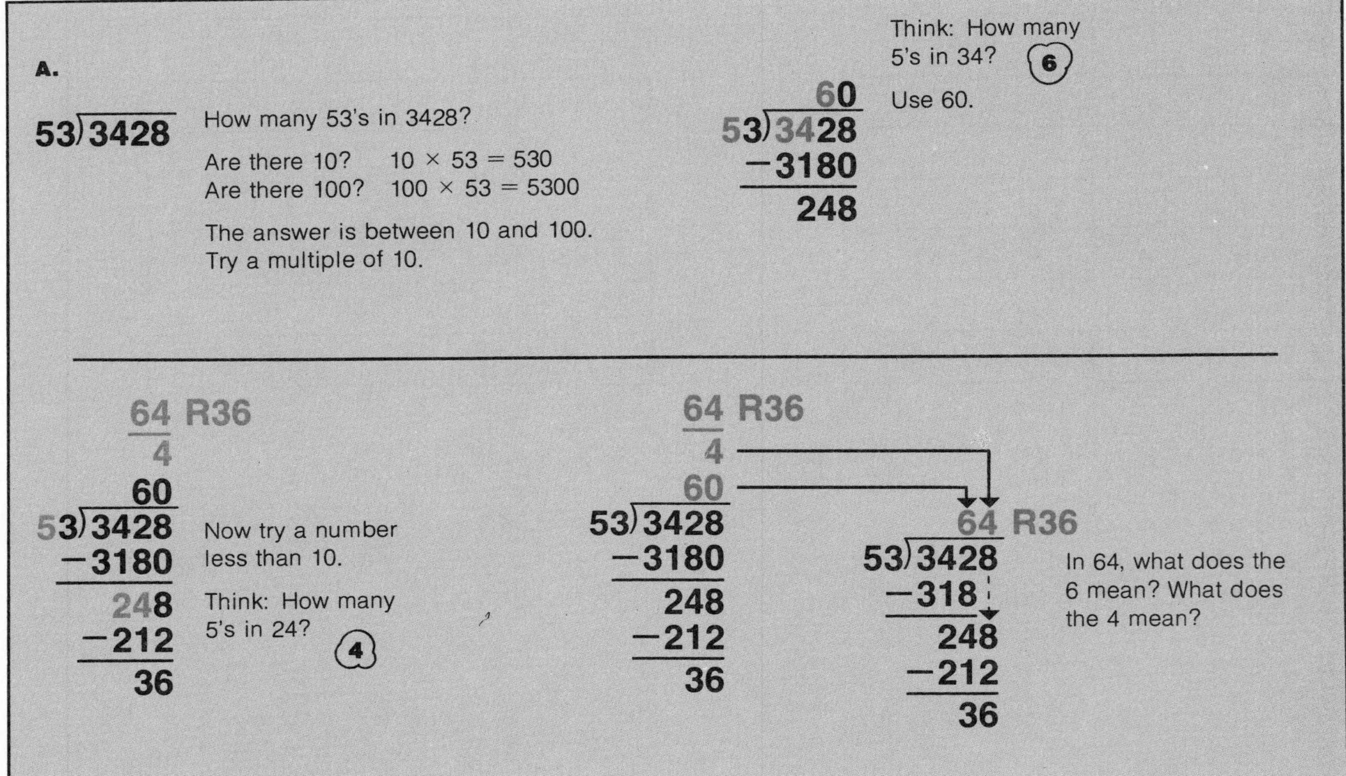

A.
53)3428
How many 53's in 3428?
Are there 10? 10 × 53 = 530
Are there 100? 100 × 53 = 5300
The answer is between 10 and 100.
Try a multiple of 10.
Think: How many 5's in 34? 6
Use 60.
60
53)3428
−3180
248
64 R36
4
60
53)3428
−3180
248
−212
36
Now try a number less than 10.
Think: How many 5's in 24? 4
64 R36
53)3428
−318
248
−212
36
In 64, what does the 6 mean? What does the 4 mean?

B. How did each student show the work?

Lisa

```
     23 R30
      3
     20
42)996
  −840
   156
  −126
    30
```

Jon

```
     23 R30
42)996
   −84
   156
  −126
    30
```

Divide.

1. 23)577
2. 30)2704
3. 62)4437
4. 85)960
5. 76)2534
6. 80)4206
7. 47)1175
8. 56)3964

Divide. First decide whether to start with a number less than 10 or with a multiple of 10.

9. 52)93
10. 71)342
11. 43)625
12. 71)3950
13. 4)266
14. 5)378
15. 44)275
16. 23)989

More practice
Set G, page 127
Set H, page 127

Using Division: Supporting Weight

When you are standing, your feet support your weight.

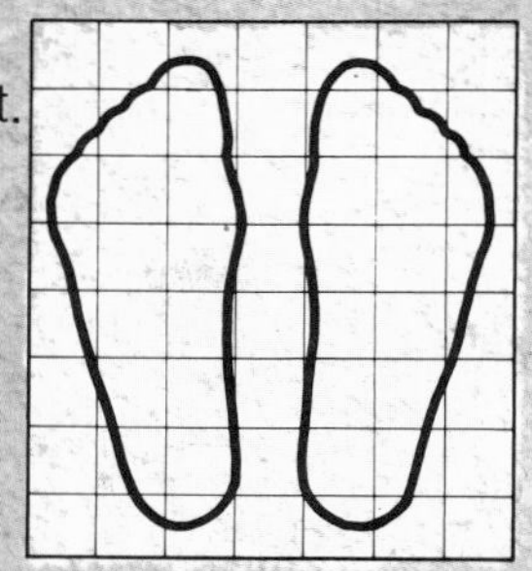

Nina weighs 84 pounds. The area of the soles of her feet is about 28 square inches. How many pounds does each square inch support?

Divide Nina's weight by the area of her feet.

$$\begin{array}{r} 3 \\ 28\overline{)84} \\ -84 \\ \hline 0 \end{array}$$

Each square inch supports 3 pounds.

Complete this table.

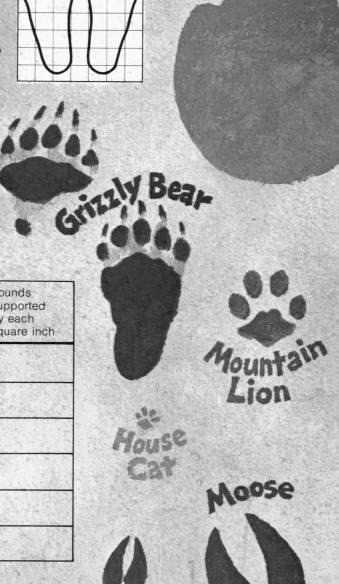

	Animal	Weight (pounds)	Area of bottom of feet (square inches)	Pounds supported by each square inch
1.	House cat	12	3	
2.	Mountain lion	176	22	
3.	Deer	240	10	
4.	Grizzly bear	820	205	
5.	Moose	1550	31	
6.	Elephant	8800	400	

7. How much do you weigh? Suppose that the area of the soles of your feet is about 26 square inches. About how many pounds does each square inch support?

Dividing: Correcting Estimates

When you start to divide, sometimes the estimate you choose is too big.

A.

$76\overline{)582}$

How many 7's in 58? (8)

Try 8.

$$\begin{array}{r} 8 \\ 76\overline{)582} \\ -608 \end{array}$$

8 is too big.
Try 7.

$$\begin{array}{r} 7 \text{ R50} \\ 76\overline{)582} \\ -532 \\ \hline 50 \end{array}$$

7 is correct.

B.

$58\overline{)3670}$

How many 5's in 36? (7)

Try 70.

$$\begin{array}{r} 70 \\ 58\overline{)3670} \\ -4060 \end{array}$$

70 is too big.
Try 60.

$$\begin{array}{r} 63 \text{ R16} \\ 3 \\ 60 \\ 58\overline{)3670} \\ -3480 \\ \hline 190 \\ -174 \\ \hline 16 \end{array}$$

or

$$\begin{array}{r} 63 \text{ R16} \\ 58\overline{)3670} \\ -348 \\ \hline 190 \\ -174 \\ \hline 16 \end{array}$$

Here is how Sheila started these problems.
For each problem, tell if she chose a number that is too big.

1. $\begin{array}{r} 4 \\ 56\overline{)203} \end{array}$
2. $\begin{array}{r} 2 \\ 47\overline{)101} \end{array}$
3. $\begin{array}{r} 50 \\ 65\overline{)3281} \end{array}$
4. $\begin{array}{r} 9 \\ 39\overline{)275} \end{array}$
5. $\begin{array}{r} 80 \\ 28\overline{)1640} \end{array}$

Divide.

6. $38\overline{)92}$
7. $78\overline{)289}$
8. $26\overline{)1834}$
9. $35\overline{)2103}$
10. $62\overline{)750}$
11. $25\overline{)60}$
12. $27\overline{)1422}$
13. $18\overline{)573}$
14. $26\overline{)2413}$
15. $35\overline{)1402}$
16. $53\overline{)2935}$
17. $67\overline{)243}$

More practice
Set I, page 127

Using Division: Predicting Adult Height

Here is a way to predict someone's adult height. This method doesn't work for everybody, because some people grow faster than others.

a. Write your present height in inches.

b. Multiply by 100.

c. Divide by the special number given for your age in the table at the right.

d. The quotient is a prediction of your adult height.

Susan
Age : 12 years
Height: 59 inches

59

59×100=5900

$93\overline{)5900}$

Predicted adult height: 63 inches

Age (years)	Special number	
	Boys	Girls
8	72	78
9	75	81
10	78	84
11	81	88
12	84	93
13	87	97

Complete the table.

	Name	Age (years)	Present height (inches)	Predicted adult height (inches)
1.	Julio	8	49	
2.	Mark	11	57	
3.	Joyce	10	58	
4.	Roger	12	60	
5.	Ernie	13	61	
6.	Karen	12	60	
7.	Jack	10	54	
8.	Rita	9	53	
9.	Peter	11	61	

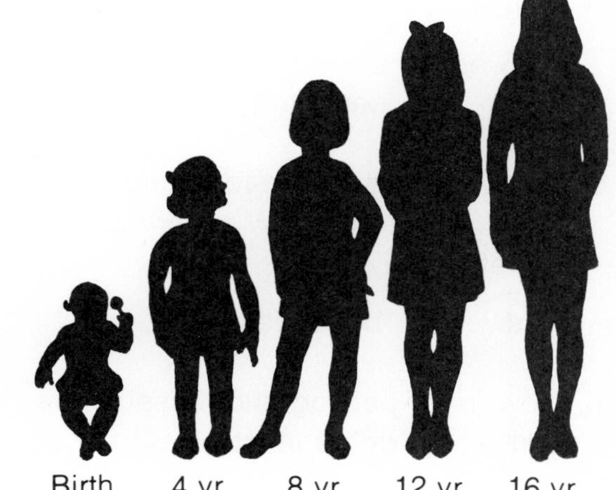

10. Predict your own adult height. Remember, this is only a prediction. It might not come true.

Interpreting Remainders

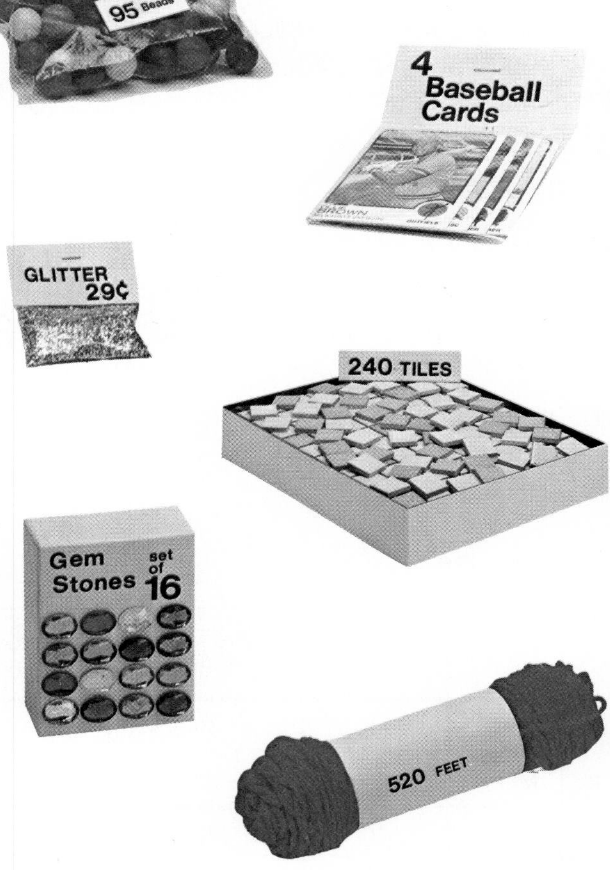

María did the same division for each problem below. But she gave a different answer to each problem. Study the problems to see why.

$$\begin{array}{r} 23 \text{ R3} \\ 4\overline{)95} \end{array}$$

A. How many 4-inch candlewicks can be cut from the long wick?

Answer: 23 candlewicks

B. How many sheets of cardboard can you buy with 95¢? Will any money be left?

Answer: ▒ sheets of cardboard
▒ cents left

C. If you divided the beads equally among 4 people, how many beads would be left over?

Answer: ▒ beads left over

D. How many packages of baseball cards must you buy to get at least 95 cards?

Answer: ▒ packages

Why is "23 packages" not the correct answer?

1. How many packages of glitter can you buy with 85¢?
2. If you divide the box of tiles equally among 7 children, how many tiles will be left over?
3. How many sets of stones must you buy if you need 150 stones?
4. How many 15-foot lengths of yarn can you get from one package?

19¢

two for 89¢

5. How many paintbrushes can you buy with 90¢? How much money will you have left?

6. If it takes 25 tiles to cover a coaster, how many coasters can you make with one box of tiles?

7. Suppose you save $2 per week. How many weeks will it take to get enough money for the chemistry set?

8. How much would you expect to pay for one bottle of glue?

Time Out

If it takes 12 minutes to cut a log into 3 pieces, how long would it take to cut a log into 4 pieces?

Using Division: Changing Measures

A. Smallest plane ever flown

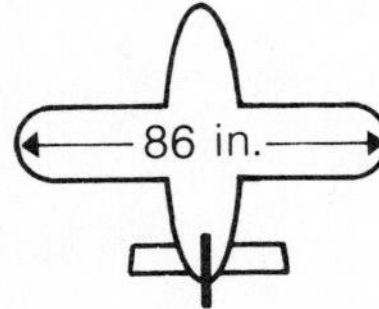

86 inches = ▒ feet ▒ inches

There are 12 inches in 1 foot.
How many groups of 12 in 86?

$$\begin{array}{r} 7 \\ 12\overline{)86} \\ -84 \\ \hline 2 \end{array}$$

There are 7 groups of 12, plus 2 extra inches.

86 inches = 7 feet 2 inches

B. First solo flight around the world

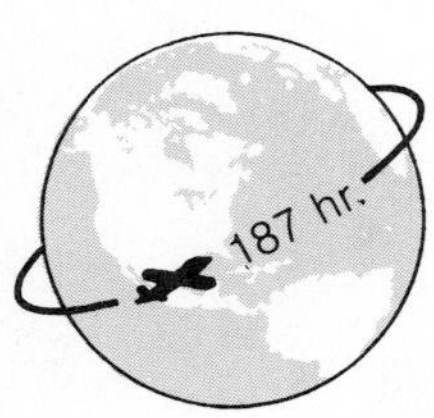

187 hours = ▒ days ▒ hours

There are 24 hours in 1 day.
How many groups of 24 in 187?

$$\begin{array}{r} 7 \\ 24\overline{)187} \\ -168 \\ \hline 19 \end{array}$$

187 hours = 7 days 19 hours

Measures

Length

1 foot (ft.)	= 12 inches (in.)
1 yard (yd.)	= 3 feet (ft.)
1 yard (yd.)	= 36 inches (in.)

Capacity

1 cup (c.)	= 8 fluid ounces (fl. oz.)
1 pint (pt.)	= 2 cups (c.)
1 quart (qt.)	= 2 pints (pt.)
1 gallon (gal.)	= 4 quarts (qt.)

Weight

1 pound (lb.)	= 16 ounces (oz.)

Time

1 minute (min.)	= 60 seconds (sec.)
1 hour (hr.)	= 60 minutes (min.)
1 day (da.)	= 24 hours (hr.)
1 week (wk.)	= 7 days (da.)
1 year (yr.)	= 12 months (mo.)

Use the table of measures to help you find the missing numbers.

1. 134 inches = ▒ feet ▒ inches
2. 97 days = ▒ weeks ▒ days
3. 153 quarts = ▒ gallons ▒ quarts
4. 246 feet = ▒ yards
5. 94 ounces = ▒ pounds ▒ ounces
6. 42 months = ▒ years ▒ months
7. 250 minutes = ▒ hours ▒ minutes
8. 180 inches = ▒ feet
9. 39 cups = ▒ pints ▒ cups
10. 280 inches = ▒ yards ▒ inches

Use the table of measures on page 86 to help you find the answers.

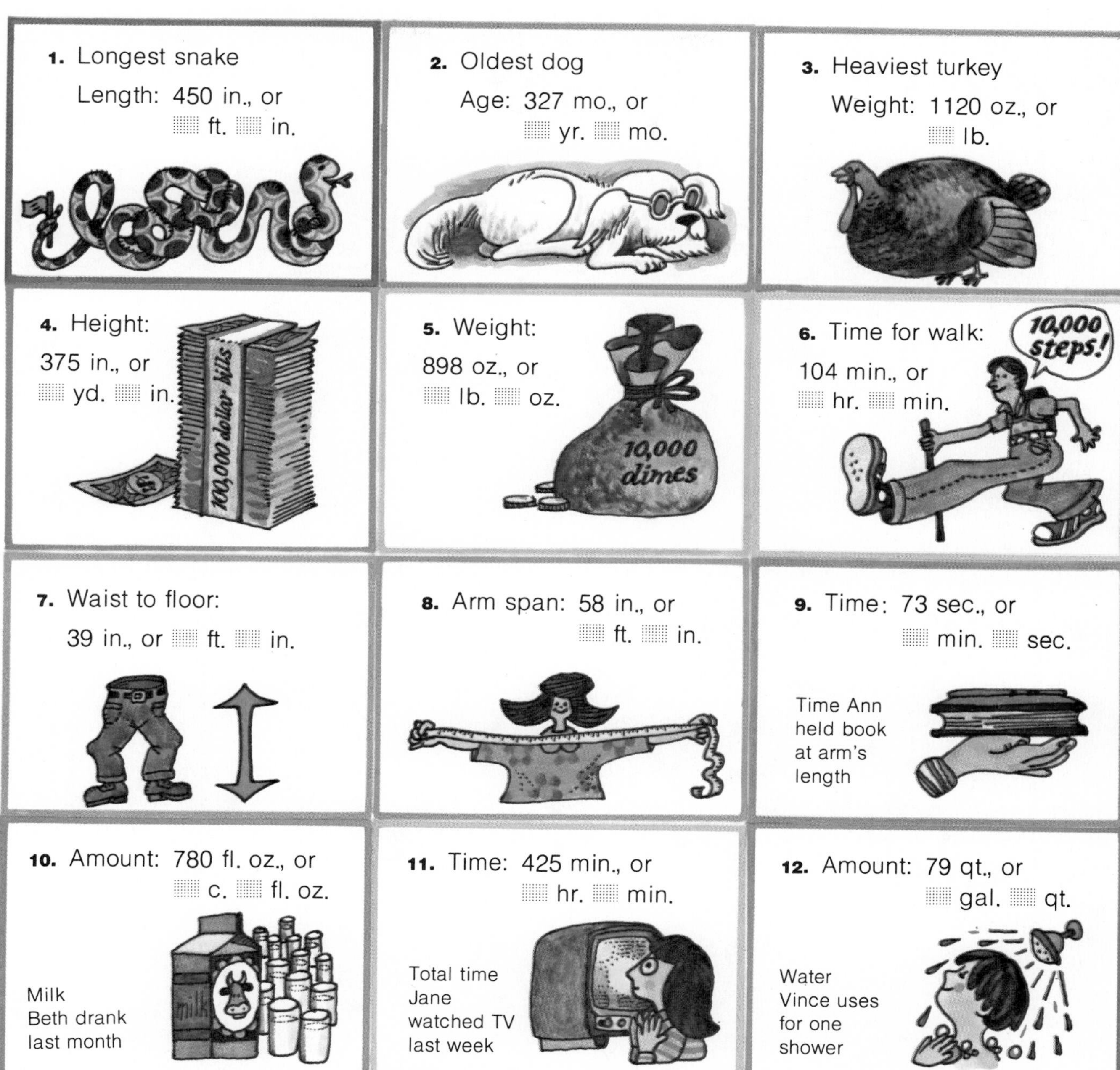

1. Longest snake
   Length: 450 in., or ▒ ft. ▒ in.

2. Oldest dog
   Age: 327 mo., or ▒ yr. ▒ mo.

3. Heaviest turkey
   Weight: 1120 oz., or ▒ lb.

4. Height: 375 in., or ▒ yd. ▒ in.

5. Weight: 898 oz., or ▒ lb. ▒ oz.

6. Time for walk: 104 min., or ▒ hr. ▒ min.

7. Waist to floor: 39 in., or ▒ ft. ▒ in.

8. Arm span: 58 in., or ▒ ft. ▒ in.

9. Time: 73 sec., or ▒ min. ▒ sec.
   Time Ann held book at arm's length

10. Amount: 780 fl. oz., or ▒ c. ▒ fl. oz.
    Milk Beth drank last month

11. Time: 425 min., or ▒ hr. ▒ min.
    Total time Jane watched TV last week

12. Amount: 79 qt., or ▒ gal. ▒ qt.
    Water Vince uses for one shower

Number Tricks

Do Charlie's number trick starting with each of these numbers. Give your answers.

1. 7 **2.** 15 **3.** 100 **4.** 750 **5.** Any number of your choice

6. Use the number trick below. What is the answer if you pick 5?

Pick a number.	5
Add 15.	20
Multiply by 4.	80
Subtract 12.	▒
Divide by 4.	▒
Subtract the number picked.	▒

7. Do you get the same answer if you start with 14? With 82? With any number?

8. Use the number trick below. What is the answer if you pick 2?

Pick a number.	2
Add 30.	32
Multiply by 7.	▒
Subtract the number picked.	▒
Divide by 6.	▒
Subtract the number picked.	▒

9. Do you get the same answer if you start with 61? With 400? With any number?

Solving Equations with Missing Factors

A. You can use an equation to describe the picture.

12 12 12 12 12

60 coins altogether

Number of stacks		Number per stack		Total number
5	$\times$	**12**	$=$	**60**
Factor		Factor		Product

B. This equation uses n for a missing factor.

How many stacks of 13?

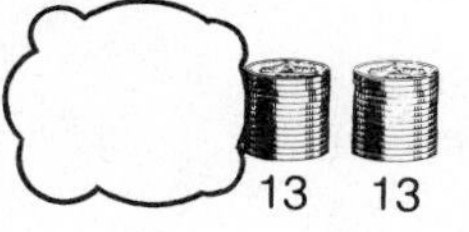

52 coins altogether

$$n \times 13 = 52$$

$$n = 4$$

There are 4 stacks.

Divide to find n.

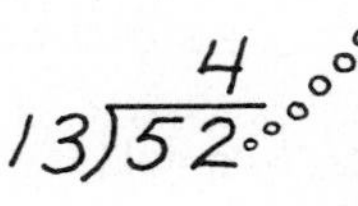

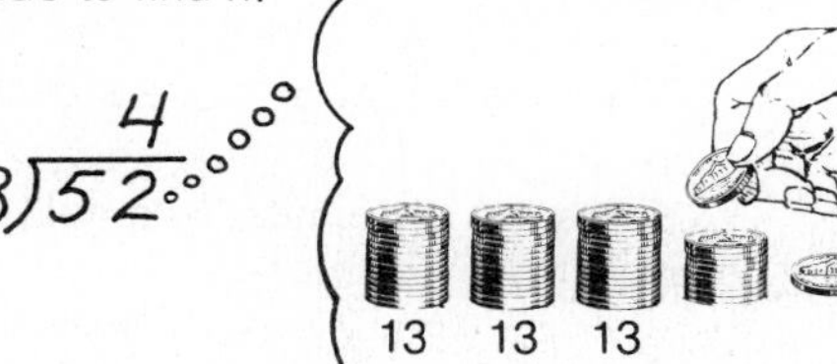

C. This equation also has a missing factor.

How many coins per stack?

42 coins altogether

$$3 \times n = 42$$

$$n = 14$$

There are 14 coins per stack.

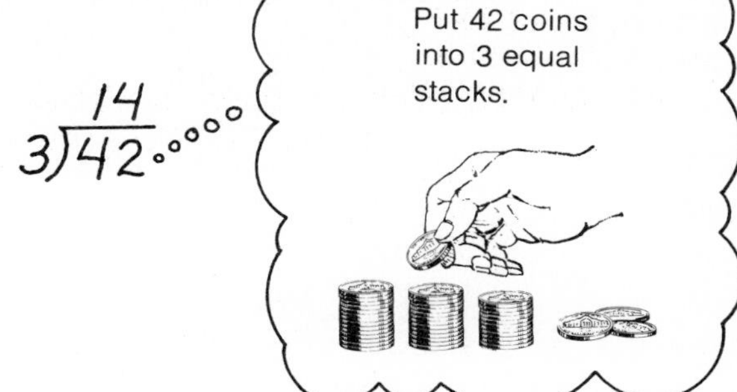

■ *You can divide to find a missing factor.*

$n \times 23 = 115$

$$23 \overline{)115} = 5, \quad 115 - 115 = 0$$

$n = 5$

$42 \times n = 336$

$$42 \overline{)336} = 8, \quad 336 - 336 = 0$$

$n = 8$

Find the number for n.

1. $26 \times n = 338$

2. $n \times 18 = 486$

3. $n \times 13 = 299$

4. $38 \times n = 988$

5. $n \times 13 = 117$

6. $n \times 85 = 680$

7. $56 \times n = 672$

8. $n \times 49 = 2450$

Using Equations to Solve Problems

You can use equations to help you solve problems.

Twelve girls picked up 72 pine cones.
They shared the cones equally.
How many pine cones did each girl get?

	Number of girls		Number of pine cones per girl		Total number of pine cones
Write an equation.	**12**	×	***n***	=	**72**
Find the number for *n*.			***n***	=	**6**

$$\begin{array}{r} 6 \\ 12\overline{)72} \\ -72 \\ \hline 0 \end{array}$$

Answer the question. Each girl got 6 pine cones.

Follow the same steps to solve the problems on this page and the next page.

1. The 21 cabins at the camp have the same number of campers in each. There are 252 campers in all. How many campers are in each cabin?

Number of cabins		Number of campers per cabin		Total number of campers
21	×	***n***	=	**252**

2. One day, 56 people went on a canoe trip. Four people were assigned to each canoe. How many canoes were needed?

Number of canoes		Number of people per canoe		Total number of people
n	×	**4**	=	**56**

3. If the trail is marked into 25-foot sections, how many sections will there be?

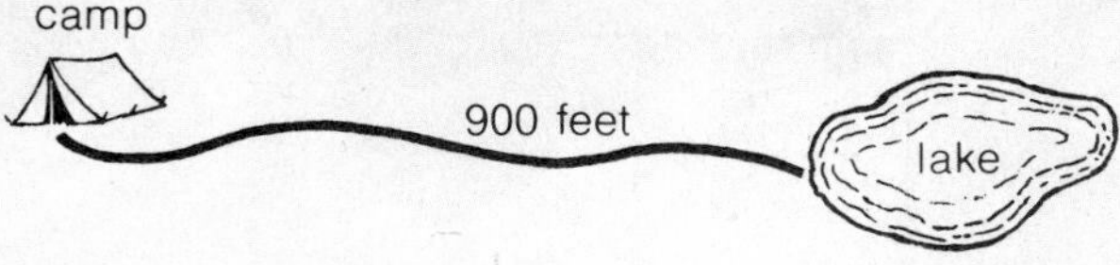

4. There were 198 campers in archery classes, with 18 campers in each class. How many archery classes were there?

5. The camp cook expected 285 people for lunch. He cooked 3 ears of corn for each person. How many ears of corn did he cook?

6. One day, 112 people separated into 8 equal groups to go hiking. How many people were in each group?

7. There were 31 swimming classes, with 16 children in each class. How many children took swimming?

8. If the campers share the marshmallows equally, how many marshmallows will each camper have?

Using Pictures to Solve Problems

Start with 12 points. Draw straight lines to connect each point with all the other points.

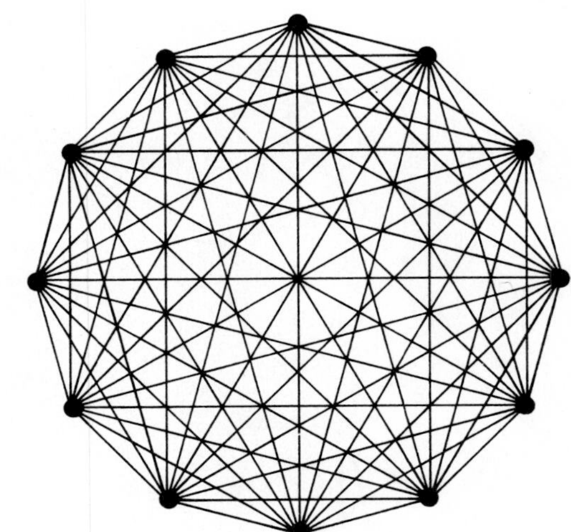

1. Without counting, guess the number of lines.

To find the exact number of lines, first look at some simpler problems.

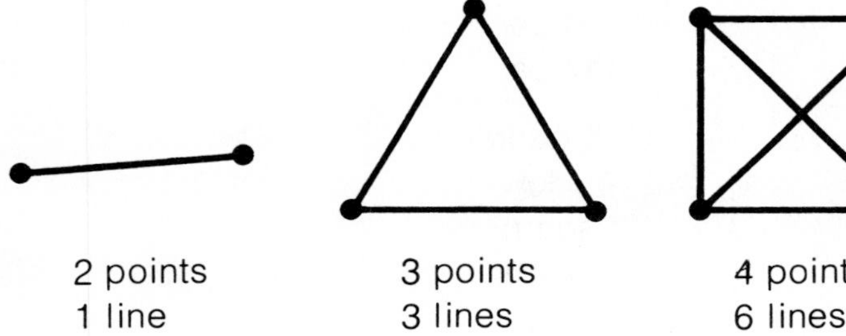

2. Draw points and count lines
   a. for 5 points.
   b. for 6 points.
   c. for 7 points.

3. Record your results in a table like the one shown at the right.

4. Find a pattern. Complete the table to find the number of lines for 12 points.

5. How many lines for 15 points? For 20 points? For 24 points?

Number of points	Number of lines	
2	1	
3	3	+ 2
4	6	+ 3
5		+ 4
6		+
7		
8		
9		
10		
11		
12		

Check Yourself
Dividing Whole Numbers, Pages 66–92

Basic facts, pages 66–67

Give the quotient.

1. $56 \div 8$ **2.** $54 \div 6$ **3.** $72 \div 9$

Dividing: one-digit divisor, pages 68, 70, 72, 73–75, 88

Find the quotient and the remainder.

4. $6\overline{)43}$

5. $8\overline{)66}$

6. $4\overline{)39}$

7. $5\overline{)42}$

8. $3\overline{)92}$

9. $5\overline{)323}$

10. $8\overline{)601}$

11. $6\overline{)5209}$

12. Multiply and add to check which answer is correct.

$\begin{array}{r} 27 \text{ R1} \\ 4\overline{)110} \end{array}$ $\begin{array}{r} 27 \text{ R2} \\ 4\overline{)110} \end{array}$ $\begin{array}{r} 27 \text{ R3} \\ 4\overline{)110} \end{array}$

Dividing: two-digit divisor, pages 78, 80, 82

Divide.

13. $52\overline{)387}$

14. $40\overline{)3872}$

15. $84\overline{)2275}$

16. $73\overline{)4645}$

Tell whether the quotient tried in each exercise is correct or too big.

17. $\begin{array}{r} 4 \\ 37\overline{)134} \end{array}$

18. $\begin{array}{r} 5 \\ 66\overline{)340} \end{array}$

19. $\begin{array}{r} 8 \\ 54\overline{)425} \end{array}$

20. $\begin{array}{r} 4 \\ 75\overline{)291} \end{array}$

Problem solving, pages 69, 71, 76, 77, 79, 81, 83–87, 89–91

21. Find the average height of these three students.

Dan	144 centimeters
Ellen	138 centimeters
Ted	147 centimeters

22. Divide 86 pennies equally among 4 people. How many pennies will each person have? How many will be left over?

23. There are 3 feet in 1 yard.
14 feet = $\square$ yards $\square$ feet

24. There are 16 ounces in 1 pound.
50 ounces = $\square$ pounds $\square$ ounces

25. Find *n*.

$35 \times n = 735$

26. Kiyo is putting 96 cookies into bags of 6 cookies each. How many bags does he need?

Writing Ratios

You can use a pair of numbers called a *ratio* to describe each picture.

A.

Pencils ⟶ 6
Cents ⟶ 19

The ratio "6 to 19" tells the price of the pencils.

B.

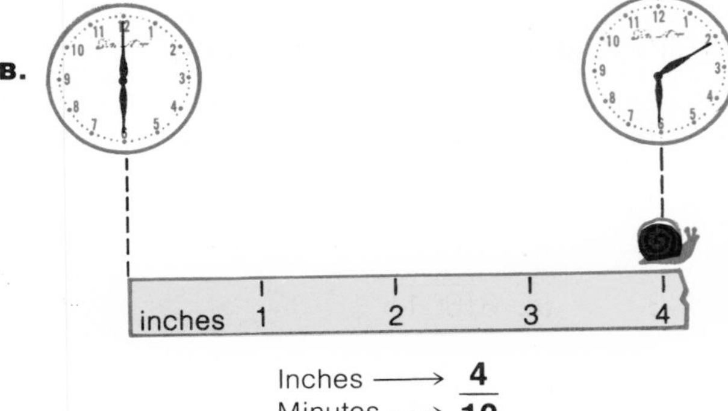

Inches ⟶ 4
Minutes ⟶ 10

The ratio "4 to 10" tells the snail's speed.

Write a ratio for each picture.

1.

Records ⟶ ▒
Dollars ⟶ ▒

2.

Ounces ⟶ ▒
Calories ⟶ ▒

3.

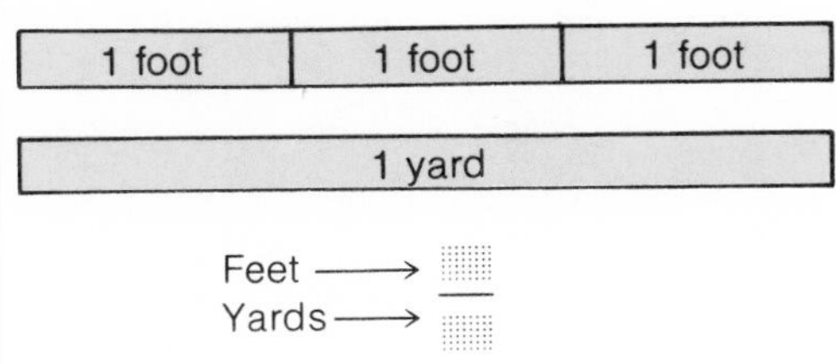

Feet ⟶ ▒
Yards ⟶ ▒

4.

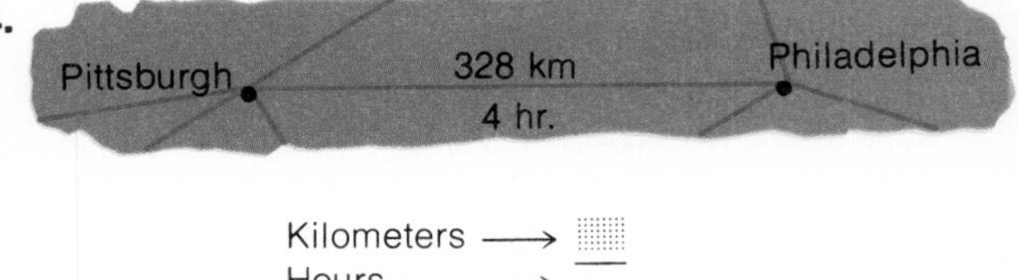

Kilometers ⟶ ▒
Hours ⟶ ▒

5.

Cups of pancake mix ⟶ ▒
Cups of milk ⟶ ▒

6.

Apples ⟶ ▒
Pounds ⟶ ▒

7.

Ounces of peanuts ⟶ ▒
Ounces of cashews ⟶ ▒

8.

Arms ⟶ ▒
Legs ⟶ ▒

Write a ratio for each situation.

9. Sue walked 3 miles in 70 minutes.
10. Your heart pumps 10 pints of blood in 30 seconds.
11. Twelve Mexican pesos are worth one U.S. dollar.
12. Donna's wristwatch gains 3 minutes every 4 days.
13. Gail earns $82 in 5 days.
14. There are 16 tablespoons in 1 cup.
15. The basketball team scored 10 points in 8 minutes.
16. Andy read 185 pages in 3 hours.
17. Four roller-coaster rides cost 50¢.
18. Five dimes are worth two quarters.
19. A 12-pound turkey cooks in 3 hours.
20. Mix 2 cups of sugar with 4 eggs.

Finding Equal Ratios Through Pictures

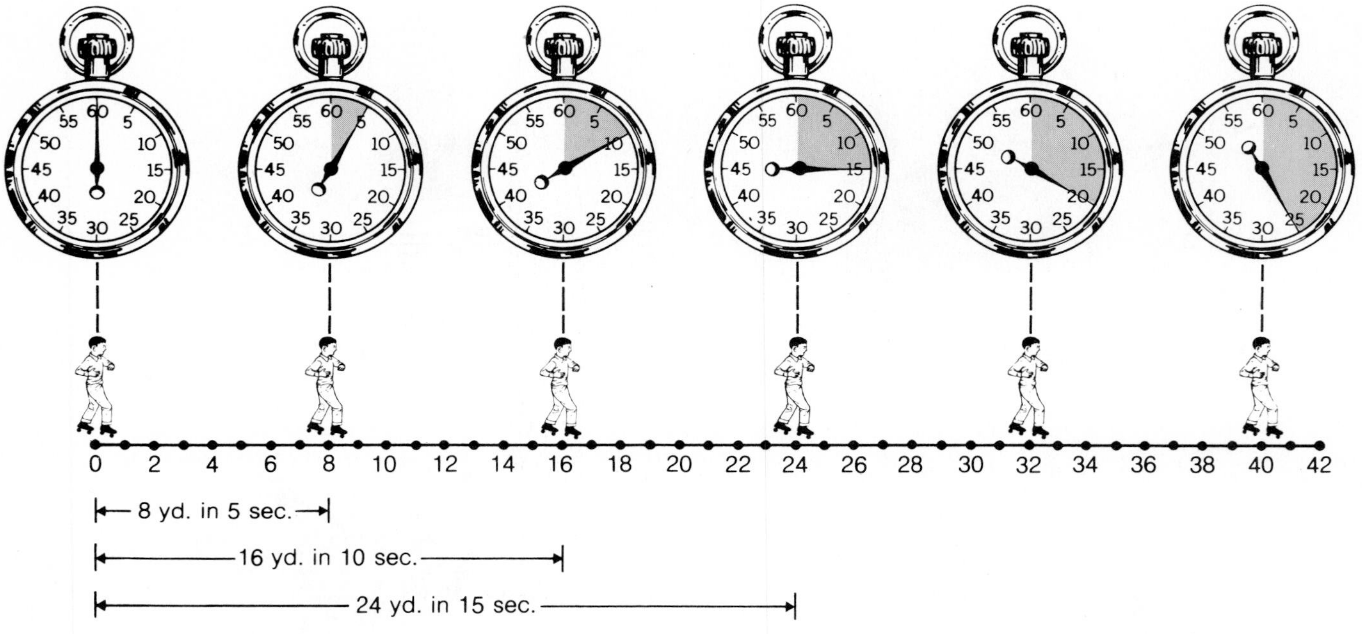

Each ratio below tells the skater's speed.
His speed stayed the same. The ratios are equal.

Yards ⟶
Seconds ⟶ $\frac{\mathbf{8}}{\mathbf{5}} = \frac{\mathbf{16}}{\mathbf{10}} = \frac{\mathbf{24}}{\mathbf{15}} = \frac{\mathbf{32}}{\mathbf{20}} = \frac{\mathbf{40}}{\mathbf{25}}$

Complete each list of equal ratios.

1. There are 3 teaspoons in 1 tablespoon.

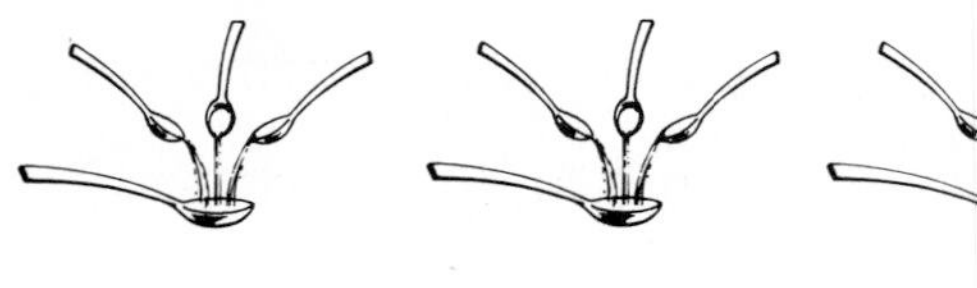

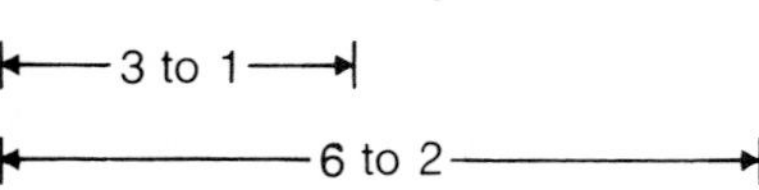

Teaspoons ⟶
Tablespoons ⟶ $\frac{3}{1} = \frac{6}{\square} = \frac{\square}{3} = \frac{\square}{4} = \frac{15}{\square}$

2.

 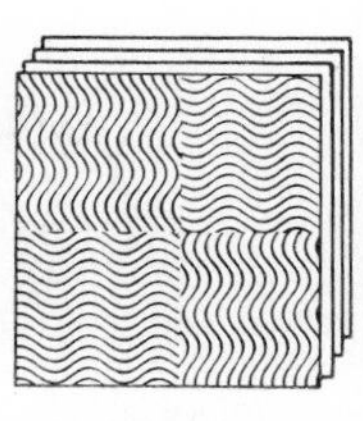   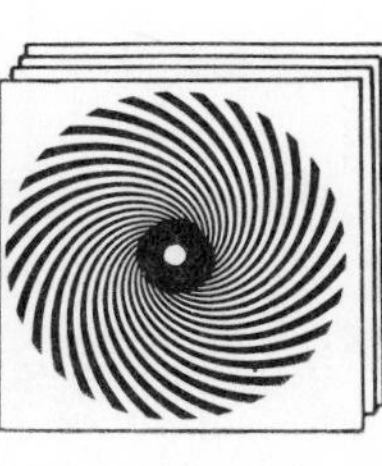

4 for 5

8 for ▒

Posters → Dollars →

$\frac{4}{5} = \frac{8}{▒} = \frac{▒}{15} = \frac{16}{▒} = \frac{20}{▒}$

3. To get Groovy Green, you mix:

3 cans of True Blue
4 cans of Mellow Yellow

3 to 4

6 to ▒

Cans of True Blue → Cans of Mellow Yellow →

$\frac{3}{4} = \frac{6}{▒} = \frac{9}{▒} = \frac{▒}{16} = \frac{15}{▒}$

4. Two of Al's footprints measure 15 inches.

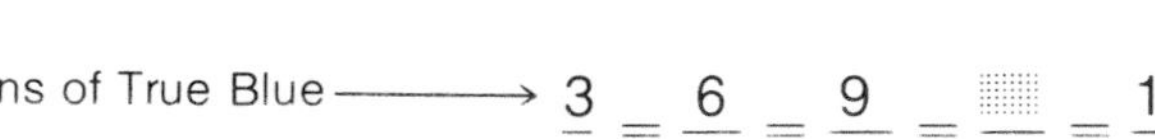

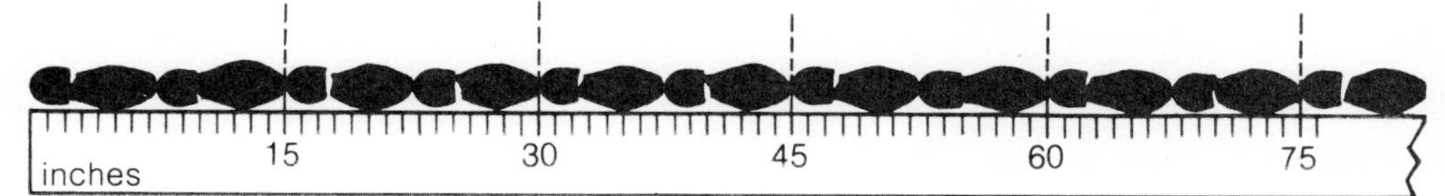

Footprints → Inches →

$\frac{2}{15} = \frac{4}{▒} = \frac{6}{▒} = \frac{▒}{60} = \frac{▒}{75}$

Finding Equal Ratios by Multiplying

You can find equal ratios by multiplying.

Pennies → 4, Inches → 3

$$\frac{4}{3} = \overset{4 \times 2}{\underset{3 \times 2}{\frac{8}{6}}} = \overset{4 \times 3}{\underset{3 \times 3}{\frac{12}{9}}} = \overset{4 \times 4}{\underset{3 \times 4}{\frac{16}{12}}} = \overset{4 \times 5}{\underset{3 \times 5}{\frac{20}{15}}}$$

Harriet's class did experiments that produced ratios.
Multiply to complete the list shown for each experiment.

1. 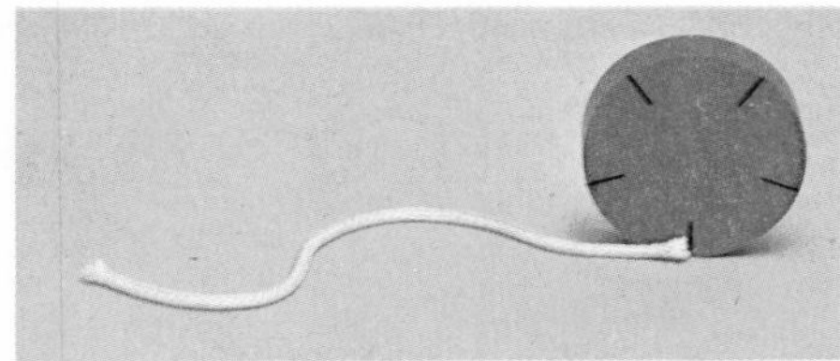

Complete turns → 1, Distance rolled (cm) → 5

$$\frac{1}{5} = \overset{1 \times 2}{\underset{5 \times 2}{\frac{\square}{\square}}} = \overset{1 \times 3}{\underset{5 \times 3}{\frac{\square}{\square}}} = \overset{1 \times 4}{\underset{5 \times 4}{\frac{\square}{\square}}} = \overset{1 \times 5}{\underset{5 \times 5}{\frac{\square}{\square}}}$$

2. 

Water (cups) → 2, Time (seconds) → 7

$$\frac{2}{7} = \overset{2 \times 2}{\underset{7 \times 2}{\frac{\square}{\square}}} = \overset{2 \times 3}{\underset{7 \times 3}{\frac{\square}{\square}}} = \overset{2 \times 4}{\underset{7 \times 4}{\frac{\square}{\square}}} = \overset{2 \times 5}{\underset{7 \times 5}{\frac{\square}{\square}}}$$

3. 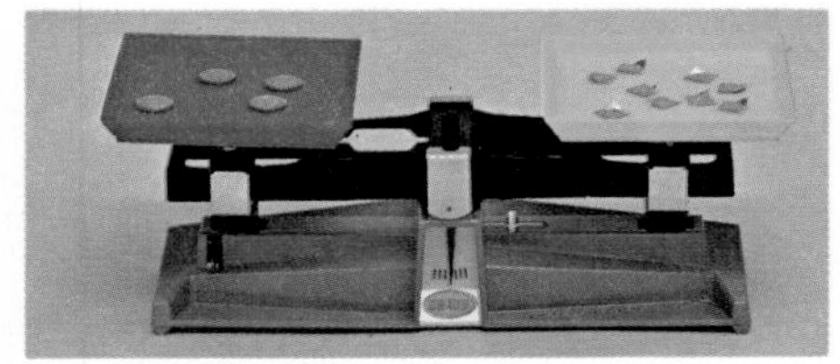

Dimes → 4, Grams → 9

$$\frac{4}{9} = \overset{4 \times 2}{\underset{9 \times 2}{\frac{\square}{\square}}} = \overset{4 \times 3}{\underset{9 \times 3}{\frac{\square}{\square}}} = \overset{4 \times 4}{\underset{9 \times 4}{\frac{\square}{\square}}} = \overset{4 \times 5}{\underset{9 \times 5}{\frac{\square}{\square}}}$$

For each exercise, continue the list of equal ratios until you find the answer.

4.

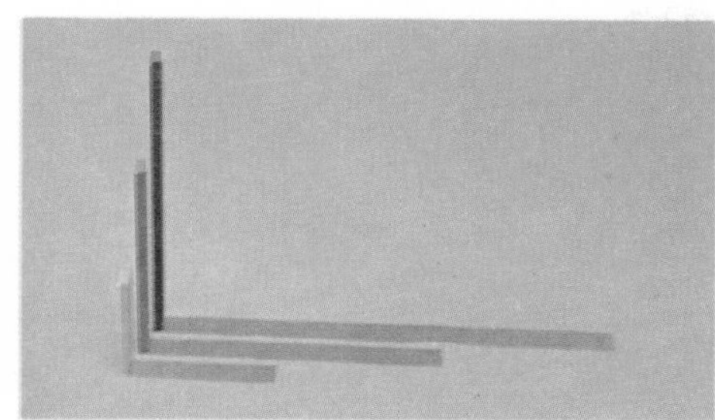

How long is the shadow of a 60-centimeter stick?

Height of stick (cm) ⟶
Length of shadow (cm) ⟶ $\frac{10}{13} = \frac{20}{26} = \frac{30}{39} =$

5.

How many turns of the red gear for 18 turns of the blue gear?

Turns of red gear ⟶
Turns of blue gear ⟶ $\frac{2}{3} = \frac{4}{6} = \frac{6}{9} =$

6.

Give the distance along the ramp for a height of 12 cm above the floor.

Distance along ramp (cm) ⟶
Height above floor (cm) ⟶ $\frac{5}{2} = \frac{10}{4} = \frac{15}{6} =$

7.

How many pennies would stretch the rubber band 10 centimeters?

Pennies in cup ⟶
Amount of stretch (cm) ⟶ $\frac{6}{2} = \frac{12}{4} = \frac{18}{6} =$

More practice
Set J, page 127

Finding Cross-Products

These ratios are equal. $\frac{2}{3} = \frac{4}{6} = \frac{6}{9} = \frac{8}{12} = \frac{10}{15} = \frac{12}{18}$

$$\frac{2}{3} = \frac{8}{12} \qquad \begin{matrix} 3 \times 8 \\ 2 \times 12 \end{matrix}$$

2×12 and 3×8 are called ***cross-products.***

$$2 \times 12 = 24$$
$$3 \times 8 = 24$$

The cross-products are equal.

Are the cross-products for these ratios equal?

$\frac{4}{6} = \frac{6}{9}$ $\quad 6 \times 6$, 4×9

$\frac{2}{3} = \frac{12}{18}$ $\quad 3 \times 12$, 2×18

$\frac{10}{15} = \frac{8}{12}$ $\quad 15 \times 8$, 10×12

■ *If two ratios are equal,*
their cross-products are equal.

Equal ratios are given.
Show that the cross-products are equal.

Here's how

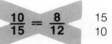

$\frac{2}{5} = \frac{4}{10}$

2X10=20
5X4=20

1. $\frac{6}{8} = \frac{9}{12}$

2. $\frac{4}{5} = \frac{8}{10}$

3. $\frac{10}{6} = \frac{25}{15}$

4. $\frac{24}{30} = \frac{4}{5}$

5. $\frac{9}{1} = \frac{108}{12}$

6. $\frac{7}{8} = \frac{42}{48}$

7. $\frac{6}{11} = \frac{42}{77}$

8. $\frac{16}{28} = \frac{8}{14}$

9. $\frac{18}{30} = \frac{21}{35}$

You can use cross-products to check if two ratios are equal.

$\frac{9}{12}$ $\frac{15}{20}$

$9 \times 20 = 180$
$12 \times 15 = 180$

The cross-products are equal, so the ratios are equal.

$\frac{4}{6}$ $\frac{10}{12}$

$4 \times 12 = 48$
$6 \times 10 = 60$

The cross-products are not equal, so the ratios are not equal.

Tell whether the ratios are equal.
Find cross-products to help you decide.

10. $\frac{2}{5}$ $\frac{3}{6}$

11. $\frac{2}{3}$ $\frac{7}{10}$

12. $\frac{30}{9}$ $\frac{40}{12}$

13. $\frac{6}{8}$ $\frac{15}{20}$

14. $\frac{9}{12}$ $\frac{12}{16}$

15. $\frac{30}{36}$ $\frac{20}{24}$

16. $\frac{10}{15}$ $\frac{16}{20}$

17. $\frac{4}{7}$ $\frac{32}{56}$

18. $\frac{1}{5}$ $\frac{13}{65}$

19. $\frac{8}{3}$ $\frac{27}{10}$

20. $\frac{18}{63}$ $\frac{4}{14}$

21. $\frac{40}{160}$ $\frac{8}{30}$

Keeping Skillful

Divide.

1. $5\overline{)65}$

2. $8\overline{)136}$

3. $9\overline{)207}$

4. $65\overline{)390}$

5. $47\overline{)517}$

Find the number for *n*.

6. $3 \times n = 42$

7. $n \times 4 = 108$

8. $9 \times n = 333$

9. $12 \times n = 600$

10. $n \times 25 = 125$

Finding Missing Numbers in Equal Ratios

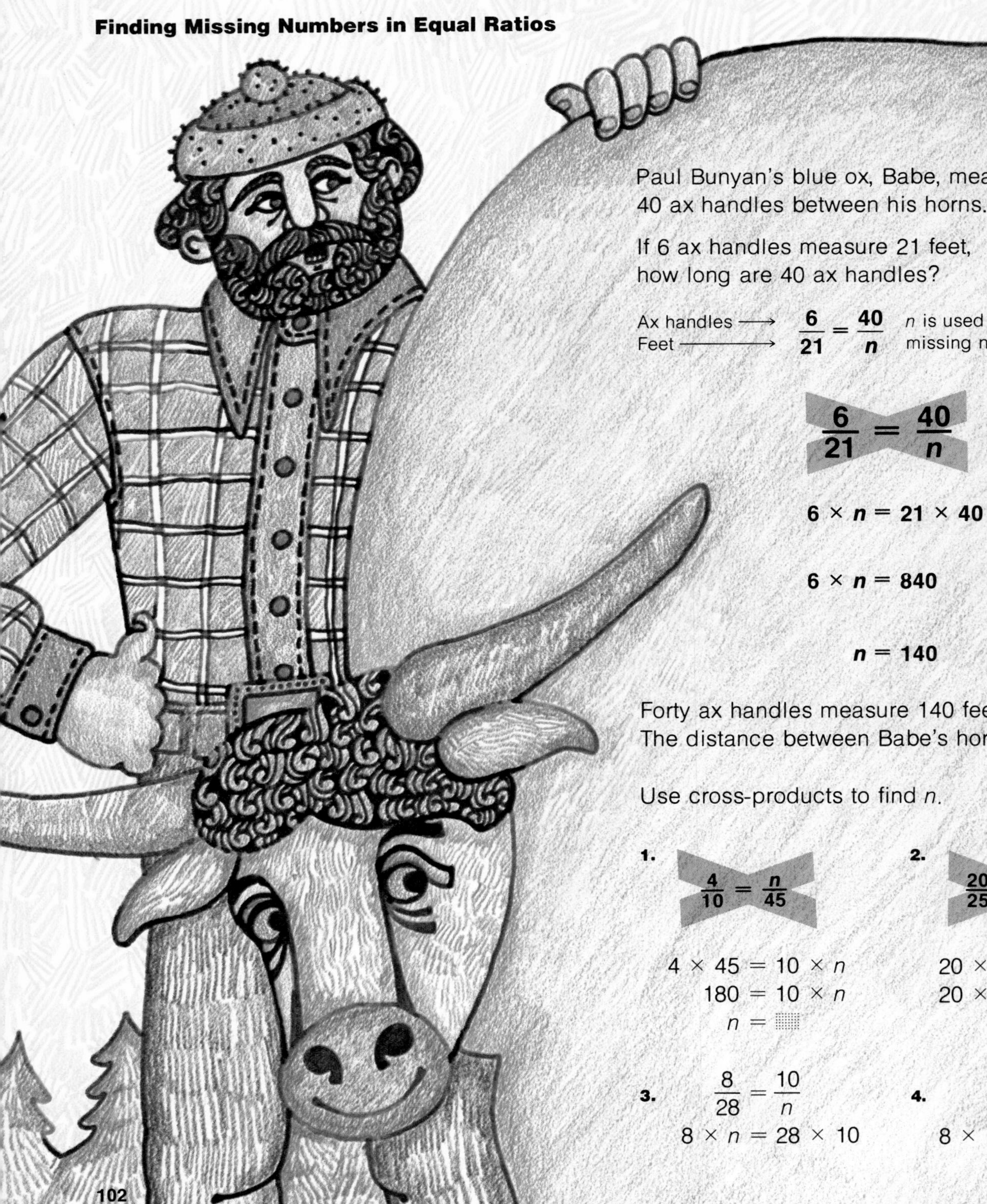

Paul Bunyan's blue ox, Babe, measured 40 ax handles between his horns.

If 6 ax handles measure 21 feet, how long are 40 ax handles?

Ax handles ⟶ Feet ⟶ $\frac{6}{21} = \frac{40}{n}$ n is used for the missing number.

$$\frac{6}{21} = \frac{40}{n}$$

21 × 40

6 × *n*

6 × *n* = 21 × 40   The cross-products are equal.

6 × *n* = 840   Divide to find the missing factor.

***n* = 140** $6\overline{)840}$

Forty ax handles measure 140 feet.
The distance between Babe's horns was 140 feet.

Use cross-products to find *n*.

1. $\frac{4}{10} = \frac{n}{45}$

$4 \times 45 = 10 \times n$
$180 = 10 \times n$
$n = \square$

2. $\frac{20}{25} = \frac{36}{n}$

$20 \times n = 25 \times 36$
$20 \times n = 900$
$n = \square$

3. $\frac{8}{28} = \frac{10}{n}$

$8 \times n = 28 \times 10$

4. $\frac{8}{3} = \frac{n}{12}$

$8 \times 12 = 3 \times n$

5. $\frac{2}{3} = \frac{n}{42}$

6. $\frac{4}{1} = \frac{52}{n}$

7. $\frac{24}{28} = \frac{18}{n}$

8. $\frac{10}{6} = \frac{n}{15}$

9. $\frac{20}{25} = \frac{12}{n}$

10. $\frac{7}{9} = \frac{n}{36}$

11. $\frac{9}{4} = \frac{108}{n}$

12. $\frac{18}{4} = \frac{n}{10}$

13. $\frac{12}{28} = \frac{18}{n}$

14. $\frac{1}{6} = \frac{n}{78}$

15. $\frac{8}{50} = \frac{20}{n}$

16. $\frac{10}{4} = \frac{n}{22}$

17. $\frac{16}{24} = \frac{n}{27}$

18. $\frac{10}{16} = \frac{25}{n}$

19. $\frac{12}{8} = \frac{54}{n}$

20. $\frac{19}{57} = \frac{n}{9}$

21. $\frac{17}{1} = \frac{51}{n}$

22. $\frac{75}{100} = \frac{30}{n}$

More practice
Set K, page 127

Time Out!

Copy the regions shown below.

How can you cut the red region into three pieces to make it exactly fit the blue region?

How can you cut the red region into two pieces to make it exactly fit?

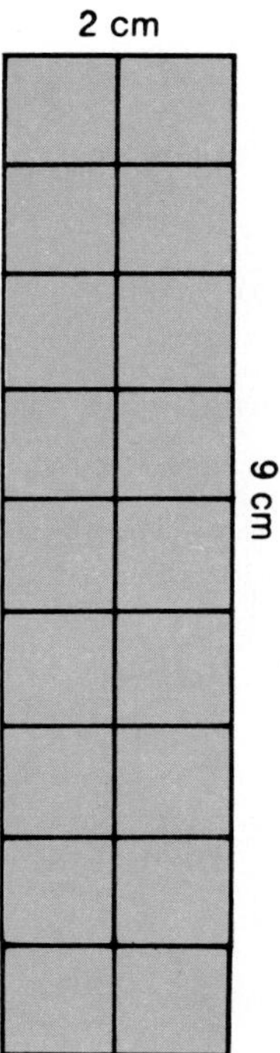

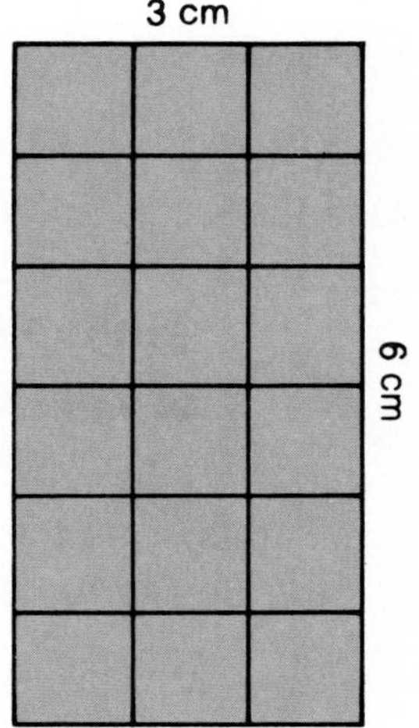

Using Ratios to Solve Problems

Isabel and María have a puppy named Snoopy.

At this price, how much would 6 cans of Snoopy's food cost?

Write equal ratios. Use n for the missing number.

$$\frac{4}{58} = \frac{6}{n} \begin{array}{l} \longleftarrow \text{Cans} \\ \longleftarrow \text{Cents} \end{array}$$

Write the cross-products.

$$4 \times n = 58 \times 6$$
$$4 \times n = 348$$

Find n.

$$n = 87$$

Answer the question. Six cans would cost 87¢.

Use the steps above to help you solve these problems.

1. **Snoopy's speed:**
30 yards in 12 seconds

At this speed, how long would it take the dog to run 100 yards?

$$\frac{30}{12} = \frac{100}{n} \begin{array}{l} \longleftarrow \text{Yards} \\ \longleftarrow \text{Seconds} \end{array}$$

2. **Snoopy's pulse:**
28 heartbeats in 15 seconds

At this rate, how many times would the dog's heart beat in 60 seconds?

$$\frac{28}{15} = \frac{n}{60} \begin{array}{l} \longleftarrow \text{Heartbeats} \\ \longleftarrow \text{Seconds} \end{array}$$

3. **Snoopy's Special Diet**
Mix: 4 oz. of hamburger
6 oz. of dog food

How much hamburger should Isabel mix with 3 ounces of dog food?

4. **6 Doggy Chews for 51¢**

At this price, how many doggy chews can María buy with 85¢?

Using Ratios with Measures

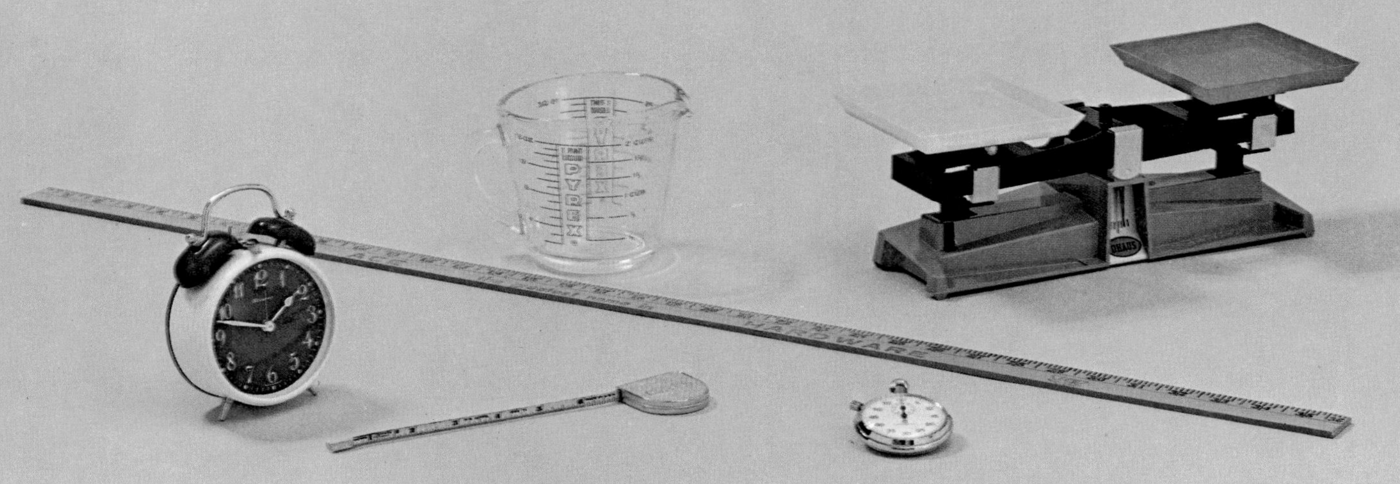

You can use ratios when you work with measures.
Write equal ratios to help you solve each problem.

1. 2 cups is 1 pint.
How many cups is 12 pints?

$\frac{2}{1} = \frac{n}{12}$ ⟵ Cups / ⟵ Pints

2. 12 inches is 1 foot.
How many feet is 72 inches?

$\frac{12}{1} = \frac{72}{n}$ ⟵ Inches / ⟵ Feet

3. 7 days is 1 week.
How many days is 20 weeks?

$\frac{7}{1} = \frac{n}{20}$ ⟵ Days / ⟵ Weeks

4. 16 ounces is 1 pound.
How many ounces is 8 pounds?

5. 4 quarts is 1 gallon.
How many gallons is 68 quarts?

6. 12 months is 1 year.
How many years is 180 months?

7. 8 fluid ounces is 1 cup.
How many fluid ounces is 14 cups?

8. 36 inches is 1 yard.
How many inches is 9 yards?

9. 60 seconds is 1 minute.
How many seconds is 10 minutes?

10. 3 feet is 1 yard.
How many yards is 87 feet?

Using Ratios: Space Travel

The chart shows that Ed weighs 100 pounds on Earth but would weigh 264 pounds on the planet Jupiter. Ed would weigh more on Jupiter because Jupiter has a stronger force of gravity.

Ed's weight	
On Earth	100 lb.
On the moon	17 lb.
On Mercury	28 lb.
On Venus	86 lb.
On Mars	38 lb.
On Jupiter	264 lb.
On Saturn	120 lb.
On Uranus	92 lb.
On Neptune	110 lb.
On Pluto	70 lb.

Ed's father weighs 175 pounds on Earth. How much would he weigh on Jupiter?

Write equal ratios to find out.

Ed Father

$$\frac{100}{264} = \frac{175}{n} \quad \begin{matrix} \leftarrow \text{Weight on Earth} \\ \leftarrow \text{Weight on Jupiter} \end{matrix}$$

$$n = 462$$

Ed's father would weigh 462 pounds on Jupiter.

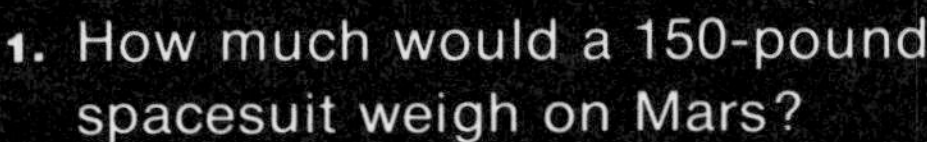

Write equal ratios to help you solve each problem. Use the chart for Ed's weight.

1. How much would a 150-pound spacesuit weigh on Mars?

   Ed Spacesuit

   $$\frac{100}{38} = \frac{150}{n} \quad \begin{matrix} \leftarrow \text{Weight on Earth} \\ \leftarrow \text{Weight on Mars} \end{matrix}$$

2. How much would Ed's 175-pound father weigh on Uranus?
3. How much would a 10-pound cat weigh on Neptune?
4. How much would a 300-pound piano weigh on the moon?
5. How much would a 25-pound TV set weigh on Jupiter?
6. How much would a 250-pound refrigerator weigh on Mars?
7. How much would a 30-pound poodle weigh on Pluto?
8. How much would a 2000-pound car weigh on Mercury?

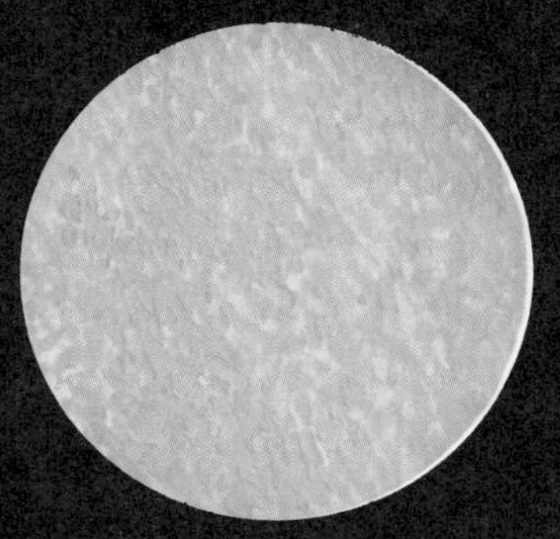

When astronauts travel between planets, they will be in a spaceship for many months.

Write equal ratios to help you solve these problems.

9. If a spaceship travels 20 miles in 3 seconds, how long does it take the spaceship to travel 500 miles?

10. If the spaceship burns 6 tons of fuel in 4 days, how many tons of fuel are needed for 90 days?

11. Before blastoff, water is stored on the spaceship. Three gallons of water weigh 25 pounds. How much do 60 gallons of water weigh?

12. Under stress, one astronaut's heart beat 10 times in 5 seconds. At this rate, how many times would it beat in 60 seconds?

13. Space Breakfast
Pang Instant Orange Drink

Mix: 2 teaspoons Pang
6 ounces water

How many teaspoons of Pang should you mix with 15 ounces of water?

14. Suppose that it takes 6 months to travel 35 million miles to Mars. At this speed, how many months would it take to travel 385 million miles to Jupiter?

Using Mathematics: Floor Plans

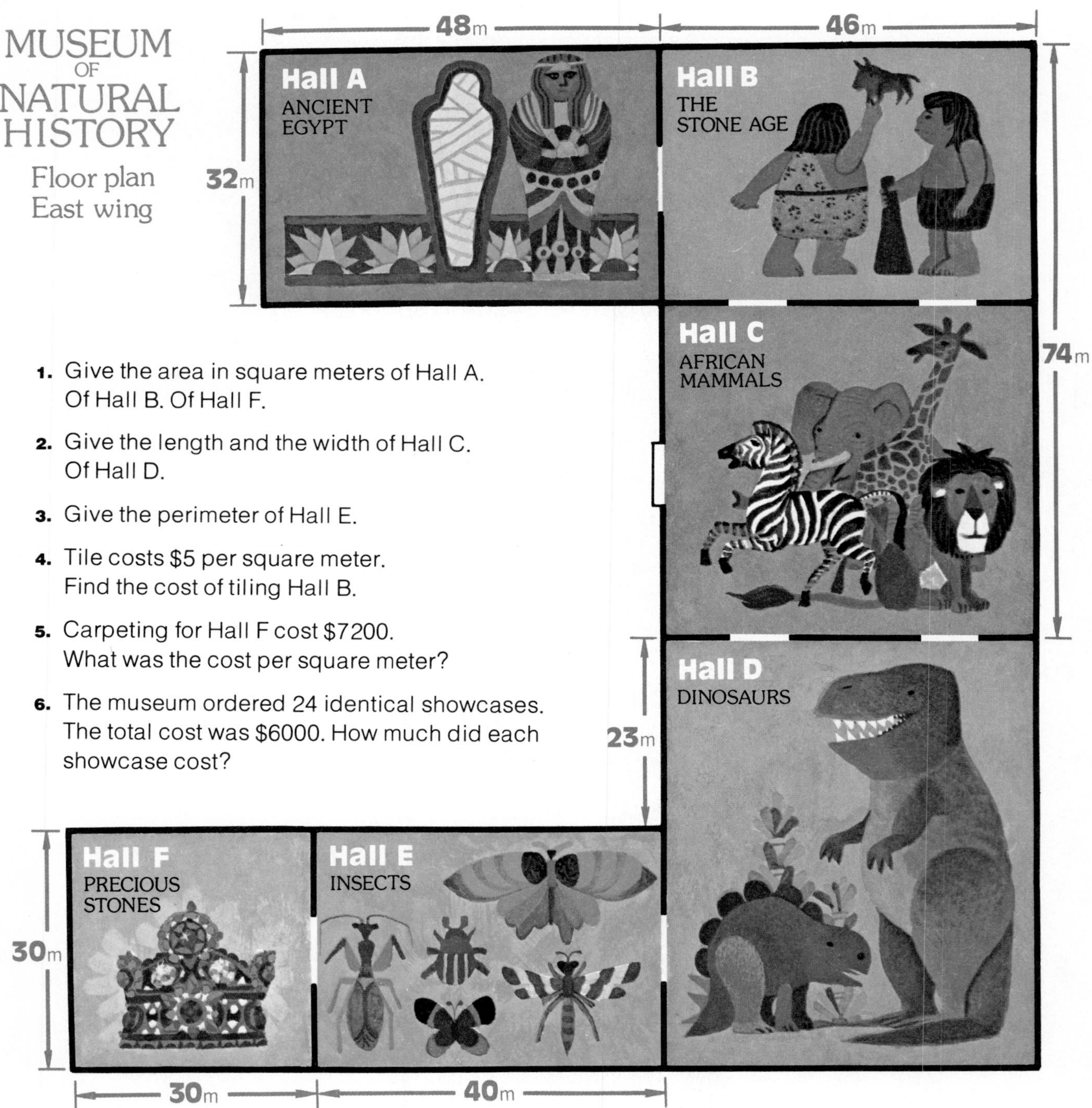

1. Give the area in square meters of Hall A. Of Hall B. Of Hall F.
2. Give the length and the width of Hall C. Of Hall D.
3. Give the perimeter of Hall E.
4. Tile costs $5 per square meter. Find the cost of tiling Hall B.
5. Carpeting for Hall F cost $7200. What was the cost per square meter?
6. The museum ordered 24 identical showcases. The total cost was $6000. How much did each showcase cost?

Check Yourself
Ratio, Pages 94 - 108

Writing ratios, pages 94–95

1. Write a ratio.

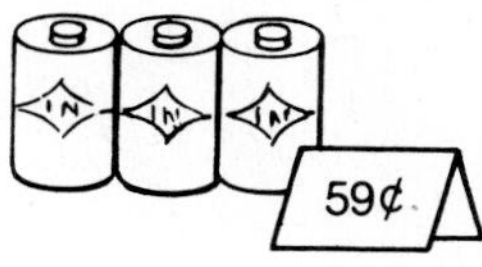

Batteries ⟶ ▒
Cents ⟶ ▒

Finding equal ratios, pages 96–101

Write three more equal ratios for each list.

2. $\frac{4}{5} = \frac{8}{10} = \frac{12}{15}$

3. $\frac{2}{9} = \frac{4}{18} = \frac{6}{27}$

4. $\frac{3}{1} = \frac{6}{2} = \frac{9}{3}$

Tell whether the ratios are equal.

5. $\frac{4}{10}$ $\frac{14}{35}$

6. $\frac{12}{5}$ $\frac{25}{10}$

7. $\frac{9}{12}$ $\frac{12}{15}$

8. $\frac{6}{8}$ $\frac{9}{12}$

Finding missing numbers in equal ratios, pages 102–103

Find *n*.

9. $\frac{6}{9} = \frac{10}{n}$

10. $\frac{8}{36} = \frac{n}{27}$

11. $\frac{25}{20} = \frac{40}{n}$

12. $\frac{21}{12} = \frac{n}{8}$

Problem solving, pages 94–99, 104–107

13. There are 3 feet in 1 yard. How many feet is 18 yards?

14. There are 7 days in 1 week. How many weeks is 14 days?

15. At this price, how much would 6 basketballs cost?

16. A car traveled 12 miles in 15 minutes. At that speed, how far would the car travel in 35 minutes?

Geometric Figures and Volume, Pages 110–124

Recognizing Geometric Figures

Name other objects that are shaped like the figures on this page.

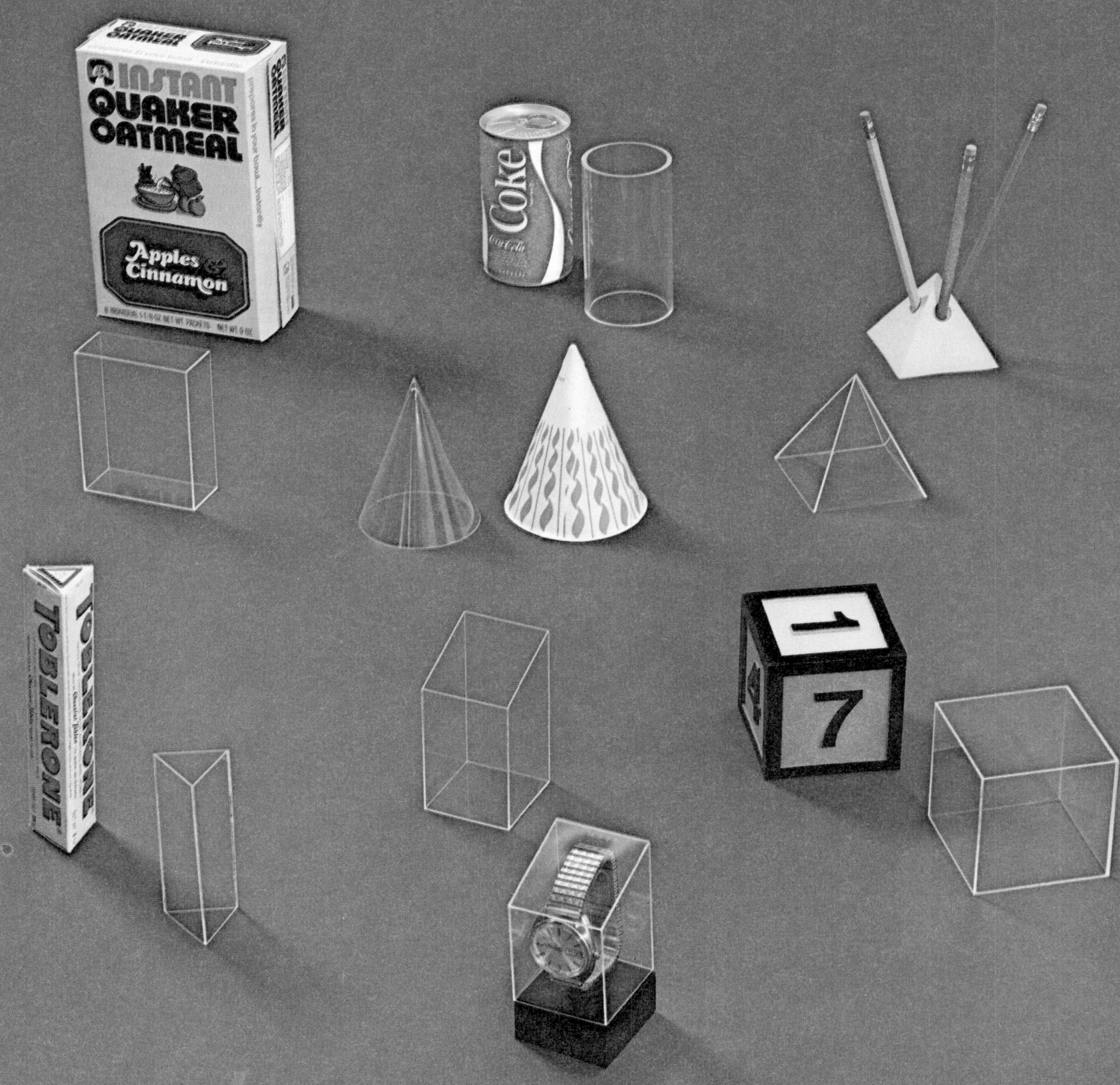

Counting Faces, Vertices, and Edges

Study the pictures of the cube below.
Count to find the number of faces, vertices, and edges.

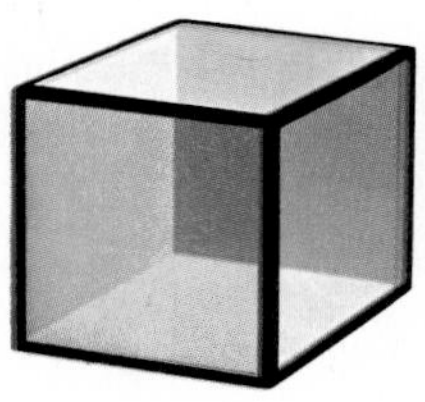

The 6 ***faces*** are the flat surfaces.

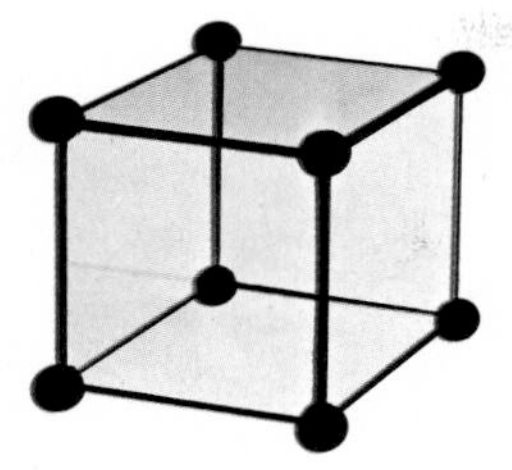

There are 8 ***vertices***.

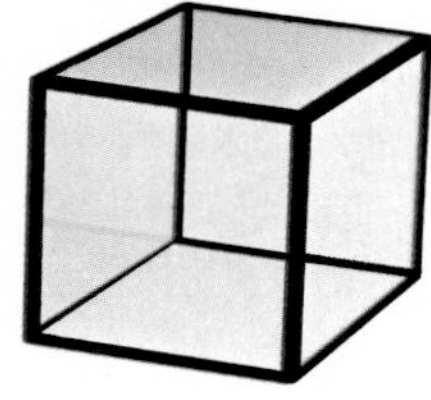

There are 12 ***edges***.

Complete the table for each geometric figure.

	Geometric figure	Number of faces	Number of vertices	Number of edges
1.		4		
2.			5	
3.				12
4.				
5.				

Matching Faces with Geometric Figures

Shirley traced around the edges of the box to see what all the faces looked like.

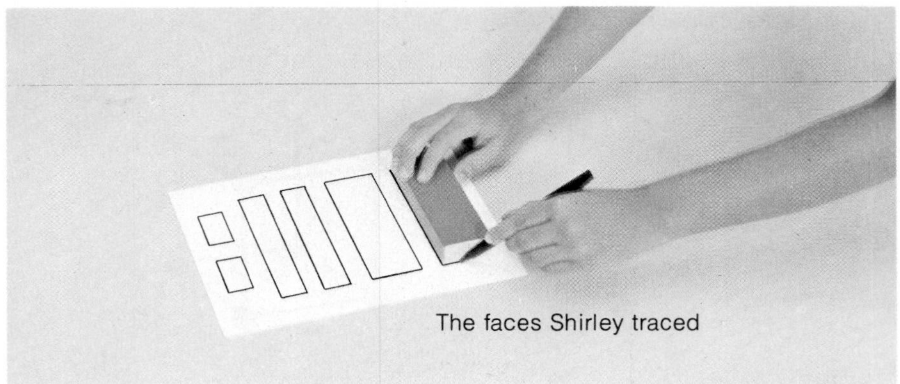

The faces Shirley traced

In each exercise, match the faces with the correct geometric figure. Write the letter for the figure.

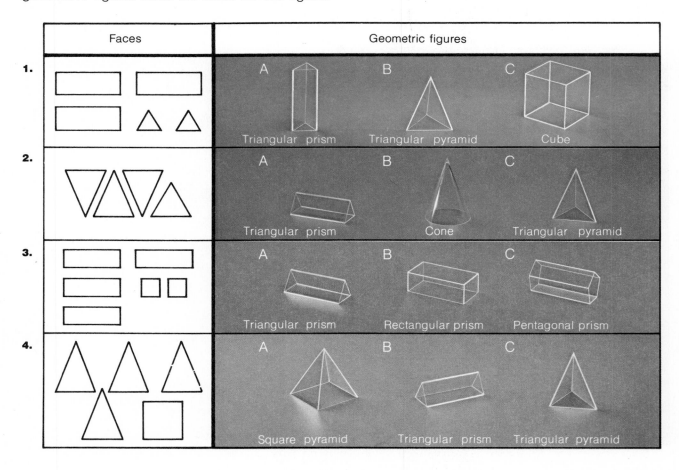

	Faces	Geometric figures		
1.		A Triangular prism	B Triangular pyramid	C Cube
2.		A Triangular prism	B Cone	C Triangular pyramid
3.		A Triangular prism	B Rectangular prism	C Pentagonal prism
4.		A Square pyramid	B Triangular prism	C Triangular pyramid

Making Patterns for Geometric Figures

Joel used squared paper to draw a pattern for a ***rectangular prism.***

Joel's pattern forms a prism like this one.

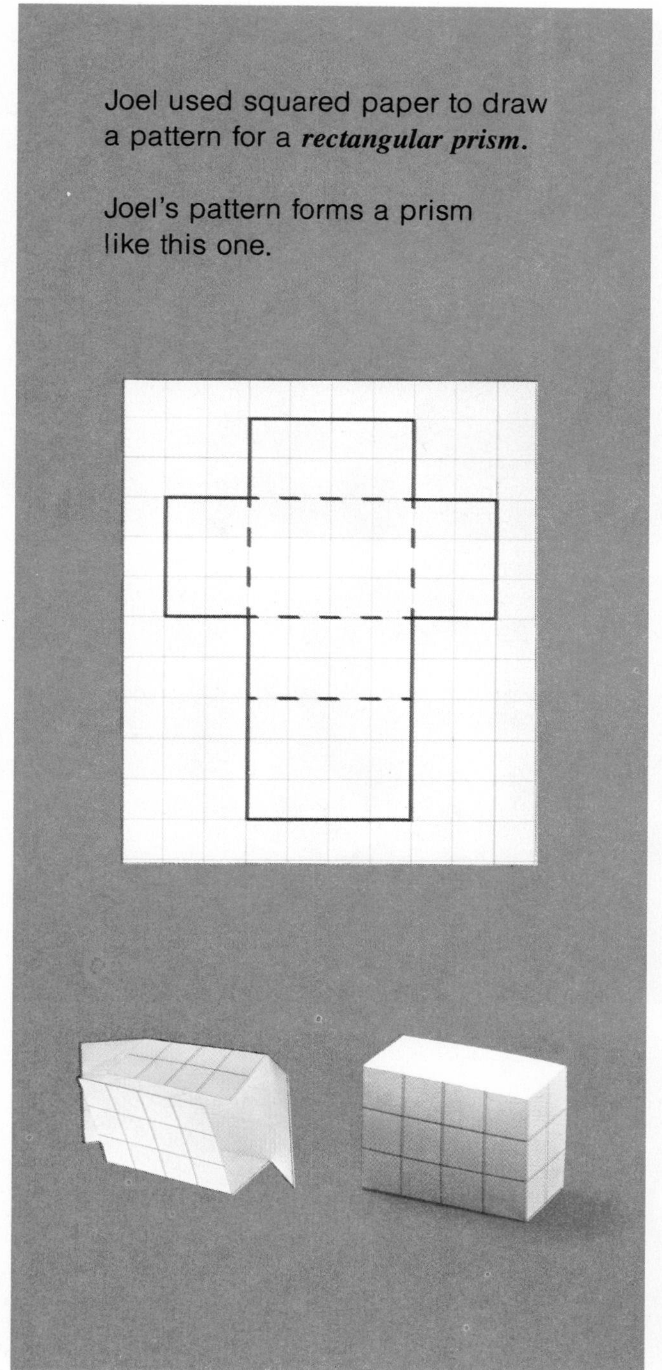

Draw each pattern.
Then make the figure by cutting and folding.

1.

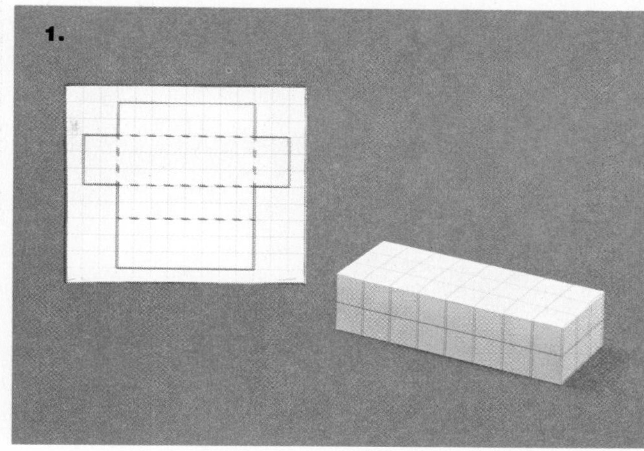

2.

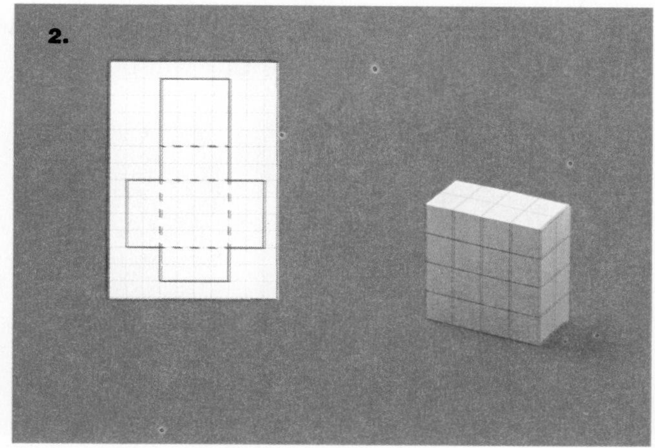

3. Make a pattern for this prism.

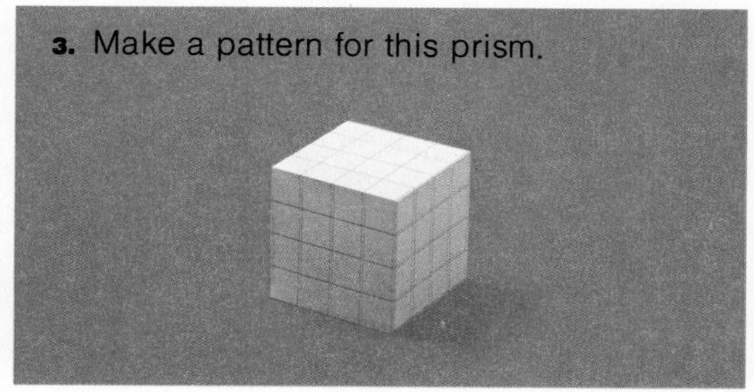

Counting Cubes to Find Volume

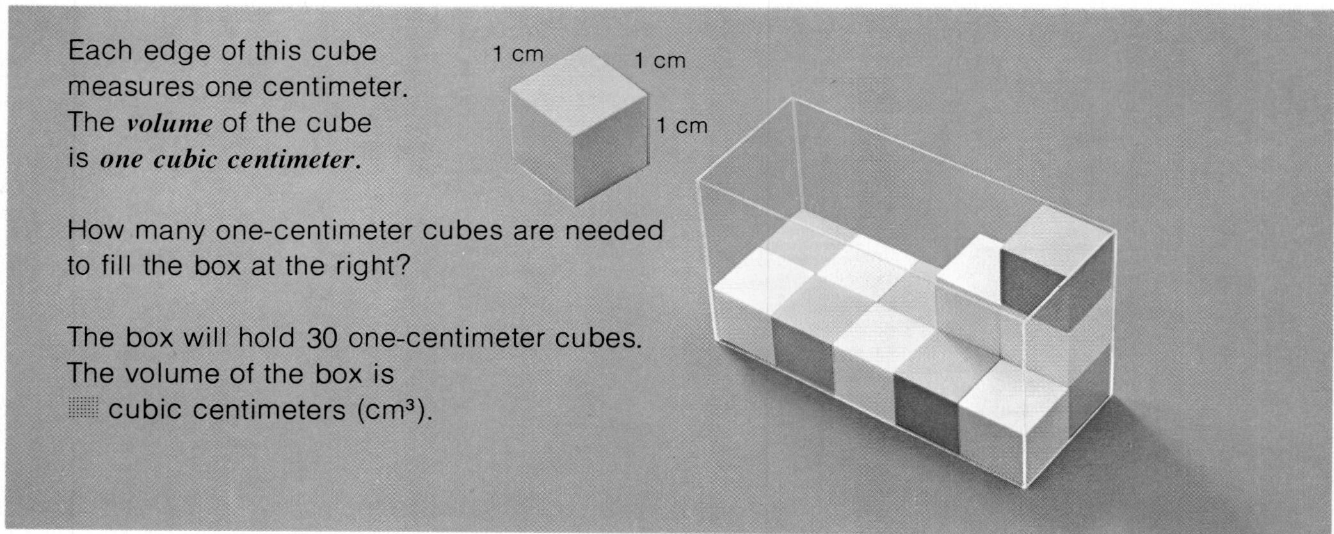

Each edge of this cube measures one centimeter. The *volume* of the cube is ***one cubic centimeter.***

How many one-centimeter cubes are needed to fill the box at the right?

The box will hold 30 one-centimeter cubes. The volume of the box is ▒ cubic centimeters (cm^3).

Give the volume of each box in cubic centimeters. Think of how many cubes the box will hold.

1.

2.

3.

4.

5.

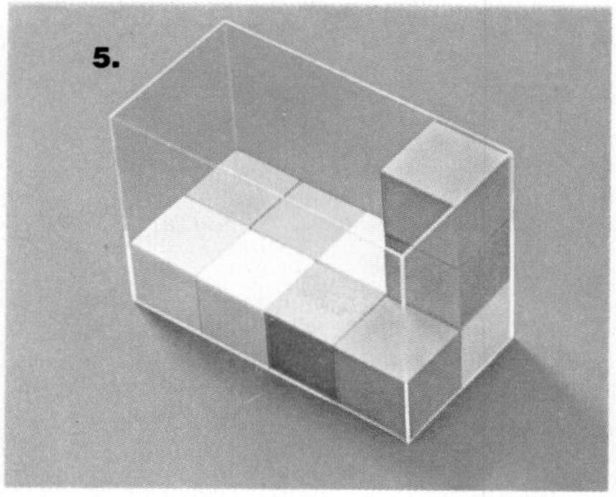

6.

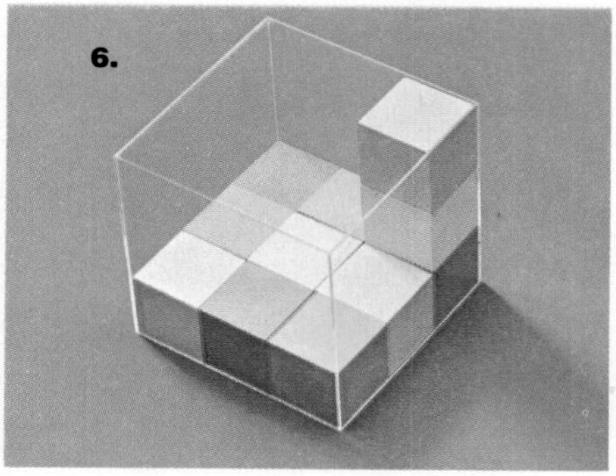

The figures on this page are made up of one-centimeter cubes. Count the cubes and give the volumes in cubic centimeters.

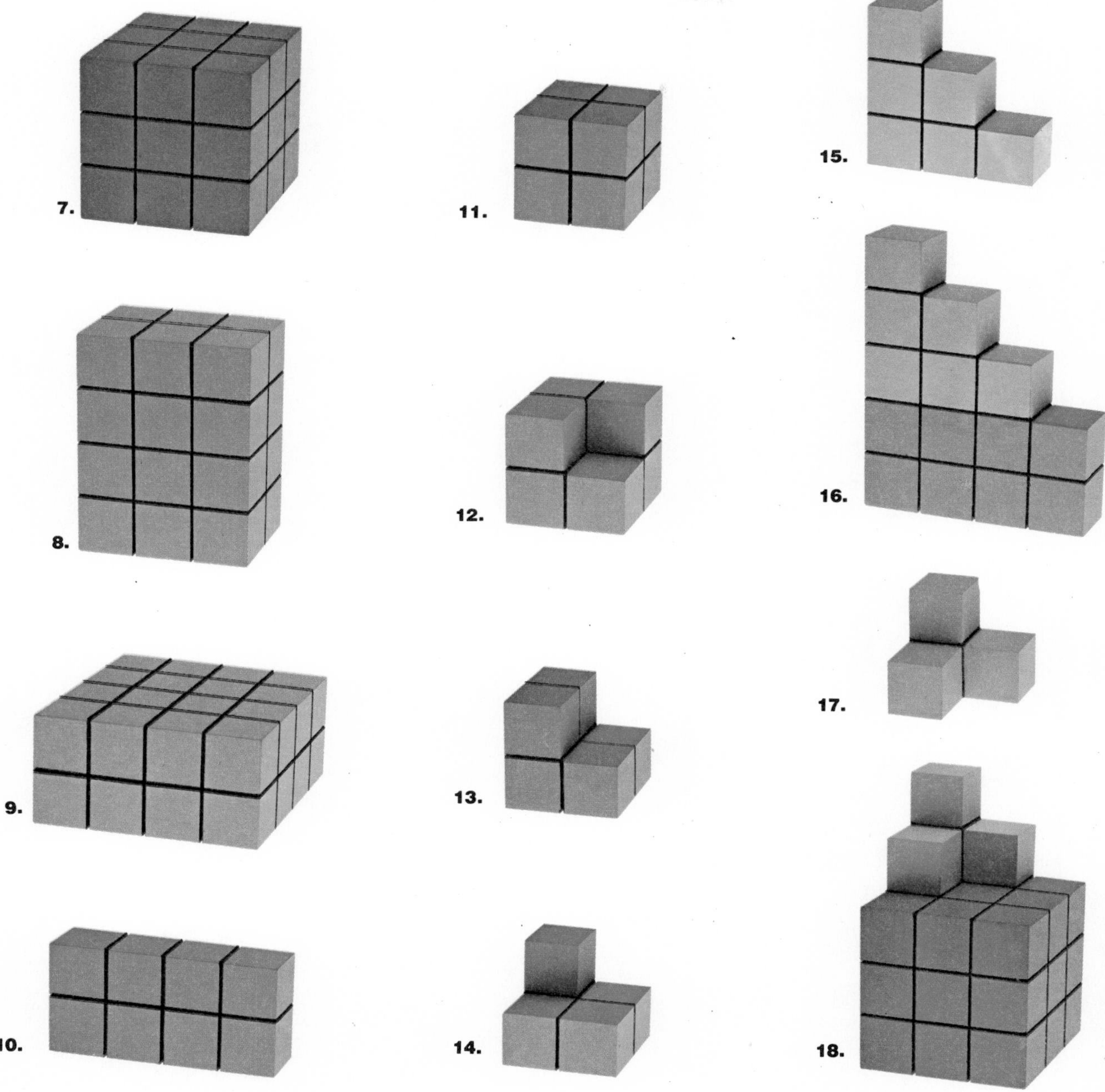

Multiplying to Find Volume

A. You can find the volume of a rectangular prism by multiplying.

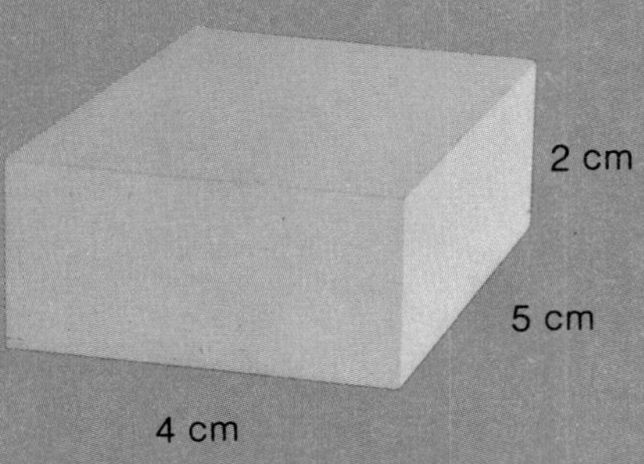

Imagine filling the prism with one-centimeter cubes.

How many cubes are in one layer? ($4 \times 5 = 20$)
How many layers of cubes are there? (2)

Cubes per layer		Number of layers		Volume
(4 × 5)	×	**2**	=	**40**

The volume is 40 cm^3.

B. Find the volume of this prism by multiplying.

Cubes per layer		Number of layers		
(4 × 5)	×	**3**	=	▒ **cm^3**

In exercises 1 through 8, give the volumes in cubic centimeters.

1.

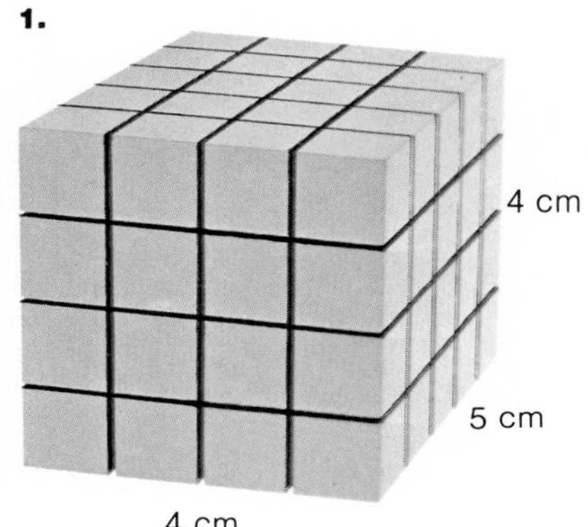

2.

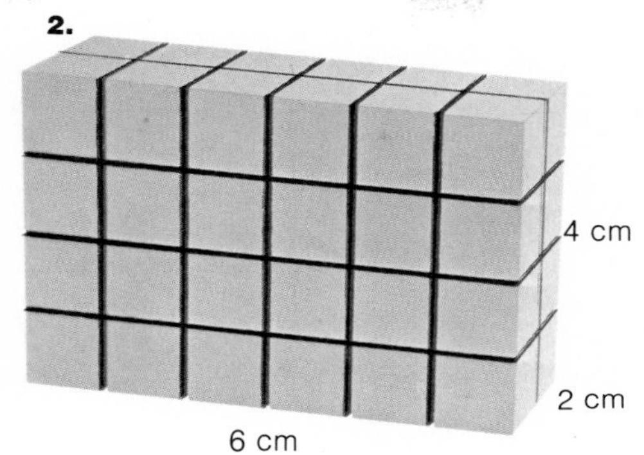

3.

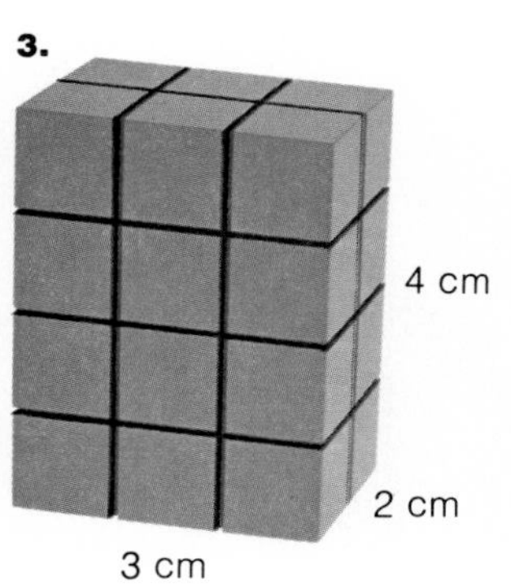

4.

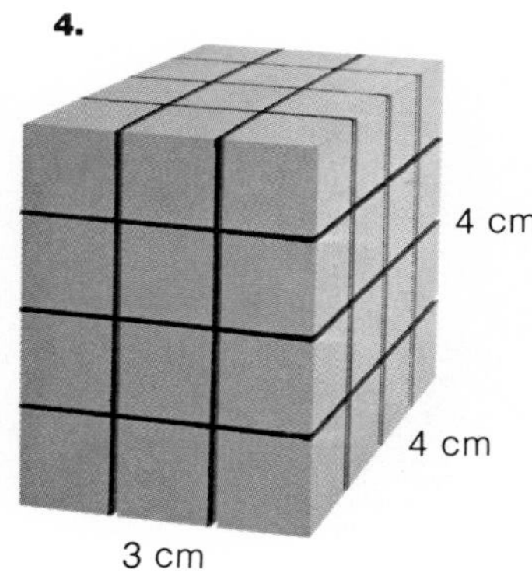

5.

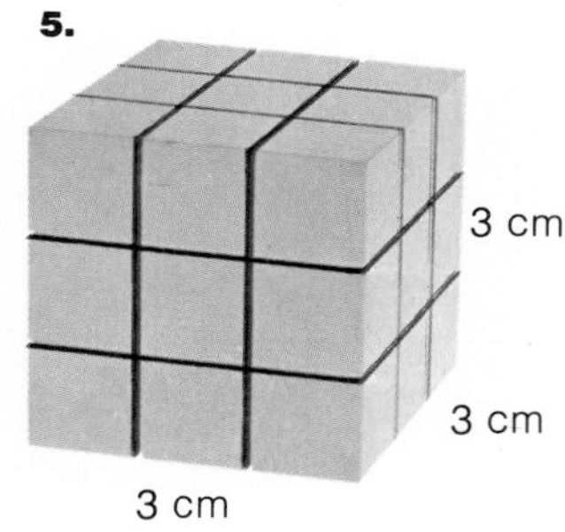

6.

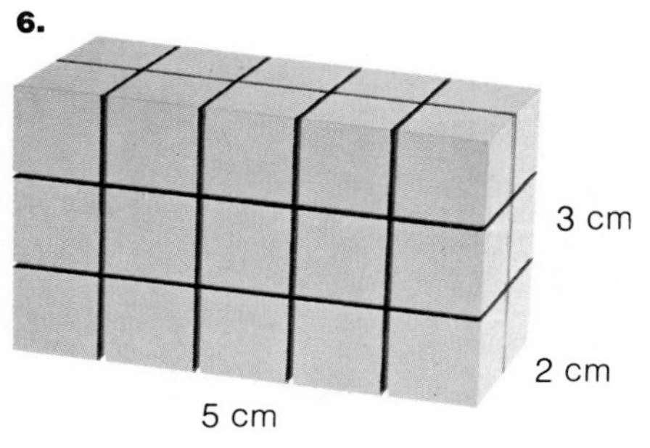

7.

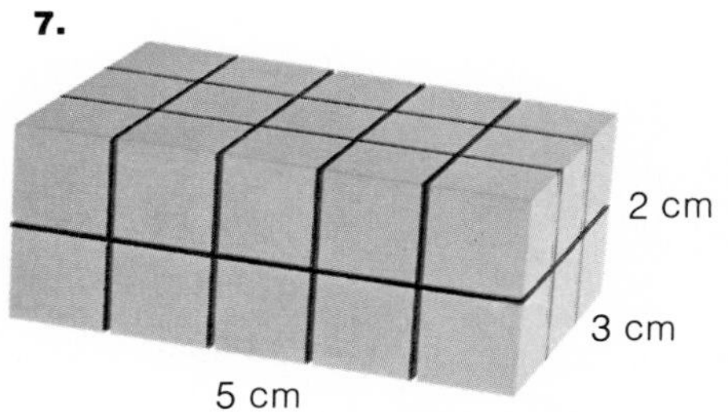

8.

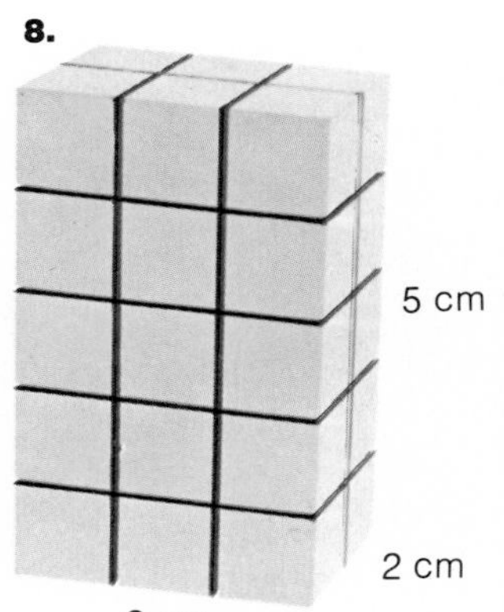

Keeping Skillful

Divide.

1. $9\overline{)45}$

2. $7\overline{)63}$

3. $4\overline{)92}$

4. $5\overline{)81}$

5. $6\overline{)837}$

6. $9\overline{)396}$

7. $20\overline{)740}$

8. $60\overline{)840}$

9. $35\overline{)624}$

10. $12\overline{)506}$

11. $41\overline{)1680}$

12. $22\overline{)484}$

13. $33\overline{)1099}$

14. $52\overline{)2704}$

15. $71\overline{)1541}$

Finding the Volume of Rectangular Prisms

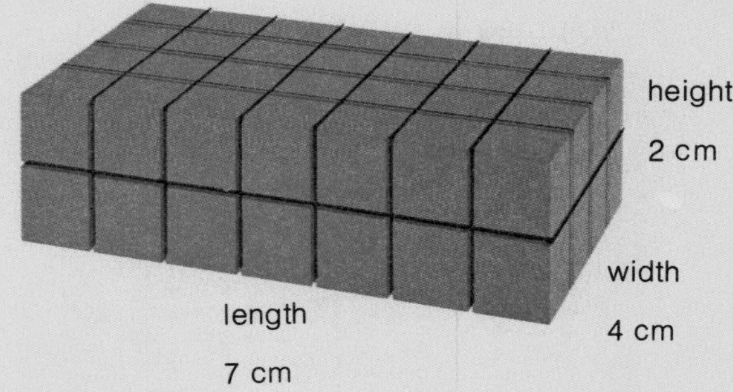

■ *To find the volume of a rectangular prism, multiply*

length × width × height.

Volume = 7 × 4 × 2
Volume = 56 cm^3

Give the volume of each prism in cubic centimeters.

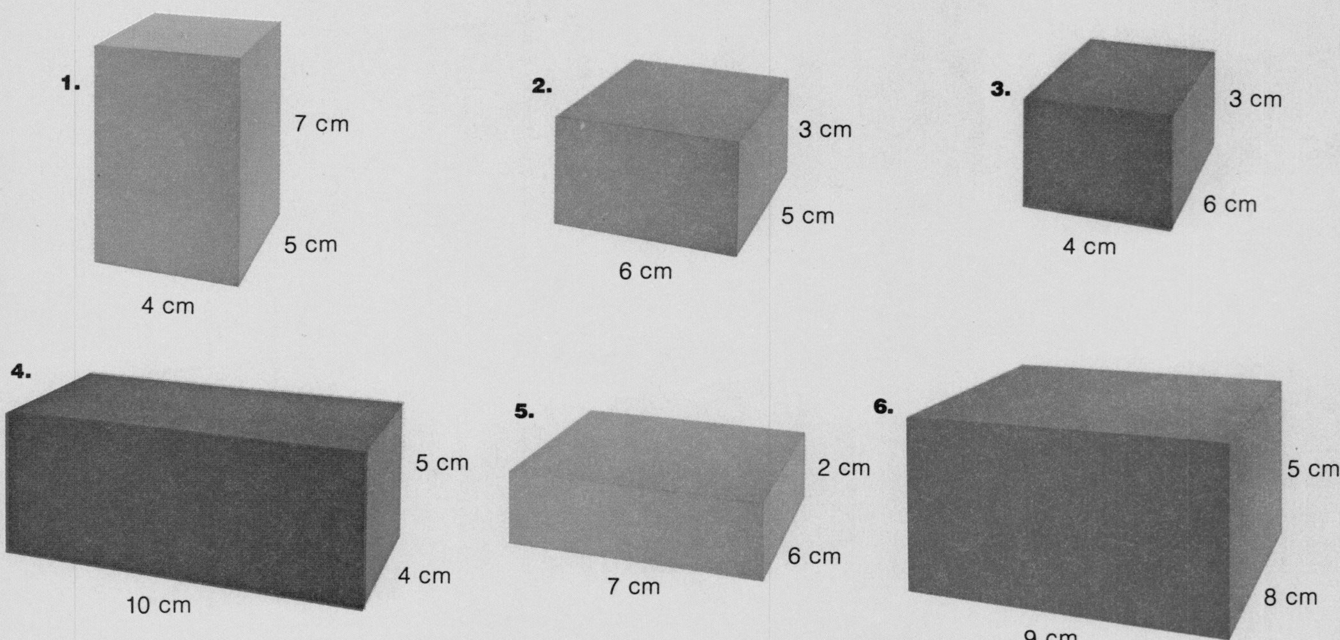

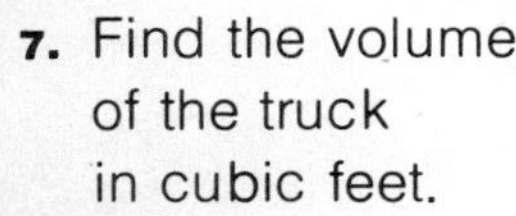

7. Find the volume of the truck in cubic feet.

8. Find the volume of the telephone booth in cubic feet.

9. Find the volume of the briefcase in cubic centimeters.

10. Find the volume of the tool chest in cubic centimeters.

11. Find the volume in cubic centimeters.

Using Volume to Solve Problems

A. Mr. Harris rented a truck. The van had 324 cubic feet of space. What was the height of the van?

Volume = length × width × height

$$324 = (9 \times 6) \times h$$
$$324 = 54 \times h$$
$$h = ▒$$

$$54\overline{)324}$$

The height of the van was ▒ feet.
Would a $6\frac{1}{2}$-foot bookcase stand upright in the van?

B. Irv's pet frog can jump 9 inches above the ground. Irv has a box with 528 cubic inches of space. Can the frog jump out?

Volume = length × width × height

$$528 = (8 \times 6) \times h$$
$$528 = 48 \times h$$
$$h = ▒$$

$$48\overline{)528}$$

The box is ▒ inches high. Can the frog jump out?

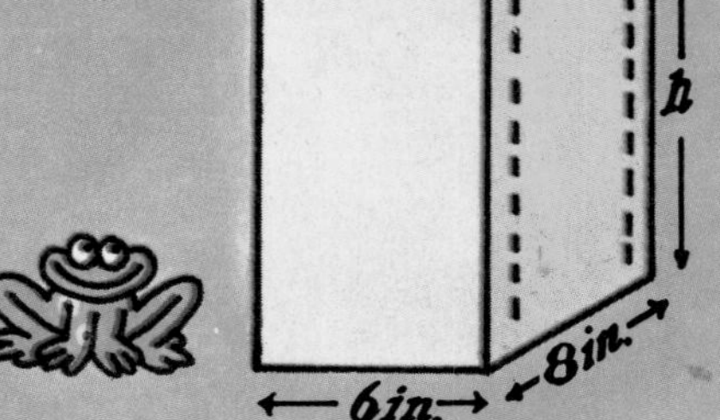

Solve problems 1 and 2.

1. The tree house in the Lindgrens' yard has 150 cubic feet of space. Hilda is $4\frac{3}{4}$ feet tall. Can she stand up straight in the tree house?

   Hilda's brother is $5\frac{1}{2}$ feet tall. Can he stand up straight in the tree house?

2. Nate's clubhouse has 216 cubic feet of space. Nate has a cot that is $5\frac{1}{2}$ feet long. Will the cot fit into the clubhouse?

Volume = length × width × height

$$216 = \ell \times (4 \times 6)$$
$$216 = \ell \times 24$$
$$\ell = \blacksquare$$

$24\overline{)216}$

The clubhouse is ▒ feet long. Will the cot fit?

EXPLORE

Run water into a glass fish tank until the height of the water is 10 centimeters. Find the volume of the water.

Put a rock in the water and find the new volume.

What is the volume of the rock?

Finding the Volume of Halves of Prisms

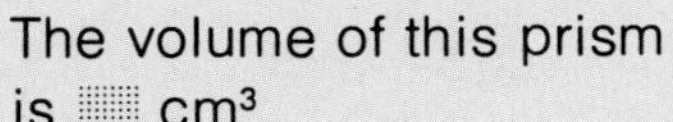

The volume of this prism is ▒ cm^3.

What is the volume of each half of the prism?

Give the volume of each figure below in cubic centimeters. Use the idea of one-half of a prism to help you find the answers.

1.

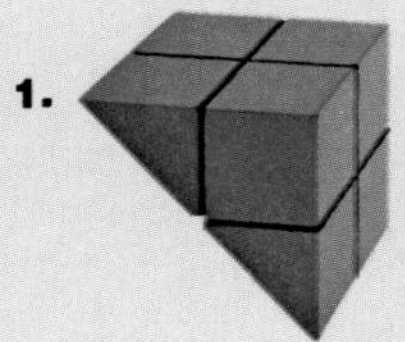

2.

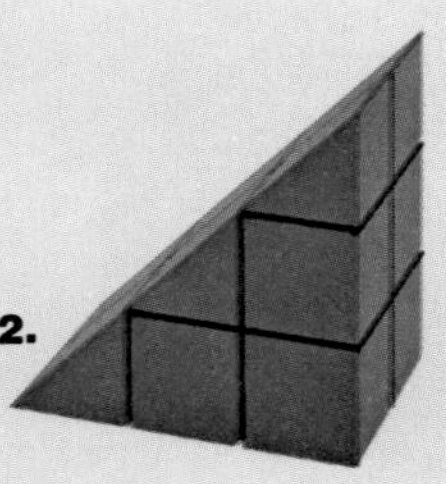

3.

4.

★5.

★6.

SIDE TRIP Ancient Numerals

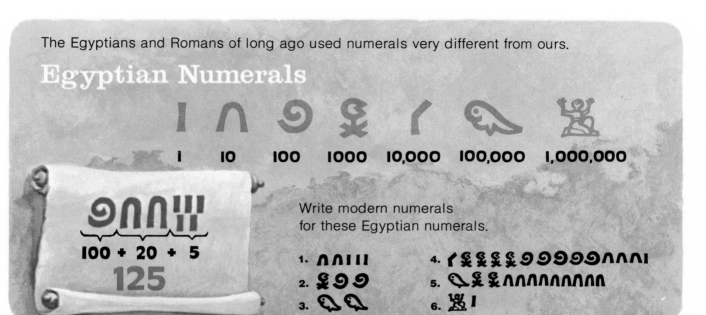

The Egyptians and Romans of long ago used numerals very different from ours.

Egyptian Numerals

𓏺	𓎆	𓍢	𓆼	𓂭	𓆐	𓁨
1	10	100	1000	10,000	100,000	1,000,000

𓍢𓎆𓎆𓏺𓏺𓏺𓏺𓏺

100 + 20 + 5

125

Write modern numerals for these Egyptian numerals.

1. 𓎆𓎆𓏺𓏺𓏺
2. 𓆼𓍢𓍢
3. 𓆐𓆐
4. 𓂭𓆼𓆼𓆼𓆼𓍢𓍢𓍢𓍢𓍢𓎆𓎆𓎆𓏺
5. 𓆐𓆼𓆼𓎆𓎆𓎆𓎆𓎆𓎆𓎆𓎆𓎆
6. 𓁨𓏺

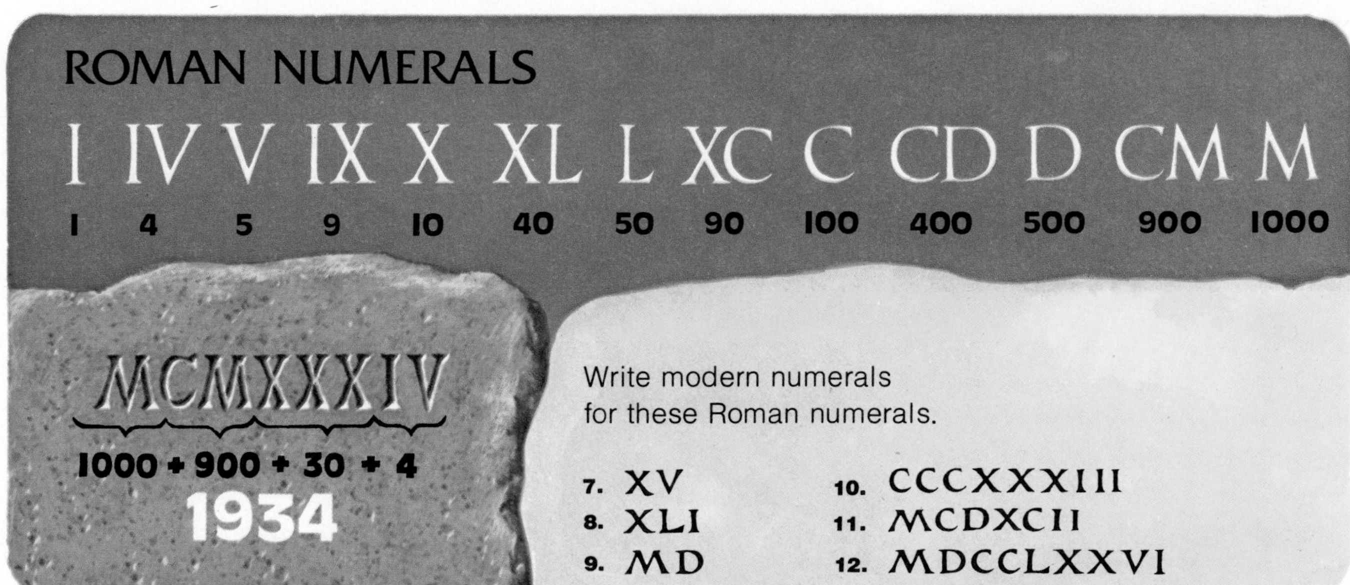

ROMAN NUMERALS

I	IV	V	IX	X	XL	L	XC	C	CD	D	CM	M
1	4	5	9	10	40	50	90	100	400	500	900	1000

MCMXXXIV

1000 + 900 + 30 + 4

1934

Write modern numerals for these Roman numerals.

7. XV
8. XLI
9. MD
10. CCCXXXIII
11. MCDXCII
12. MDCCLXXVI

Write the following numbers as Egyptian numerals and also as Roman numerals.

13. Your age
14. The current year
15. The year you were born

Check Yourself
Geometric Figures and Volume, Pages 110–123

Geometric figures, pages 110–113

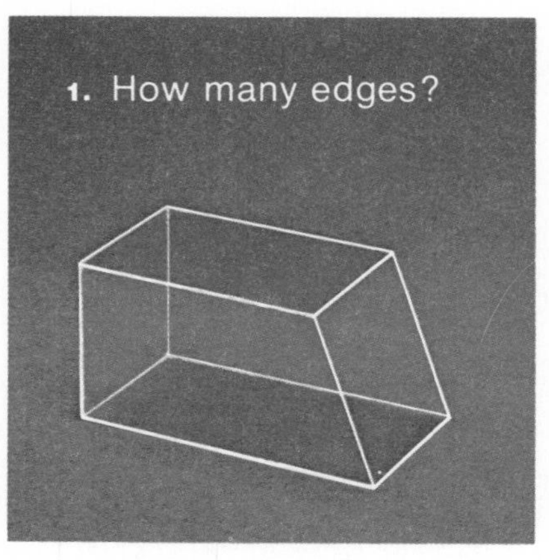

1. How many edges?

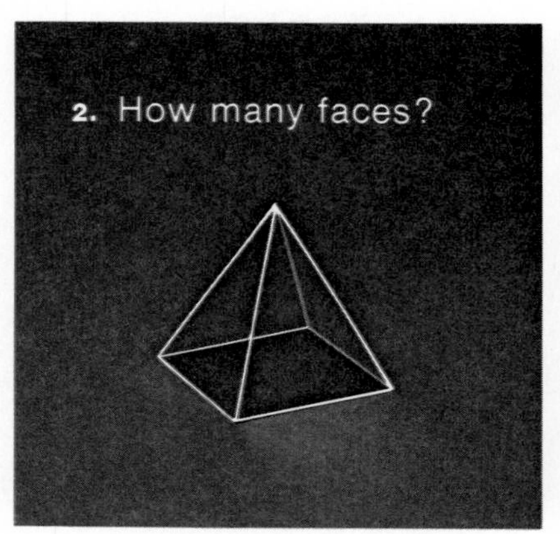

2. How many faces?

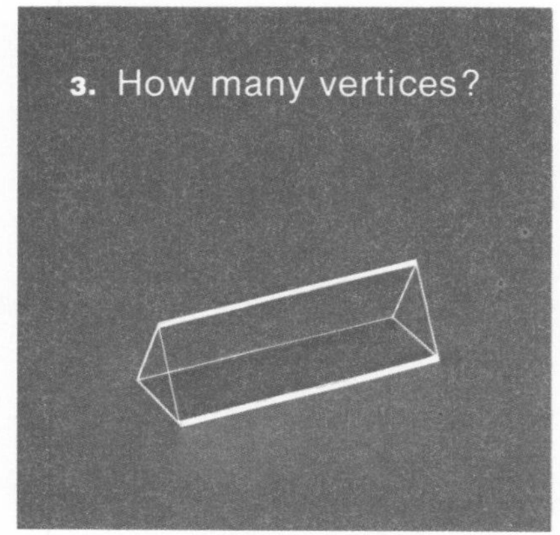

3. How many vertices?

Finding volume, pages 114–122

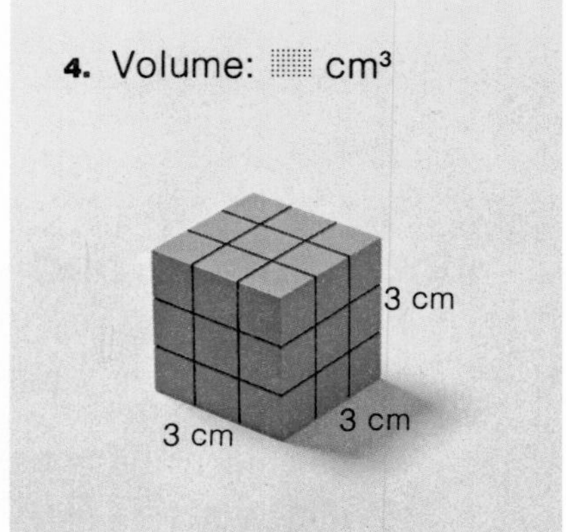

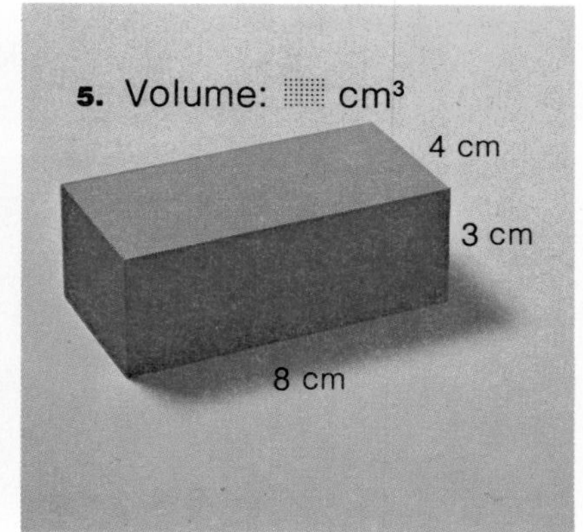

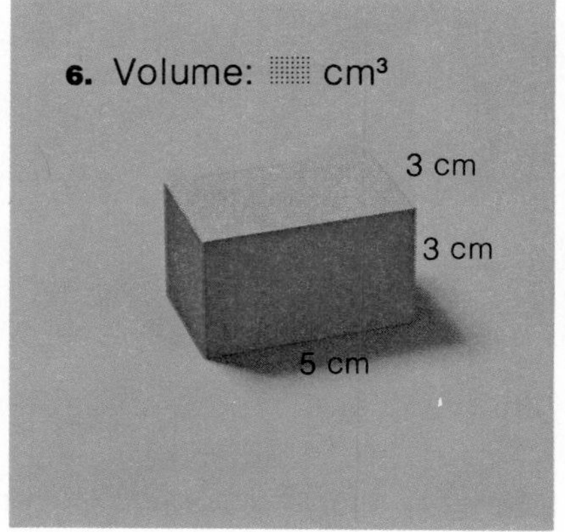

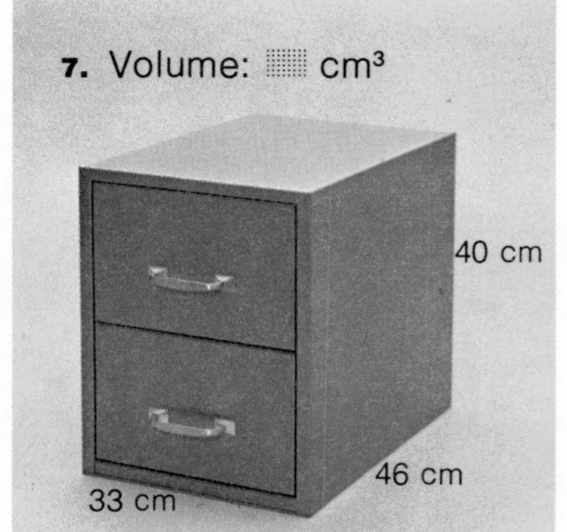

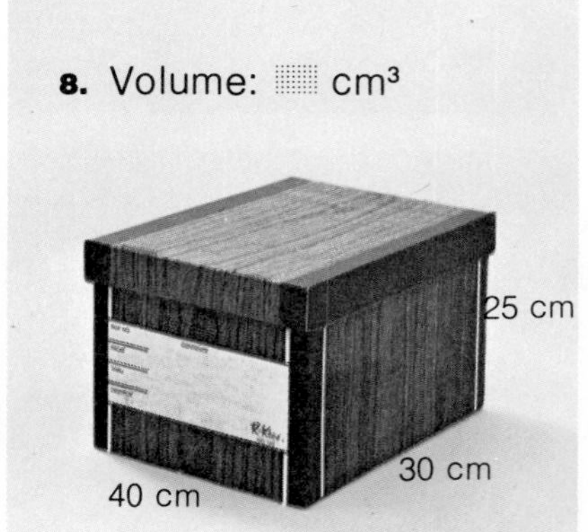

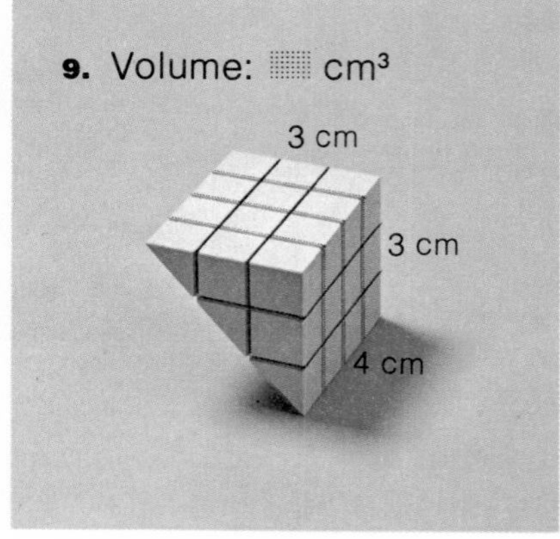

Check Yourself: Level 26

Dividing: one-digit divisors, pages 66–77

1. $7\overline{)61}$

2. $4\overline{)93}$

3. $6\overline{)318}$

4. $3\overline{)983}$

5. $9\overline{)3083}$

Dividing: two-digit divisors, pages 78–87

6. $32\overline{)168}$

7. $42\overline{)2436}$

8. $38\overline{)950}$

Problem solving, pages 71, 76, 77, 79, 81, 83–92

9. How many hair ribbons 60 cm long can be cut from a 1500-cm roll of ribbon?

10. Find the average length of the four fish.

    34 cm 42 cm
    26 cm 38 cm

11. If you divide 262 baseball cards equally among 6 people, how many cards will be left over?

12. 366 days = ▒ weeks ▒ days

13. Find n.

    $8 \times n = 128$

14. Lois filled 15 packages with tennis balls. She put the same number of balls in each package. She packaged 90 balls in all. How many balls did she put in each package?

Ratios, pages 94–107

Find n.

15. $\frac{3}{5} = \frac{n}{40}$ 16. $\frac{2}{9} = \frac{34}{n}$

17. A machine makes 5 widgets in 3 hours. How many widgets does it make in 24 hours?

18. Susan walked 4 blocks in 9 minutes. At this speed, how many minutes does it take her to walk 56 blocks?

19. 16 ounces is 1 pound. How many ounces is 12 pounds?

Volume, pages 114–122

20. Find the volume.

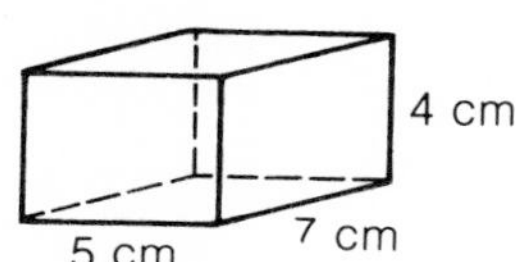

More Practice

Set A

1. $4\overline{)30}$ **2.** $6\overline{)44}$ **3.** $7\overline{)51}$ **4.** $5\overline{)37}$ **5.** $4\overline{)35}$

6. $8\overline{)67}$ **7.** $5\overline{)48}$ **8.** $7\overline{)66}$ **9.** $6\overline{)35}$ **10.** $4\overline{)37}$

Give only the remainder.

11. $58 \div 9$ **12.** $60 \div 9$ **13.** $62 \div 9$

14. $67 \div 9$ **15.** $70 \div 9$ **16.** $75 \div 9$

Set B

1. $2\overline{)45}$ **2.** $5\overline{)71}$ **3.** $3\overline{)65}$ **4.** $7\overline{)86}$ **5.** $6\overline{)85}$ **6.** $4\overline{)73}$ **7.** $2\overline{)73}$ **8.** $3\overline{)76}$

9. $5\overline{)88}$ **10.** $6\overline{)93}$ **11.** $8\overline{)98}$ **12.** $4\overline{)90}$ **13.** $3\overline{)89}$ **14.** $9\overline{)96}$ **15.** $6\overline{)97}$ **16.** $7\overline{)99}$

Set C

1. $3\overline{)100}$ **2.** $3\overline{)150}$ **3.** $4\overline{)100}$ **4.** $4\overline{)150}$ **5.** $5\overline{)100}$

6. $5\overline{)150}$ **7.** $6\overline{)200}$ **8.** $6\overline{)300}$ **9.** $7\overline{)200}$ **10.** $7\overline{)300}$

Choose the correct answer.

11. $6\overline{)429}$ **a.** 7 R9 **b.** 70 R9 **c.** 71 R3

12. $8\overline{)604}$ **a.** 70 R44 **b.** 75 R4 **c.** 75

13. $5\overline{)482}$ **a.** 96 **b.** 96 R2 **c.** 90 R2

14. $9\overline{)829}$ **a.** 92 R1 **b.** 90 R19 **c.** 92

15. $7\overline{)446}$ **a.** 50 R96 **b.** 63 **c.** 63 R5

16. $9\overline{)702}$ **a.** 80 **b.** 78 **c.** 70 R2

17. $8\overline{)700}$ **a.** 87 R4 **b.** 87 **c.** 80 R4

Set D

When you divide, which is the sensible number to start with?

1. 30 or 300? $9\overline{)350}$

2. 30 or 300? $2\overline{)628}$

3. 20 or 200? $3\overline{)716}$

4. 800 or 8000? $4\overline{)3219}$

5. 600 or 6000? $6\overline{)3800}$

6. 400 or 4000? $7\overline{)3159}$

Divide.

7. $2\overline{)1256}$ **8.** $4\overline{)999}$ **9.** $5\overline{)3159}$ **10.** $7\overline{)902}$ **11.** $6\overline{)2000}$ **12.** $6\overline{)4000}$

13. $9\overline{)936}$ **14.** $9\overline{)6747}$ **15.** $8\overline{)4075}$ **16.** $8\overline{)5032}$ **17.** $9\overline{)7643}$ **18.** $7\overline{)2755}$

Set E

1. 4×30 **2.** 4×32 **3.** 5×30 **4.** 5×32 **5.** 3×50

6. 3×54 **7.** 6×80 **8.** 6×85 **9.** 7×60 **10.** 7×63

More Practice

Set F

1. $31\overline{)220}$
2. $40\overline{)85}$
3. $20\overline{)170}$
4. $30\overline{)100}$
5. $42\overline{)215}$
6. $35\overline{)81}$
7. $23\overline{)139}$
8. $54\overline{)270}$
9. $37\overline{)149}$
10. $63\overline{)196}$
11. $45\overline{)278}$
12. $90\overline{)556}$
13. $71\overline{)150}$
14. $84\overline{)350}$
15. $75\overline{)300}$
16. $75\overline{)600}$

Set G

Multiply.

1. 10×42
2. 10×55
3. 20×42
4. 20×55
5. 30×42
6. 30×55
7. 20×56
8. 40×33
9. 70×54
10. 60×41

Subtract.

11. $\begin{array}{r} 968 \\ -\ 840 \\ \hline \end{array}$
12. $\begin{array}{r} 3900 \\ -\ 3780 \\ \hline \end{array}$
13. $\begin{array}{r} 1883 \\ -\ 1650 \\ \hline \end{array}$
14. $\begin{array}{r} 2713 \\ -\ 2460 \\ \hline \end{array}$

Set H

1. $21\overline{)899}$
2. $20\overline{)750}$
3. $30\overline{)666}$
4. $30\overline{)900}$
5. $40\overline{)1660}$
6. $52\overline{)1718}$
7. $47\overline{)1175}$
8. $32\overline{)1628}$
9. $42\overline{)956}$
10. $70\overline{)2385}$
11. $54\overline{)3948}$
12. $66\overline{)2799}$
13. $55\overline{)2750}$
14. $63\overline{)3250}$
15. $86\overline{)975}$
16. $73\overline{)4684}$

Set I

Tell whether or not the number tried in the quotient is too big.

1. $37\overline{)141}$ (quotient tried: 4)
2. $18\overline{)36}$ (quotient tried: 3)
3. $44\overline{)93}$ (quotient tried: 2)
4. $15\overline{)45}$ (quotient tried: 4)
5. $29\overline{)118}$ (quotient tried: 5)
6. $35\overline{)1402}$ (quotient tried: 40)
7. $58\overline{)2425}$ (quotient tried: 40)
8. $47\overline{)3852}$ (quotient tried: 80)
9. $25\overline{)1000}$ (quotient tried: 50)
10. $66\overline{)4500}$ (quotient tried: 70)

Set J

Write five more equal ratios for each list.

1. $\frac{3}{5} = \frac{6}{10} = \frac{9}{15}$
2. $\frac{4}{3} = \frac{8}{6} = \frac{12}{9}$
3. $\frac{2}{7} = \frac{4}{14} = \frac{6}{21}$
4. $\frac{5}{6} = \frac{10}{12} = \frac{15}{18}$
5. $\frac{4}{9} = \frac{8}{18} = \frac{12}{27}$
6. $\frac{11}{20} = \frac{22}{40} = \frac{33}{60}$

Set K

Find n.

1. $\frac{1}{4} = \frac{n}{48}$
2. $\frac{3}{7} = \frac{n}{91}$
3. $\frac{5}{2} = \frac{n}{28}$
4. $\frac{2}{5} = \frac{28}{n}$
5. $\frac{8}{3} = \frac{24}{n}$
6. $\frac{4}{5} = \frac{n}{75}$
7. $\frac{3}{8} = \frac{51}{n}$
8. $\frac{2}{30} = \frac{n}{45}$
9. $\frac{2}{35} = \frac{70}{n}$
10. $\frac{8}{9} = \frac{n}{333}$

Check Yourself Answers: Level 26

Check Yourself, page 93

1. 7
2. 9
3. 8
4. 7 R1
5. 8 R2
6. 9 R3
7. 8 R2
8. 30 R2
9. 64 R3
10. 75 R1
11. 868 R1
12. 27 R2
13. 7 R23
14. 96 R32
15. 27 R7
16. 63 R46
17. Too big
18. Correct
19. Too big
20. Too big
21. 143
22. 21 per person
    2 left over
23. 4 yards 2 feet
24. 3 pounds 2 ounces
25. $n = 21$
26. 16 bags

Check Yourself, page 109

1. $\frac{3}{59}$

Answers may vary for exercises 2–4.

2. $\frac{16}{20}, \frac{20}{25}, \frac{24}{30}, \frac{28}{35}, \frac{32}{40}, \cdots$
3. $\frac{8}{36}, \frac{10}{45}, \frac{12}{54}, \frac{14}{63}, \frac{16}{72}, \cdots$
4. $\frac{12}{4}, \frac{15}{5}, \frac{18}{6}, \frac{21}{7}, \frac{24}{8}, \cdots$
5. Yes
6. No
7. No
8. Yes
9. 15
10. 6
11. 32
12. 14
13. 54 feet
14. 2 weeks
15. $21
16. 28 miles

Check Yourself, page 124

1. 12
2. 5
3. 6
4. 27 cm^3
5. 96 cm^3
6. 45 cm^3
7. 60,720 cm^3
8. 30,000 cm^3
9. 18 cm^3

Check Yourself: Level 26, page 125

1. 8 R5
2. 23 R1
3. 53
4. 327 R2
5. 342 R5
6. 5 R8
7. 58
8. 25
9. 25 ribbons
10. 35 cm
11. 4 cards
12. 52 weeks 2 days
13. 16
14. 6 balls
15. 24
16. 153
17. 40 widgets
18. 126 minutes
19. 192 ounces
20. 140 cm^3

Level 27

Decimals and Metric Measures, Pages 130–153

Writing Decimals: Tenths

A. Put 10 ones together to make 1 ten.

1 ten = 10 ones

Divide 1 one into 10 equal parts. Each part is 1 tenth.

1 one = 10 tenths

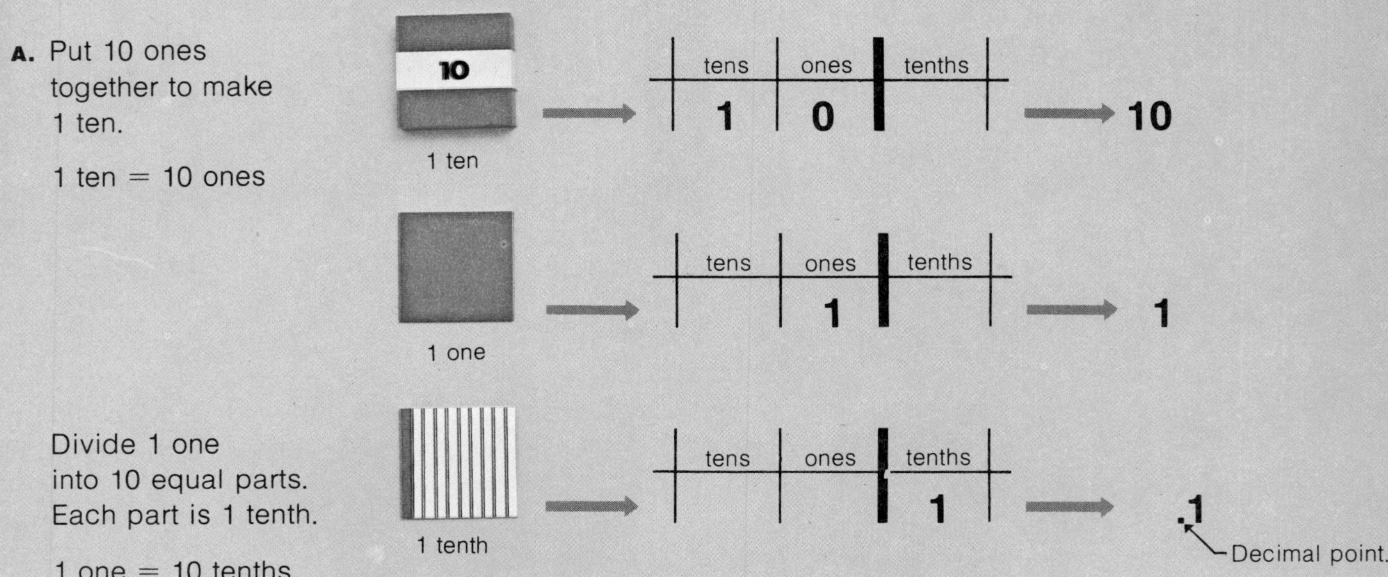

B.

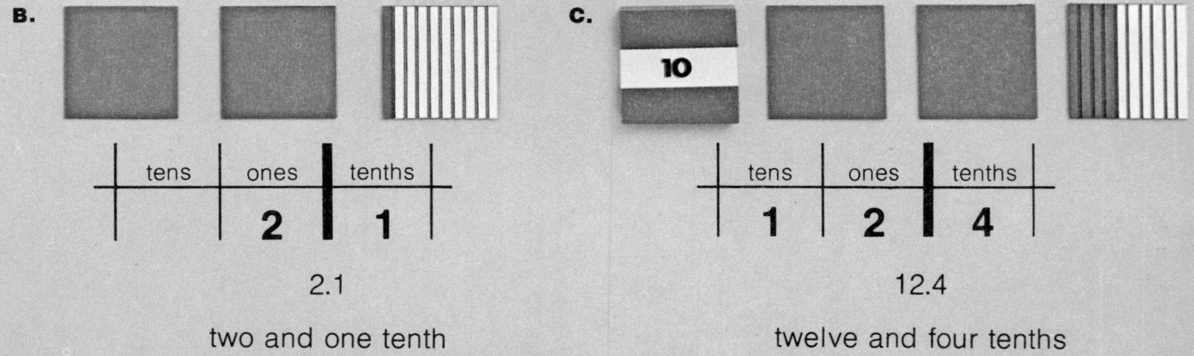

tens	ones	tenths
	2	1

2.1

two and one tenth

C.

tens	ones	tenths
1	2	4

12.4

twelve and four tenths

Numbers like .1, 2.1, and 12.4 are called ***decimals***.

In each exercise, write a decimal for the amount shown in red.

Here's how

2.6

.3

1.

2.

3.

4.

5.

10

6.

10 10 10

Miguel saw these decimals on his way to school.
Read each number. Tell what each 7 means.

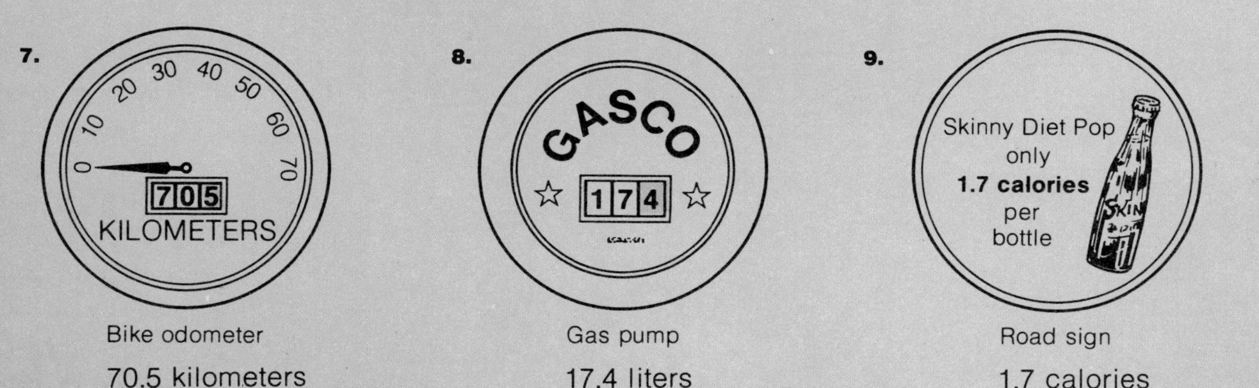

Bike odometer

70.5 kilometers

Gas pump

17.4 liters

Road sign

1.7 calories

Writing Decimals: Hundredths

A. Put 10 tens together to make 1 hundred.

1 hundred = 10 tens

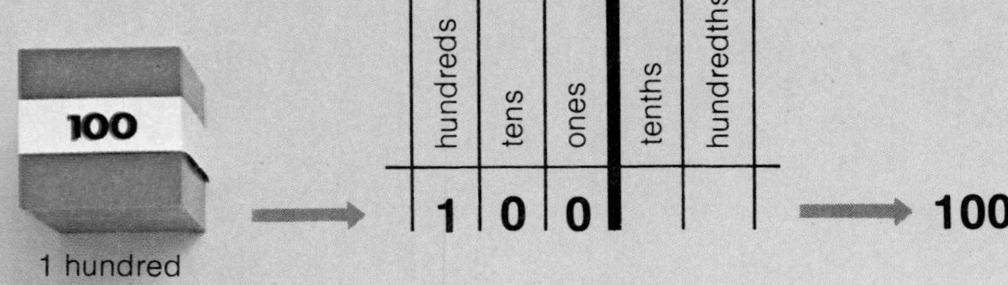

1 hundred

hundreds	tens	ones	tenths	hundredths
1	0	0		

→ **100**

1 ten

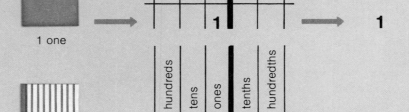

hundreds	tens	ones	tenths	hundredths
	1	0		

→ **10**

1 one

hundreds	tens	ones	tenths	hundredths
		1		

→ **1**

1 tenth

hundreds	tens	ones	tenths	hundredths
			1	

→ **.1**

Divide each tenth into 10 equal parts. Each part is 1 hundredth.

1 tenth = 10 hundredths

1 hundredth

hundreds	tens	ones	tenths	hundredths
			0	1

→ **.01**

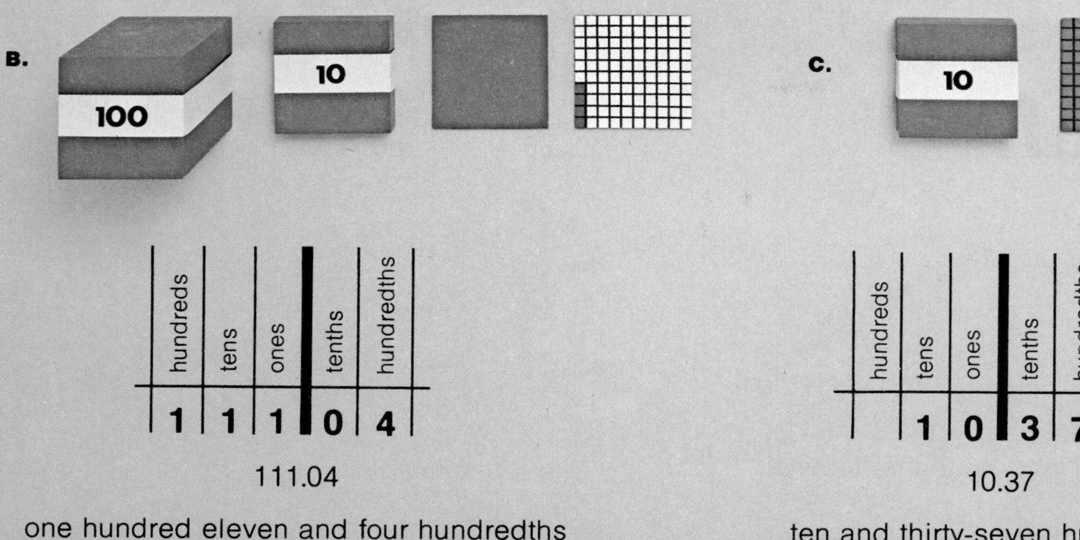

B.

hundreds	tens	ones	tenths	hundredths
1	1	1	0	4

111.04

one hundred eleven and four hundredths

C.

hundreds	tens	ones	tenths	hundredths
	1	0	3	7

10.37

ten and thirty-seven hundredths

Give a decimal for each picture.

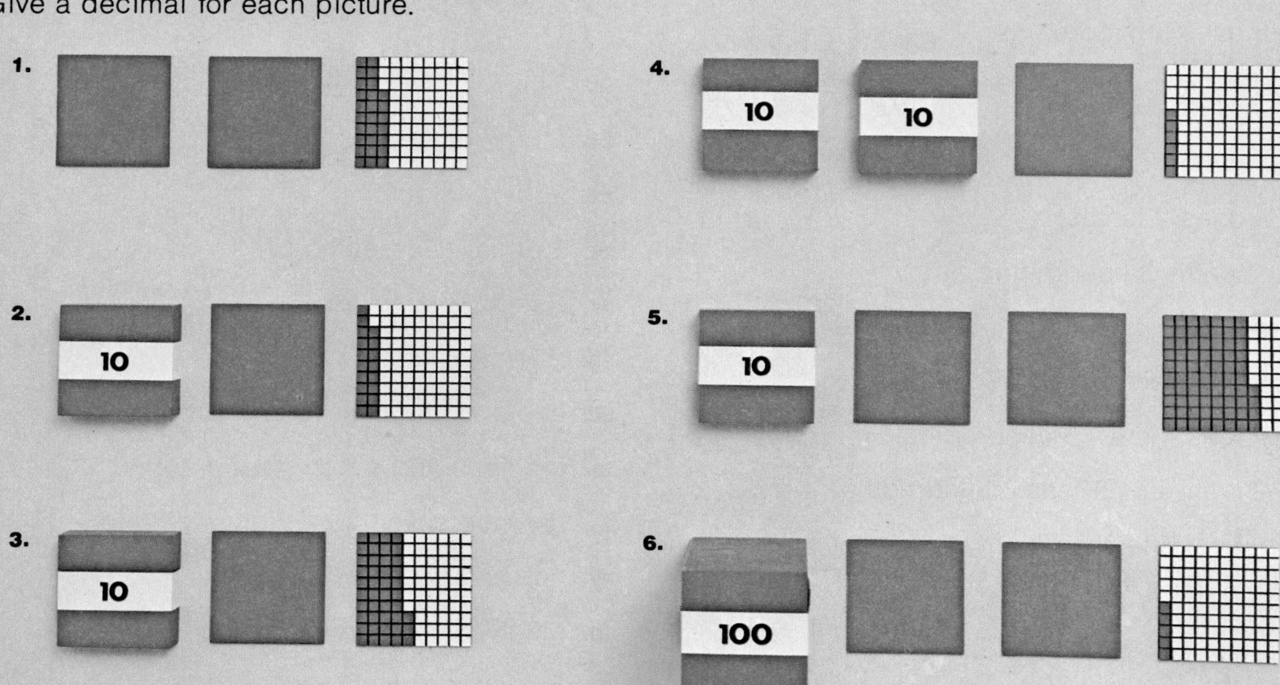

Writing Decimals: Tenths and Hundredths

Tell what each 4 means.

Here's how

1.42 *4 tenths*

1. 16.4
2. 98.47
3. 100.04
4. 34.73
5. 7.54
6. 476.8

For each exercise, imagine the digits in a place-value chart. Write the decimal.

Here's how

6 ones 5 hundredths

6.05

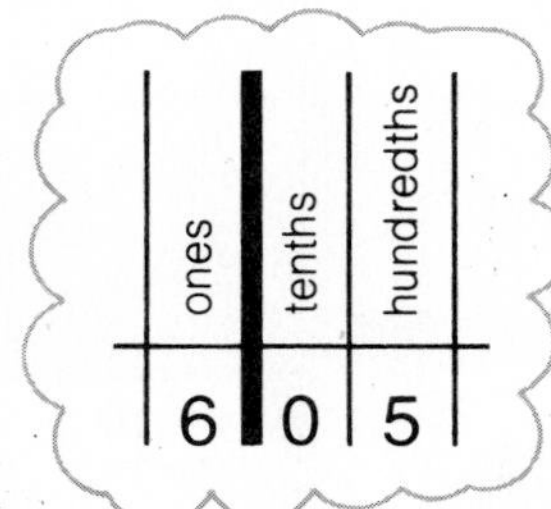

7. 4 tenths
8. 3 ones 2 tenths
9. 5 tenths 3 hundredths
10. 4 ones 2 tenths 5 hundredths
11. 7 hundredths
12. 2 tens 4 ones 5 hundredths
13. 3 hundreds 9 tens 6 hundredths
14. 6 tens 6 tenths

Write the missing numbers.

15. .26 = ▒ hundredths
16. .60 = ▒ hundredths
17. .06 = ▒ hundredths
18. .2 = ▒ tenths
19. .20 = ▒ hundredths
20. .02 = ▒ hundredths

Write a decimal.

Here's how

4 and 5 hundredths *4.05*

one and sixty-two hundredths *1.62*

21. 5 hundredths
22. 25 hundredths
23. 2 and 5 hundredths
24. 2 and 50 hundredths
25. 2 and 5 tenths
26. one and eighty-seven hundredths
27. eighteen and seventy hundredths
28. one and seven hundredths
29. one and seventy hundredths
30. eighty-seven hundredths

Using Decimals: Money

There are 100 cents in one dollar.

1¢
1 hundredth of a dollar
$.01

5¢
5 hundredths of a dollar
$.05

10¢
10 hundredths of a dollar
$.10

25¢
25 hundredths of a dollar
$.25

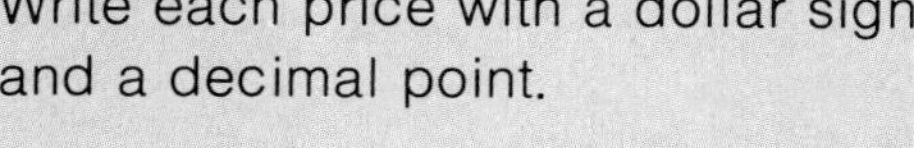

Write each price with a dollar sign and a decimal point.

1. 

2. 

3. 

4. 

5. 

6. 

7. 

8. 

9. 

10. eight dollars and sixty-seven cents
11. ninety-three cents
12. fifteen dollars and six cents
13. four dollars and nine cents
14. twenty-seven dollars and ninety cents
15. forty dollars and fifty-nine cents
16. eight hundred dollars and ten cents
17. one dollar and four cents
18. five hundred five dollars and five cents
19. two dollars and sixty-three cents
20. ninety dollars and nine cents

Writing Decimals: Thousandths

A. Divide 1 hundredth into 10 equal parts.
Each part is 1 thousandth.

1 hundredth = 10 thousandths

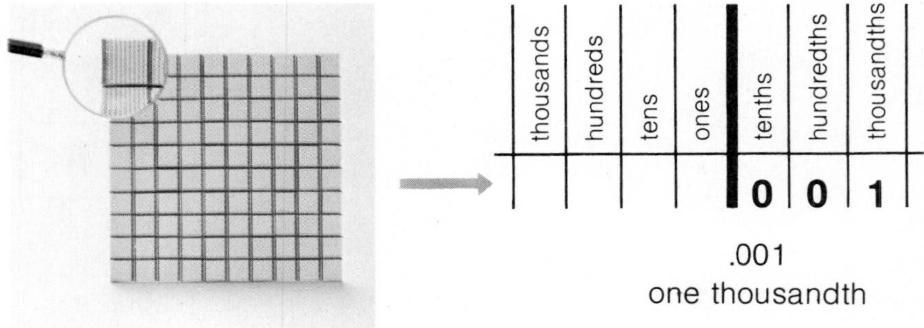

1 thousandth

.001
one thousandth

B.

thousands	hundreds	tens	ones	tenths	hundredths	thousandths
				0	0	3

.003

three thousandths

C.

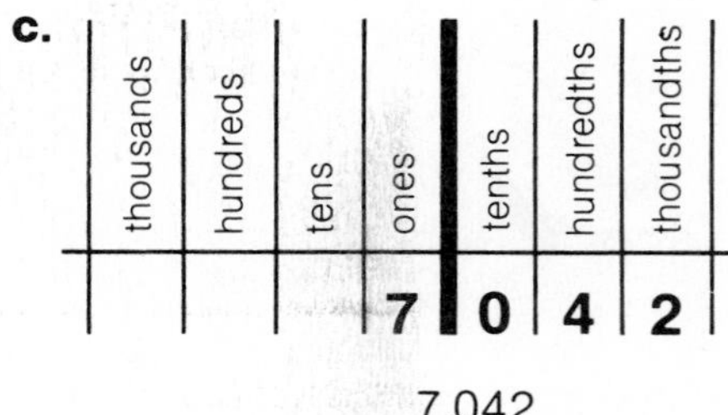

7.042

seven and forty-two thousandths

D.

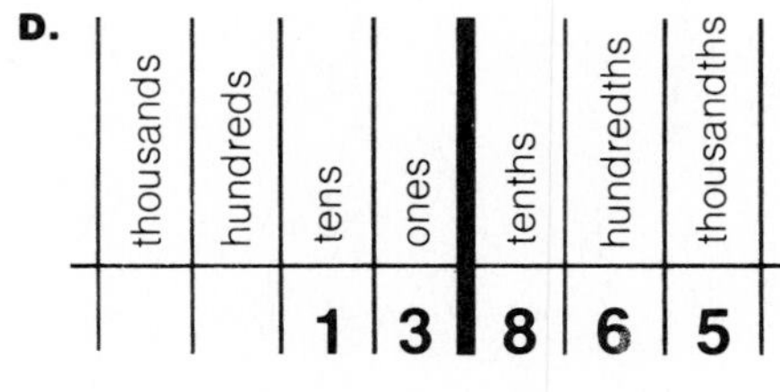

13.865

thirteen and eight hundred sixty-five thousandths

Tell what each 7 means.

Here's how

80.427 *7 thousandths*

1. 57.28 **2.** 725.36 **3.** 9.273 **4.** 34.007

5. 21.397 **6.** 75.059 **7.** 26.782 **8.** 99.078

Each exercise describes a number in a place-value chart. Write the decimal.

Here's how

6 ones 2 tenths 3 thousandths 6.203

9. 8 tens 6 ones 2 tenths 4 hundredths 1 thousandth

10. 2 tens 3 ones 7 thousandths

11. 6 hundreds 3 tens 4 ones 2 hundredths 8 thousandths

12. 5 thousands 2 hundreds 7 ones 2 tenths 6 thousandths

13. 4 thousands 3 tens 8 ones 9 thousandths

14. 8 thousands 9 hundreds 6 tens 7 hundredths 8 thousandths

Write the missing numbers.

15. .333 = ▒ thousandths

16. .330 = ▒ thousandths

17. .300 = ▒ thousandths

18. .66 = ▒ hundredths

19. .70 = ▒ hundredths

20. .700 = ▒ thousandths

Write the decimal.

Here's how

92 thousandths .092

four and forty-one thousandths 4.041

21. 8 thousandths

22. 28 thousandths

23. 628 thousandths

24. 6 and 28 thousandths

25. 62 and 800 thousandths

26. four thousandths

27. fourteen thousandths

28. three hundred fourteen thousandths

29. three and one hundred forty thousandths

30. thirty-one and four thousandths

Keeping Skillful

For each exercise, put the numbers in order from least to greatest.

1. 80
79
101
81

2. 398
409
389
410

3. 1009
899
900
1010

4. 1975
1896
2002
1984

Find each quotient.

5. $6\overline{)85}$

6. $6\overline{)850}$

7. $60\overline{)850}$

8. $60\overline{)8500}$

9. $600\overline{)8500}$

Ordering Decimals

For each exercise, give the missing numbers for A, B, C, and D.

1. 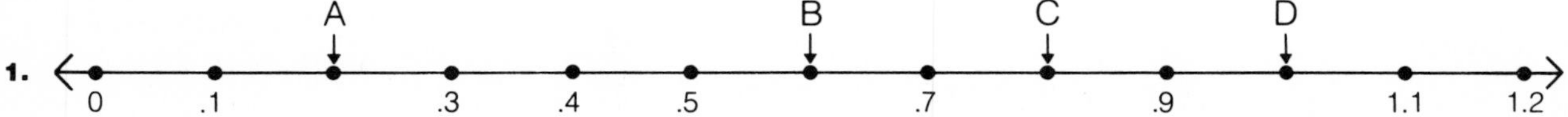

2. 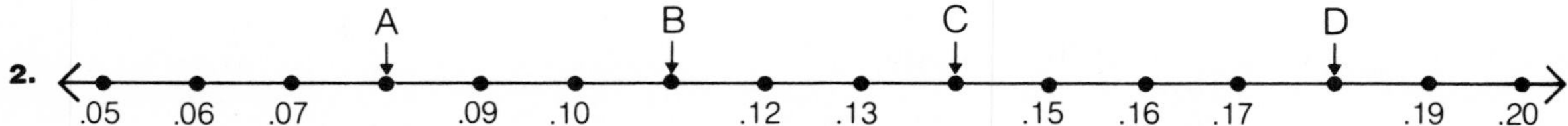

3. 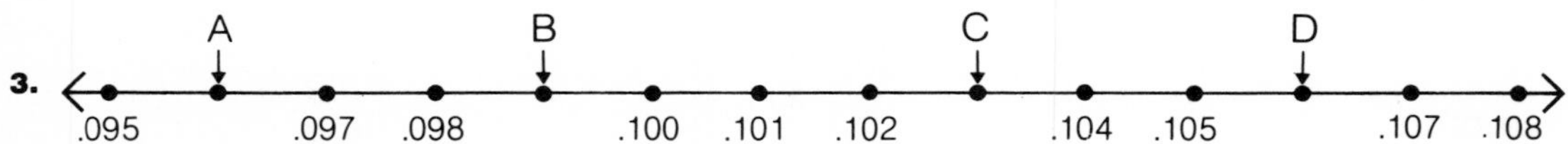

4. 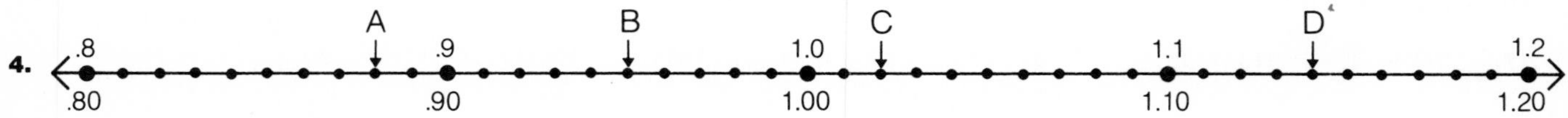

5. 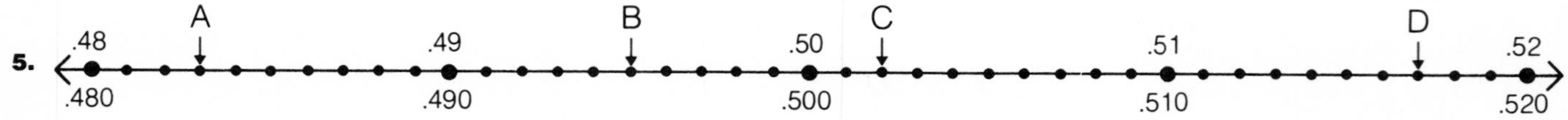

★ 6. 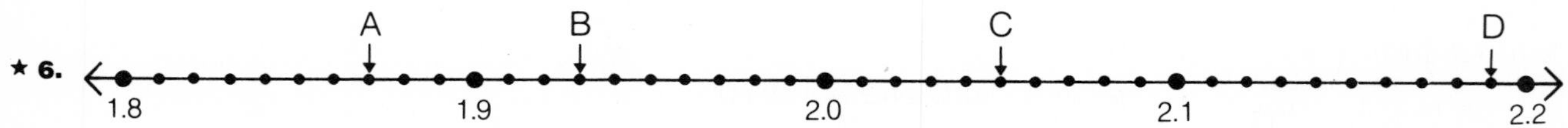

Study the patterns.
Then give the missing numbers.

7. 3.8 3.9 4.0 4.1 ____ ____ ____

8. 2.5 2.6 2.7 2.8 ____ ____ ____

9. .55 .56 .57 .58 ____ ____ ____

10. 1.36 1.37 1.38 1.39 ____ ____ ____

11. .095 .096 .097 .098 ____ ____ ____

12. 3.720 3.721 3.722 ____ ____ ____

Give the number that is 1 tenth greater.

13. 2.5

14. 2.41

15. 2.385

16. 3.715

17. 3.840

★ **18.** 3.925

Give the number that is 1 hundredth greater.

19. 2.54

20. 3.142

21. 4.667

22. 1.175

23. 1.183

★ **24.** 1.195

Give the number that is 1 thousandth greater.

25. 3.142

26. 8.125

27. 6.667

28. 3.157

29. 3.158

★ **30.** 3.159

Time Out!

All six faces of the large cube were painted. Then the cube was cut into 27 smaller cubes.

1. How many of the small cubes are painted on all six faces?

2. Painted on three faces?

3. Painted on two faces?

4. Painted on one face?

5. Not painted at all?

6. How many times was the large cube cut to make the 27 smaller cubes?

Comparing Decimals

A. Compare .8 and .6.
Use > or <.

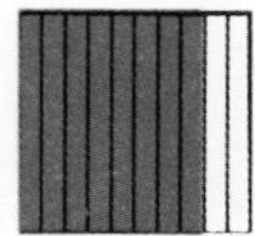

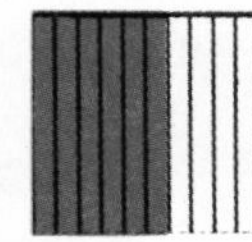

8 tenths is greater than 6 tenths.

.8 > .6

B. Compare .29 and .32.

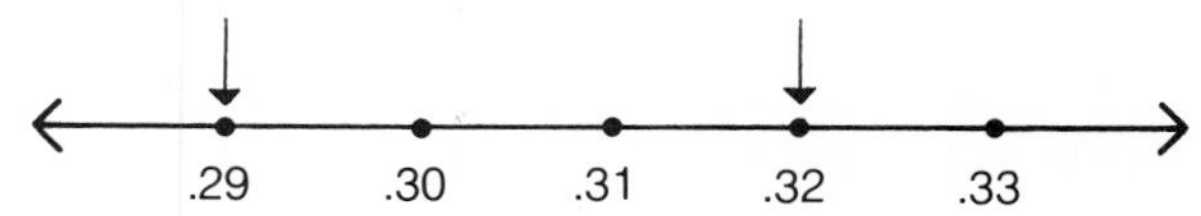

29 hundredths is less than 32 hundredths.

.29 < .32

Compare these decimals. Replace ● with > or <.

1. .56 ● .38

2. .481 ● .610

3. .5 ● .9

4. .09 ● .65

5. .72 ● .80

6. .568 ● .921

7. .490 ● .049

8. .500 ● .005

9. 1.4 ● 1.8

10. 3.6 ● 3.4

11. 2.76 ● 2.92

12. 8.67 ● 8.72

13. 9.036 ● 9.360

14. 8.278 ● 8.782

15. List the pitchers and their lifetime earned run averages in order. Begin with the pitcher with the lowest average.

Baseball pitcher	Earned run average
Mudcat Grant	3.72
Dazzy Vance	3.24
Wild Bill Donovan	2.70
Schoolboy Rowe	3.87
Dizzy Trout	3.23
Blue Moon Odom	3.37
Sad Sam Jones	3.84

Equal Decimals

A. Compare .2 and .20.

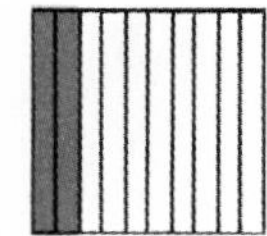

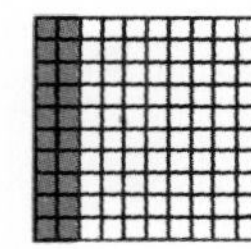

2 tenths = 20 hundredths

.2 = .20

B. Compare .610 and .61.

61 hundredths = 610 thousandths

.61 = .610

Give an equal decimal in hundredths.

Here's how

.3 *.3 = .30*

1. .2 **6.** .5

2. .4 **7.** 3.5

3. .6 **8.** 35.0

4. .8 **9.** 3.1

5. 1.0 **10.** 1.3

Give an equal decimal in tenths.

Here's how

3.90 *3.90 = 3.9*

11. 2.10 **14.** 8.50

12. 5.40 **15.** 8.500

13. 7.30 **16.** 85.500

Give an equal decimal in thousandths.

Here's how

.65 *.65 = .650*

17. .98 **21.** .75

18. .8 **22.** 7.5

19. .80 **23.** 75.0

20. .08 **24.** .05

On each computer tape, find the number that is not equal to the other numbers.

25. .500
.050
.5

26. 3.007
3.700
3.7

27. 1.08
1.080
1.008

28. 5.045
5.450
5.45

Comparing Decimals

A. Compare .47 and .5.

$.47 < .50$ **.5 = .50**

$.47 < .5$

B. Compare .32 and .246.

$.320 > .246$ **.32 = .320**

$.32 > .246$

Compare these decimals.
Replace ● with $>$, $<$, or $=$.

1. .6 ● .60
2. .78 ● .6
3. .58 ● .6
4. .5 ● .58
5. .4 ● .04
6. .4 ● .40
7. .18 ● .2
8. .59 ● .590
9. .612 ● .590
10. .612 ● .59
11. .04 ● .300
12. .300 ● .004
13. .040 ● .30
14. .3 ● .04
15. .3 ● .300
16. .67 ● .076
17. .67 ● .667
18. .067 ● .6
19. .06 ● .016
20. .080 ● .79

More practice
Set A, page 175

Keeping Skillful

Add.

1. 46 + 32 **2.** 25 + 78 **3.** 92 + 48

4. 127 + 96 **5.** 189 + 376

Rename to get 10 more ones.

	thousands	hundreds	tens	ones
		2	$\overset{2}{\cancel{3}}$	$\overset{17}{\cancel{7}}$
6.			6	8
7.		1	7	6
8.		5	3	4
9.		3	2	0
10.		1	4	3

Rename to get 10 more tens.

	thousands	hundreds	tens	ones
	6	$\overset{2}{\cancel{3}}$	$\overset{15}{\cancel{5}}$	8
11.		5	6	2
12.		3	4	9
13.		2	1	7
14.		9	0	6
15.	1	2	0	5

Subtract.

16. 47 − 18 **17.** 567 − 219 **18.** 724 − 386

19. 502 − 196 **20.** 600 − 284

SIDE TRIP Clock Addition

You know that $11 + 3 = 14$.
But when you add on a clock, then $11 \oplus 3 = 2$.

A. To find $11 \oplus 3$ on a clock, start with the hour hand at 11. Then move the hand forward 3 hours.

$11 \oplus 3 = 2$

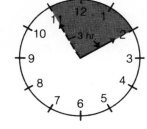

B. To find $8 \oplus 9$ on a clock, start at 8. Move the hand forward 9 hours.

$8 \oplus 9 = 5$

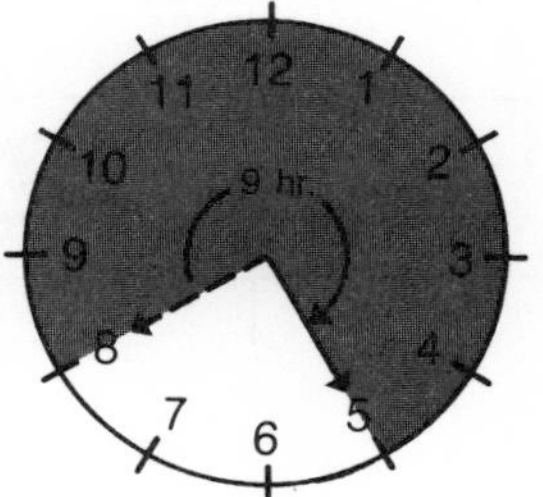

Give the clock sums. Use a clock face to help you.

1. $10 \oplus 4$
2. $10 \oplus 3$
3. $10 \oplus 2$
4. $10 \oplus 1$
5. $7 \oplus 7$
6. $7 \oplus 3$
7. $10 \oplus 10$
8. $11 \oplus 5$
9. $12 \oplus 5$
10. $5 \oplus 12$

11. Complete a clock-addition table like the one below.

Number of hours later

Starting time

⊕	12	1	2	3	4	5	6	7	8	9	10	11
12	*12*			*3*					*8*			
1		*2*										
2									*10*		*12*	*1*
3				*6*					*11*			
4	*4*											
5												
6												
7								*2*				
8												
9	*9*	*10*		*12*	*1*							
10												
11												*10*

12. Is $7 \oplus 9$ the same as $9 \oplus 7$?

13. When 12 is one addend, what do you know about the sum and the other addend?

14. Try this: $(3 \oplus 5) \oplus 6$. Add the numbers in parentheses first.

15. Is $(4 \oplus 7) \oplus 9$ the same as $4 \oplus (7 \oplus 9)$?

★ 16. List three number patterns from rows, columns, and diagonals in your clock-addition table.

Metric Units of Length

1 meter (m)

There are 10 *decimeters* (10 dm) in 1 meter.

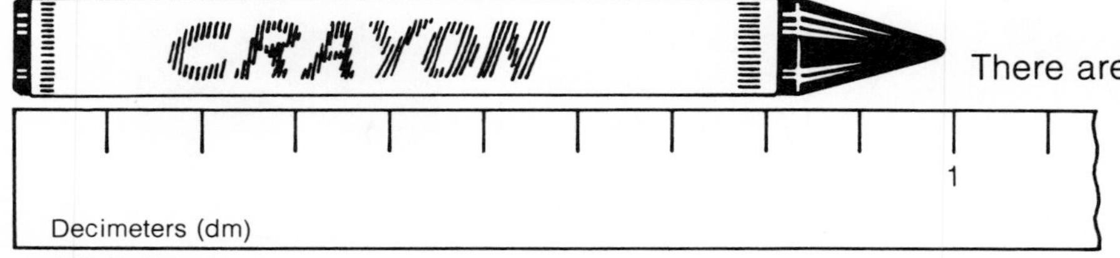

ACTUAL SIZE

There are 100 *centimeters* (100 cm) in 1 meter.

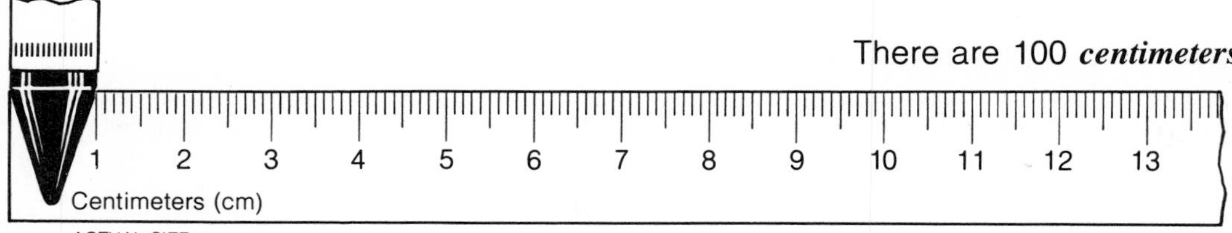

ACTUAL SIZE

There are 1000 *millimeters* (1000 mm) in 1 meter.

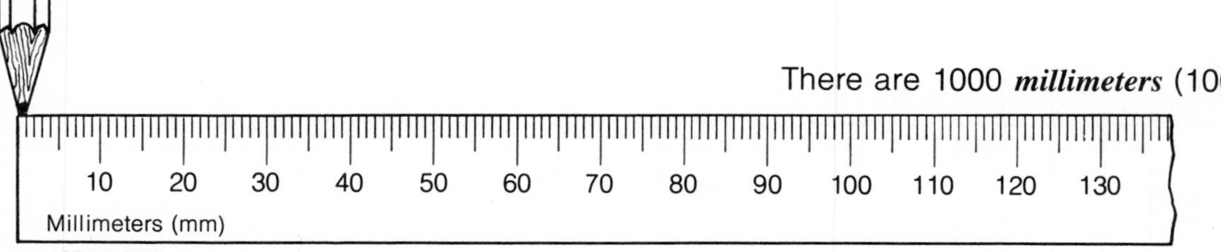

ACTUAL SIZE

Give the missing numbers.
Use the pictures to help you.

1. 1 m = ▒ dm

2. 1 dm = ▒ cm

3. 1 cm = ▒ mm

Choose the best measure.

4. Width of a door	1 mm	1 cm	1 m
5. Length of a pencil	180 mm	180 cm	180 m
6. Width of a room	8 mm	8 cm	8 m
7. Height of a woman	160 mm	160 cm	160 m
8. Length of a key	54 mm	54 cm	54 m

Meter and Centimeter

There are 100 centimeters in 1 meter. *Centi-* means "hundredth."

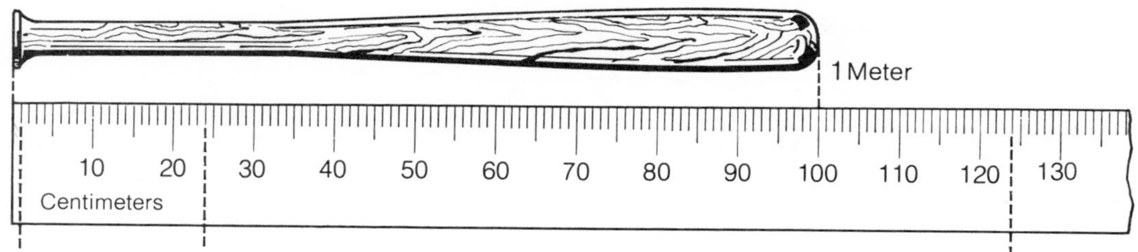

A. 1 centimeter is
1 hundredth meter.

1 cm = 0.01 m

B. 24 centimeters is
24 hundredths meter.

24 cm = 0.24 m

C. 124 centimeters is
1 and 24 hundredths meters.

124 cm = 1.24 m

Give each missing number.

1. 8 cm = ▒ m

2. 9 cm = ▒ m

3. 10 cm = ▒ m

4. 11 cm = ▒ m

5. 75 cm = ▒ m

6. 98 cm = ▒ m

7. 100 cm = ▒ m

8. 101 cm = ▒ m

9. 25 cm = ▒ m

10. 125 cm = ▒ m

11. 225 cm = ▒ m

12. 325 cm = ▒ m

Explore

Are you as wide as you are tall?

Measure your height in centimeters.
Measure your arm span in centimeters.
Are the two measures nearly the same?

Meter and Millimeter

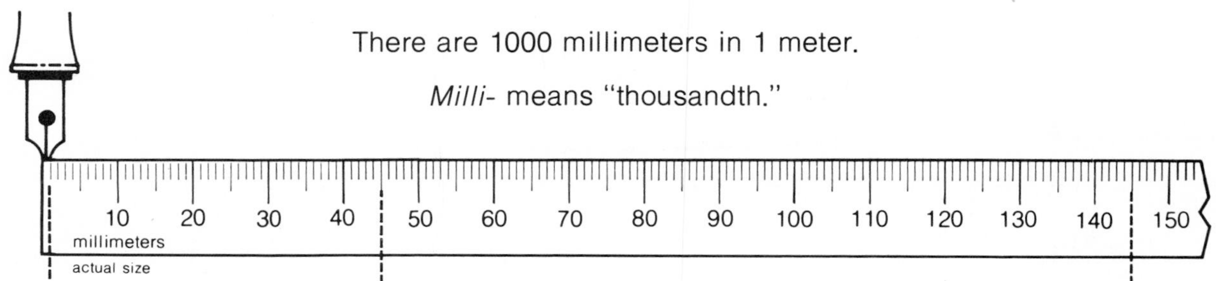

There are 1000 millimeters in 1 meter.

Milli- means "thousandth."

A. 1 millimeter is 1 thousandth meter.

1 mm = 0.001 m

B. 45 millimeters is 45 thousandths meter.

45 mm = 0.045 m

C. 145 millimeters is 145 thousandths meter.

145 mm = 0.145 m

Give each missing number.

1. 8 mm = ____ m
2. 9 mm = ____ m
3. 10 mm = ____ m
4. 11 mm = ____ m
5. 98 mm = ____ m
6. 99 mm = ____ m
7. 100 mm = ____ m
8. 101 mm = ____ m
9. 50 mm = ____ m
10. 150 mm = ____ m
11. 250 mm = ____ m
12. 350 mm = ____ m

PEANUTS
WE'RE GOING TO HAVE TO LEARN THE METRIC SYSTEM, FRANKLIN..
11-19
BY THE TIME WE GROW UP, THE METRIC SYSTEM WILL PROBABLY BE OFFICIAL..
ONE INCH IS 2.54 CENTIMETERS.. ONE FOOT IS 0.3048 METERS AND ONE MILE IS 1.609 KILOMETERS...

I'LL NEVER MEASURE ANYTHING AGAIN AS LONG AS I LIVE!

Centimeter and Millimeter

There are 10 millimeters in 1 centimeter.

mm
10 20 30 40 50 60 70 80 90 100 110 120 130 140 150
1 2 3 4 5 6 7 8 9 10 11 12 13 14 15
cm
actual size

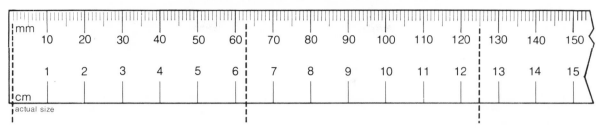

A. 1 millimeter is
1 tenth centimeter.

1 mm = 0.1 cm

B. 63 millimeters is
6 and 3 tenths centimeters.

63 mm = 6.3 cm

C. 125 millimeters is
12 and 5 tenths centimeters.

125 mm = 12.5 cm

Give each missing number.

1. 5 mm = ▒ cm
2. 8 mm = ▒ cm
3. 9 mm = ▒ cm
4. 10 mm = ▒ cm
5. 98 mm = ▒ cm
6. 99 mm = ▒ cm
7. 100 mm = ▒ cm
8. 101 mm = ▒ cm
9. 35 mm = ▒ cm
10. 135 mm = ▒ cm
11. 235 mm = ▒ cm
12. 335 mm = ▒ cm

Give each measure in millimeters.
Then give each measure in centimeters.

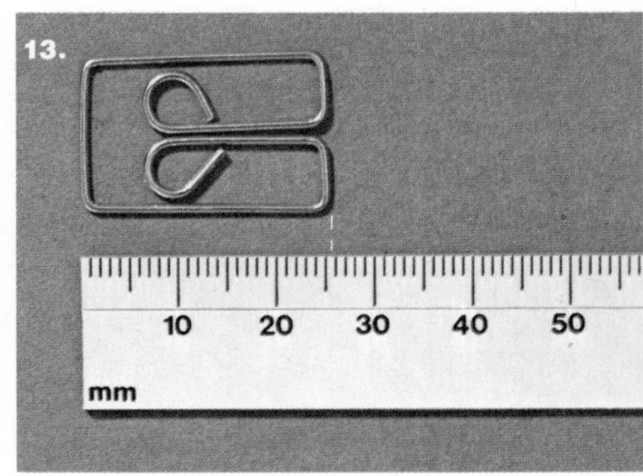

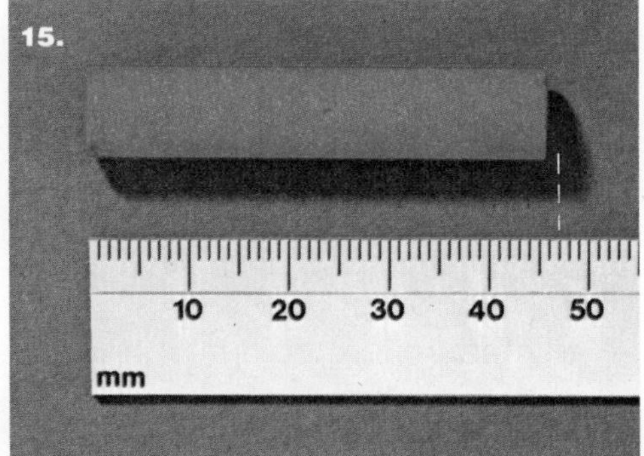

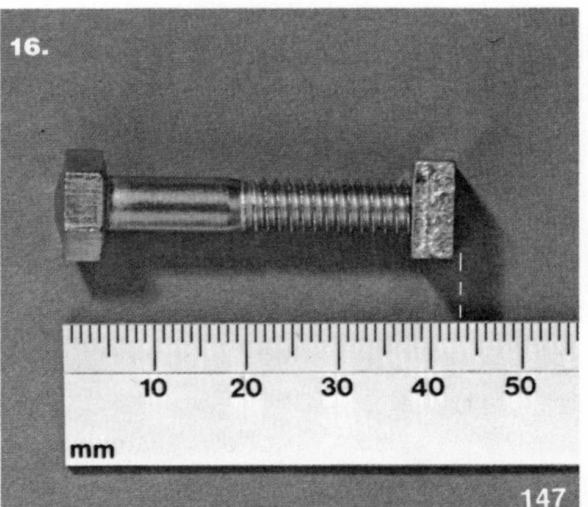

Capacity: Liter and Milliliter

A.

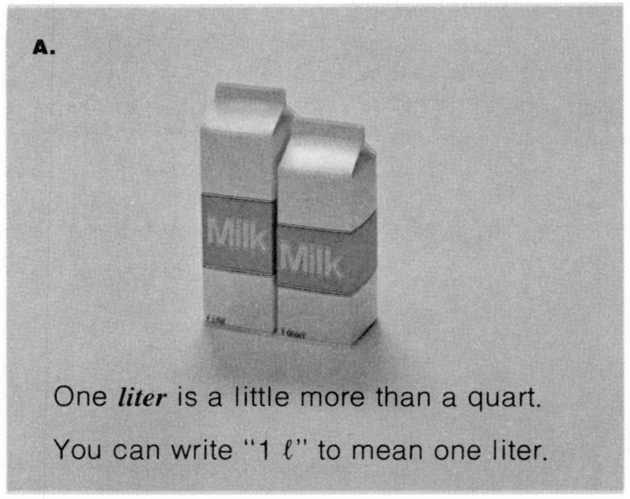

One ***liter*** is a little more than a quart.

You can write "1 ℓ" to mean one liter.

This large bottle holds about 19 liters (19 ℓ).

B.

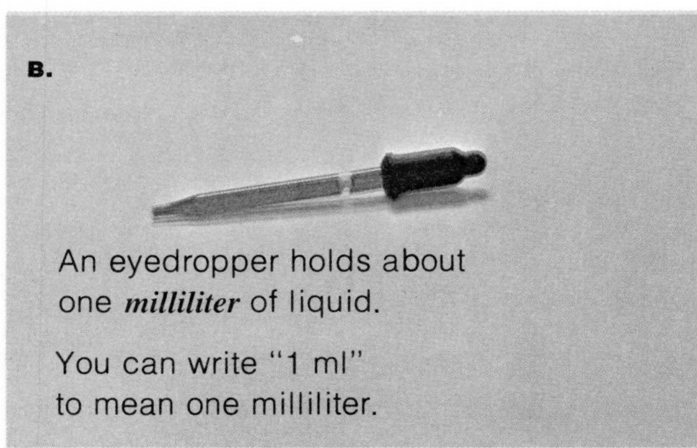

An eyedropper holds about one ***milliliter*** of liquid.

You can write "1 ml" to mean one milliliter.

A glass of milk is about 250 milliliters (250 ml).

For each object, choose the best measure.

1. 1 ml
10 ml
100 ml

2. 5 ml
50 ml
500 ml

3. 8 ℓ
80 ℓ
800 ℓ

4. 17 ml
17 ℓ

c. There are 1000 milliliters in 1 liter.

Remember, *milli-* means "thousandth."

1 milliliter is 1 thousandth liter.	345 milliliters is 345 thousandths liter.
1 ml = 0.001 ℓ	345 ml = 0.345 ℓ

Give each measure in liters.

5. 2 ml **6.** 20 ml **7.** 200 ml **8.** 2000 ml

9. 45 ml **10.** 875 ml **11.** 1250 ml **12.** 600 ml

13. 360 ml

14. 720 ml

15. 165 ml

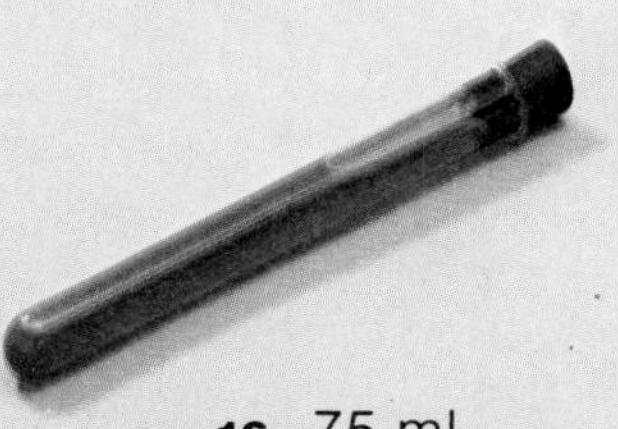

16. 75 ml

17. 235 ml

18. 1000 ml

Weight: Gram and Kilogram

A.

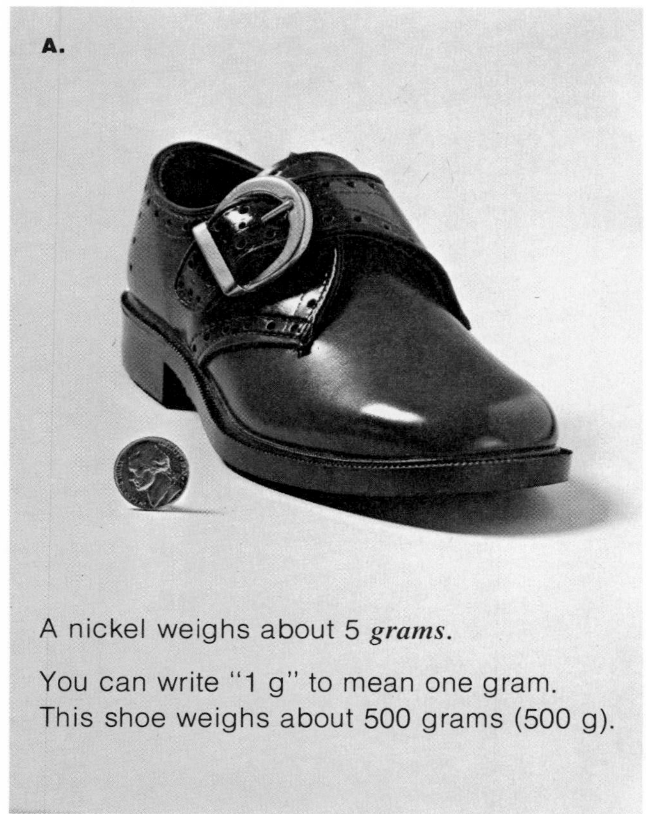

A nickel weighs about 5 grams.
You can write "1 g" to mean one gram.
This shoe weighs about 500 grams (500 g).

B.

Janet has about 1 kilogram of butter, a little more than 2 pounds.
You can write "1 kg" to mean one kilogram.
Janet weighs about 40 kilograms (40 kg).
Burghard's
BUTTER

Choose the better measure.

1. 5 g
5 kg

2. 70 g
70 kg

3. 305 g
305 kg

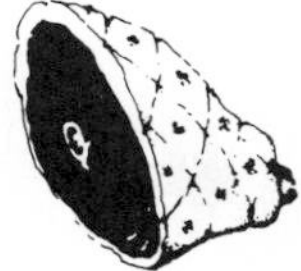

4. 3 g
3 kg

Temperature: Fahrenheit and Celsius

Some thermometers measure temperature in degrees ***Fahrenheit*** (° F).
Some other thermometers measure temperature in degrees ***Celsius*** (° C).

Which temperature is sensible?

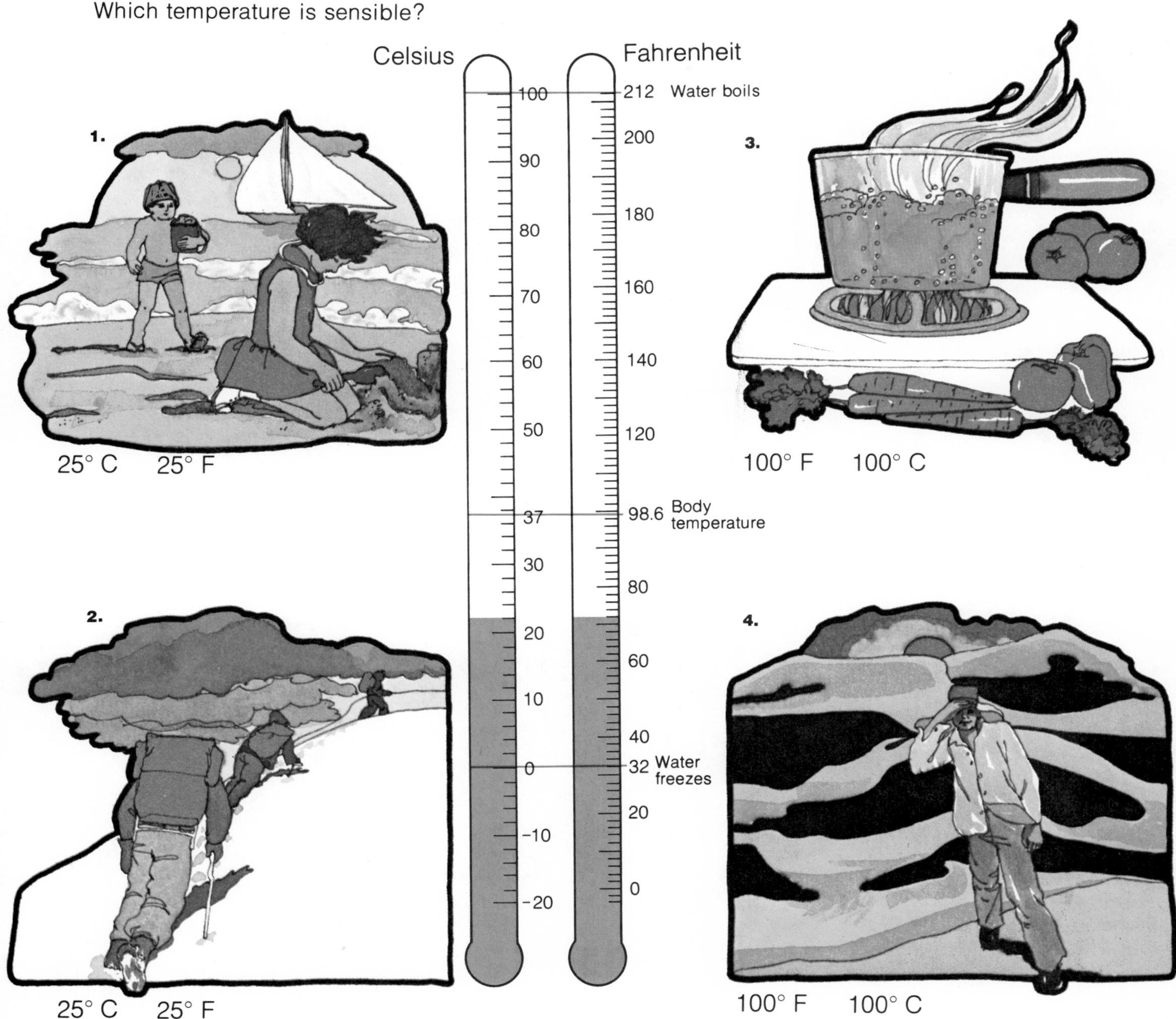

Using Mathematics: Nutrition

Carlos has three favorite cereals.

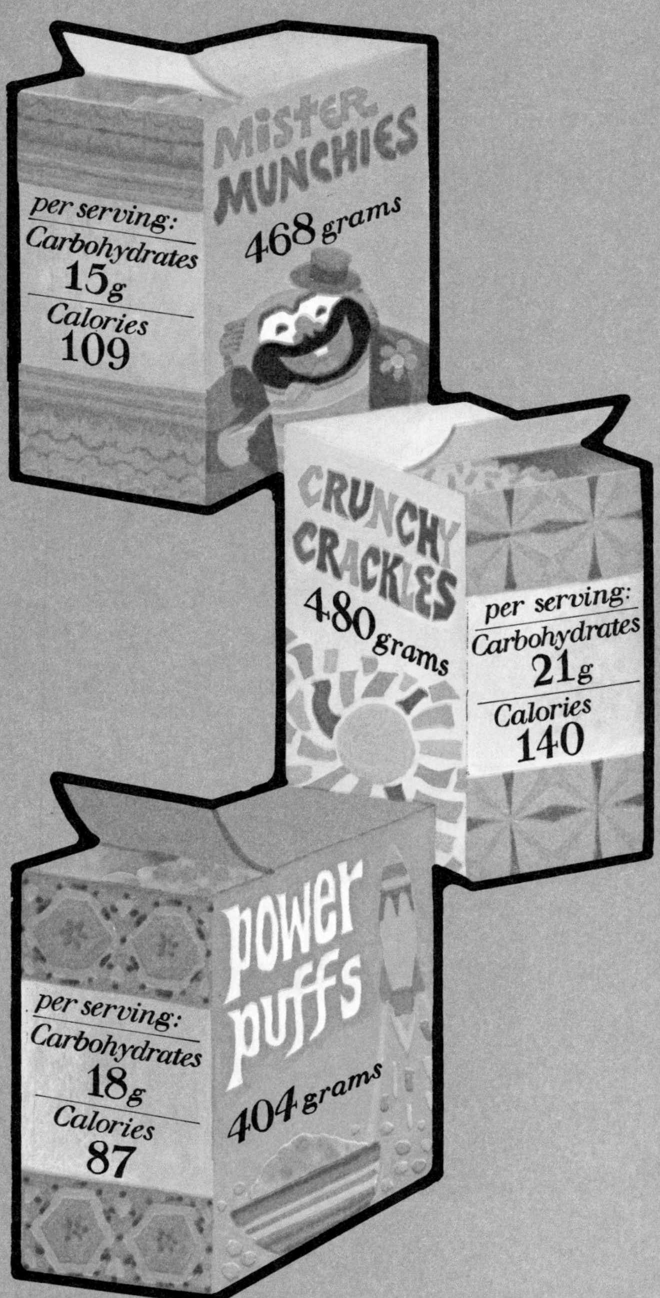

1. How many more grams of cereal are in a box of Crunchy Crackles than in a box of Mister Munchies?
2. How many grams of cereal are in 12 boxes of Power Puffs?
3. There are 18 servings in a box of Mister Munchies. How many grams of cereal are in one serving?
4. There are 16 servings in a box of Crunchy Crackles. How many grams of cereal are in one serving?

For five days, Carlos kept a record of how many servings he ate for breakfast.

Monday:	2 Mr. Munchies
Tuesday:	1 Mr. Munchies 1 Crunchy Crackles
Wednesday:	1 Crunchy Crackles 1 Power Puffs
Thursday:	3 Power Puffs
Friday:	1 Mr. Munchies 1 Power Puffs

5. Tell how many grams of carbohydrate were in his cereal on each of the days. Use the side panels of the cereal boxes to help you.
6. Tell how many calories were in his cereal on each of the days.

Check Yourself
Decimals and Metric Measures, Pages 130–152

Reading and writing decimals, pages 130–137

Tell what each 3 means.

1. 27.3 **2.** .803 **3.** 4.13

Write each decimal.

4. 96 hundredths

5. 3 and 6 hundredths

6. 142 thousandths

7. 5 and 12 thousandths

8. 4 and 3 thousandths

Ordering decimals, pages 138–139

Give the missing numbers for A and B.

9.

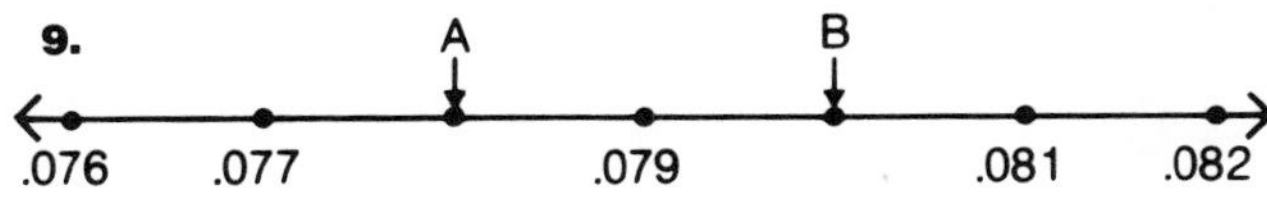

10.

Give the missing number for each ▒.

11. 6.5 6.6 6.7 6.8 ▒ ▒ ▒

12. 1.36 1.37 1.38 ▒ ▒ ▒

Comparing decimals, pages 140–142

Replace ● with $<$, $>$, or $=$.

13. 6.36 ● 6.29

14. .49 ● .5

15. .019 ● .19

16. .800 ● .80

Metric measures, pages 144–151

Choose the best measure.

17.

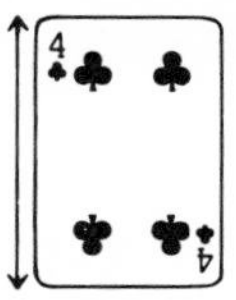

90 mm
90 cm
90 m

19.

10 ml
100 ml
1000 ml

18.

450 g
450 kg

20.

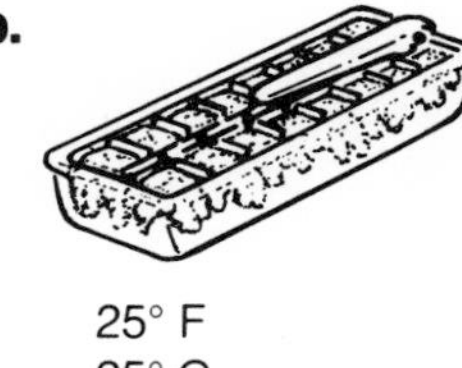

25° F
25° C

21. 57 cm is ▒ meter.

22. Give the measure to the nearest millimeter.

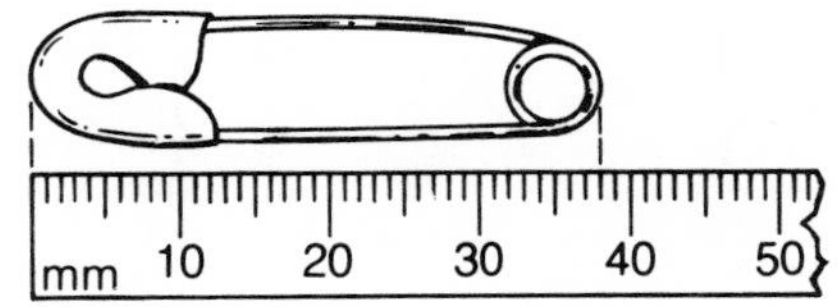

Adding Decimals

A.

What is the total weight of the two packages of chicken?

Find 3.75 + 2.48.

ones	tenths	hundredths

$$\begin{array}{r} \scriptstyle 1 \\ 3.75 \\ +\,2.48 \\ \hline 3 \end{array}$$

Add the hundredths.

13 hundredths = 1 tenth 3 hundredths

$$\begin{array}{r} \scriptstyle 1\;\;1 \\ 3.75 \\ +\,2.48 \\ \hline .23 \end{array}$$

Add the tenths.

12 tenths = 1 one 2 tenths

$$\begin{array}{r} \scriptstyle 1\;\;1 \\ 3.75 \\ +\,2.48 \\ \hline 6.23 \end{array}$$

Add the ones.

The total weight is 6.23 pounds.

B. When you add decimals, line up the decimal points and the numerals in their proper places.

Find 2.78 + 5.91.

$$\begin{array}{r} 2.78 \\ +\,5.91 \\ \hline 8.69 \end{array}$$

Find 6.3 + 9.54.

$$\begin{array}{r} 6.3 \\ +\,9.54 \\ \hline 15.84 \end{array}$$

This is how Lucy added 7.3 and 8.64. Correct her mistake.

$$\begin{array}{r} 7.3 \\ +\,8.64 \\ \hline 9.37 \end{array}$$

Find each sum.

1. 7.5 + 1.3

2. 8.1 + 6.6

3. 1.8 + .6

4. 7.5 + 5.7

5. 6.28 + 3.14

6. 8.37 + .67

7. 2.54 + 1.67

8. 80.75 + 57.08

9. 34.25 + 52.43

10. 3.45 + .976

11. 35.4 + 4.35

12. 5.32 + .085

13. 2.5 + 13.7 + 8.9

14. 3.0 + 11.8 + .76

15. \$4.89 + \$9.16

16. 3.63 + 36.3

17. 45.9 + 5.63 + 1.4

18. .159 + .875

19. 1.667 + 3.333

20. 3.05 + 50.3

21. 20.555 + 25.54

22. 7.35 + 4.12 + 5.25

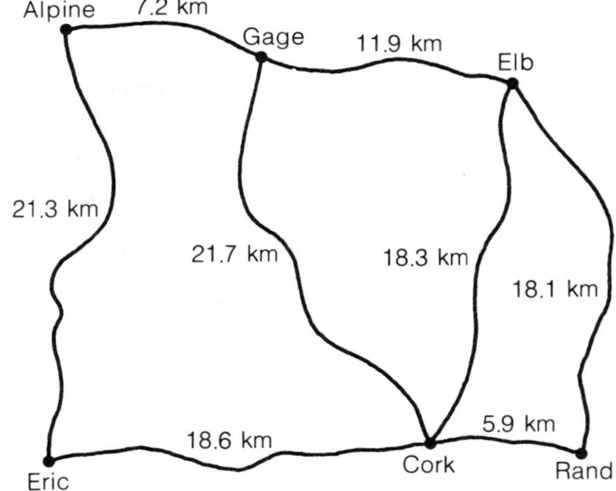

Find the shortest distance along the highways for each trip. The distance between each two cities is given in kilometers.

23. Alpine to Elb

24. Elb to Eric

25. Eric to Gage

26. Gage to Rand

27. Rand to Alpine

28. Alpine to Cork

More practice
Set B, page 175
Set C, page 175

Using Addition of Decimals: Metric Measurement

1. How many kilograms of meat in all?

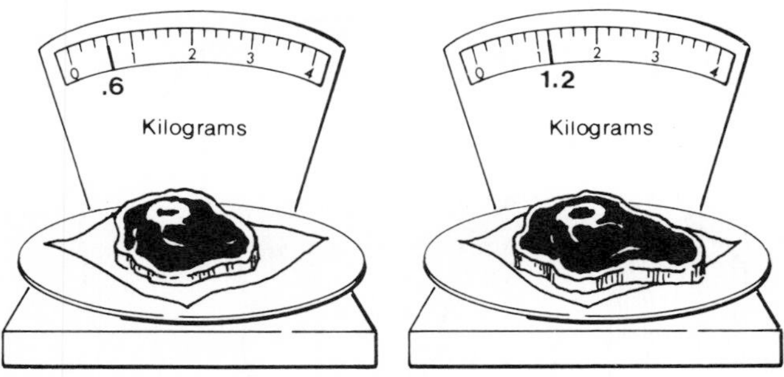

2. How many kilograms of cheese in all?

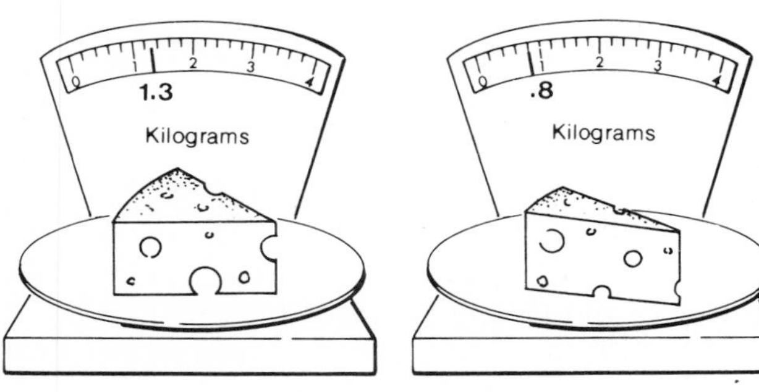

3. How many liters of juice in all?

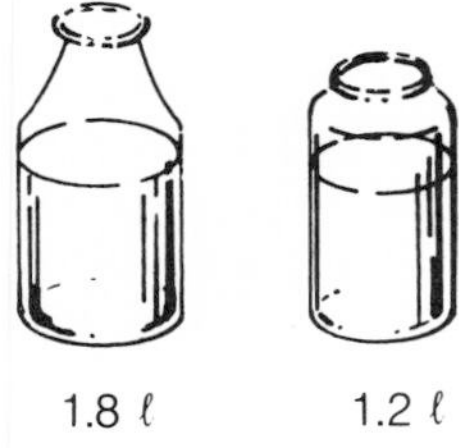

4. What is the distance from home to the art museum?

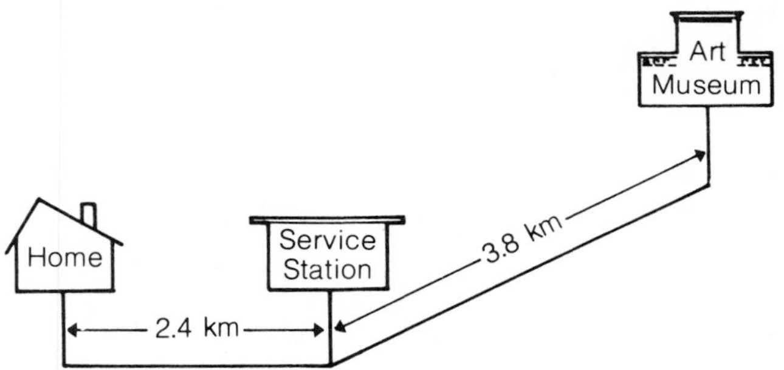

5. What is the distance around the lake?

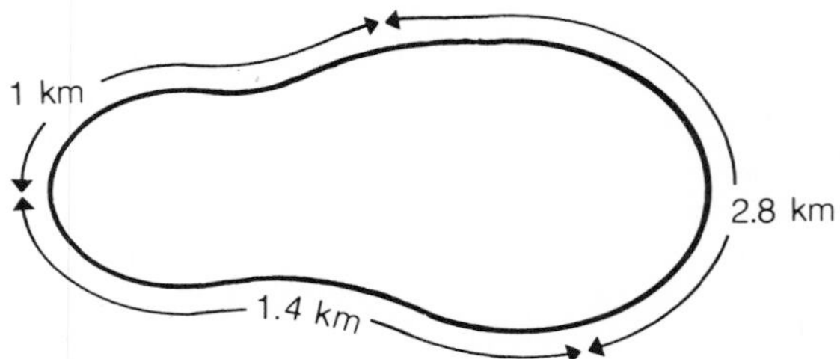

6. What is the distance across all four coins?

Practicing Addition of Decimals: Palindromes

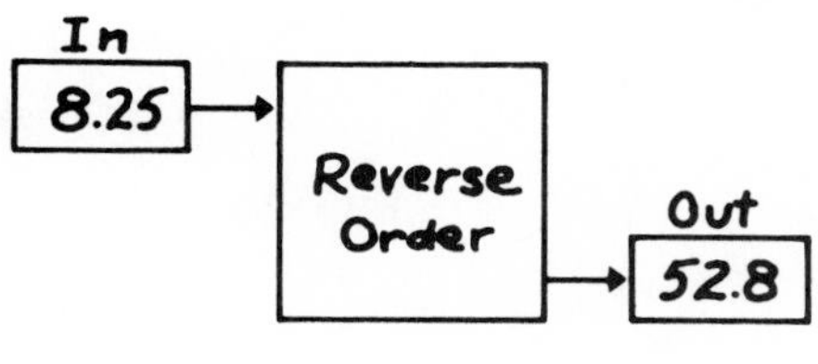

Complete the table. Which numbers did not change when you reversed them?

In	Out
24.7	7.42
38.83	38.83
5.47	
6.6	
384.483	

Numbers like 38.83, 6.6, and 384.483 are called palindromes. Palindrome decimals do not change when you reverse them.

Give the reverse of each number below. Which of these numbers are palindromes?

1. 6.49 **2.** 89.98 **3.** 52.4 **4.** 30.06 **5.** 904.409

A palindrome can be made from a decimal by adding.

3.2	Write the number.
+ 2.3	Reverse it and add.
5.5	The sum is a palindrome.

Sometimes you have to repeat the steps to get a palindrome.

7.5	Write the number.
+ 5.7	Reverse it and add.
13.2	This sum is not a palindrome.
+ 2.31	Reverse the sum and add.
15.51	This sum is a palindrome.

Use addition to get a palindrome from each of these decimals.

6. 3.4 **7.** 1.53 **8.** 4.09 **9.** 8.4 **10.** 3.9

11. 37.2 **12.** 13.8 **13.** 37.2 **14.** 52.17 ★ **15.** 16.9

Subtracting Decimals

A. Barometric pressure

Before the tornado	29.36 in.
During the tornado	27.45 in.

By how much did the pressure change?

Find 29.36 − 27.45.

$$\begin{array}{r} 29.36 \\ -\ 27.45 \\ \hline 1 \end{array}$$

Subtract the hundredths.

$$\begin{array}{r} 2\overset{8}{\not9}.\overset{13}{\not3}6 \\ -\ 27.45 \\ \hline .91 \end{array}$$

Rename to get 10 more tenths.

9 ones 3 tenths = 8 ones 13 tenths

Subtract the tenths.

$$\begin{array}{r} 2\overset{8}{\not9}.\overset{13}{\not3}6 \\ -\ 27.45 \\ \hline 1.91 \end{array}$$

Subtract the ones.

The barometric pressure changed by 1.91 in.

B. When you subtract decimals, line up the decimal points and the numerals in their proper places.

Find 6.78 − 4.51.

$$\begin{array}{r} 6.78 \\ -\ 4.51 \\ \hline 2.27 \end{array}$$

Find 9.36 − 2.1.

$$\begin{array}{r} 9.36 \\ -\ 2.1 \\ \hline \end{array} \rightarrow \begin{array}{r} 9.36 \\ -\ 2.10 \\ \hline 7.26 \end{array}$$

Find 8.7 − 1.31.

$$\begin{array}{r} 8.7 \\ -\ 1.31 \\ \hline \end{array} \rightarrow \begin{array}{r} 8.70 \\ -\ 1.31 \\ \hline 7.39 \end{array}$$

Find each difference.

1. $\begin{array}{r} 6.7 \\ -\ 2.5 \\ \hline \end{array}$

2. $\begin{array}{r} 6.3 \\ -\ .7 \\ \hline \end{array}$

3. $\begin{array}{r} 17.1 \\ -\ 2.8 \\ \hline \end{array}$

4. $\begin{array}{r} .60 \\ -\ .41 \\ \hline \end{array}$

5. $\begin{array}{r} 6.28 \\ -\ 3.14 \\ \hline \end{array}$

6. $\begin{array}{r} 2.57 \\ -\ .81 \\ \hline \end{array}$

7. $\begin{array}{r} 3.24 \\ -\ 1.99 \\ \hline \end{array}$

8. $\begin{array}{r} 8.26 \\ -\ 3.38 \\ \hline \end{array}$

9. $\begin{array}{r} 4.25 \\ -\ 1.70 \\ \hline \end{array}$

10. $\begin{array}{r} .75 \\ -\ .5 \\ \hline \end{array}$

11. $\begin{array}{r} 6.70 \\ -\ 3.33 \\ \hline \end{array}$

12. $\begin{array}{r} 6.7 \\ -\ 1.91 \\ \hline \end{array}$

13. $\begin{array}{r} 10.33 \\ -\ 8.5 \\ \hline \end{array}$

14. $\begin{array}{r} 1.11 \\ -\ .9 \\ \hline \end{array}$

15. $\begin{array}{r} 8.375 \\ -\ 4.125 \\ \hline \end{array}$

16. $\begin{array}{r} 6.667 \\ -\ 1.875 \\ \hline \end{array}$

17. 32.7 − 29.73

18. 54.25 − 5.4

19. 10.6 − 3.51

20. 31.4 − 27.53

Find the difference between the two records given.

21. Barometric pressure, world records

Highest	32.00 in.
Lowest	25.91 in.

22. Rainfall in 24 hours

World record	73.62 in.
U.S. record	38.2 in.

23. Highest recorded temperature

World record	136.4° F
U.S. record	134.0° F

24. Wind speed
Mt. Washington, New Hampshire

Highest	231.0 mph
Average	35.3 mph

More practice
Set D, page 175
Set E, page 175
Set F, page 175

Using Decimals: Automobile Speed Records

LAND SPEED RECORDS FOR ONE MILE

1904 Henry Ford 91.370 mph

1970 Gary Gabelich 622.407 mph

1. The record speed in 1970 was how much greater than the record speed in 1904?

By how much did each driver increase his speed?

2.

Major H. O. D. Segrave

1927 203.790 mph
1929 231.446 mph

3.

Donald Campbell

1933 272.109 mph
1935 301.13 mph

4.

John Cobb

1939 368.9 mph
1947 394.2 mph

5.

Craig Breedlove

1963 407.45 mph
1965 600.601 mph

Indianapolis 500

Year	Winner	Average speed (mph)
1911	Ray Harroun	74.59
1939	Wilbur Shaw	115.035
1940	Wilbur Shaw	114.277
1947	Mauri Rose	116.338
1954	Bill Vukovich	130.840
1961	A. J. Foyt	139.130
1967	A. J. Foyt	151.207
1973	Gordon Johncock	159.014

6. How much faster was the winning speed in 1973 than in 1911?

7. How much slower was Wilbur Shaw's winning speed in 1940 than in 1939?

8. How much faster was A. J. Foyt's winning speed in 1967 than in 1961?

9. Mauri Rose's winning speed was 3.476 mph faster in 1948 than in 1947. What was his speed in 1948?

10. Bill Vukovich won the race in 1953. His average speed that year was 2.100 mph faster than in 1954. What was his winning speed in 1953?

★ 11. Make up two more problems about the speed records.

Keeping Skillful

Subtract. Then check your answer by adding.

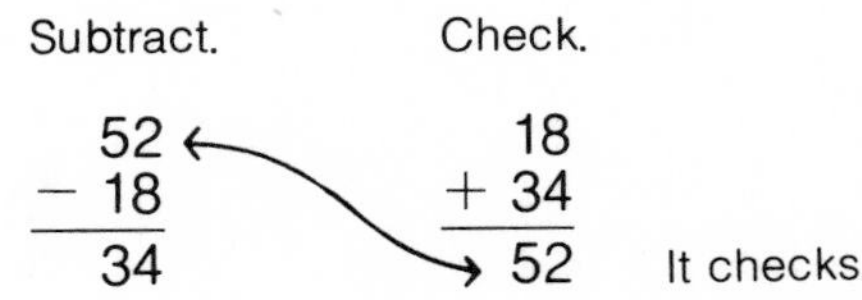

1. $\begin{array}{r} 28 \\ -\ 13 \\ \hline \end{array}$

2. $\begin{array}{r} 75 \\ -\ 48 \\ \hline \end{array}$

3. $\begin{array}{r} 100 \\ -\ 62 \\ \hline \end{array}$

4. $\begin{array}{r} 803 \\ -\ 90 \\ \hline \end{array}$

5. $\begin{array}{r} 1001 \\ -\ 189 \\ \hline \end{array}$

6. $\begin{array}{r} 3025 \\ -\ 667 \\ \hline \end{array}$

Find the missing numbers.

7. $\begin{array}{r} 9 \\ +\ \square \\ \hline 16 \end{array}$

8. $\begin{array}{r} 16 \\ -\ 9 \\ \hline \square \end{array}$

9. $\begin{array}{r} \square \\ +\ 20 \\ \hline 45 \end{array}$

10. $\begin{array}{r} 45 \\ -\ 20 \\ \hline \square \end{array}$

11. $\begin{array}{r} 89 \\ +\ \square \\ \hline 176 \end{array}$

12. $\begin{array}{r} 176 \\ -\ 89 \\ \hline \square \end{array}$

13. $\begin{array}{r} 152 \\ +\ \square \\ \hline 300 \end{array}$

14. $\begin{array}{r} 300 \\ -\ 152 \\ \hline \square \end{array}$

Using Decimals: Money

Find the total cost of each student's purchase. Then tell how much change each will get from a ten-dollar bill.

1. Gail: Planet of the Apes
   bird
2. Bob: jet
   helicopter
3. Adrienne: Porsche
   Dracula
4. Peggy: submarine
   '30 Ford
   Porsche
5. Brian: bicycle
   Dracula
   Frankenstein

Solve each problem.

6. Melvyn had \$6.25. He bought the jet and the helicopter. How much money did he have left?
7. Barbara had \$5.50. She bought the Porsche and the bird. How much money did she have left?
8. Ken had \$7.83. He bought the jet, the helicopter, and the submarine. How much money did he have left?
9. Denise has \$6.00. Does she have enough money to buy Dracula and the Planet of the Apes?
10. Rita has \$6.00. Does she have enough money to buy the bicycle, the '30 Ford, and Frankenstein?

Using Decimals: Installment Buying

1.

Radio	$20.50
Tax	1.03
Delivery	3.55
Finance Charge	1.87
TOTAL	$26.95

Larry is buying a radio on the installment plan. He must pay $3.85 each month for seven months.

Complete the table to find the new balance for each month.

Month	Balance	Payment	New balance	
1	$26.95	$3.85	$23.10 ←	*$26.95 − $3.85*
2	$23.10	$3.85	←	*$23.10 − $3.85*
3		$3.85		
4		$3.85		
5		$3.85		
6		$3.85		
7		$3.85		

2.

Television	$349.95
Tax	17.50
Finance Charge	6.70
TOTAL	$374.15

Mr. LeBlanc pays $74.83 per month for a television set.

Complete the table.

Month	Balance	Payment	New balance	
1	$374.15	$74.83	←	*$374.15−$74.83*
2		$74.83		
3		$74.83		
4		$74.83		
5		$74.83		

Time Out!

How many lines are used to form each figure?
How many different triangles of any size are in each figure?

All the answers you need are on the chalkboard. Find the sums without computing.

The order in which you add decimals does not change the sum.

.5 + .2 = .7
.2 + .5 = .7

The way in which you group decimals does not change the sum.

(.2 + .3) + .4 = .9
.2 + (.3 + .4) = .9

Answers:

3.4 + 2.5 = 5.9
7.8 + 5.4 = 13.2
.33 + .75 = 1.08
8.33 + 3.14 = 11.47
8.76 + 2.16 = 10.92
.125 + .675 = .800
.258 + .833 = 1.091

2.7 + (1.5 + 1.4) = 5.6
1.2 + (8.6 + 5.9) = 15.7
(.16 + .25) + .34 = .75
(.83 + .66) + .75 = 2.24
2.54 + (6.67 + 3.14) = 12.35
9.25 + (7.33 + 9.83) = 26.41
(.375 + .875) + .125 = 1.375

1. 5.4 + 7.8

2. 2.16 + 8.76

3. .75 + .33

4. 2.5 + 3.4

5. .833 + .258

6. 3.14 + 8.33

7. .83 + (.66 + .75)

8. (.83 + .75) + .66

9. .75 + (.83 + .66)

10. (2.7 + 1.5) + 1.4

11. (2.7 + 1.4) + 1.5

12. 1.4 + (2.7 + 1.5)

13. (.25 + .34) + .16

14. (.875 + .125) + .375

15. (3.14 + 2.54) + 6.67

16. (.16 + .34) + .25

17. .875 + (.375 + .125)

★ **18.** (3.4 + 2.5) + 1.2 + 8.6

Solving Equations with Missing Addends

Mrs. Klein had 3.2 pounds of ground beef in the freezer. She sent Ted to the store for more. Then she had 5.9 pounds of ground beef. How much did Ted buy?

	Number of pounds in freezer		Number of pounds bought		Total number of pounds
Write an equation, using n for the missing addend.	**3.2**	**+**	***n***	**=**	**5.9**
Subtract to find n.			***n***	**=**	**2.7**

$$\begin{array}{r} 5.9 \\ -3.2 \\ \hline 2.7 \end{array}$$

Answer the question. Ted bought 2.7 pounds of ground beef.

Solve each equation.

1. $2.8 + n = 3.4$
   $n = $ ▒
2. $n + 1.7 = 4.2$
   $n = $ ▒
3. $1.76 + n = 3.04$
   $n = $ ▒
4. $n + 3.92 = 4.28$
   $n = $ ▒
5. $n + 9.8 = 10.3$
   $n = $ ▒
6. $n + 2.96 = 5.01$
   $n = $ ▒
7. $n + 6.4 = 12.9$
   $n = $ ▒
8. $2.9 + n = 7.4$
   $n = $ ▒
9. $1.09 + n = 3.26$
10. $9.64 + n = 20.90$
11. $n + .8 = 4.1$
12. $n + .38 = 1.91$
13. $n + 7.26 = 11.63$
14. $2.38 + n = 7.25$
15. $37.4 + n = 100.2$
16. $n + 45.71 = 72.35$
17. $8.066 + n = 9.412$
18. $n + 3.334 = 6.125$

Using Equations to Solve Problems

On Saturday, Karin and her brother Arnie drove 1.6 miles to the theater. After the movie, they drove to the grocery store. They drove 3.5 miles in all. How far is the grocery store from the theater?

	Number of miles to theater		Number of miles to grocery store		Total number of miles
Write an equation.	**1.6**	**+**	***n***	**=**	**3.5**
Find *n*.			***n***	**=**	**1.9**

$$\begin{array}{r} 3.5 \\ -1.6 \\ \hline 1.9 \end{array}$$

Answer the question. The grocery store is 1.9 miles from the theater.

Use the steps above to help you solve these problems.

1. First Karin bought 12.6 gallons of gasoline to fill her car's fuel tank. The tank holds 15.2 gallons. How much gasoline was already in the tank?

$n + 12.6 = 15.2$

$n =$ ▒

2. Karin's movie ticket cost \$1.25. The two tickets cost \$1.85. How much did Arnie's ticket cost?

$1.25 + n = 1.85$

$n =$ ▒

3. Arnie spent \$.37 for popcorn. He also bought some candy. He spent \$.63 in all. How much did the candy cost?

4. On the way from the theater to the grocery store, Karin and Arnie passed the zoo. How far is the zoo from the theater?

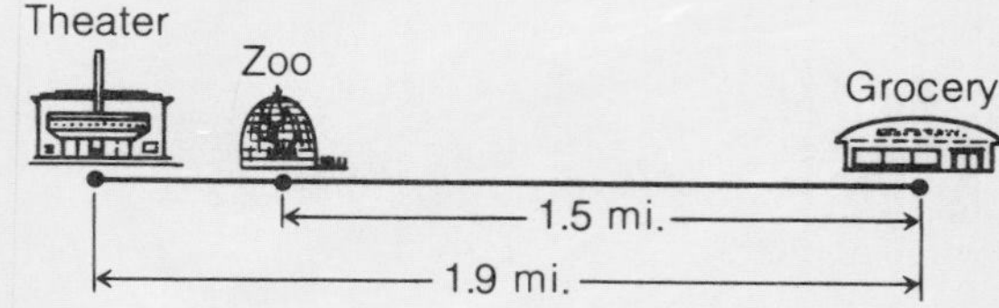

5. How much pot roast did Karin buy if she bought both pieces?

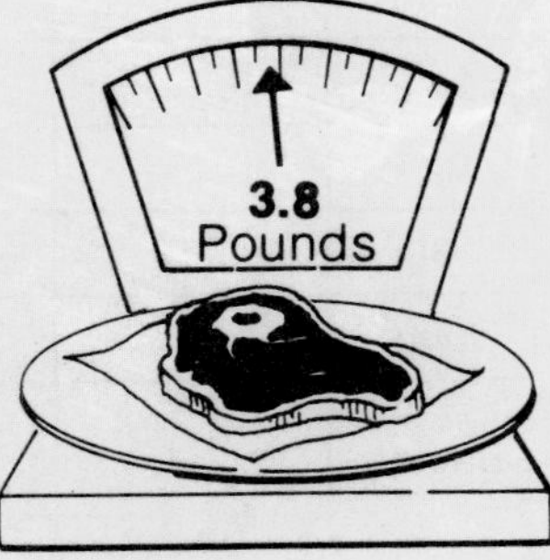

6. Karin bought two packages of fish. Together, the packages weighed 3.4 pounds. One weighed 1.6 pounds. How much did the other package weigh?

7. Karin spent $3.40 for the packages of fish. One package cost $1.60. How much did the other package cost?

8. Arnie spent $1.62 at the grocery store. The total bill was $16.38. How much did Karin spend?

Making Tables to Solve Problems

King Henry hired Tom the Tailor to make him some new clothes. He offered Tom two methods of payment.

Method A

Tom would be paid $.01 for the first day of work. Each day after the first, he would receive twice the amount of the previous day.

Method B

Tom would be paid $.50 for the first day. Each day after the first, he would receive $.10 more than on the previous day.

1. Guess which method pays Tom more money on the seventh day. On the fourteenth day.
2. If Tom works for 14 days, which method do you think pays the greater total amount?
3. Complete the table to see which method pays more money.
4. Which method pays more on the seventh day? How much more?
5. Which method pays more on the fourteenth day? How much more?
6. Which method pays the greater total amount for 14 days' work? How much greater?
7. How much would method A pay on the twentieth day?

Day	Method A	Method B
1st	$.01	$.50
2nd	.02	.60
3rd	.04	.70
4th		
5th		
6th		
7th		
8th		
9th		
10th		
11th		
12th		
13th		
14th		
Total earnings		

The king was so pleased with his new clothes that he made Tom his Royal Tailor. He ordered printed announcements of the news.

The printer offered two plans of payment to the king.

Plan X

The printer would be paid $.05 per copy.

Plan Y

The printer would be paid $.50 for the first copy and $.02 for each additional copy.

Number of copies	Plan X cost	Plan Y cost
1	$.05	$.50
2	.10	.52
3	.15	.54
4	.20	.56
5		
6		
7		
8		
9		
10		
11		
12		
13		
14		
15		
16		
17		
18		
19		
20		

1. Complete the table to find the cost of each plan.
2. Under which plan would ten copies cost more? How much more?
3. Under which plan would fifteen copies cost more? How much more?
4. Under which plan would twenty copies cost more? How much more?
5. When would the two plans cost the same amount?
6. Suppose that the king wanted one hundred copies printed. Which plan would cost less?

SIDE TRIP Logic Patterns

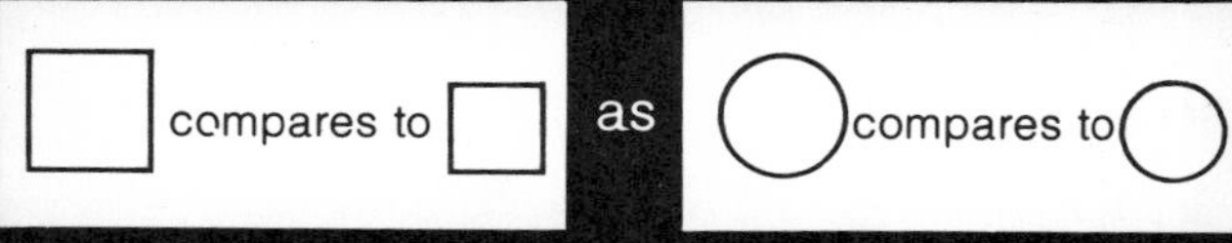

Choose the answer you think is correct.

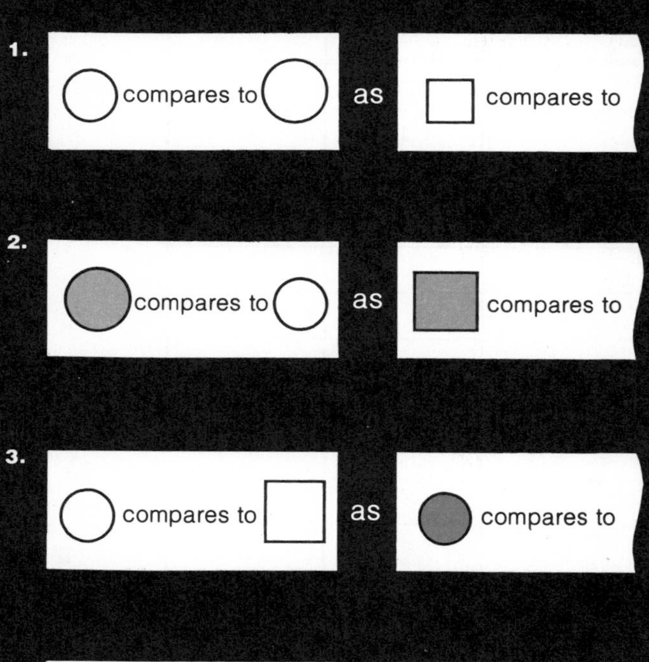

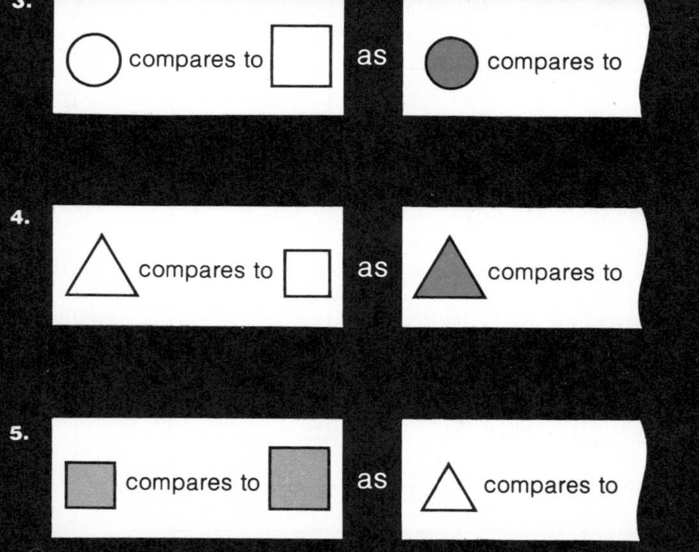

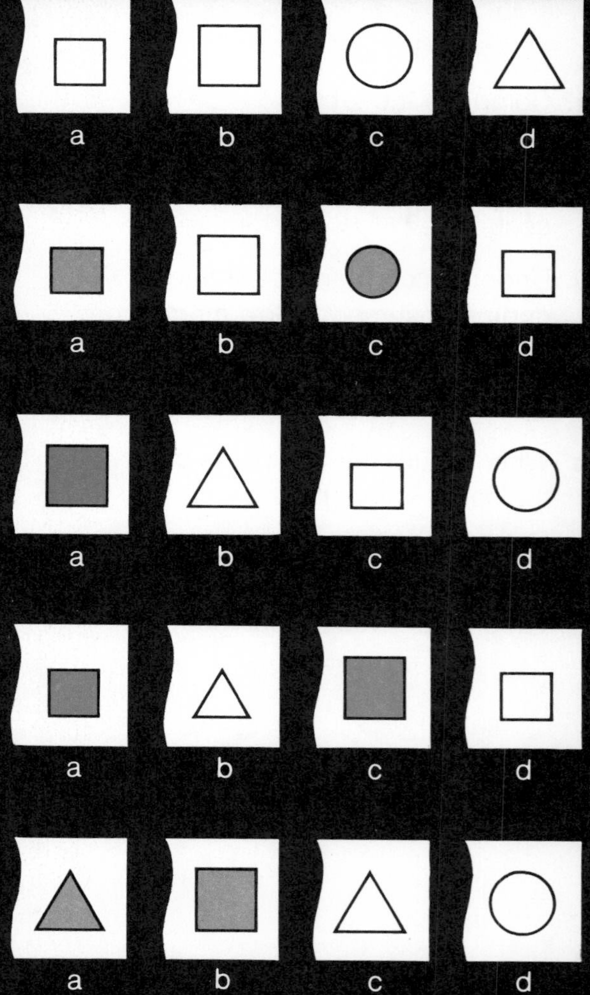

Check Yourself
Adding and Subtracting Decimals, Pages 154–170

Adding decimals, pages 154–155, 157, 164

Add.

1. $\begin{array}{r} 6.7 \\ +\ 5.2 \\ \hline \end{array}$ **2.** $\begin{array}{r} 5.86 \\ +\ 4.01 \\ \hline \end{array}$ **3.** $\begin{array}{r} 9.3 \\ +\ 4.8 \\ \hline \end{array}$

4. $\begin{array}{r} 7.46 \\ +\ 3.79 \\ \hline \end{array}$ **5.** $\begin{array}{r} 3.66 \\ +\ 8.59 \\ \hline \end{array}$ **6.** $\begin{array}{r} .07 \\ +\ .398 \\ \hline \end{array}$

7. 1.7 + 2.5

8. 2.4 + 3.68

9. 3.67 + .095

Subtracting decimals, pages 158–159

Subtract.

10. $\begin{array}{r} 7.8 \\ -\ 3.5 \\ \hline \end{array}$ **11.** $\begin{array}{r} 5.36 \\ -\ 3.24 \\ \hline \end{array}$ **12.** $\begin{array}{r} 9.3 \\ -\ 8.4 \\ \hline \end{array}$

13. $\begin{array}{r} 8.42 \\ -\ 4.37 \\ \hline \end{array}$ **14.** $\begin{array}{r} 9.32 \\ -\ 6.57 \\ \hline \end{array}$ **15.** $\begin{array}{r} .78 \\ -\ .193 \\ \hline \end{array}$

16. 7.1 − 6.8

17. 6.82 − 5.3

18. 8.5 − 3.27

Problem solving, pages 156, 160–163, 165–169

19. Give the total cost of both models.

Sports car	$1.97
Airplane	$2.19

20. How many kilograms of fish?

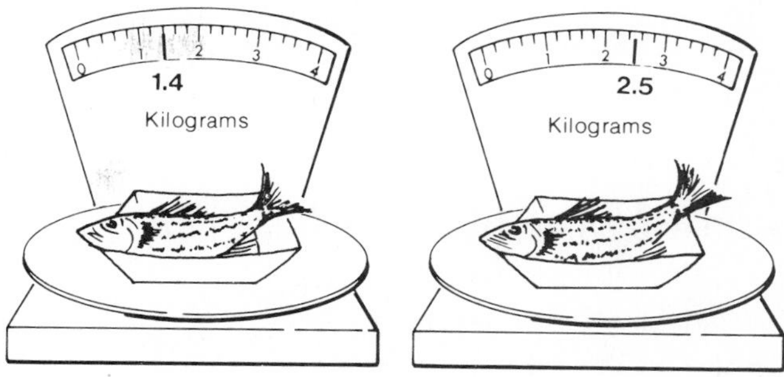

21. How far is it from home to the post office?

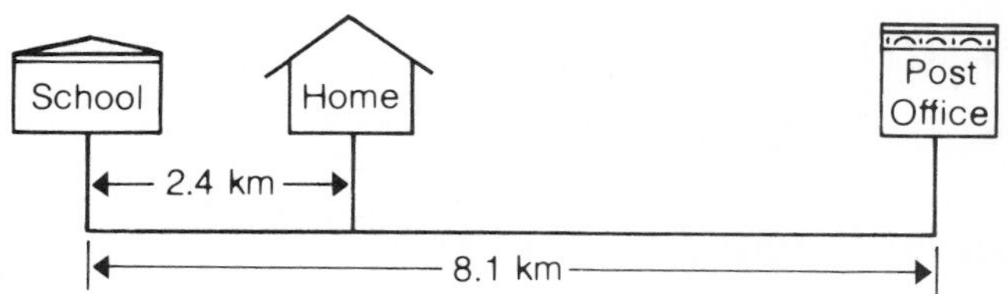

22. Find the change in barometric pressure.

Thursday	31.09 in.
Friday	29.32 in.

23. How much faster was Al Unser's winning speed in 1971 than in 1970?

Indianapolis 500

Year	Winner	Speed (mph)
1970	Al Unser	155.749
1971	Al Unser	157.735

24. Give the number for n.

$n + 2.7 = 4.6$

25. Debbie spent $.29 for a ball-point pen and some money for chalk. She spent $.44 in all. How much did she spend for chalk?

Check Yourself: Level 27

Reading and writing decimals, pages 130–137

Write a decimal.

1. 8 and 9 tenths

2. 19 and 17 hundredths

3. 10 and 58 thousandths

Comparing decimals, pages 140–142

Replace ● with >, <, or =.

4. 7.54 ● 7.28

5. .600 ● .6

6. .04 ● .40

Metric measures, pages 144–151

Choose the better measure.

7.  25 ml / 250 ml

8. 

1 kg / 1 g

9.  100° F / 100° C

Adding decimals, pages 154–157

10. $\begin{array}{r} 17.5 \\ +\ 18.3 \\ \hline \end{array}$ **11.** $\begin{array}{r} 14.2 \\ +\ 11.9 \\ \hline \end{array}$ **12.** $\begin{array}{r} 5.89 \\ +\ 7.26 \\ \hline \end{array}$

13. 19.38 + 16.2

Subtracting decimals, pages 158–163

14. $\begin{array}{r} 14.3 \\ -\ 9.6 \\ \hline \end{array}$ **15.** $\begin{array}{r} 9.46 \\ -\ 6.38 \\ \hline \end{array}$ **16.** $\begin{array}{r} 83.76 \\ -\ 52.49 \\ \hline \end{array}$

17. 9.3 − 3.72

Problem solving, pages 156, 160–163, 165–169

18. Give the total cost of both games.

I Win $6.75
Polyhedron-rummy $1.75

19. Rachel weighed 37.8 kilograms. She gained 1.9 kilograms. Then how much did she weigh?

20. How much greater was the land speed record in 1970 than in 1965?

Year	Driver	Speed (mph)
1965	Breedlove	600.601
1970	Gabelich	622.407

21. Give the number for n.

$1.6 + n = 4.2$

22. Mary had $25.36 in the bank. After making a deposit, she had $31.62. How much did she deposit?

Evaluation: Levels 25–27
Part A

Adding whole numbers, pages 8–15, 22–24

Add.

1. $\begin{array}{r} 35 \\ +\ 26 \\ \hline \end{array}$ **2.** $\begin{array}{r} 57 \\ +\ 84 \\ \hline \end{array}$ **3.** $\begin{array}{r} 486 \\ +\ 307 \\ \hline \end{array}$

4. 875 + 349

5. 116 + 1398 + 27

6. Find the perimeter.

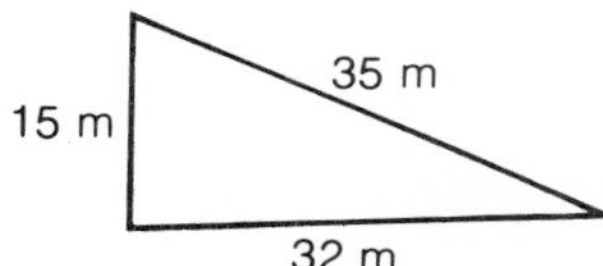

Subtracting whole numbers, pages 16–24

Subtract.

7. $\begin{array}{r} 54 \\ -\ 27 \\ \hline \end{array}$ **8.** $\begin{array}{r} 372 \\ -\ 148 \\ \hline \end{array}$ **9.** $\begin{array}{r} 954 \\ -\ 785 \\ \hline \end{array}$

10. $\begin{array}{r} 705 \\ -\ 427 \\ \hline \end{array}$ **11.** $\begin{array}{r} 4035 \\ -\ 3952 \\ \hline \end{array}$ **12.** $\begin{array}{r} 1532 \\ -\ 965 \\ \hline \end{array}$

13. Marilyn is how much taller than Eleanor?

161 cm

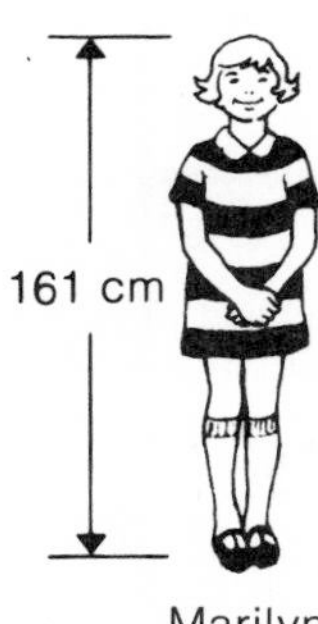

Marilyn

152 cm

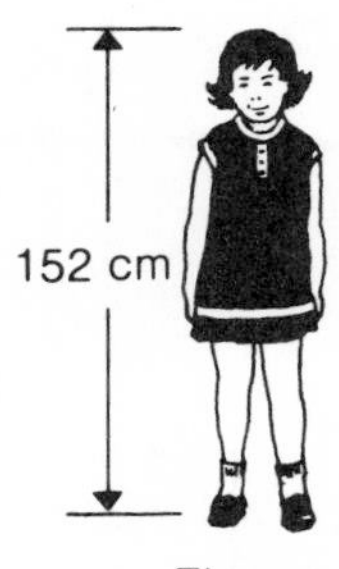

Eleanor

Multiplying whole numbers, pages 32–49

Multiply.

14. $\begin{array}{r} 86 \\ \times\ 4 \\ \hline \end{array}$ **15.** $\begin{array}{r} 276 \\ \times\ 8 \\ \hline \end{array}$ **16.** $\begin{array}{r} 65 \\ \times\ 79 \\ \hline \end{array}$

17. 382 × 47

18. 275 × 369

19. 5 × 25 × 200

20. The principal bought 12 chess sets for the chess club. There are 32 chess pieces in a set. How many pieces in 12 sets?

Dividing whole numbers, pages 68–91

Divide.

21. $5\overline{)72}$ **24.** $32\overline{)268}$

22. $3\overline{)87}$ **25.** $96\overline{)1167}$

23. $4\overline{)630}$ **26.** $39\overline{)8639}$

27. The 117 band members march in 9 equal rows. How many band members in each row?

28. Find the average height of the girls.

Janice:	160 cm
Linda:	149 cm
Mary Lou:	153 cm

Evaluation: Levels 25–27
Part B

Ratio, pages 94–107

Find *n*.

1. $\frac{2}{3} = \frac{16}{n}$ **2.** $\frac{10}{4} = \frac{n}{22}$

3. Suppose that your heart beats 40 times in 30 seconds. At this rate, how many times will it beat in 21 seconds?

Volume, pages 114–122

4. Find the volume.

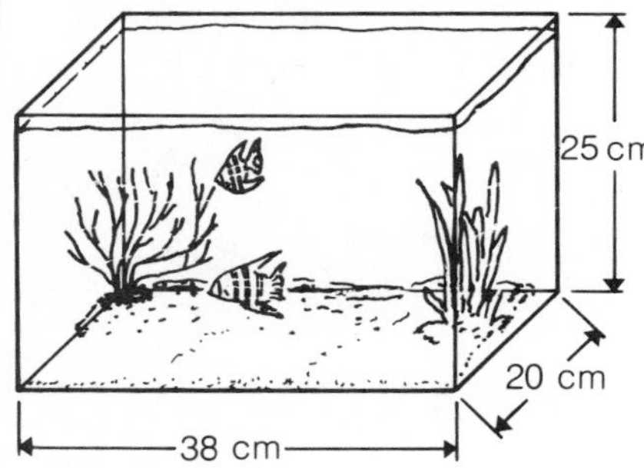

Metric measures, pages 144–151

Choose the best measure.

5.

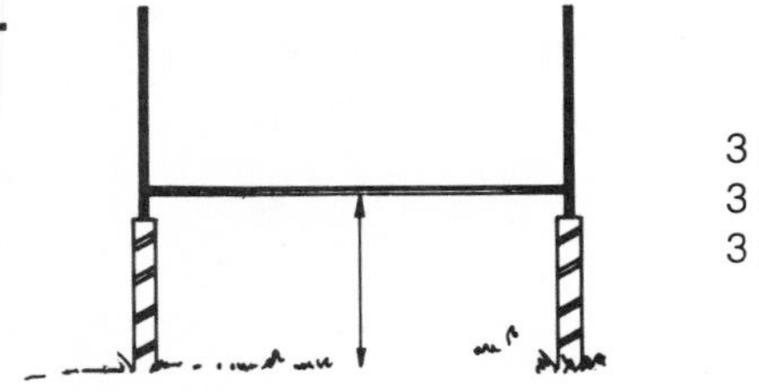

3 mm
3 cm
3 m

6.

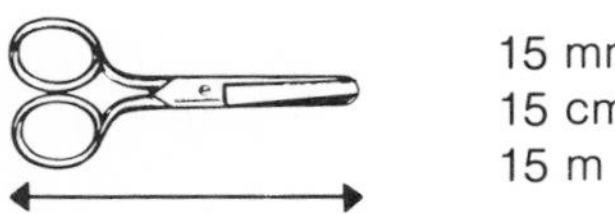

15 mm
15 cm
15 m

Adding decimals, pages 154–157

Add.

7. $\begin{array}{r} 63.7 \\ +\ 25.6 \\ \hline \end{array}$ **8.** $\begin{array}{r} 80.63 \\ +\ 29.41 \\ \hline \end{array}$ **9.** $\begin{array}{r} 1.333 \\ +\ 8.775 \\ \hline \end{array}$

10. .125 + .875 + .625

11. How far is it from Elderberry Ridge to Blueberry Hill?

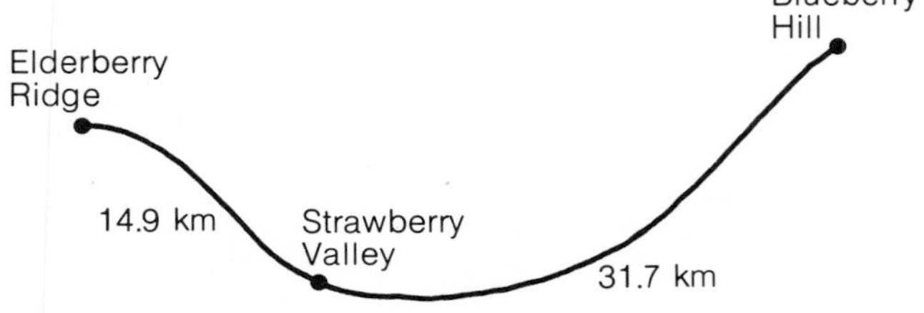

Subtracting decimals, pages 158–163

Subtract.

12. $\begin{array}{r} 48.2 \\ -\ 29.6 \\ \hline \end{array}$ **13.** $\begin{array}{r} 6.30 \\ -\ 4.15 \\ \hline \end{array}$ **14.** $\begin{array}{r} 8.614 \\ -\ 5.279 \\ \hline \end{array}$

15. 14.25 − 6.31

16. What was the cost of the bat?

Receipt	
Baseball	$2.98
Bat	
TOTAL	$12.95

More Practice

Set A

Compare these decimals.
Replace ● with $>$, $<$, or $=$.

1. 4.9 ● 4.7
2. 4.90 ● 4.70
3. .008 ● .8
4. .800 ● .8
5. 21.6 ● 21.63
6. .50 ● .5
7. .02 ● .002
8. .33 ● .333

Set B

Add.

1. $\begin{array}{r} 8.5 \\ +\ 5.8 \\ \hline \end{array}$
2. $\begin{array}{r} 6.38 \\ +\ 2.05 \\ \hline \end{array}$
3. $\begin{array}{r} 1.39 \\ +\ 7.84 \\ \hline \end{array}$
4. $\begin{array}{r} .65 \\ +\ .35 \\ \hline \end{array}$
5. $\begin{array}{r} 17.6 \\ +\ 24.9 \\ \hline \end{array}$
6. $\begin{array}{r} \$2.30 \\ +\ \ 6.70 \\ \hline \end{array}$
7. 15.3 + 17.9
8. 3.28 + 5.72
9. 9.04 + 6.38
10. $3.49 + $4.95

Set C

Add.

1. $\begin{array}{r} .375 \\ +\ .875 \\ \hline \end{array}$
2. $\begin{array}{r} .4 \\ +\ .92 \\ \hline \end{array}$
3. $\begin{array}{r} .367 \\ .592 \\ +\ .485 \\ \hline \end{array}$
4. $\begin{array}{r} 1.608 \\ +\ 3.175 \\ \hline \end{array}$
5. $\begin{array}{r} .726 \\ +\ .09 \\ \hline \end{array}$
6. $\begin{array}{r} 2.345 \\ 9.2 \\ +\ 6.78 \\ \hline \end{array}$
7. .125 + .375 + .625
8. .389 + .1 + .72
9. .3 + .333 + .33
10. 1.414 + 1.414 + 3.14

Set D

Subtract.

1. $\begin{array}{r} 7.6 \\ -\ 3.8 \\ \hline \end{array}$
2. $\begin{array}{r} 9.45 \\ -\ 6.07 \\ \hline \end{array}$
3. $\begin{array}{r} 7.03 \\ -\ 1.26 \\ \hline \end{array}$
4. $\begin{array}{r} .74 \\ -\ .36 \\ \hline \end{array}$
5. $\begin{array}{r} 34.8 \\ -\ 29.5 \\ \hline \end{array}$
6. $\begin{array}{r} \$3.25 \\ -\ \ 1.98 \\ \hline \end{array}$
7. 49.6 − 18.3
8. 3.42 − 1.54
9. 8.05 − 6.27
10. $12.59 − $8.75

Set E

Subtract.

1. $\begin{array}{r} .725 \\ -\ .165 \\ \hline \end{array}$
2. $\begin{array}{r} .333 \\ -\ .125 \\ \hline \end{array}$
3. $\begin{array}{r} 3.109 \\ -\ 2.341 \\ \hline \end{array}$
4. $\begin{array}{r} .106 \\ -\ .095 \\ \hline \end{array}$
5. $\begin{array}{r} .833 \\ -\ .167 \\ \hline \end{array}$
6. $\begin{array}{r} 9.382 \\ -\ 7.684 \\ \hline \end{array}$
7. .625 − .333
8. .801 − .526
9. 2.667 − 1.675
10. 8.003 − 6.247

Set F

Subtract.

1. $\begin{array}{r} .875 \\ -\ .375 \\ \hline \end{array}$
2. $\begin{array}{r} 9.437 \\ -\ 6.908 \\ \hline \end{array}$
3. $\begin{array}{r} .875 \\ -\ .75 \\ \hline \end{array}$
4. $\begin{array}{r} 7.642 \\ -\ 5.386 \\ \hline \end{array}$
5. $\begin{array}{r} 7.001 \\ -\ 2.385 \\ \hline \end{array}$
6. $\begin{array}{r} 9.6 \\ -\ \ .67 \\ \hline \end{array}$
7. .999 − .99
8. 402.5 − 75.25
9. 8.003 − 5.248
10. 8.5 − 2.667

Check Yourself Answers: Level 27

Check Yourself, page 153

1. 3 tenths
2. 3 thousandths
3. 3 hundredths
4. .96
5. 3.06
6. .142
7. 5.012
8. 4.003
9. .078 .080
10. .684 .706
11. 6.9 7.0 7.1
12. 1.39 1.40 1.41
13. 6.36 > 6.29
14. .49 < .5
15. .019 < .19
16. .800 = .80
17. 90 mm
18. 450 g
19. 1000 ml
20. 25° F
21. .57 m
22. 38 mm

Check Yourself, page 171

1. 11.9
2. 9.87
3. 14.1
4. 11.25
5. 12.25
6. .468
7. 4.2
8. 6.08
9. 3.765
10. 4.3
11. 2.12
12. .9
13. 4.05
14. 2.75
15. .587
16. .3
17. 1.52
18. 5.23
19. $4.16
20. 3.9 kg
21. 5.7 km
22. 1.77 in.
23. 1.986 mph
24. 1.9
25. $.15

Check Yourself: Level 27, page 172

1. 8.9
2. 19.17
3. 10.058
4. 7.54 > 7.28
5. .600 = .6
6. .04 < .40
7. 250 ml
8. 1 kg
9. 100° C
10. 35.8
11. 26.1
12. 13.15
13. 35.58
14. 4.7
15. 3.08
16. 31.27
17. 5.58
18. $8.50
19. 39.7 kg
20. 21.806 mph
21. 2.6
22. $6.26

Level 28

Meaning of Fractions, Pages 178–203

Fraction of an Object

A. Mario cuts his pizzas into 8 equal pieces, or eighths.

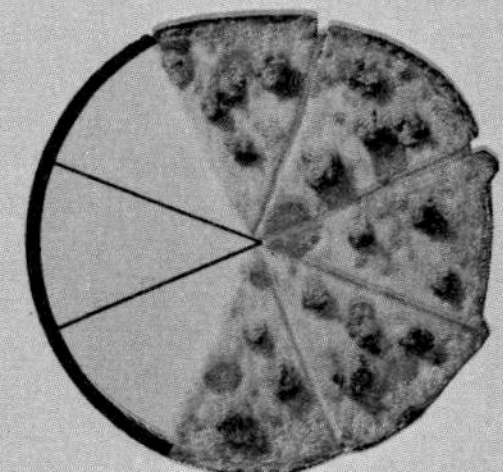

Julie ate 3 pieces. She ate $\frac{3}{8}$ of the pizza.

Denominator: number of equal pieces ⟶ $\frac{3}{8}$ ⟵ *Numerator:* number of pieces eaten

three-eighths

B. What fraction of the cake is left?

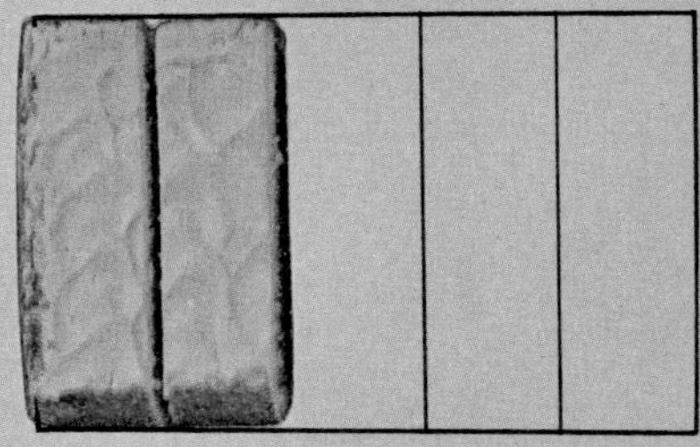

▒ ⟵ Number of pieces left
▒ ⟵ Number of equal pieces

two-fifths

Numbers like $\frac{3}{8}$ and $\frac{2}{5}$ are called ***fractions.***

Give the fractions for exercises 1 through 8.

1. ▒ of the spinner is red.

2. ▒ of the cloth is red.

3. ▒ of the spinner is blue.

▒ of the spinner is yellow.

4. ▒ of the hour has passed.

5. 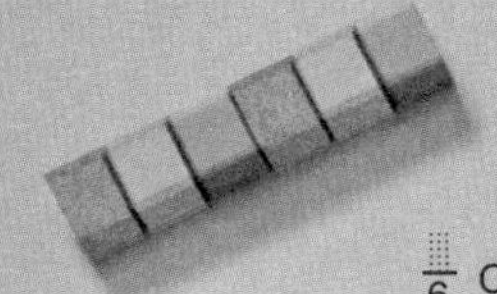

$\frac{\square}{6}$ of the bar is blue.

$\frac{0}{6} = 0$

6. 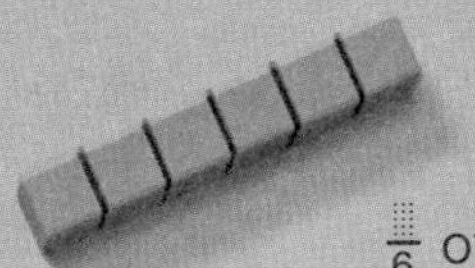

$\frac{\square}{6}$ of the bar is blue.

$\frac{6}{6} = 1$

7. 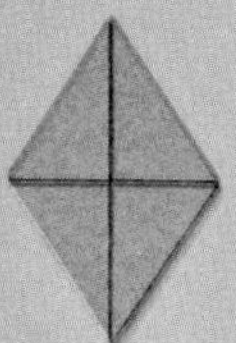

$\square$ of the figure is red.

8. 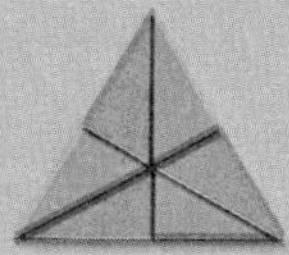

$\square$ of the triangle is yellow.

This pizza is cut into eight parts.
The parts are not equal,
so they are not eighths.

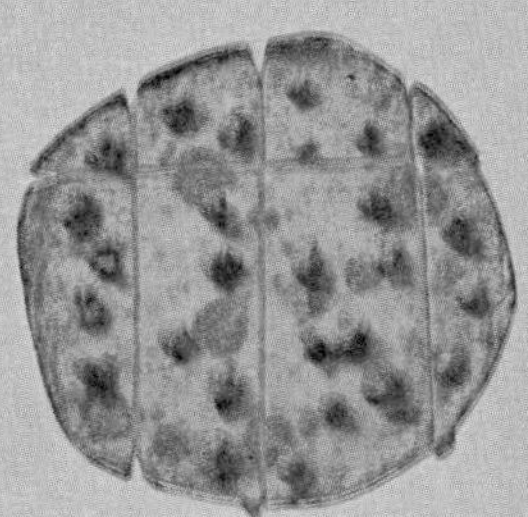

9. Which show one-fourth?

a. 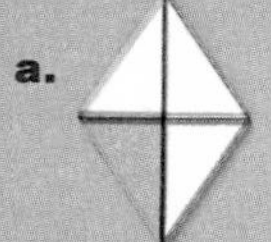
b. 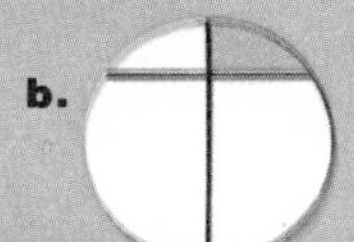
c. 

10. Which show one-half?

a. 
b. 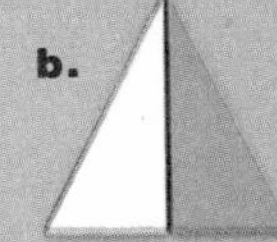
c. 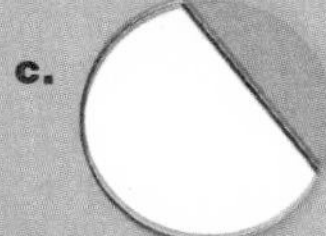

11. Which show two-thirds?

a. 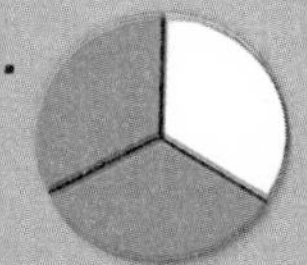
b. 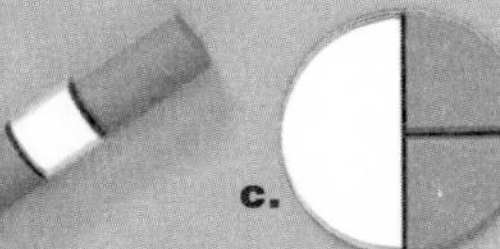
c.

12. Which show three-fifths?

a. 
b. 
c. 

Fraction of a Set

What fraction of the bottles in this carton are empty?

$\frac{4}{6}$ ← Number of empty bottles

Number of bottles → 6

Give a fraction for each exercise.

1. ____ of the coins are pennies.

2. ____ of the rabbits are gray.

3. ____ of the marbles are green.

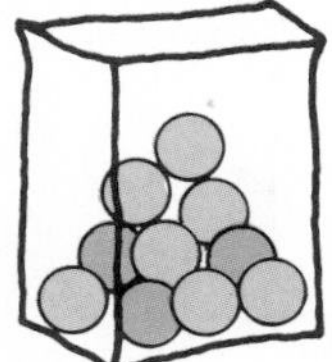

4. ____ of the balls are baseballs.

5. ____ of the balls are footballs.

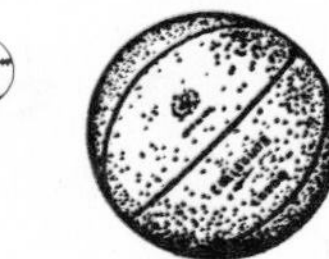
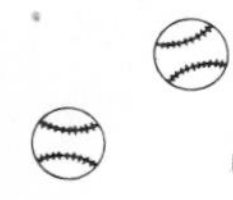
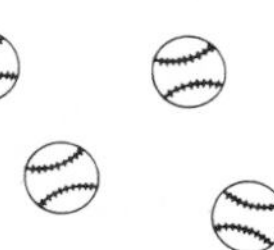

6. ____ of the eggs are broken.

7. ____ of the dimes show heads.

8. ____ of the apples are red.

9. ____ of the cards are red.

10. ____ of the cards are hearts.

Stan wrote the first ten Roman numerals like this.

I II III IV V VI VII VIII IX X

He wrote the numeral I with three line segments.

He wrote the numeral II with four segments.

What fraction of the first ten Roman numerals did he write with

11. four segments?

12. five segments?

13. six segments?

14. seven segments?

15. fewer than five segments?

16. more than four segments?

EXPERIMENT

1. Put two cards like this into a bag.

2. Shake the bag.
3. Draw one card without looking.
4. Record whether the letter is A or B.
5. Return the card to the bag.
6. Repeat 20 times.

17. If you did the experiment, do you think you would draw more A's, more B's, or about the same number of each?

Larry did the experiment. His results are shown.

18. What fraction of the letters he drew were A's? Is this fraction close to $\frac{1}{2}$?

19. What fraction of the letters he drew were B's? Is this fraction close to $\frac{1}{2}$?

20. Do the experiment yourself. What fraction of the letters you drew were A's? B's? Are your fractions close to $\frac{1}{2}$?

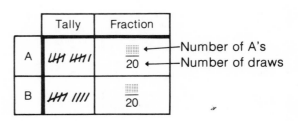

	Tally	Fraction
A	HHT HHT I	$\frac{\square}{20}$
B	HHT IIII	$\frac{\square}{20}$

Number of A's (numerator) — Number of draws (denominator)

Using Fractions in Measurement

Give each length to the nearest $\frac{1}{8}$ inch.

1. 

2. 

3. 

4. 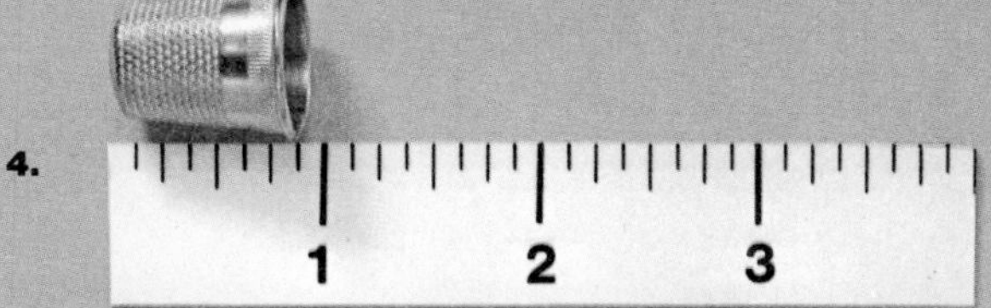

5. 

6. 

7. 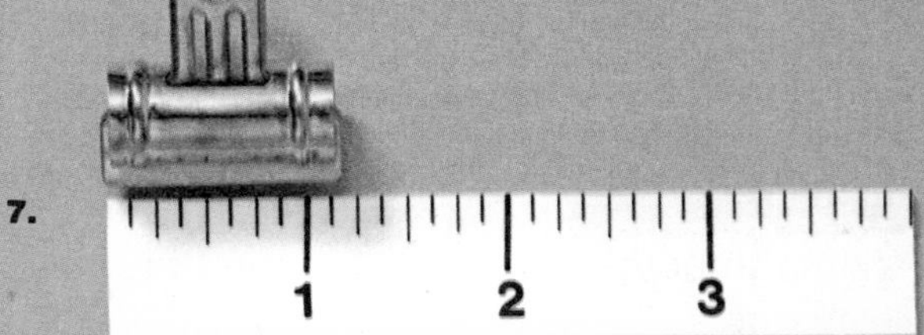

8. 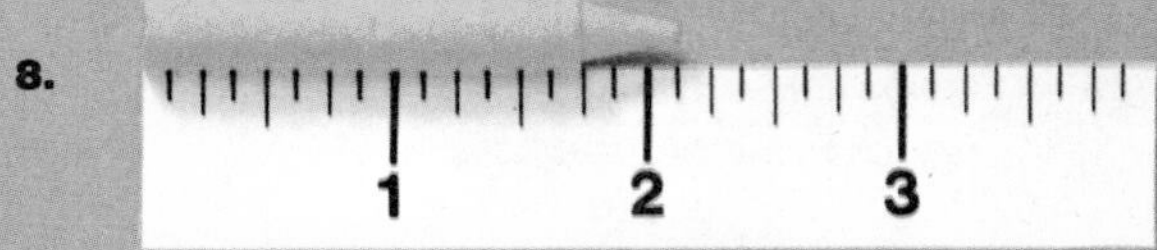

9. 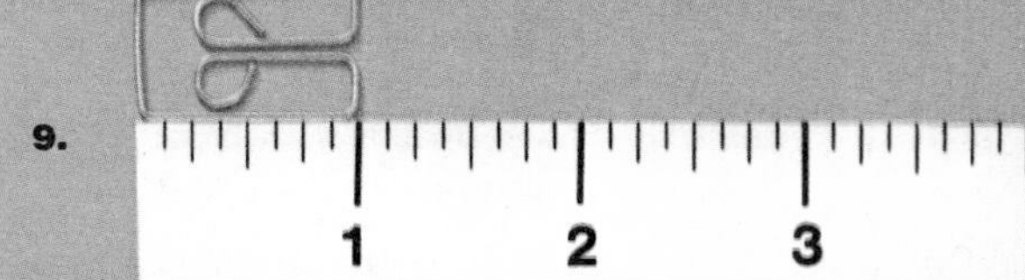

10. 

Give a fraction for each exercise.

11. ▒ of the race completed

12. ▒ of a mile walked

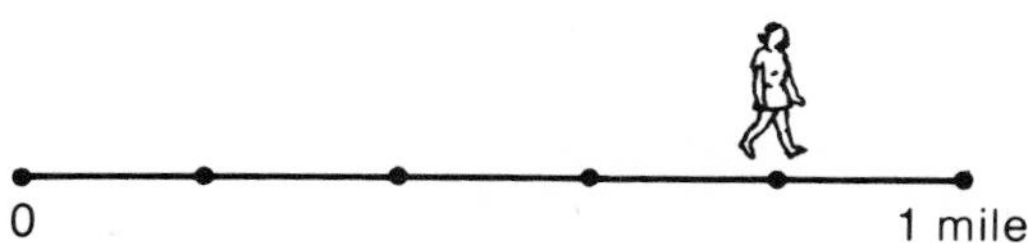

13. ▒ cup of punch

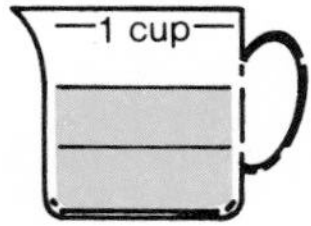

14. ▒ pound of tomatoes

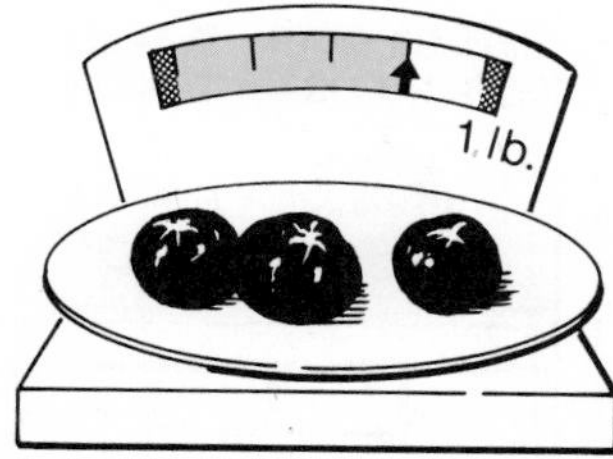

15. ▒ tank of gasoline

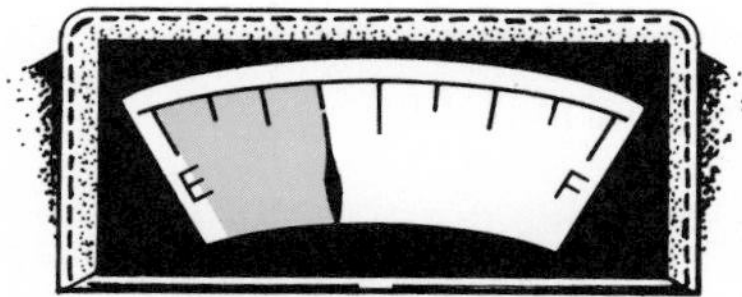

16. ▒ inch of liquid

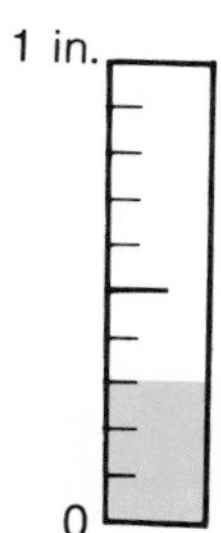

17. ▒ yard of cloth

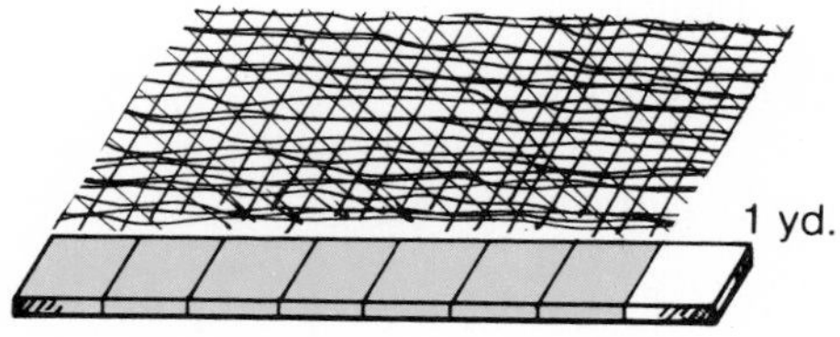

18. ▒ ounce

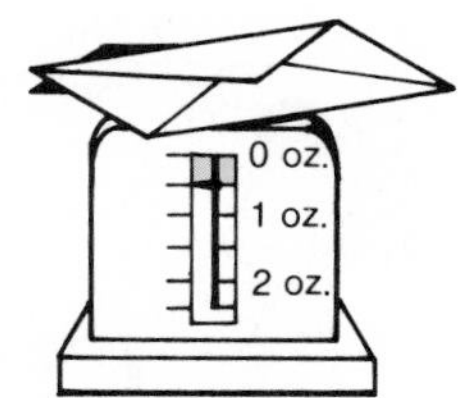

Using Fractions in Measurement

Replace ▒ with a fraction.

one foot

0 1 2 3 4 5 6 7 8 9 10 11 12
inches

one yard

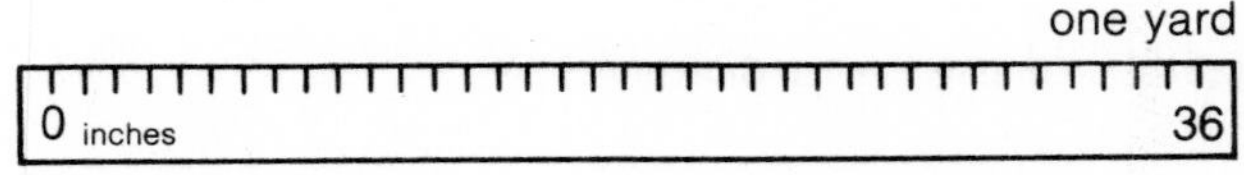

1. There are 12 inches in 1 foot.

   1 inch = $\frac{1}{12}$ foot

   a. 5 inches = ▒ foot

   b. 7 inches = ▒ foot

   c. 10 inches = ▒ foot

2. There are 36 inches in 1 yard.

   1 inch = $\frac{1}{36}$ yard

   a. 5 inches = ▒ yard

   b. 12 inches = ▒ yard

   c. 17 inches = ▒ yard

   d. 23 inches = ▒ yard

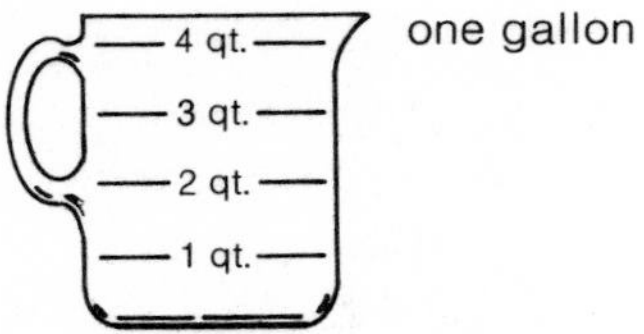

one gallon

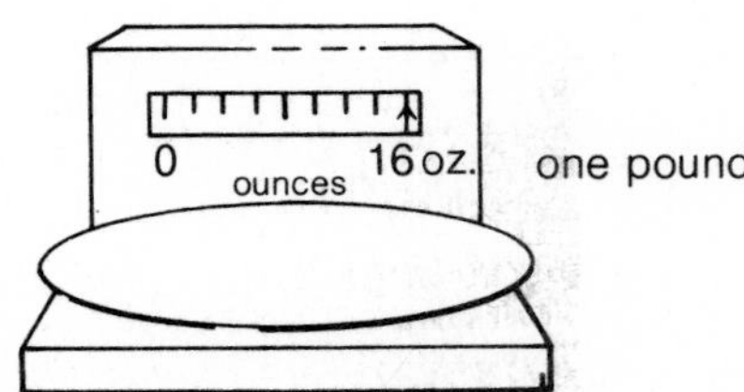

one pound

3. There are 4 quarts in 1 gallon.

   1 quart = $\frac{1}{4}$ gallon

   a. 2 quarts = ▒ gallon

   b. 3 quarts = ▒ gallon

4. There are 16 ounces in 1 pound.

   1 ounce = $\frac{1}{16}$ pound

   a. 5 ounces = ▒ pound

   b. 8 ounces = ▒ pound

   c. 11 ounces = ▒ pound

   d. 15 ounces = ▒ pound

SUN	MON	TUES	WED	THUR	FRI	SAT
					1	2
3	4	5	6	7	8	9
10	11	12	13	14	15	16
17	18	19	20	21	22	23
24	25	26	27	28	29	30

5. There are 7 days in 1 week.

 1 day = $\frac{1}{7}$ week

 a. 2 days = ▒ week

 b. 4 days = ▒ week

 c. 5 days = ▒ week

6. There are 24 hours in 1 day.

 1 hour = $\frac{1}{24}$ day

 a. 5 hours = ▒ day

 b. 11 hours = ▒ day

 c. 23 hours = ▒ day

7. There are 60 minutes in 1 hour.

 1 minute = $\frac{1}{60}$ hour

 a. 15 minutes = ▒ hour

 b. 25 minutes = ▒ hour

 c. 40 minutes = ▒ hour

8. There are 60 seconds in 1 minute.

 1 second = $\frac{1}{60}$ minute

 a. 10 seconds = ▒ minute

 b. 12 seconds = ▒ minute

 c. 45 seconds = ▒ minute

Finding Equal Fractions Through Pictures

The same amount is shaded in each picture.

$\frac{1}{2}$

$\frac{2}{4}$

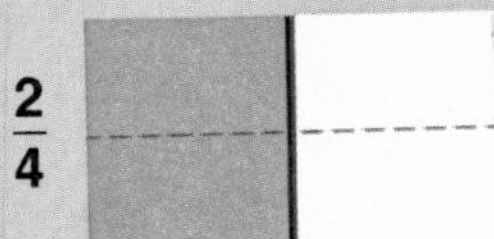

$$\frac{1}{2} = \frac{2}{4}$$

Give the equal fractions for the amount shaded.

1\.

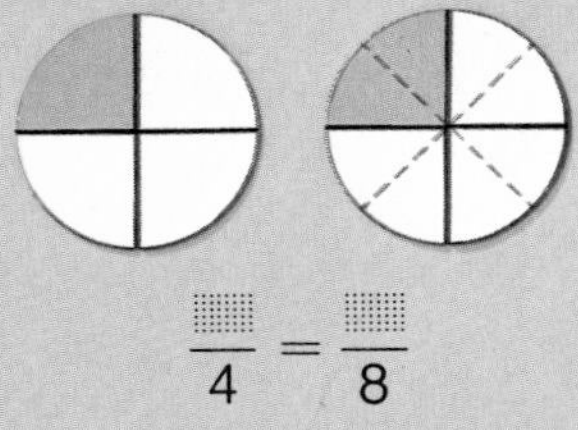

$\frac{\square}{4} = \frac{\square}{8}$

2\.

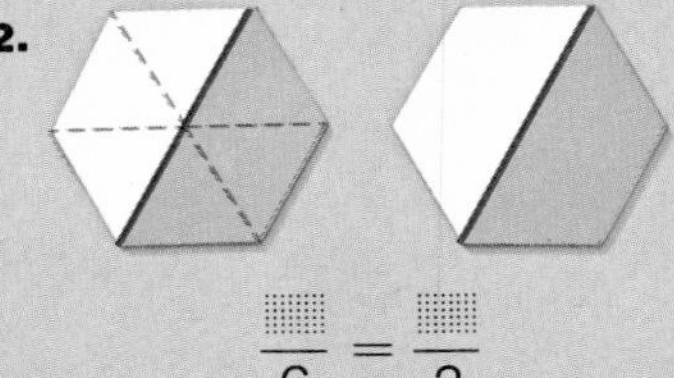

$\frac{\square}{6} = \frac{\square}{2}$

3\.

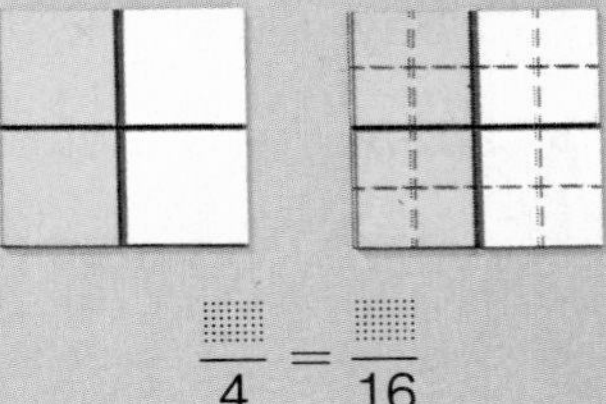

$\frac{\square}{4} = \frac{\square}{16}$

4\.

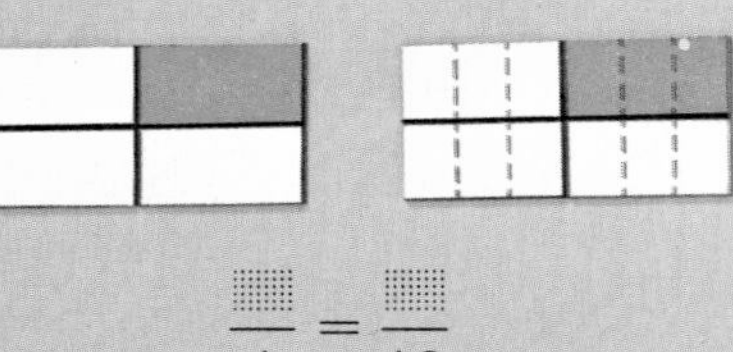

$\frac{\square}{4} = \frac{\square}{12}$

5\.

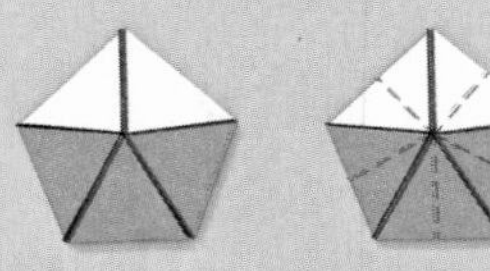

$\frac{\square}{5} = \frac{\square}{10}$

6\.

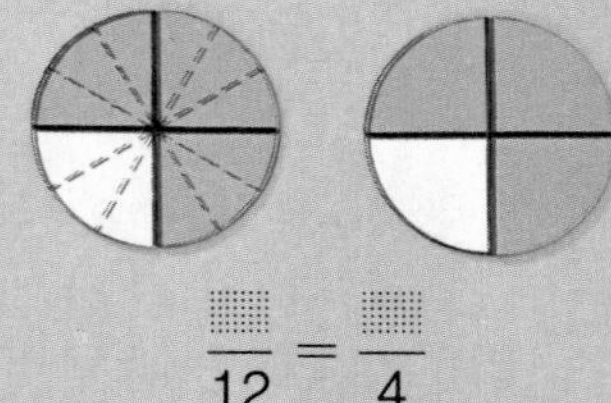

$\frac{\square}{12} = \frac{\square}{4}$

7\.

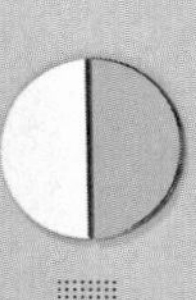

$\frac{\square}{2} = \frac{\square}{4} = \frac{\square}{6} = \frac{\square}{8} = \frac{\square}{10}$

8\.

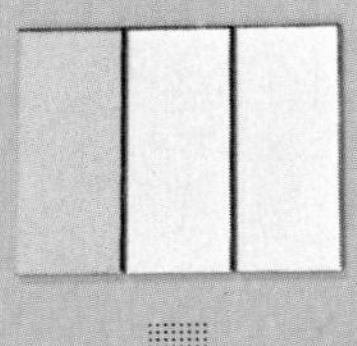
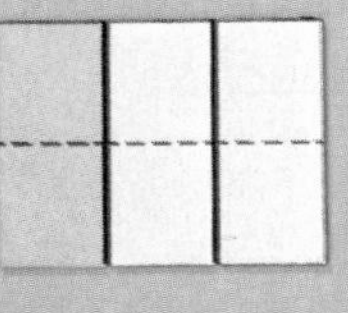
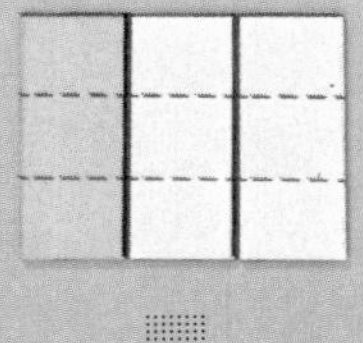

$\frac{\square}{3} = \frac{\square}{6} = \frac{\square}{9} = \frac{\square}{12} = \frac{\square}{15}$

Finding Equal Fractions for Equal Measures

Give the equal fractions.

1.

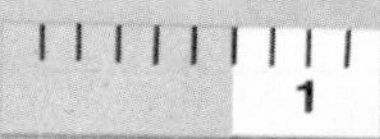

$\frac{\square}{4}$ in. $=$ $\frac{\square}{8}$ in.

2.

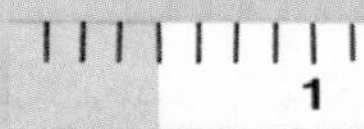

$\frac{\square}{2}$ in. $=$ $\frac{\square}{8}$ in.

3.

$\frac{\square}{4}$ ft. $=$ $\frac{\square}{12}$ ft.

4.

$\frac{\square}{6}$ ft. $=$ $\frac{\square}{12}$ ft.

5.

$\frac{\square}{3}$ yd. $=$ $\frac{\square}{36}$ yd.

6.

$\frac{\square}{36}$ yd. $=$ $\frac{\square}{2}$ yd.

7.

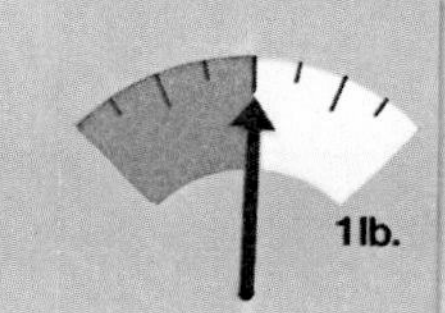

$\frac{\square}{8}$ lb. $=$ $\frac{\square}{16}$ lb.

8.

$\frac{\square}{16}$ lb. $=$ $\frac{\square}{4}$ lb.

Finding Equal Fractions on the Number Line

Use the number lines to complete the lists of equal fractions.

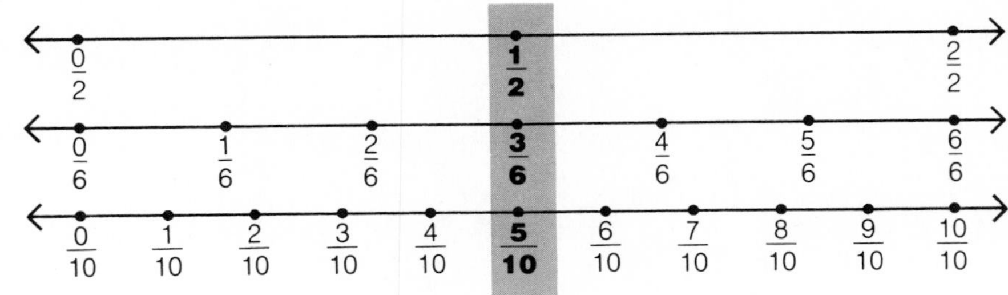

Here's how

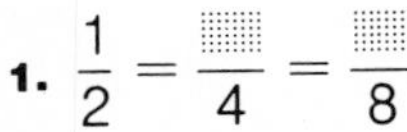

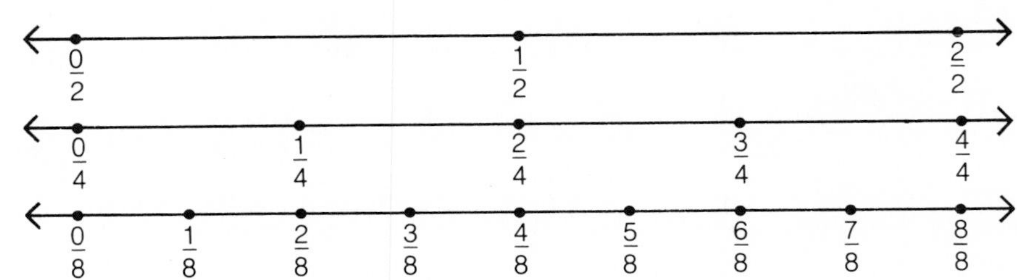

1. $\frac{1}{2} = \frac{\square}{4} = \frac{\square}{8}$

2. $\frac{3}{4} = \frac{\square}{\square}$

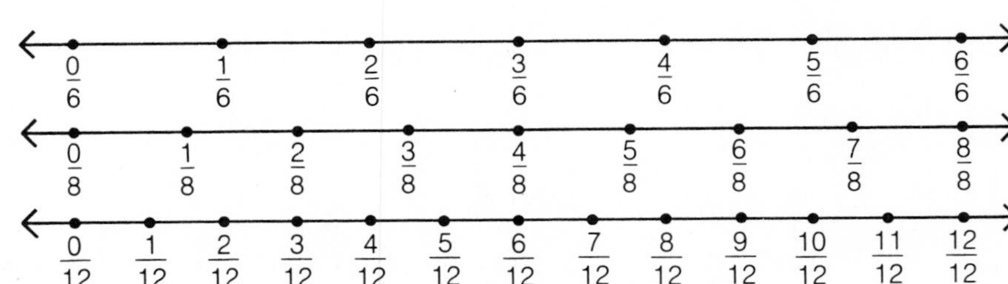

3. $\frac{3}{6} = \frac{\square}{\square} = \frac{\square}{\square}$

4. $\frac{4}{6} = \frac{\square}{\square}$

5. $\frac{6}{8} = \frac{\square}{\square}$

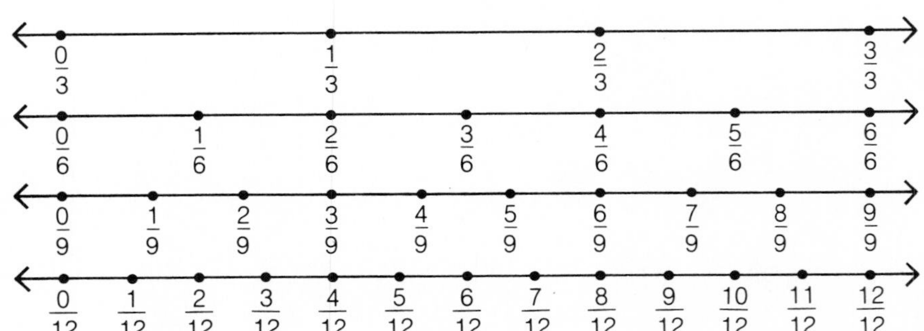

6. $\frac{2}{3} = \frac{\square}{\square} = \frac{\square}{\square} = \frac{\square}{\square}$

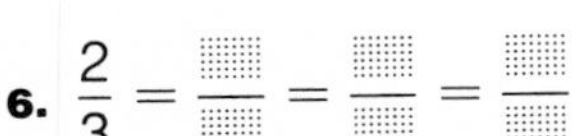

7. $\frac{3}{9} = \frac{\square}{3} = \frac{\square}{6} = \frac{\square}{12}$

8. $\frac{5}{6} = \frac{\square}{\square}$

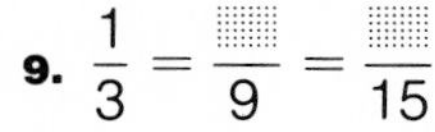

9. $\frac{1}{3} = \frac{\square}{9} = \frac{\square}{15}$

10. $\frac{2}{3} = \frac{\square}{\square} = \frac{\square}{\square}$

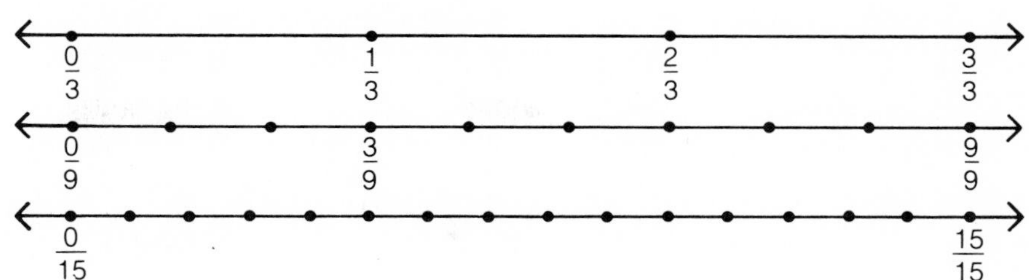

11. $\frac{3}{5} = \frac{\square}{\square} = \frac{\square}{\square}$

12. $\frac{1}{5} = \frac{\square}{\square} = \frac{\square}{\square}$

13. $\frac{5}{5} = \frac{\square}{\square} = \frac{\square}{\square}$

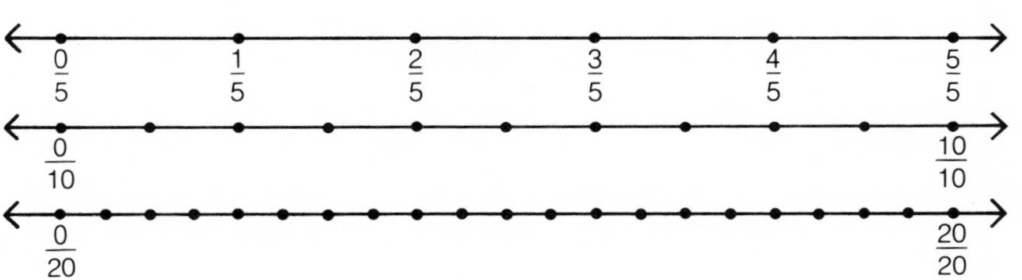

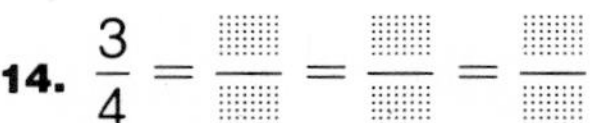

14. $\frac{3}{4} = \frac{\square}{\square} = \frac{\square}{\square} = \frac{\square}{\square}$

15. $\frac{2}{4} = \frac{\square}{\square} = \frac{\square}{\square} = \frac{\square}{\square}$

16. $\frac{5}{8} = \frac{\square}{\square}$

17. $\frac{3}{12} = \frac{\square}{\square} = \frac{\square}{\square} = \frac{\square}{\square}$

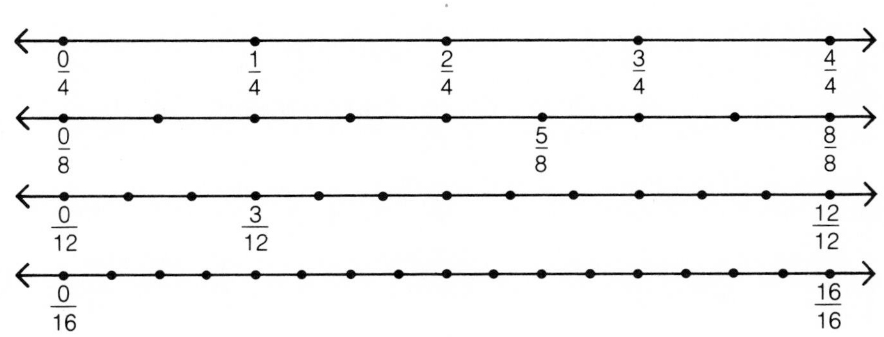

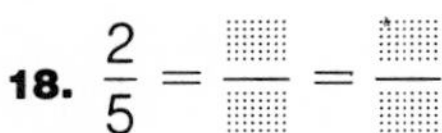

18. $\frac{2}{5} = \frac{\square}{\square} = \frac{\square}{\square}$

19. $\frac{4}{5} = \frac{\square}{\square} = \frac{\square}{\square}$

20. $\frac{0}{5} = \frac{\square}{\square} = \frac{\square}{\square}$

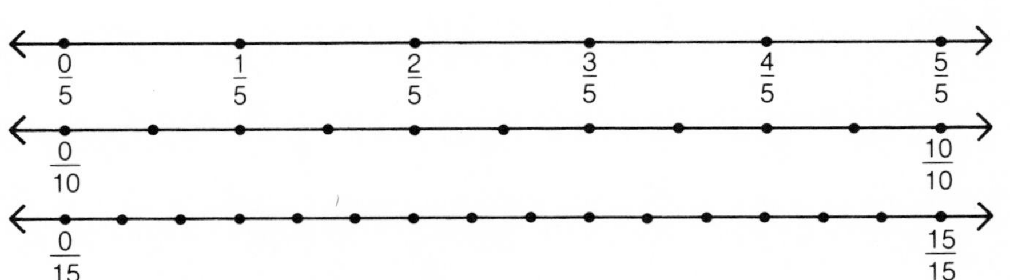

Finding Equal Fractions by Multiplying

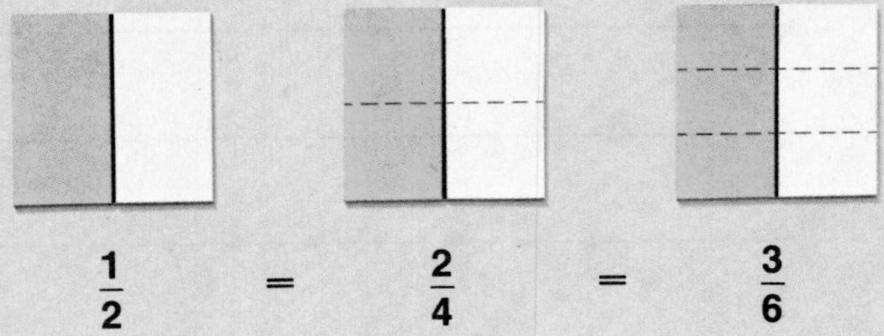

You can multiply to find fractions equal to $\frac{1}{2}$.

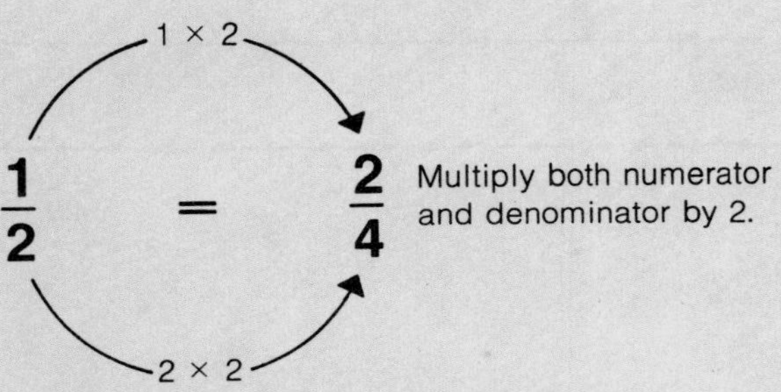

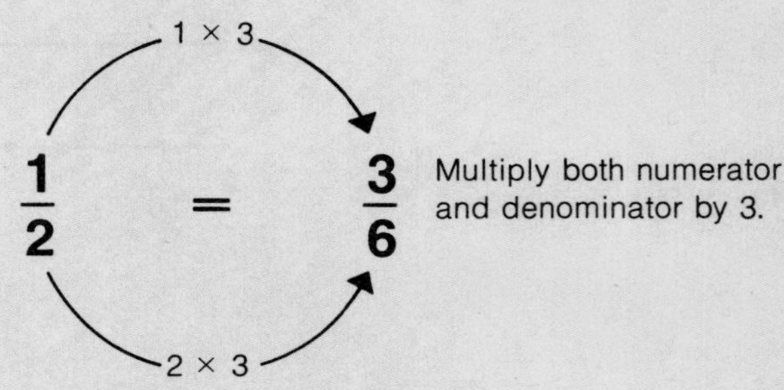

■ *You can multiply both numerator and denominator of a fraction by the same number to find an equal fraction.*

Complete each list of equal fractions.

1. $\frac{2}{3} = \frac{\square}{6} = \frac{\square}{\square} = \frac{\square}{\square} = \frac{\square}{\square} = \frac{\square}{\square}$ (numerators: 2 × 2, 2 × 3, 2 × 4, 2 × 5, 2 × 6; denominators: 3 × 2, 3 × 3, 3 × 4, 3 × 5, 3 × 6)

2. $\frac{3}{4} = \frac{\square}{\square} = \frac{\square}{\square} = \frac{\square}{\square} = \frac{\square}{\square} = \frac{\square}{\square}$

3. $\frac{1}{5} = \frac{\square}{\square} = \frac{\square}{\square} = \frac{\square}{\square} = \frac{\square}{\square} = \frac{\square}{\square}$

4. $\frac{4}{5} = \frac{\square}{\square} = \frac{\square}{\square} = \frac{\square}{\square} = \frac{\square}{\square} = \frac{\square}{\square}$

For each fraction, list five equal fractions.

5. $\frac{3}{5}$	**8.** $\frac{5}{9}$	**11.** $\frac{7}{8}$	**14.** $\frac{3}{10}$
6. $\frac{6}{7}$	**9.** $\frac{2}{7}$	**12.** $\frac{4}{9}$	**15.** $\frac{5}{6}$
7. $\frac{5}{8}$	**10.** $\frac{3}{8}$	**13.** $\frac{1}{6}$	**16.** $\frac{8}{9}$

More practice
Set A, page 238

Finding Missing Numbers in Equal Fractions

Find the number that makes the fractions equal.

A.

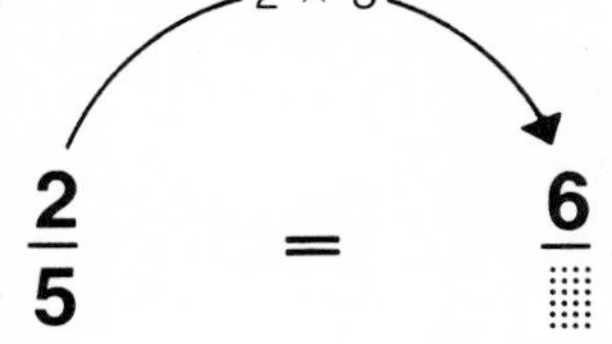

2 was multiplied by 3 to get 6.

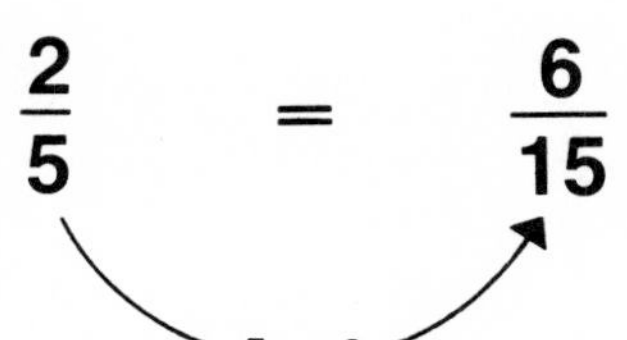

Multiply 5 by 3 to get 15.

B.

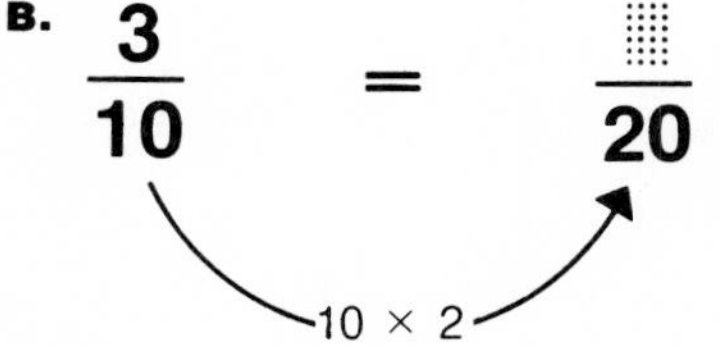

10 was multiplied by 2 to get 20.

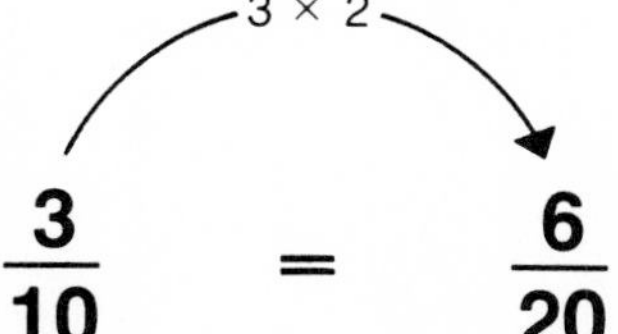

Multiply 3 by 2 to get 6.

What number makes the fractions equal?

1. $\frac{1}{3} = \frac{\square}{6}$ **4.** $\frac{2}{5} = \frac{4}{\square}$ **7.** $\frac{3}{4} = \frac{\square}{8}$ **10.** $\frac{2}{3} = \frac{6}{\square}$ **13.** $\frac{1}{6} = \frac{\square}{12}$

2. $\frac{1}{5} = \frac{\square}{15}$ **5.** $\frac{3}{4} = \frac{9}{\square}$ **8.** $\frac{5}{2} = \frac{\square}{10}$ **11.** $\frac{9}{10} = \frac{18}{\square}$ **14.** $\frac{3}{5} = \frac{12}{\square}$

3. $\frac{5}{8} = \frac{\square}{16}$ **6.** $\frac{7}{2} = \frac{14}{\square}$ **9.** $\frac{5}{8} = \frac{\square}{24}$ **12.** $\frac{5}{3} = \frac{\square}{9}$ **15.** $\frac{5}{6} = \frac{15}{\square}$

Keeping Skillful

Round to the nearest hundred.

1. 512 **3.** 258 **5.** 97

2. 386 **4.** 197 **6.** 997

Round each number to the nearest hundred. Estimate the sum.

7. $\begin{array}{r} 416 \\ +\ 389 \\ \hline \end{array}$ **9.** $\begin{array}{r} 675 \\ +\ 131 \\ \hline \end{array}$

8. $\begin{array}{r} 186 \\ +\ 221 \\ \hline \end{array}$ **10.** $\begin{array}{r} 295 \\ 88 \\ +\ 415 \\ \hline \end{array}$

Divide. Check your answer by multiplying and adding.

11. $5\overline{)87}$ **14.** $9\overline{)141}$

12. $7\overline{)613}$ **15.** $51\overline{)666}$

13. $3\overline{)835}$ **16.** $62\overline{)1555}$

Finding Equal Fractions by Dividing

A. You can divide to find a fraction equal to $\frac{9}{12}$.

$$\frac{9}{12} = \frac{3}{4}$$

9 ÷ 3

12 ÷ 3

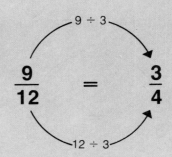

Divide both numerator and denominator by 3.

■ *You can divide both numerator and denominator of a fraction by the same number to find an equal fraction.*

What number makes the fractions equal?

B.

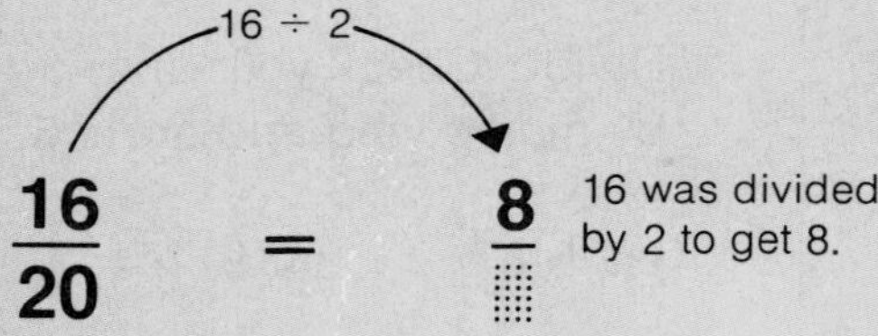

16 was divided by 2 to get 8.

$$\frac{16}{20} = \frac{8}{10}$$

20 ÷ 2

Divide 20 by 2 to get 10.

C.

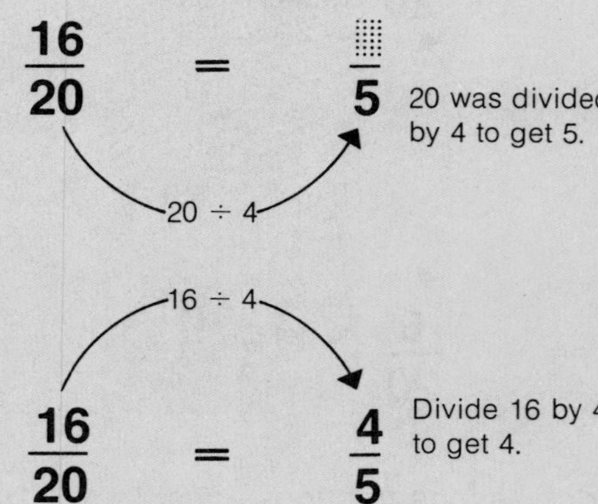

20 was divided by 4 to get 5.

Divide 16 by 4 to get 4.

Give the number that makes the fractions equal.

1. $\frac{8}{12} = \frac{\square}{6}$ **2.** $\frac{3}{9} = \frac{1}{\square}$ **3.** $\frac{6}{24} = \frac{\square}{4}$ **4.** $\frac{7}{14} = \frac{\square}{2}$ **5.** $\frac{4}{6} = \frac{\square}{3}$ **6.** $\frac{15}{20} = \frac{3}{\square}$

7. $\frac{9}{18} = \frac{\square}{6}$ **8.** $\frac{8}{16} = \frac{\square}{4}$ **9.** $\frac{14}{16} = \frac{\square}{8}$ **10.** $\frac{10}{15} = \frac{2}{\square}$ **11.** $\frac{9}{18} = \frac{1}{\square}$ **12.** $\frac{24}{30} = \frac{12}{\square}$

More practice Set B, page 238

Renaming Fractions in Lowest Terms

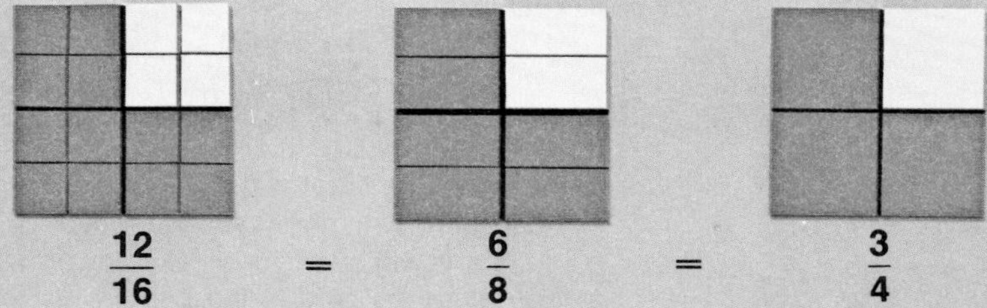

$\frac{12}{16} = \frac{6}{8} = \frac{3}{4}$

A. To ***rename*** $\frac{12}{16}$, find an equal fraction with a smaller denominator.

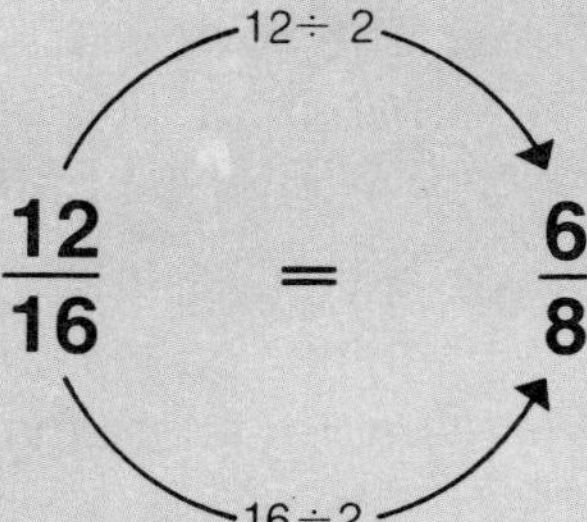

Rename $\frac{6}{8}$.

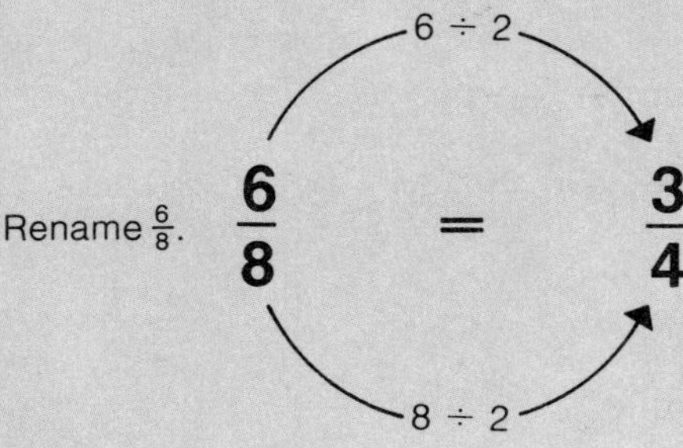

Can you rename $\frac{3}{4}$?

$\frac{3}{4}$ is in ***lowest terms.***

■ *A fraction is in lowest terms when it cannot be renamed.*

B. Rename $\frac{32}{40}$ in lowest terms.

To shorten your work, divide numerator and denominator by the biggest number you can.

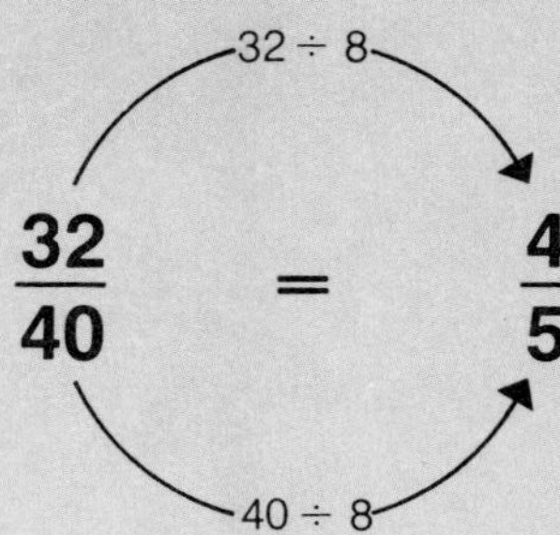

Rename these fractions in lowest terms.

1. $\frac{5}{15}$ **2.** $\frac{4}{12}$ **3.** $\frac{10}{25}$ **4.** $\frac{9}{15}$ **5.** $\frac{9}{18}$ **6.** $\frac{6}{10}$ **7.** $\frac{3}{21}$ **8.** $\frac{8}{12}$

9. $\frac{6}{9}$ **10.** $\frac{10}{16}$ **11.** $\frac{15}{50}$ **12.** $\frac{16}{24}$ **13.** $\frac{12}{32}$ **14.** $\frac{30}{36}$ **15.** $\frac{35}{40}$ **16.** $\frac{12}{20}$

More practice
Set C, page 238

Using Equal Fractions

For each exercise, tell whether the amounts are equal.

1. $\frac{1}{2}$ pound of chocolate

$\frac{8}{16}$ pound of chocolate

2. $\frac{6}{8}$ yard of material

$\frac{3}{4}$ yard of material

3. $\frac{1}{6}$ dozen eggs

$\frac{3}{12}$ dozen eggs

4. $\frac{2}{8}$ mile

$\frac{1}{4}$ mile

5. $\frac{9}{10}$ ounce of perfume

$\frac{4}{5}$ ounce of perfume

6. $\frac{15}{60}$ minute

$\frac{1}{4}$ minute

7. $\frac{6}{10}$ kilometer

$\frac{3}{5}$ kilometer

8. $\frac{5}{8}$ pound of sugar

$\frac{1}{2}$ pound of sugar

EXPERIMENT

1. Put cards like this into a bag.

2. Shake the bag
3. Draw one letter without looking.
4. Record whether or not the letter is a vowel.
5. Return the card to the bag.
6. Make 24 draws.

9. The vowels are A, E, I, O, and U. What fraction of the letters of TRIANGLE are vowels?

10. If you did the experiment, do you think you would draw more vowels or more letters that are not vowels?

11. Alec did the experiment. His results are shown.

	Tally	Fraction
Vowels	𝍸 ||||	$\frac{▒}{24}$
Not vowels	𝍸 𝍸 𝍸	$\frac{▒}{24}$

Number of vowels (numerator); Number of draws (denominator)

What fraction of the letters he drew were vowels? Is this fraction close to $\frac{3}{8}$?

12. Do the experiment yourself. What fraction of the letters you drew were vowels? Is your fraction close to $\frac{3}{8}$?

Fraction Rummy

A game for two or three players

Object: To match cards that show equal fractions

Rules:

1. Deal five cards to each player. Place the remaining cards face down in a center pile. Turn over the top card to start a discard row.
2. The player to the left of the dealer plays first. For a turn, each player
   a. draws the top card of the center pile or a card from the discard row.
   b. looks for three or more cards showing equal fractions. These matching cards are placed face up on the table in front of the player.
   c. discards a card from the hand. The player puts this card face up in the discard row so that all cards in the row are visible. Then the next player takes a turn.
3. A player may take any card from the discard row but must take all cards discarded before the desired card.
4. Suppose player A has a card that matches cards played by an opponent. This card can be placed face up in front of player A during A's turn.
5. Play continues until all the cards have been used from either a player's hand or the center pile.

Scoring:

Each player receives one point for each card played.

Each player subtracts one point for each card remaining in the hand.

Any player who has played all the cards receives two additional points.

The player with the most points is the winner.

Making the deck:

You need 36 cards.
Make one card for each of the following fractions.

$\frac{10}{20}$	$\frac{10}{40}$	$\frac{1}{12}$	$\frac{1}{8}$	$\frac{1}{6}$	$\frac{2}{3}$
$\frac{2}{16}$	$\frac{1}{10}$	$\frac{2}{24}$	$\frac{1}{3}$	$\frac{1}{4}$	$\frac{1}{2}$
$\frac{2}{12}$	$\frac{2}{10}$	$\frac{2}{20}$	$\frac{1}{5}$	$\frac{3}{9}$	$\frac{4}{6}$
$\frac{3}{36}$	$\frac{3}{24}$	$\frac{3}{18}$	$\frac{2}{8}$	$\frac{4}{8}$	$\frac{2}{6}$
$\frac{4}{12}$	$\frac{3}{15}$	$\frac{4}{20}$	$\frac{6}{9}$	$\frac{3}{30}$	$\frac{4}{16}$
$\frac{5}{10}$	$\frac{4}{48}$	$\frac{4}{32}$	$\frac{4}{24}$	$\frac{8}{12}$	$\frac{5}{50}$

Comparing Fractions with Common Denominators

Both $\frac{3}{8}$ and $\frac{5}{8}$ have the same denominator.
We say they have a ***common denominator***.

A. Compare $\frac{3}{8}$ and $\frac{5}{8}$.

There are fewer red parts than blue parts.

3 eighths is less than 5 eighths.

$$\mathbf{\frac{3}{8} < \frac{5}{8}}$$

B. Compare $\frac{7}{10}$ and $\frac{5}{10}$.

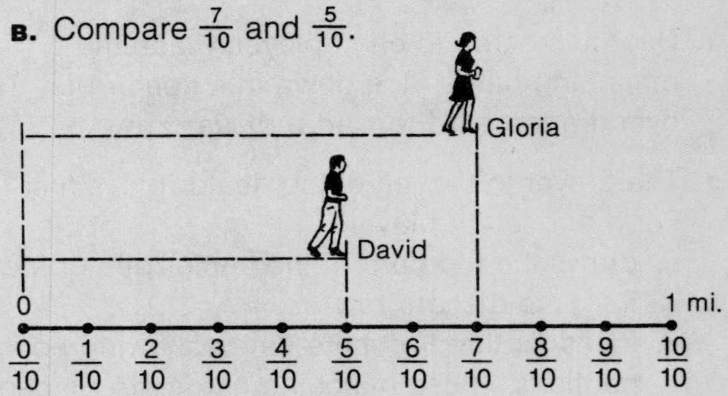

Gloria walked farther than David.

7 tenths is greater than 5 tenths.

$$\mathbf{\frac{7}{10} > \frac{5}{10}}$$

■ *You can compare fractions with a common denominator by comparing the numerators.*

Compare these fractions. Replace ● with > or <.

1. $\frac{1}{3}$ ● $\frac{2}{3}$

2. $\frac{4}{5}$ ● $\frac{5}{5}$

3. $\frac{7}{10}$ ● $\frac{3}{10}$

4. $\frac{5}{9}$ ● $\frac{2}{9}$

5. $\frac{9}{8}$ ● $\frac{13}{8}$

6. $\frac{6}{12}$ ● $\frac{11}{12}$

7. $\frac{17}{18}$ ● $\frac{7}{18}$

8. $\frac{15}{15}$ ● $\frac{7}{15}$

9. $\frac{5}{6}$ ● $\frac{1}{6}$

10. $\frac{20}{20}$ ● $\frac{19}{20}$

11. $\frac{0}{25}$ ● $\frac{15}{25}$

12. $\frac{99}{100}$ ● $\frac{98}{100}$

13. $\frac{5}{16}$ ● $\frac{0}{16}$

14. $\frac{66}{100}$ ● $\frac{68}{100}$

15. $\frac{11}{20}$ ● $\frac{14}{20}$

16. $\frac{49}{50}$ ● $\frac{50}{50}$

Comparing Fractions with Different Denominators

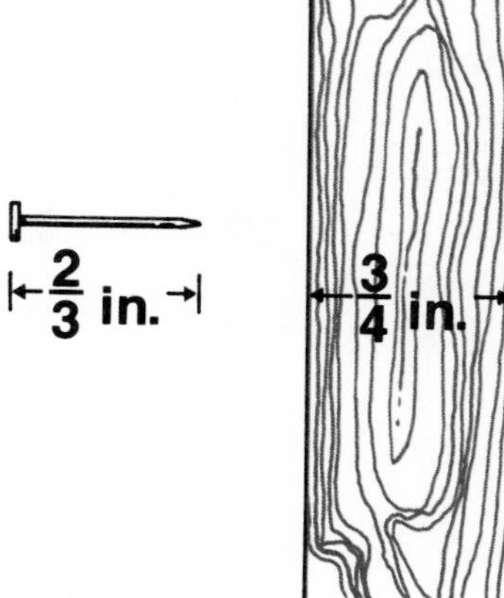

Is the nail long enough to go through the board?

Compare $\frac{2}{3}$ and $\frac{3}{4}$.

First find fractions that are equal to $\frac{2}{3}$ and to $\frac{3}{4}$ and that have a common denominator.

$$\frac{2}{3} = \frac{4}{6} = \frac{6}{9} = \frac{8}{12}$$

$$\frac{3}{4} = \frac{6}{8} = \frac{9}{12}$$

Then compare the numerators of the new fractions.

$$\frac{8}{12} < \frac{9}{12}$$

$$\frac{2}{3} < \frac{3}{4}$$

The nail is not long enough to go through the board.

Compare these fractions. Replace ● with >, <, or =.

Here's how

$\frac{4}{5}$ ● $\frac{1}{3}$

$$\frac{4}{5} = \frac{8}{10} = \frac{12}{15}$$

$$\frac{1}{3} = \frac{2}{6} = \frac{3}{9} = \frac{4}{12} = \frac{5}{15}$$

$$\frac{12}{15} > \frac{5}{15} \text{ so } \frac{4}{5} > \frac{1}{3}$$

1. $\frac{1}{2}$ ● $\frac{1}{3}$

2. $\frac{2}{3}$ ● $\frac{2}{5}$

3. $\frac{2}{6}$ ● $\frac{1}{3}$

4. $\frac{3}{5}$ ● $\frac{1}{2}$

5. $\frac{3}{4}$ ● $\frac{4}{5}$

6. $\frac{7}{10}$ ● $\frac{3}{5}$

7. $\frac{5}{6}$ ● $\frac{3}{4}$

8. $\frac{1}{3}$ ● $\frac{3}{8}$

9. $\frac{7}{9}$ ● $\frac{5}{6}$

10. $\frac{2}{10}$ ● $\frac{3}{15}$

11. $\frac{5}{8}$ ● $\frac{10}{16}$

12. $\frac{2}{3}$ ● $\frac{5}{8}$

Comparing Fractions with Different Denominators

Will the pencil fit in the sharpener?

Compare $\frac{1}{4}$ and $\frac{5}{16}$.

$$\frac{1}{4} = \frac{2}{8} = \frac{3}{12} = \frac{4}{16}$$

$$\frac{5}{16}$$

$$\frac{5}{16} > \frac{4}{16}$$

$$\frac{5}{16} > \frac{1}{4}$$

The pencil will fit in the sharpener.

Is 16 a multiple of 4?
Is 16 a common denominator for $\frac{1}{4}$ and $\frac{5}{16}$?

If one denominator is a multiple of the other, the larger denominator can be used as a common denominator.

For each pair of fractions, give a common denominator. First see if one denominator is a multiple of the other.

1. $\frac{1}{10}, \frac{1}{5}$
2. $\frac{4}{7}, \frac{16}{28}$
3. $\frac{7}{12}, \frac{3}{8}$
4. $\frac{7}{15}, \frac{4}{5}$
5. $\frac{5}{8}, \frac{11}{16}$
6. $\frac{2}{3}, \frac{5}{12}$
7. $\frac{2}{5}, \frac{8}{20}$
8. $\frac{3}{10}, \frac{1}{3}$
9. $\frac{5}{21}, \frac{2}{7}$
10. $\frac{2}{5}, \frac{4}{15}$

Replace ● with >, <, or =.

11. $\frac{1}{2}$ ● $\frac{3}{4}$
12. $\frac{2}{3}$ ● $\frac{5}{6}$
13. $\frac{5}{8}$ ● $\frac{4}{8}$
14. $\frac{2}{3}$ ● $\frac{7}{9}$
15. $\frac{7}{10}$ ● $\frac{9}{10}$
16. $\frac{3}{4}$ ● $\frac{7}{12}$
17. $\frac{7}{10}$ ● $\frac{4}{5}$
18. $\frac{2}{3}$ ● $\frac{8}{12}$
19. $\frac{3}{4}$ ● $\frac{7}{16}$
20. $\frac{1}{4}$ ● $\frac{3}{8}$
21. $\frac{3}{7}$ ● $\frac{9}{21}$
22. $\frac{4}{9}$ ● $\frac{2}{9}$

More practice
Set D, page 238

Keeping Skillful

Replace ● with >, <, or =.

1. .69 ● .71
2. .11 ● .09
3. .4 ● .40
4. .58 ● .40
5. .41 ● .4
6. .7 ● .70
7. .77 ● .770
8. .7 ● .75
9. .70 ● .07
10. .075 ● .70

Add.

11. $\begin{array}{r} 2.3 \\ +\ 6.1 \\ \hline \end{array}$

12. $\begin{array}{r} 16.67 \\ +\ 10.19 \\ \hline \end{array}$

13. $\begin{array}{r} 2.54 \\ +\ 5.08 \\ \hline \end{array}$

14. $\begin{array}{r} 6.5 \\ 2.7 \\ +\ 2.3 \\ \hline \end{array}$

15. $\begin{array}{r} 1.159 \\ +\ 1.167 \\ \hline \end{array}$

16. $\begin{array}{r} .875 \\ +\ .125 \\ \hline \end{array}$

17. $\begin{array}{r} 3.333 \\ +\ 6.28 \\ \hline \end{array}$

18. $\begin{array}{r} 8.79 \\ 7.9 \\ +\ 12.87 \\ \hline \end{array}$

Subtract.

19. $\begin{array}{r} 8.4 \\ -\ 6.1 \\ \hline \end{array}$

20. $\begin{array}{r} 6.86 \\ -\ 1.67 \\ \hline \end{array}$

21. $\begin{array}{r} 7.12 \\ -\ 5.08 \\ \hline \end{array}$

22. $\begin{array}{r} 1.0 \\ -\ .5 \\ \hline \end{array}$

23. $\begin{array}{r} 2.326 \\ -\ .159 \\ \hline \end{array}$

24. $\begin{array}{r} 9.61 \\ -\ 6.28 \\ \hline \end{array}$

25. $\begin{array}{r} 1.000 \\ -\ .333 \\ \hline \end{array}$

26. $\begin{array}{r} 1.000 \\ -\ .875 \\ \hline \end{array}$

Time Out!

Arrange 17 toothpicks as shown.

Move 3 toothpicks to make 5 squares that are the same size.

Again make the pattern shown above.

Remove 5 toothpicks so that exactly 3 squares remain.

Ordering Fractions

Three students took a final exam.
José finished the test in $\frac{3}{4}$ hour, Marcia in $\frac{2}{3}$ hour, and Linda in $\frac{5}{6}$ hour.
In what order did they finish the test?

To find out, put the fractions $\frac{3}{4}$, $\frac{2}{3}$, and $\frac{5}{6}$ in order.

First find fractions that are equal to $\frac{3}{4}$, $\frac{2}{3}$, and $\frac{5}{6}$ and that have a common denominator.

$$\frac{3}{4} = \frac{6}{8} = \frac{9}{12}$$

$$\frac{2}{3} = \frac{4}{6} = \frac{6}{9} = \frac{8}{12}$$

$$\frac{5}{6} = \frac{10}{12}$$

Marcia finished first. Who finished second? Third?

In each exercise, give the fractions in order from least to greatest.

1. $\frac{1}{2}, \frac{1}{6}, \frac{1}{3}$

2. $\frac{1}{2}, \frac{3}{4}, \frac{1}{4}$

3. $\frac{1}{4}, \frac{2}{3}, \frac{5}{6}$

4. $\frac{1}{3}, \frac{2}{3}, \frac{5}{9}$

5. $\frac{5}{6}, \frac{7}{9}, \frac{11}{18}$

6. $\frac{1}{3}, \frac{2}{3}, \frac{1}{4}$

7. $\frac{1}{2}, \frac{2}{3}, \frac{1}{6}$

8. $\frac{1}{2}, \frac{3}{4}, \frac{5}{8}$

9. $\frac{1}{3}, \frac{1}{6}, \frac{5}{8}$

10. $\frac{5}{12}, \frac{1}{4}, \frac{1}{3}$

11. $\frac{1}{2}, \frac{1}{10}, \frac{1}{5}$

12. $\frac{5}{12}, \frac{1}{2}, \frac{1}{6}$

13. $\frac{1}{3}, \frac{1}{4}, \frac{1}{6}$

★ **14.** $\frac{7}{10}, \frac{2}{5}, \frac{3}{4}, \frac{1}{2}$

★ **15.** $\frac{2}{3}, \frac{7}{8}, \frac{3}{4}, \frac{5}{12}$

Here are the times of the winners in six different races. For each race, list the students in the order in which they finished.

16. First race

Lucy $\frac{3}{5}$ minute

Ida $\frac{1}{2}$ minute

Barb $\frac{2}{5}$ minute

17. Second race

Mark $\frac{1}{2}$ minute

Chang $\frac{2}{5}$ minute

Warren $\frac{7}{10}$ minute

18. Third race

Gina $\frac{5}{6}$ minute

Wanda $\frac{2}{3}$ minute

Chris $\frac{1}{2}$ minute

19. Fourth race

Sam $\frac{2}{3}$ minute

Larry $\frac{3}{4}$ minute

Fred $\frac{1}{2}$ minute

20. Fifth race

Millie $\frac{3}{4}$ minute

Jane $\frac{2}{3}$ minute

Amy $\frac{5}{6}$ minute

★ **21.** Sixth race

Carlos $\frac{5}{6}$ minute

Sol $\frac{3}{5}$ minute

Nick $\frac{2}{3}$ minute

Time Out!

Copy this drawing.

Find a path that starts in one room, passes through each door once and only once, and ends in another room.

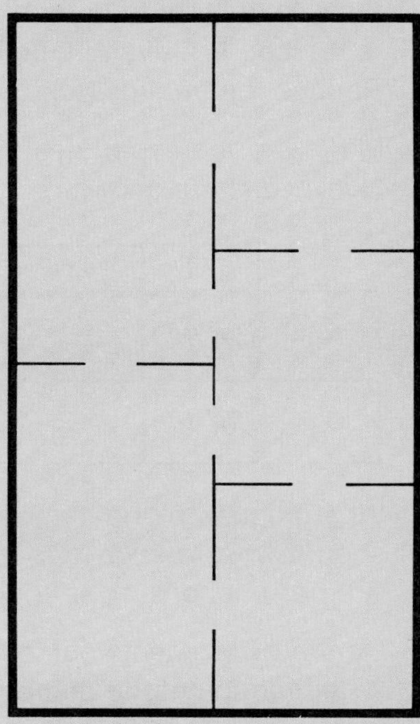

Using Fractions in Experiments

EXPERIMENT
1. Put cards like this into a bag.

2. Shake the bag.
3. Draw one card without looking.
4. Record whether the number is even or odd.
5. Return the card to the bag.
6. Make 20 draws.

1. If you do the experiment, do you think you will draw more even numbers, more odd numbers, or about the same number of each?

2. What fraction of the numbers in the bag are even? Odd? Reduce the fractions to lowest terms.

3. María did the experiment. Her results are shown.

	Tally	Fraction
Even	~~||||~~ ~~||||~~ |	$\frac{\square}{20}$
Odd	~~||||~~ ||||	$\frac{\square}{20}$

What fraction of the numbers she drew were even? Odd? Are her fractions close to $\frac{1}{2}$?

4. Do the experiment yourself. What fraction of the numbers you drew were even? Odd? Are your fractions close to $\frac{1}{2}$?

Explore

EXPERIMENT
1. Put five green marbles and three red marbles into a bag.
2. Shake the bag.
3. Draw one marble without looking.
4. Record whether the marble is green or red.
5. Return the marble to the bag.
6. Make 24 draws.

1. If you do the experiment, do you think you will draw more green marbles, more red marbles, or about the same number of each?

2. Do the experiment. Record your results in a table.

	Tally	Fraction
Green		
Red		

3. Is your fraction for green marbles close to $\frac{5}{8}$?

4. Is your fraction for red marbles close to $\frac{3}{8}$?

5. Compare your results with those of your classmates.

Check Yourself
Meaning of Fractions, Pages 178 – 202

Meaning of fractions, pages 178 – 185

1. What fraction of the pie has been eaten?

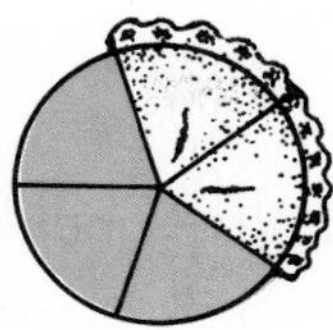

2. What fraction of the dozen eggs are dyed blue?

3. Give the length to the nearest $\frac{1}{8}$ inch.

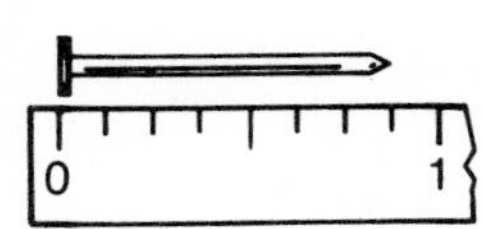

4. What fraction of the cup is filled?

Equal fractions, pages 186 – 195

Give the equal fractions.

5.

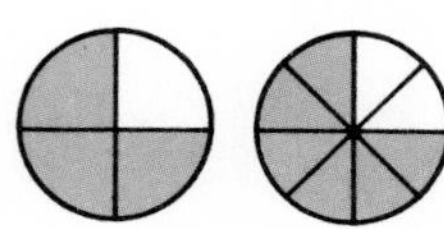

$$\frac{3}{4} = \frac{\square}{8}$$

6.

0 1 in.

0 1 in.

$$\frac{1}{2} = \frac{\square}{4}$$

7. $\frac{3}{5} = \frac{\square}{15}$

8. $\frac{2}{3} = \frac{16}{\square}$

9. $\frac{8}{12} = \frac{\square}{3}$

Rename in lowest terms.

10. $\frac{12}{20}$

11. $\frac{18}{24}$

Comparing fractions, pages 196 – 198, 200 – 201

For each pair of fractions, give a common denominator.

12. $\frac{5}{6}, \frac{3}{4}$

13. $\frac{2}{5}, \frac{1}{3}$

Replace $\square$ with $>$ or $<$.

14. $\frac{3}{4} \quad \square \quad \frac{2}{3}$

15. $\frac{7}{10} \quad \square \quad \frac{3}{5}$

16. Give the fractions in order from least to greatest.

$\frac{5}{6}, \frac{2}{3}, \frac{7}{12}$

Adding Fractions: Same Denominator

A. Ruth walked $\frac{1}{8}$ mile to Ted's house.
Then she rode $\frac{5}{8}$ mile to school.
How far did she travel?

Find $\frac{1}{8} + \frac{5}{8}$.

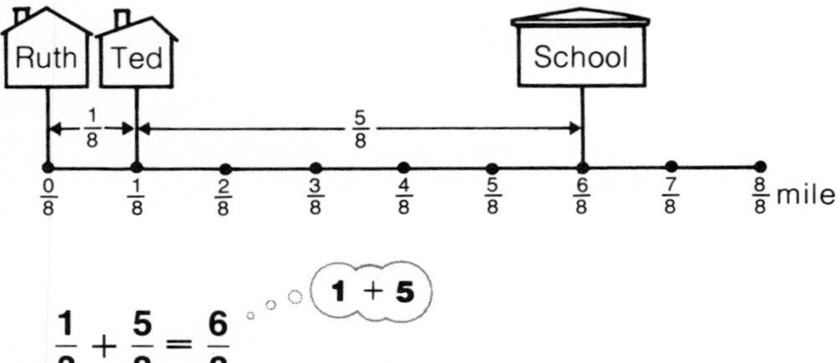

$$\frac{1}{8} + \frac{5}{8} = \frac{6}{8}$$

1 + 5

Ruth traveled $\frac{6}{8}$ mile.

B. It rained $\frac{3}{10}$ inch on Monday.
It rained $\frac{6}{10}$ inch on Tuesday.
How much rain fell on the two days?

Find $\frac{3}{10} + \frac{6}{10}$.

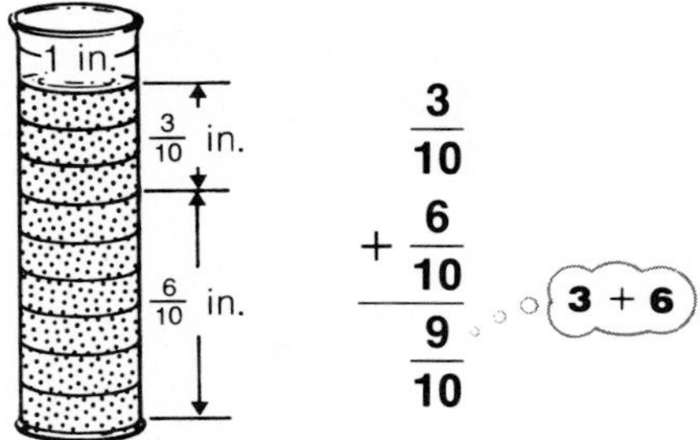

$\frac{9}{10}$ inch of rain fell on the two days.

Add.

1. $\frac{4}{6}$ $\frac{1}{6}$

$\frac{0}{6}$ $\frac{1}{6}$ $\frac{2}{6}$ $\frac{3}{6}$ $\frac{4}{6}$ $\frac{5}{6}$ $\frac{6}{6}$

$\frac{4}{6} + \frac{1}{6} = \frac{\square}{6}$

2. $\frac{3}{5} + \frac{1}{5} = \frac{\square}{5}$

3. $\frac{3}{8} + \frac{4}{8} = \frac{\square}{8}$

4. $\frac{3}{16} + \frac{5}{16} = \frac{\square}{16}$

5. $\frac{5}{12} + \frac{4}{12}$

6. $\frac{1}{6} + \frac{2}{6}$

7. $\frac{2}{7} + \frac{4}{7}$

8. $\frac{3}{5} + \frac{2}{5}$

9. $\frac{2}{3} + \frac{2}{3}$

10. $\frac{4}{10} + \frac{7}{10}$

More practice
Set E, page 238

Subtracting Fractions: Same Denominator

A. Nancy had $\frac{7}{8}$ yard of wool.
She used $\frac{5}{8}$ yard to make a vest.
What fraction of a yard was left?
Find $\frac{7}{8} - \frac{5}{8}$.

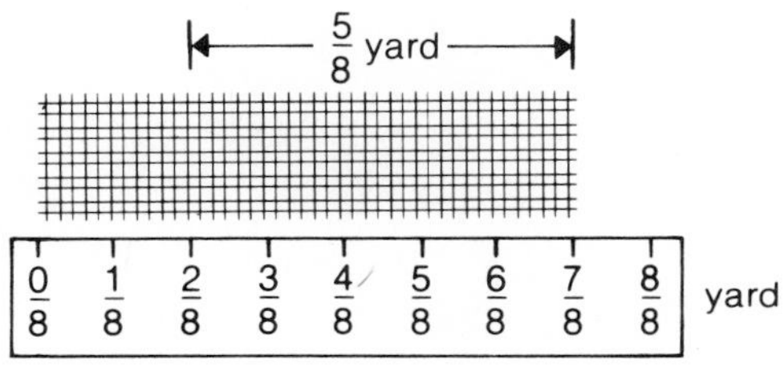

$$\frac{7}{8} - \frac{5}{8} = \frac{2}{8}$$ (7 − 5)

Nancy had $\frac{2}{8}$ yard left.

B. Jennifer had $\frac{3}{4}$ of a pie.
She ate $\frac{1}{4}$ of the whole pie for lunch.
What fraction of the pie was left?
Find $\frac{3}{4} - \frac{1}{4}$.

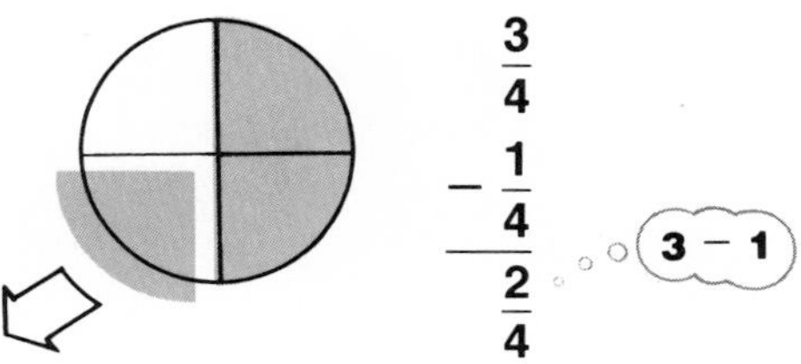

Jennifer had $\frac{2}{4}$ of the whole pie left.

Subtract.

1. 8/10, 5/10

0/10 1/10 2/10 3/10 4/10 5/10 6/10 7/10 8/10 9/10 10/10

$\frac{8}{10} - \frac{5}{10} = \frac{\square}{10}$

2. $\frac{7}{8} - \frac{2}{8} = \frac{\square}{8}$

3. $\frac{5}{6} - \frac{1}{6} = \frac{\square}{6}$

4. $\frac{6}{7} - \frac{2}{7} = \frac{\square}{7}$

5. $\frac{5}{3} - \frac{4}{3} = \frac{\square}{3}$

6. $\frac{11}{16} - \frac{7}{16} = \frac{\square}{16}$

7. $\frac{5}{5} - \frac{3}{5}$

8. $\frac{7}{8} - \frac{4}{8}$

9. $\frac{6}{9} - \frac{1}{9}$

10. $\frac{8}{5} - \frac{4}{5}$

11. $\frac{7}{10} - \frac{4}{10}$

12. $\frac{11}{12} - \frac{6}{12}$

13. $\frac{13}{8} - \frac{7}{8}$

14. $\frac{17}{12} - \frac{14}{12}$

More practice
Set I, page 239

Adding Fractions: Different Denominators

A. Art worked on his model airplane for $\frac{2}{3}$ hour.
He worked on his train set for $\frac{1}{4}$ hour.
What fraction of an hour did he spend on these hobbies?

Find $\frac{2}{3} + \frac{1}{4}$.

$$\begin{array}{r} \frac{2}{3} \\ + \frac{1}{4} \\ \hline \end{array}$$

Find a common denominator for $\frac{2}{3}$ and $\frac{1}{4}$.

Use multiples of the two denominators.

$\frac{2}{3} \rightarrow 3 \quad 6 \quad 9 \quad 12$

$\frac{1}{4} \rightarrow 4 \quad 8 \quad 12$

A common multiple of the denominators can be used as a common denominator.

$$\begin{array}{r} \frac{2}{3} = \frac{8}{12} \\ + \frac{1}{4} = \frac{3}{12} \\ \hline \frac{11}{12} \end{array}$$

Find equal fractions with a common denominator.

Add.

Art spent $\frac{11}{12}$ hour on these hobbies.

Add.

Here's how

$\frac{1}{3} \quad 3 \quad 6 \quad 9 \quad 12 \quad 15$

$+\frac{2}{5} \quad 5 \quad 10 \quad 15$

$$\begin{array}{r} \frac{1}{3} = \frac{5}{15} \\ + \frac{2}{5} = \frac{6}{15} \\ \hline \frac{11}{15} \end{array}$$

1. $\frac{1}{4} + \frac{1}{3}$

2. $\frac{1}{2} + \frac{2}{5}$

3. $\frac{1}{3} + \frac{1}{2}$

4. $\frac{1}{3} + \frac{3}{5}$

5. $\frac{2}{4} + \frac{1}{3}$

6. $\frac{1}{4} + \frac{2}{5}$

7. $\frac{2}{3} + \frac{1}{2}$

8. $\frac{1}{6} + \frac{1}{4}$

9. $\frac{5}{8} + \frac{1}{6}$

10. $\frac{1}{5} + \frac{2}{3}$

11. $\frac{3}{4} + \frac{1}{5}$

12. $\frac{3}{4} + \frac{1}{6}$

B. If one denominator is a multiple of the other, it can be used as a common denominator.

$$\begin{array}{r} \frac{2}{3} \\ + \frac{1}{12} \\ \hline \end{array}$$

12 is a common multiple of 3 and 12.
12 is a common denominator.

$$\begin{array}{rcl} \frac{2}{3} & = & \frac{8}{12} \\ + \frac{1}{12} & = & \frac{1}{12} \\ \hline & & \frac{9}{12} \end{array}$$

C. The product of the two denominators can always be used as a common denominator.

$$\begin{array}{r} \frac{3}{4} \\ + \frac{1}{6} \\ \hline \end{array}$$

$4 \times 6 = 24$
24 is a common multiple of 4 and 6.
24 is a common denominator.

$$\begin{array}{rcl} \frac{3}{4} & = & \frac{18}{24} \\ + \frac{1}{6} & = & \frac{4}{24} \\ \hline & & \frac{22}{24} \end{array}$$

Add.

13. $\frac{3}{10} + \frac{1}{3}$

14. $\frac{1}{6} + \frac{1}{2}$

15. $\frac{1}{5} + \frac{5}{6}$

16. $\frac{7}{10} + \frac{1}{4}$

17. $\frac{5}{8} + \frac{1}{4}$

18. $\frac{3}{5} + \frac{4}{15}$

19. $\frac{3}{4} + \frac{1}{12}$

20. $\frac{3}{4} + \frac{1}{2}$

21. $\frac{1}{3} + \frac{4}{9}$

22. $\frac{2}{3} + \frac{1}{12}$

23. $\frac{1}{3} + \frac{5}{7}$

24. $\frac{1}{5} + \frac{5}{8}$

25. $\frac{1}{3} + \frac{3}{8}$

26. $\frac{4}{5} + \frac{1}{4}$

27. $\frac{11}{12} + \frac{2}{3}$

28. $\frac{3}{5} + \frac{3}{10}$

More practice
Set F, page 238
Set G, page 239

Adding Fractions: Puzzles

Add across. Add down.

1.

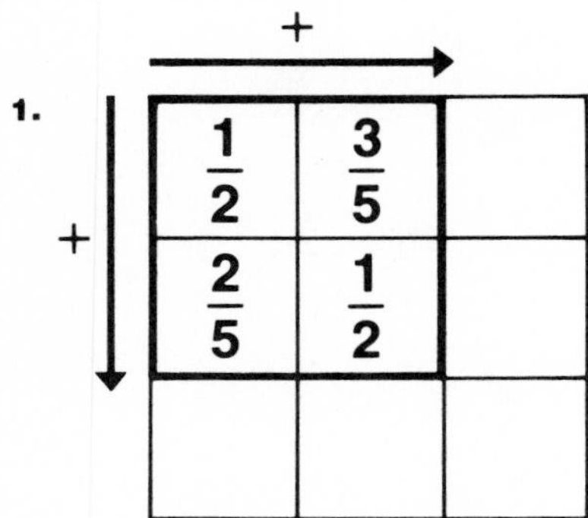

$\frac{1}{2}$	$\frac{3}{5}$	
$\frac{2}{5}$	$\frac{1}{2}$	

2.

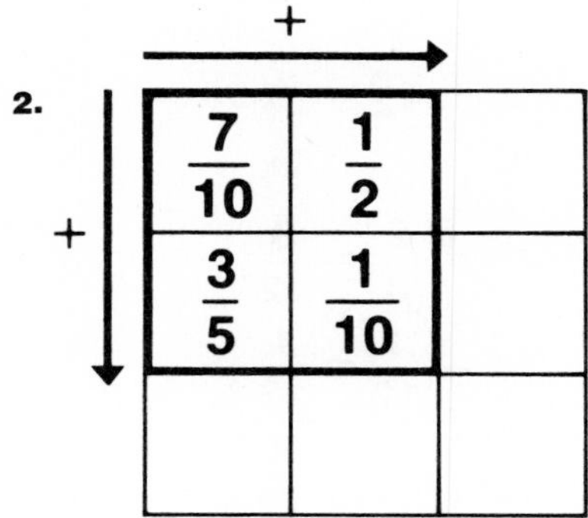

$\frac{7}{10}$	$\frac{1}{2}$	
$\frac{3}{5}$	$\frac{1}{10}$	

3.

$\frac{1}{3}$	$\frac{5}{6}$	
$\frac{1}{2}$	$\frac{1}{6}$	

4.

$\frac{1}{8}$	$\frac{3}{4}$	
$\frac{1}{2}$	$\frac{5}{8}$	

5.

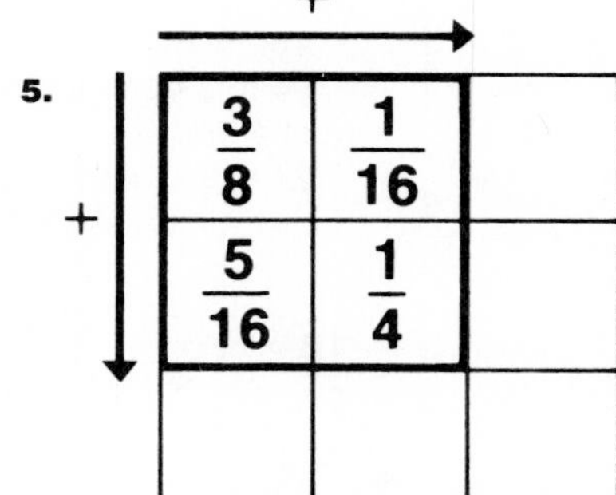

$\frac{3}{8}$	$\frac{1}{16}$	
$\frac{5}{16}$	$\frac{1}{4}$	

6.

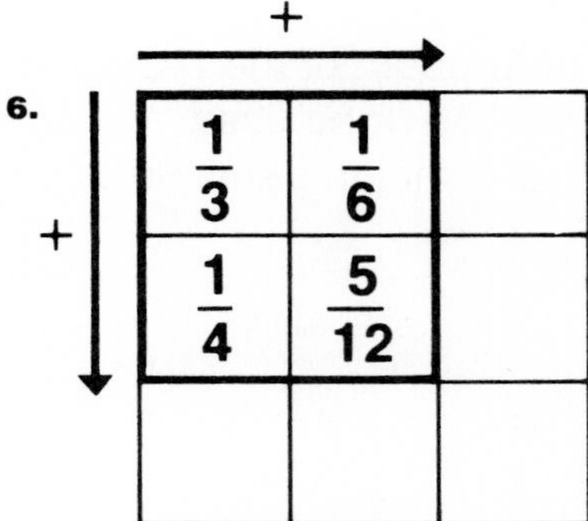

$\frac{1}{3}$	$\frac{1}{6}$	
$\frac{1}{4}$	$\frac{5}{12}$	

In this dart game, the score is the sum of the rings hit in two throws.

7. Find each score.

8. Who had the highest score?

9. Who had the lowest score?

★ **10.** What is the highest possible score?

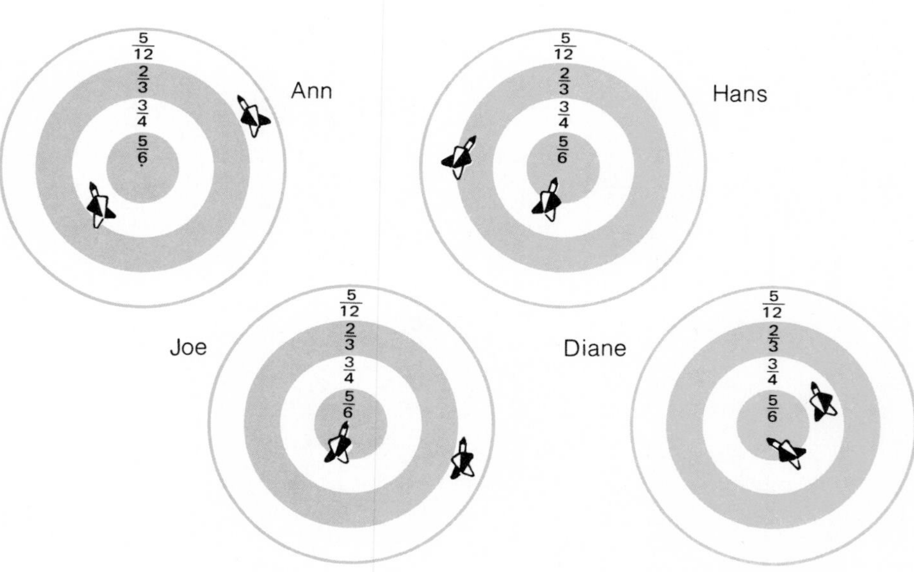

Adding Three Fractions

Find the sum. $\frac{3}{10} + \frac{1}{4} + \frac{2}{5}$

Find a common denominator.

Find equal fractions with a common denominator. Then add.

$$\begin{array}{rcl} \frac{3}{10} & = & \frac{6}{20} \\ \frac{1}{4} & = & \frac{5}{20} \\ + \frac{2}{5} & = & \frac{8}{20} \\ \hline & & \frac{19}{20} \end{array}$$

Add.

1. $\frac{1}{4} + \frac{5}{4} + \frac{3}{4}$
2. $\frac{1}{3} + \frac{5}{6} + \frac{2}{3}$
3. $\frac{3}{5} + \frac{1}{5} + \frac{7}{10}$
4. $\frac{1}{2} + \frac{3}{5} + \frac{1}{10}$
5. $\frac{1}{2} + \frac{1}{4} + \frac{1}{8}$
6. $\frac{1}{2} + \frac{1}{3} + \frac{5}{6}$
7. $\frac{5}{8} + \frac{1}{4} + \frac{3}{4}$

Find the perimeters.

8.

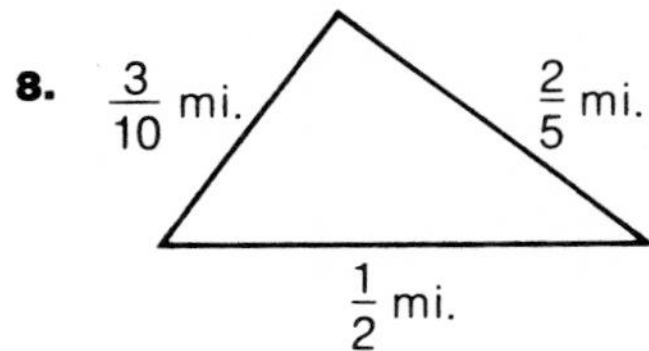

9.

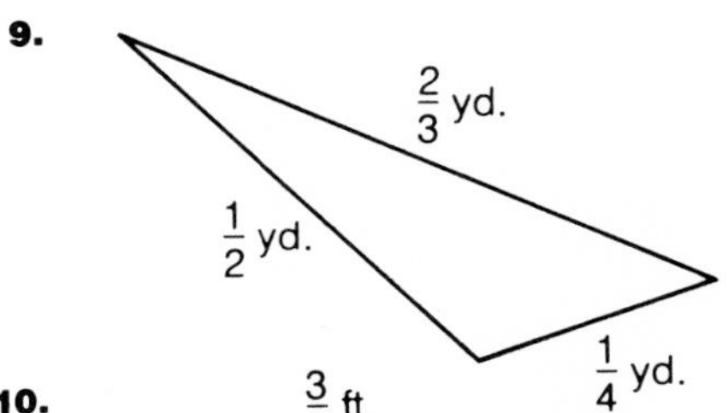

10.

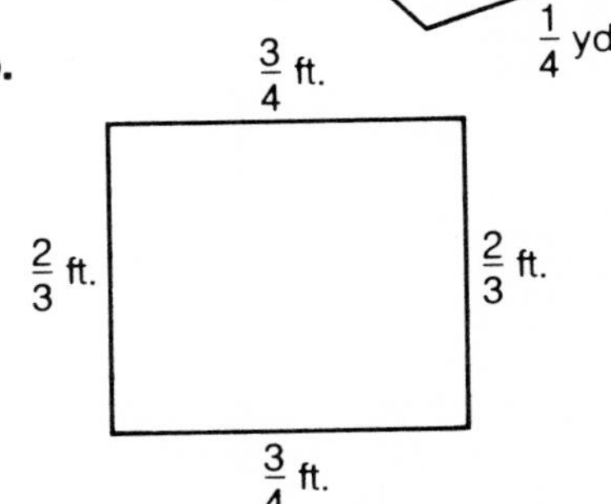

More practice
Set H, page 239

Keeping Skillful

Give the least common multiple for each pair of numbers.

1. 2 and 4
2. 3 and 6
3. 4 and 3
4. 8 and 4
5. 4 and 6
6. 8 and 3
7. 3 and 7
8. 9 and 5
9. 3 and 9
10. 2 and 3
11. 12 and 8
12. 4 and 10
13. 10 and 5
14. 4 and 5
15. 6 and 8
16. 6 and 5
17. 10 and 6
18. 3 and 5
19. 5 and 7
20. 4 and 12
21. 7 and 4
22. 9 and 6

Subtracting Fractions: Different Denominators

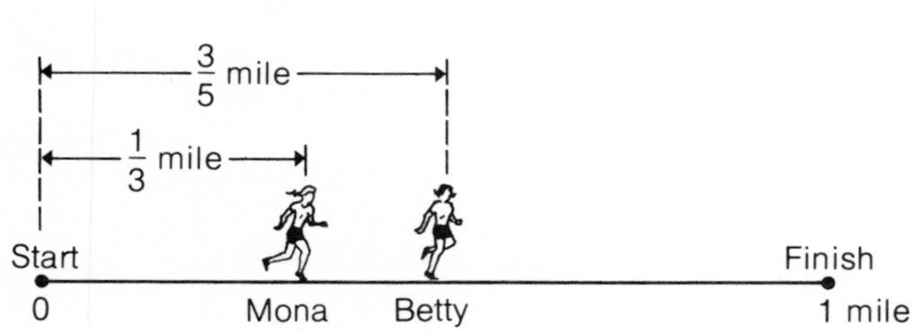

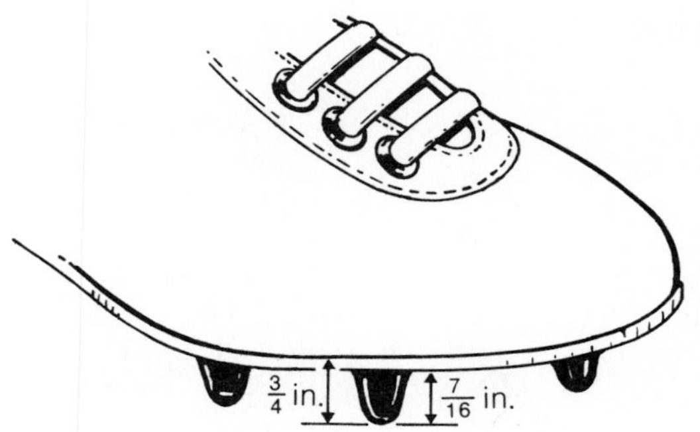

A. Betty is how far ahead of Mona?

Find $\frac{3}{5} - \frac{1}{3}$.

$$\frac{3}{5} - \frac{1}{3}$$

$$\frac{9}{15} - \frac{5}{15}$$ Find equal fractions with a common denominator.

$$\frac{4}{15}$$ Subtract.

Betty is $\frac{4}{15}$ mile ahead of Mona.

B. How thick is the sole?

Find $\frac{3}{4} - \frac{7}{16}$.

$$\begin{array}{r} \frac{3}{4} = \frac{12}{16} \\ -\frac{7}{16} = \frac{7}{16} \\ \hline \frac{5}{16} \end{array}$$

The sole is $\frac{5}{16}$ inch thick.

Subtract.

1. $\frac{11}{12} - \frac{3}{4}$

2. $\frac{5}{8} - \frac{1}{2}$

3. $\frac{2}{3} - \frac{1}{6}$

4. $\frac{4}{5} - \frac{1}{2}$

5. $\frac{2}{3} - \frac{7}{12}$

6. $\frac{1}{2} - \frac{1}{3}$

7. $\frac{3}{4} - \frac{1}{6}$

8. $\frac{5}{6} - \frac{1}{2}$

9. $\frac{5}{6} - \frac{2}{3}$

10. $\frac{5}{9} - \frac{1}{3}$

11. $\begin{array}{r} \frac{5}{8} \\ -\frac{1}{6} \\ \hline \end{array}$

12. $\begin{array}{r} \frac{2}{3} \\ -\frac{3}{8} \\ \hline \end{array}$

13. $\begin{array}{r} \frac{4}{5} \\ -\frac{1}{3} \\ \hline \end{array}$

14. $\begin{array}{r} \frac{7}{10} \\ -\frac{2}{5} \\ \hline \end{array}$

15. $\begin{array}{r} \frac{7}{8} \\ -\frac{1}{3} \\ \hline \end{array}$

16. $\begin{array}{r} \frac{3}{5} \\ -\frac{1}{6} \\ \hline \end{array}$

More practice
Set J, page 239
Set K, page 239

$\frac{7}{8}$ lb. $\frac{9}{16}$ lb.

17. How much more does the football weigh?

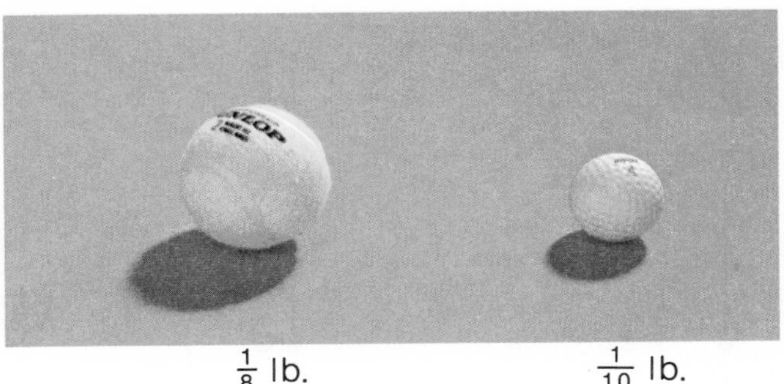

$\frac{1}{8}$ lb. $\frac{1}{10}$ lb.

19. How much more does the tennis ball weigh?

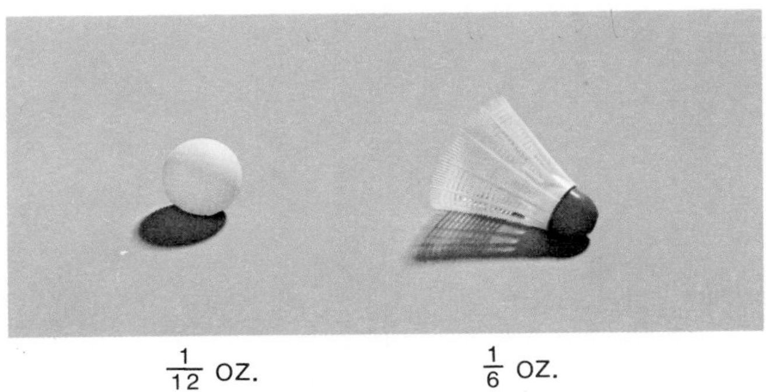

$\frac{1}{12}$ oz. $\frac{1}{6}$ oz.

18. How much more does the shuttlecock weigh?

$\frac{15}{16}$ lb. $\frac{3}{8}$ lb.

20. How much more does the soccer ball weigh?

Time Out!

1. On each sheet of paper, three lines divide the paper into parts. How many parts in A? In B? In C? In D? In E?

2. What is the greatest number of parts for three lines?

3. Show how you would draw four lines to divide a sheet of paper into the greatest number of parts.

A 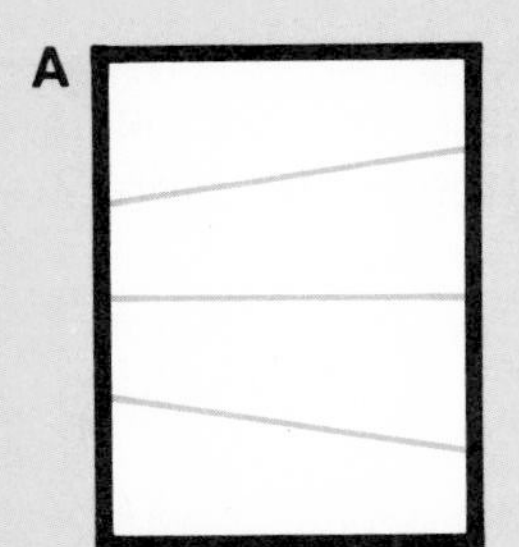

B 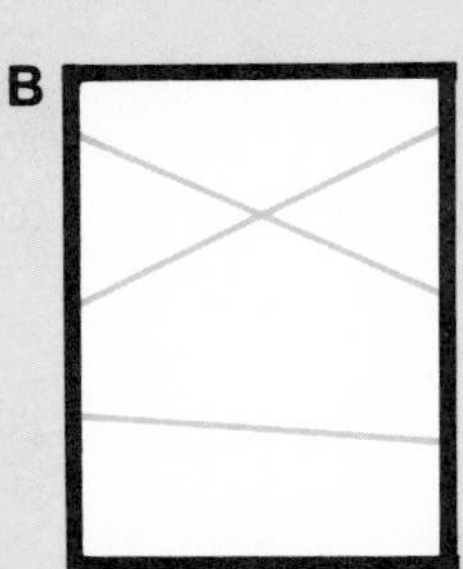

C 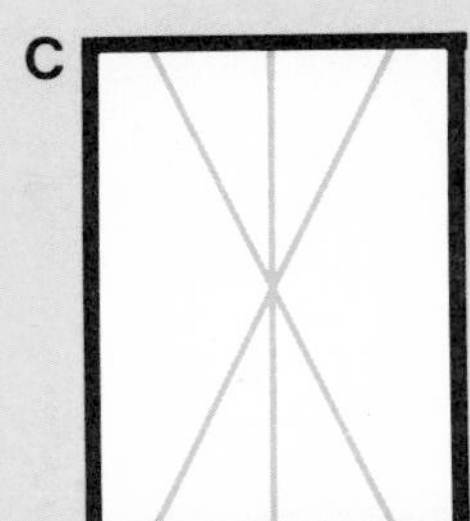

D 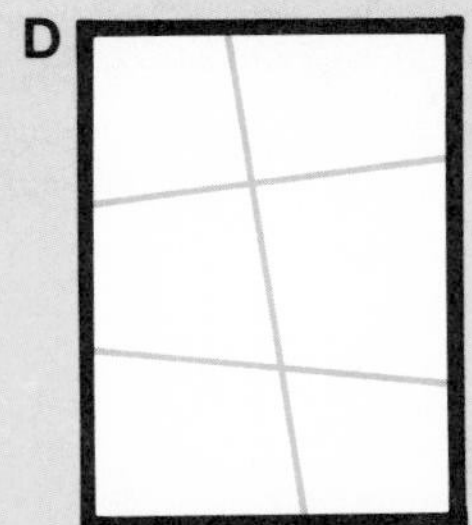

E 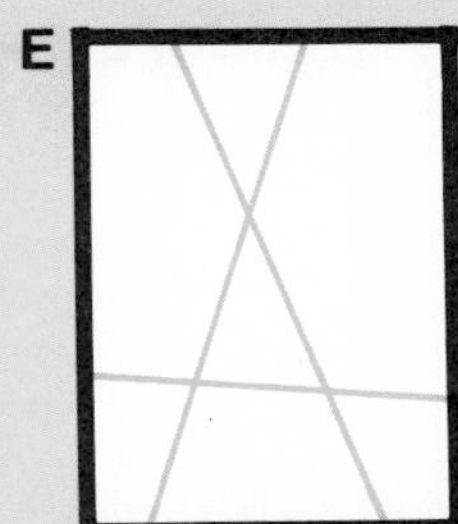

Using a Nomograph to Add and Subtract Fractions

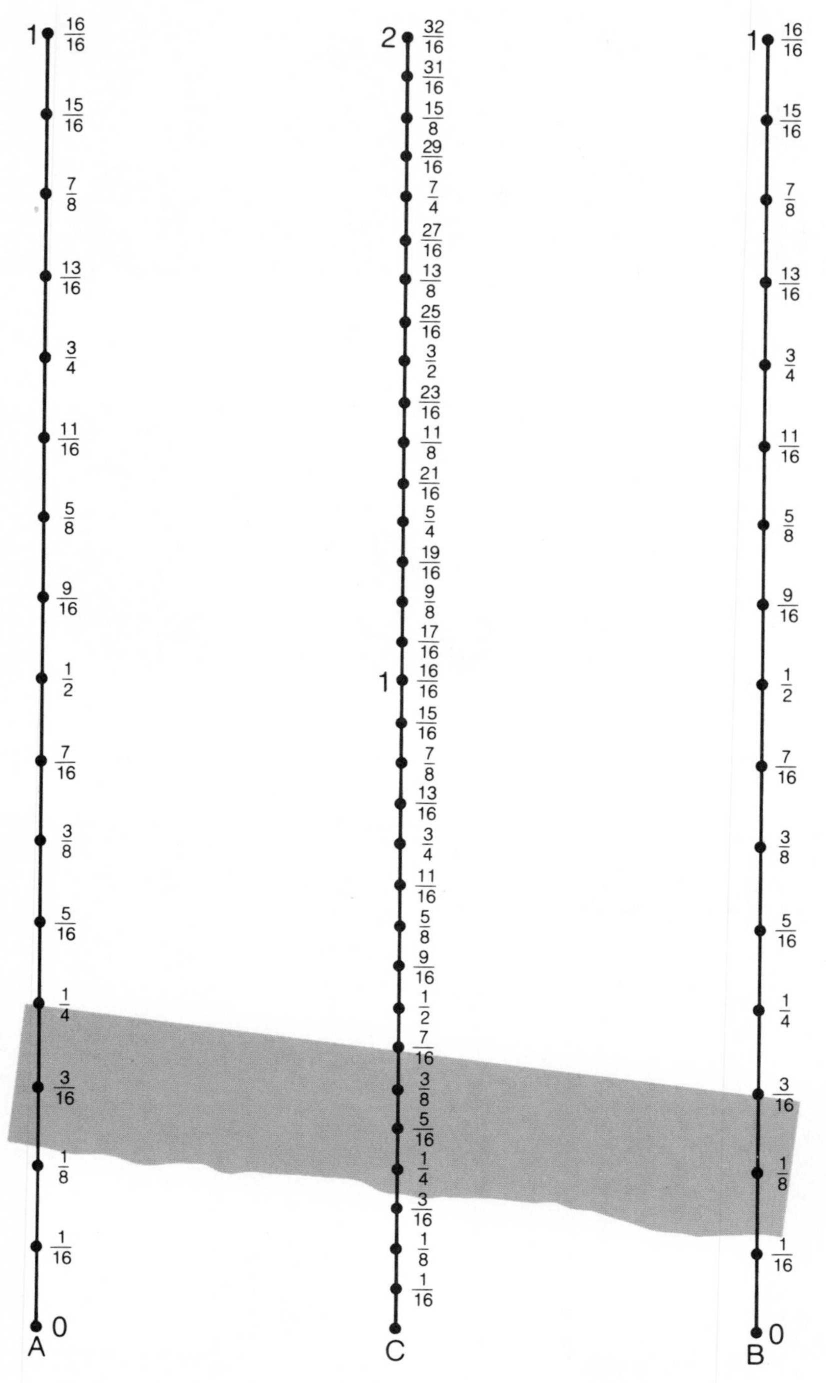

Use this nomograph to add fractions. The edge of the card shows this sum:

$$\frac{1}{4} + \frac{3}{16} = \frac{7}{16}$$

Add. Then place a ruler or a card on the nomograph to check each sum.

1. $\frac{1}{4} + \frac{5}{8}$

2. $\frac{1}{2} + \frac{3}{4}$

3. $\frac{3}{8} + \frac{13}{16}$

4. $\frac{1}{4} + \frac{3}{8}$

5. $\frac{7}{8} + \frac{3}{4}$

6. $\frac{13}{16} + \frac{1}{2}$

7. $\frac{1}{4} + \frac{9}{16}$

8. $\frac{5}{8} + \frac{3}{16}$

9. $\frac{3}{4} + \frac{7}{16}$

10. $\frac{5}{16} + \frac{3}{8}$

● **Discuss** How can you use the nomograph to subtract fractions?

On the nomograph, the edge of the card also shows these differences:

$$\frac{7}{16} - \frac{1}{4} = \frac{3}{16}$$
$$\frac{7}{16} - \frac{3}{16} = \frac{1}{4}$$

Subtract. Check by placing a ruler or a card on the nomograph.

11. $\frac{5}{16} - \frac{3}{16}$

12. $\frac{3}{8} - \frac{1}{4}$

13. $\frac{5}{8} - \frac{9}{16}$

14. $\frac{3}{4} - \frac{1}{16}$

15. $\frac{1}{2} - \frac{3}{16}$

16. $\frac{7}{8} - \frac{1}{2}$

17. $\frac{1}{4} - \frac{1}{8}$

18. $\frac{3}{4} - \frac{11}{16}$

19. $\frac{5}{8} - \frac{1}{4}$

20. $\frac{15}{16} - \frac{1}{4}$

21. $\frac{11}{16} - \frac{3}{8}$

22. $1 - \frac{3}{8}$

SMALLEST DIFFERENCE GAME

A game for two players

Object: To get the most cards

Rules:

1. Deal three cards to each player.
2. From the three cards, each player chooses two cards that will give the smallest difference.
3. Players compare their answers. The player with the smaller difference gets the four cards and places them face down. If there is a tie, the cards go to the winner of the next round.
4. Both players draw two cards and repeat rules 2 and 3.
5. When only two cards remain in the deck, each player draws one card to play the last round.
6. If there is a tie on the last round, the players keep their own cards.

Scoring: The player with more cards wins.

To make the deck, make four cards for each of these fractions.

$\frac{1}{2}$ $\frac{1}{3}$ $\frac{2}{3}$ $\frac{1}{4}$ $\frac{3}{4}$ $\frac{1}{6}$ $\frac{5}{6}$ $\frac{1}{12}$ $\frac{5}{12}$ $\frac{7}{12}$ $\frac{11}{12}$

Using Addition and Subtraction of Fractions: Travel

Give the distance for each trip along the shortest route.

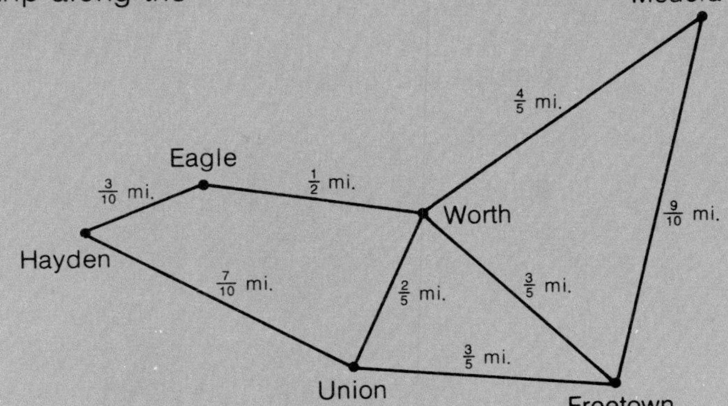

1. Union to Medora
2. Hayden to Worth
3. Eagle to Freetown
4. Freetown to Hayden
5. Medora to Eagle
6. Medora to Hayden

Solve each problem.

7.

$\frac{1}{8}$ full
Before

$\frac{3}{4}$ full
After

What fraction of a tank of gas was added to the car?

9.

$\frac{7}{8}$ full
Morning

$\frac{1}{4}$ full
Evening

What fraction of a tank was used during the day?

8.

$\frac{3}{4}$ full
Morning

$\frac{1}{3}$ full
Evening

What fraction of a tank was used during the day?

10.

$\frac{2}{3}$ full
Morning

$\frac{1}{2}$ full
Evening

What fraction of a tank was used during the day?

Subtract to find the distance between the expressway exits.

11. Central Ave. and Adams St.

Central Ave.	$\frac{3}{8}$ **mi.**
Adams St.	$\frac{3}{4}$ **mi.**

12. Belmont Ave. and Chicago Ave.

Belmont Ave.	$\frac{1}{4}$ **mi.**
Chicago Ave.	$\frac{2}{3}$ **mi.**

13. King Blvd. and Kennedy Ave.

King Blvd.	$\frac{1}{8}$ **mi.**
Kennedy Ave.	$\frac{1}{2}$ **mi.**

14. Wisconsin St. and Ohio St.

Wisconsin St.	$\frac{1}{3}$ **mi.**
Ohio St.	$\frac{5}{8}$ **mi.**

Solve each problem.

15. Of all the cars, trucks, and buses in the world, about $\frac{4}{9}$ are in the United States. About $\frac{1}{18}$ are in France. What fraction of the cars, trucks, and buses are in France and the United States combined?

16. About $\frac{3}{10}$ of the cars in the United States are less than 3 years old. About $\frac{3}{10}$ are between 3 and 5 years old. What fraction of the cars in the United States are less than 5 years old?

★ **17.** About $\frac{1}{9}$ of the cars in the United States are in California. About $\frac{1}{15}$ of the cars are in New York State. What fraction of the cars in the United States are in California and New York combined?

Subtracting from One

A. Cut one pie into thirds.
How many thirds are in one pie?

$$1 = \frac{3}{3}$$

B. Cut one pie into eighths.
How many eighths are in one pie?

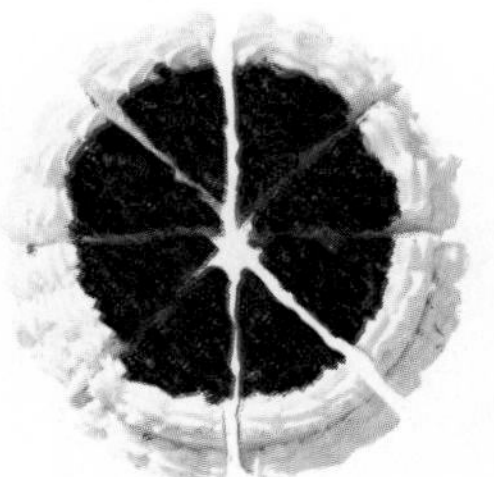

$$1 = \frac{\square}{8}$$

Give the missing numbers.

1. $1 = \frac{\square}{5}$

2. $1 = \frac{\square}{2}$

3. $1 = \frac{\square}{6}$

4. $1 = \frac{\square}{4}$

5. $1 = \frac{\square}{9}$

6. $1 = \frac{\square}{12}$

7. $1 = \frac{\square}{30}$

8. $1 = \frac{\square}{15}$

9. $1 = \frac{\square}{10}$

10. $1 = \frac{\square}{7}$

11. $1 = \frac{\square}{20}$

12. $1 = \frac{\square}{18}$

Subtract.

Here's how

$1 - \frac{1}{3}$ $\quad 1 - \frac{1}{3}$

$\frac{3}{3} - \frac{1}{3} = \frac{2}{3}$

$$\begin{array}{r} 1 \\ - \frac{5}{6} \\ \hline \end{array} \qquad \begin{array}{rl} 1 & = \frac{6}{6} \\ - \frac{5}{6} & = \frac{5}{6} \\ \hline & \frac{1}{6} \end{array}$$

13. $1 - \frac{3}{5}$

$\frac{\square}{5} - \frac{3}{5}$

14. $1 - \frac{3}{8}$

$\frac{\square}{8} - \frac{3}{8}$

15. $1 - \frac{2}{3}$

16. $1 - \frac{5}{9}$

17. $1 - \frac{3}{7}$

18. $1 - \frac{4}{5}$

19. $1 - \frac{5}{12}$

20. $1 - \frac{7}{10}$

21. $\begin{array}{rl} 1 & = \frac{\square}{4} \\ - \frac{3}{4} & = \frac{3}{4} \\ \hline \end{array}$

22. $\begin{array}{r} 1 \\ - \frac{4}{15} \\ \hline \end{array}$

23. $\begin{array}{r} 1 \\ - \frac{7}{18} \\ \hline \end{array}$

Using Subtraction of Fractions: Geography

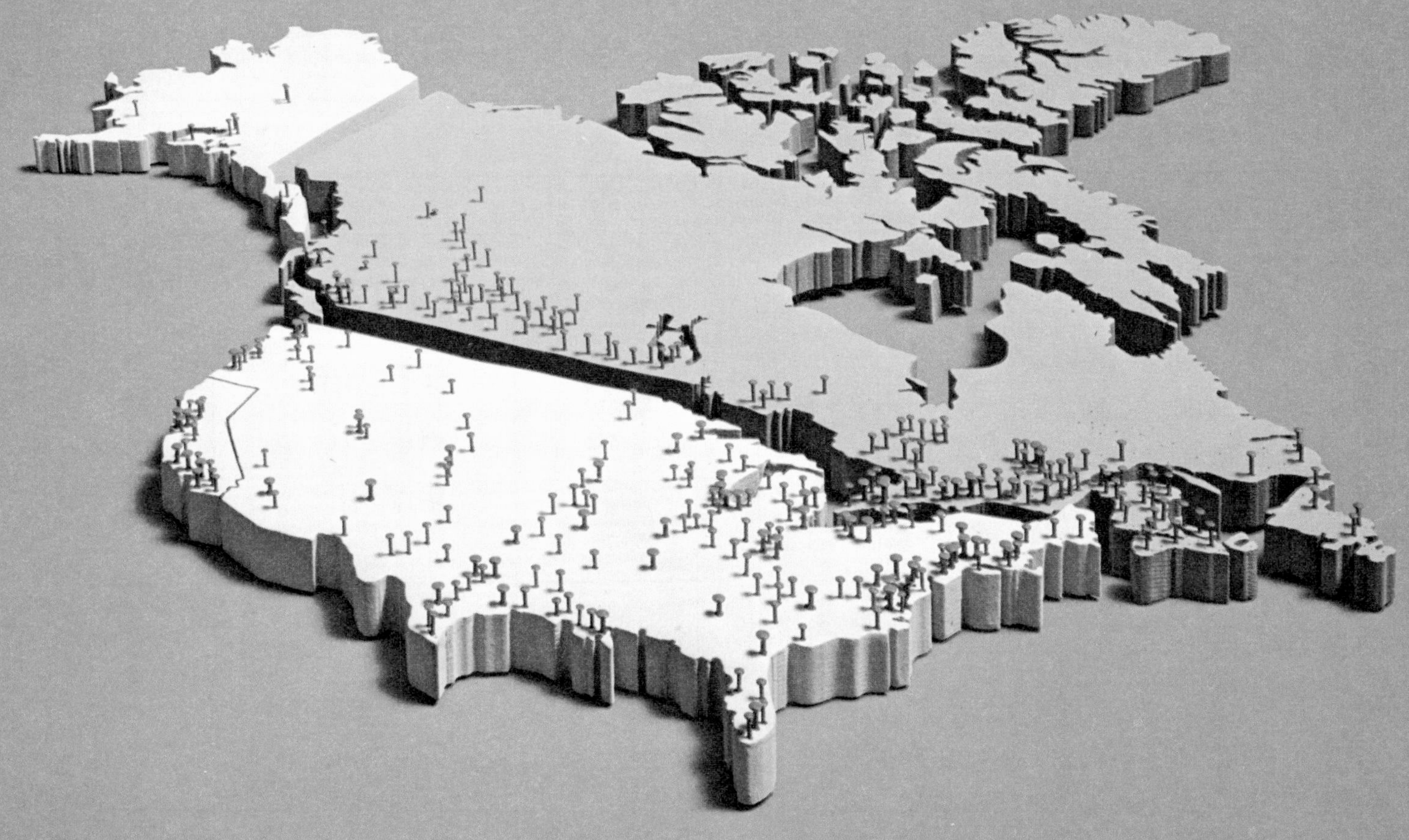

1. About $\frac{1}{4}$ of the people in the United States live in rural areas. What fraction do not live in rural areas?

2. About $\frac{1}{10}$ of the people in the United States live in California. What fraction live in the other 49 states?

3. About $\frac{1}{18}$ of the people in the world live in the United States. What fraction live outside the United States?

4. About $\frac{1}{6}$ of the land in the United States is in Alaska. What fraction is in the other 49 states?

5. About $\frac{3}{50}$ of the land in the world is in the United States. What fraction is outside the United States?

6. About $\frac{5}{7}$ of the earth's surface is water. What fraction of the earth's surface is land?

Using Fractions in Experiments

In each experiment, find the missing number.

1. Dan tossed a penny 20 times.
He recorded the outcome of each toss.

Outcome	Tally	Fraction
Heads	卌 卌 ||	$\frac{12}{20}$
Tails	卌 |||	$\frac{8}{20}$
Total	20	$\frac{\square}{20}$

2. Vera made 40 spins.

Outcome	Tally	Fraction
Green	卌 卌	$\frac{10}{40}$
Yellow	卌 卌 卌 ||	$\frac{17}{40}$
Black	卌 卌 |||	$\frac{13}{40}$
Total	40	$\frac{\square}{40}$

3. Jill tossed a three-colored cube 60 times.

Outcome	Tally	Fraction
Red	卌 卌 卌 卌 卌 卌 卌 |	$\frac{36}{60}$
Blue	卌 ||||	$\frac{9}{60}$
Green	卌 卌 卌	$\frac{15}{60}$
Total	60	$\frac{\square}{60}$

4. Vera tossed a thumbtack 100 times.

Outcome	Tally	Fraction
Side	卌 卌 卌 卌 卌 卌 卌 ||	$\frac{\square}{100}$
Top	卌 卌 卌 卌 卌 卌 卌 卌 卌 卌 卌 卌 |||	$\frac{63}{100}$
Total	100	$\frac{100}{100}$

5. Inger pulled cards out of a bag 30 times.

Outcome	Tally	Fraction
A	𝍸 𝍸 𝍸 ||	$\frac{17}{30}$
B	𝍸 𝍸 |||	$\frac{\square}{\square}$
Total	30	$\frac{30}{30}$

6. Laura tossed a dime 40 times.

Outcome	Tally	Fraction
Heads	𝍸 𝍸 𝍸 ||||	$\frac{\square}{\square}$
Tails	𝍸 𝍸 𝍸 𝍸 |	$\frac{21}{40}$
Total	40	$\frac{40}{40}$

7. Toss a nickel 30 times. Record your results in a table like the one below.

Repeat the experiment. Do you get the same results?

Outcome	Tally	Fraction
Heads		
Tails		
Total		

8. Toss a thumbtack 50 times. Record your results in a table like the one below.

Repeat the experiment. Do you get the same results?

Outcome	Tally	Fraction
Side		
Top		
Total		

SIDE TRIP Making Designs with Straight Lines

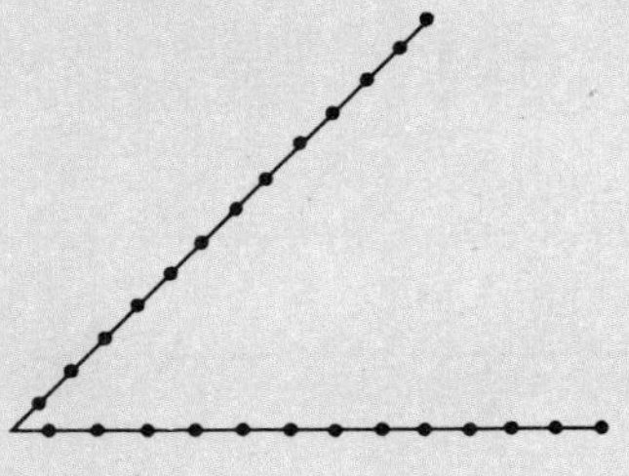

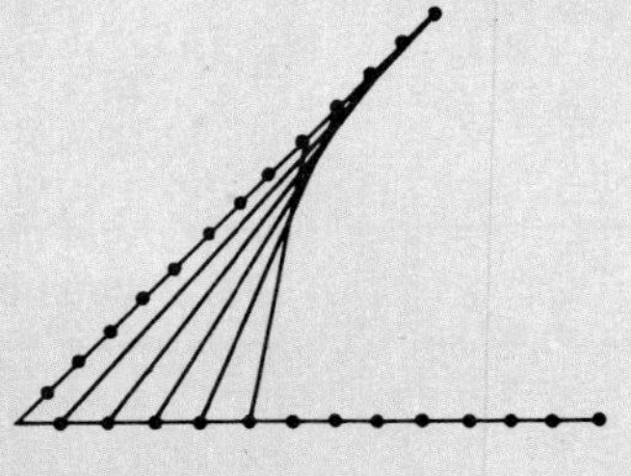

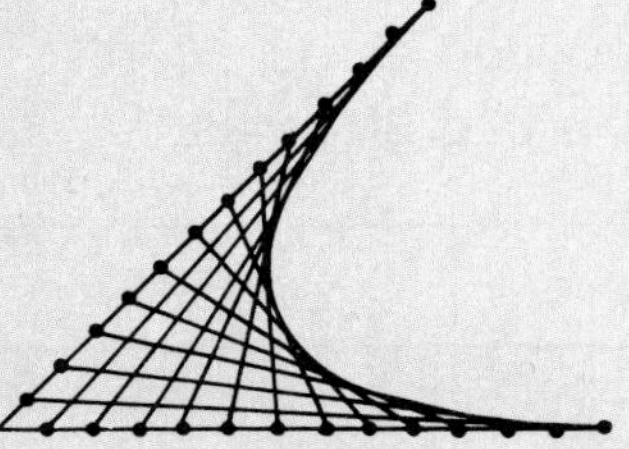

Start with two or more lines. Draw dots along the lines so they are evenly spaced.

Connect the dots with straight lines. Follow a pattern.

Try these.

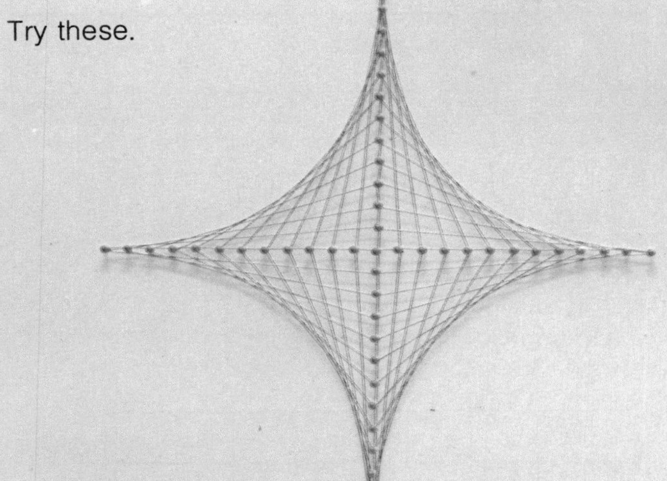

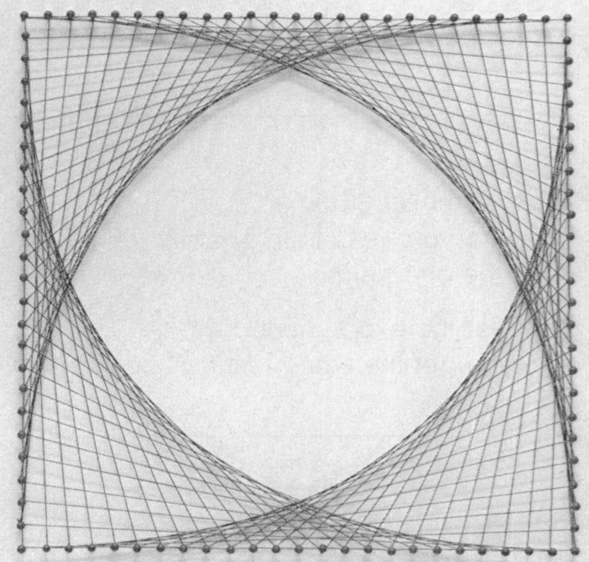

Use your ruler and pencil to make other designs like these.

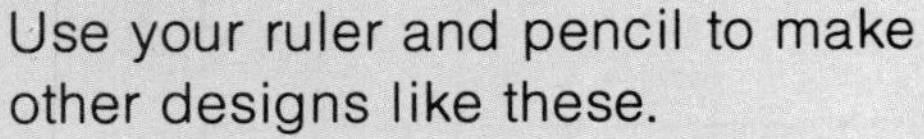

When line designs like these are stitched with colored thread, they are called ***curve stitchings.***

Check Yourself
Adding and Subtracting Fractions, Pages 204–220

Adding fractions, pages 204, 206–209, 212–213

Add.

1. $\frac{2}{7} + \frac{3}{7}$ **2.** $\frac{3}{8} + \frac{1}{4}$

3. $\frac{1}{2} + \frac{1}{3}$ **4.** $\frac{2}{3} + \frac{1}{4}$

5. $\frac{3}{5} + \frac{1}{5}$ **6.** $\frac{3}{8} + \frac{7}{16}$ **7.** $\frac{3}{4} + \frac{1}{6}$

8. $\frac{1}{6} + \frac{1}{3} + \frac{1}{2}$

Subtracting fractions, pages 205, 210–213, 216

Subtract.

9. $\frac{7}{9} - \frac{5}{9}$ **10.** $\frac{5}{6} - \frac{1}{3}$ **11.** $\frac{2}{3} - \frac{1}{4}$

12. $\frac{6}{10} - \frac{3}{10}$ **13.** $\frac{11}{12} - \frac{1}{4}$ **14.** $\frac{5}{6} - \frac{3}{8}$

15. $1 - \frac{1}{4} = \frac{\square}{4}$ **16.** $1 - \frac{5}{6} = \frac{\square}{6}$

Problem solving, pages 214–215, 217–219

17. How far is Jack's house from the dentist?

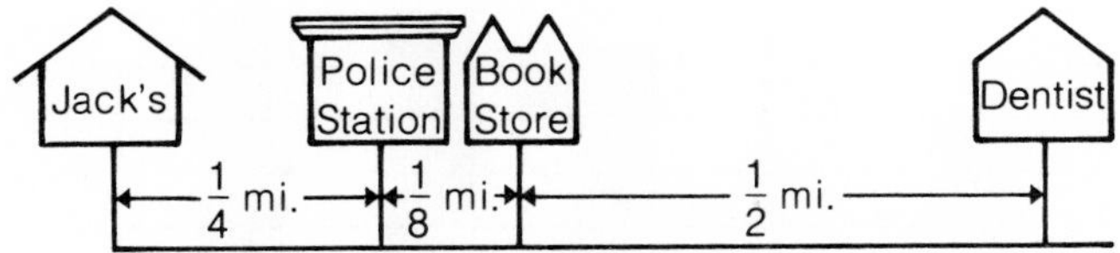

18. The bolt is how much longer than the tack?

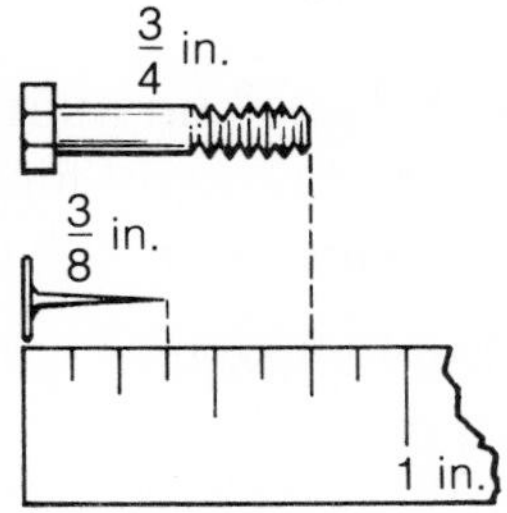

19. $\frac{7}{10}$ of the students have pets. What fraction do not have pets?

20. Luis tossed a coin 30 times. Give the missing number in the table.

Outcome	Tally	Fraction
Heads	𝍸 𝍸 ///	$\frac{13}{30}$
Tails	𝍸 𝍸 𝍸 //	$\frac{\square}{30}$
Total	30	$\frac{30}{30}$

Using Bar Graphs

Each day for one week, Miss Lupa kept a record of how many students had brought lunch to school. The table and the ***bar graph*** show her results.

How does the bar graph show how many students brought lunch each day?

Day	Number of students who brought lunch
Monday	4
Tuesday	7
Wednesday	3
Thursday	5
Friday	8

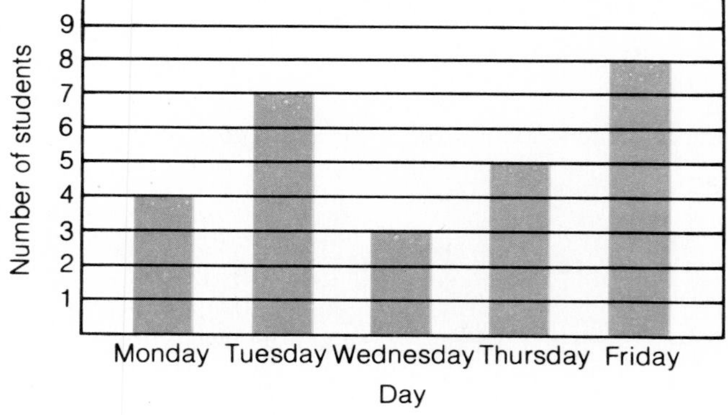

Miss Lupa also made a bar graph to show how many students rode bikes to school each day for one week.

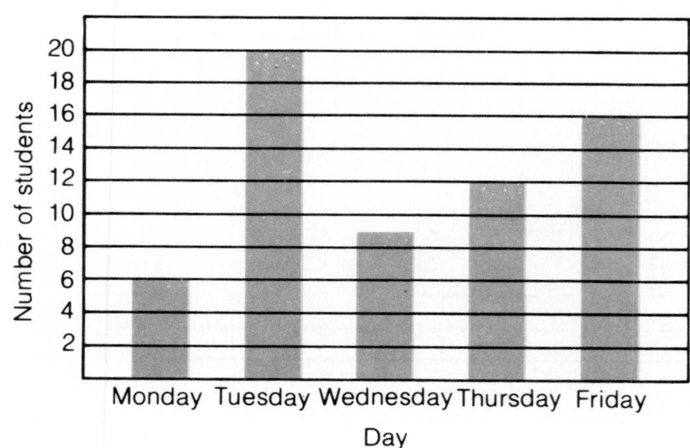

1. Tell how many students rode bikes on each day.
2. On which day did the most students ride bikes?
3. On which day did the fewest students ride bikes?
4. On which day did 9 students ride bikes?
5. How many more students rode bikes on Friday than on Monday?
6. How many more students rode bikes on Tuesday than on Thursday?

This bar graph shows the heights of five students.

7. Give the height of each student.

8. Who is tallest?

9. Who is shortest?

10. Who is 57 inches tall?

11. How much taller than Pam is Jay?

12. How much taller than Kim is Leo?

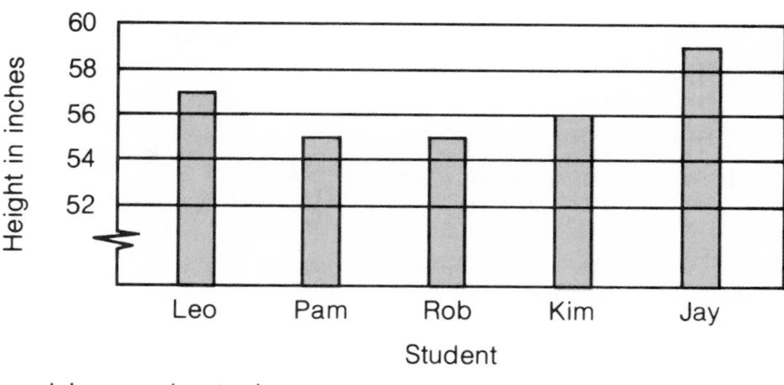

13. Make a bar graph to show the distance jumped by each student. Start your bar graph like the one shown below.

Student	Distance jumped (inches)
Leo	52
Pam	45
Rob	46
Kim	48
Jay	54

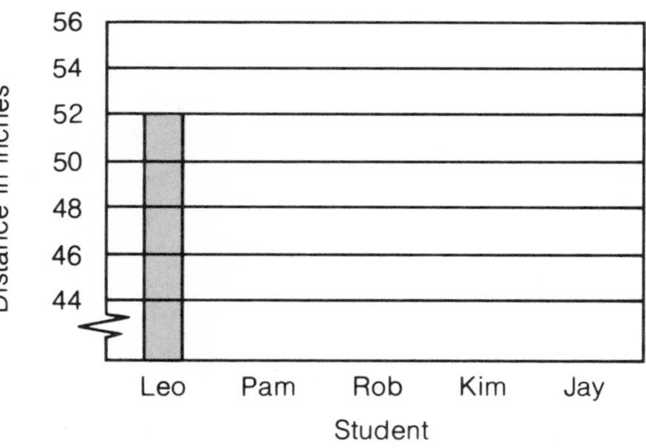

Explore

Work with four other students.
Make a bar graph of your heights.

Reading Bar Graphs

Terry made a bar graph of the lengths of the words in the paragraph at the right.

Use his bar graph to answer these questions.

1. How many words had

a. 4 letters?

b. 7 letters?

c. 10 letters?

2. Which word length occurred

a. most often?

b. least often?

Clouds are usually classified in three main groups according to their appearance. The clouds that form billowing heaps are called cumulus clouds. This name comes from Latin and means "heaped." Those clouds that look like feathery streaks are called cirrus clouds. In Latin, *cirrus* means "curl." And those clouds that form flat, unbroken sheets are called stratus clouds. In Latin, *stratus* means "layer."

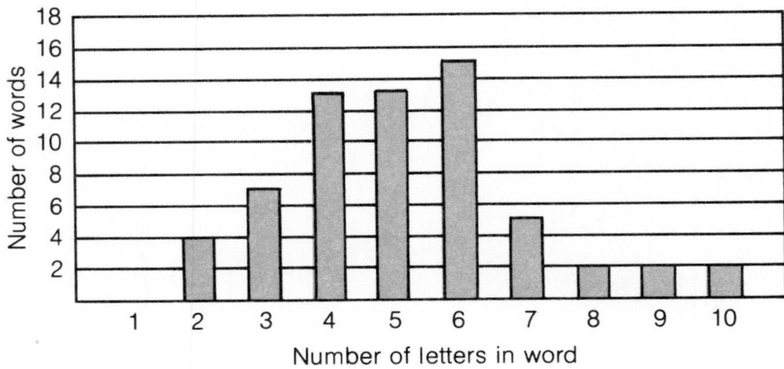

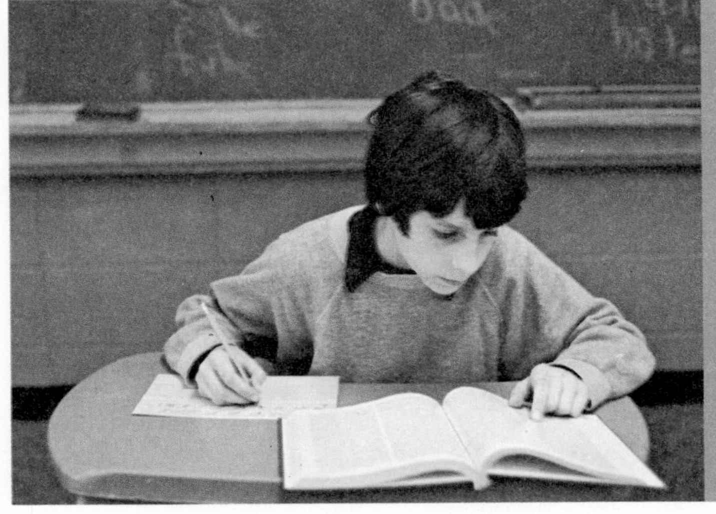

Explore

Choose a short paragraph in one of your books. Make a bar graph like Terry's to show the lengths of the words.

You could also make a bar graph to show how often each letter of the alphabet is used in the paragraph.

Reading Double Bar Graphs

Rita polled students in the fifth and sixth grades to see which colors they liked best. The graph shows her results.

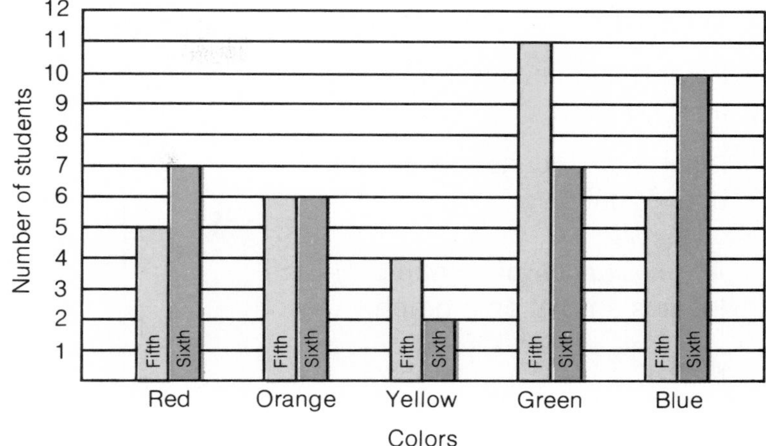

1. How many fifth graders chose red? Orange?
2. How many sixth graders chose yellow? Green?
3. Which color did the fifth-grade students like best? Least?
4. Which color did the sixth-grade students like best? Least?

Allen earned money by doing outdoor chores during the summer.
The graph shows what he earned and spent each week for five weeks.

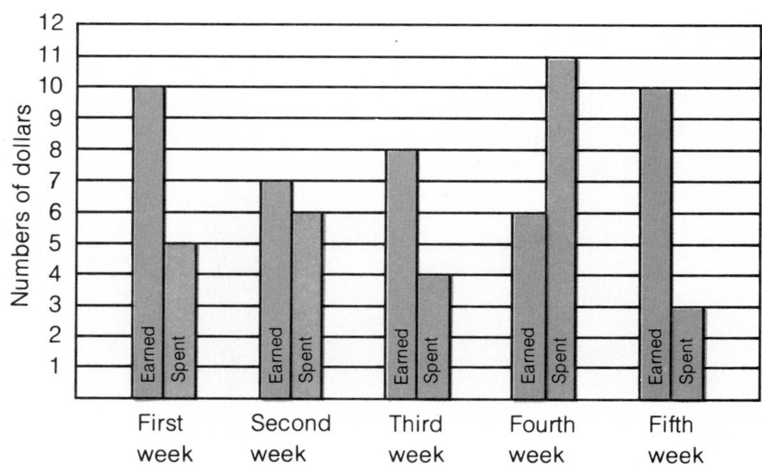

5. How much did he earn the first week?
6. How much did he spend the first week?
7. During which week did he spend more than he earned?
8. How much did he earn in five weeks?
9. How much did he spend in five weeks?
10. In the five weeks, he earned how much more than he spent?

Locating Points with Ordered Pairs

Use the red and the blue number lines to locate points on the graph.

Point R is 3 units to the right and 4 units up.

Point S is ▒ units to the right and ▒ units up.

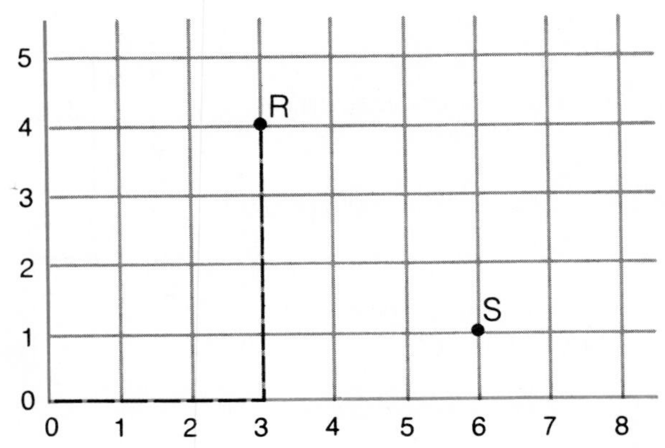

An ***ordered pair*** of numbers locates a point on a graph.

Number of units to the right → **R (3, 4)** ← Number of units up

S (6, 1)

The ordered pair for point A is (2, 1).

1. For each of the points B through H, give an ordered pair.

2. What letter names the point

a. for (4, 2)?

b. for (2, 4)?

3. Do (4, 2) and (2, 4) locate different points?

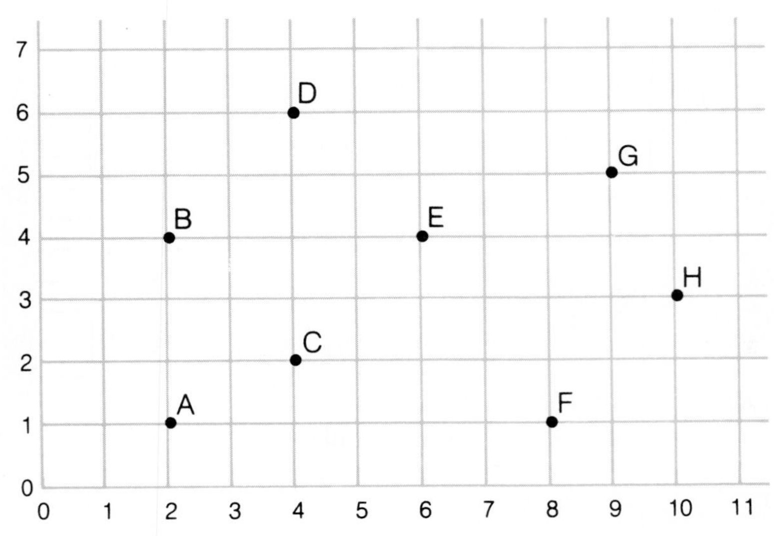

4. Locate these points on a graph like the one below.

A (2, 2)	J (7, 8)	S (5, 2)
B (5, 8)	K (4, 2)	T (12, 8)
C (9, 2)	L (12, 5)	U (12, 2)
D (13, 5)	M (2, 8)	V (7, 2)
E (9, 8)	N (14, 2)	W (11, 2)
F (6, 6)	P (8, 8)	X (4, 8)
G (2, 5)	Q (4, 5)	
H (14, 8)	R (8, 2)	

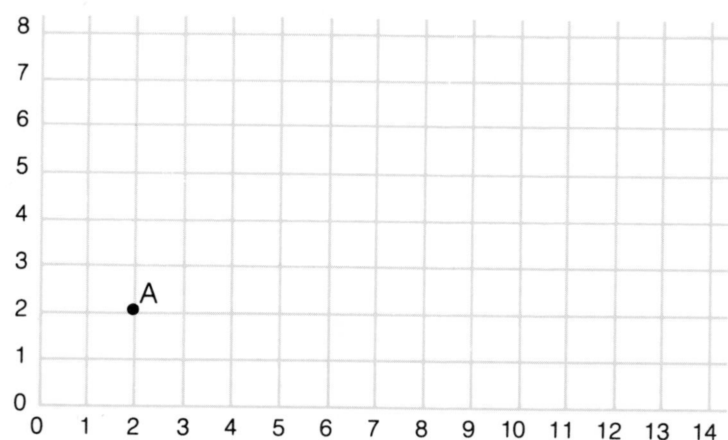

5. Draw the following segments on your graph.

AK RP TH BF MG CW GQ LD JV

EC UL BS QK TL FJ UN MX

6. What word did you graph?

Keeping Skillful

Multiply.

1. 12×20

2. 50×18

3. 60×12

4. 13×70

5. 15×60

6. 100×18

7. 200×19

8. 400×15

Divide.

9. $12\overline{)256}$

10. $18\overline{)982}$

11. $13\overline{)937}$

12. $15\overline{)943}$

13. $12\overline{)784}$

14. $19\overline{)3810}$

15. $15\overline{)6871}$

16. $18\overline{)2054}$

Graphing Pictures

Mark a dot for each ordered pair.
Connect the dots in order.
Start with the first column.

Mark your graph paper like this for each picture.

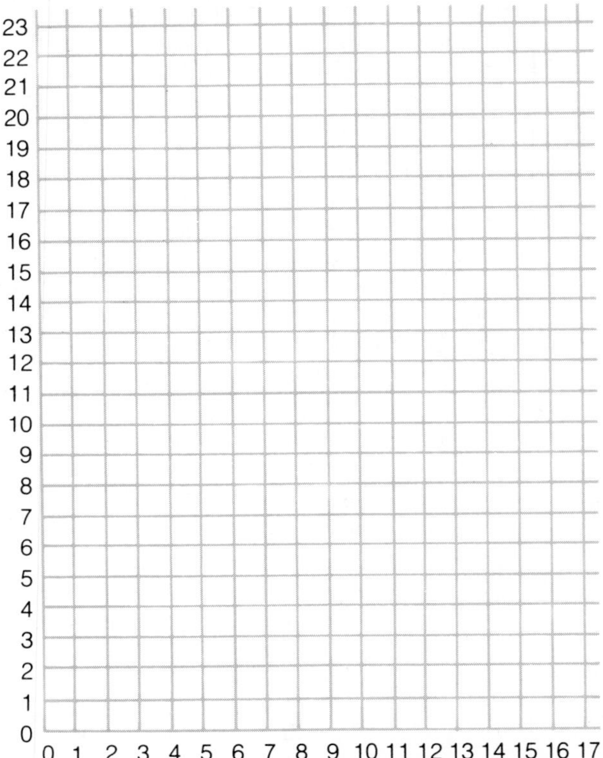

1. What shines brightly in the sky on a clear night?

(1, 1)	(14, 8)	(0, 8)
(6, 4)	(8, 8)	(3, 5)
(11, 0)	(7, 12)	(1, 1)
(9, 5)	(5, 8)	

2. What is most useful when it is used up?

(8, 10)	(8, 2)	(9, 18)
(8, 3)	(9, 3)	(8, 18)
(7, 3)	(9, 10)	(6, 17)
(7, 4)	(15, 10)	(4, 15)
(6, 4)	(14, 13)	(3, 13)
(6, 3)	(13, 15)	(2, 10)
(7, 2)	(11, 17)	(9, 10)

★ **3.** He carries a comb with him every place he goes.

(4, 0)	(5, 9)	(4, 21)	(8, 19)	(17, 13)	(14, 6)
(5, 1)	(6, 13)	(5, 21)	(8, 18)	(15, 10)	(12, 5)
(8, 0)	(5, 17)	(5, 22)	(7, 17)	(17, 11)	(11, 5)
(11, 1)	(4, 17)	(6, 21)	(8, 13)	(15, 9)	(12, 2)
(9, 5)	(5, 18)	(7, 22)	(9, 12)	(17, 9)	(11, 1)
(8, 5)	(4, 19)	(7, 21)	(14, 12)	(15, 8)	(9, 0)
(6, 6)	(5, 19)	(8, 21)	(16, 16)	(17, 8)	(4, 0)
(5, 8)	(5, 20)	(7, 20)	(15, 11)	(15, 7)	

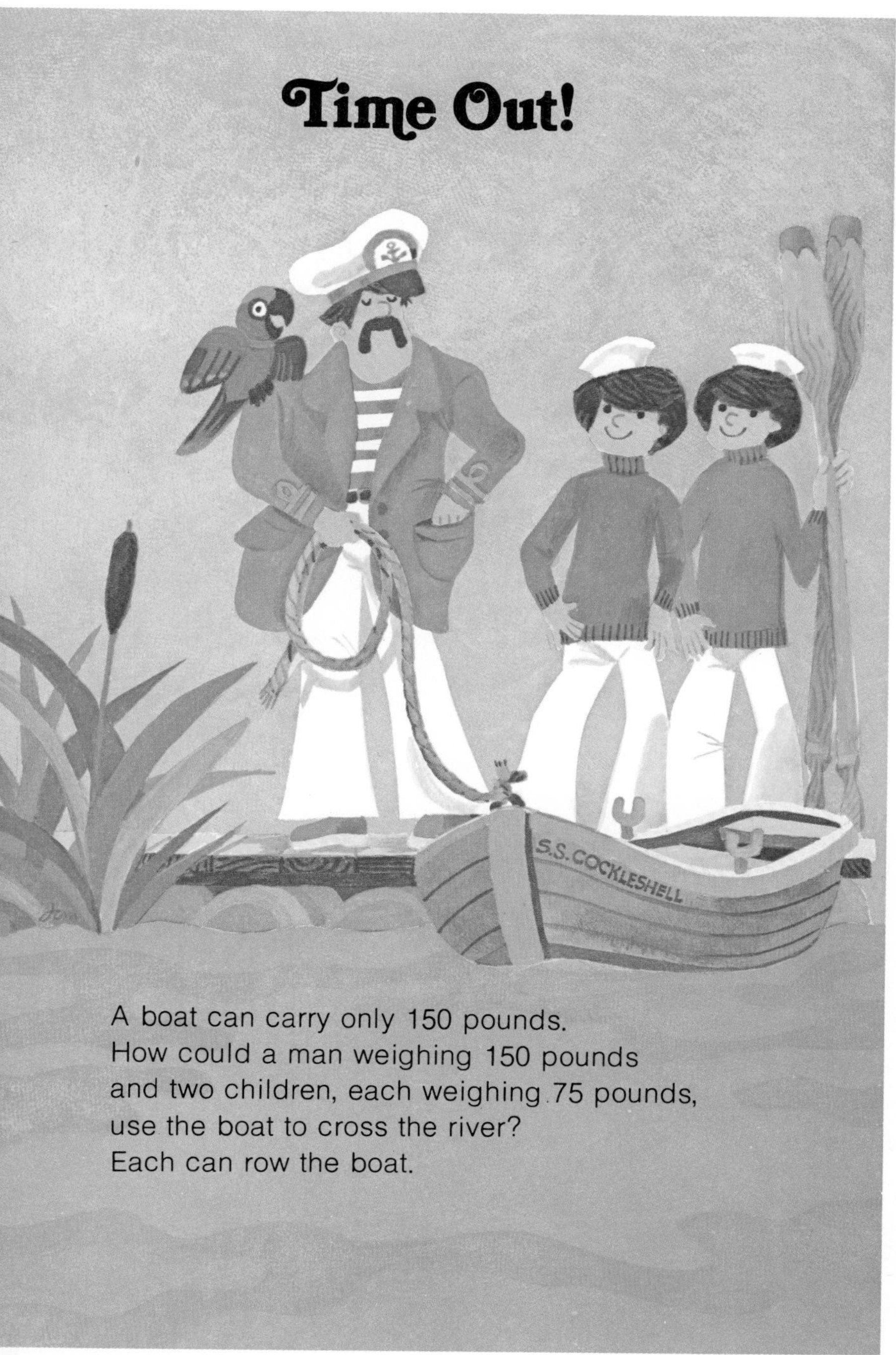

A boat can carry only 150 pounds.
How could a man weighing 150 pounds
and two children, each weighing 75 pounds,
use the boat to cross the river?
Each can row the boat.

Keeping Skillful

Compute.

1. 57 + 78
2. 205 + 348 + 729
3. \$79.43 − \$23.76
4. 9 × 764
5. 93 ÷ 23
6. \$42.68 + \$35.72
7. 76 ÷ 21
8. 7943 − 2984
9. 47 × 23
10. 707 + 9285
11. 385 ÷ 29
12. \$104.35 − \$76.19
13. 578 + 723
14. 79 × 46
15. 48 × 27
16. 476 − 294
17. 1395 − 843
18. 792 ÷ 41
19. \$4.38 + \$.95
20. 58 × 382
21. 485 ÷ 39
22. \$7.28 − \$4.66
23. 951 × 38

Using Graphs: Growth Curves

This ***line graph*** shows the growth of a German shepherd puppy.

Age ↓ Weight ↓

(9, 20)

The point (9, 20) tells you that when the puppy was 9 weeks old, it weighed 20 pounds.

1. Use the points on the graph to complete the table.

Age in weeks	Weight in pounds	Ordered pair (Age, Weight)
0	1	(0, 1)
1	2	(1,)
2	3	(, 3)
4	7	
	16	
9		
10		
		(12,)
	32	
		(16,)

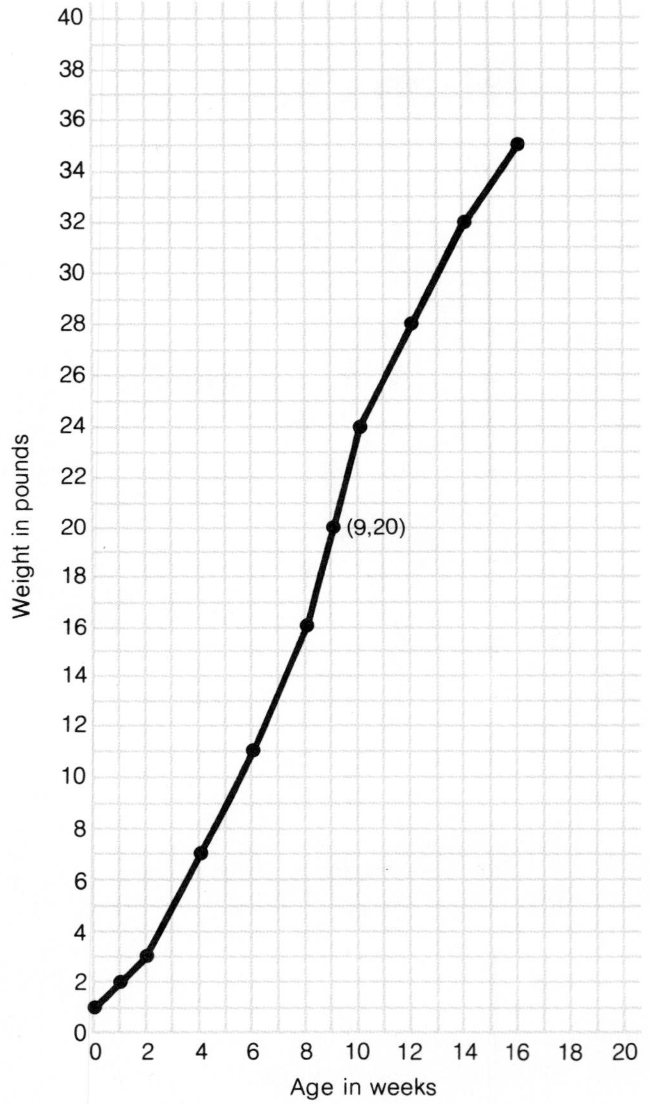

2. How much did the puppy weigh at 6 weeks?

3. The puppy weighed 24 pounds at how many weeks of age?

4. How much weight did the puppy gain between 2 weeks and 4 weeks?
Between 8 weeks and 10 weeks?

This table shows the growth of a baby mouse.

5. Complete the table.

Age in weeks	Weight in grams	Ordered pair (Age, Weight)
2	4	(2, 4)
4	12	
6	18	
8	22	
10	24	
12	26	
14	27	
16	27	
20	30	
24	31	

6. Make a graph to show the growth of the mouse. Start your graph like this.

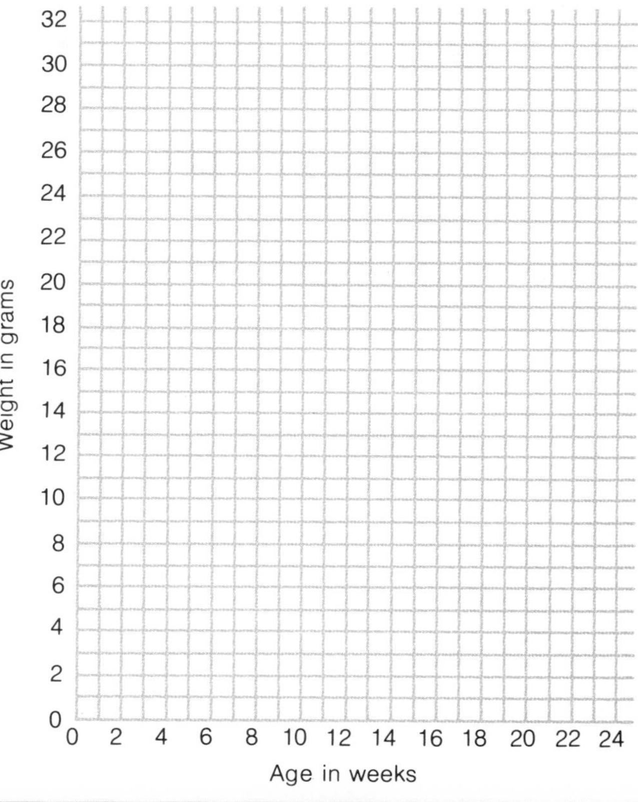

Explore

Plant two or three fast-growing seeds, such as beans, in a small flowerpot. Set the pot in sunlight. Keep the soil warm and moist.

The first day that you can see the plant is day 1. Measure the height of the plant every two days. Keep a record of the plant's height on a graph.

Reading Line Graphs

This line graph shows what Marla earns selling cookies.

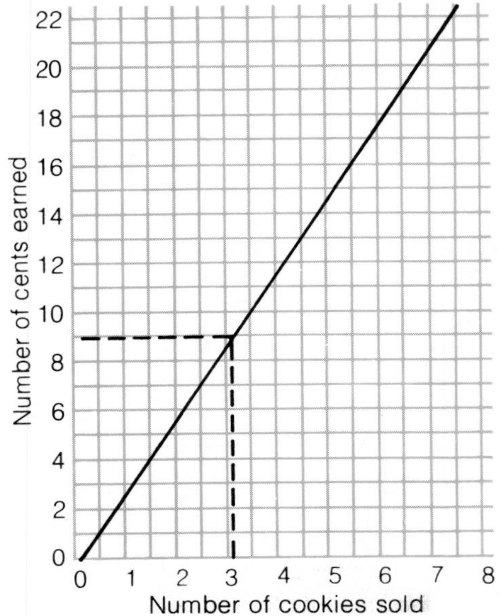

1. How much will she earn if she sells
   - a. 2 cookies?
   - b. 6 cookies?
2. How many cookies must she sell to earn 12 cents?
3. How much will she earn if she sells
   - a. 3 cookies?
   - b. 7 cookies?
   - c. 1 cooky?

This line graph shows what Tom can earn selling comic books.

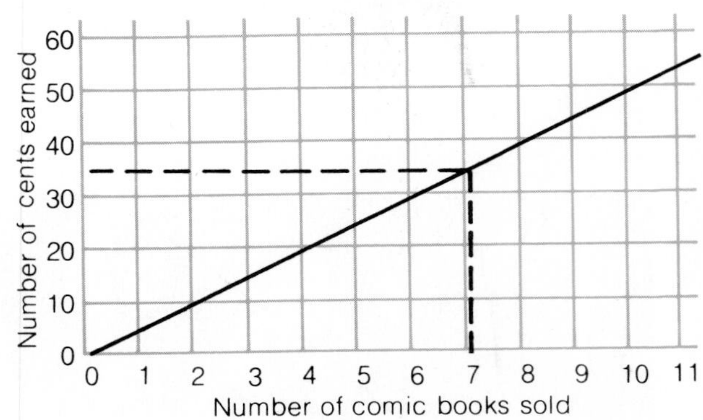

4. How many comics must he sell to earn
   - a. 50 cents?
   - b. 20 cents?
5. How much can he earn if he sells
   - a. 6 comic books?
   - b. 2 comic books?
6. If Tom sold 7 comics, the amount earned would be about halfway between 30 and 40 cents. Tom would earn about ▒ cents.

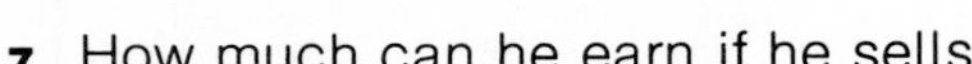

7. How much can he earn if he sells
   - a. 9 comic books?
   - b. 3 comic books?
   - c. 5 comic books?

This graph shows how long it takes Lynn to jog a certain number of laps around the playground.

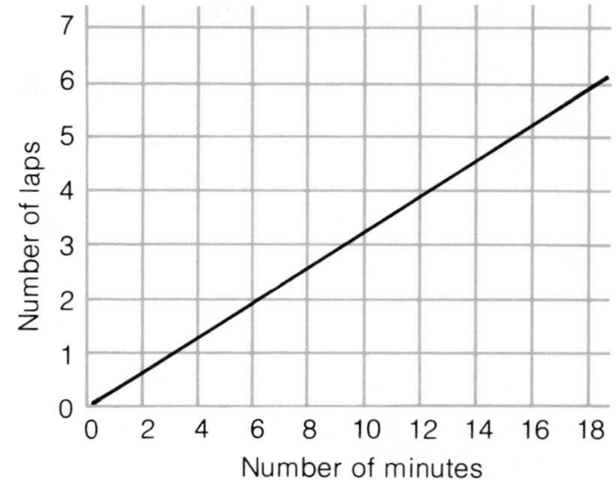

8. How many laps does she jog in

a. 6 minutes? **c.** 12 minutes?

b. 9 minutes?

9. In how many minutes does she jog

a. 1 lap? **c.** 6 laps?

b. 5 laps?

This graph shows Irene's height from age 7 to age 18.

10. How tall was Irene when she was

a. 15 years old? **c.** 8 years old?

b. 13 years old?

11. How old was she when she was

a. 51 inches tall?

b. 58 inches tall?

c. 62 inches tall?

★ **12.** How old was she when she was

a. 57 inches tall?

b. 61 inches tall?

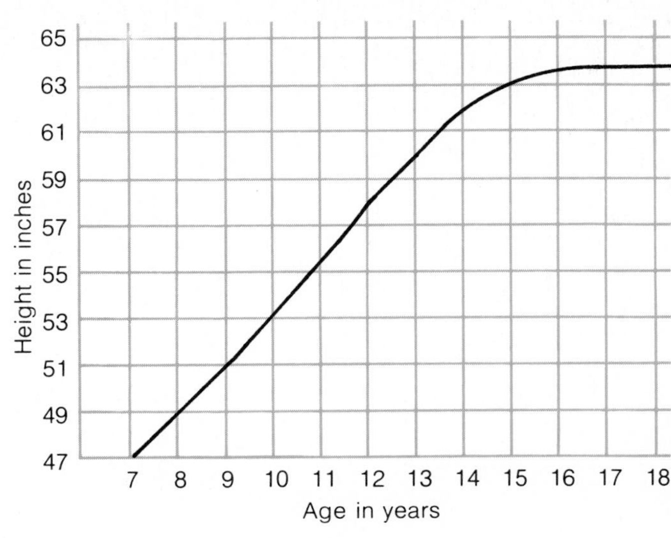

13. How old are you? How tall?
When Irene was your age, was she shorter or taller than you are?

Making Graphs

Pedro took his pulse to time his heartbeat.
His heart beat 20 times in 15 seconds.

1. Complete the table to show his pulse if it continued at the same rate.

Number of seconds	Number of beats
15	20
30	40
45	
60	
75	
90	
105	
120	

2. Use your table to make a graph. Start your graph like this.

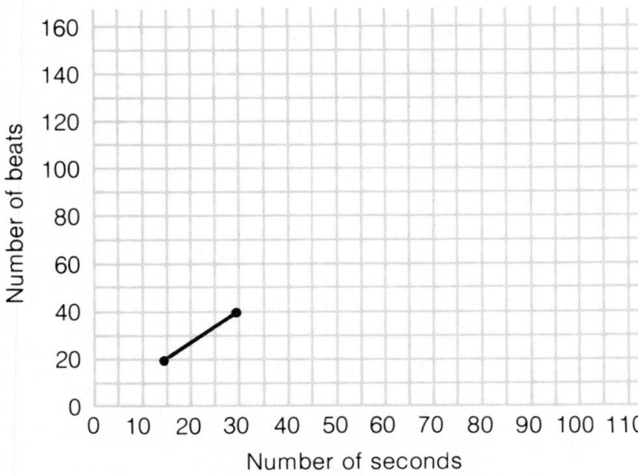

3. How many times did Pedro's heart beat in 1 minute (60 seconds)?

4. How many times would Pedro's heart beat in 4 minutes?

★ **5.** Pedro ran in place for 2 minutes and took his pulse again. This time his heart beat 23 times in 15 seconds. At this rate, how many times would it beat in 1 minute?

Marie sat quietly and counted the number of breaths she took in 1 minute. She breathed 15 times in 1 minute.

6. Complete the table to show her breathing if it continued at the same rate.

Number of minutes	Number of breaths
1	15
2	30
3	
4	
5	
6	

7. Use your table of exercise 6 to make a graph. Start your graph like this.

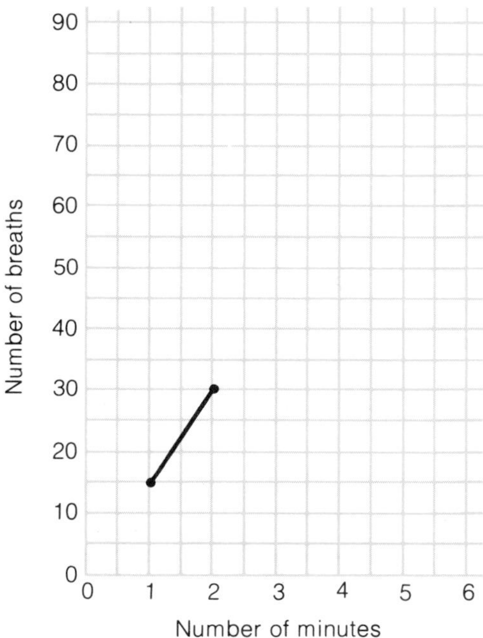

8. How many times did Marie breathe in 5 minutes?

9. At this rate, how many times would she breathe in 1 hour (60 minutes)?

10. Marie ran the 100-yard dash. Then she counted the number of breaths for 1 minute. This time she breathed 25 times in 1 minute. At this rate, how many times would she breathe in 3 minutes?

Explore

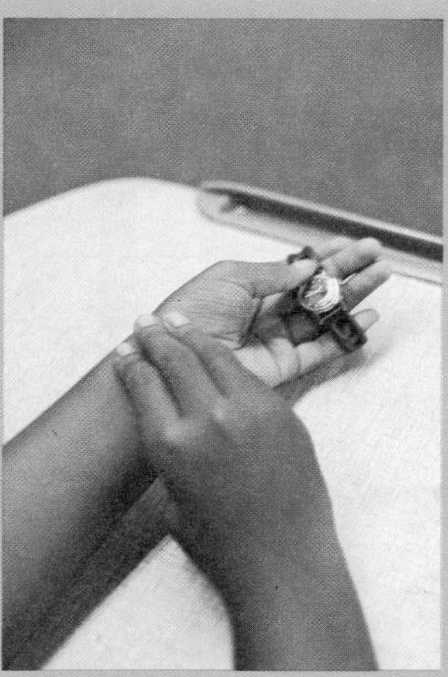

Take your own pulse.
Make a table and a graph like Pedro's to show your pulse rate.

Exercise for 2 minutes.
Take your pulse.
How much faster is your heart beating?

Compare your results with those of your classmates.

Check Yourself
Graphing, Pages 222–235

Bar graphs, pages 222–225

This bar graph shows the average life span of five kinds of animals.

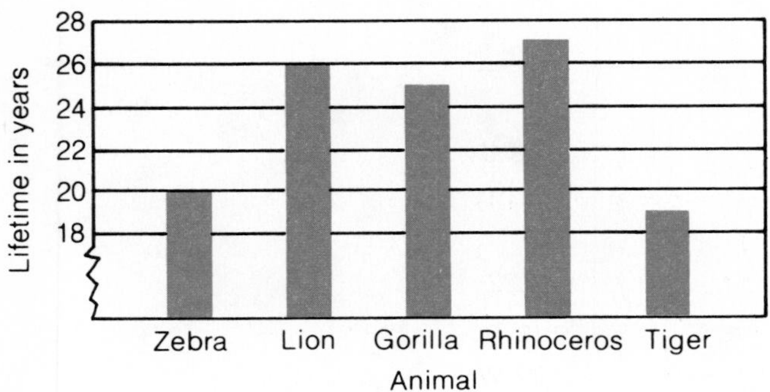

1. Which animal has the longest life?
2. Which animal has the shortest life?
3. How much longer does the lion live than the tiger?

This bar graph shows how many planes arrived and departed at an airport.

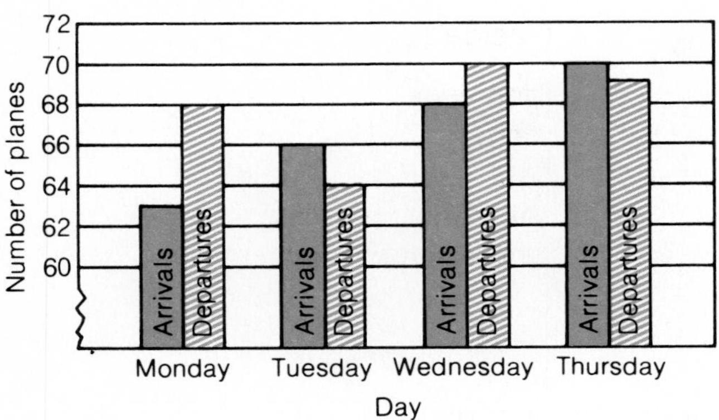

4. How many planes arrived on Tuesday?
5. How many planes departed on Thursday?
6. On which day were there the fewest arrivals?

Ordered pairs and line graphs, pages 226–228, 230–235

Give the ordered pair for each point.

7. A
8. B
9. C
10. D
11. E
12. F

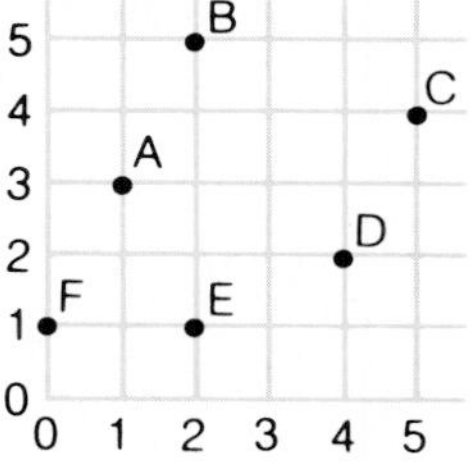

Name the point for each ordered pair.

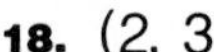

13. (4, 1)
14. (3, 5)
15. (1, 2)
16. (0, 4)
17. (3, 0)
18. (2, 3)

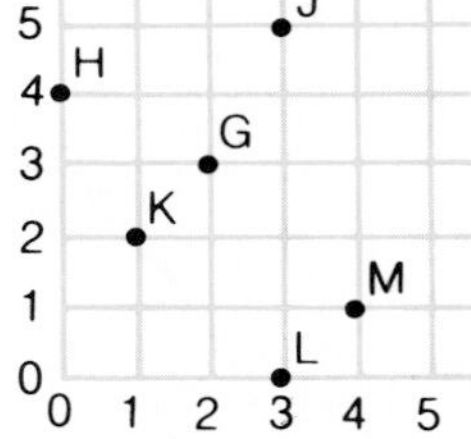

This line graph tells how far Ms. Shelby's car traveled per hour.

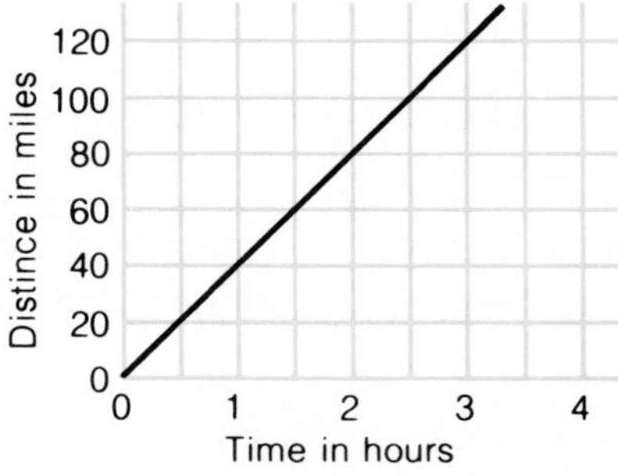

19. How many miles did her car travel in 2 hours?
20. How many miles in 3 hours?

Check Yourself: Level 28

Meaning of fractions, pages 178–202, 218–219

Replace ▒ with a fraction.

1. ▒ of the disk is blue.

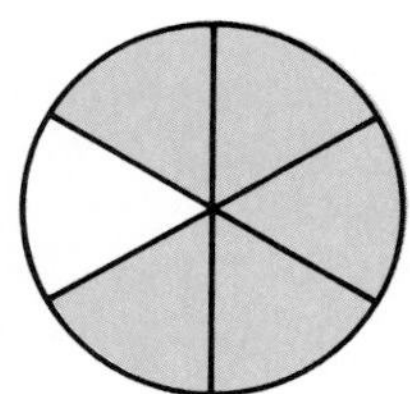

2. ▒ inch

3. ▒ of the dogs are brown.

Give the equal fractions.

4. $\frac{3}{5} = \frac{▒}{25}$ **5.** $\frac{16}{24} = \frac{8}{▒}$

Compare these fractions. Use > or <.

6. 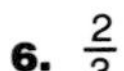 $\frac{2}{3}$  $\frac{11}{15}$ **7.** $\frac{4}{5}$  $\frac{3}{4}$

Adding fractions, pages 204, 206–209, 212, 214

Add.

8. $\frac{3}{5} + \frac{1}{5}$ **9.** 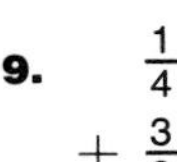 $\frac{1}{4} + \frac{3}{8}$ **10.** $\frac{2}{3} + \frac{3}{4}$

11. Find the perimeter.

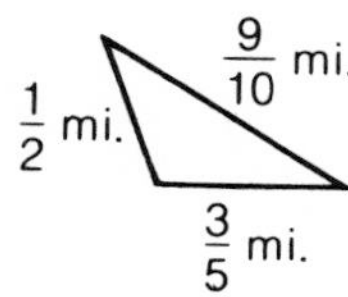

Subtracting fractions, pages 205, 210–211, 213–217

Subtract.

12. $\frac{7}{10} - \frac{6}{10}$ **13.** $\frac{5}{12} - \frac{1}{4}$ **14.** $\frac{3}{4} - \frac{1}{6}$ **15.** $\frac{7}{8} - \frac{3}{4}$

16. How wide is the white stripe on the bike tire?

$\frac{5}{8}$ in. $\frac{1}{4}$ in.

Graphing, pages 222–235

This graph tells how old three U.S. Presidents were when they were inaugurated.

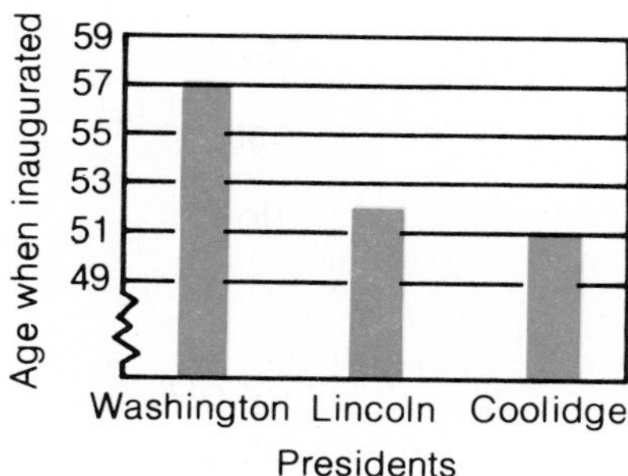

17. Which President was youngest?

18. Washington was how many years older than Lincoln when inaugurated?

This graph tells how much gasoline is used by a certain make of car.

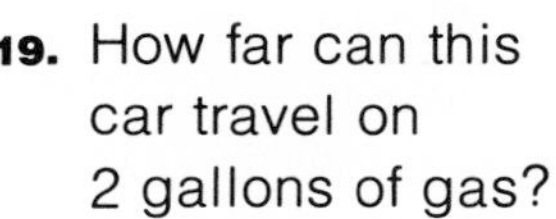
19. How far can this car travel on 2 gallons of gas?

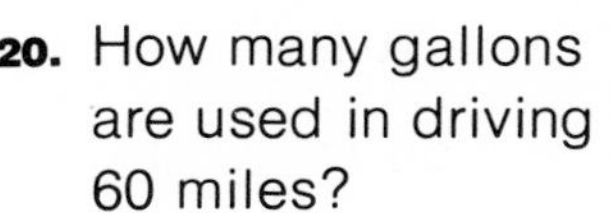
20. How many gallons are used in driving 60 miles?

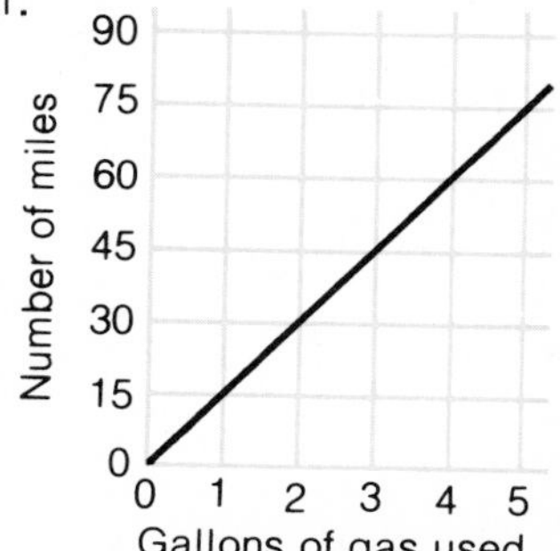

More Practice

Set A

For each fraction, write three equal fractions.

1. $\frac{1}{2}$
2. $\frac{2}{3}$
3. $\frac{4}{5}$
4. $\frac{1}{4}$
5. $\frac{3}{8}$
6. $\frac{1}{10}$
7. $\frac{1}{3}$
8. $\frac{3}{4}$
9. $\frac{5}{6}$

Set B

Give the number that makes the fractions equal.

1. $\frac{1}{2} = \frac{\square}{10}$
2. $\frac{3}{5} = \frac{6}{\square}$
3. $\frac{18}{8} = \frac{9}{\square}$
4. $\frac{3}{4} = \frac{9}{\square}$
5. $\frac{4}{5} = \frac{\square}{20}$
6. $\frac{21}{24} = \frac{\square}{8}$
7. $\frac{16}{18} = \frac{8}{\square}$
8. $\frac{2}{3} = \frac{10}{\square}$
9. $\frac{12}{10} = \frac{\square}{5}$
10. $\frac{5}{6} = \frac{\square}{24}$

Set C

Rename these fractions in lowest terms.

1. $\frac{4}{12}$
2. $\frac{8}{16}$
3. $\frac{6}{10}$
4. $\frac{6}{18}$
5. $\frac{3}{21}$
6. $\frac{8}{10}$
7. $\frac{6}{9}$
8. $\frac{25}{10}$
9. $\frac{12}{16}$

Set D

For each pair of fractions, give a common denominator.

1. $\frac{2}{3}, \frac{5}{6}$
2. $\frac{3}{4}, \frac{2}{3}$
3. $\frac{2}{3}, \frac{1}{2}$
4. $\frac{4}{15}, \frac{2}{5}$
5. $\frac{1}{4}, \frac{3}{8}$
6. $\frac{7}{10}, \frac{2}{3}$
7. $\frac{4}{5}, \frac{9}{10}$
8. $\frac{1}{3}, \frac{3}{5}$
9. $\frac{8}{21}, \frac{3}{7}$
10. $\frac{3}{4}, \frac{5}{6}$

Set E

1. $\frac{1}{6} + \frac{4}{6}$
2. $\frac{2}{5} + \frac{4}{5}$
3. $\frac{1}{3} + \frac{2}{3}$
4. $\frac{6}{10} + \frac{2}{10}$
5. $\frac{5}{7} + \frac{3}{7}$
6. $\frac{3}{4} + \frac{2}{4}$
7. $\frac{1}{8} + \frac{6}{8}$
8. $\frac{5}{16} + \frac{4}{16}$
9. $\frac{5}{12} + \frac{2}{12}$

Set F

1. $\frac{1}{3} + \frac{1}{2}$
2. $\frac{3}{8} + \frac{1}{2}$
3. $\frac{1}{5} + \frac{3}{10}$
4. $\frac{3}{4} + \frac{1}{3}$
5. $\frac{2}{5} + \frac{1}{2}$
6. $\frac{5}{8} + \frac{3}{16}$
7. $\frac{1}{4} + \frac{2}{5}$
8. $\frac{1}{4} + \frac{3}{8}$
9. $\frac{5}{6} + \frac{1}{4}$
10. $\frac{2}{3} + \frac{7}{12}$
11. $\frac{2}{3} + \frac{1}{5}$
12. $\frac{1}{3} + \frac{3}{7}$
13. $\frac{2}{5} + \frac{7}{10}$
14. $\frac{1}{8} + \frac{2}{3}$

More Practice

Set G

1. $\frac{3}{5} + \frac{1}{10}$
2. $\frac{1}{4} + \frac{2}{3}$
3. $\frac{3}{4} + \frac{1}{6}$
4. $\frac{2}{5} + \frac{1}{3}$
5. $\frac{2}{3} + \frac{1}{6}$
6. $\frac{3}{5} + \frac{7}{10}$
7. $\frac{1}{4} + \frac{5}{8}$
8. $\frac{2}{3} + \frac{1}{2}$
9. $\frac{2}{5} + \frac{1}{4}$
10. $\frac{3}{8} + \frac{1}{6}$

Set H

1. $\frac{3}{10} + \frac{1}{2} + \frac{2}{5}$
2. $\frac{2}{3} + \frac{1}{4} + \frac{1}{2}$
3. $\frac{1}{2} + \frac{3}{8} + \frac{3}{4}$
4. $\frac{1}{3} + \frac{1}{2} + \frac{3}{4}$
5. $\frac{1}{3} + \frac{3}{4} + \frac{1}{6}$

Set I

1. $\frac{2}{3} - \frac{1}{3}$
2. $\frac{5}{6} - \frac{4}{6}$
3. $\frac{4}{5} - \frac{2}{5}$
4. $\frac{9}{10} - \frac{2}{10}$
5. $\frac{6}{8} - \frac{3}{8}$
6. $\frac{11}{12} - \frac{6}{12}$

Set J

1. $\frac{5}{6} - \frac{2}{3}$
2. $\frac{2}{3} - \frac{1}{2}$
3. $\frac{7}{10} - \frac{3}{5}$
4. $\frac{3}{4} - \frac{2}{3}$
5. $\frac{7}{8} - \frac{1}{2}$
6. $\frac{3}{4} - \frac{1}{6}$
7. $\frac{3}{5} - \frac{1}{3}$
8. $\frac{4}{5} - \frac{1}{2}$
9. $\frac{7}{9} - \frac{2}{3}$
10. $\frac{11}{12} - \frac{3}{4}$
11. $\frac{2}{3} - \frac{1}{12}$
12. $\frac{7}{8} - \frac{3}{4}$
13. $\frac{5}{6} - \frac{3}{8}$
14. $\frac{4}{5} - \frac{1}{6}$
15. $\frac{2}{3} - \frac{3}{8}$
16. $\frac{11}{12} - \frac{5}{6}$

Set K

1. $\frac{3}{4} - \frac{3}{8}$
2. $\frac{5}{6} - \frac{2}{3}$
3. $\frac{3}{4} - \frac{1}{3}$
4. $\frac{1}{2} - \frac{1}{3}$
5. $\frac{9}{10} - \frac{4}{5}$
6. $\frac{7}{12} - \frac{1}{6}$
7. $\frac{1}{2} - \frac{2}{5}$
8. $\frac{2}{3} - \frac{3}{5}$
9. $\frac{5}{6} - \frac{3}{4}$
10. $\frac{11}{12} - \frac{2}{3}$
11. $\frac{3}{4} - \frac{7}{12}$
12. $\frac{5}{6} - \frac{3}{5}$
13. $\frac{7}{8} - \frac{2}{3}$
14. $\frac{7}{8} - \frac{11}{16}$
15. $\frac{5}{6} - \frac{2}{9}$

Check Yourself Answers: Level 28

Check Yourself, page 203

1. $\frac{3}{5}$
2. $\frac{5}{12}$
3. $\frac{7}{8}$ in.
4. $\frac{3}{4}$ cup
5. $\frac{3}{4} = \frac{6}{8}$
6. $\frac{1}{2} = \frac{2}{4}$
7. $\frac{3}{5} = \frac{9}{15}$
8. $\frac{2}{3} = \frac{16}{24}$
9. $\frac{8}{12} = \frac{2}{3}$
10. $\frac{3}{5}$
11. $\frac{3}{4}$
12. 12
13. 15
14. $\frac{3}{4} > \frac{2}{3}$
15. $\frac{7}{10} > \frac{3}{5}$
16. $\frac{7}{12}, \frac{2}{3}, \frac{5}{6}$

Check Yourself, page 221

1. $\frac{5}{7}$
2. $\frac{5}{8}$
3. $\frac{5}{6}$
4. $\frac{11}{12}$
5. $\frac{4}{5}$
6. $\frac{13}{16}$
7. $\frac{11}{12}$
8. $\frac{6}{6} = 1$
9. $\frac{2}{9}$
10. $\frac{3}{6} = \frac{1}{2}$
11. $\frac{5}{12}$
12. $\frac{3}{10}$
13. $\frac{8}{12} = \frac{2}{3}$
14. $\frac{11}{24}$
15. $\frac{3}{4}$
16. $\frac{1}{6}$
17. $\frac{7}{8}$ mi.
18. $\frac{3}{8}$ in.
19. $\frac{3}{10}$
20. $\frac{17}{30}$

Check Yourself, page 236

1. Rhinoceros
2. Tiger
3. 7 yr.
4. 66
5. 69
6. Monday
7. (1, 3)
8. (2, 5)
9. (5, 4)
10. (4, 2)
11. (2, 1)
12. (0, 1)
13. M
14. J
15. K
16. H
17. L
18. G
19. 80 mi.
20. 120 mi.

Check Yourself: Level 28, page 237

1. $\frac{5}{6}$
2. $\frac{7}{8}$
3. $\frac{2}{5}$
4. $\frac{3}{5} = \frac{15}{25}$
5. $\frac{16}{24} = \frac{8}{12}$
6. $\frac{2}{3} < \frac{11}{15}$
7. $\frac{4}{5} > \frac{3}{4}$
8. $\frac{4}{5}$
9. $\frac{5}{8}$
10. $\frac{17}{12}$
11. $\frac{20}{10}$ mi.
12. $\frac{1}{10}$
13. $\frac{2}{12} = \frac{1}{6}$
14. $\frac{7}{12}$
15. $\frac{1}{8}$
16. $\frac{3}{8}$ in.
17. Coolidge
18. 5 yr.
19. 30 mi.
20. 4 gal.

Level 29

Meaning of Mixed Numbers, Pages 242–257

Mixed Numbers

A. How many cakes are shown?

There are $2\frac{3}{4}$ cakes.

B. How many cartons of cola are shown?

There are $1\frac{5}{6}$ cartons of cola.

Numbers like $2\frac{3}{4}$ and $1\frac{5}{6}$ are called ***mixed numbers.***
A mixed number is made up of a whole number and a fraction.

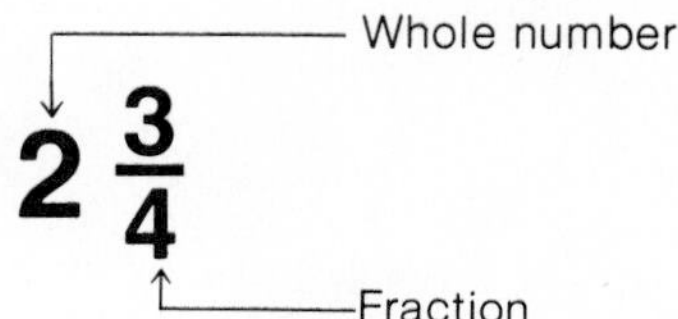

Give a mixed number for each amount shown.

1. How many coffeecakes?

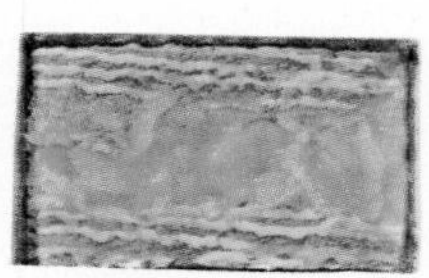

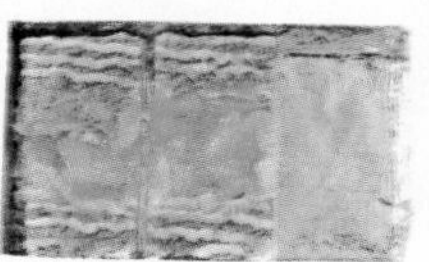

2. How many chocolate bars?

3. How many pies?

4. How many glasses of tea?

5. How many cups of punch?

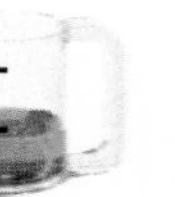

6. How many gallons of cider?

7. How many cartons of root beer?

8. How many packages of cakes?

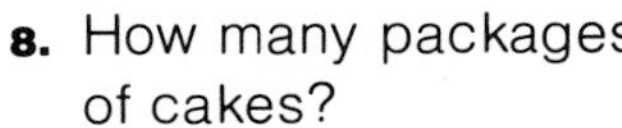
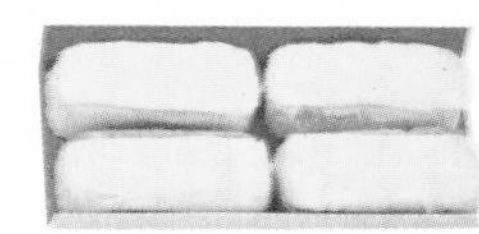

9. How many boxes of candy?

10. How many dozen eggs?

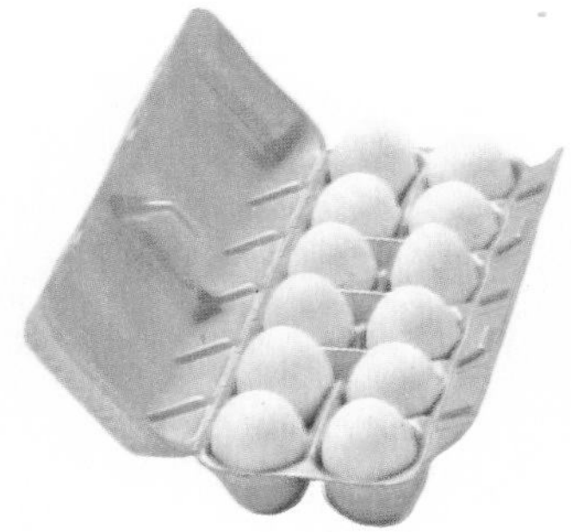

Mixed Numbers on the Number Line

Each mile shown is marked in 4 equal parts. Each part is $\frac{1}{4}$ mile.

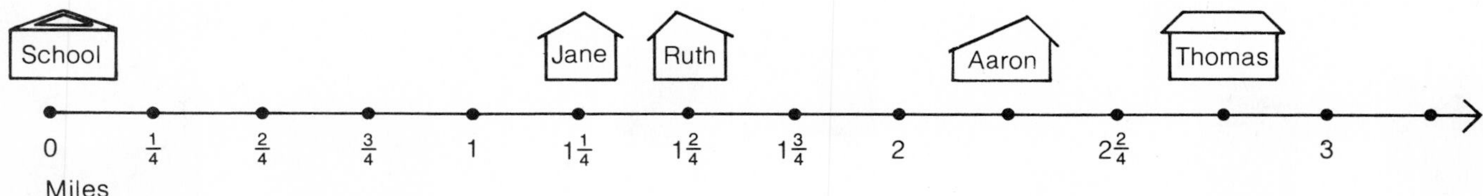

A. Jane lives $1\frac{1}{4}$ miles from school.
Is $1\frac{1}{4}$ miles farther than 1 mile? How much farther?

B. How far from school does Ruth live?

C. How far from school does Aaron live?

D. Who lives $2\frac{3}{4}$ miles from school?

1. Each mile shown is marked in 5 equal parts. Each part is $\frac{1}{5}$ mile.
How far from the store does each person live?

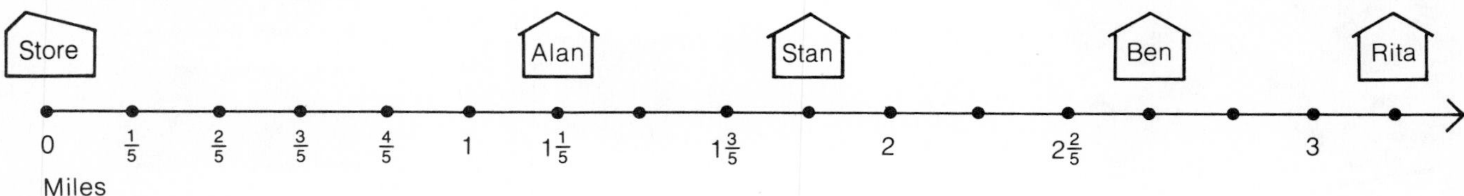

2. Give a mixed number for each point that has a letter.

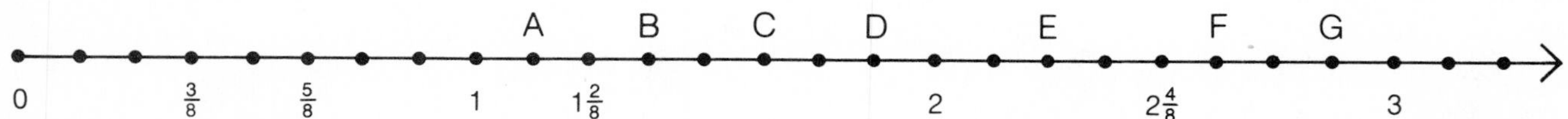

3. Each mile on the map is marked in 4 equal parts.
Each part is ▒ mile.

4. Give the distance from Carefree Camp to each of these places.

a. Caterpillar Creek	f. Badger Bridge
b. Horrid Hollow	g. Muskrat Mountain
c. Cougar Cave	h. Rabbit Ravine
d. Gopher Gulch	i. Soupy Swamp
e. Moose Mill	j. Sweetwater Slough

1 mile

Start

Carefree Camp

a. Caterpillar Creek

b. Horrid Hollow

c. Cougar Cave

d. Gopher Gulch

e. Moose Mill

f. Badger Bridge

g. Muskrat Mountain

h. Rabbit Ravine

i. Soupy Swamp

j. Sweetwater Slough

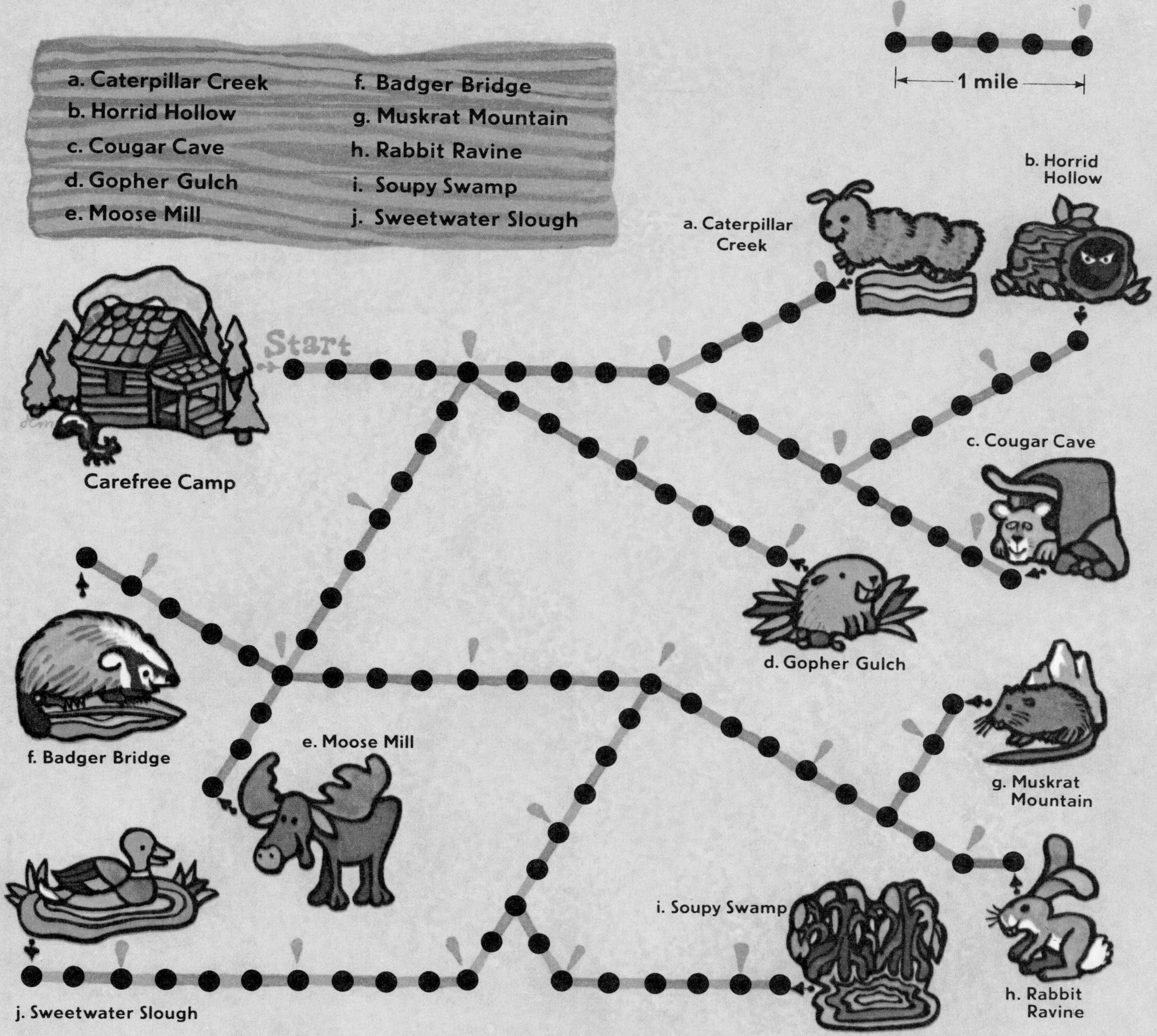

Using Mixed Numbers in Measurement

Each inch is marked in 4 equal parts. Each part is $\frac{1}{4}$ inch.
With this ruler you can measure to the nearest $\frac{1}{4}$ inch.

These objects were measured to the nearest $\frac{1}{4}$ inch.

The pen is 5 inches long.

The pencil is $3\frac{1}{4}$ inches long.

The nail is $1\frac{2}{4}$ inches long.

A.

inches

ACTUAL SIZE

Give each length to the nearest $\frac{1}{4}$ inch.

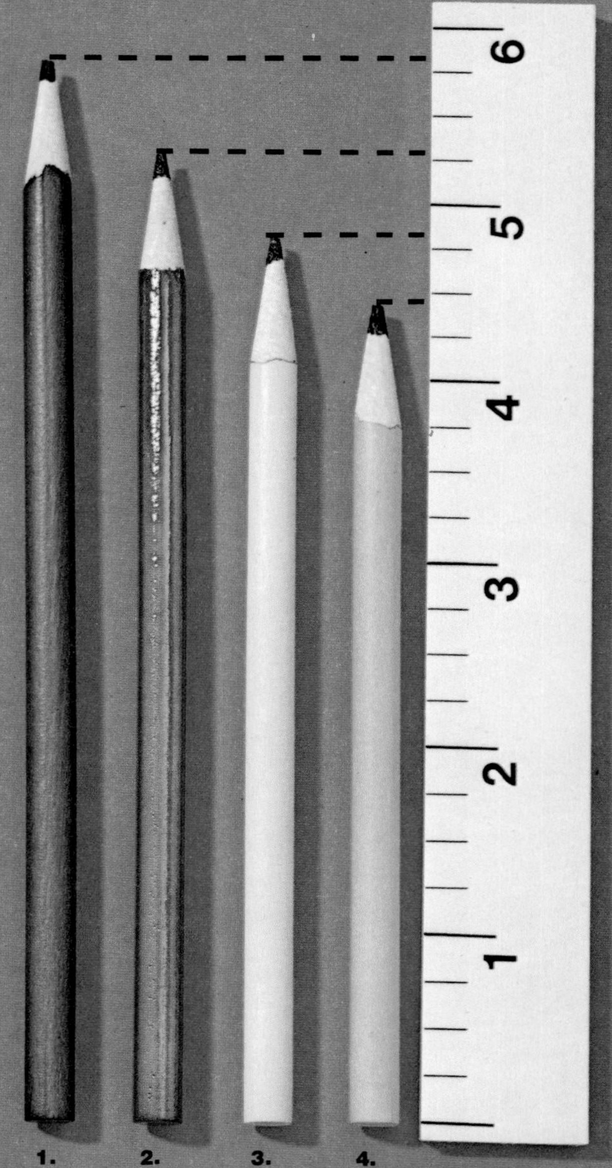

Each inch is marked in 8 equal parts. Each part is $\frac{1}{8}$ inch.
With this ruler you can measure to the nearest $\frac{1}{8}$ inch.

The same objects were measured to the nearest $\frac{1}{8}$ inch.

The pen is $4\frac{7}{8}$ inches long.

The pencil is $3\frac{2}{8}$ inches long.

The nail is $1\frac{3}{8}$ inches long.

B.

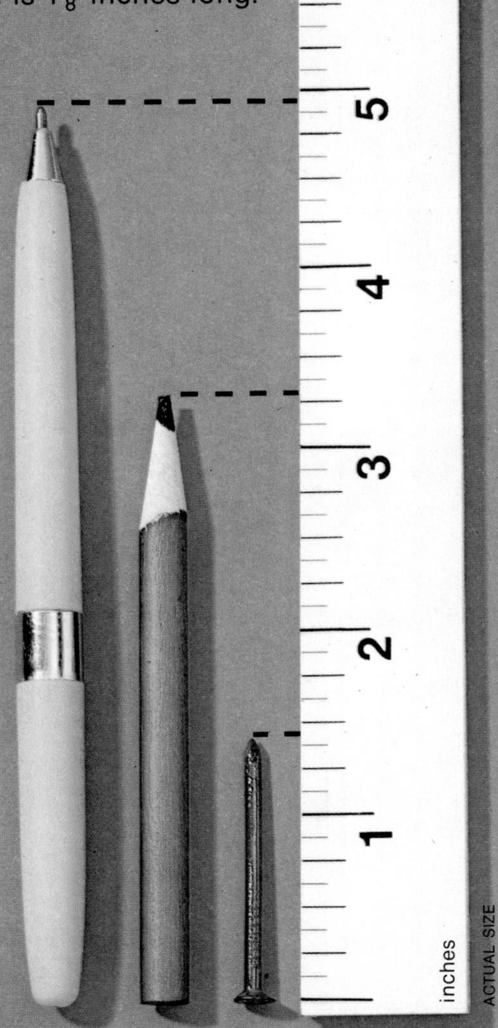

Give each length to the nearest $\frac{1}{8}$ inch.

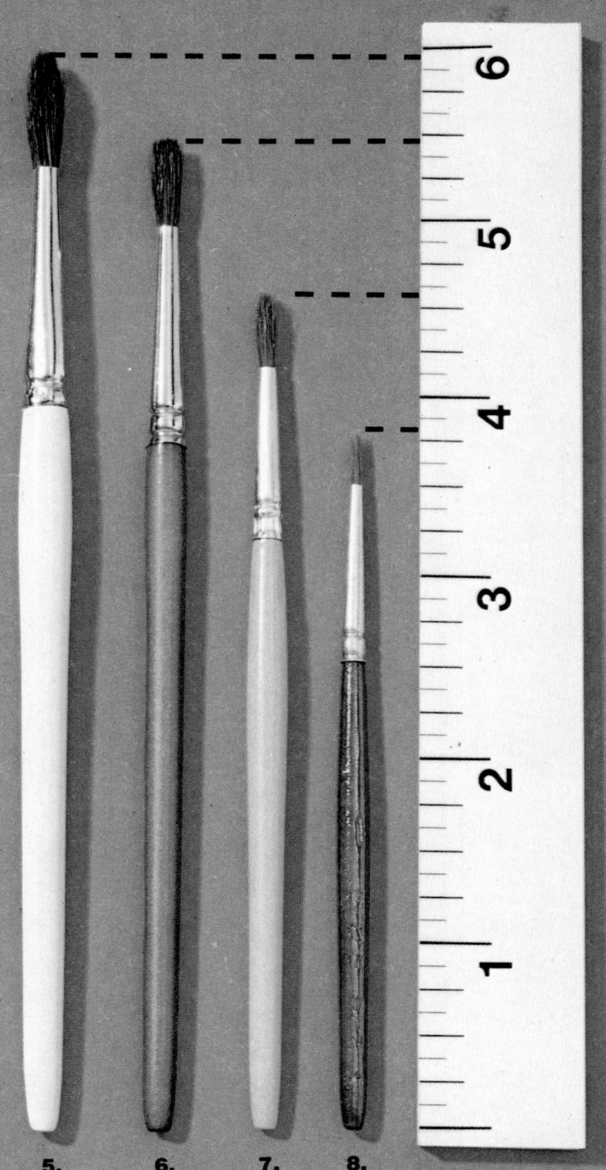

5. **6.** **7.** **8.**

Comparing Mixed Numbers: Baseball

Which length is greater?

A.

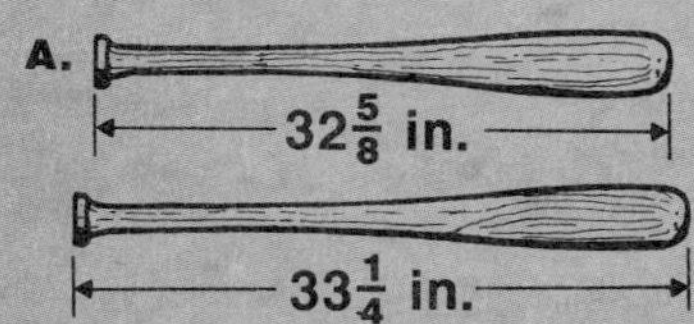

Compare $32\frac{5}{8}$ and $33\frac{1}{4}$.

Compare the whole numbers.

$$33\frac{1}{4} > 32\frac{5}{8}$$

B.

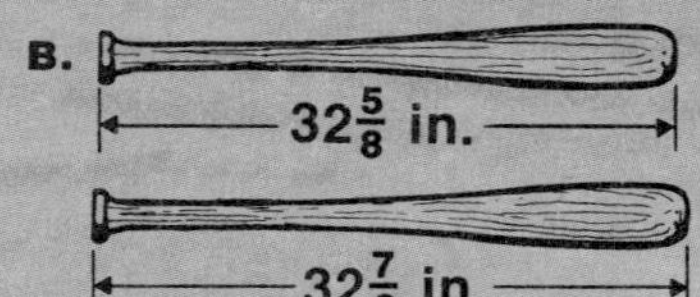

Compare $32\frac{5}{8}$ and $32\frac{7}{8}$.

The whole numbers are equal. Compare the fractions.

$$32\frac{7}{8} > 32\frac{5}{8}$$

C.

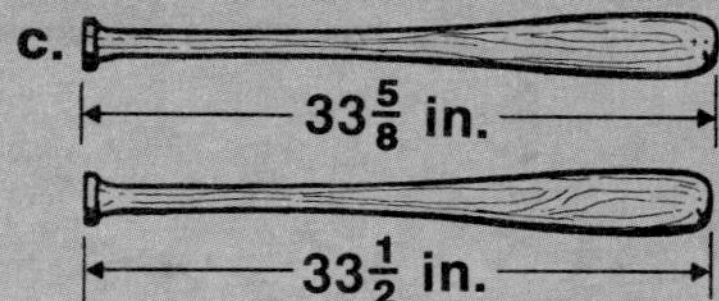

Compare $33\frac{5}{8}$ and $33\frac{1}{2}$.

The whole numbers are equal. Compare the fractions. First find a common denominator.

$$33\frac{5}{8} \bigcirc 33\frac{1}{2}$$

$$33\frac{5}{8} > 33\frac{4}{8}$$

$$33\frac{5}{8} > 33\frac{1}{2}$$

Which length is greater?

1.

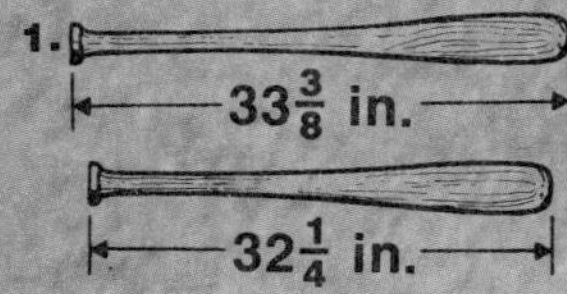

2.

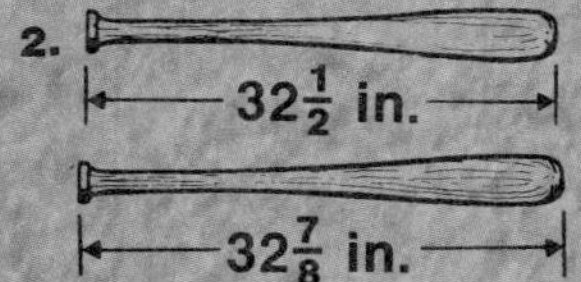

3.

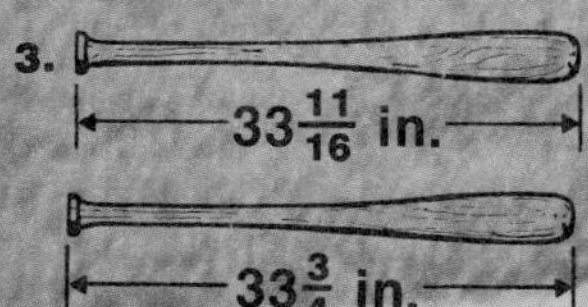

Which weight is greater?

4.

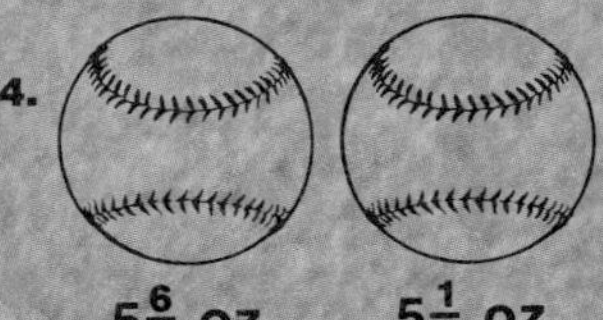

5.

6.

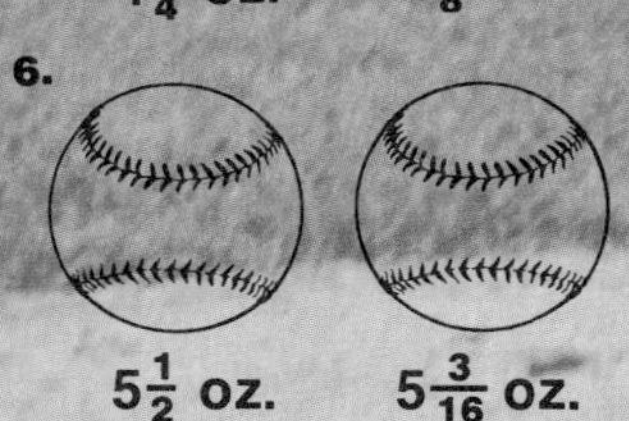

7. In professional baseball, the ball must weigh at least 5 ounces, but not more than $5\frac{1}{4}$ ounces.

Which of these baseballs cannot be used in a professional game?

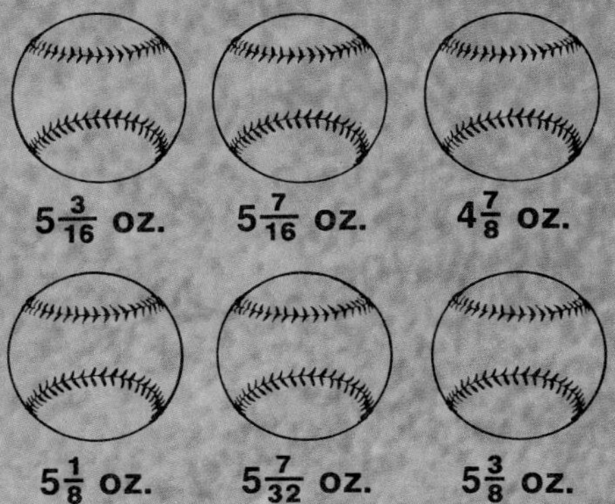

$5\frac{3}{16}$ oz. $5\frac{7}{16}$ oz. $4\frac{7}{8}$ oz.

$5\frac{1}{8}$ oz. $5\frac{7}{32}$ oz. $5\frac{3}{8}$ oz.

8. In professional baseball, the distance around the ball must be at least 9 inches, but not more than $9\frac{1}{4}$ inches.

Which of these baseballs cannot be used in a professional game?

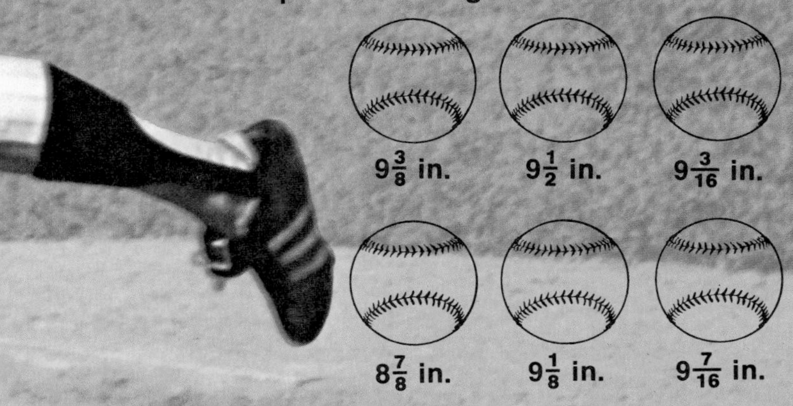

$9\frac{3}{8}$ in. $9\frac{1}{2}$ in. $9\frac{3}{16}$ in.

$8\frac{7}{8}$ in. $9\frac{1}{8}$ in. $9\frac{7}{16}$ in.

Time Out!

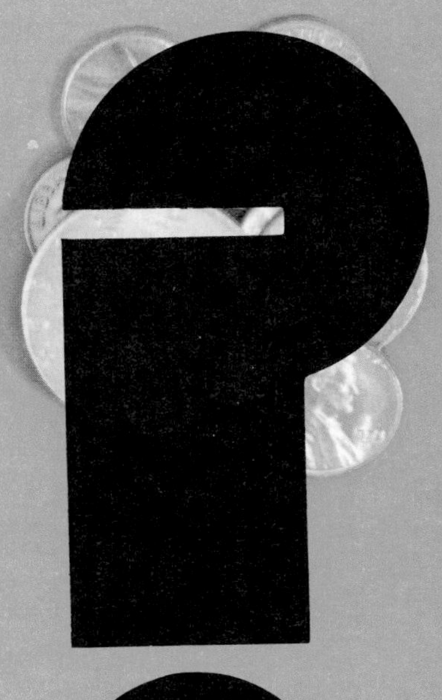

Dolores has some change in her purse.
She has no silver dollars.
She cannot make change for a nickel, dime, quarter, half dollar, or dollar.
What is the greatest amount of money she can have?

Mixed Numbers and Improper Fractions

For every whole number or mixed number, you can find equal fractions.

A. Use the number lines to find equal fractions.

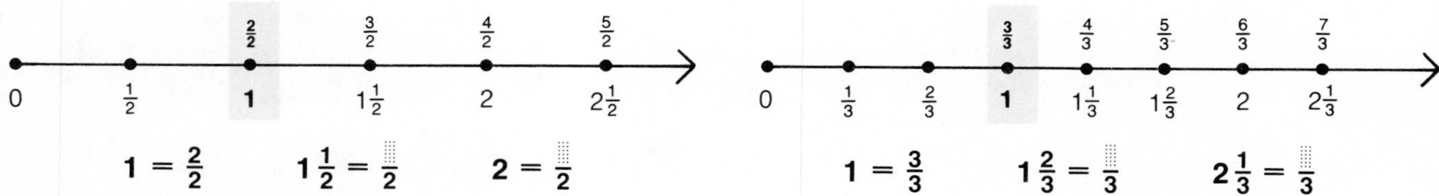

$1 = \frac{2}{2}$ $\quad 1\frac{1}{2} = \frac{\square}{2}$ $\quad 2 = \frac{\square}{2}$ $\quad 1 = \frac{3}{3}$ $\quad 1\frac{2}{3} = \frac{\square}{3}$ $\quad 2\frac{1}{3} = \frac{\square}{3}$

Fractions like $\frac{2}{2}$, $\frac{3}{2}$, $\frac{4}{2}$, $\frac{3}{3}$, $\frac{5}{3}$, and $\frac{7}{3}$ are ***improper fractions.***
The numerator is greater than or equal to the denominator.

B. Which of these are improper fractions?

$\frac{2}{3}$ $\quad \frac{5}{2}$ $\quad \frac{9}{6}$ $\quad \frac{11}{4}$ $\quad \frac{1}{8}$ $\quad \frac{6}{7}$ $\quad \frac{8}{7}$ $\quad \frac{15}{5}$ $\quad \frac{43}{10}$ $\quad \frac{8}{8}$

Give a mixed number and an improper fraction for each point that has a letter.

1.

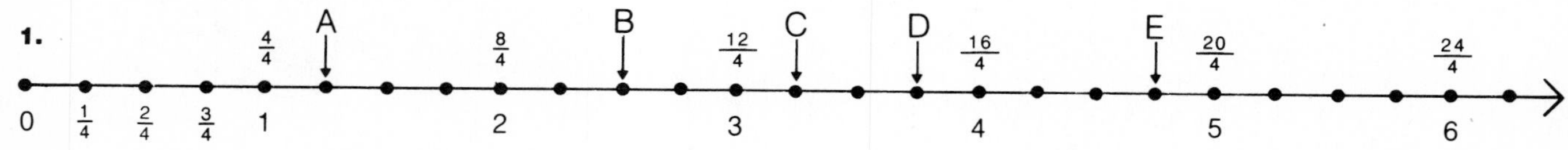

2.

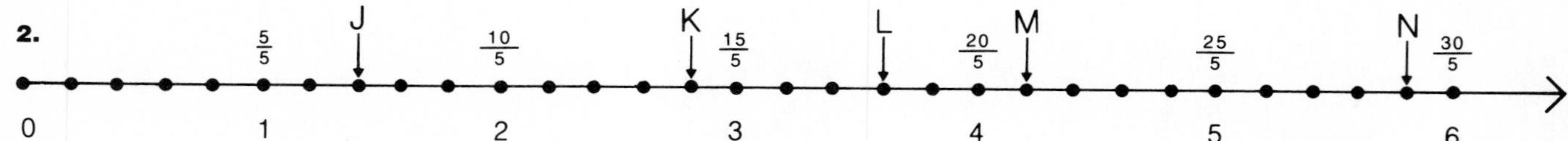

3. The cross-country trail is more than 4 kilometers long.
Each kilometer is marked in 10 equal parts.
Each part is $\frac{1}{10}$ kilometer.

Give a mixed number and an improper fraction
for the distance each person has jogged.

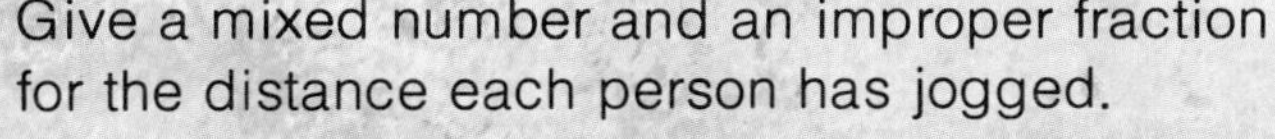

Divide.

1. $5\overline{)347}$
2. $7\overline{)296}$
3. $8\overline{)672}$
4. $9\overline{)4329}$
5. $4\overline{)379}$
6. $6\overline{)3471}$
7. $21\overline{)446}$
8. $32\overline{)419}$
9. $43\overline{)7862}$
10. $54\overline{)1289}$
11. $67\overline{)3490}$
12. $78\overline{)6298}$

Dividing to Find Mixed Numbers

In shop class, Ramona had to saw a 31-inch board into two equal pieces. How long was each piece?

Ramona divided and wrote her answer as a mixed number.

$$2\overline{)31}\quad 15\text{ R}1$$

$15\frac{1}{2}$ ← Remainder (1), ← Divisor (2)

Each piece was $15\frac{1}{2}$ inches long.

Divide. Express your answers as mixed numbers.

1. $2\overline{)45}$
2. $2\overline{)13}$
3. $2\overline{)59}$
4. $3\overline{)92}$
5. $4\overline{)31}$
6. $5\overline{)81}$
7. $12\overline{)75}$
8. $10\overline{)53}$
9. $10\overline{)153}$
10. $8\overline{)66}$
11. $3\overline{)32}$
12. $3\overline{)35}$
13. $3\overline{)38}$
14. $3\overline{)41}$
15. $3\overline{)44}$
16. A 17-inch piece of wire must be cut into 4 equal pieces. How long will each piece be?
17. A 32-meter piece of rope must be cut into 10 equal pieces. How long will each piece be?

More practice
Set A, page 302

Changing Improper Fractions to Mixed Numbers

A. Use the number line to find a mixed number for $\frac{14}{3}$.

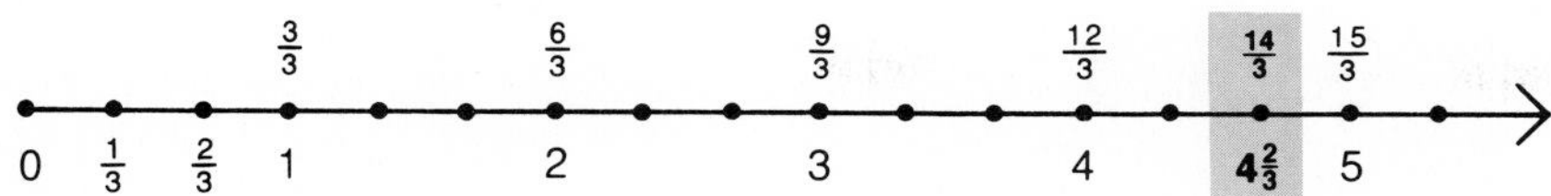

$$\frac{14}{3} = 4\frac{2}{3}$$

You can divide to find a mixed number for $\frac{14}{3}$.
Find 14 ÷ 3.

$$\begin{array}{r} 4 \\ 3\overline{)14} \\ -12 \\ \hline 2 \end{array} \quad 4\frac{2}{3}$$

You can think of $\frac{14}{3}$ as 14 ÷ 3.

B. Use the number line to find a whole number for $\frac{15}{5}$.

$\frac{5}{5}$ $\frac{10}{5}$ $\frac{15}{5}$ $\frac{20}{5}$ $\frac{25}{5}$

0 $\frac{1}{5}$ $\frac{2}{5}$ $\frac{3}{5}$ $\frac{4}{5}$ 1 2 3 4 5

$$\frac{15}{5} = 3$$

Divide to find a whole number for $\frac{15}{5}$.

15 ÷ 5 = 3

You can think of $\frac{15}{5}$ as 15 ÷ 5.

■ *You can divide the numerator by the denominator to find a mixed number or a whole number equal to an improper fraction.*

Write each improper fraction as a mixed number or a whole number.

1. $\frac{35}{3}$ **9.** $\frac{50}{6}$

2. $\frac{39}{4}$ **10.** $\frac{60}{2}$

3. $\frac{49}{10}$ **11.** $\frac{28}{4}$

4. $\frac{27}{2}$ **12.** $\frac{29}{4}$

5. $\frac{27}{3}$ **13.** $\frac{30}{4}$

6. $\frac{41}{8}$ **14.** $\frac{31}{4}$

7. $\frac{28}{5}$ **15.** $\frac{32}{4}$

8. $\frac{25}{6}$ **16.** $\frac{55}{12}$

More practice
Set B, page 302

Using the Remainder in Division Problems

When you divide to solve a problem, you need to decide whether a mixed number is a sensible answer.

A. Mr. Wood is making bookshelves. He has to saw a 75-inch board into 2 equal pieces. How long will each piece be?

A mixed number is a sensible answer to this problem.

$$2\overline{)75} = 37 \text{ R1}$$

$$37\frac{1}{2}$$

Each piece will be $37\frac{1}{2}$ inches long.

B. Mrs. Reed has 150 books to divide equally among 4 classrooms. How many books should she give to each room?

A mixed number is not a sensible answer to this problem.

$$4\overline{)150} = 37 \text{ R2}$$

She can give 37 books to each room. There will be 2 books left over.

Solve each problem. Give the answer as a mixed number only if it makes sense.

1. Mrs. Bowman cut 53 inches of ribbon into 4 equal pieces. How long was each piece?
2. Mr. Cutler has 76 pairs of scissors to distribute equally among 3 classrooms. How many pairs can he give to each room?
3. There are 90 students in Ms. Poole's swimming classes. She teaches 6 classes, all the same size. How many students are in each class?
4. Mr. Cleaver put 45 pounds of sausage into 12 equal packages. How much did he put into each package?

5. In 5 days, Mr. Wheeler drives 362 miles on his regular bus route. How many miles does he drive each day?

6. Mr. Silverman used 100 ounces of silver to make 16 identical spoons. How much silver did he use for each spoon?

7. Mrs. Burns and her cafeteria staff have prepared 325 meatballs for lunch. How many people can she serve if each person gets 3 meatballs?

8. Mr. Taylor is sewing buttons on sweaters. He has 100 buttons. Each sweater takes 6 buttons. How many sweaters can Mr. Taylor complete?

9. Mrs. Saddler has 180 pounds of feed to divide equally among 16 horses. How much feed can she give each horse?

10. Mrs. Burgher ordered 430 pounds of ground beef. She will send equal amounts to her 4 restaurants. How much will each restaurant get?

Keeping Skillful

Add.

1. $\frac{1}{3} + \frac{1}{3}$
2. $\frac{2}{8} + \frac{3}{8}$
3. $\frac{1}{5} + \frac{3}{5}$
4. $\frac{7}{10} + \frac{2}{10}$
5. $\frac{1}{3} + \frac{1}{6}$
6. $\frac{1}{2} + \frac{3}{8}$
7. $\frac{3}{10} + \frac{2}{5}$
8. $\frac{1}{5} + \frac{1}{4}$
9. $\frac{2}{3} + \frac{1}{4}$
10. $\frac{2}{5} + \frac{1}{3}$
11. $\frac{5}{6} + \frac{1}{8}$
12. $\frac{1}{9} + \frac{1}{12}$

Subtract.

13. $\frac{7}{8} - \frac{2}{8}$
14. $\frac{1}{2} - \frac{1}{2}$
15. $\frac{5}{5} - \frac{2}{5}$
16. $\frac{4}{3} - \frac{2}{3}$
17. $\frac{7}{8} - \frac{1}{4}$
18. $\frac{6}{10} - \frac{1}{5}$
19. $\frac{4}{3} - \frac{6}{9}$
20. $\frac{1}{6} - \frac{1}{9}$
21. $\frac{2}{3} - \frac{1}{2}$
22. $\frac{7}{10} - \frac{1}{2}$
23. $\frac{6}{5} - \frac{1}{2}$
24. $\frac{5}{4} - \frac{2}{3}$

Mixo-Fracto Game

A game for two to four players

Object: To match cards that show a mixed number and a fraction equal to the mixed number

Matching pair

Rules:

1. Deal five cards to each player. Place the remaining cards face down in a center pile. Turn the top card over to start the discard pile.
2. The person to the left of the dealer plays first. On a turn, each player
   - a. draws the top card from either the center pile or the discard pile.
   - b. looks for matching pairs and places each pair face up on the table.
   - c. puts one card on the discard pile. Then the next player takes a turn.
3. Suppose you incorrectly match a pair and someone challenges you. You must keep the pair in your hand and lose your next turn.
4. The game ends when a player has no more cards or when all the cards in the center pile have been used.

Scoring:

The first person to play all the cards is the winner. If the cards in the center pile are used before anyone goes out, the player who has the greatest number of pairs is the winner.

Make two cards for each of these numbers.

$\frac{7}{3}$	$2\frac{1}{3}$
$\frac{8}{3}$	$2\frac{2}{3}$
$\frac{9}{4}$	$2\frac{1}{4}$
$\frac{11}{4}$	$2\frac{3}{4}$

Make three cards for each of these numbers.

$\frac{3}{2}$	$1\frac{1}{2}$
$\frac{5}{2}$	$2\frac{1}{2}$
$\frac{4}{3}$	$1\frac{1}{3}$
$\frac{5}{3}$	$1\frac{2}{3}$
$\frac{5}{4}$	$1\frac{1}{4}$
$\frac{7}{4}$	$1\frac{3}{4}$

Check Yourself
Meaning of Mixed Numbers, Pages 242–256

Meaning of mixed numbers, pages 242–247

1. How many cakes are shown?

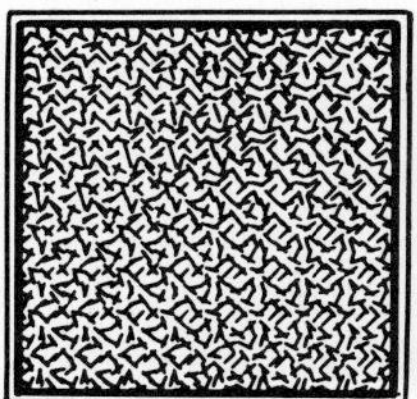

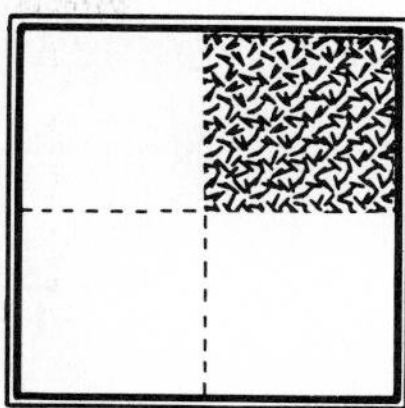

2. How many cartons of cola are shown?

3. Give the length of the paper clip to the nearest $\frac{1}{4}$ inch.

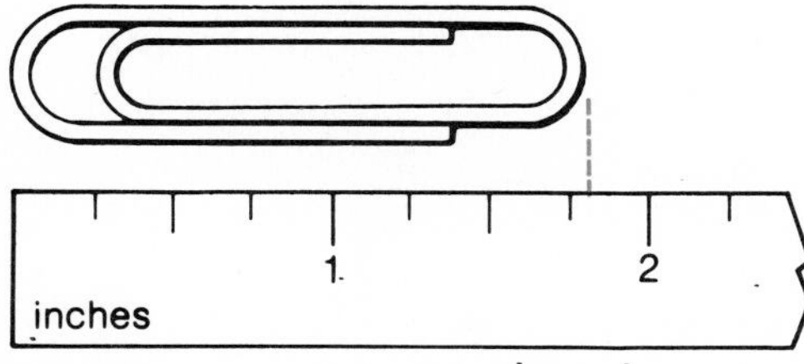

4. Give the length of the eraser to the nearest $\frac{1}{8}$ inch.

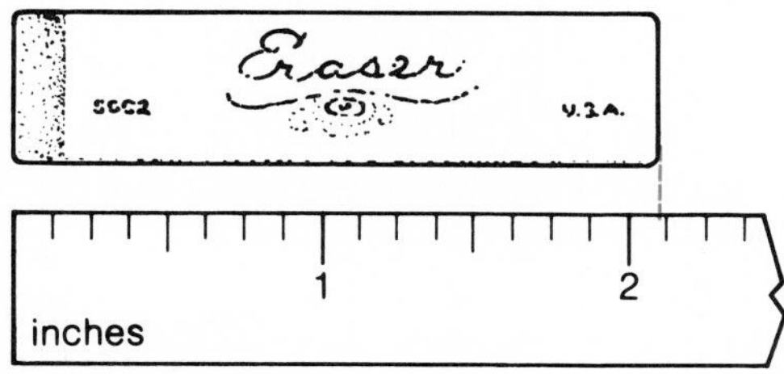

Comparing mixed numbers, pages 248–249

5. Which weight is greater?

$4\frac{7}{8}$ oz. $5\frac{1}{4}$ oz.

6. Sheila walked $3\frac{7}{10}$ miles.
Lynn walked $3\frac{2}{5}$ miles.
Who walked farther?

Dividing to get mixed numbers, pages 252, 254–255

Give your answers as mixed numbers.

7. $10\overline{)37}$

8. Mr. Cable cut a rope 125 yards long into 3 equal pieces. How long was each piece?

Changing improper fractions, pages 250–251, 253, 256

Give each improper fraction as a whole number or a mixed number.

9. $\frac{27}{5}$ **10.** $\frac{18}{3}$

Adding Mixed Numbers: Same Denominator

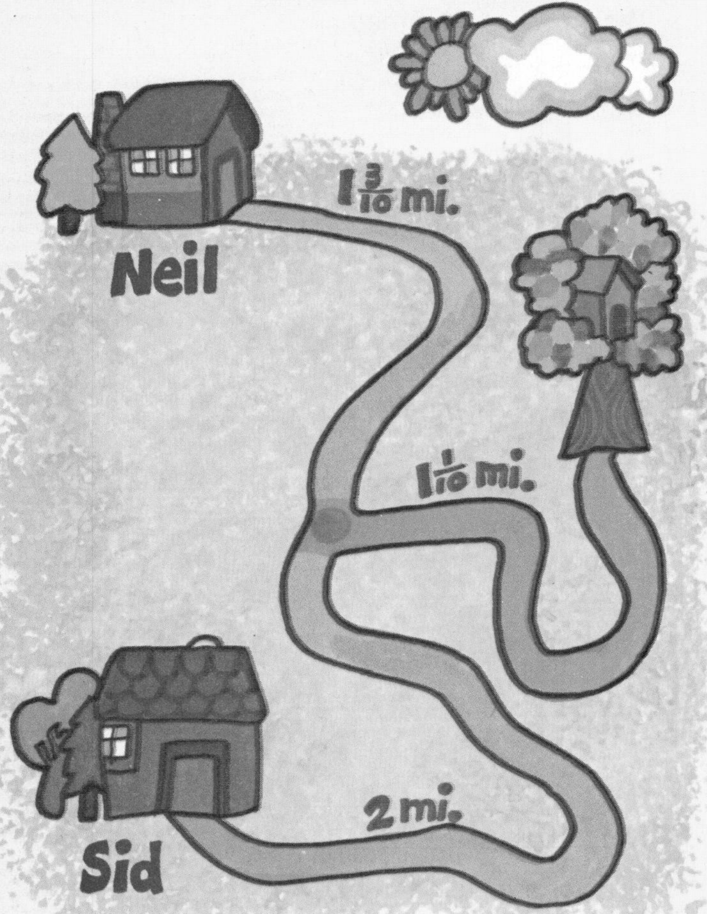

A. How far does Neil bicycle from his home to the tree house?

Find $1\frac{3}{10} + 1\frac{1}{10}$.

$$\begin{array}{r} 1\frac{3}{10} \\ +\,1\frac{1}{10} \\ \hline 2\frac{4}{10} = 2\frac{2}{5} \end{array}$$

Add the fractions.
Then add the whole numbers.

Neil bicycles $2\frac{4}{10}$, or $2\frac{2}{5}$, miles.

B. How far does Sid bicycle from his home to the tree house?

Find $2 + 1\frac{1}{10}$.

$$\begin{array}{r} 2 \\ +\,1\frac{1}{10} \\ \hline 3\frac{1}{10} \end{array}$$

Sid bicycles $3\frac{1}{10}$ miles.

Find each sum.

1. $\begin{array}{r} 2\frac{1}{3} \\ +\,1\frac{1}{3} \\ \hline \end{array}$ **2.** $\begin{array}{r} 5\frac{1}{4} \\ +\,2\frac{1}{4} \\ \hline \end{array}$ **3.** $\begin{array}{r} 1\frac{2}{7} \\ +\,2\frac{3}{7} \\ \hline \end{array}$ **4.** $\begin{array}{r} 2\frac{1}{6} \\ +\,\frac{4}{6} \\ \hline \end{array}$ **5.** $\begin{array}{r} 2\frac{2}{3} \\ +\,7 \\ \hline \end{array}$

6. $9\frac{3}{8} + 5\frac{4}{8}$

7. $\frac{3}{10} + 6\frac{4}{10}$

8. $4\frac{2}{5} + 4\frac{2}{5}$

9. $6\frac{1}{4} + 3\frac{2}{4}$

10. $7\frac{4}{9} + 8\frac{2}{9}$

11. $13\frac{7}{10} + 9\frac{1}{10}$

12. $3\frac{1}{3} + \frac{1}{3}$

13. $10\frac{1}{8} + 12\frac{5}{8}$

14. $29\frac{1}{3} + 58\frac{1}{3}$

15. $4\frac{5}{7} + 6$

16. $34 + 18\frac{4}{5}$

17. $9\frac{1}{16} + 100\frac{1}{16}$

More practice
Set C, page 302

Find the total amount.

18.

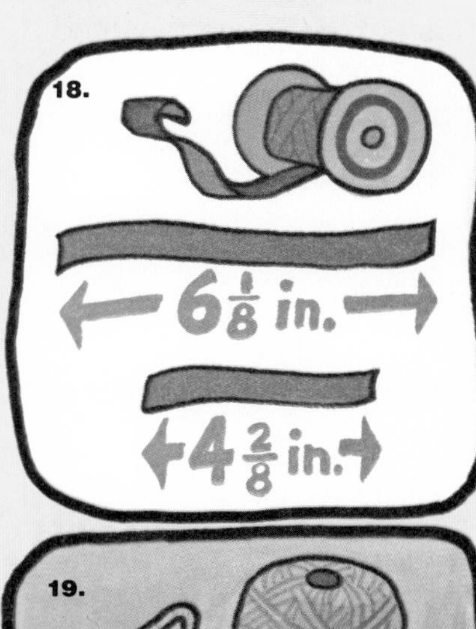

19.

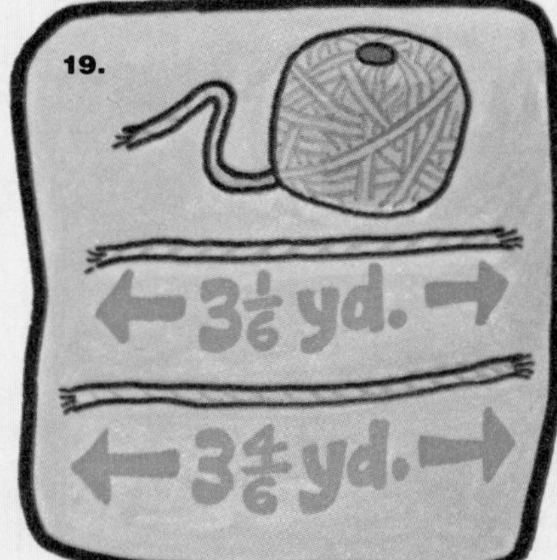

20.

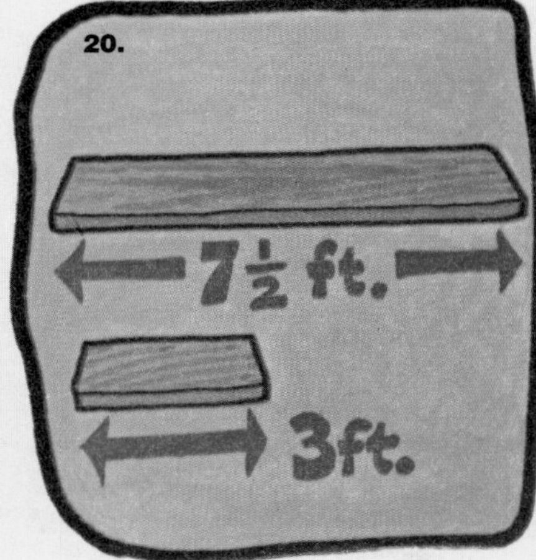

21.

22.

23.

24.

25. How far is the top of Sid's head from the floor?

Adding Mixed Numbers: Renaming the Sum

A. Tracie added to find how much sugar she used. Then she renamed the sum.

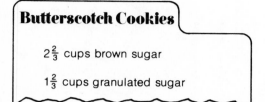

Butterscotch Cookies

$2\frac{2}{3}$ cups brown sugar

$1\frac{2}{3}$ cups granulated sugar

$$\begin{array}{r} 2\frac{2}{3} \\ +\ 1\frac{2}{3} \\ \hline 3\frac{4}{3} = 4\frac{1}{3} \end{array}$$

This is how Tracie renamed $3\frac{4}{3}$.

$3\frac{4}{3}$

$3 + \frac{4}{3}$

$3 + 1\frac{1}{3}$

$4\frac{1}{3}$

Tracie used $4\frac{1}{3}$ cups of sugar.

Here are two more sums. Rename them.

B. $3\frac{4}{4}$

$3 + \frac{4}{4}$

$3 + 1$

$\square$

C. $2\frac{7}{5}$

$2 + \frac{7}{5}$

$2 + 1\frac{\square}{5}$

$\square$

Rename these mixed numbers. The fraction part in your answer must be less than 1.

1. $4\frac{3}{2} = 5\frac{\square}{2}$

2. $9\frac{5}{3} = 10\frac{\square}{3}$

3. $8\frac{7}{5} = \square\frac{2}{5}$

4. $7\frac{11}{6} = \square\frac{5}{6}$

5. $3\frac{11}{8} = 4\frac{\square}{8}$

6. $2\frac{5}{5} = \square$

7. $2\frac{3}{3}$

8. $2\frac{8}{8}$

9. $1\frac{6}{4}$

10. $99\frac{13}{10}$

11. $5\frac{19}{12}$

12. $20\frac{16}{16}$

Add. Rename each sum.

13. $3\frac{1}{2} + 2\frac{1}{2}$

14. $5\frac{2}{3} + 7\frac{2}{3}$

15. $5\frac{3}{4} + 8\frac{1}{4}$

16. $1\frac{4}{5} + 1\frac{3}{5}$

17. $\frac{5}{7} + 8\frac{6}{7}$

18. $6\frac{1}{5} + 3\frac{4}{5}$

19. $3\frac{7}{10} + 1\frac{4}{10}$

20. $22\frac{5}{6} + \frac{1}{6}$

21. $12\frac{5}{8} + 17\frac{6}{8}$

Add. Rename each sum.

22. $9\frac{3}{4} + 5\frac{3}{4}$

23. $9\frac{9}{12} + 5\frac{9}{12}$

24. $14\frac{1}{3} + 6\frac{2}{3}$

25. $12\frac{5}{8} + 8\frac{5}{8}$

26. $1\frac{7}{9} + 1\frac{3}{9}$

27. $11\frac{2}{3} + 5\frac{2}{3}$

28. $3\frac{4}{5} + 7\frac{2}{5}$

29. $40\frac{7}{10} + 11\frac{9}{10}$

30. $6\frac{3}{4} + 7\frac{1}{4}$

31. $13\frac{1}{2} + 24\frac{1}{2}$

32. $6\frac{9}{10} + 5\frac{3}{10}$

33. $3\frac{7}{16} + 5\frac{9}{16}$

Tracie wants to try both recipes for apricot bread.
For each ingredient, find the total amount she needs.

34. Honey **35.** Apricot juice **36.** Mashed apricots **37.** Baking powder

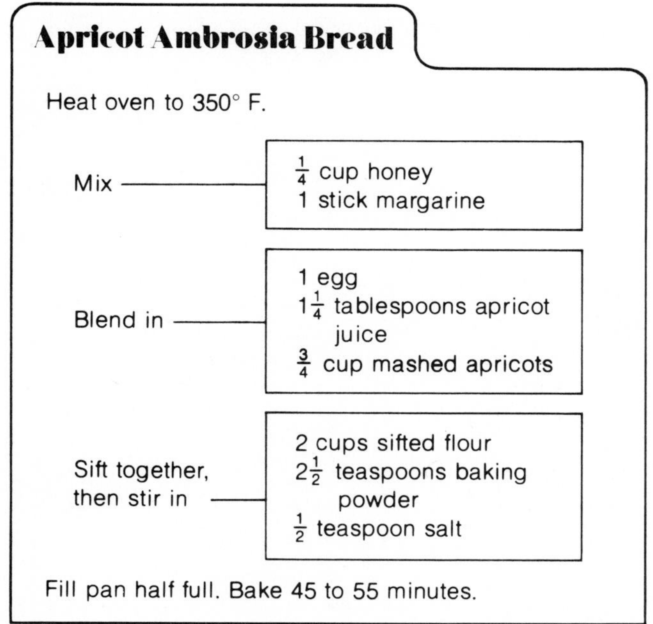

Apricot Ambrosia Bread

Heat oven to 350° F.

Mix — $\frac{1}{4}$ cup honey; 1 stick margarine

Blend in — 1 egg; $1\frac{1}{4}$ tablespoons apricot juice; $\frac{3}{4}$ cup mashed apricots

Sift together, then stir in — 2 cups sifted flour; $2\frac{1}{2}$ teaspoons baking powder; $\frac{1}{2}$ teaspoon salt

Fill pan half full. Bake 45 to 55 minutes.

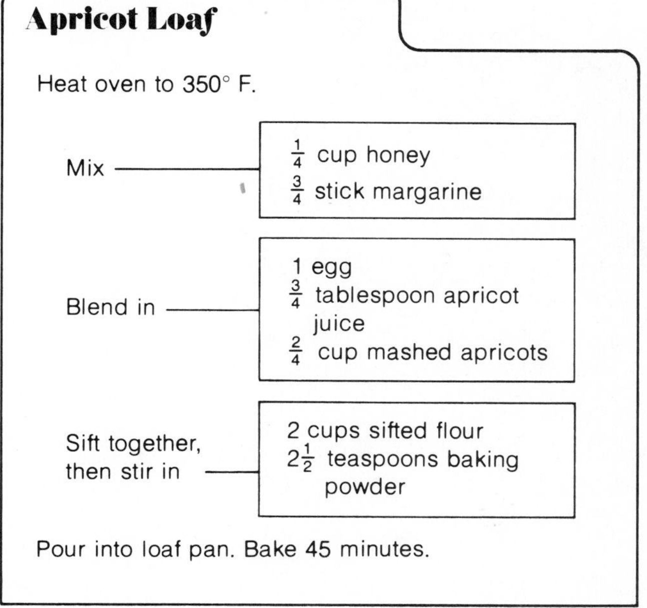

Apricot Loaf

Heat oven to 350° F.

Mix — $\frac{1}{4}$ cup honey; $\frac{3}{4}$ stick margarine

Blend in — 1 egg; $\frac{3}{4}$ tablespoon apricot juice; $\frac{2}{4}$ cup mashed apricots

Sift together, then stir in — 2 cups sifted flour; $2\frac{1}{2}$ teaspoons baking powder

Pour into loaf pan. Bake 45 minutes.

More practice
Set D, page 302

Adding Mixed Numbers: Different Denominators

Doug played a game. He tossed two paper clips into an egg carton with numbers on it. What was his total score?

Find $5\frac{1}{4} + 1\frac{7}{8}$.

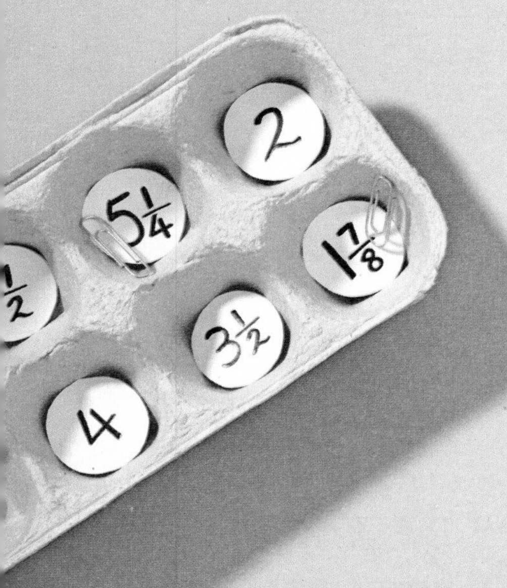

Before you add the fractions, you need a common denominator.

$$\begin{array}{r} 5\frac{1}{4} = 5\frac{2}{8} \\ +\ 1\frac{7}{8} = 1\frac{7}{8} \\ \hline 6\frac{9}{8} = 7\frac{1}{8} \end{array}$$

Doug's total score was $7\frac{1}{8}$.

Add. Rename the sum if necessary.

1. $\begin{array}{r} 4\frac{5}{6} = 4\frac{5}{6} \\ +\ 1\frac{2}{3} = 1\frac{\square}{6} \\ \hline \end{array}$

2. $\begin{array}{r} 6\frac{4}{5} = 6\frac{\square}{10} \\ +\ 7\frac{1}{2} = 7\frac{\square}{10} \\ \hline \end{array}$

3. $\begin{array}{r} 5\frac{1}{4} = 5\frac{\square}{12} \\ +\ 2\frac{2}{3} = 2\frac{\square}{12} \\ \hline \end{array}$

4. $\begin{array}{r} 1\frac{1}{6} = 1\frac{\square}{24} \\ +\ 1\frac{7}{8} = 1\frac{\square}{24} \\ \hline \end{array}$

5. $\begin{array}{r} 12\frac{3}{10} \\ +\ 8\frac{1}{2} \\ \hline \end{array}$

6. $\begin{array}{r} 4\frac{1}{2} \\ +\ 6\frac{1}{3} \\ \hline \end{array}$

7. $\begin{array}{r} 8\frac{1}{4} \\ +\ 7\frac{1}{3} \\ \hline \end{array}$

8. $\begin{array}{r} 11\frac{9}{16} \\ +\ 3\frac{1}{4} \\ \hline \end{array}$

9. $\begin{array}{r} 7\frac{1}{2} \\ +\ 2\frac{5}{8} \\ \hline \end{array}$

10. $\begin{array}{r} 2\frac{3}{4} \\ +\ 1\frac{2}{5} \\ \hline \end{array}$

11. $6\frac{3}{5} + 4\frac{1}{10}$

12. $2\frac{1}{3} + 4\frac{1}{2}$

13. $7\frac{3}{4} + 3\frac{1}{2}$

14. $3\frac{7}{12} + 5\frac{1}{4}$

15. $12\frac{1}{2} + 14\frac{7}{10}$

16. $8\frac{3}{4} + 12\frac{1}{3}$

17. $2\frac{1}{3} + 9\frac{3}{8}$

18. $10\frac{5}{16} + 10\frac{1}{2}$

More practice
Set E, page 302

Find each player's total score.

19. Virginia

20. Marcie

21. Alan

Add.

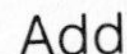

22. (+ across, + down)

$23\frac{1}{5}$	$19\frac{1}{2}$	
$16\frac{1}{2}$	$39\frac{1}{5}$	

23. (+ across, + down)

$15\frac{2}{3}$	$35\frac{1}{4}$	
$21\frac{5}{6}$	$48\frac{1}{2}$	

24. (+ across, + down)

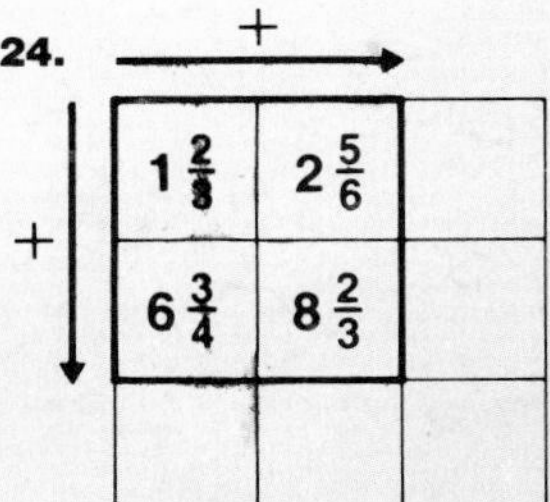

$1\frac{2}{3}$	$2\frac{5}{6}$	
$6\frac{3}{4}$	$8\frac{2}{3}$	

Using Addition of Mixed Numbers: Bicycle Trips

Last summer, Eric bicycled around Flat Country. The distances between towns and Eric's traveling times are given on the map.

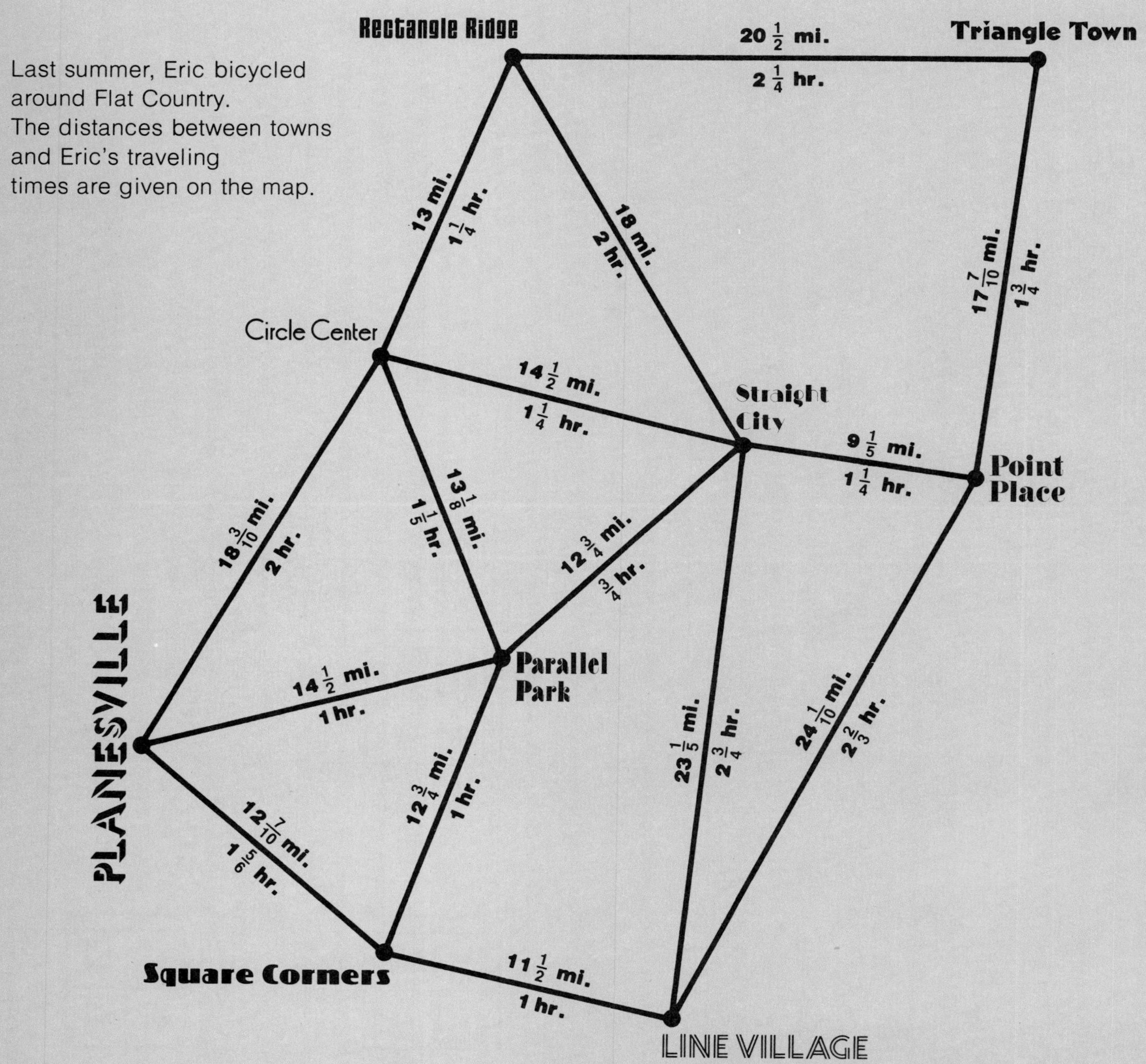

A. How many miles was the trip from Circle Center to Straight City to Point Place?

$$\begin{array}{r} 14\frac{1}{2} = 14\frac{5}{10} \\ +\ 9\frac{1}{5} = \ 9\frac{2}{10} \\ \hline 23\frac{7}{10} \end{array}$$

The distance was $23\frac{7}{10}$ miles.

B. How much time did this trip take?

$$\begin{array}{r} 1\frac{1}{4} \\ +\ 1\frac{1}{4} \\ \hline 2\frac{2}{4} = 2\frac{1}{2} \end{array}$$

The traveling time was $2\frac{1}{2}$ hours.

Eric kept a record of his travels.
Find the distance for each trip.
Then find the traveling time.

		Distance	Time
1.	Rectangle Ridge to Triangle Town to Point Place		
2.	Circle Center to Straight City to Line Village		
3.	Rectangle Ridge to Straight City to Parallel Park		
4.	Planesville to Square Corners to Line Village		
5.	Straight City to Point Place to Line Village		
6.	Rectangle Ridge to Circle Center to Planesville		
7.	Straight City to Parallel Park to Square Corners		
8.	Planesville to Parallel Park to Straight City		
9.	Circle Center to Parallel Park to Square Corners		
10.	Triangle Town to Point Place to Line Village		
11.	Parallel Park to Square Corners to Line Village		
12.	Triangle Town to Point Place to Straight City		

Adding Three Mixed Numbers

What is the perimeter of this triangle?

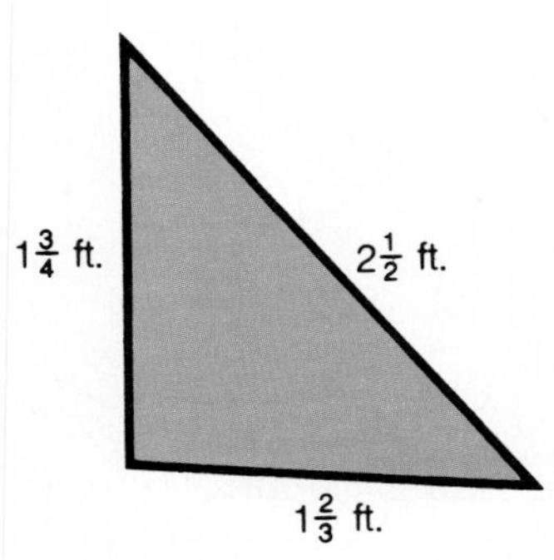

Find $1\frac{3}{4} + 1\frac{2}{3} + 2\frac{1}{2}$.

Find a common denominator for the fractions. Then add.

$$\begin{array}{r} 1\frac{3}{4} = 1\frac{9}{12} \\ 1\frac{2}{3} = 1\frac{8}{12} \\ +\ 2\frac{1}{2} = 2\frac{6}{12} \\ \hline 4\frac{23}{12} = 5\frac{11}{12} \end{array}$$

The perimeter is $5\frac{11}{12}$ feet.

Find each sum.

1. $1\frac{2}{3} = 1\frac{\square}{12}$, $1\frac{1}{4} = 1\frac{\square}{12}$, $+\ 3\frac{1}{2} = 3\frac{\square}{12}$

2. $2\frac{5}{8} = 2\frac{\square}{8}$, $1\frac{1}{4} = 1\frac{\square}{8}$, $+\ 3\frac{1}{2} = 3\frac{\square}{8}$

3. $9\frac{7}{8} = 9\frac{\square}{24}$, $3\frac{1}{6} = 3\frac{\square}{24}$, $+\ 2\frac{1}{2} = 2\frac{\square}{24}$

4. $7\frac{1}{3}$, $3\frac{3}{4}$, $+\ 6\frac{1}{2}$

5. $4\frac{3}{4}$, $1\frac{1}{2}$, $+\ 5\frac{2}{3}$

6. $2\frac{1}{2}$, $4\frac{1}{4}$, $+\ 6\frac{3}{8}$

7. $9\frac{1}{2}$, $4\frac{7}{8}$, $+\ 6\frac{3}{4}$

8. $7\frac{1}{6}$, $7\frac{1}{2}$, $+\ 7\frac{5}{8}$

9. $5\frac{1}{2}$, $2\frac{3}{8}$, $+\ 3\frac{5}{6}$

10. $7\frac{2}{3} + 4\frac{1}{2} + 3\frac{1}{6}$

11. $4\frac{3}{8} + 6\frac{3}{4} + 2\frac{1}{2}$

12. $6\frac{1}{2} + 3\frac{1}{4} + 4\frac{1}{3}$

13. $3\frac{1}{4} + 2\frac{5}{6} + 7\frac{1}{2}$

14. $4\frac{4}{5} + 2\frac{1}{2} + 8\frac{7}{10}$

15. $10\frac{5}{6} + 10\frac{7}{8} + 10\frac{1}{2}$

More practice
Set F, page 302

Find the perimeter of each polygon.

16.

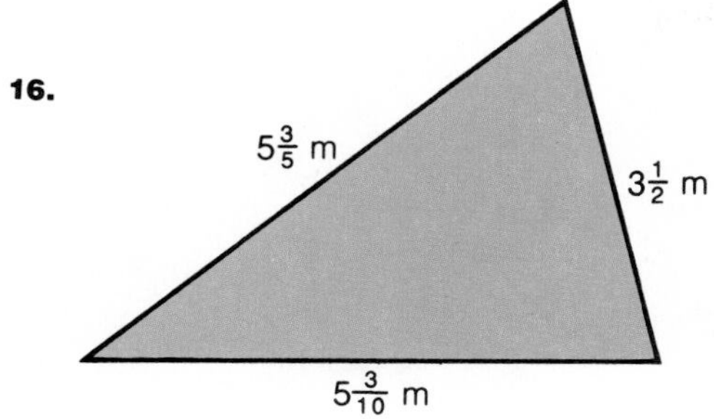

17.

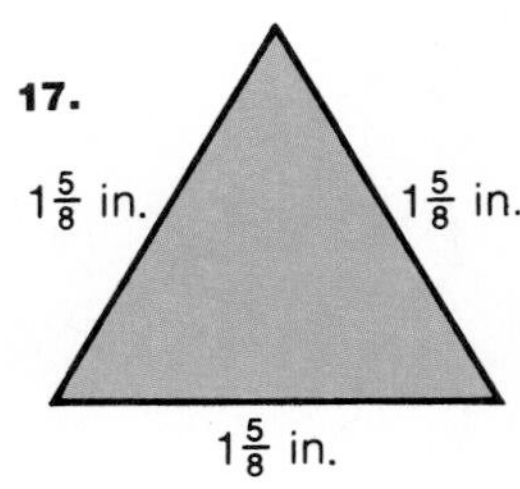

18.

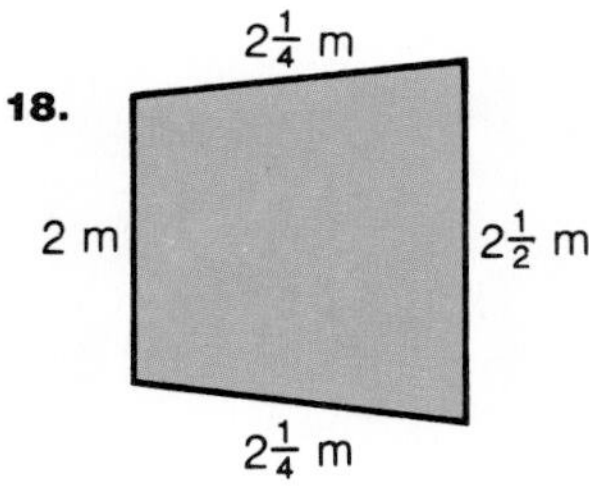

19.

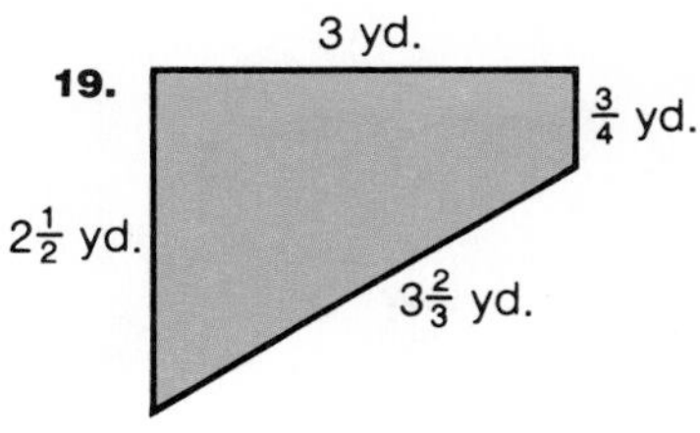

20.

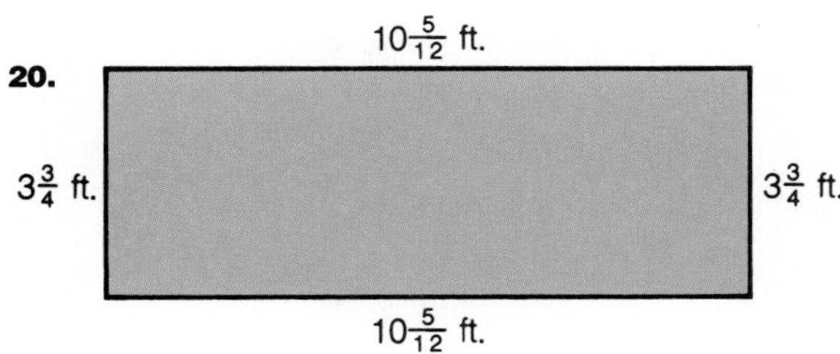

Time Out!

In the mirror,
Alice can see
the reflection
of a clock
in another room.

What times are shown?

1. 

2. 

3. 

4. 

Subtracting Mixed Numbers: Same Denominator

How far has Willa Worm stretched beyond her normal length?

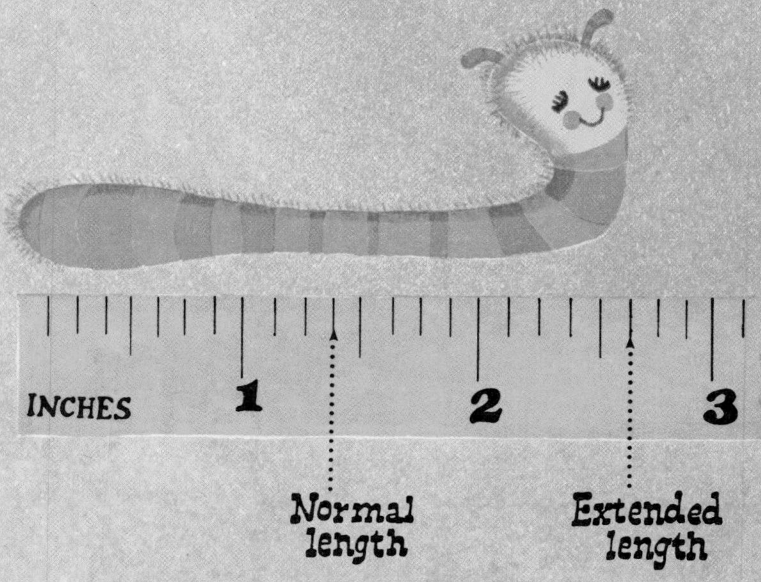

Find $2\frac{5}{8} - 1\frac{3}{8}$.

Subtract the fractions.
Then subtract the whole numbers.

$$\begin{array}{r} 2\frac{5}{8} \\ -\ 1\frac{3}{8} \\ \hline 1\frac{2}{8} = 1\frac{1}{4} \end{array}$$

Willa has stretched $1\frac{1}{4}$ inches.

Subtract.

1. $14\frac{3}{5} - 6\frac{1}{5}$

2. $8\frac{4}{6} - 3\frac{2}{6}$

3. $14\frac{3}{4} - 7\frac{1}{4}$

4. $7\frac{9}{10} - 3$

5. $9\frac{2}{3} - 9\frac{1}{3}$

6. $7\frac{10}{12} - 2\frac{3}{12}$

7. $38\frac{6}{7} - 17\frac{4}{7}$

8. $16\frac{7}{9} - 7\frac{5}{9}$

9. $29\frac{9}{10} - 16\frac{6}{10}$

10. $6\frac{5}{8} - 2\frac{1}{8}$

11. $6\frac{2}{3} - 4\frac{1}{3}$

12. $17\frac{3}{4} - 12$

13. $5\frac{4}{9} - 5\frac{1}{9}$

14. $12\frac{5}{7} - 6$

15. $25\frac{11}{16} - 5\frac{7}{16}$

16. $10\frac{5}{6} - 4\frac{1}{6}$

17. $3\frac{4}{5} - \frac{2}{5}$

18. $68\frac{5}{10} - 43\frac{2}{10}$

19. $14\frac{9}{16} - 14\frac{3}{16}$

More practice
Set G, page 303

Find the difference between the heights of

20. Gerry and Kate.

21. Gerry and Andrea.

22. Gerry and Paul.

23. Kate and Andrea.

24. Kate and Paul.

25. Andrea and Paul.

Find the difference between the weights of

26. Gerry and Kate.

27. Gerry and Andrea.

28. Gerry and Paul.

29. Kate and Andrea.

30. Kate and Paul.

31. Andrea and Paul.

Renaming to Subtract Mixed Numbers

A. Sometimes you need to rename a whole number before you subtract.

Find $8 - 2\frac{3}{4}$.

How can you subtract $\frac{3}{4}$?

$$\begin{array}{r} 8 \\ -\ 2\frac{3}{4} \\ \hline \end{array}$$

You need a fraction.
Rename 8.

$$8 = 7\frac{\square}{4}$$

$8 = 7 + 1$

$\quad = 7 + \frac{4}{4}$

$\quad = 7\frac{4}{4}$

$$8 = 7\frac{4}{4}$$

Subtract.

$$\begin{array}{rcl} 8 & = & 7\frac{4}{4} \\ -\ 2\frac{3}{4} & = & 2\frac{3}{4} \\ \hline & & 5\frac{1}{4} \end{array}$$

Rename these whole numbers.

1. $3 = 2\frac{\square}{2}$

2. $6 = 5\frac{\square}{3}$

3. $7 = 6\frac{\square}{10}$

4. $7 = 6\frac{\square}{4}$

5. $7 = 6\frac{\square}{8}$

6. $4 = 3\frac{\square}{5}$

7. $2 = 1\frac{\square}{8}$

8. $1 = \frac{\square}{7}$

9. $5 = 4\frac{\square}{3}$

10. $12 = 11\frac{\square}{5}$

Subtract.

11. $\begin{array}{rcl} 6 & = & 5\frac{\square}{2} \\ -\ 4\frac{1}{2} & = & 4\frac{1}{2} \\ \hline \end{array}$

12. $\begin{array}{rcl} 7 & = & 6\frac{\square}{4} \\ -\ 2\frac{3}{4} & = & 2\frac{3}{4} \\ \hline \end{array}$

13. $\begin{array}{rcl} 2 & = & 1\frac{\square}{8} \\ -\ 1\frac{5}{8} & = & 1\frac{5}{8} \\ \hline \end{array}$

14. $\begin{array}{rcl} 9 & = & 8\frac{\square}{10} \\ -\ 3\frac{3}{10} & = & 3\frac{3}{10} \\ \hline \end{array}$

15. $\begin{array}{r} 5 \\ -\ 1\frac{1}{2} \\ \hline \end{array}$

16. $\begin{array}{r} 4 \\ -\ 2\frac{5}{6} \\ \hline \end{array}$

17. $\begin{array}{r} 11 \\ -\ 6\frac{3}{5} \\ \hline \end{array}$

18. $\begin{array}{r} 20 \\ -\ 14\frac{2}{3} \\ \hline \end{array}$

19. $16 - 9\frac{1}{3}$

20. $8 - 2\frac{1}{2}$

21. $10 - 3\frac{3}{4}$

22. $25 - 5\frac{7}{12}$

23. $17 - 16\frac{2}{5}$

24. $42 - 41\frac{3}{8}$

25. $32 - 9\frac{7}{10}$

B. Sometimes you need to rename a mixed number.

Find $4\frac{1}{5} - 1\frac{2}{5}$.

How can you subtract the fractions?

$$\begin{array}{r} 4\frac{1}{5} \\ -\,1\frac{2}{5} \\ \hline \end{array}$$

Rename $4\frac{1}{5}$.

$$4\frac{1}{5} = 3\frac{\square}{5}$$

$4\frac{1}{5} = 4 + \frac{1}{5}$

$= 3\frac{5}{5} + \frac{1}{5}$

$= 3\frac{6}{5}$

$$4\frac{1}{5} = 3\frac{6}{5}$$

Subtract.

$$\begin{array}{rr} 4\frac{1}{5} = & 3\frac{6}{5} \\ -\,1\frac{2}{5} = & 1\frac{2}{5} \\ \hline & 2\frac{4}{5} \end{array}$$

Rename these mixed numbers.

1. $5\frac{1}{2} = 4\frac{\square}{2}$
2. $6\frac{3}{10} = 5\frac{\square}{10}$
3. $2\frac{1}{6} = 1\frac{\square}{6}$
4. $9\frac{2}{4} = 8\frac{\square}{4}$
5. $7\frac{1}{3} = 6\frac{\square}{3}$
6. $7\frac{1}{8} = 6\frac{\square}{8}$
7. $8\frac{1}{3} = 7\frac{\square}{3}$
8. $10\frac{4}{5} = 9\frac{\square}{5}$
9. $4\frac{7}{16} = 3\frac{\square}{16}$
10. $13\frac{5}{6} = 12\frac{\square}{6}$

Subtract.

11. $\begin{array}{rr} 6\frac{3}{10} = & 5\frac{\square}{10} \\ -\,4\frac{7}{10} = & 4\frac{7}{10} \\ \hline \end{array}$

12. $\begin{array}{rr} 9\frac{1}{6} = & 8\frac{\square}{6} \\ -\,3\frac{5}{6} = & 3\frac{5}{6} \\ \hline \end{array}$

13. $\begin{array}{rr} 18\frac{1}{3} = & 17\frac{\square}{3} \\ -\,17\frac{2}{3} = & 17\frac{2}{3} \\ \hline \end{array}$

14. $\begin{array}{rr} 11\frac{3}{8} = & 10\frac{\square}{8} \\ -\,6\frac{7}{8} = & 6\frac{7}{8} \\ \hline \end{array}$

15. $\begin{array}{r} 9\frac{1}{4} \\ -\,1\frac{3}{4} \\ \hline \end{array}$

16. $\begin{array}{r} 15\frac{2}{5} \\ -\,7\frac{4}{5} \\ \hline \end{array}$

17. $\begin{array}{r} 30\frac{1}{8} \\ -\,19\frac{7}{8} \\ \hline \end{array}$

18. $\begin{array}{r} 8\frac{1}{10} \\ -\,5\frac{5}{10} \\ \hline \end{array}$

19. $8\frac{1}{3} - 2\frac{2}{3}$
20. $7\frac{1}{4} - 5\frac{3}{4}$
21. $4\frac{2}{10} - 3\frac{7}{10}$
22. $50\frac{1}{5} - 39\frac{3}{5}$
23. $4\frac{3}{16} - 1\frac{7}{16}$
24. $28\frac{5}{8} - 3\frac{6}{8}$
25. $18\frac{3}{10} - 7\frac{9}{10}$

More practice
Set H, page 303

Subtracting Mixed Numbers: Different Denominators

Sometimes you need to find a common denominator before you subtract mixed numbers.

A. Find $2\frac{3}{5} - 1\frac{1}{2}$.

$$\begin{array}{r} 2\frac{3}{5} = 2\frac{6}{10} \\ -\ 1\frac{1}{2} = 1\frac{5}{10} \\ \hline 1\frac{1}{10} \end{array}$$

B. Find $6\frac{1}{2} - 2\frac{3}{8}$.

$$\begin{array}{r} 6\frac{1}{2} = 6\frac{4}{8} \\ -\ 2\frac{3}{8} = 2\frac{3}{8} \\ \hline 4\frac{1}{8} \end{array}$$

Subtract.

1. $12\frac{4}{5} = 12\frac{\square}{10}$; $-\ 6\frac{1}{2} = 6\frac{\square}{10}$

2. $11\frac{2}{3} = 11\frac{\square}{6}$; $-\ 4\frac{1}{2} = 4\frac{\square}{6}$

3. $6\frac{7}{8} = 6\frac{7}{8}$; $-\ 5\frac{1}{2} = 5\frac{\square}{8}$

4. $3\frac{5}{6} = 3\frac{\square}{12}$; $-\ 1\frac{3}{4} = 1\frac{\square}{12}$

5. $17\frac{3}{5} - 3\frac{1}{2}$

6. $19\frac{9}{10} - 12\frac{3}{5}$

7. $15\frac{1}{2} - 8\frac{1}{3}$

8. $14\frac{5}{6} - 6\frac{2}{3}$

9. $26\frac{3}{4} - 12\frac{3}{8}$

10. $10\frac{1}{2} - 7\frac{1}{8}$

11. $16\frac{1}{2} - 11\frac{2}{5}$

12. $9\frac{2}{3} - 8\frac{1}{2}$

13. $10\frac{5}{8} - 2\frac{1}{4}$

14. $7\frac{1}{2} - 4\frac{3}{8}$

15. $6\frac{2}{3} - 4\frac{1}{4}$

16. $12\frac{1}{4} - 9\frac{1}{6}$

17. $8\frac{3}{4} - 5\frac{2}{3}$

18. $4\frac{5}{6} - 1\frac{2}{3}$

19. $9\frac{3}{4} - 7\frac{1}{2}$

20. $29\frac{5}{8} - 13\frac{1}{16}$

More practice
Set I, page 303

During February, six different swimming teams are recording the number of miles they swim. Each team has a goal.

Use the table below. How many miles does each team have left to swim?

	Team	Goal (miles)	Miles recorded
21.	Sea Stars	$30\frac{7}{10}$	$20\frac{2}{5}$
22.	Electric Eels	$25\frac{4}{5}$	$17\frac{3}{10}$
23.	Tiger Sharks	$25\frac{4}{5}$	$12\frac{1}{2}$
24.	Swim Fiends	$20\frac{1}{2}$	$15\frac{2}{5}$
25.	Dog Paddlers	$18\frac{9}{10}$	$10\frac{1}{2}$
26.	Water Whizzes	$16\frac{1}{2}$	$6\frac{1}{5}$

27. Which two teams have the same goal?

28. Which team has the shortest distance left to swim?

29. Which team has the longest distance left to swim?

30. Which two teams have the same distance left to swim?

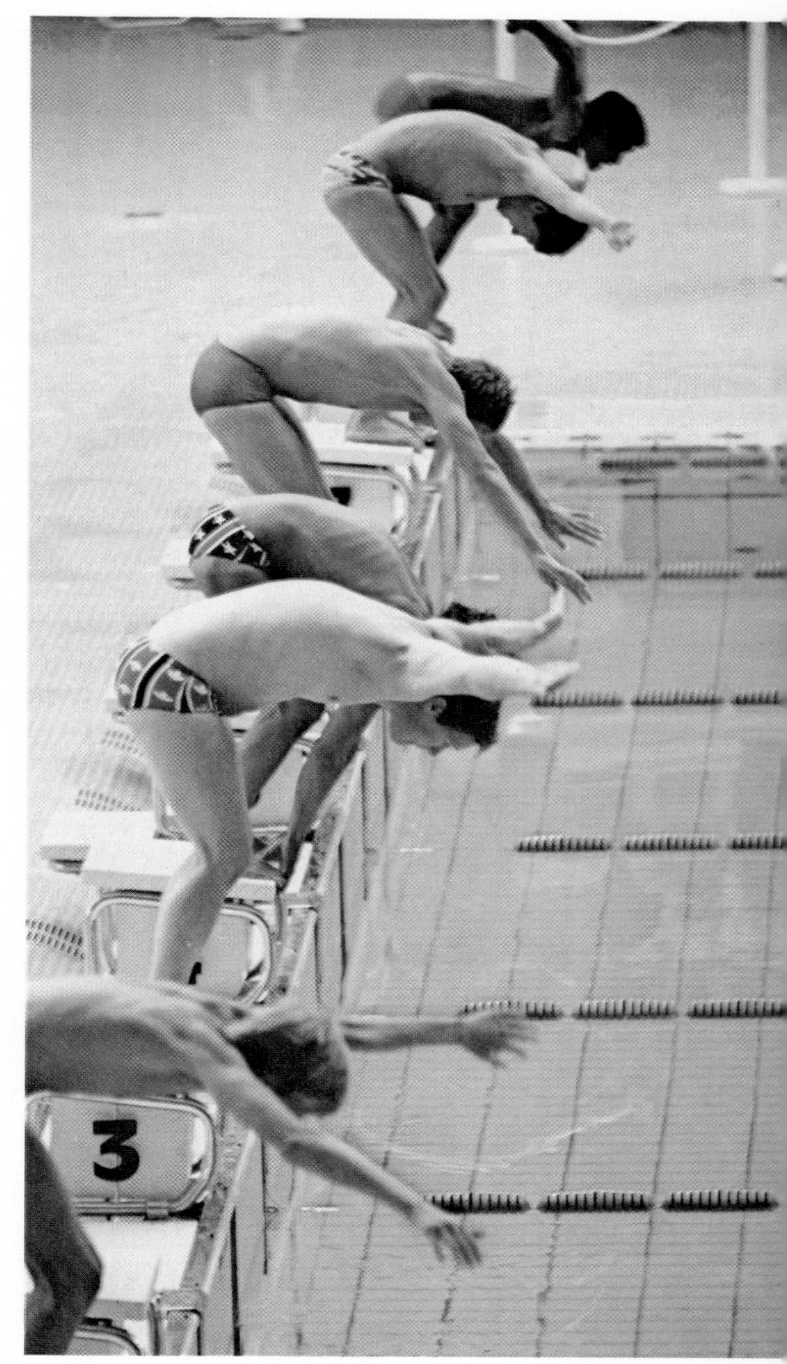

Subtracting Mixed Numbers: Different Denominators and Renaming

After you find a common denominator, you may need to rename before you subtract.

A. Find $3\frac{1}{4} - 1\frac{1}{2}$.

Find a common denominator. Rename $3\frac{1}{4}$ to get more fourths.

$$\begin{array}{r} 3\frac{1}{4} = 3\frac{1}{4} = 2\frac{5}{4} \\ -\ 1\frac{1}{2} = 1\frac{2}{4} = 1\frac{2}{4} \\ \hline 1\frac{3}{4} \end{array}$$

B. Find $7\frac{1}{5} - 2\frac{1}{2}$.

Find a common denominator. Rename $7\frac{2}{10}$ to get more tenths.

$$\begin{array}{r} 7\frac{1}{5} = 7\frac{2}{10} = 6\frac{12}{10} \\ -\ 2\frac{1}{2} = 2\frac{5}{10} = 2\frac{5}{10} \\ \hline 4\frac{7}{10} \end{array}$$

Subtract.

1. $6\frac{1}{2} = 6\frac{\square}{4} = 5\frac{\square}{4}$; $-\ 2\frac{3}{4} = 2\frac{3}{4} = 2\frac{3}{4}$
2. $7\frac{1}{4} = 7\frac{\square}{8} = 6\frac{\square}{8}$; $-\ 4\frac{3}{8} = 4\frac{3}{8} = 4\frac{3}{8}$
3. $5\frac{1}{4} = 5\frac{\square}{12} = 4\frac{\square}{12}$; $-\ 1\frac{2}{3} = 1\frac{\square}{12} = 1\frac{\square}{12}$
4. $7\frac{1}{4} - 4\frac{1}{2}$
5. $12\frac{1}{2} - 8\frac{3}{4}$
6. $9\frac{1}{4} - 6\frac{3}{8}$
7. $12\frac{5}{8} - 7\frac{3}{4}$
8. $14\frac{1}{3} - 8\frac{3}{4}$
9. $6\frac{1}{4} - 5\frac{2}{3}$
10. $8\frac{1}{3} - 6\frac{5}{6}$
11. $9\frac{1}{6} - 4\frac{1}{4}$
12. $16\frac{1}{10} - 8\frac{1}{2}$
13. $7\frac{3}{10} - 5\frac{3}{5}$
14. $6\frac{1}{2} - 2\frac{4}{5}$
15. $25\frac{1}{2} - 11\frac{9}{10}$
16. $12\frac{3}{16} - 7\frac{3}{4}$
17. $10\frac{1}{2} - 9\frac{3}{5}$
18. $5\frac{1}{3} - 2\frac{1}{2}$
19. $4\frac{1}{3} - 1\frac{3}{4}$
20. $7\frac{1}{6} - 3\frac{5}{8}$

More practice
Set J, page 303

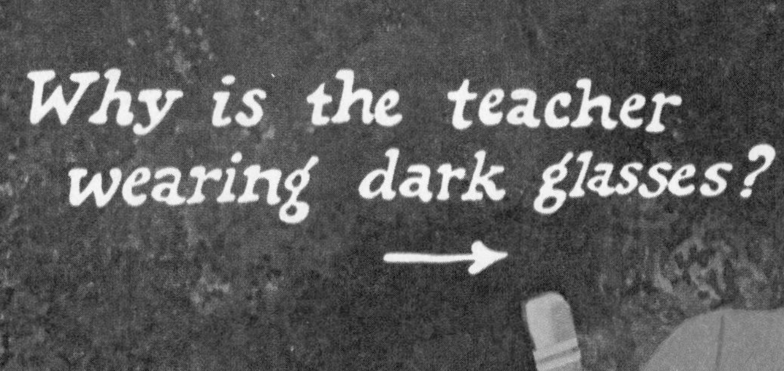
Why is the teacher wearing dark glasses?

To decode the message, first subtract.
Write each answer in lowest terms.
Then match each answer with its letter in the code table.

$1\frac{5}{6}$	$2\frac{5}{12}$	$3\frac{5}{8}$	$4\frac{2}{3}$	$5\frac{5}{12}$	$6\frac{2}{9}$	$6\frac{3}{8}$	$6\frac{3}{4}$	$7\frac{1}{2}$	$8\frac{11}{12}$	$18\frac{7}{8}$	$4\frac{1}{24}$
I	E	A	H	L	B	R	T	C	S	O	G

21. $12\frac{1}{2} - 5\frac{3}{4}$

22. $8\frac{1}{6} - 3\frac{1}{2}$

23. $7\frac{1}{6} - 4\frac{3}{4}$

24. $15\frac{1}{3} - 7\frac{5}{6}$

25. $9\frac{1}{4} - 3\frac{5}{6}$

26. $6\frac{7}{8} - 3\frac{1}{4}$

27. $13\frac{3}{4} - 4\frac{5}{6}$

28. $17\frac{2}{3} - 8\frac{3}{4}$

29. $5\frac{2}{3} - 3\frac{5}{6}$

30. $10\frac{1}{4} - 1\frac{1}{3}$

31. $25\frac{1}{2} - 16\frac{7}{12}$

32. $33\frac{1}{4} - 14\frac{3}{8}$

33. $18\frac{2}{3} - 12\frac{4}{9}$

34. $23\frac{1}{8} - 16\frac{3}{4}$

35. $42\frac{1}{3} - 40\frac{1}{2}$

36. $6\frac{1}{6} - 2\frac{1}{8}$

37. $34 - 29\frac{1}{3}$

38. $26\frac{1}{4} - 19\frac{1}{2}$

Using Subtraction of Mixed Numbers: A School Fair

LET JODY guess your weight
If she misses by more than 5 pounds, you win a prize!

Find the difference between the heights reached by

1. Sandy and Carol.
2. Sandy and Ian.
3. Sandy and Dave.
4. Sandy and Naomi.
5. Carol and Ian.
6. Carol and Dave.
7. Carol and Naomi.
8. Ian and Dave.
9. Ian and Naomi.
10. Dave and Naomi.

Find the difference between Jody's guess and the actual weight of each person.

	Name	Jody's guess (pounds)	Actual weight (pounds)
11.	Tim	83	$78\frac{3}{4}$
12.	Alex	87	$96\frac{1}{4}$
13.	Ellen	$75\frac{1}{2}$	$80\frac{1}{4}$
14.	Claire	68	$72\frac{1}{2}$
15.	Jack	93	$91\frac{1}{4}$
16.	Leslie	$73\frac{1}{2}$	$75\frac{1}{2}$
17.	Michael	89	$86\frac{1}{2}$

18. Who won a prize?

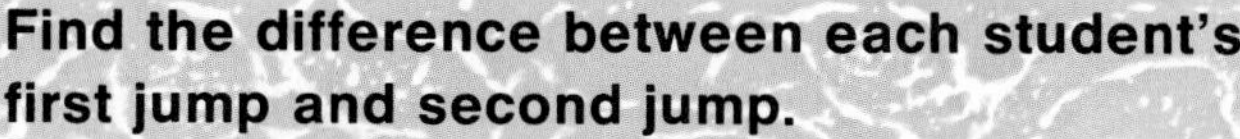

Find the difference between each student's first jump and second jump.

	Name	First jump (inches)	Second jump (inches)
19.	Lila	$34\frac{1}{2}$	36
20.	Marty	$39\frac{1}{8}$	46
21.	Robin	$42\frac{3}{4}$	$37\frac{1}{4}$
22.	Jeffrey	$46\frac{5}{8}$	$41\frac{1}{2}$
23.	Nelson	$35\frac{3}{4}$	$27\frac{3}{4}$
24.	Denise	$30\frac{1}{2}$	$41\frac{1}{8}$
25.	Joanne	$28\frac{1}{4}$	$36\frac{1}{2}$

26. Who jumped farthest?

For each item given, subtract to find how much was sold during the day.

	Ice cream	Gallons to begin with	Gallons left over
27.	Vanilla	5	$2\frac{1}{2}$
28.	Chocolate	3	$1\frac{3}{4}$
29.	Strawberry	$2\frac{1}{2}$	$1\frac{1}{2}$
30.	Peppermint	$2\frac{1}{4}$	1
31.	Peach	$1\frac{3}{4}$	$1\frac{1}{8}$

	Topping	Cups to begin with	Cups left over
32.	Strawberry	5	$1\frac{1}{3}$
33.	Chocolate	5	$1\frac{1}{4}$
34.	Marshmallow	5	$2\frac{1}{2}$
35.	Pineapple	5	$3\frac{2}{3}$

Using Addition and Subtraction of Mixed Numbers

Alvin kept a record of the number of hours he spent on several activities during one school week.

Day	Hours				
	Model cars	Basketball	Television	School	Sleep
Monday	$1\frac{1}{3}$		$1\frac{2}{3}$	$6\frac{1}{2}$	$8\frac{1}{2}$
Tuesday		$1\frac{3}{4}$		$6\frac{1}{2}$	$9\frac{3}{4}$
Wednesday		$1\frac{1}{2}$	$1\frac{1}{4}$	$6\frac{1}{2}$	8
Thursday	$\frac{3}{4}$		$2\frac{1}{2}$	$6\frac{1}{2}$	$8\frac{3}{4}$
Friday	$1\frac{2}{3}$	$2\frac{1}{4}$		$6\frac{1}{2}$	$9\frac{1}{2}$

1. Find the total number of hours that Alvin spent on each activity.

2. Find the difference between the total times Alvin spent on

a. model cars and basketball.

b. model cars and television.

c. basketball and television.

d. basketball and school.

e. television and school.

3. Find the difference between the time Alvin spent sleeping and the time he spent in school on

a. Monday.

b. Tuesday.

c. Wednesday.

d. Thursday.

e. Friday.

One Saturday morning,
Jane, Heidi, and Alvin went fishing.

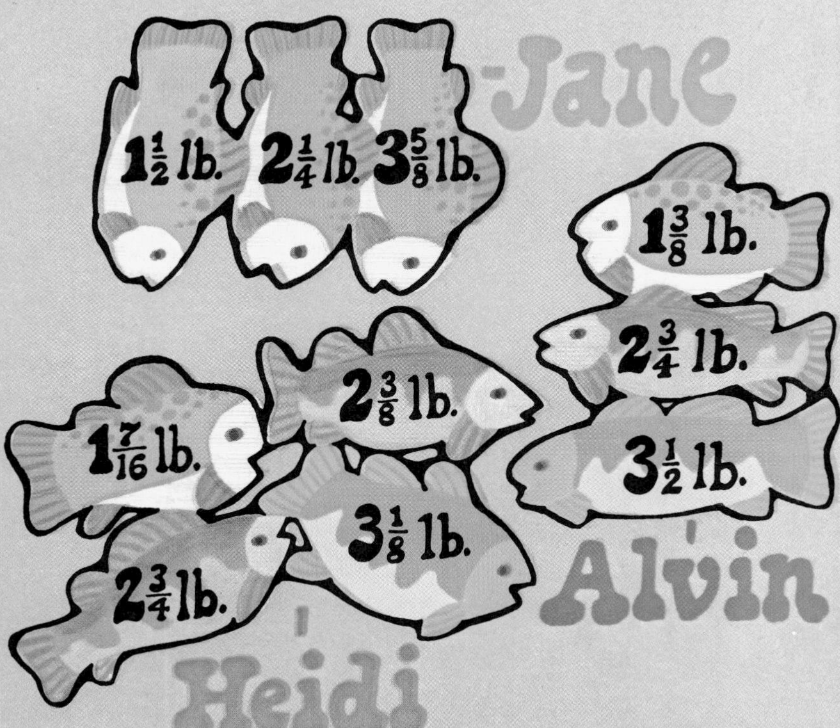

4. Find the total weight of

a. Jane's fish.

b. Heidi's fish.

c. Alvin's fish.

5. Find the difference between the weights of the heaviest fish and the lightest fish caught by

a. Jane.

b. Heidi.

c. Alvin.

Keeping Skillful

Add.

1. 45 + 45 + 90

2. 53 + 37 + 90

3. 60 + 60 + 60

4. 120 + 30 + 30

5. 120 + 35 + 25

Subtract.

6. 90 − 72

7. 90 − 11

8. 90 − 45

9. 180 − 60

10. 180 − 135

11. 180 − 90

Give the area of each rectangle in square meters.

	Rectangle	Length (meters)	Width (meters)
12.	A	100	56
13.	B	10	10
14.	C	482	100
15.	D	1000	327

Using Mathematics: Facts About Texas

1. The city of San Antonio was founded in 1718. Houston became a city 119 years later. In what year did Houston become a city?

2. San Antonio belonged to Spain from 1718 until the Mexican Revolution in 1821. For how long did San Antonio belong to Spain?

3. When Mexico won independence from Spain in 1821, Texas became part of the republic of Mexico. Texas won independence from Mexico in 1836. For how long was Texas a part of Mexico?

4. In 1836, Texas became an independent republic. After 9 years of independence, Texas became the twenty-eighth state. In what year did Texas become a state?

5. In 1850, the year of the first federal census, the population of Texas was 212,592. In 1970, the population was 11,196,730. By how much did the population increase?

Check Yourself
Adding and Subtracting Mixed Numbers, Pages 258–280

Adding mixed numbers, pages 258–263, 266–267

Find each sum.

1. $7\frac{3}{10} + 3\frac{4}{10}$

2. $18 + 6\frac{5}{8}$

3. $9\frac{4}{5} + 8\frac{3}{5}$

4. $6\frac{5}{8} + 7\frac{1}{4}$

5. $2\frac{2}{3} + 9\frac{1}{2}$

6. $1\frac{1}{2} + 6\frac{2}{3} + 3\frac{1}{4}$

Subtracting mixed numbers, pages 268–275

Find each difference.

7. $5\frac{6}{7} - 3\frac{2}{7}$

8. $10\frac{3}{4} - 6$

9. $14 - 8\frac{1}{3}$

10. $8\frac{1}{4} - 5\frac{3}{4}$

11. $18\frac{4}{5} - 11\frac{1}{2}$

12. $23\frac{1}{4} - 9\frac{2}{3}$

Problem solving, pages 258–261, 264–265, 272–273, 276–279

13. Denise bought two packages of meat.
One package weighed $1\frac{3}{4}$ pounds.
The other package weighed $2\frac{5}{8}$ pounds.
How many pounds of meat did she buy?

14. Find the perimeter.

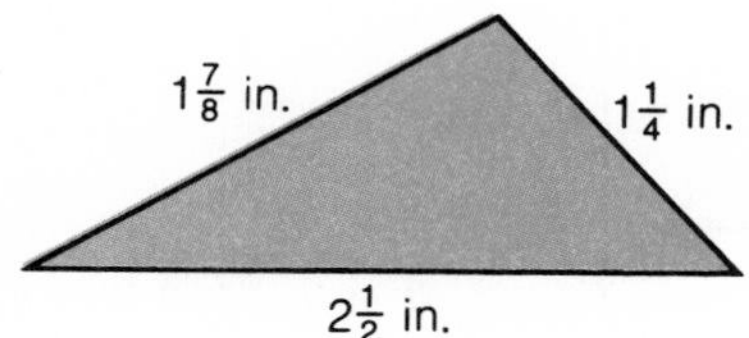

15. How much farther has Kevin walked than Lenny?

Lenny — $3\frac{7}{8}$ miles

Kevin — $6\frac{1}{4}$ miles

16. Brenda jumped $4\frac{1}{3}$ feet, and
Craig jumped $3\frac{5}{6}$ feet.
How much longer was Brenda's jump?

Lines and Parts of Lines

Objects in the world around you suggest ideas in geometry. The tip of your pencil suggests a point. The edge of your ruler suggests a segment.

Look at the photographs on page 283. Which objects remind you of the following geometric ideas?

1. A point
2. A line
3. A segment
4. A ray
5. Intersecting lines
6. Parallel lines

• **Discuss** Find objects in your classroom that suggest points, lines, segments, and rays.

Diagram	Name
• A	Point A
⟷ C D	Line CD
C D	Segment CD
C D →	Ray CD
	Intersecting lines
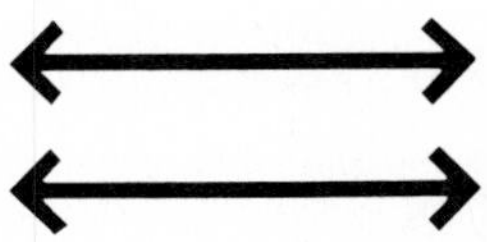	Parallel lines

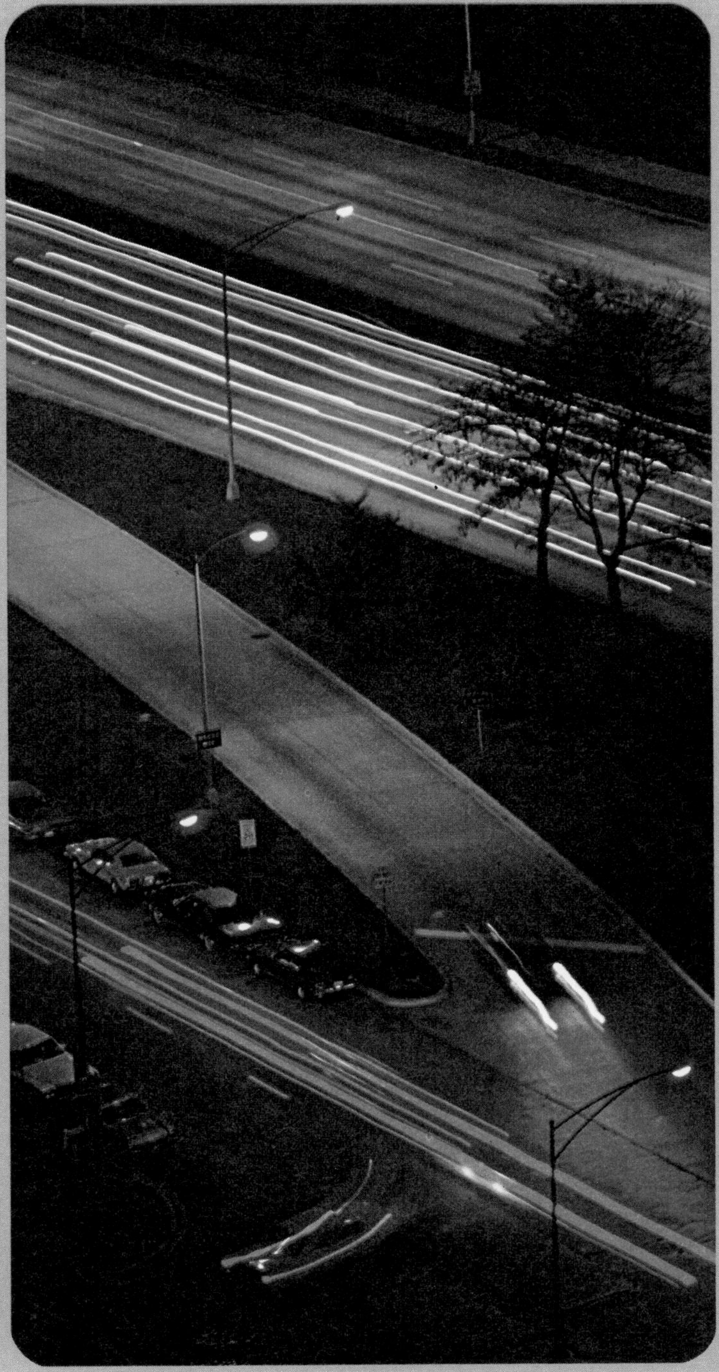

Angles

Ray BA and ray BC have the same endpoint.
The rays form an ***angle.***
The endpoint is the ***vertex*** of the angle.

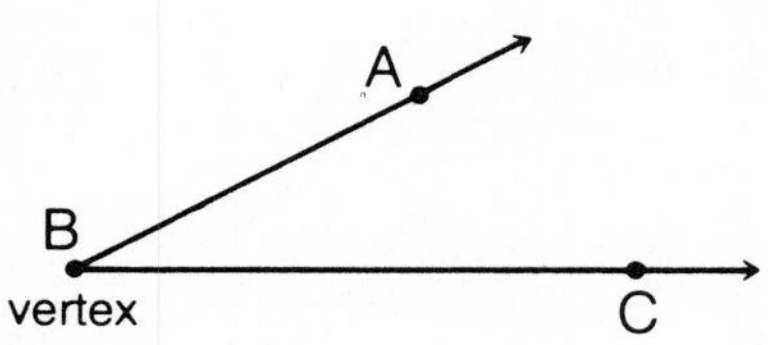

You can use three letters to name an angle. The letter for the vertex is given between the other two.

Angle ABC, or angle CBA
∠ABC, or ∠CBA

Sometimes people use only the letter for the vertex to name the angle.

∠B

Use three letters to name each angle.

1.

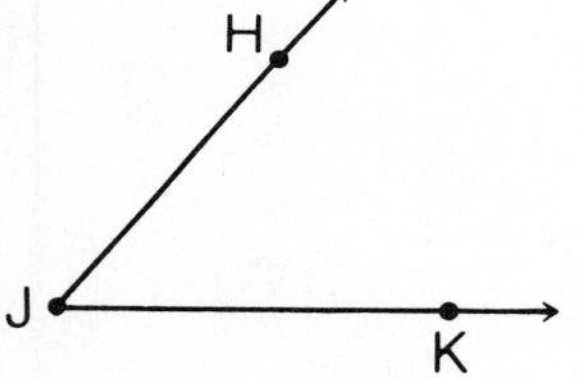

2.

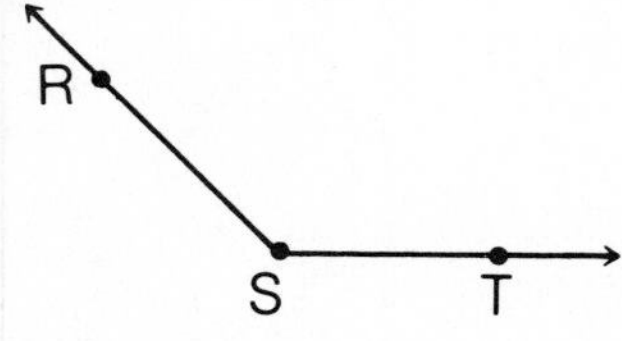

3.

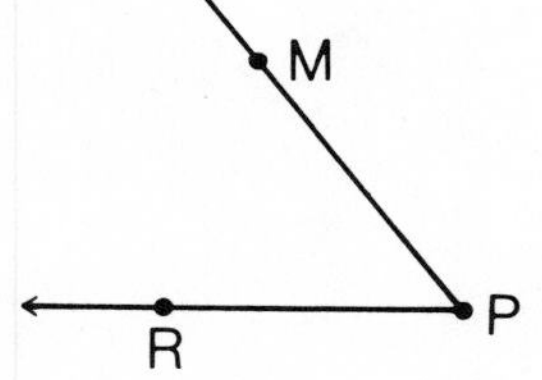

4.

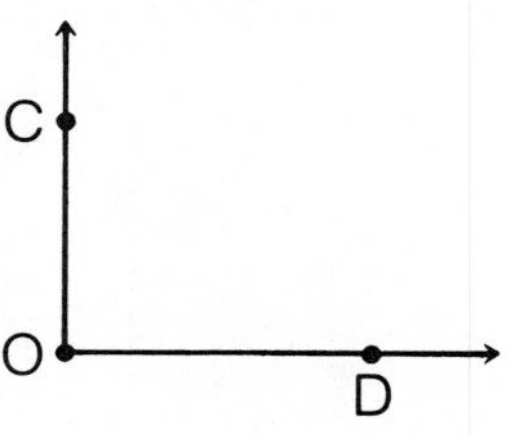

5.

6.

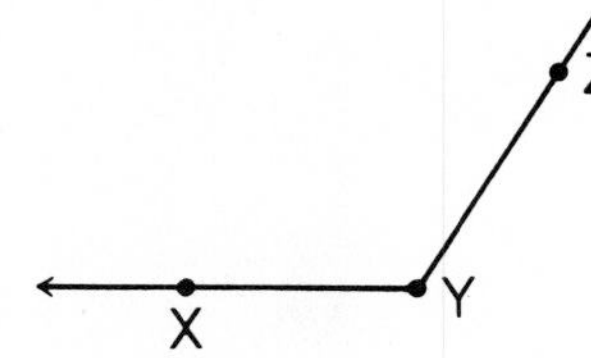

7. List all the angles you can find in the picture below. The list is started for you.

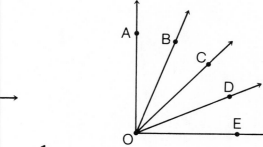

∠AOB
∠AOC

Right, Acute, and Obtuse Angles

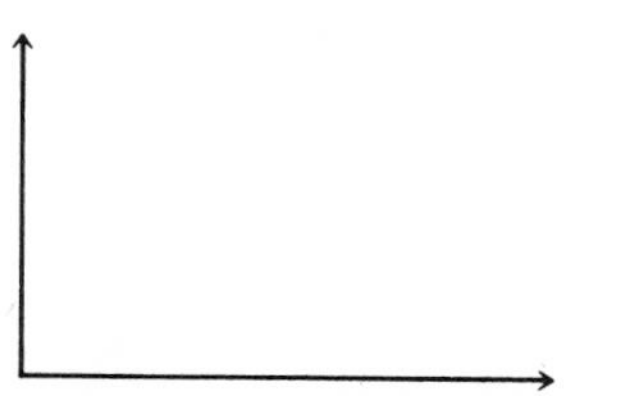

A ***right angle*** looks like a square corner.

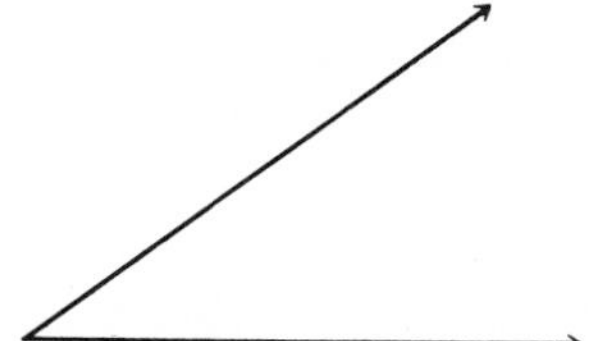

An ***acute angle*** is smaller than a right angle.

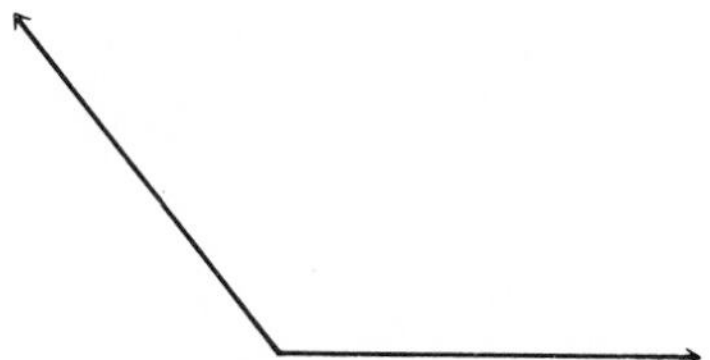

An ***obtuse angle*** is larger than a right angle.

Tell whether each angle is right, acute, or obtuse.
You can use a square corner to help you decide.

1.

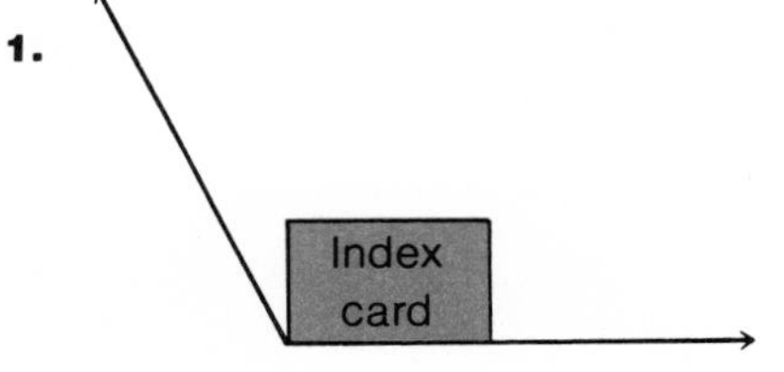

2.

3.

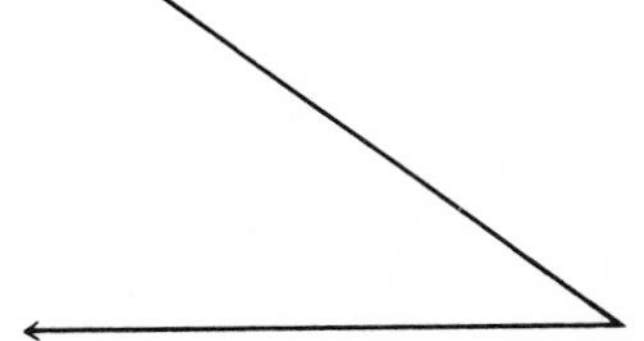

4.

5.

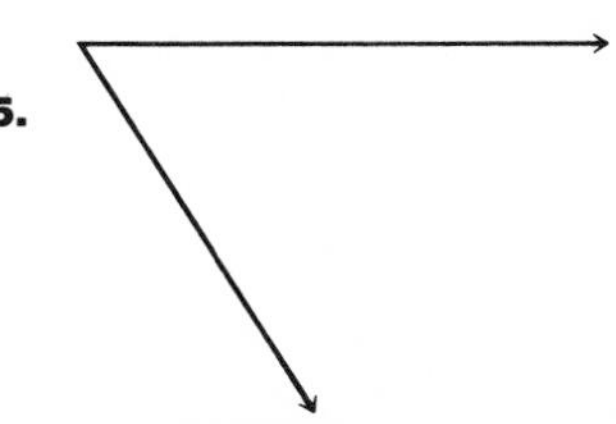

6.

7. List all the angles you can find in the picture below. Tell whether each angle is right, acute, or obtuse.

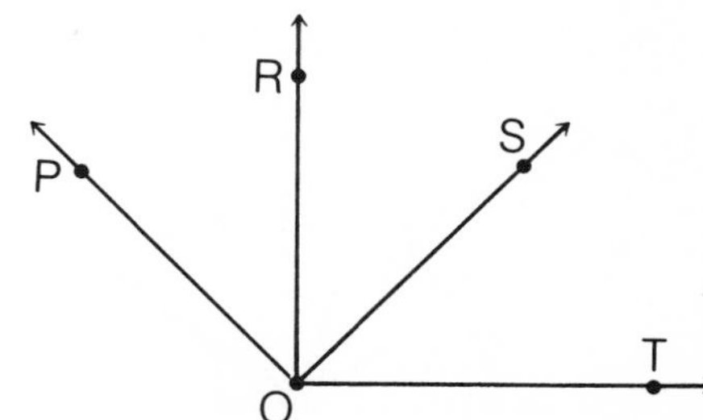

Measuring Angles

Janet Bradley drew a unit angle.
She called the unit one Bradley.

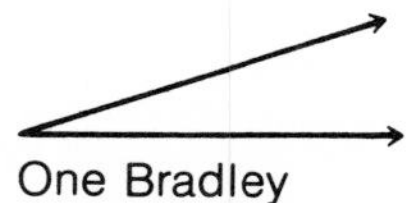

She traced the angle 10 times
on a sheet of plastic.
Then she could measure other angles.

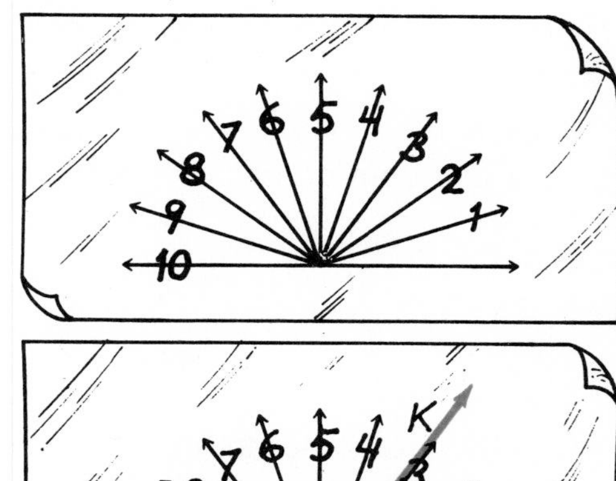

The measure of $\angle$KOR is 3 Bradleys.

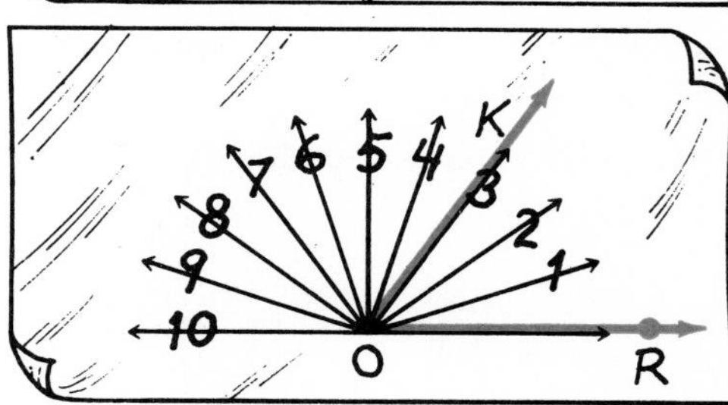

Give the measure of each angle in Bradleys.

1. 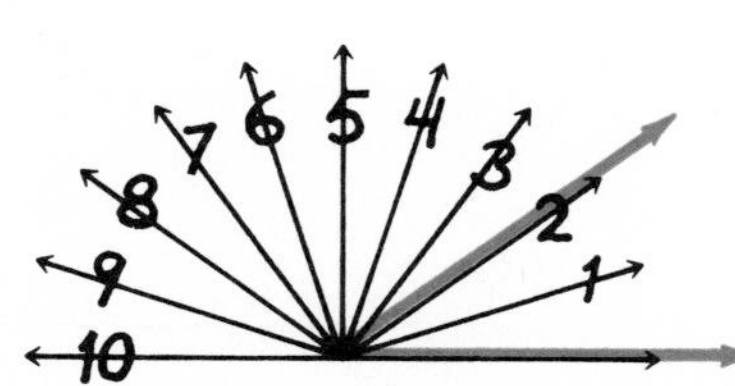

2. 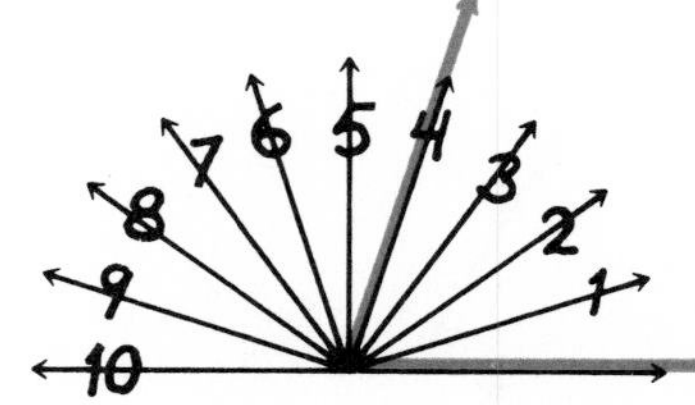

3. 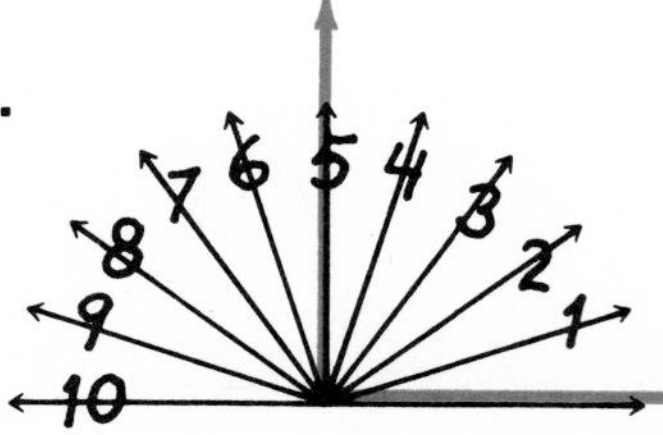

4. 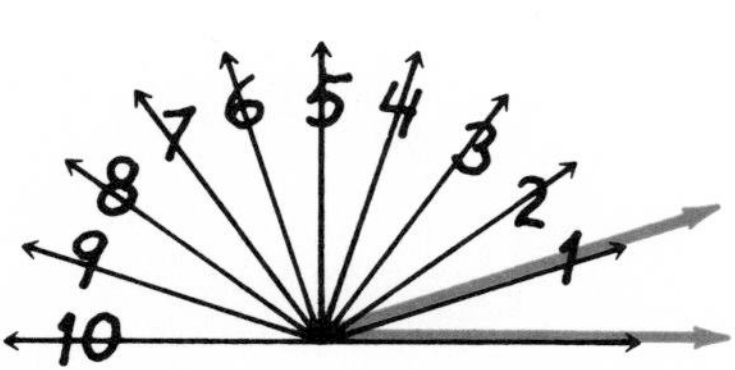

5. 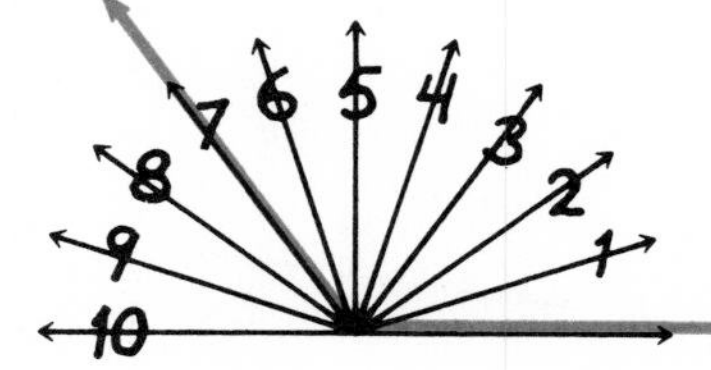

6. 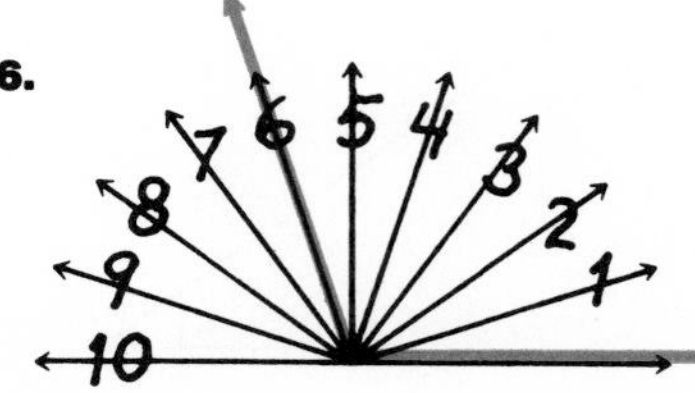

About 4000 years ago, the Sumerians developed a unit angle called the ***degree.*** People still use the degree as the most common unit of angle measure.

One degree 1°

A ***protractor*** shows 180°. It is used to measure angles.

The measure of ∠ABC is about 35°.

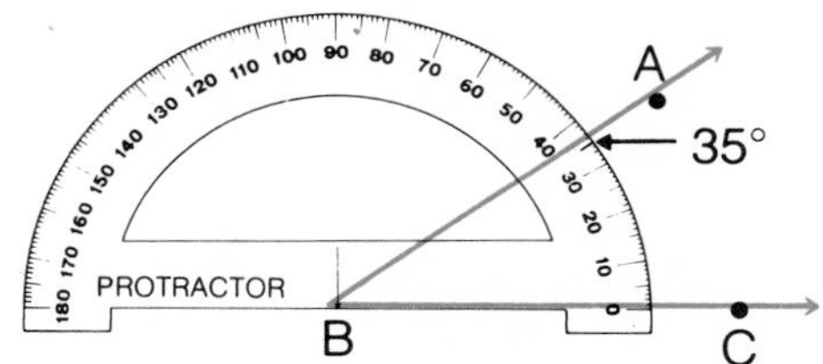

Give the measure of each angle to the nearest degree.

7. ∠ACE

8. ∠BDF

9. ∠LMN

10. ∠GHJ

11. ∠WBC

12. ∠DEF

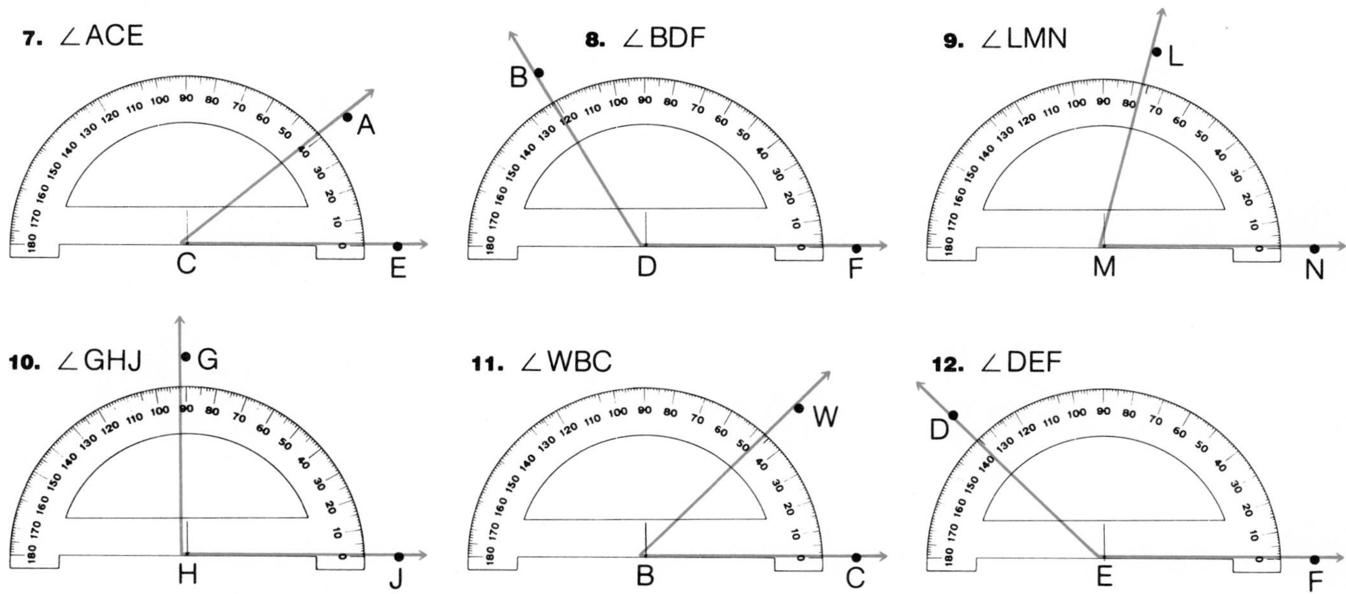

13. Which angle shown is a right angle?

14. What is the measure of a right angle?

Using a Protractor

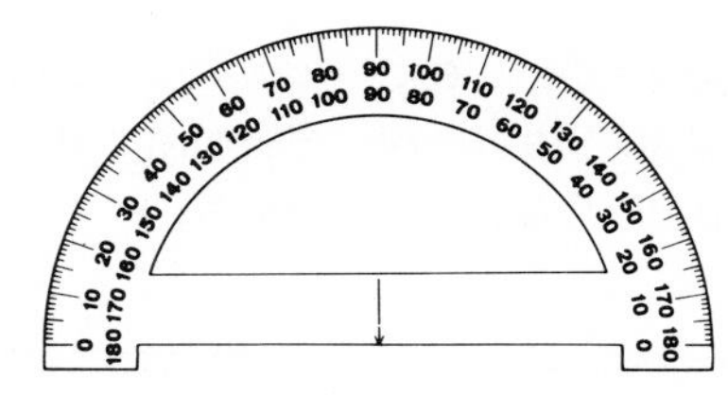

Most protractors have two scales. To measure an angle, you need to decide which scale to use.

Study examples A and B.
Remember, the measure of a right angle is 90°.

A. Is the measure of ∠GHQ 50° or 130°?

The angle is smaller than a right angle, so the measure is less than 90°.
The measure of ∠GHQ is 50°.

B. Is the measure of ∠RST 145° or 35°?

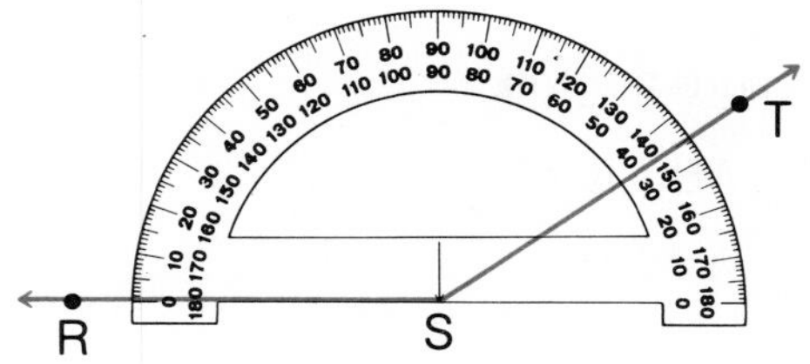

The angle is larger than a right angle, so the measure is greater than 90°.
The measure of ∠RST is 145°.

Give the measure of each angle to the nearest degree.

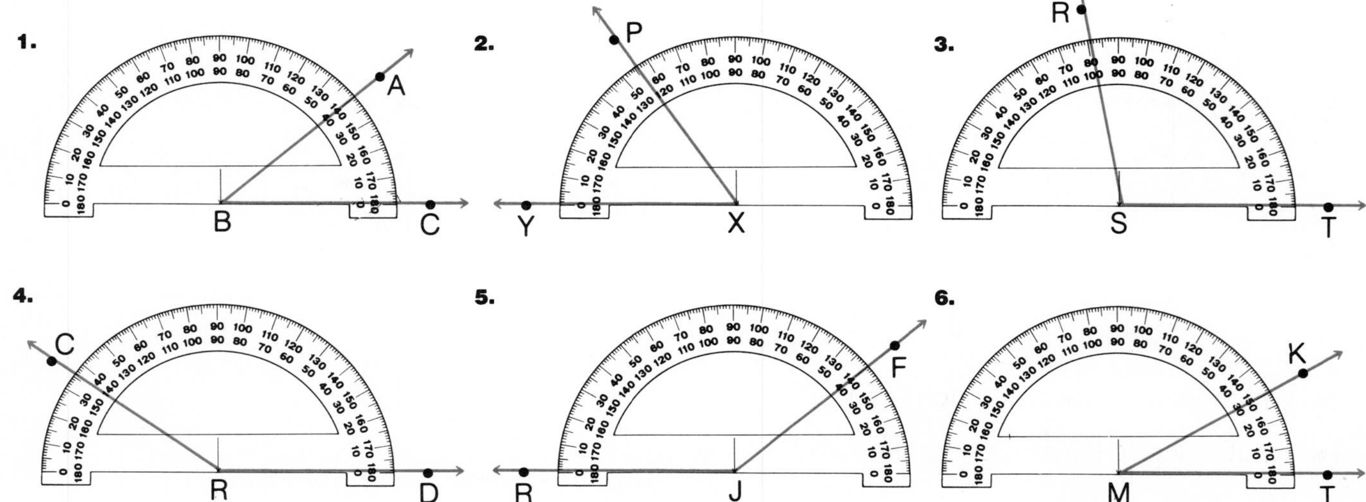

When you use your protractor, place the center mark of the protractor on the vertex of the angle.

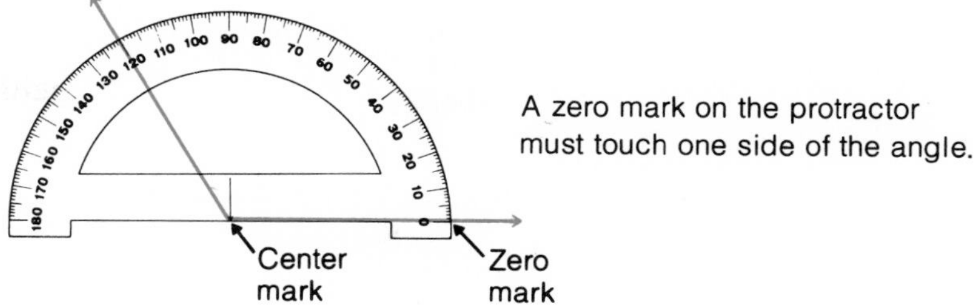

7. Use your protractor to measure each angle to the nearest degree.

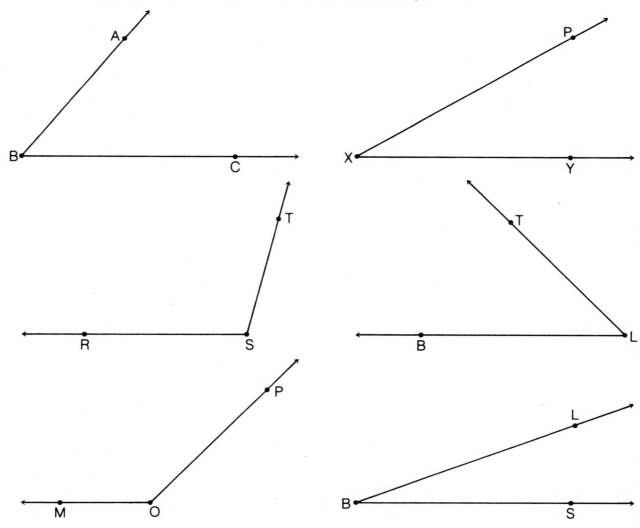

Drawing Angles

You can use your protractor to help you draw angles.
Here is how to draw an angle whose measure is 60°.

Draw ray ST.

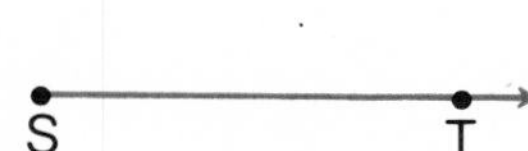

Put the center mark of the protractor on point S.
Put a zero mark on ray ST.
Mark point R at 60°.

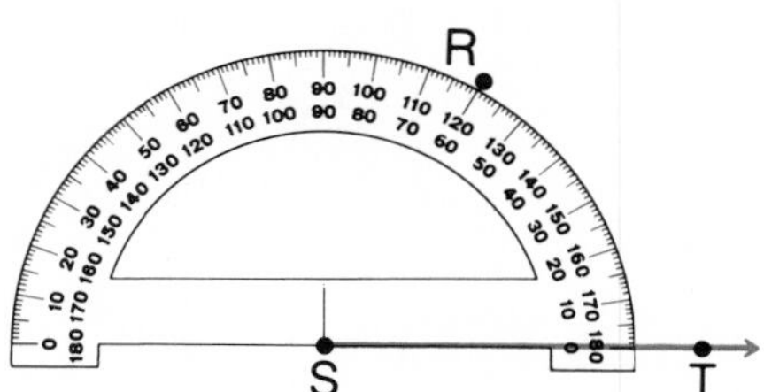

Draw ray SR.
The measure of ∠RST is 60°.

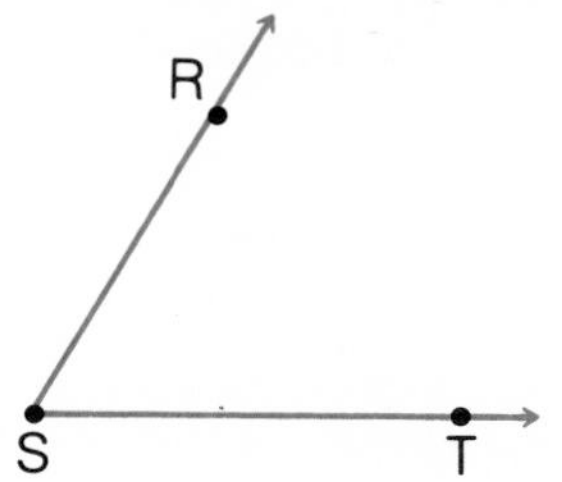

Draw an angle for each measure that is given.

1. 30°	**4.** 75°	**7.** 95°
2. 55°	**5.** 20°	**8.** 120°
3. 130°	**6.** 155°	**9.** 80°

Intersecting lines that form right angles are called ***perpendicular lines.***

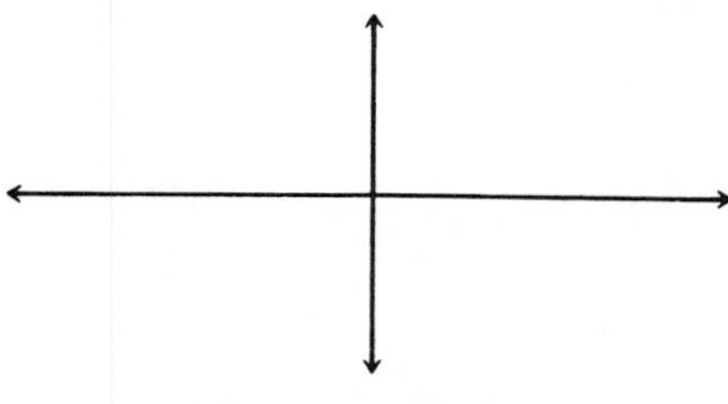

Perpendicular lines

10. Use your protractor to draw two perpendicular lines.

SIDE TRIP Making Circle Designs

You can use your protractor to draw a circle.

Draw around the outside edge of the protractor.

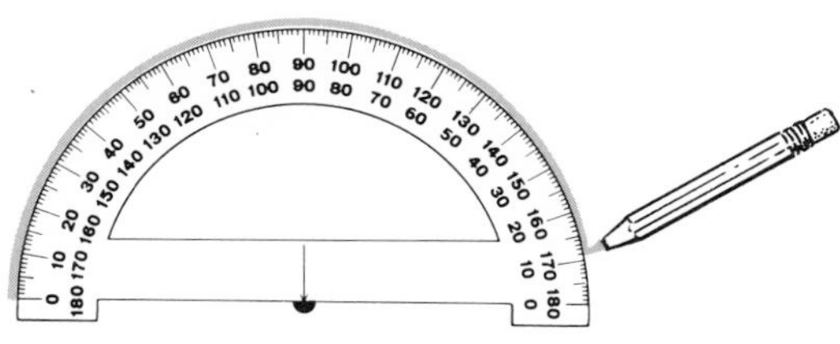

Place the protractor as shown. Draw around the outside edge to complete the circle.

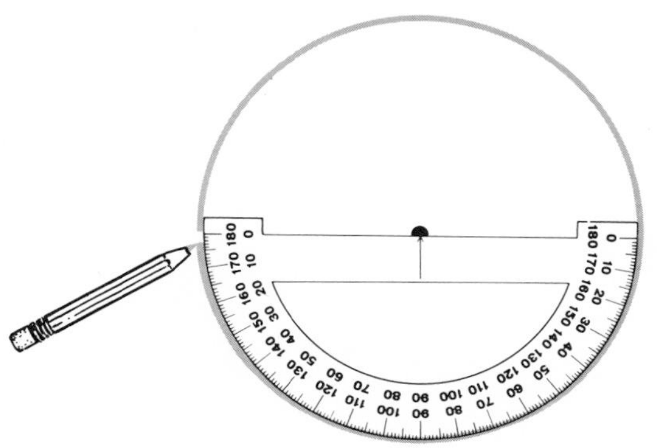

Before you try the designs, practice making circles with your protractor.

Design A

1. Use your protractor to mark off every 60° on a circle. Number the marks as shown.

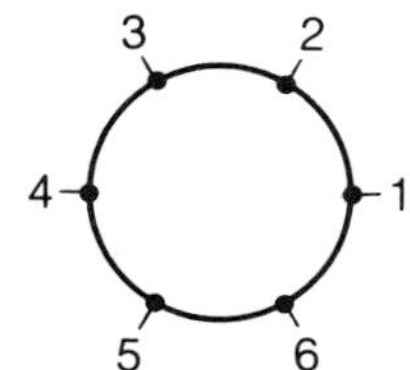

2. Connect points in this order.

a. 1 to 3 to 5 to 1

b. 2 to 4 to 6 to 2

3. How many triangles are in your design?

4. What other geometric shapes can you see?

Design B

5. Mark off every 45° on a circle. Number the marks as shown.

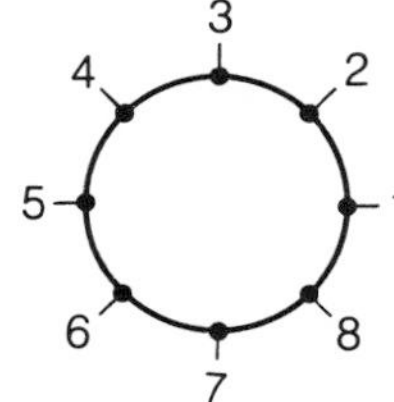

6. Connect points in this order.

a. 1 to 3 to 5 to 7 to 1

b. 2 to 4 to 6 to 8 to 2

7. Name two geometric shapes in the design.

Design C

8. Mark off every 45° on a circle. Number the marks as you did for design B.

9. Connect points in this order.

1 to 4 to 7 to 2
to 5 to 8 to 3 to 6 to 1

10. Name three geometric shapes in the design.

Congruent Angles

Angles that have the same measure are ***congruent angles.***

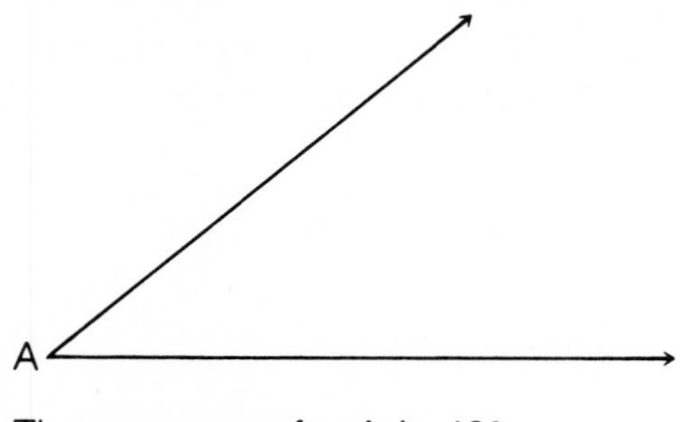

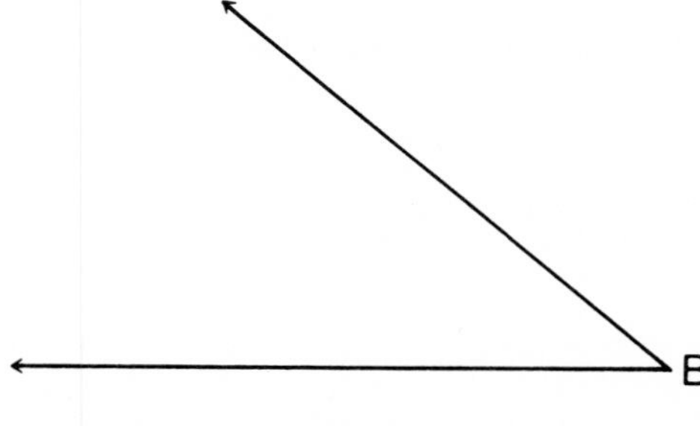

The measure of ∠A is 40°.

The measure of ∠B is 40°.

∠A and ∠B are congruent.

1. Use your protractor to find the measure of each angle.

2. Which angles seem to be congruent?

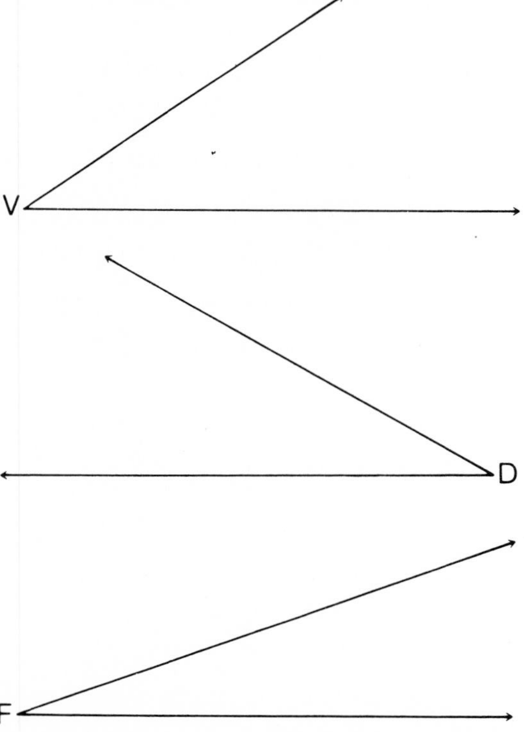

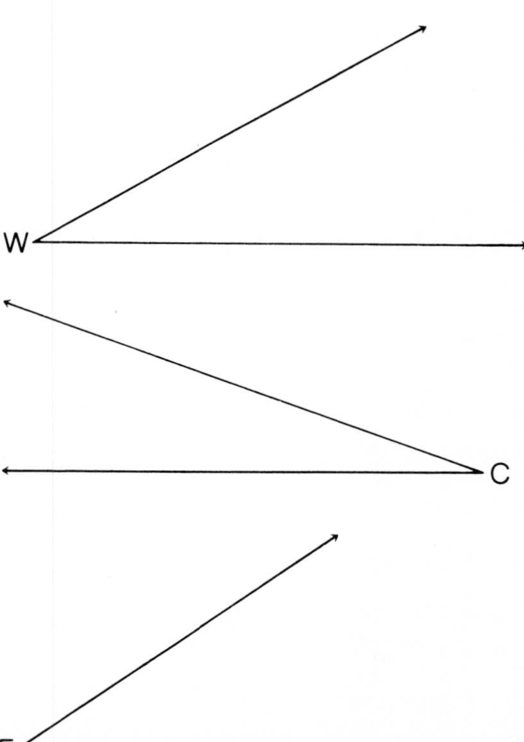

Congruent Angles in a Triangle

1. Measure each angle of triangle ABC.
2. Are any angles congruent?
3. Measure each angle of triangle HJK.
4. Which angles seem to be congruent?

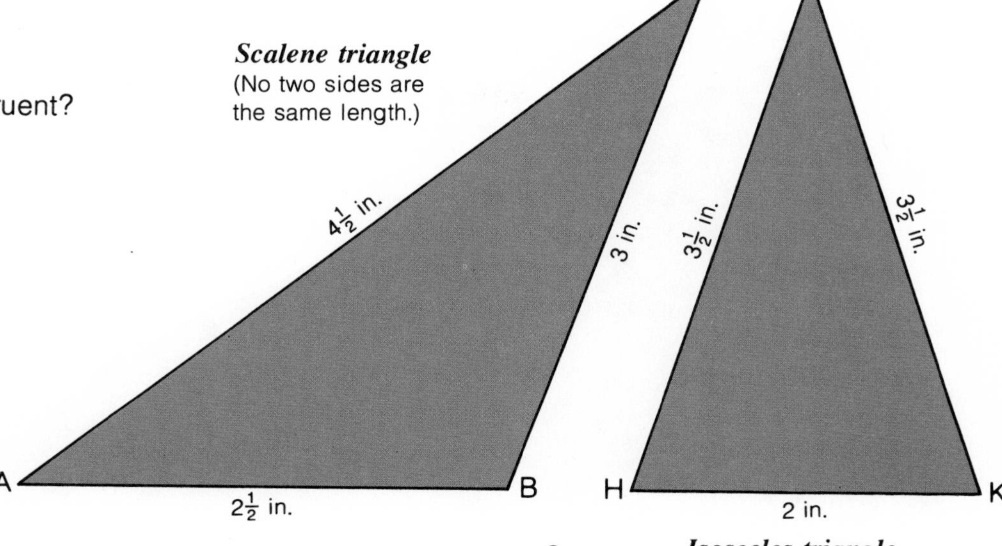

5. Measure each angle of triangle RST.
6. Which angles seem to be congruent?

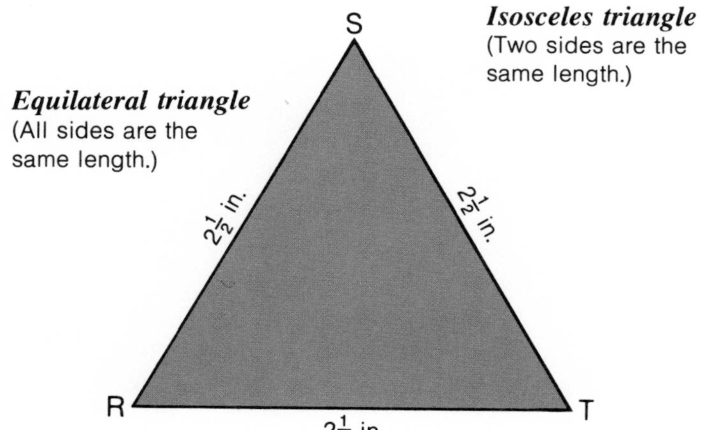

Explore

Draw an isosceles triangle XYZ with two sides each 4 inches long. Measure each angle. Which angles seem to be congruent?

Draw three more isosceles triangles. Does each triangle have a pair of congruent angles?

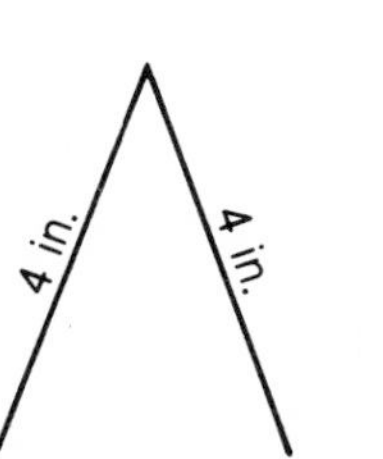

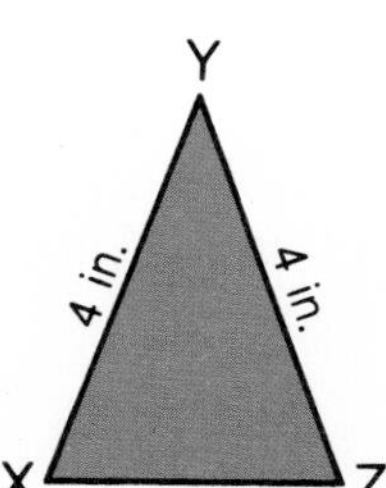

Adding the Measures of the Angles of a Triangle

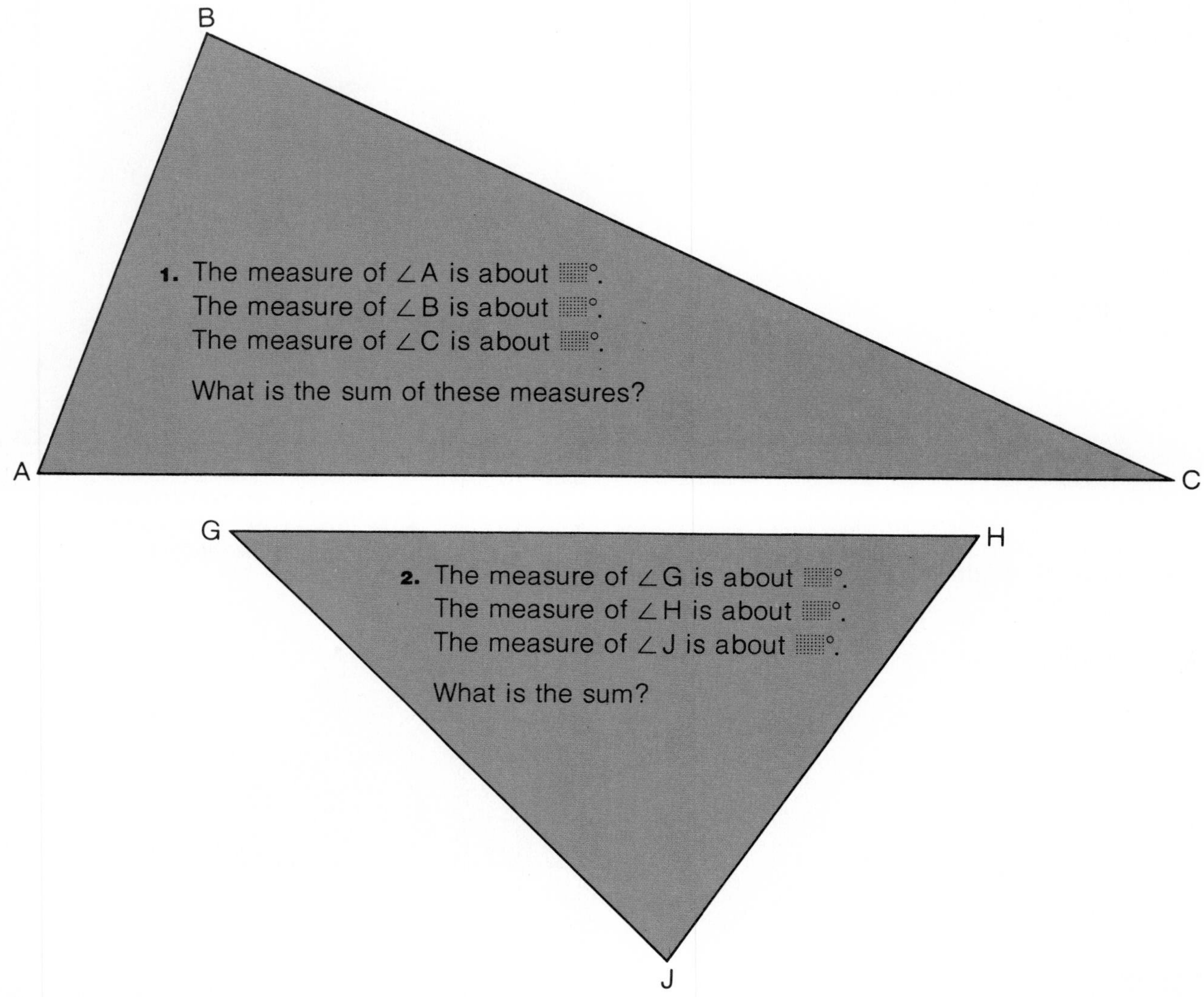

1. The measure of ∠A is about ▒°.
   The measure of ∠B is about ▒°.
   The measure of ∠C is about ▒°.

   What is the sum of these measures?

2. The measure of ∠G is about ▒°.
   The measure of ∠H is about ▒°.
   The measure of ∠J is about ▒°.

   What is the sum?

3. Draw two large triangles. Measure each angle. For each triangle, find the sum of the numbers you obtained by these measurements.

■ *In any triangle, the sum of the measures of the angles is 180°.*

4. Draw a large triangle and cut it out. Label the corners and tear them off.

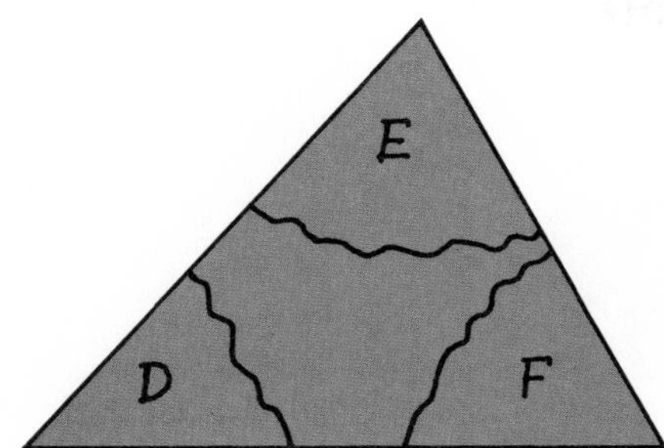

5. Place the corners together, as shown.

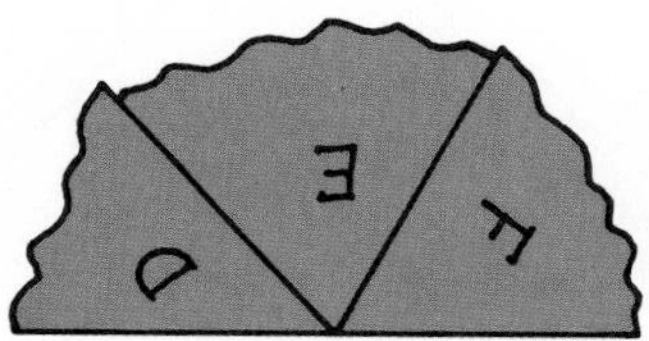

Do the angles fit on a straight line?

6. Place your protractor on the angles.

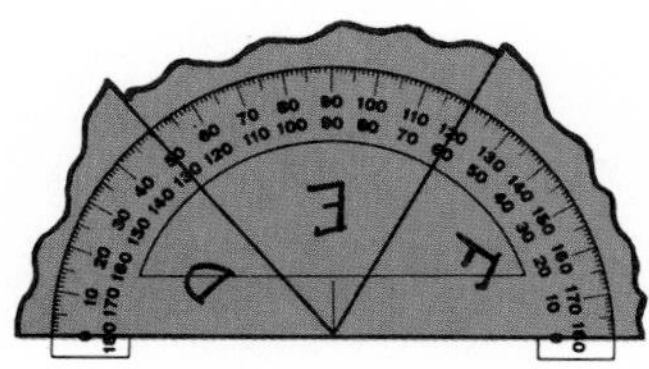

How many degrees are in the three angles?

Keeping Skillful

Multiply.

1. 25×83
2. 19×72
3. 112×39
4. 216×138
5. 16×10
6. 16×100
7. 16×1000
8. $16 \times 10{,}000$

Divide.

9. $10\overline{)880}$
10. $20\overline{)880}$
11. $40\overline{)880}$
12. $80\overline{)880}$
13. $31\overline{)775}$
14. $29\overline{)667}$
15. $83\overline{)913}$
16. $98\overline{)1078}$

Write each improper fraction as a mixed number or a whole number.

17. $\frac{7}{5}$
18. $\frac{11}{4}$
19. $\frac{21}{10}$
20. $\frac{32}{7}$
21. $\frac{51}{8}$
22. $\frac{36}{9}$
23. $\frac{61}{10}$
24. $\frac{72}{5}$
25. $\frac{96}{12}$

Triangles and Quadrilaterals

Remember, quadrilaterals are polygons with four sides. You can use triangles to make quadrilaterals.

Trace these triangles. Cut them out and letter them.

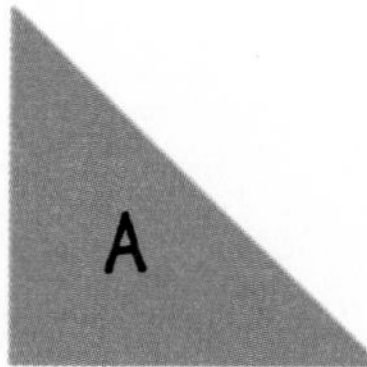

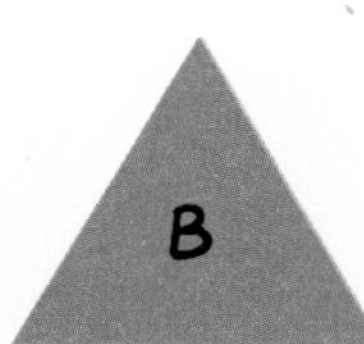

1. Trace this square.
   How many times do you use triangle A to cover the square?

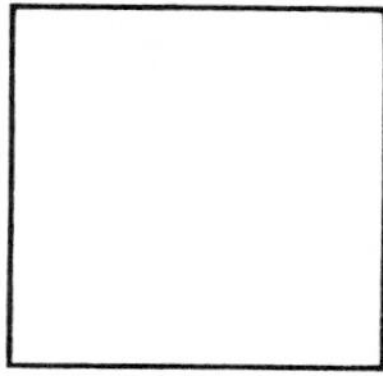

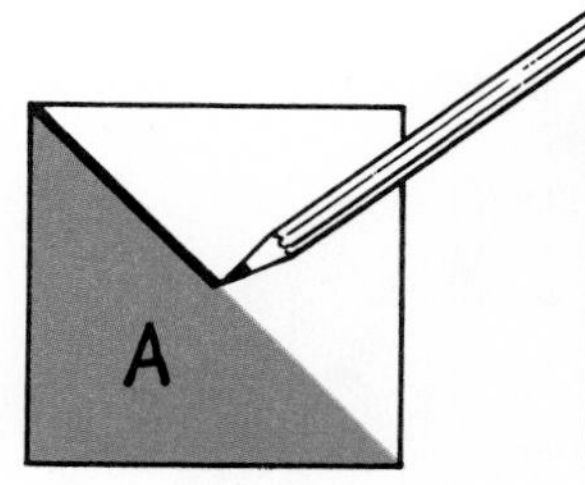

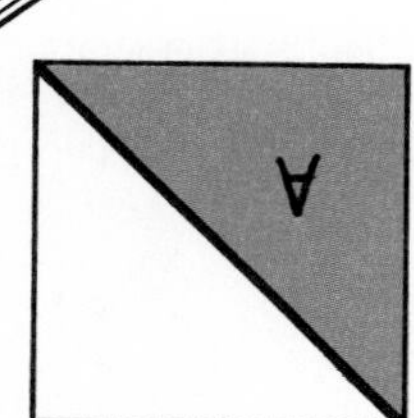

2. Trace this rectangle.
   Choose one of the triangles.
3. How many times should you use the triangle to cover the rectangle exactly?
4. Sketch how this can be done.

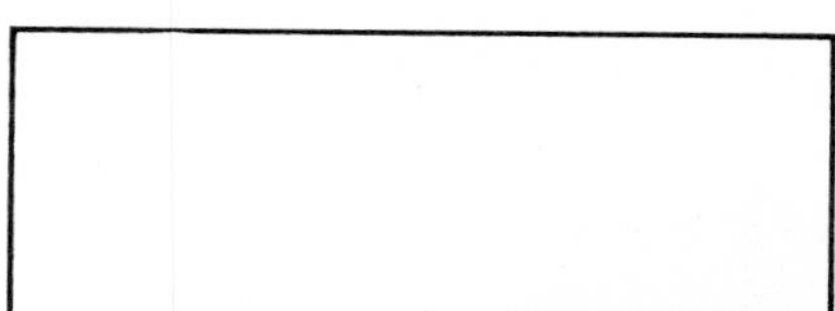

Four-sided polygons whose opposite sides are parallel are ***parallelograms.***

5. Trace this parallelogram.
   Choose one of the triangles.
6. How many times should you use the triangle to cover the parallelogram exactly?
7. Sketch how this can be done.

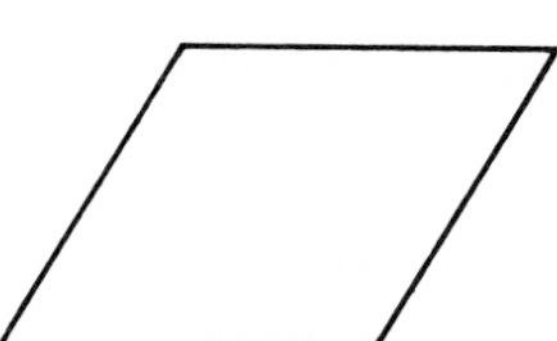

● **Discuss** How many triangles did you need to cover the square? The rectangle? The parallelogram?

What is the sum of the measures of the angles of a triangle?

What is the sum of the measures of the angles of the square? Of the rectangle? Of the parallelogram?

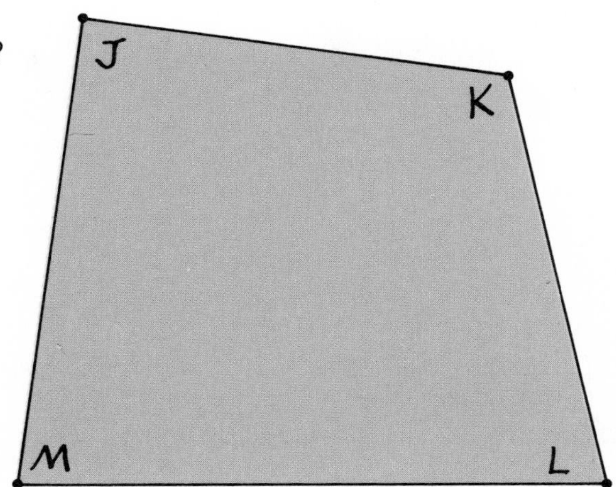

8. Draw any quadrilateral and cut it out. Label the corners.

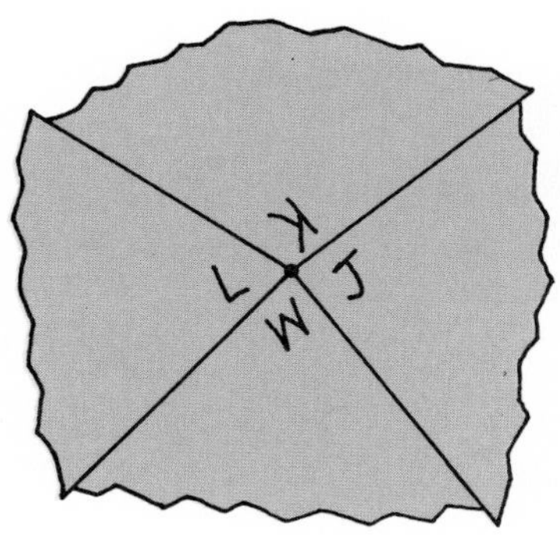

9. Tear off the corners. Can you fit them together around a point?

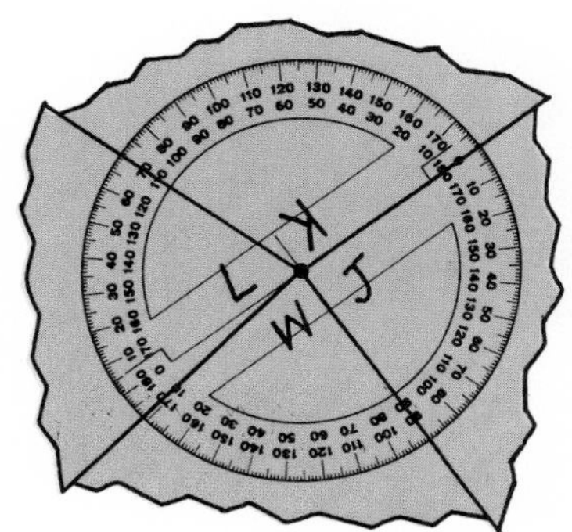

10. Place two protractors on the angles. What is the sum of the measures of the angles?

■ *In any quadrilateral, the sum of the measures of the angles is 360°.*

Finding Angle Measures

Find the missing measures.

1.

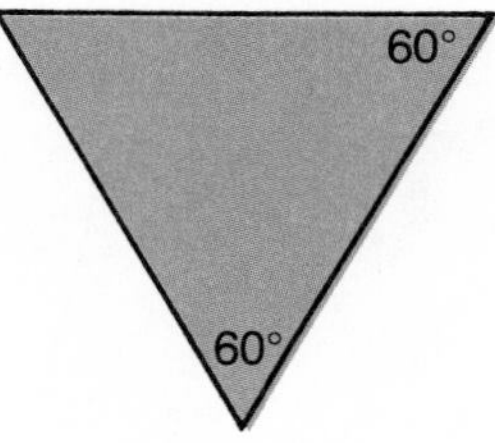

2.

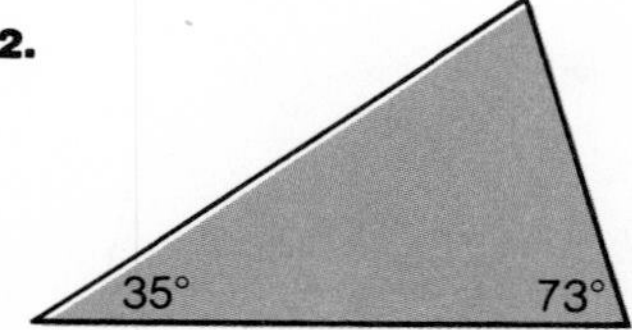

3.

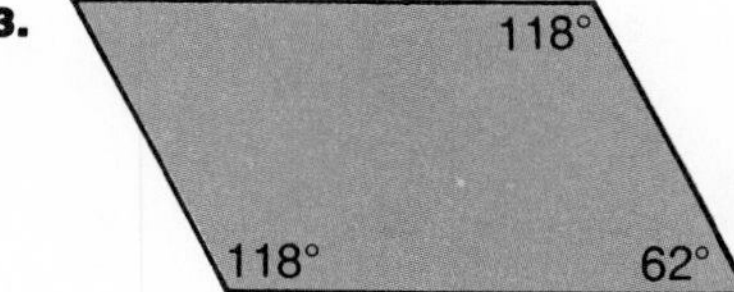

4.

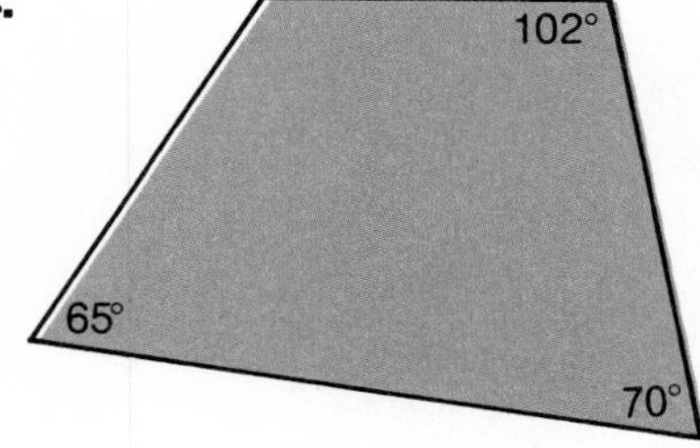

5.

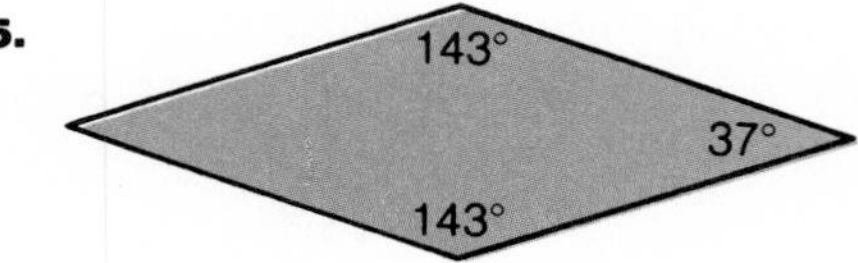

6.

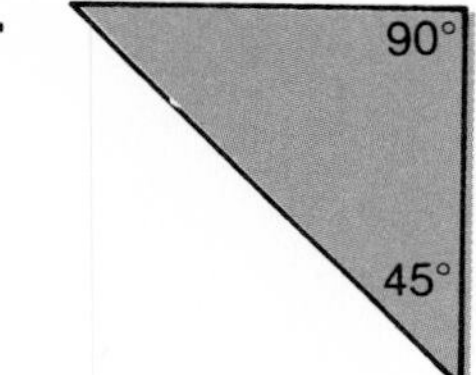

7.

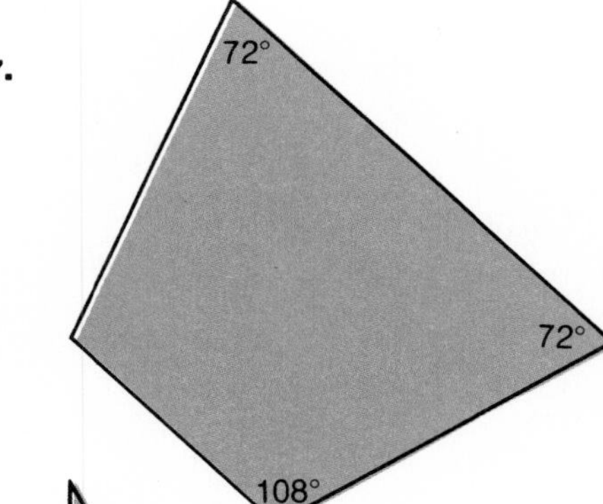

8.

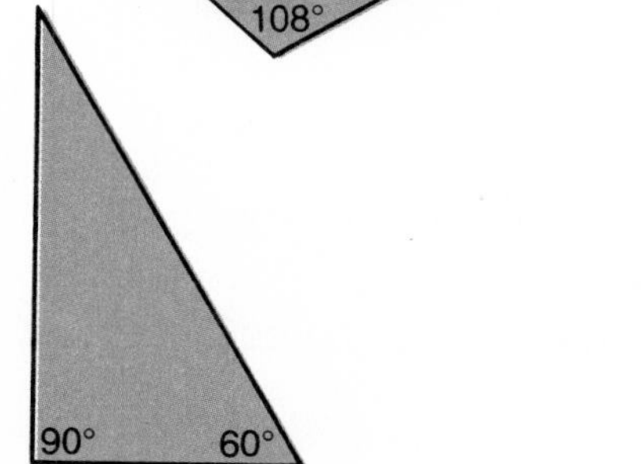

SIDE TRIP Diagonals of Polygons

Mr. Le Blanc's class recorded the number of diagonals that certain polygons have.

Number of sides	3 sides	4 sides	5 sides	6 sides	7 sides	8 sides
Number of diagonals	0	2	5	9		

Roger thought he could guess the next number without drawing the diagonals. He guessed "14."

0 1 2 3 4 5 6 7 8 9 10 11 12 13 14 15 16 17 18 19 20 21 22

1. Copy this polygon and draw all the diagonals. Was Roger's guess correct?

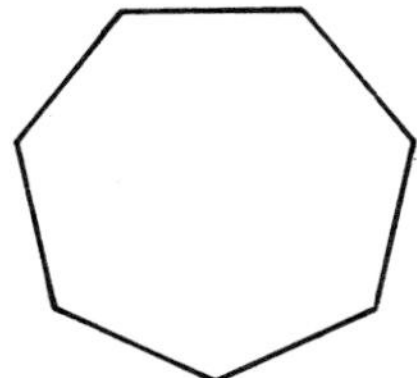

Find the pattern. Use it to answer these questions.

2. How many diagonals does an 8-sided polygon have?
3. How many diagonals does a 9-sided polygon have?
★4. How many diagonals does a 10-sided polygon have?

Check Yourself
Measuring Angles, Pages 282–299

Angles, pages 284–285

1. Use three letters to name this angle.

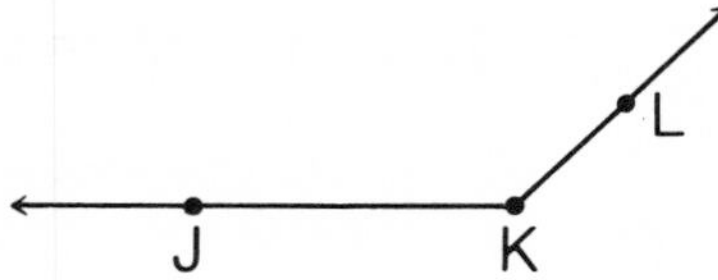

2. Which angle below is a right angle?

3. Which angle below is greater than a right angle?

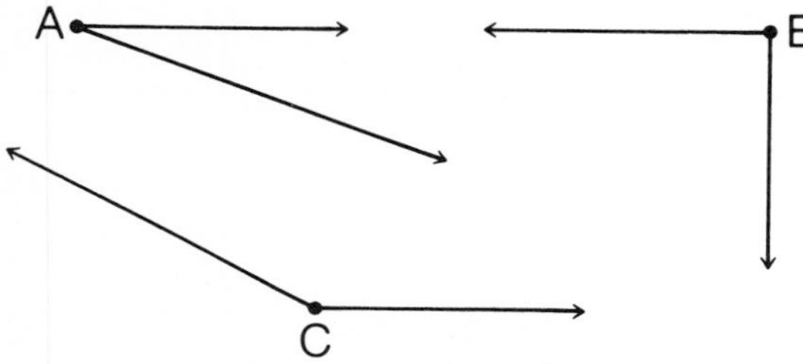

Measuring angles, pages 286–290

4. Give the measure of ∠DEF in degrees.

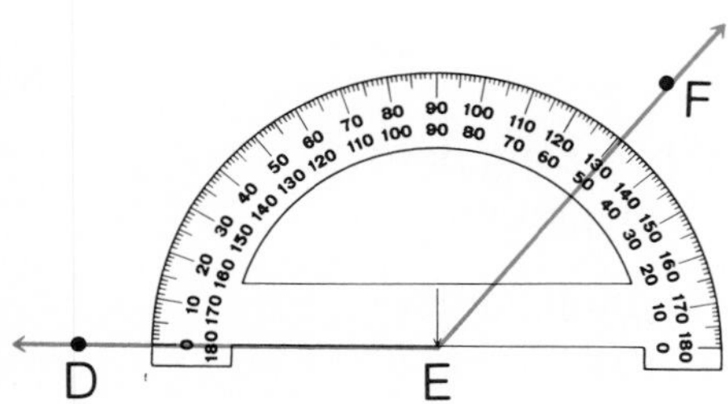

5. Use your protractor to find the measure of angle F to the nearest degree.

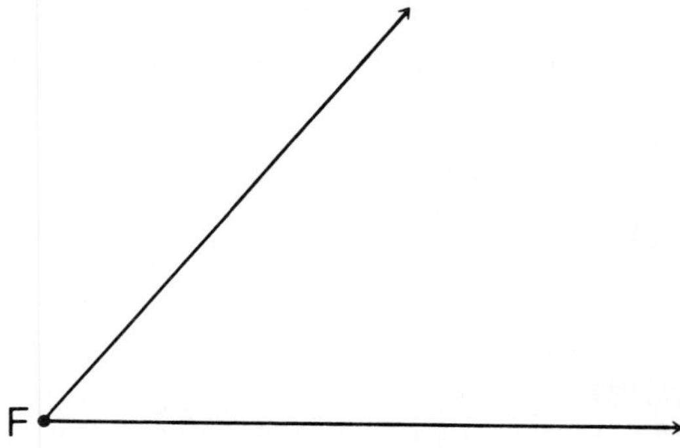

6. Draw an angle whose measure is 65°.

Angles of polygons, pages 292–298

Find the missing angle measures.

7.

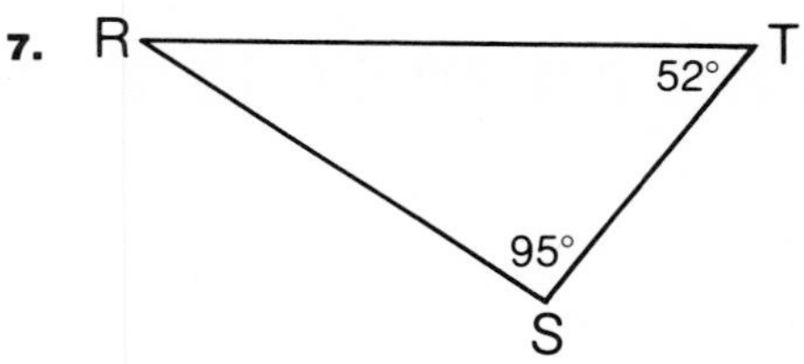

8.

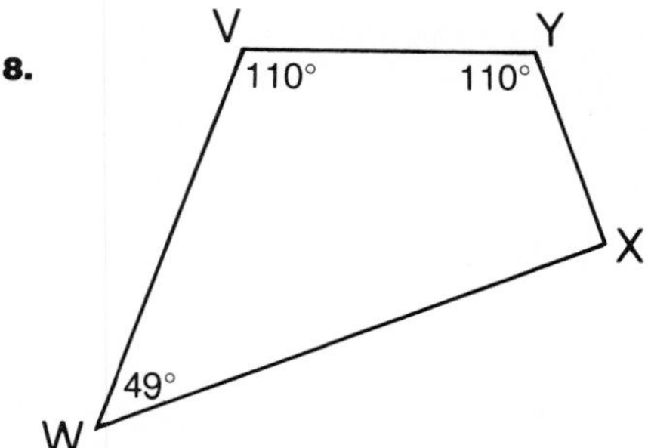

9. Which angles of the quadrilateral are congruent?

Check Yourself: Level 29

Meaning of mixed numbers, pages 242–253

1. Give the length of the nail to the nearest $\frac{1}{4}$ inch.

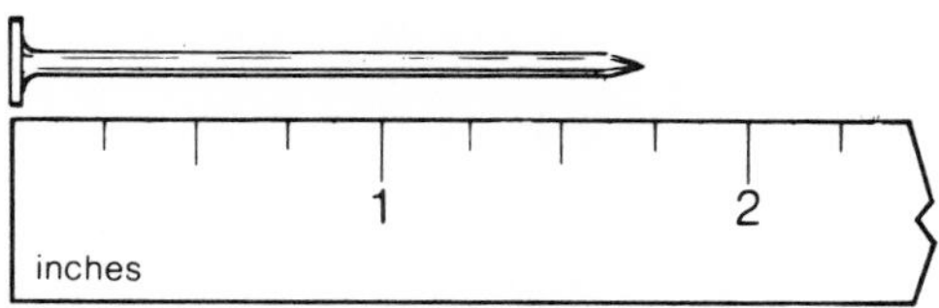

2. Use < or >. $2\frac{5}{8}$ ● $2\frac{1}{4}$

3. A 93-inch piece of tape was cut into 8 equal pieces. How long was each piece?

Write each improper fraction as a mixed number or a whole number.

4. $\frac{29}{2}$ **5.** $\frac{42}{7}$

Adding mixed numbers, pages 258–267

Find each sum.

6. $6\frac{3}{8} + 4\frac{1}{8}$ **7.** $32\frac{1}{5} + 17$ **8.** $9 + 8\frac{3}{4}$

9. $6\frac{1}{3} + 2\frac{1}{4}$ **10.** $2\frac{7}{10} + 9\frac{3}{5}$ **11.** $1\frac{1}{2} + 1\frac{1}{6} + 1\frac{1}{3}$

12. A beagle puppy weighed $5\frac{1}{4}$ pounds. A collie puppy weighed $7\frac{5}{8}$ pounds. Find their total weight.

Subtracting mixed numbers, pages 268–279

Find each difference.

13. $14\frac{2}{3} - 5\frac{1}{3}$ **14.** $25\frac{1}{6} - 11$ **15.** $19 - 3\frac{5}{8}$

16. $9\frac{1}{4} - 7\frac{3}{4}$ **17.** $12\frac{3}{5} - 1\frac{1}{2}$ **18.** $8\frac{2}{3} - 2\frac{5}{6}$

19. How much farther did Kathy bicycle on Monday?

Monday: $13\frac{7}{10}$ mi. Tuesday: $5\frac{2}{5}$ mi.

Measuring angles, pages 282–300

20. Give the measure of ∠RST in degrees.

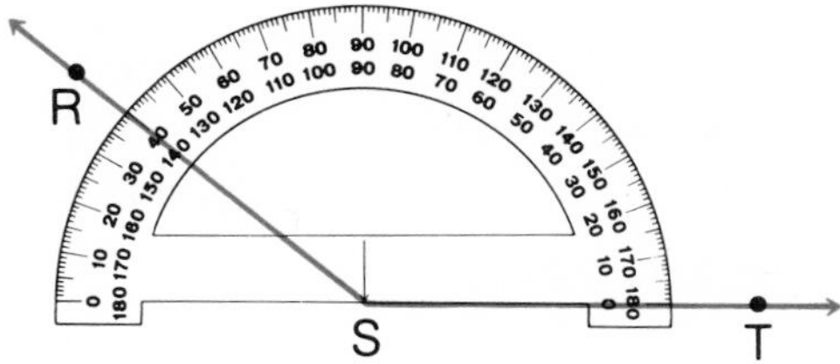

Find the missing angle measures.

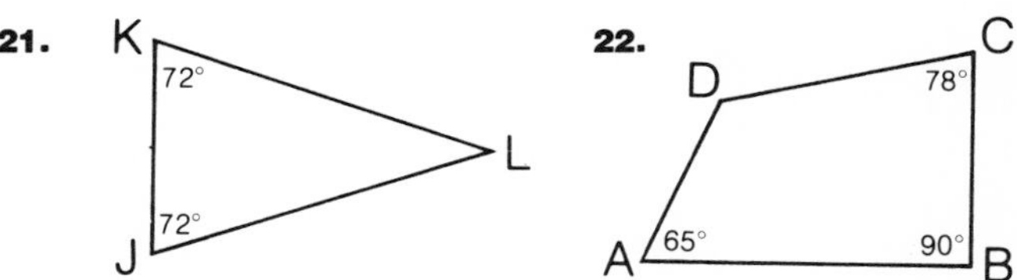

23. Which angles of the triangle are congruent?

24. Which angle of the quadrilateral is a right angle?

More Practice

Set A

Express each answer as a mixed number.

1. $5\overline{)37}$
2. $8\overline{)123}$
3. $4\overline{)89}$
4. $3\overline{)41}$
5. $10\overline{)119}$
6. $6\overline{)41}$
7. $2\overline{)27}$
8. $12\overline{)63}$
9. $10\overline{)57}$
10. $16\overline{)132}$

Set B

Write each improper fraction as a mixed number or a whole number.

1. $\frac{65}{8}$
2. $\frac{33}{3}$
3. $\frac{77}{6}$
4. $\frac{19}{4}$
5. $\frac{45}{5}$
6. $\frac{81}{10}$
7. $\frac{55}{2}$
8. $\frac{27}{5}$
9. $\frac{72}{4}$
10. $\frac{13}{6}$
11. $\frac{23}{7}$
12. $\frac{7}{2}$
13. $\frac{15}{3}$
14. $\frac{35}{8}$

Set C

1. $\begin{array}{r} 1 \\ +\ 2\frac{1}{3} \\ \hline \end{array}$
2. $\begin{array}{r} 7\frac{2}{8} \\ +\ 3\frac{5}{8} \\ \hline \end{array}$
3. $\begin{array}{r} 4\frac{2}{4} \\ +\ \frac{1}{4} \\ \hline \end{array}$
4. $\begin{array}{r} 8\frac{4}{9} \\ +\ 2\frac{4}{9} \\ \hline \end{array}$
5. $3 + 6\frac{3}{10}$
6. $46 + 4\frac{2}{6}$
7. $5\frac{1}{5} + 4\frac{4}{5}$
8. $3\frac{3}{12} + 16\frac{7}{12}$

Set D

Rename each sum.

1. $3\frac{2}{3} + 1\frac{2}{3}$
2. $4\frac{5}{6} + 3\frac{1}{6}$
3. $6\frac{7}{8} + 5\frac{5}{8}$
4. $16\frac{5}{12} + 7\frac{11}{12}$
5. $29\frac{4}{5} + 15\frac{2}{5}$
6. $7\frac{3}{4} + 6\frac{1}{4}$
7. $\frac{1}{2} + 4\frac{1}{2}$
8. $13\frac{3}{8} + 12\frac{7}{8}$

Set E

Rename the sum if necessary.

1. $\begin{array}{r} 1\frac{2}{3} \\ +\ 3\frac{3}{4} \\ \hline \end{array}$
2. $\begin{array}{r} 6\frac{1}{6} \\ +\ 5\frac{1}{5} \\ \hline \end{array}$
3. $\begin{array}{r} 7\frac{2}{3} \\ +\ 2\frac{3}{8} \\ \hline \end{array}$
4. $\begin{array}{r} 12\frac{3}{10} \\ +\ 6\frac{4}{5} \\ \hline \end{array}$
5. $4\frac{1}{2} + 8\frac{4}{5}$
6. $9\frac{1}{4} + 1\frac{5}{8}$
7. $3\frac{1}{6} + 2\frac{5}{12}$
8. $2\frac{7}{12} + 13\frac{1}{3}$

Set F

1. $\begin{array}{r} 4\frac{3}{10} \\ 6\frac{1}{5} \\ +\ 1\frac{1}{2} \\ \hline \end{array}$
2. $\begin{array}{r} 3\frac{1}{3} \\ 2\frac{1}{4} \\ +\ 6\frac{2}{3} \\ \hline \end{array}$
3. $\begin{array}{r} \frac{5}{12} \\ 6\frac{1}{6} \\ +\ 12\frac{5}{6} \\ \hline \end{array}$
4. $\begin{array}{r} 1\frac{3}{8} \\ \frac{1}{4} \\ +\ 3\frac{1}{2} \\ \hline \end{array}$
5. $13\frac{1}{6} + 4\frac{1}{2} + 2\frac{2}{3}$
6. $4 + 3\frac{1}{3} + 6\frac{2}{5}$

More Practice

Set G

1. $23\frac{7}{8} - 14\frac{3}{8}$
2. $2\frac{3}{5} - \frac{2}{5}$
3. $13\frac{3}{4} - 7\frac{1}{4}$
4. $6\frac{7}{10} - 4\frac{1}{10}$
5. $4\frac{11}{12} - 4\frac{5}{12}$
6. $5\frac{1}{3} - 5$
7. $4\frac{5}{6} - 3\frac{1}{6}$
8. $14\frac{5}{16} - 7\frac{3}{16}$
9. $25\frac{5}{8} - \frac{1}{8}$
10. $1\frac{3}{4} - 1\frac{1}{4}$
11. $8\frac{1}{2} - 7$
12. $6\frac{11}{12} - 6\frac{5}{12}$

Set H

1. $7\frac{3}{8} - 3\frac{5}{8}$
2. $5\frac{5}{12} - 2\frac{7}{12}$
3. $13\frac{1}{6} - 4\frac{5}{6}$
4. $6\frac{1}{3} - 4\frac{2}{3}$
5. $26\frac{13}{16} - 17\frac{15}{16}$
6. $22\frac{1}{4} - 21\frac{3}{4}$
7. $1\frac{2}{5} - \frac{3}{5}$
8. $3\frac{7}{10} - 1\frac{9}{10}$
9. $46\frac{1}{12} - 29\frac{11}{12}$
10. $11\frac{3}{10} - 9\frac{7}{10}$
11. $3\frac{5}{8} - 2\frac{7}{8}$
12. $16\frac{3}{5} - 9\frac{4}{5}$

Set I

1. $6\frac{3}{8} - 4\frac{1}{4}$
2. $1\frac{5}{6} - 1\frac{2}{5}$
3. $3\frac{3}{4} - 2\frac{1}{6}$
4. $15\frac{7}{10} - 9\frac{1}{2}$
5. $9\frac{3}{4} - 7\frac{2}{3}$
6. $13\frac{5}{6} - 12\frac{5}{8}$
7. $6\frac{3}{5} - 3\frac{1}{4}$
8. $1\frac{3}{8} - \frac{3}{12}$
9. $5\frac{3}{5} - 4\frac{1}{4}$
10. $8\frac{2}{3} - 5\frac{1}{6}$
11. $6\frac{2}{3} - 1\frac{1}{8}$
12. $4\frac{5}{8} - 3\frac{1}{2}$

Set J

1. $7\frac{1}{6} - 5\frac{2}{3}$
2. $18\frac{3}{5} - 9\frac{5}{6}$
3. $6\frac{1}{3} - 4\frac{3}{8}$
4. $6\frac{3}{10} - 1\frac{3}{5}$
5. $1\frac{1}{2} - \frac{2}{3}$
6. $5\frac{3}{4} - 3\frac{4}{5}$
7. $2\frac{5}{12} - 1\frac{2}{3}$
8. $14\frac{1}{6} - 13\frac{3}{4}$
9. $7\frac{1}{4} - 3\frac{5}{6}$
10. $6\frac{1}{5} - 5\frac{1}{3}$
11. $12\frac{2}{3} - 7\frac{3}{4}$
12. $4\frac{1}{2} - 2\frac{3}{5}$

Check Yourself Answers: Level 29

Check Yourself, page 257

1. $2\frac{1}{4}$

2. $1\frac{1}{6}$

3. $1\frac{3}{4}$ in.

4. $2\frac{1}{8}$ in.

5. $5\frac{1}{4}$ oz.

6. Sheila

7. $3\frac{7}{10}$

8. $41\frac{2}{3}$ yd.

9. $5\frac{2}{5}$

10. 6

Check Yourself, page 281

1. $10\frac{7}{10}$

2. $24\frac{5}{8}$

3. $18\frac{2}{5}$

4. $13\frac{7}{8}$

5. $12\frac{1}{6}$

6. $11\frac{5}{12}$

7. $2\frac{4}{7}$

8. $4\frac{3}{4}$

9. $5\frac{2}{3}$

10. $2\frac{2}{4}$, or $2\frac{1}{2}$

11. $7\frac{3}{10}$

12. $13\frac{7}{12}$

13. $4\frac{3}{8}$ lb.

14. $5\frac{5}{8}$ in.

15. $2\frac{3}{8}$ mi.

16. $\frac{3}{6}$ ft., or $\frac{1}{2}$ ft.

Check Yourself, page 300

1. ∠ JKL, or ∠ LKJ

2. ∠B

3. ∠C

4. 130°

5. 50°

6. 65°

7. 33°

8. 91°

9. ∠V and ∠Y

Check Yourself: Level 29, page 301

1. $1\frac{3}{4}$ in.

2. >

3. $11\frac{5}{8}$ in.

4. $14\frac{1}{2}$

5. 6

6. $10\frac{4}{8}$, or $10\frac{1}{2}$

7. $49\frac{1}{5}$

8. $17\frac{3}{4}$

9. $8\frac{7}{12}$

10. $12\frac{3}{10}$

11. 4

12. $12\frac{7}{8}$ lb.

13. $9\frac{1}{3}$

14. $14\frac{1}{6}$

15. $15\frac{3}{8}$

16. $1\frac{2}{4}$, or $1\frac{1}{2}$

17. $11\frac{1}{10}$

18. $5\frac{5}{6}$

19. $8\frac{3}{10}$

20. 140°

21. 36°

22. 127°

23. ∠K and ∠J

24. ∠B

Level 30

Using Pictures to Multiply Fractions

A. Here's how to find $\frac{1}{2} \times \frac{1}{4}$.

Fold a paper into 4 equal parts as shown. Shade $\frac{1}{4}$ of the paper.

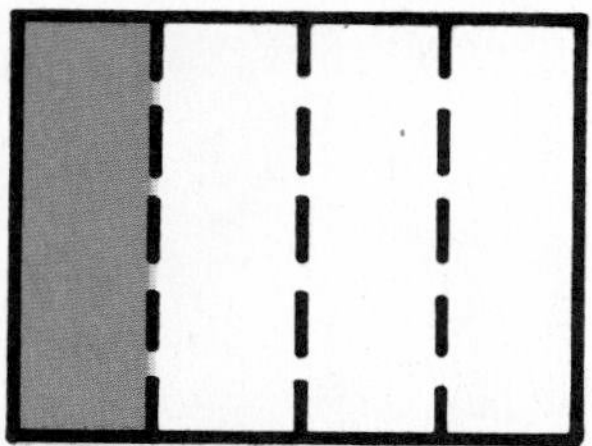

Now fold the paper in half. Darken $\frac{1}{2}$ of the shaded part.

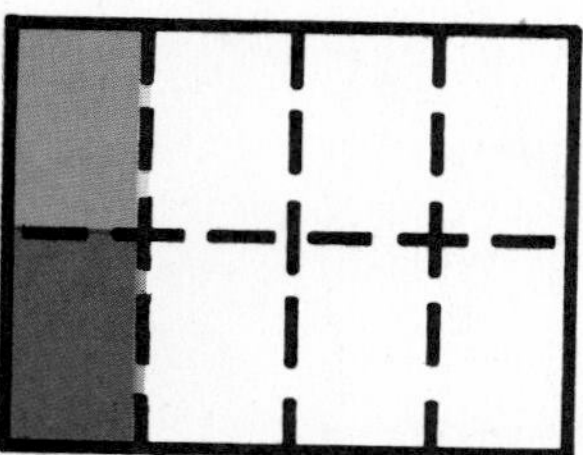

What fraction of the paper has dark shading?

$\frac{1}{2}$ of $\frac{1}{4}$ is $\frac{1}{8}$.

$\frac{1}{2} \times \frac{1}{4} = \frac{1}{8}$

B. What is $\frac{3}{4} \times \frac{3}{4}$?

Fold a paper into 4 equal parts as shown. Shade $\frac{3}{4}$ of the paper.

Now fold the paper in fourths again. Darken $\frac{3}{4}$ of the shaded part.

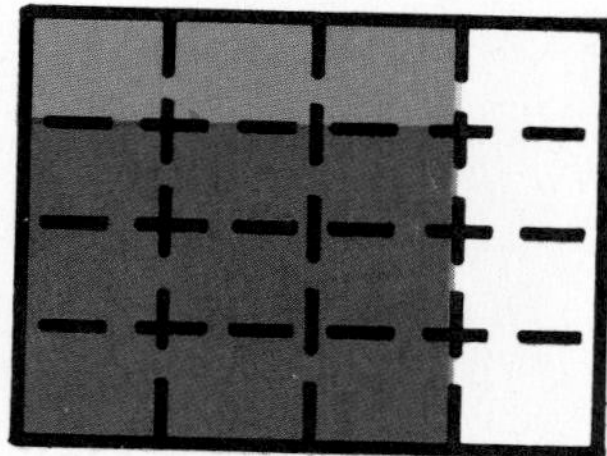

What fraction of the paper has dark shading?

$\frac{3}{4}$ of $\frac{3}{4}$ is $\frac{9}{16}$.

$\frac{3}{4} \times \frac{3}{4} = \frac{9}{16}$

In each exercise, use the picture to help you find the product.

1.

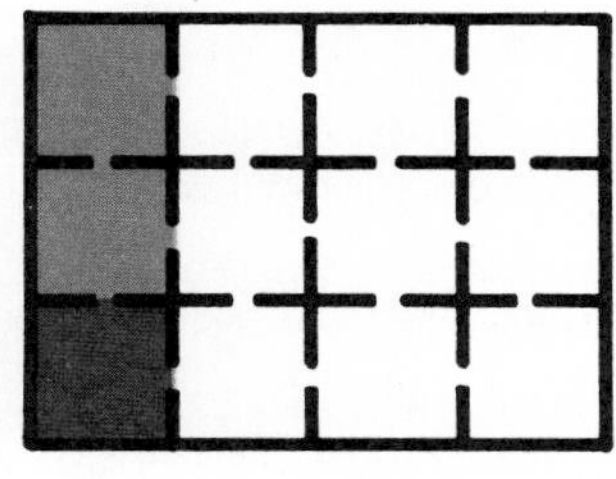

$\frac{1}{3}$ of $\frac{1}{4}$

$\frac{1}{3} \times \frac{1}{4} = \frac{\square}{\square}$

2.

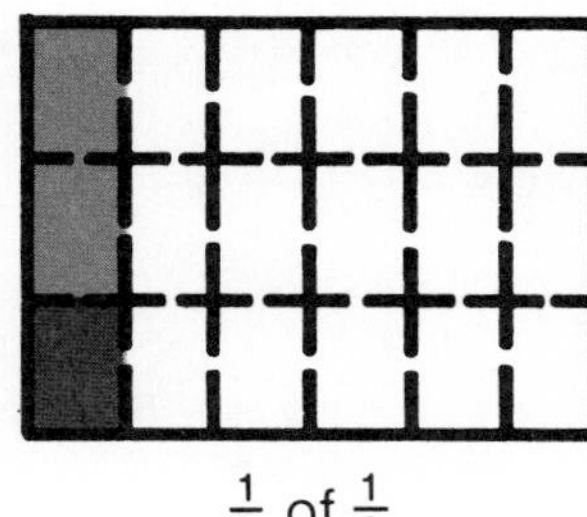

$\frac{1}{3}$ of $\frac{1}{6}$

$\frac{1}{3} \times \frac{1}{6} = \frac{\square}{\square}$

3.

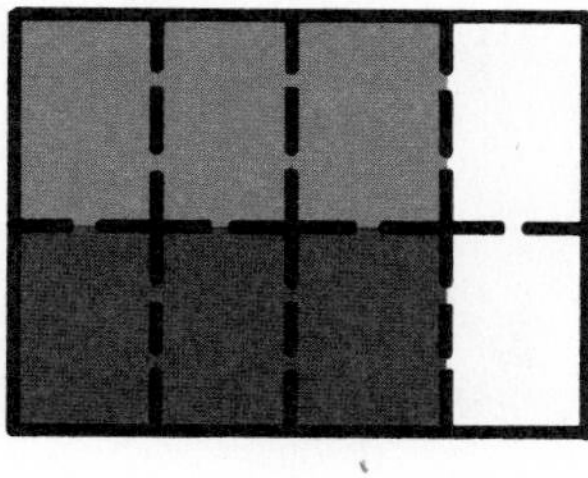

$\frac{1}{2}$ of $\frac{3}{4}$

$\frac{1}{2} \times \frac{3}{4} = \frac{\square}{\square}$

4.

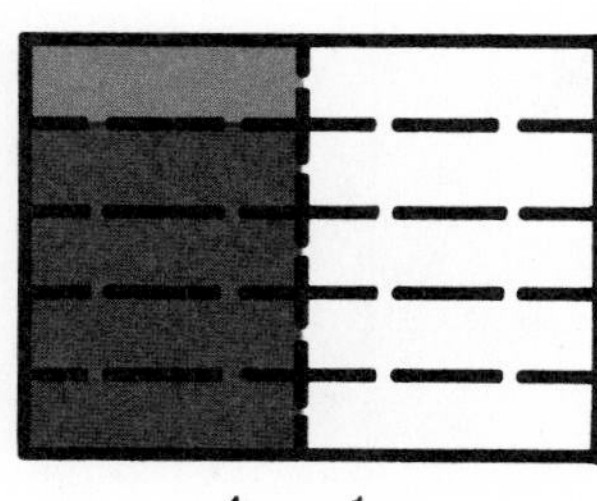

$\frac{4}{5}$ of $\frac{1}{2}$

$\frac{4}{5} \times \frac{1}{2} = \frac{\square}{\square}$

5.

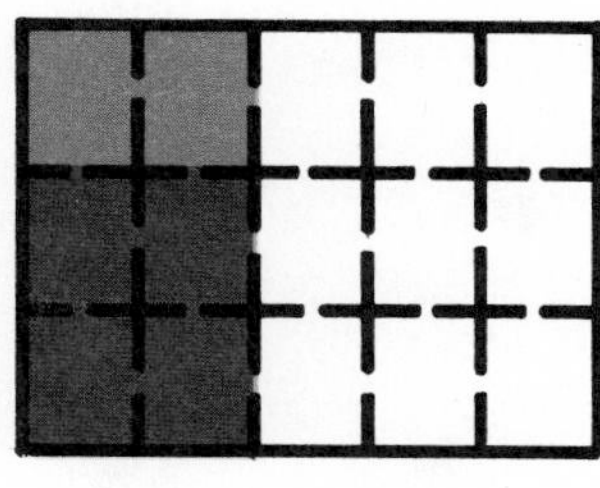

$\frac{2}{3}$ of $\frac{2}{5}$

$\frac{2}{3} \times \frac{2}{5} = \frac{\square}{\square}$

6.

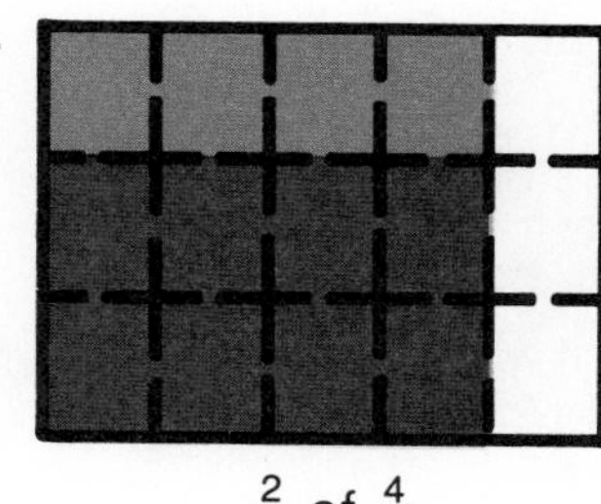

$\frac{2}{3}$ of $\frac{4}{5}$

$\frac{2}{3} \times \frac{4}{5} = \frac{\square}{\square}$

7.

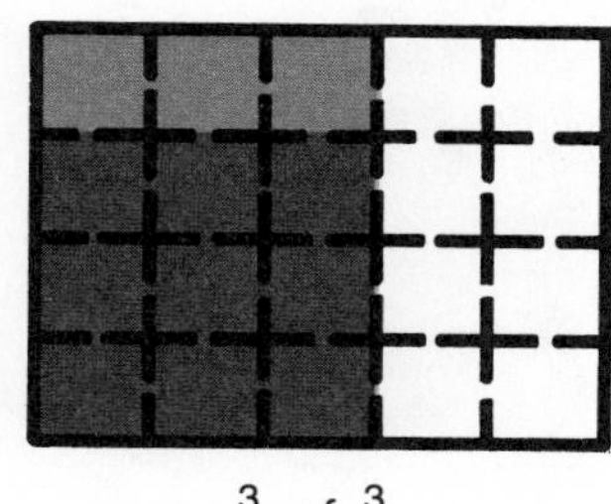

$\frac{3}{4}$ of $\frac{3}{5}$

$\frac{3}{4} \times \frac{3}{5} = \frac{\square}{\square}$

● **Discuss** How can you find $\frac{5}{7} \times \frac{2}{3}$ without using a picture?

Multiplying Fractions

To multiply fractions, first multiply the numerators. Then multiply the denominators.

$$\frac{3}{4} \times \frac{5}{7} = \frac{15}{28} \quad \begin{matrix} 3 \times 5 \\ 4 \times 7 \end{matrix}$$

Find each product.

1. $\frac{2}{3} \times \frac{4}{5}$
2. $\frac{3}{8} \times \frac{1}{2}$
3. $\frac{2}{5} \times \frac{2}{3}$
4. $\frac{3}{5} \times \frac{3}{4}$
5. $\frac{3}{5} \times \frac{7}{10}$
6. $\frac{2}{5} \times \frac{2}{7}$
7. $\frac{3}{10} \times \frac{9}{10}$
8. $\frac{1}{6} \times \frac{5}{6}$
9. $\frac{2}{7} \times \frac{3}{7}$
10. $\frac{5}{9} \times \frac{4}{3}$

Find each product. Give your answer in lowest terms.

11. $\frac{3}{4} \times \frac{2}{5} = \frac{6}{20} = \frac{}{10}$
12. $\frac{4}{5} \times \frac{1}{8} = \frac{4}{40} = \frac{1}{}$
13. $\frac{1}{4} \times \frac{2}{3}$
14. $\frac{2}{3} \times \frac{7}{8}$
15. $\frac{3}{4} \times \frac{4}{5}$
16. $\frac{3}{5} \times \frac{5}{8}$
17. $\frac{5}{6} \times \frac{1}{10}$
18. $\frac{2}{3} \times \frac{7}{8}$
19. $\frac{7}{10} \times \frac{5}{8}$
20. $\frac{3}{4} \times \frac{2}{3}$

Multiply to find each answer.

21. Land covers $\frac{2}{7}$ of the earth's surface. $\frac{1}{5}$ of the land is in Asia. What fraction of the earth's surface is land in Asia?
22. India has $\frac{1}{7}$ of the world's population. $\frac{1}{10}$ of India's population is in Bombay. What fraction of the world's population is in Bombay?
23. Africa provides $\frac{1}{8}$ of the world's petroleum. $\frac{1}{2}$ of African petroleum comes from Libya. What fraction of the world's petroleum comes from Libya?
24. The United States has $\frac{1}{18}$ of the world's population. $\frac{3}{4}$ of the United States population live in cities. What fraction of the world's population live in United States cities?
25. $\frac{3}{10}$ of the people in the United States attend school. Of these people, $\frac{3}{5}$ are in elementary school. What fraction of the people in the United States are in elementary school?

26. $\frac{1}{6}$ of the world's land is in North America, and $\frac{2}{5}$ of the land in North America is in Canada. What fraction of the world's land is in Canada?

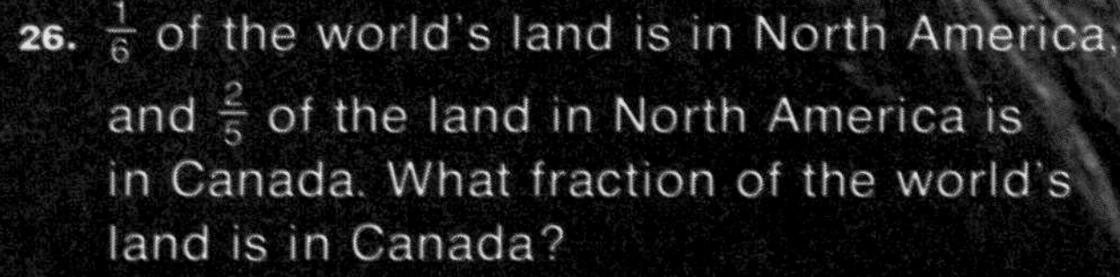

27. $\frac{1}{20}$ of the people in the United States live in Texas. In Texas, $\frac{1}{5}$ of the people are between the ages of 5 and 13. What fraction of the people in the United States are Texans between the ages of 5 and 13?

28. Water covers $\frac{5}{7}$ of the earth's surface. $\frac{19}{20}$ of this surface is salt water. What fraction of the earth's surface is salt water?

More practice
Set A, page 367

Multiplying Fractions and Whole Numbers

A. Here are 6 baby whales.
$\frac{2}{3}$ of the whales are females.
How many of the whales are females?

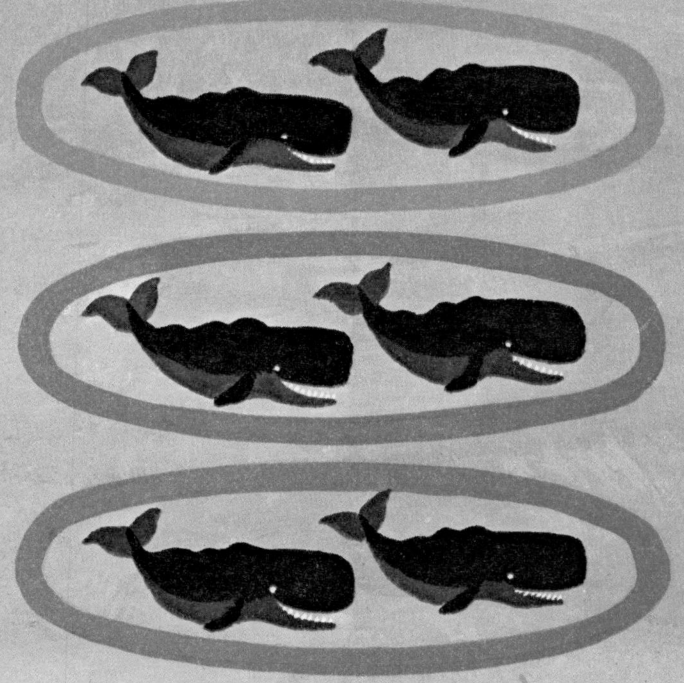

Find $\frac{2}{3}$ of 6, or $\frac{2}{3} \times 6$.

$$\frac{2}{3} \times 6$$

$$\frac{2}{3} \times \frac{6}{1} = \frac{12}{3} = 4$$

Four of the whales are females.

B. The baby whale below is 7 yards long.
Its head is $\frac{2}{5}$ of its total length.
How long is its head?

Find $\frac{2}{5}$ of 7, or $\frac{2}{5} \times 7$.

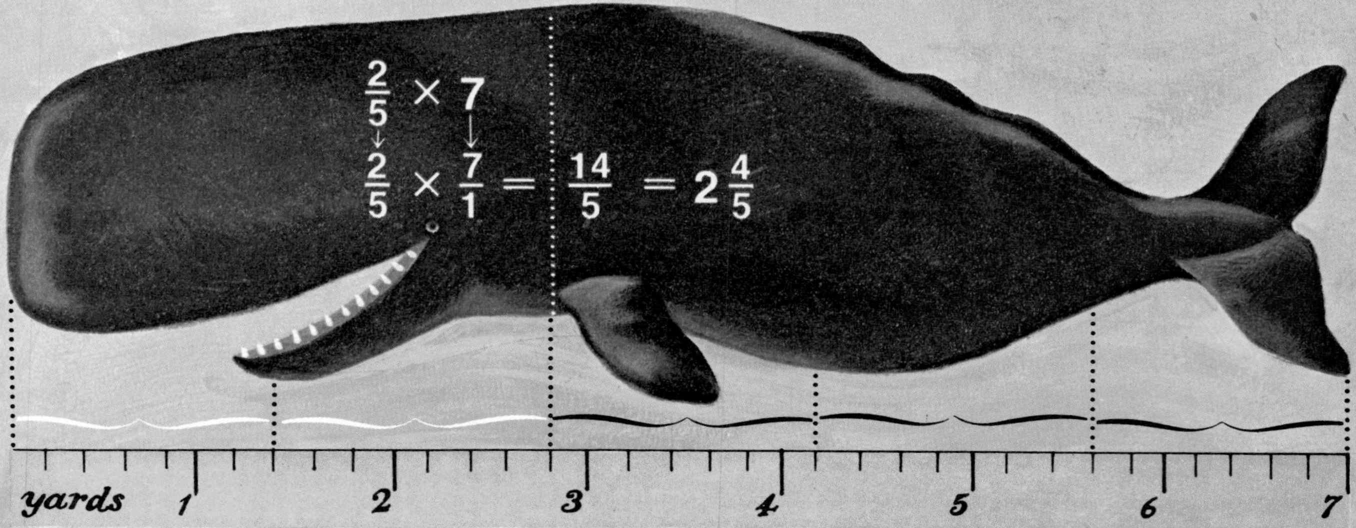

The baby whale's head is $2\frac{4}{5}$ yards long.

Multiply to find each answer.

Here's how

$\frac{3}{4}$ of 15 inches

$\frac{3}{4} \times 15$

$\frac{3}{4} \times \frac{15}{1} = \frac{45}{4} = 11\frac{1}{4}$ *inches*

1. $\frac{1}{2}$ of 4 rocks
2. $\frac{3}{5}$ of 10 grams
3. $\frac{1}{2}$ of 7 feet
4. $\frac{1}{3}$ of 16 inches
5. $\frac{2}{5}$ of 20 liters
6. $\frac{4}{5}$ of 8 ounces
7. $\frac{2}{3}$ of 12 eggs
8. $\frac{2}{5}$ of 24 yards
9. $\frac{1}{4}$ of 36 pencils
10. $\frac{3}{4}$ of 7 miles
11. $\frac{3}{10}$ of 40 meters
12. $\frac{1}{8}$ of 28 feet
13. $\frac{7}{10}$ of 6 liters
14. $\frac{1}{3}$ of 873 people

BLUE WHALE

World's largest animal
Total weight: 120 tons

Find the weight in tons for these parts of a blue whale.

15. Blubber: $\frac{5}{24}$ of total weight
16. Muscle: $\frac{5}{12}$ of total weight
17. Bones: $\frac{1}{6}$ of total weight
18. Tongue: $\frac{1}{48}$ of total weight
19. Liver: $\frac{1}{240}$ of total weight
20. Heart: $\frac{1}{300}$ of total weight

More practice
Set B, page 367

Using Multiplication of Fractions: Probability

EXPERIMENT A

Spin the pointer. Record the color on which it stops.

$\frac{1}{4}$ of the spinner is red.

You can expect about $\frac{1}{4}$ of your spins to stop on red.

If you make 20 spins, you can expect about $\frac{1}{4}$ of 20, or 5, spins to stop on red.

EXPERIMENT B

Draw a card without looking. Record its color. Put it back in the jar.

$\frac{2}{5}$ of the cards are blue.

You can expect about $\frac{2}{5}$ of your draws to be blue cards.

If you make 30 draws, you can expect about $\frac{2}{5}$ of 30, or 12, draws to be blue cards.

EXPERIMENT C

Draw a marble without looking. Record its color. Put it back in the bag.

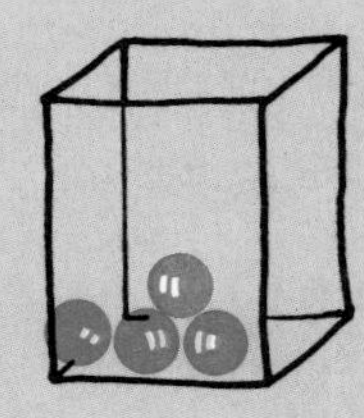

1. What fraction of the marbles are red?
2. About what fraction of your draws can you expect to be red marbles?
3. About how many draws would you expect to be red marbles if you made
   a. 40 draws?
   b. 200 draws?

EXPERIMENT D

Spin the pointer. Record the color on which it stops.

4. What fraction of the spinner is blue?
5. About what fraction of your spins can you expect to stop on blue?
6. About how many spins would you expect to stop on blue if you made
   a. 30 spins?
   b. 600 spins?

EXPERIMENT E

Place the cards face down.
Mix them up. Draw a card.
Record the letter you drew.
Put the card back. Mix again.

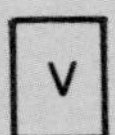

R

7. What fraction of the cards show an I?

8. About how many draws would you expect to be I's if you made

a. 35 draws?

b. 70 draws?

c. 280 draws?

EXPERIMENT F

Draw a marble
without looking.
Record its color.
Put it back in
the jar.

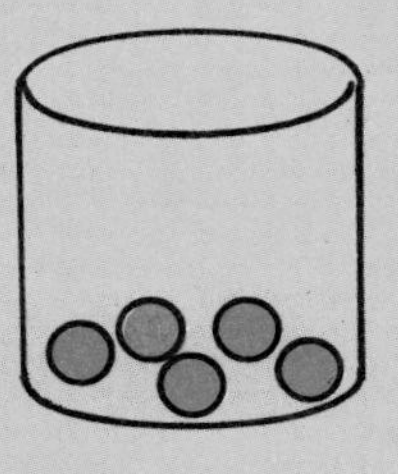

9. What fraction of the marbles are green?

10. About how many draws would you expect to be green marbles if you made

a. 50 draws?

b. 100 draws?

c. 750 draws?

EXPERIMENT G

Spin the pencil.
Record the color
of the side on which
the spinner lands.

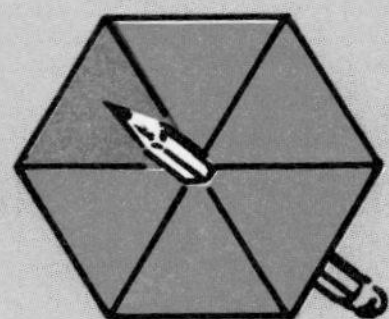

11. What fraction of the spinner is blue?

12. About how many spins would you expect to be blue if you made

a. 30 spins?

b. 150 spins?

c. 900 spins?

EXPERIMENT H

Place the cards face down.
Mix them up. Draw a card.
Record the shape on the card.
Put the card back. Mix again.

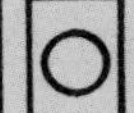

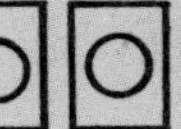

13. What fraction of the cards show triangles?

14. About how many draws would you expect to be triangles if you made

a. 40 draws?

b. 120 draws?

c. 800 draws?

Using Multiplication of Fractions: Probability

You can use the results from an experiment to predict other results of the experiment.

Julie tossed a thumbtack 50 times. She recorded her results in table 1.

Table 1

Results of tosses	Number	Fraction
Point down	19	$\frac{19}{50}$
Point up	31	$\frac{31}{50}$

Use the fractions in table 1 to make these predictions.

1. About how many times would you expect the thumbtack to land point down in

a. 100 tosses? (Find $\frac{19}{50} \times 100$.)

b. 250 tosses?

c. 400 tosses?

2. About how many times would you expect the thumbtack to land point up in

a. 100 tosses?

b. 250 tosses?

c. 400 tosses?

Ray marked four faces of a box with X's and two faces with O's. He tossed the box 80 times and recorded the letter that landed up.

Table 2

Results of tosses	Number	Fraction
X up	63	$\frac{63}{80}$
O up	17	$\frac{17}{80}$

Use the results in table 2 to make these predictions.

3. About how many times would you expect the box to land with X up in

a. 160 tosses?

b. 400 tosses?

c. 800 tosses?

4. About how many times would you expect the box to land with O up in

a. 160 tosses?

b. 400 tosses?

c. 800 tosses?

Jean took a poll of 100 students in her school to find their choice for school president. She recorded her findings in a table.

Candidates	Number	Fraction
Ann	30	$\frac{30}{100}$
Chuck	47	$\frac{47}{100}$
Henry	23	$\frac{23}{100}$

Use the results of the poll to predict the results of the election.

5. About how many votes would you expect Ann to get if

- **a.** 300 students voted?
- **b.** 500 students voted?
- **c.** 700 students voted?

6. About how many votes might Chuck get if

- **a.** 300 students voted?
- **b.** 500 students voted?
- **c.** 700 students voted?

7. About how many votes might Henry get if

- **a.** 300 students voted?
- **b.** 500 students voted?
- **c.** 700 students voted?

● **Discuss** Why can't you be sure each candidate would get the number of votes you predict?

Keeping Skillful

Find these products mentally.

1. 10 × 10

2. 20 × 10

3. 100 × 20

4. 20 × 1000

5. 200 × 100

6. 100 × 100

7. 500 × 100

8. 1000 × 500

9. 100 × 5000

10. 1000 × 500

11. 1000 × 1000

12. 7000 × 1000

13. 100 × 84

14. 840 × 100

15. 1000 × 8400

16. 84,000 × 10,000

Multiply.

17. $\begin{array}{r} 144 \\ \times\ 12 \\ \hline \end{array}$

18. $\begin{array}{r} 720 \\ \times\ 24 \\ \hline \end{array}$

19. $\begin{array}{r} 360 \\ \times\ 48 \\ \hline \end{array}$

20. $\begin{array}{r} 906 \\ \times\ 16 \\ \hline \end{array}$

21. $\begin{array}{r} 604 \\ \times\ 56 \\ \hline \end{array}$

22. $\begin{array}{r} 4008 \\ \times\ 32 \\ \hline \end{array}$

23. $\begin{array}{r} 1028 \\ \times\ 96 \\ \hline \end{array}$

24. $\begin{array}{r} 2056 \\ \times\ 808 \\ \hline \end{array}$

25. $\begin{array}{r} 2040 \\ \times\ 604 \\ \hline \end{array}$

Write each improper fraction as a mixed number or a whole number.

26. $\frac{58}{4}$

27. $\frac{58}{8}$

28. $\frac{116}{8}$

29. $\frac{48}{10}$

30. $\frac{96}{5}$

31. $\frac{230}{20}$

32. $\frac{320}{4}$

33. $\frac{264}{50}$

34. $\frac{96}{12}$

35. $\frac{256}{40}$

36. $\frac{1020}{60}$

37. $\frac{1248}{100}$

Explore

Make a square cardboard spinner like the one shown.

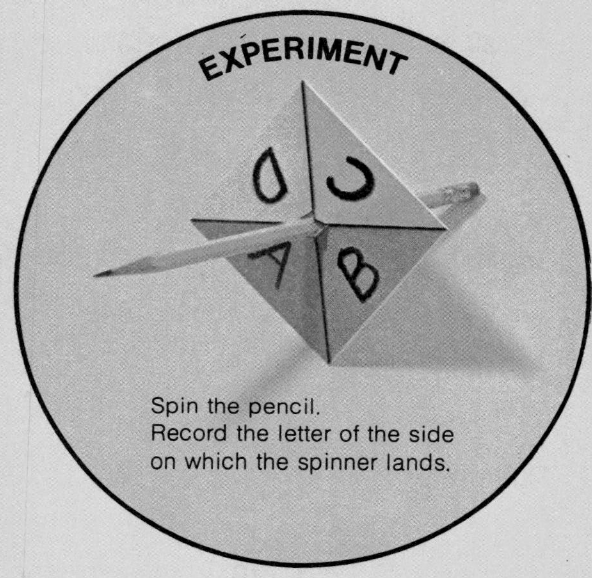

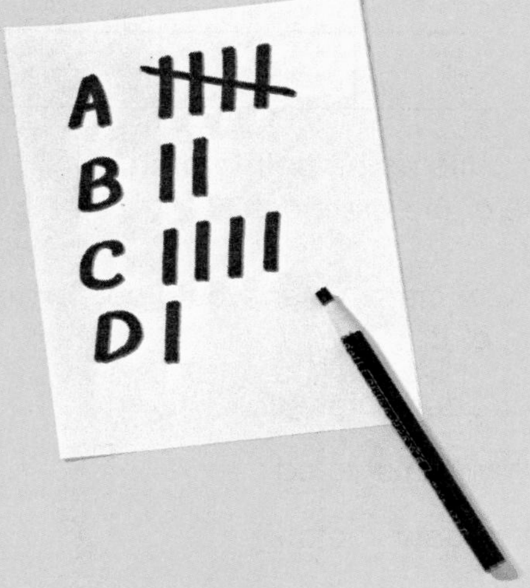

1. What fraction of the spinner is marked with A?
2. About how many spins would you expect to stop on A if you made
   a. 40 spins? b. 200 spins? c. 400 spins?
3. Do the experiment 40 times. How many times did the spinner stop on A?
4. Do the experiment 200 times. How many times did the spinner stop on A?
5. Do the experiment 400 times. How many times did the spinner stop on A?
6. Were the results of your experiments close to the results you predicted in exercise 2?

Writing Mixed Numbers as Improper Fractions

A. Write $2\frac{1}{3}$ as an improper fraction. Use the number line to help you.

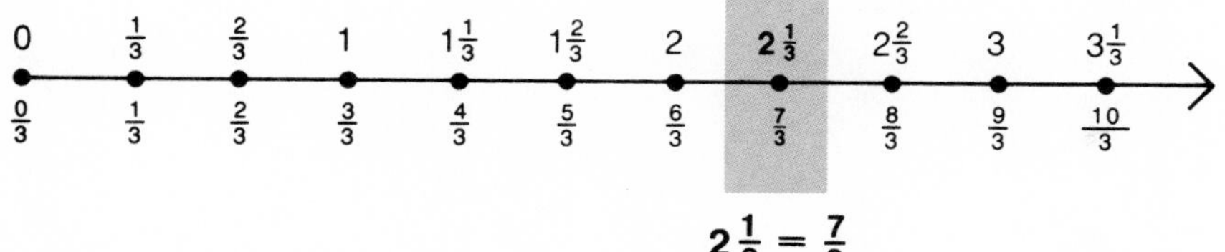

$$2\frac{1}{3} = \frac{7}{3}$$

B. Here is a way to write $2\frac{1}{3}$ as an improper fraction without using the number line.

$$2\frac{1}{3}$$

$$2 + \frac{1}{3}$$

$$\frac{6}{3} + \frac{1}{3}$$

Write 2 as a fraction with a denominator of 3. $\frac{2}{1} = \frac{6}{3}$

$$\frac{7}{3}$$

$$2\frac{1}{3} = \frac{7}{3}$$

C. Bill uses this shortcut.

$2\frac{1}{3} = \frac{7}{3}$ **Multiply 3 by 2. Then add 1.**

This is how Bill used his shortcut with $7\frac{4}{5}$.

$7\frac{4}{5} = \frac{39}{5}$ **Multiply 5 by 7. Then add 4.**

Why does Bill's shortcut work?

Write each mixed number as an improper fraction.

1. $4\frac{1}{3}$
2. $3\frac{1}{4}$
3. $8\frac{1}{2}$
4. $4\frac{1}{5}$
5. $5\frac{2}{3}$
6. $6\frac{2}{3}$
7. $3\frac{7}{8}$
8. $5\frac{3}{8}$
9. $9\frac{4}{5}$
10. $7\frac{3}{4}$
11. $8\frac{3}{5}$
12. $6\frac{7}{10}$
13. $3\frac{5}{12}$
14. $9\frac{2}{3}$
15. $7\frac{3}{8}$
16. $25\frac{1}{2}$
17. $10\frac{5}{8}$
18. $16\frac{1}{5}$
19. $33\frac{1}{3}$
20. $50\frac{3}{4}$

More practice Set C, page 367

Fluffy Biscuits	Makes 1 dozen
$1\frac{1}{4}$ cups flour	
$1\frac{1}{3}$ teaspoons baking powder	
$\frac{1}{2}$ teaspoon sugar	
2 tablespoons butter	
6 tablespoons milk	
$\frac{2}{3}$ teaspoon salt	

A. How many cups of flour do you need to make $2\frac{1}{2}$ dozen biscuits?

Find $2\frac{1}{2} \times 1\frac{1}{4}$.

$$2\frac{1}{2} \times 1\frac{1}{4}$$ Write $2\frac{1}{2}$ and $1\frac{1}{4}$ as fractions.

$$\frac{5}{2} \times \frac{5}{4} = \frac{25}{8} = 3\frac{1}{8}$$

You need $3\frac{1}{8}$ cups of flour.

B. How much butter do you need?

Find $2\frac{1}{2} \times 2$.

$$2\frac{1}{2} \times 2$$ Write $2\frac{1}{2}$ and 2 as fractions.

$$\frac{5}{2} \times \frac{2}{1} = \frac{10}{2} = 5$$

You need 5 tablespoons of butter.

Find each product.
Express the answers as mixed numbers or whole numbers.

1. $2\frac{1}{2} \times 1\frac{1}{3}$
2. $2\frac{1}{2} \times \frac{1}{2}$
3. $2\frac{1}{2} \times 6$
4. $2\frac{1}{2} \times \frac{2}{3}$
5. $3\frac{1}{2} \times 1\frac{1}{7}$
6. $1\frac{1}{6} \times 8$
7. $1\frac{2}{3} \times \frac{3}{10}$
8. $3\frac{2}{3} \times 6$
9. $2\frac{1}{2} \times 3\frac{1}{2}$
10. $1\frac{5}{8} \times 5$
11. $4\frac{1}{6} \times 1\frac{1}{5}$
12. $2\frac{1}{4} \times 2\frac{2}{5}$

13. How much of each ingredient do you need to make four cakes?

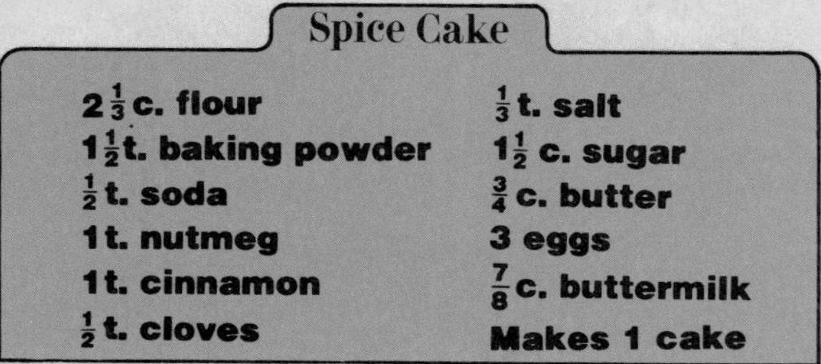

Spice Cake

$2\frac{1}{3}$ c. flour
$1\frac{1}{2}$ t. baking powder
$\frac{1}{2}$ t. soda
1 t. nutmeg
1 t. cinnamon
$\frac{1}{2}$ t. cloves
$\frac{1}{3}$ t. salt
$1\frac{1}{2}$ c. sugar
$\frac{3}{4}$ c. butter
3 eggs
$\frac{7}{8}$ c. buttermilk
Makes 1 cake

14. Rewrite this recipe to make $\frac{1}{3}$ as many pancakes.

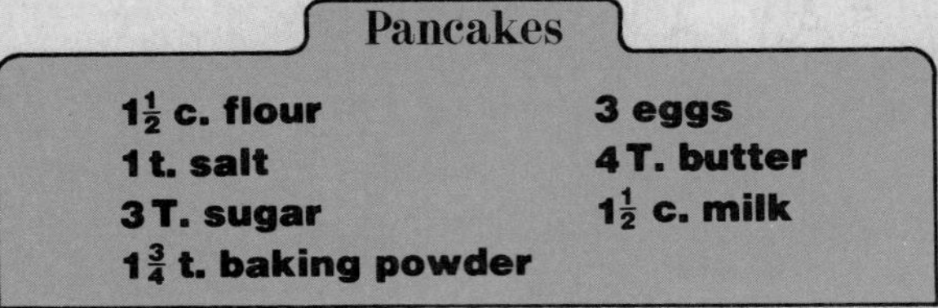

Pancakes

$1\frac{1}{2}$ c. flour
1 t. salt
3 T. sugar
$1\frac{3}{4}$ t. baking powder
3 eggs
4 T. butter
$1\frac{1}{2}$ c. milk

More practice
Set D, page 367

15. Find the food values in $2\frac{1}{2}$ cups of whole milk.

Food values in 1 cup of whole milk

Calories	166
Fat	9 grams
Protein	8 grams
Carbohydrate	12 grams

16. There are 180 calories in 1 cup of bran flakes. How many calories are in

a. $\frac{1}{2}$ cup?

b. $\frac{2}{3}$ cup?

c. $1\frac{1}{4}$ cups?

17. There are $1\frac{1}{6}$ calories in 1 ounce of diet cola. How many calories are in

a. an 8-ounce glass?

b. a 12-ounce can?

c. a 16-ounce bottle?

Using Multiplication: Facts About Animals

Find the amount of food each animal eats daily.

1. A hummingbird weighs $\frac{1}{10}$ ounce. It eats $6\frac{1}{2}$ times as much as its body weight daily.
2. A mouse weighs $\frac{7}{8}$ ounce. It eats $\frac{1}{2}$ as much as its body weight daily.
3. A collie weighs 65 pounds. It eats $\frac{1}{20}$ as much as its body weight daily.
4. A man weighs 180 pounds. He eats $\frac{1}{50}$ as much as his body weight daily.
5. An elephant weighs 9000 pounds. It eats $\frac{1}{60}$ as much as its body weight daily.

Find the amount of weight each animal can pull.

6. An ant weighs $\frac{1}{100}$ ounce. It can pull 5 times as much as its body weight.
7. An Alaskan sled dog weighs 82 pounds. It can pull $2\frac{1}{4}$ times as much as its body weight.
8. A man weighs 180 pounds. He can pull $1\frac{3}{4}$ times as much as his body weight.
9. A tiger weighs 300 pounds. It can pull $1\frac{2}{3}$ times as much as its body weight.
10. An elephant weighs 9000 pounds. It can pull $\frac{4}{9}$ as much as its body weight.

For each animal, find the weight of the baby's mother.

11. A baby mouse weighs $\frac{1}{20}$ ounce. The mother's weight is 22 times the baby's weight.

12. A baby beagle weighs $\frac{7}{8}$ pound. The mother's weight is 25 times the baby's weight.

13. A baby spider monkey weighs $2\frac{1}{5}$ pounds. The mother's weight is $6\frac{1}{2}$ times the baby's weight.

14. A baby gorilla weighs $4\frac{1}{2}$ pounds. The mother's weight is 50 times the baby's weight.

15. A baby rhinoceros weighs $72\frac{1}{2}$ pounds. The mother's weight is 28 times the baby's weight.

The average life span of a human being is 70 years. Find the average life span of these animals.

16. A box turtle lives $1\frac{3}{5}$ times as long as a human being.

17. A cockatoo lives $1\frac{1}{7}$ times as long as a human being.

18. A hippopotamus lives $\frac{4}{7}$ as long as a human being.

19. A grizzly bear lives $\frac{2}{7}$ as long as a human being.

20. A chipmunk lives $\frac{1}{28}$ as long as a human being.

Using Multiplication: Changing Measures

Length
1 foot = 12 inches
1 yard = 3 feet
1 yard = 36 inches
1 mile = 5280 feet
1 mile = 1760 yards

Weight
1 pound = 16 ounces
1 ton = 2000 pounds

Time
1 minute = 60 seconds
1 hour = 60 minutes
1 day = 24 hours
1 week = 7 days
1 year = 12 months

Capacity
1 tablespoon = 3 teaspoons
1 cup = 16 tablespoons
1 cup = 8 fluid ounces
1 pint = 2 cups
1 quart = 2 pints
1 quart = 4 cups
1 gallon = 4 quarts
1 gallon = 8 pints

A. 

inches
yards $\frac{1}{8}$ $\frac{1}{4}$ $\frac{3}{8}$ $\frac{1}{2}$ $\frac{5}{8}$ $\frac{3}{4}$ $\frac{7}{8}$ 1

$\frac{5}{8}$ yard is how many inches?

1 yard is 36 inches.

Find $\frac{5}{8}$ of 36, or $\frac{5}{8} \times 36$.

$\frac{5}{8} \times 36 = 22\frac{1}{2}$

$\frac{5}{8}$ yard is $22\frac{1}{2}$ inches.

B. 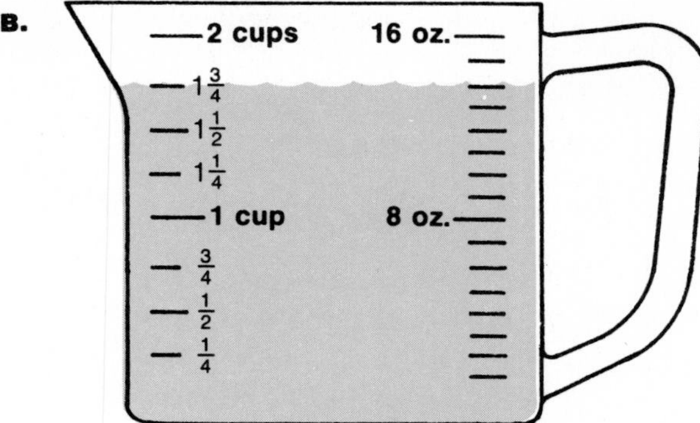

$1\frac{3}{4}$ cups is how many fluid ounces?

1 cup is 8 fluid ounces.

Find $1\frac{3}{4} \times 8$.

$1\frac{3}{4} \times 8 = 14$

$1\frac{3}{4}$ cups is 14 fluid ounces.

Multiply to find each missing number.
Use the table of measures to help you.

1. Width of wallpaper: $\frac{3}{4}$ yard, or ▒ inches
2. Length of rope: $4\frac{1}{3}$ yards, or ▒ feet
3. Distance walked to school: $\frac{1}{5}$ mile, or ▒ feet
4. Weight of pork chop: $\frac{3}{10}$ pound, or ▒ ounces
5. Weight of package: $3\frac{1}{4}$ pounds, or ▒ ounces
6. Weight of car: $\frac{4}{5}$ ton, or ▒ pounds
7. Time between eyeblinks: $\frac{1}{12}$ minute, or ▒ seconds
8. Length of movie: $2\frac{1}{5}$ hours, or ▒ minutes
9. Time in school: $\frac{3}{4}$ year, or ▒ months
10. Amount of shortening: $1\frac{1}{4}$ cups, or ▒ tablespoons
11. Amount of water: $2\frac{1}{2}$ pints, or ▒ cups
12. Amount of milk: $3\frac{1}{2}$ quarts, or ▒ cups
13. Amount of ice cream: $\frac{1}{2}$ gallon, or ▒ pints

Find each answer.

14. Clearance under bridge: $14\frac{1}{2}$ feet
    Height of truck: 170 inches
    Will the truck fit under the bridge?
15. Weight limit on road: $2\frac{1}{2}$ tons
    Weight of truck: 5800 pounds
    Should the truck use the road?

Time Out!

How many triangles?

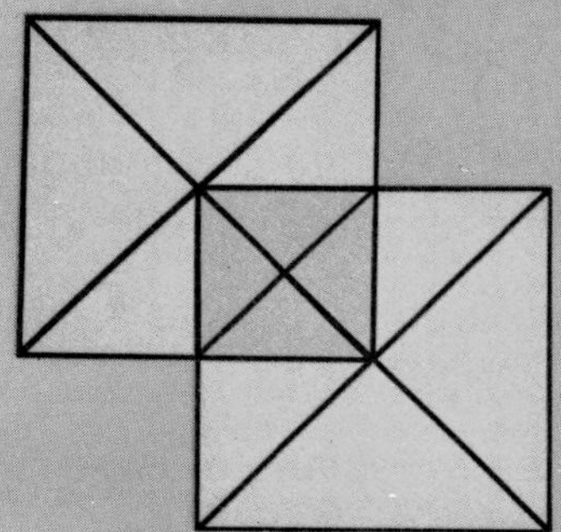

How many rectangles?

Finding the Area of a Right Triangle

Ed drew triangle A on a sheet of paper with square corners.

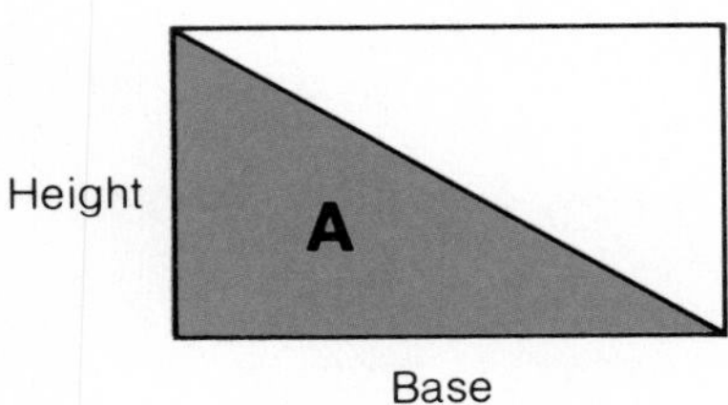

The rectangle and triangle A have the same base and the same height.

The area of triangle A is one-half the area of the rectangle.

Area of rectangle: base × height

Area of triangle: $\frac{1}{2}$ × base × height

Ed measured his triangle and found its area.

Base: 15 in.
Height: 9 in.

$\frac{1}{2} \times 15 \times 9$

$\frac{1}{2} \times \frac{15}{1} \times \frac{9}{1} = \frac{135}{2} = 67\frac{1}{2}$

Area of Ed's triangle: $67\frac{1}{2}$ sq. in.

Take a sheet of paper with square corners.
Draw a right triangle.
Find the area of your triangle.

Find the area of each right triangle.

1. $3\frac{1}{2}$ in. 12 in.

$\frac{1}{2} \times 12 \times 3\frac{1}{2}$

$\frac{1}{2} \times \frac{12}{1} \times \frac{7}{2} = \frac{84}{4} = \square$

Area: $\square$ sq. in.

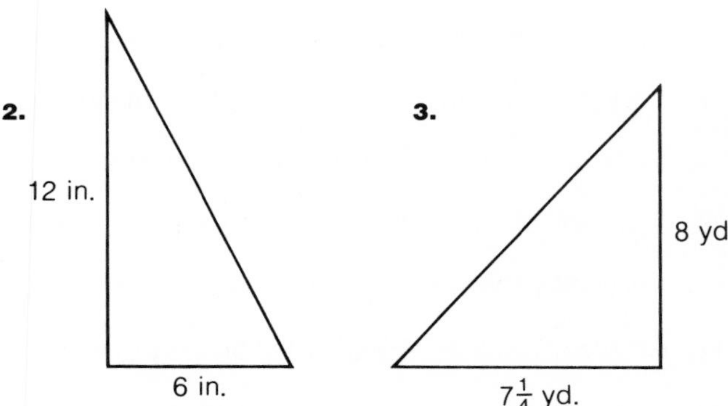

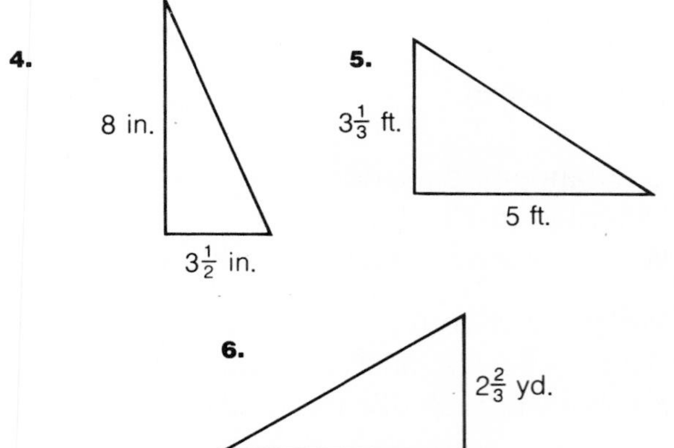

Finding the Area of a Triangle

Take a rectangular sheet of paper.
Draw a triangle like this one.

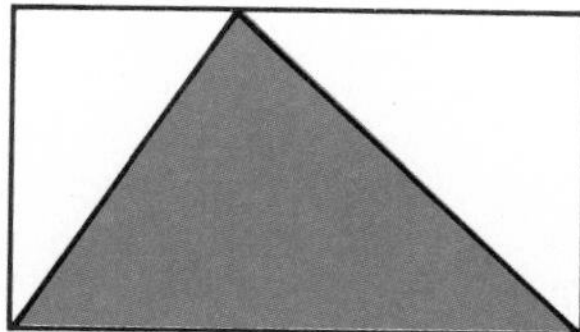

Fold the paper to show the height of the triangle. Be sure the edges match.

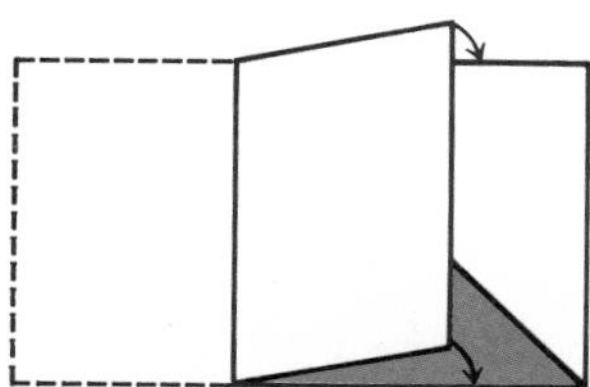

The fold separates the triangle into two triangles. The fold also separates the rectangle into two rectangles.

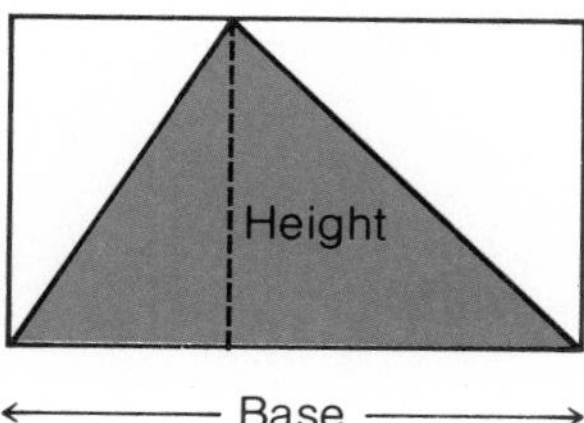

Each part of the triangle is one-half of a small rectangle.

The area of the whole triangle is one-half the area of the whole rectangle.

■ *Area of triangle:* $\frac{1}{2} \times$ *base* $\times$ *height*

Measure your triangle and find its area.

Find the area of each triangle.

1.

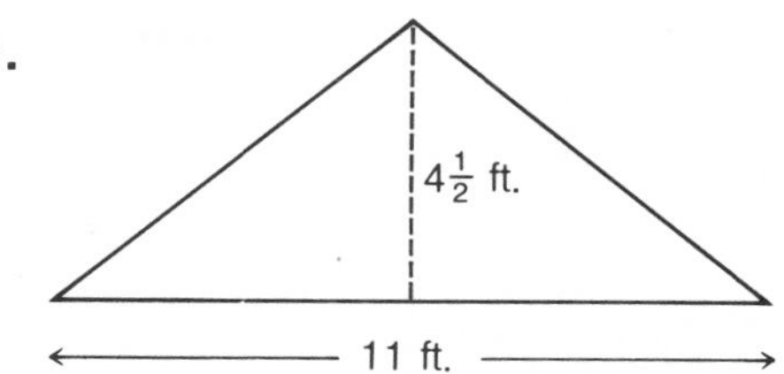

$\frac{1}{2} \times 11 \times 4\frac{1}{2}$

$\frac{1}{2} \times \frac{11}{1} \times \frac{9}{2} = \frac{99}{4} = \square$

Area: $\square$ sq. in.

2.

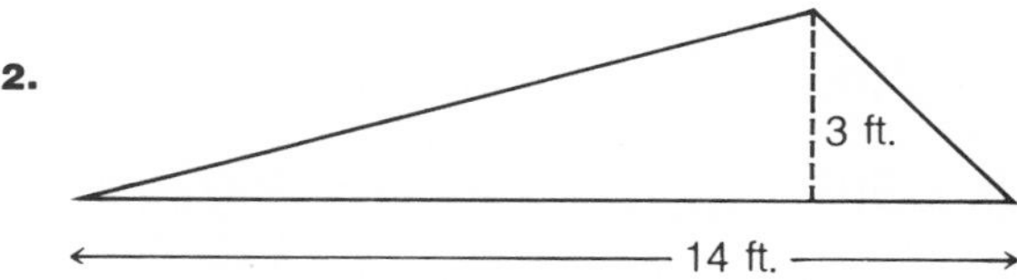

3.

$1\frac{3}{4}$ in.

8 in.

4.

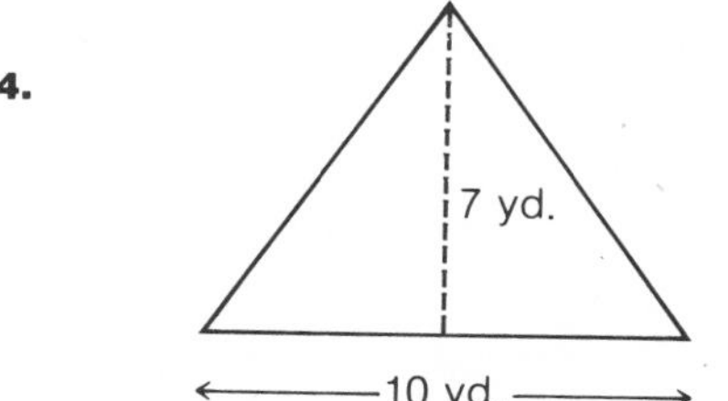

5.

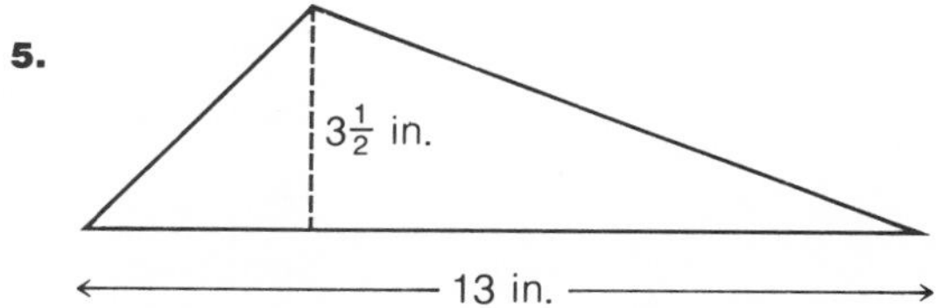

Area of a Triangle: Increasing Base and Height

Find the area of each triangle.

1. 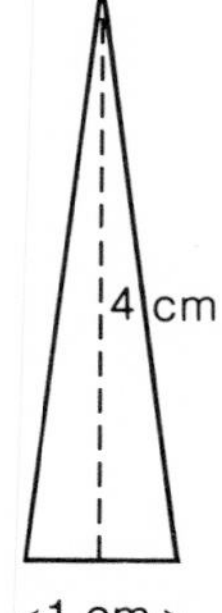

2. 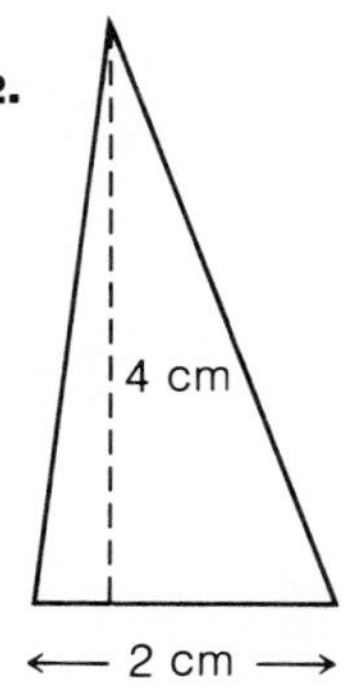

3. 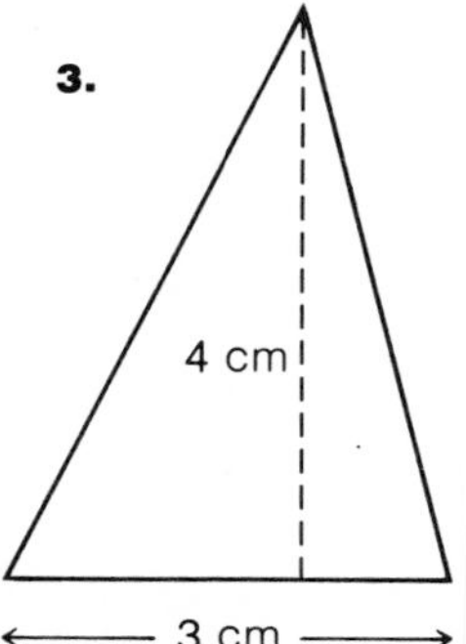

4. 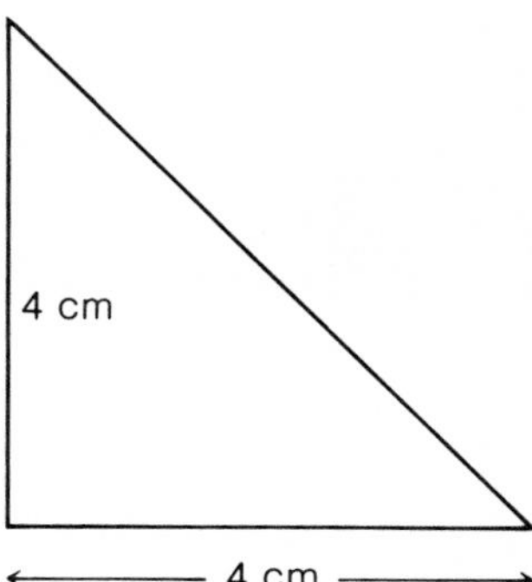

5. 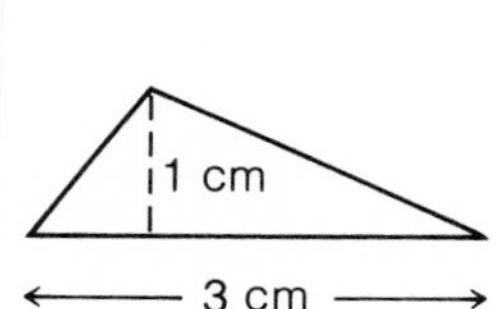

6. 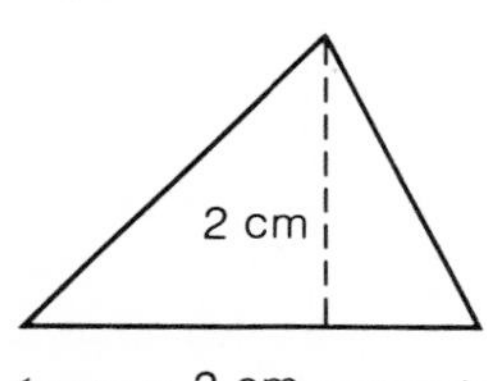

7. 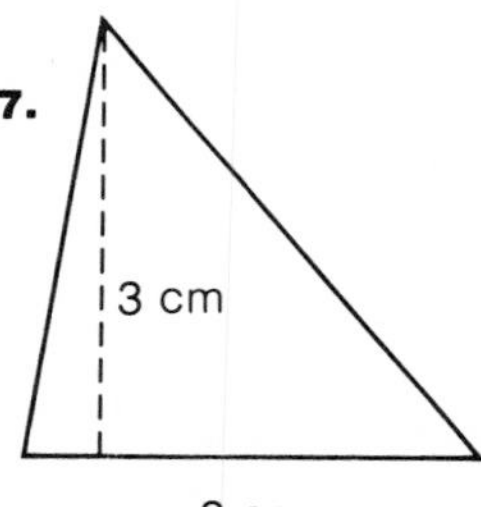

8. 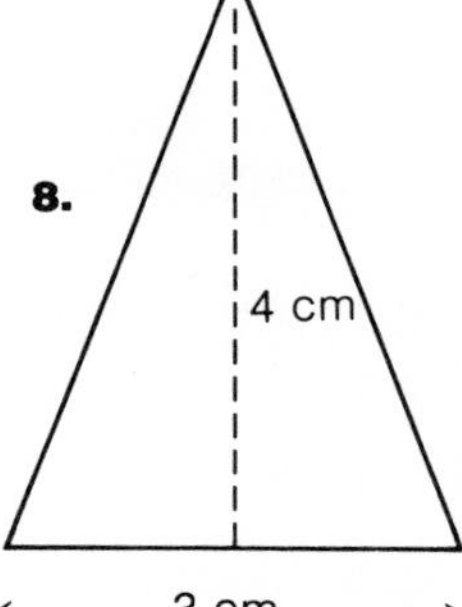

Complete the tables.

	Base (cm)	Height (cm)	Area of triangle (cm²)
9.	6	1	
10.	6	2	
11.	6	4	
12.	6	8	

	Base (cm)	Height (cm)	Area of triangle (cm²)
13.	6	1	
14.	12	1	
15.	24	1	
16.	48	1	

	Base (cm)	Height (cm)	Area of triangle (cm²)
17.	6	1	
18.	12	2	
19.	24	4	
20.	48	8	

Check Yourself
Multiplying Fractions and Mixed Numbers, Pages 306–326

Multiplying fractions and mixed numbers, pages 306–315, 317–319

Find each product. Give your answers in lowest terms.

1. $\frac{1}{2} \times \frac{4}{5}$

2. $\frac{3}{4} \times \frac{5}{6}$

3. $\frac{2}{3} \times \frac{2}{7}$

4. $\frac{3}{4} \times 8$

5. $\frac{1}{8} \times 17$

6. $\frac{4}{5} \times 10$

7. $2\frac{1}{2} \times \frac{3}{4}$

8. $\frac{2}{5} \times 3\frac{1}{10}$

9. $1\frac{2}{3} \times 6$

10. $5 \times 3\frac{1}{2}$

11. $2\frac{1}{4} \times 1\frac{1}{3}$

12. $3\frac{1}{2} \times 1\frac{2}{3}$

Problem solving, pages 308–315, 320–326

13. $\frac{1}{2}$ of the objects in a bag are marbles. $\frac{2}{3}$ of the marbles are green. What fraction of the objects are green marbles?

14. $\frac{7}{10}$ of a person's body weight is water. Ann weighs 110 pounds. Water makes up how many pounds of Ann's weight?

Hilda tossed a paper cup 80 times. Her results are shown in the table.

Results of tosses	Number	Fraction
Side	61	$\frac{61}{80}$
Top	19	$\frac{19}{80}$

15. About how many times would you expect the cup to land on its side in 160 tosses?

16. About how many times would you expect the cup to land on its side in 400 tosses?

17. A recipe for corn pudding calls for $1\frac{1}{3}$ cups of corn. How much corn is needed for a double recipe?

18. The average life span of a human being is 70 years. A deer lives $\frac{1}{7}$ as long as a human being. What is the average life span of a deer?

19. 1 day = 24 hours
Bart sleeps $\frac{1}{3}$ of the day.
How many hours does Bart sleep?

20. Find the area of this right triangle.

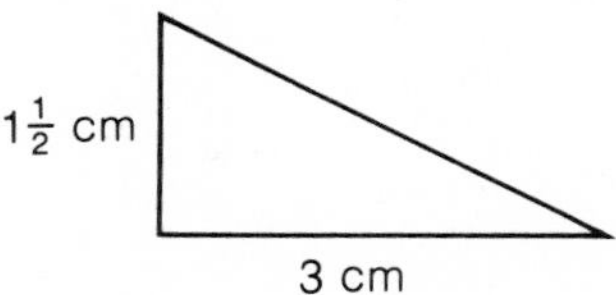

Writing Fractions as Decimals and Decimals as Fractions

A. Three-tenths of the square is shaded.

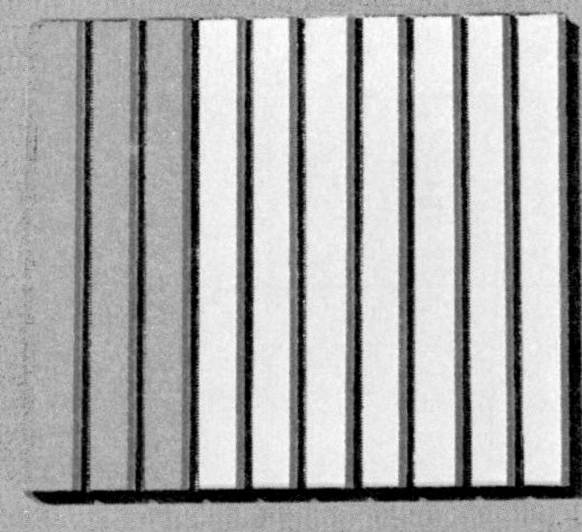

three-tenths

$$\frac{3}{10} = .3$$

B. Find 4.07 on the number line.

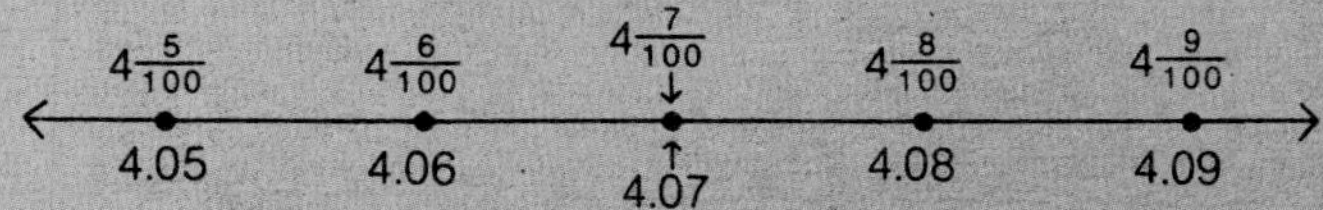

four and seven-hundredths

$$4.07 = 4\frac{7}{100}$$

Write each fraction as a decimal.

Here's how

$\frac{4}{1000}$ *.004*

1. $\frac{5}{10}$

2. $\frac{7}{10}$

3. $1\frac{7}{10}$

4. $15\frac{3}{10}$

5. $\frac{27}{100}$

6. $3\frac{67}{100}$

7. $\frac{2}{100}$

8. $2\frac{9}{100}$

9. $\frac{285}{1000}$

10. $\frac{72}{1000}$

11. $\frac{9}{1000}$

12. $6\frac{49}{100}$

13. $\frac{783}{1000}$

14. $15\frac{15}{100}$

Write each decimal as a fraction.

Here's how

2.37 *$2\frac{37}{100}$*

15. .9

16. .8

17. .24

18. 1.6

19. .76

20. .81

21. .03

22. 4.9

23. 5.06

24. 7.47

25. .605

26. .084

27. 21.2

28. 17.89

29. 32.83

30. .70

31. 9.4

32. 36.1

Multiplying Decimals by Using Fractions

A. Find 2 × 1.3.

$$2 \times 1\frac{3}{10}$$

$$\frac{2}{1} \times \frac{13}{10} = \frac{26}{10} = 2\frac{6}{10} \longrightarrow \begin{array}{r} 1.3 \\ \times \quad 2 \\ \hline 2.6 \end{array}$$

The answer is in tenths.

B. Find .4 × 1.6.

$$\frac{4}{10} \times 1\frac{6}{10}$$

$$\frac{4}{10} \times \frac{16}{10} = \frac{64}{100} \longrightarrow \begin{array}{r} 1.6 \\ \times \ .4 \\ \hline .64 \end{array}$$

The answer is in hundredths.

C. Find .7 × .38.

$$\frac{7}{10} \times \frac{38}{100} = \frac{266}{1000} \longrightarrow \begin{array}{r} .38 \\ \times \ .7 \\ \hline .266 \end{array}$$

The answer is in thousandths.

Find each product.

1. .6 × 3
2. 6 × .3
3. .6 × .3
4. .06 × 3
5. .03 × 6
6. 7 × .4
7. 2.1 × .4
8. .9 × .6
9. 8.6 × 3
10. .51 × 8
11. .16 × .8
12. 45 × .5
13. .07 × 7
14. 3.8 × .2
15. 91 × .01
16. 7.4 × .3
17. .61 × 8
18. .25 × .9

Counting Decimal Places

To find how many ***decimal places*** a numeral has, count all the digits to the right of the decimal point.

A. These numerals have 3 decimal places.

.003
5.172
28.000
6.100

B. These numerals have 2 decimal places.

.09
5.78
34.00
6.10

C. These numerals have 1 decimal place.

.7
206.3
19.0
6.1

D. These numerals have 0 decimal places.

5
240
67,311
61

In exercises 1–22, tell how many decimal places in each numeral.

1. 5.2
2. 6.98
3. .008
4. 467.0
5. 35.9
6. 18.009
7. 92
8. .90
9. 875
10. 4872.5
11. 5.00
12. 98.6
13. .035
14. 56.007
15. 76,000
16. .75
17. 22.0
18. .09736
19. 3.1416
20. .000008
21. 45.00958
22. 156.781334

Use these same digits. Place a decimal point to show a numeral with 1 decimal place.

Here's how

672 67.2

23. 943
24. 27
25. 8
26. 874
27. 604
28. 5723
29. 40
30. 5
31. 7000
32. 89
33. 7
34. 9621
35. 3062
36. 10400

Use these same digits. Place a decimal point to show 2 decimal places.

Here's how

429 4.29

37. 625
38. 110
39. 59
40. 12
41. 700
42. 5619
43. 4002

Place a decimal point to show 3 decimal places.

Here's how

310 .310

44. 925
45. 7496
46. 300
47. 78009
48. 5000
49. 106
50. 40800

Multiplying Decimals

Here is a quick way to multiply decimals.

Multiply as you do with whole numbers.

Count the total number of decimal places in the factors.

Count off the same number of decimal places in the answer.

A.

$$\begin{array}{r} .26 \\ \times \quad .8 \\ \hline .208 \end{array} \quad \begin{array}{l} \longleftarrow \text{2 decimal places} \\ \longleftarrow \text{1 decimal place} \\ \longleftarrow \text{3 decimal places} \end{array}$$

B.

$$\begin{array}{r} 316 \\ \times \quad .04 \\ \hline 12.64 \end{array} \quad \begin{array}{l} \longleftarrow \text{0 decimal places} \\ \longleftarrow \text{2 decimal places} \\ \longleftarrow \text{2 decimal places} \end{array}$$

C.

$$\begin{array}{r} 8.72 \\ \times \quad .19 \\ \hline 7848 \\ 8720 \\ \hline 1.6568 \end{array} \quad \begin{array}{l} \longleftarrow \text{2 decimal places} \\ \longleftarrow \text{2 decimal places} \\ \\ \\ \longleftarrow \text{4 decimal places} \end{array}$$

Find each product.

1. 19.7 × 8

2. 19.7 × .8

3. 19.7 × .08

4. 19.7 × .008

5. 1.97 × 8

6. 1.97 × .8

7. 1.97 × .08

8. .197 × 8

9. .197 × .8

10. .31 × .9

11. 6.4 × .8

12. 7.1 × .05

13. 856 × .06

14. 32.4 × .9

15. .62 × .94

16. 8.9 × .75

17. 5.82 × 4.3

18. 45.7 × 2.6

19. 32 × 4.6

20. 3.2 × 4.6

21. .32 × 4.6

22. 32 × .46

23. 3.2 × .46

24. .32 × .46

25. .005 × 83

26. .2 × 6.8

27. .03 × 25.9

28. .7 × 7.48

29. .8 × 523

30. .009 × 62.1

31. 6 × .803

32. .09 × 1.876

33. .15 × .93

34. 5.6 × 17.8

35. 94 × .347

More practice
Set E, page 367

Multiplying Decimals: Zeros in the Product

When you multiply decimals, sometimes you need to write one or more zeros in the product.

A.

$$\begin{array}{r l} .4 & \longleftarrow \text{1 decimal place} \\ \times\ .2 & \longleftarrow \text{1 decimal place} \\ \hline .08 & \longleftarrow \text{2 decimal places} \end{array}$$

B.

$$\begin{array}{r l} .026 & \longleftarrow \text{3 decimal places} \\ \times\ \ .07 & \longleftarrow \text{2 decimal places} \\ \hline .00182 & \longleftarrow \text{5 decimal places} \end{array}$$

Multiply.

1. .7 × .3

2. .07 × .3

3. .007 × 3

4. .007 × .03

5. .007 × .003

6. .3 × .2

7. .006 × .03

8. .00009 × 9

9. .08 × .04

10. .05 × .7

11. .0029 × .01

12. .005 × .05

13. .013 × .001

14. .008 × 7

15. 1.25 × .001

16. .007 × .7

17. .0006 × .04

18. .37 × .1

19. .012 × .3

20. .25 .7

21. .46 × .02

22. .018 × .06

23. 2.9 × .03

24. .125 × .5

25. 6.43 × .009

26. 7.531 × .0024

27. .0198 × .0038

Five-in-a-Row

Two or more people can play this game.

Each player makes a 5-by-5 grid like this.

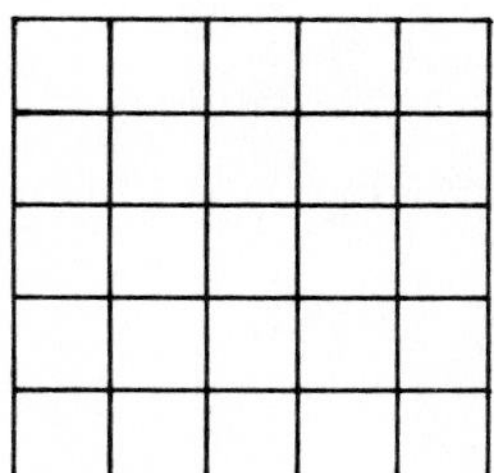

These numbers are written on the grid in any order, with one number in each square.

.002 .036 .063 .4
.004 .04 .064 .42
.006 .042 .072 .48
.009 .045 .09 .56
.012 .054 .12
.015 .056 .24
.024 .06 .36

Someone reads the exercises at the right. Each player finds the answer on the card and marks it or crosses it out. The first player to get five squares in a row, in a column, or in a diagonal wins the game.

Exercises

a. .04 × .1

b. 2 × .006

c. .07 × .8

d. 1.2 × .3

e. .07 × .9

f. .3 × .4

g. 1.5 × .01

h. .006 × 9

i. .03 × .3

j. 2.1 × .02

k. .003 × 2

l. .09 × .5

m. 6 × .08

n. .09 × .4

o. .08 × .8

p. 6 × .07

q. .2 × .2

r. .08 × .9

s. .1 × .6

t. 5.6 × .1

u. .006 × 4

John and Alfred made these grids. Who won the game when the exercises were called in the order given?

John

<table>
<tr><td>.24</td><td>.56</td><td>.48</td><td>.4</td><td>.004</td></tr>
<tr><td>.072</td><td>.063</td><td>.036</td><td>.009</td><td>.042</td></tr>
<tr><td>.06</td><td>.064</td><td>.002</td><td>.42</td><td>.006</td></tr>
<tr><td>.12</td><td>.36</td><td>.04</td><td>.054</td><td>.024</td></tr>
<tr><td>.045</td><td>.09</td><td>.012</td><td>.056</td><td>.015</td></tr>
</table>

Alfred

<table>
<tr><td>.002</td><td>.06</td><td>.056</td><td>.009</td><td>.09</td></tr>
<tr><td>.04</td><td>.004</td><td>.24</td><td>.042</td><td>.072</td></tr>
<tr><td>.045</td><td>.054</td><td>.006</td><td>.4</td><td>.12</td></tr>
<tr><td>.012</td><td>.063</td><td>.015</td><td>.036</td><td>.024</td></tr>
<tr><td>.36</td><td>.42</td><td>.48</td><td>.56</td><td>.064</td></tr>
</table>

Fried Chicken Dinner
$2.65

Ham & Cheese Platter
$1.70

Tuna Salad Bowl
$2.15

Burger Palace Platter
$1.60

Special Bacon Cheeseburger
$1.45

Burger Palace Menu

Sandwiches

Hamburger	.75
Frankfurter	.45
Hot Turkey	1.85
Hot Beef	1.75
Tuna Fish	.95
Cheese	.50
Egg Salad	.85

Side Orders

French Fries	.45
Onion Rings	.85
Cole Slaw	.40
Cottage Cheese	.40
Chili	.75

Fountain Favorites

Banana Split	.85
Hot Fudge Sundae	.75
Strawberry Sundae	.75
Ice Cream Soda	.45
Thick Shakes	.55
Cola (small)	.25
(large)	.35

Desserts

Apple pie	.50
Pecan Pie	.55
Fudge Cake	.40
Rice Pudding	.35

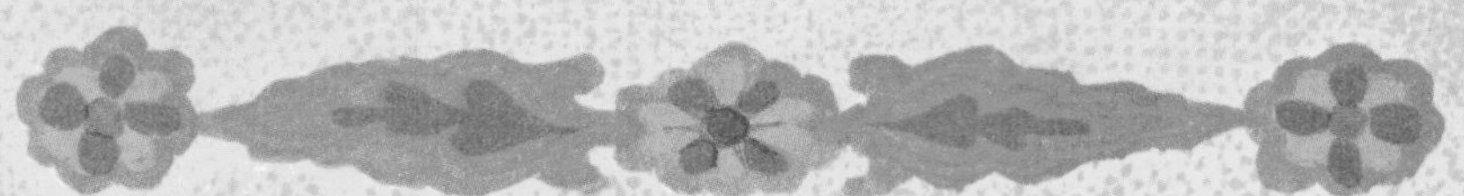

Complete each Burger Palace check.

1.

Items	Cost
2 hot fudge sundaes	1.50
2 banana splits	
3 chocolate shakes	
1 rice pudding	
4 french fries	
Waitress 2 | Guests 8 | Date 7/8 | TOTAL:	

2.

Items	Cost
5 Burger Palace platters	
3 colas (large)	
2 ice cream sodas	
3 onion rings	
2 apple pies	
2 pecan pies	
Waitress 5 | Guests 5 | Date 7/8 | TOTAL:	

3.

Items	Cost
1 fried chicken dinner	
3 bacon cheeseburgers	
2 hot turkey sandwiches	
5 french fries	
3 colas (large)	
3 colas (small)	
Waitress 4 | Guests 6 | Date 7/9 | TOTAL:	

4.

Items	Cost
2 frankfurters	
3 ham and cheese platters	
2 tuna salad bowls	
3 french fries	
2 cole slaws	
2 onion rings	
5 colas (large)	
2 chocolate shakes	
Waitress 2 | Guests 7 | Date 7/10 | TOTAL:	

Using Multiplication of Decimals: Earning Money

Some students in Ann's school spent two Saturdays earning money to buy sports equipment.

The students' goal was $90. Complete their records to see if they made their goal.

1.

WORK RECORD	Sat., May 7
WORK DONE	Money earned
2 cars washed	2.50
1 car waxed	
10 windows washed	
3 lawns mowed	
3 lawns weeded	
TOTAL:	

2.

WORK RECORD	Sat., May 14
WORK DONE	Money earned
3 cars washed	
1 car waxed	
9 windows washed	
4 lawns mowed	
1 lawn weeded	
2 lawns raked	
TOTAL:	

3.

SALES RECORD	Sat., May 7
ITEMS SOLD	Money earned
3 cakes	
8 pies	
5 dozen cookies	
20 brownies	
5 potholders	
2 wallets	
TOTAL:	

4.

SALES RECORD	Sat., May 14
ITEMS SOLD	Money earned
5 cakes	
2 pies	
6 dozen cookies	
12 brownies	
1 belt	
3 wallets	
TOTAL:	

Multiplying Decimals by 10, 100, or 1000

Find each product. Look for a quick way to find the answers.

A. 10 × .26 = 2.6 ⟵
$$\begin{array}{r} .26 \\ \times\ 10 \\ \hline 2.60 \end{array}$$ or 2.6

10 × .47 = ▒

10 × 9.3 = ▒

10 × .7 = ▒

10 × .081 = ▒

B. 100 × .26 = 26 ⟵
$$\begin{array}{r} .26 \\ \times\ 100 \\ \hline 26.00 \end{array}$$ or 26

100 × .47 = ▒

100 × 9.3 = ▒

100 × .7 = ▒

100 × .081 = ▒

C. 1000 × .26 = 260 ⟵
$$\begin{array}{r} .26 \\ \times\ 1000 \\ \hline 260.00 \end{array}$$ or 260

1000 × .47 = ▒

1000 × 9.3 = ▒

1000 × .7 = ▒

1000 × .081 = ▒

● **Discuss** What is a quick way to multiply a decimal by 10? By 100? By 1000?

Find each product.

1. 10 × .4
2. 100 × .4
3. 1000 × .4
4. 10 × 5.36
5. 100 × 5.36
6. 1000 × 5.36
7. 10 × .03
8. 100 × .03
9. 1000 × .03
10. 1000 × .0008
11. 100 × .629
12. 100 × 75.3
13. 10 × 8.901
14. 1000 × .043
15. .006 × 100
16. 57.4 × 1000
17. 100 × .4251
18. 1000 × .4251
19. ★ 10,000 × .4251
20. ★ 100,000 × .4251
21. ★ 1,000,000 × .4251

More practice
Set F, page 367

22. In each exercise, think of the items placed end to end in a row. Guess how the rows should be arranged in order from shortest to longest.

    a. 10,000 paper clips

    b. 100 guitars

    c. 10 Volkswagens

    d. 1000 bathtubs

    e. 10,000 pennies

    f. 1,000,000 human cells

23. In each exercise, think of the items piled in a stack. Guess how the stacks should be arranged in order from shortest to tallest.

    a. 1000 math books

    b. 100 stories of a tall building

    c. 10,000 coffee cans

    d. 100,000 dollar bills

24. Use the following data to compute the lengths in exercise 22. List your answers in order from least to greatest.

    a. Paper clip: 0.034 meter long

    b. Guitar: 0.9 meter long

    c. Volkswagen: 4.06 meters long

    d. Bathtub: 1.5 meters long

    e. Penny: 0.018 meter across

    f. Human cell: 0.000006 meter long

25. Use the following data to compute the heights in exercise 23. List your answers in order from least to greatest.

    a. Math book: 0.022 meter thick

    b. One story of tall building: 3.44 meters tall

    c. Coffee can: 0.178 meter tall

    d. Dollar bill: 0.0000952 meter thick

Using Multiplication of Decimals: Changing Metric Measures

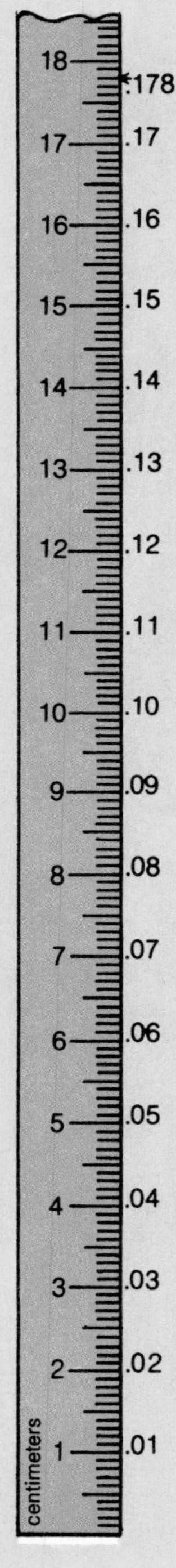

A. The high-jump record for a flea is 0.178 meter. Find this distance in centimeters.

Find 100 × .178.

100 × .178 = 17.8

The flea jumped 17.8 centimeters.

B. The long-jump record for three frog-jumps in a row is 0.0098 kilometer. Find this distance in meters.

Find 1000 × .0098.

1000 × .0098 = 9.8

The frog jumped 9.8 meters.

1 kilometer (km) = 1000 meters (m)
1 meter = 100 centimeters (cm)
1 meter = 1000 millimeters (mm)
1 centimeter = 10 millimeters

Multiply to find each missing number.

1. Longest steel-arch bridge:
   0.504 km, or ▒ m
2. Longest tightrope walk:
   0.246 km, or ▒ m
3. Longest submarine:
   0.126 km, or ▒ m
4. Highest ocean wave:
   0.0336 km, or ▒ m
5. Longest fingernail:
   0.569 m, or ▒ cm
6. Longest snail:
   0.27 m, or ▒ cm
7. Shortest frog:
   0.0123 m, or ▒ mm
8. Shortest fish:
   0.0088 m, or ▒ m
9. Thickness of human hair:
   0.005 cm, or ▒ mm
10. Thickness of paper:
    0.0075 cm, or ▒ mm

1 kilogram (kg) = 1000 grams (g)

Multiply to find each missing number.

11. Baseball:
0.141 kg, or ▒ g

12. Chimpanzee's brain:
0.325 kg, or ▒ g

13. Owl's daily food intake:
0.16 kg, or ▒ g

14. Star of Africa diamond:
0.106 kg, or ▒ g

15. Newborn kitten:
0.098 kg, or ▒ g

16. World's smallest mouse:
0.0042 kg, or ▒ g

1 liter (ℓ) = 1000 milliliters (ml)

17. Milk in baby's bottle:
0.24 ℓ, or ▒ ml

18. Water a small dog drinks daily:
0.7 ℓ, or ▒ ml

19. Sodium chloride in a test tube:
0.025 ℓ, or ▒ ml

20. Perspiration in one day:
0.94 ℓ, or ▒ ml

21. Water in largest raindrop:
0.00012 ℓ, or ▒ ml

22. Penicillin in a syringe:
0.003 ℓ, or ▒ ml

23.

Will a full carton of milk fit in the pitcher?

24.

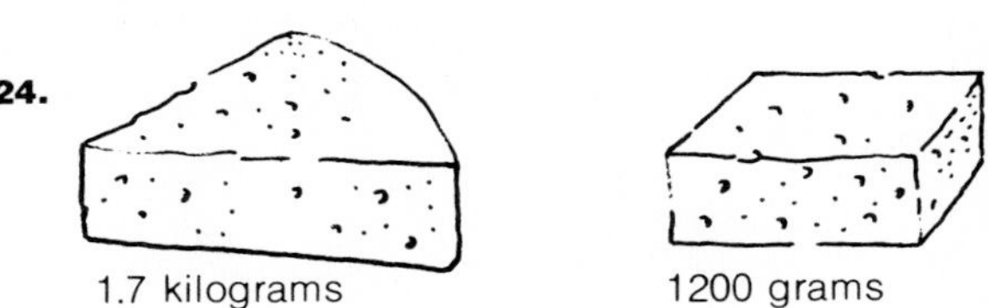

Which piece of cheese weighs more?

25.

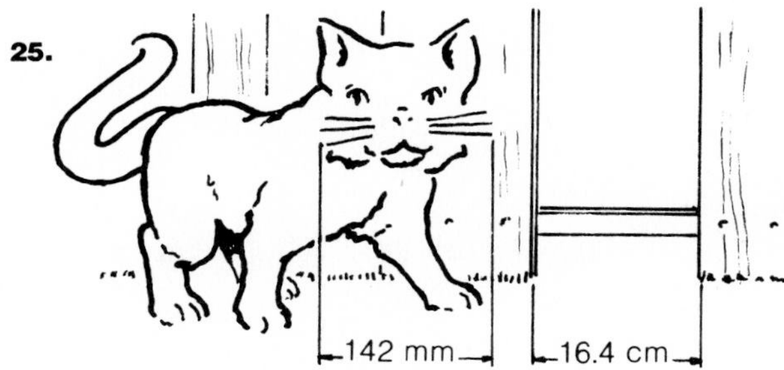

Will the cat's whiskers touch the fence when the cat walks through the fence?

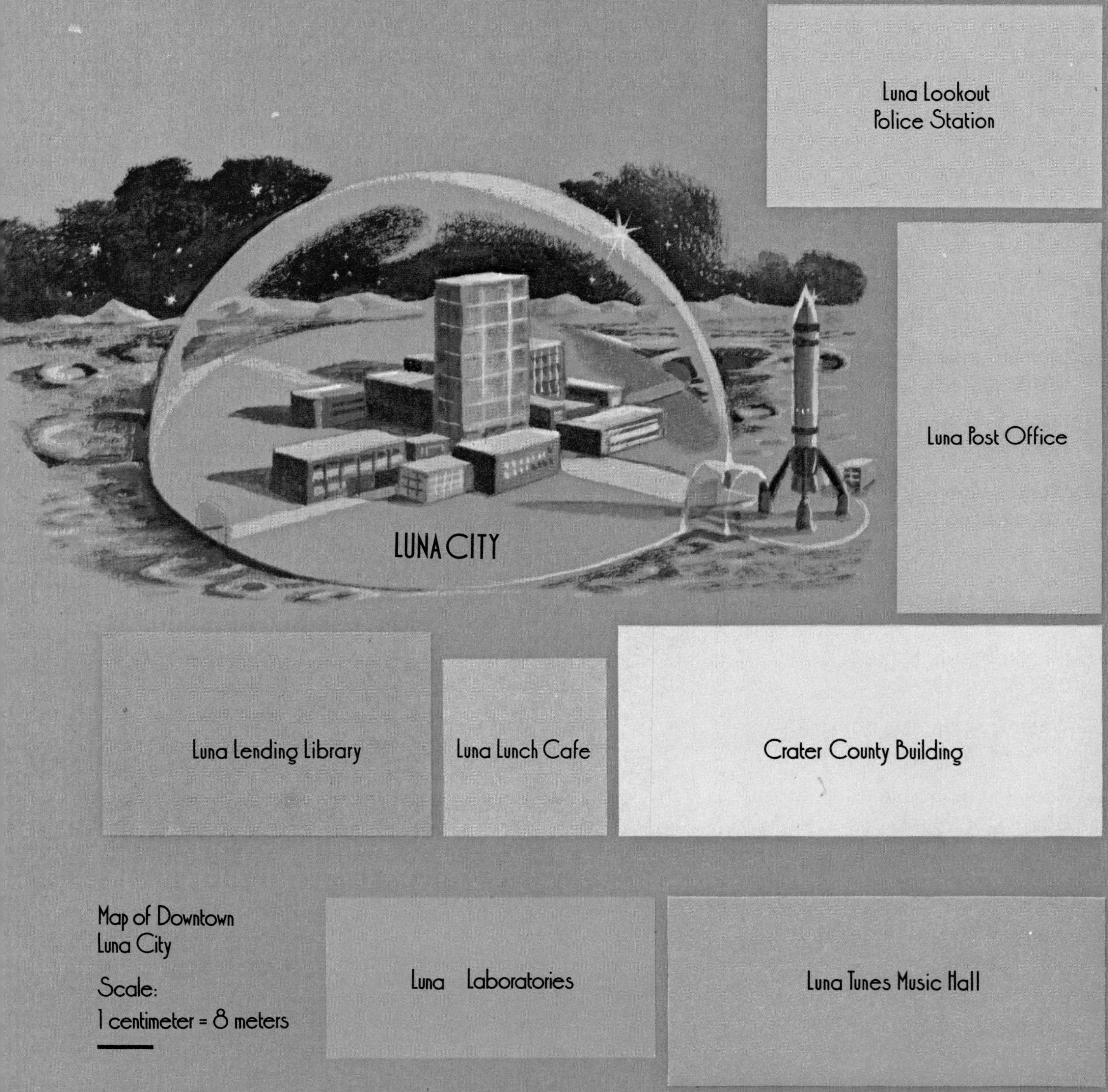

Luna Lookout
Police Station

Luna Post Office

LUNA CITY

Luna Lending Library

Luna Lunch Cafe

Crater County Building

Map of Downtown
Luna City

Scale:
1 centimeter = 8 meters

Luna Laboratories

Luna Tunes Music Hall

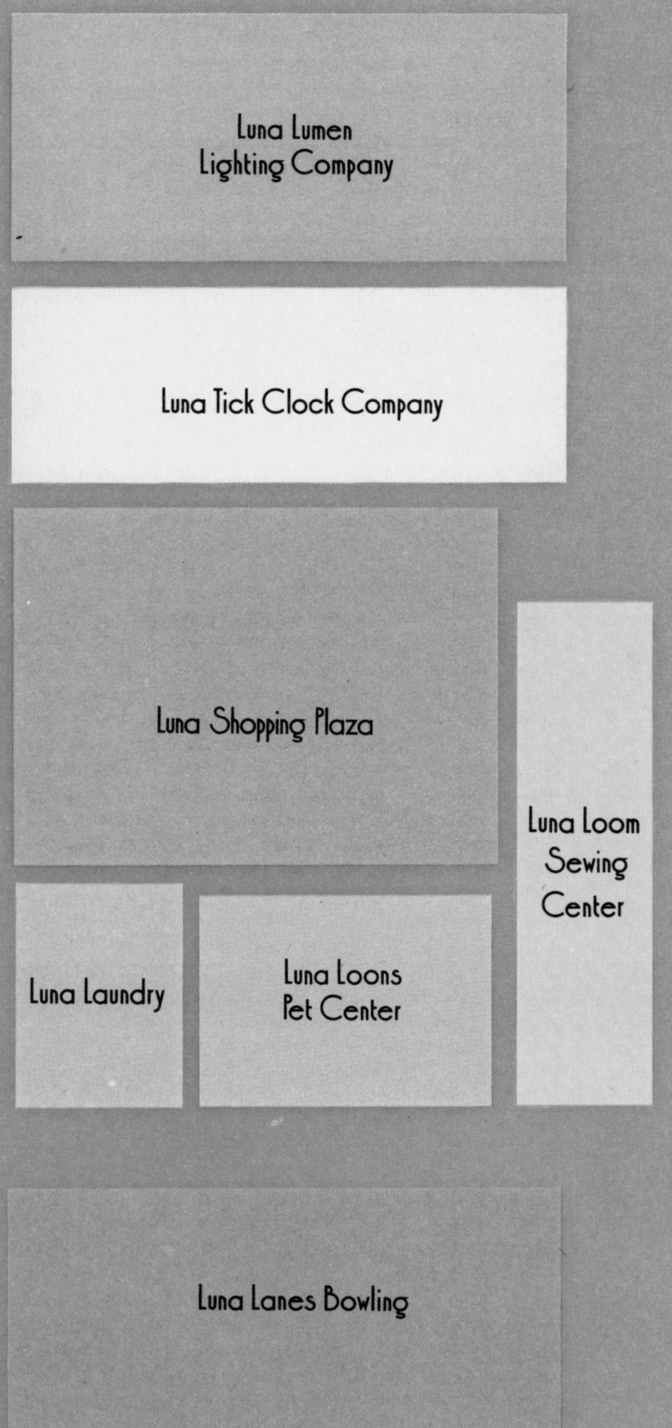

On the map, 1 centimeter represents 8 meters.

Find the actual length and width of each of these buildings. First measure on the map to the nearest tenth of a centimeter. Then multiply by 8.

1. Luna Laboratories
   Actual length: 8 × 5.8, or ▒, meters
   Actual width: 8 × 2.9, or ▒, meters
2. Luna Shopping Plaza
3. Luna Lookout Police Station
4. Luna Lumen Lighting Company
5. Luna Tick Clock Company
6. Luna Lunch Cafe
7. Luna Loons Pet Center
8. Luna Lanes Bowling
9. Luna Post Office
10. Luna Lending Library
11. Luna Laundry
12. Crater County Building
13. Luna Loom Sewing Center
14. Luna Tunes Music Hall

Using Multiplication of Decimals: A Beam Balance

Weight of button: 0.9 gram
Distance from center: 6.4 centimeters

Weight of ring: 1.6 grams
Distance from center: 3.6 centimeters

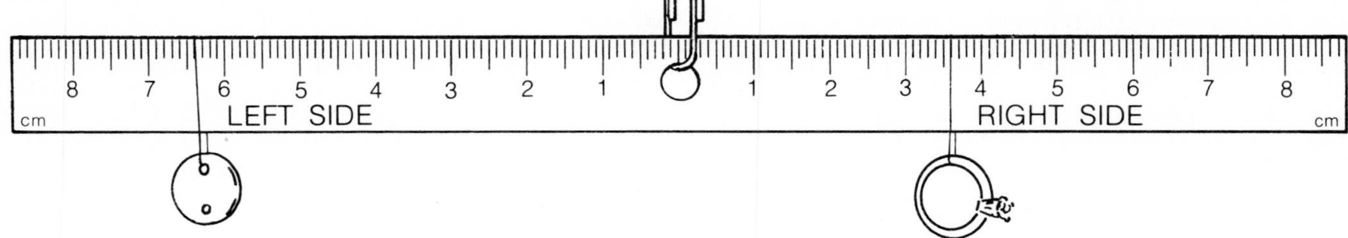

The beam balances when "weight times distance" on the left side equals "weight times distance" on the right side.

LEFT SIDE			RIGHT SIDE		
Weight of object		Distance from center	Weight of object		Distance from center
.9	×	6.4 = 5.76	1.6	×	3.6 = 5.76

$$.9 \times 6.4 = 5.76 \qquad 1.6 \times 3.6 = 5.76$$

Complete the table.

	LEFT SIDE			RIGHT SIDE			
	Weight of object	Distance from center	Weight times distance	Weight of object	Distance from center	Weight times distance	Will the beam balance?
	Paper clip: 0.9 g	7.0 cm	*6.30*	Sugar cube: 2.1 g	3.0 cm	*6.30*	*Yes*
	Eraser: 11.3 g	2.1 cm	*23.73*	Pencil: 4.9 g	4.6 cm	*22.54*	*No*
1.	Earring: 1.5 g	4.5 cm		Ring: 2.5 g	2.7 cm		
2.	Paper: 4.8 g	1.2 cm		Tissue: 1.8 g	3.2 cm		
3.	Eraser: 11.3 g	1.3 cm		Dime: 2.3 g	5.4 cm		
4.	Nickel: 5.0 g	7.2 cm		Paper: 4.8 g	2.6 cm		
5.	Button: 0.6 g	4.2 cm		Sugar cube: 2.1 g	1.2 cm		
6.	Eraser: 8.0 g	4.5 cm		Nickel: 5.0 g	7.2 cm		
7.	Earring: 0.8 g	7.5 cm		Ring: 2.4 g	2.5 cm		
8.	Button: 0.6 g	7.2 cm		Tissue: 1.8 g	1.6 cm		
9.	Nickel: 5.0 g	6.3 cm		Paper: 4.3 g	6.9 cm		
10.	Paper clip: 0.9 g	3.5 cm		Button: 0.5 g	6.3 cm		

Multiplying Decimals: Order and Grouping

- *The order in which you multiply decimals does not change the product.*

  3.4 × .2 = .68
  .2 × 3.4 = .68

- *The way in which you group decimals does not change the product.*

  (.4 × 1.6) × .2 = .128
  .4 × (1.6 × .2) = .128

Find each product. Order and group the numbers in a way that makes your work easier.

1. .2 × 8.7 × 5
   1 × 8.7

2. 3.6 × .4 × 20
   3.6 × 8

3. .5 × 8.79 × .2
   .1 × 8.79

4. 25 × 4 × 6.1
   100 × 6.1

5. .97 × .3 × .2
   .97 × .06

6. .5 × .76 × 2

7. .4 × 5 × .83

8. 4 × .69 × 25

9. .74 × 2 × 50

10. 500 × .02 × .29

11. .8 × 3.6 × 50

12. 4 × .95 × 25

13. .4 × 2.5 × .67

14. .02 × 7.47 × 50

15. .6 × .5 × 9.3

16. 250 × .04 × .19

17. .88 × .80 × 5

18. .05 × 6.3 × 200

19. 500 × .74 × .08

20. .5 × 15.8 × 40

Keeping Skillful

Divide.

1. 6)403
2. 7)470
3. 8)537
4. 9)604
5. 15)358
6. 21)716
7. 33)1432
8. 53)2864

Add or subtract.

9. .49 + .81

10. .78 + .64

11. 8.5 − 2.7

12. 13.6 + 2.9 + 4.9

13. .6 + 6.6 + 66.6

14. 3.77 − .89

15. 3.21 + 4.58 + 6.63

16. 4.04 − 2.75

17. .49 − .271

18. .35 + .729 + .91

19. .333 − .277

20. 3.05 − 1.69

21. 6.924 + 7.287 + .256

22. .506 − .25

23. .404 + .073 + .536

24. .49 − .271

25. .215 + .425 + .835

SIDE TRIP Taxicab Geometry

In Union City, the shortest distance along city streets from corner A to the red taxi is 4 blocks.

The red taxi is also 4 blocks from corner B. This taxi is "equal taxi distance" from corners A and B.

The blue taxi is equal taxi distance (5 blocks) from corners A and B.

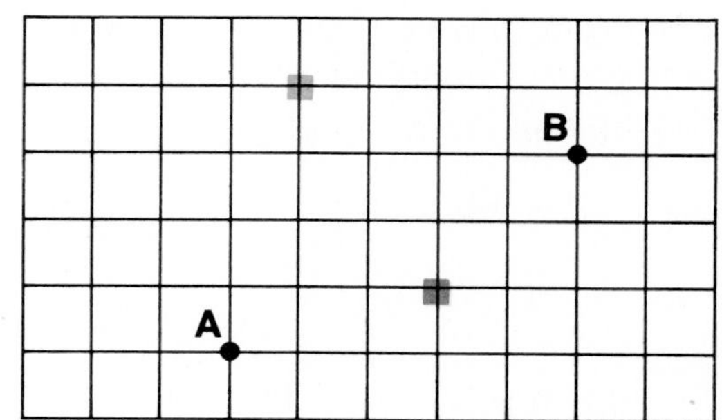

For each exercise, copy the grid.

1. Mark all corners that are 2 blocks from corner C.

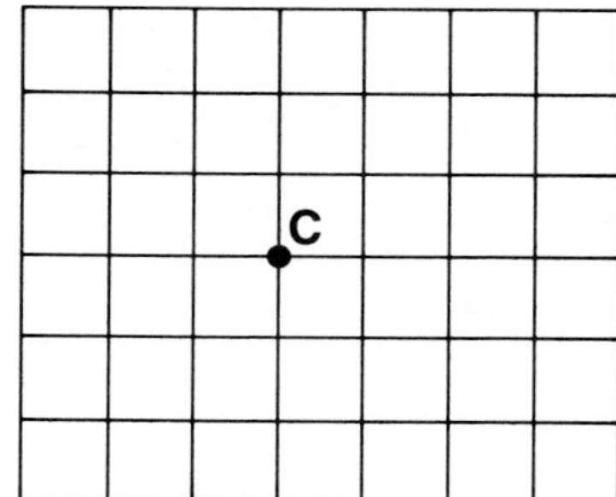

2. Mark all corners that are 3 blocks from corner D.

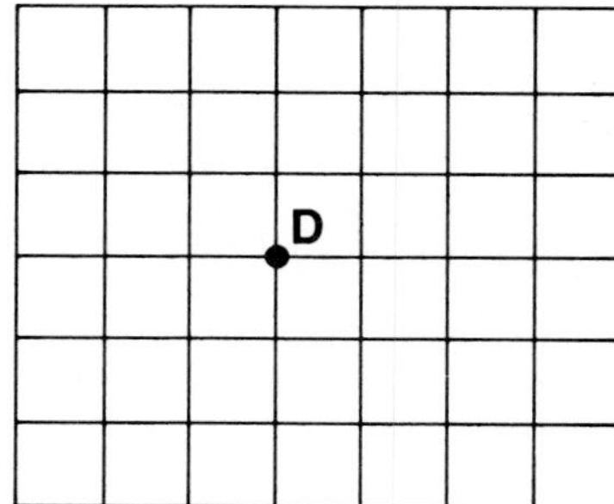

3. Mark all corners that are equal taxi distance from corners E and F.

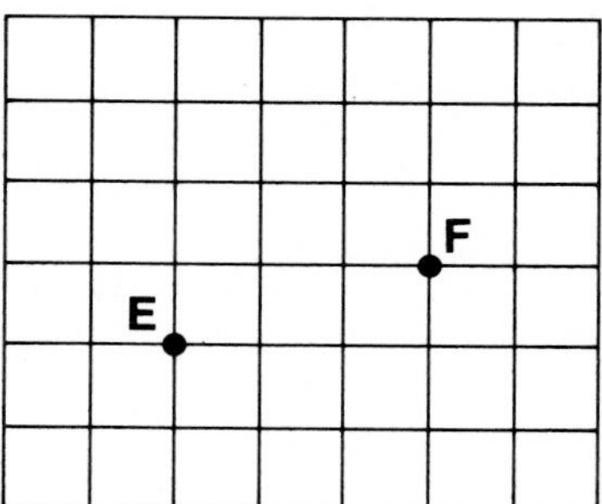

4. Mark all corners that are equal taxi distance from corners G and H.

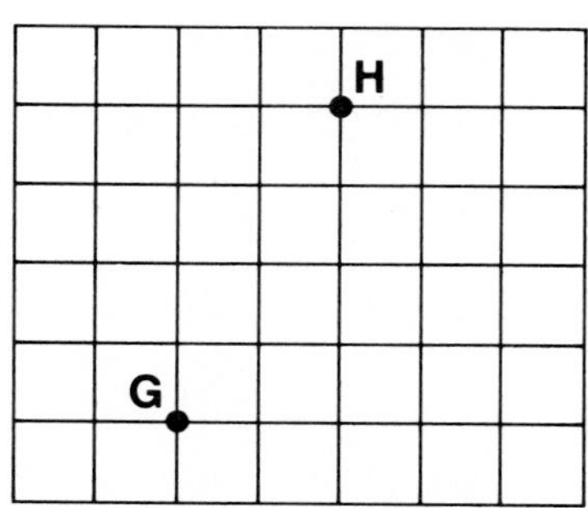

5. Mark all corners that are equal taxi distance from corners J and K.

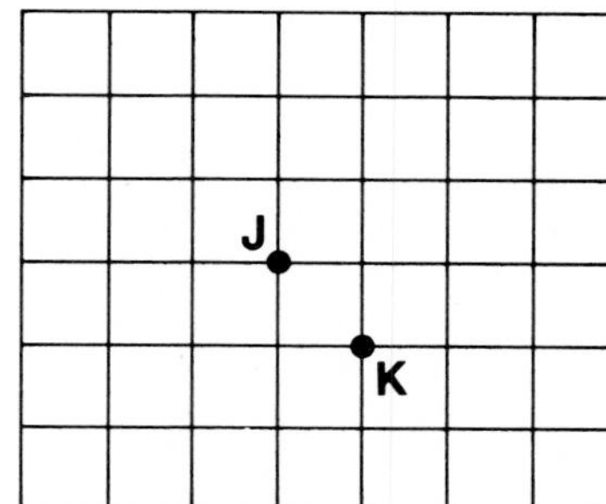

6. Mark all corners that are equal taxi distance from corners L and M.

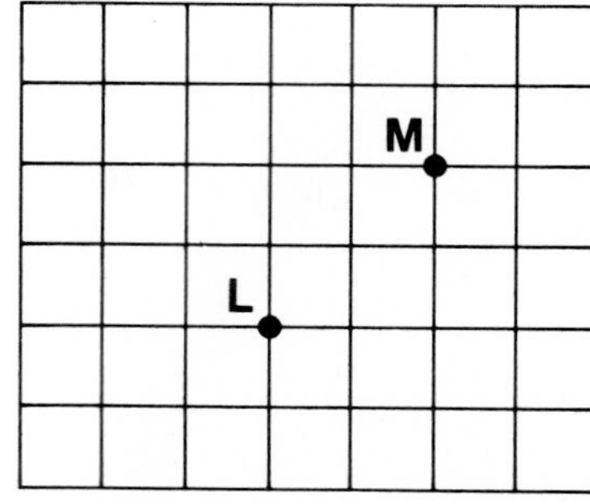

Check Yourself
Multiplying Decimals, Pages 328–346

Multiplying decimals,
pages 329, 331–333, 338–339, 345

Multiply.

1. $.8 \times 4$

2. $4.3 \times .6$

3. $3.1 \times .07$

4. $.19 \times 6$

5. $1.73 \times .09$

6. $5.6 \times .12$

7. 7.8×59

8. $.25 \times .17$

9. $68.3 \times .84$

10. $.08 \times .6$

11. $.025 \times .003$

12. $.12 \times .14$

13. $100 \times .07$

14. 1000×4.27

15. $.8605 \times 10$

Problem solving, pages 334–344

16. The Wilsons bought 5 chicken dinners for $2.65 each. What was the total cost?

17. Linda earns $4.50 a week delivering papers. How much will she earn in 4 weeks?

18. A badge is 0.04 meter wide. How long is a row of 1000 badges?

19. 1 kilometer = 1000 meters
The longest vehicle in the world is a trailer 0.174 kilometer long. How many meters long is this trailer?

20. In the picture, 1 centimeter represents 8 meters. Find the actual length of the Luna City Cinema in meters.

e.

Matching Puzzle Pieces

Tell which puzzle piece fits into each empty space.

a.

1.

3.

b.

4.

2.

5.

c.

d.

f.
7.
g.
6.
h.
8.
i.
9.
j.
10.

Finding Congruent Figures

Figures that have the same size and shape are *congruent.*
These four figures are congruent.

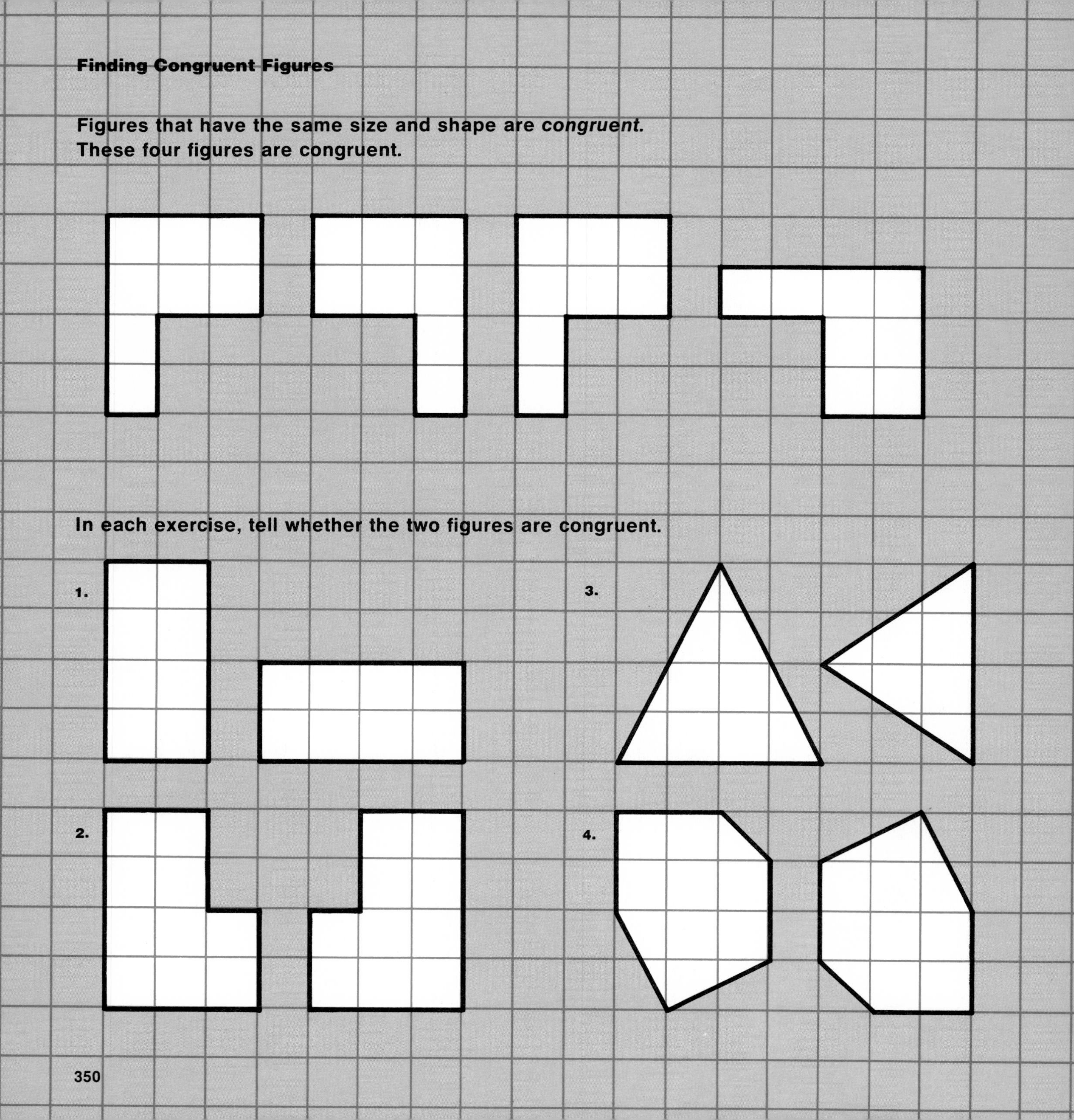

In each exercise, tell whether the two figures are congruent.

1.

2.

3.

4.

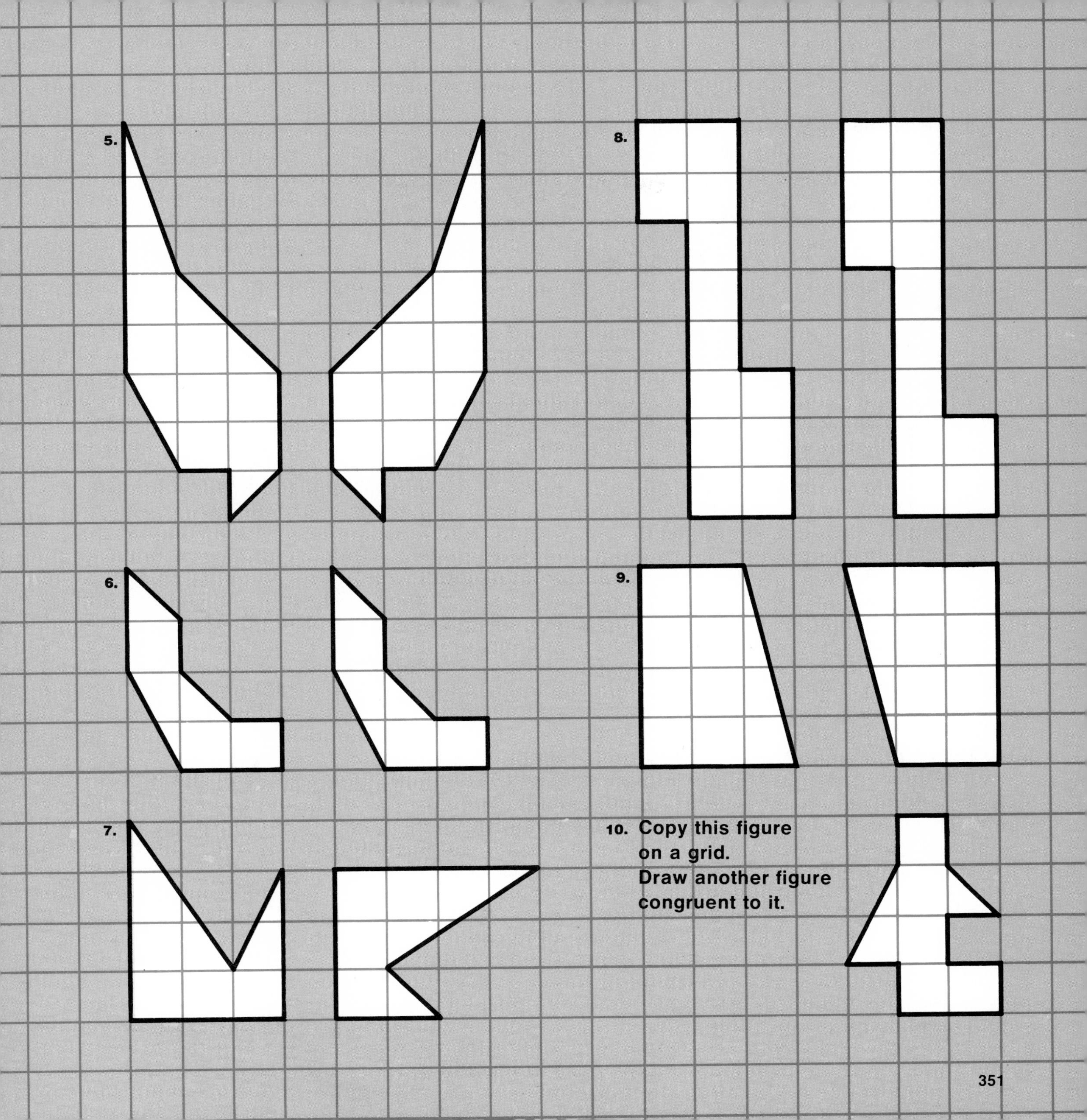
5.
6.
7.
8.
9.
10. Copy this figure
on a grid.
Draw another figure
congruent to it.

Finding Congruent Parts

Tell whether the diagonal divides the figure into congruent parts.

1. 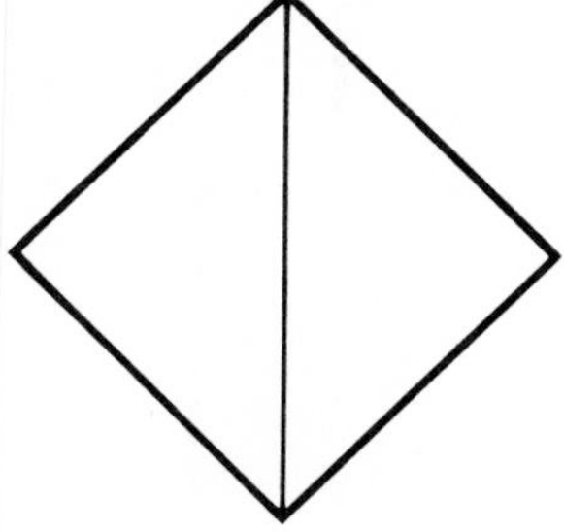

2. 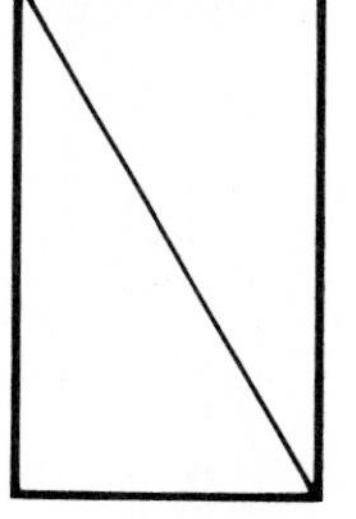

3. 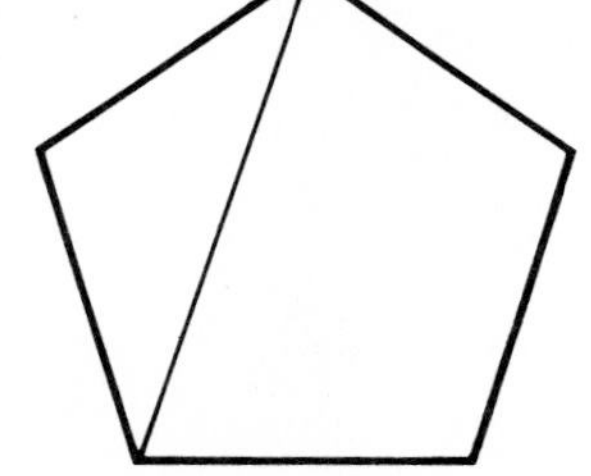

4. 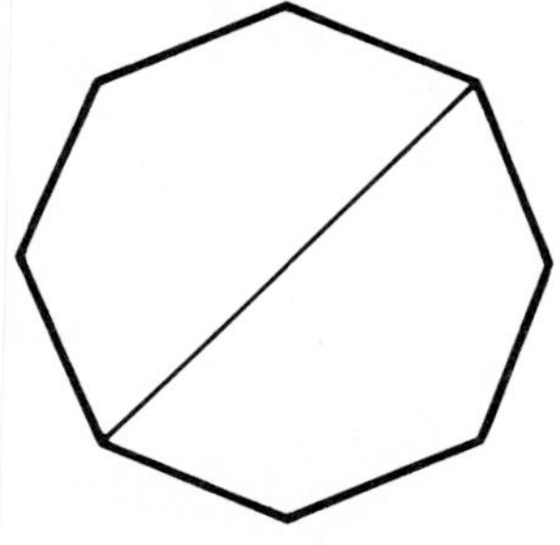

Tell whether each rectangle is divided into congruent parts.

5. 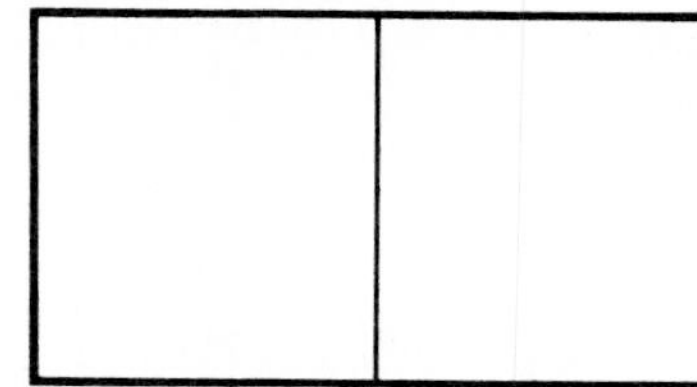

6. 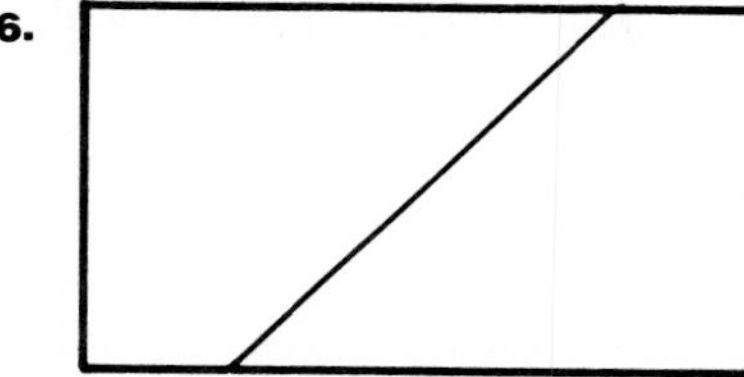

7. 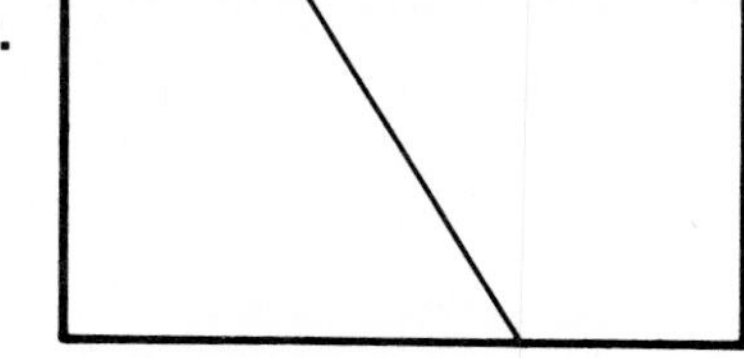

8. Draw a rectangle. Show another way to divide it into two congruent parts.

Copy these three figures.

9. Divide this figure into two congruent parts. Three congruent parts. Six congruent parts.

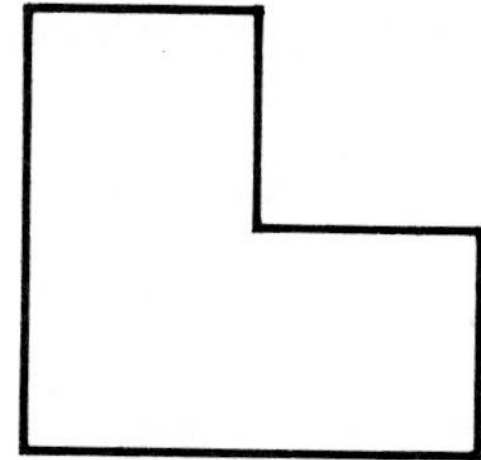

10. Divide this figure into two congruent parts. Three congruent parts. Six congruent parts.

11. Divide this figure into two congruent parts. Four congruent parts. Six congruent parts.

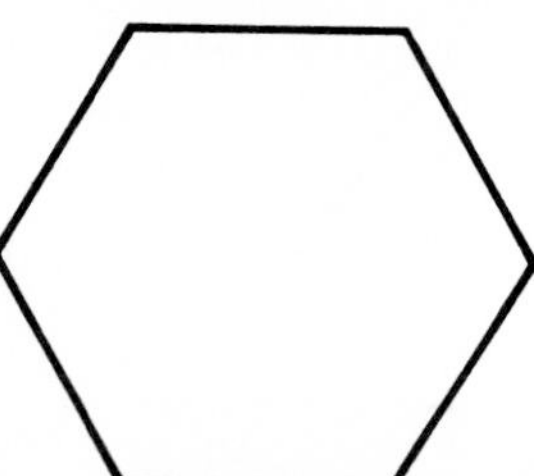

TIME OUT!

In each exercise, tell whether the figures in red are congruent.

1.

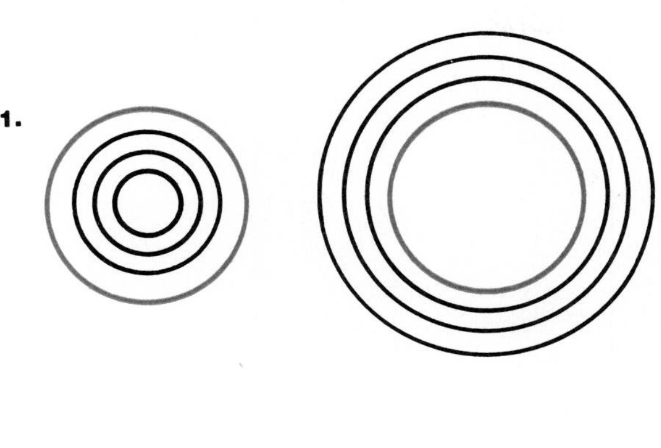

4.

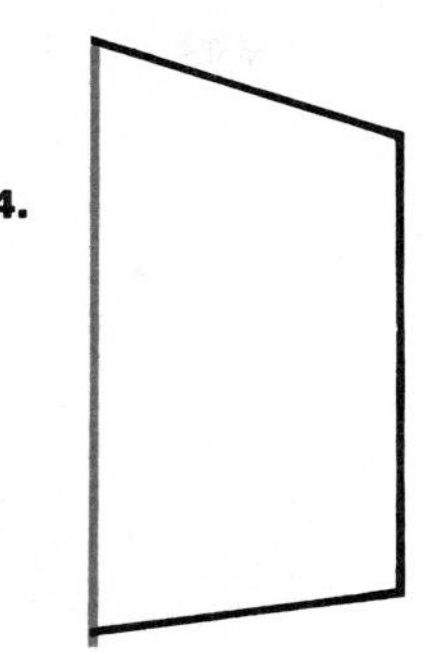

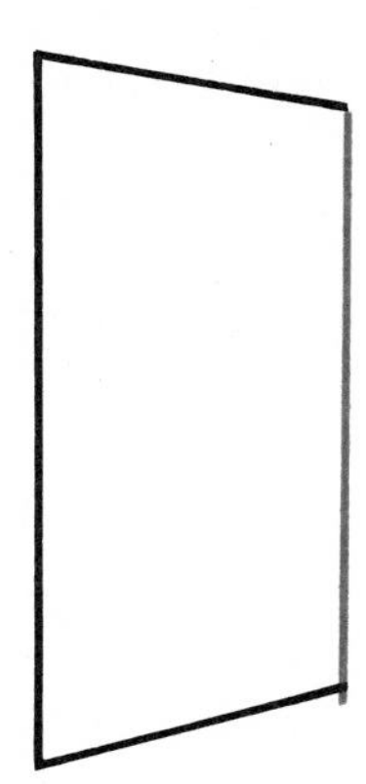

2.

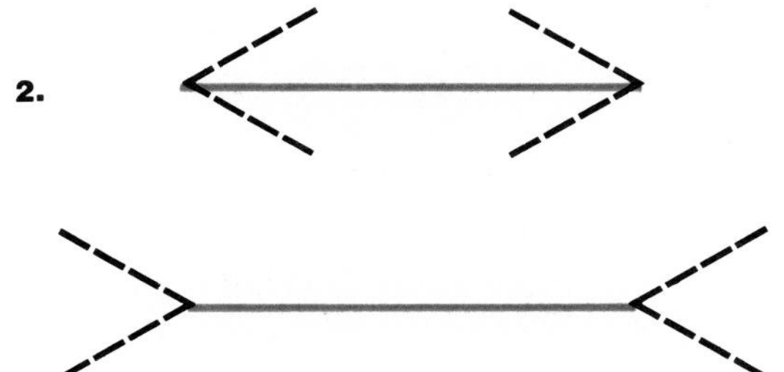

5.

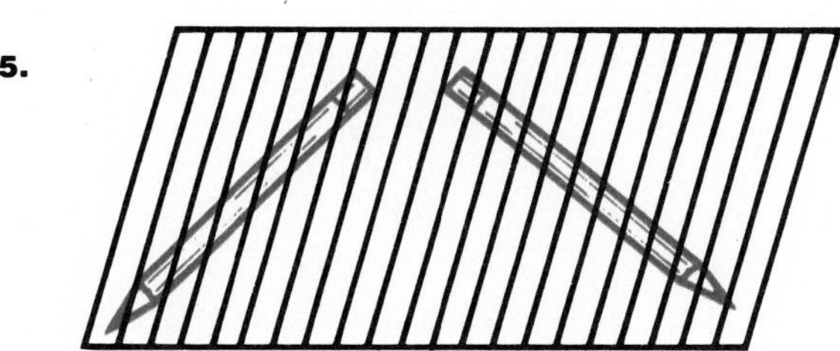

3.

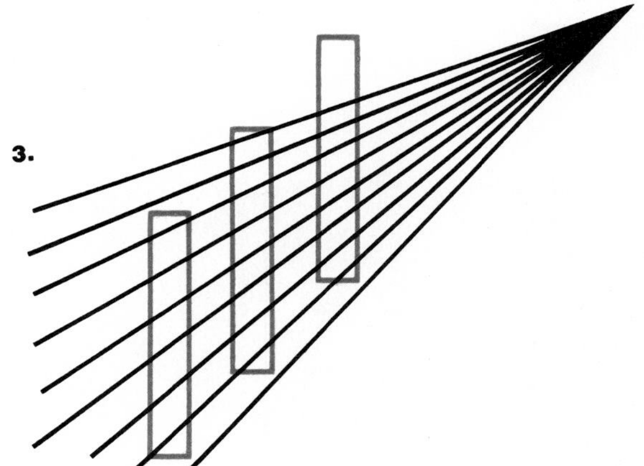

6.

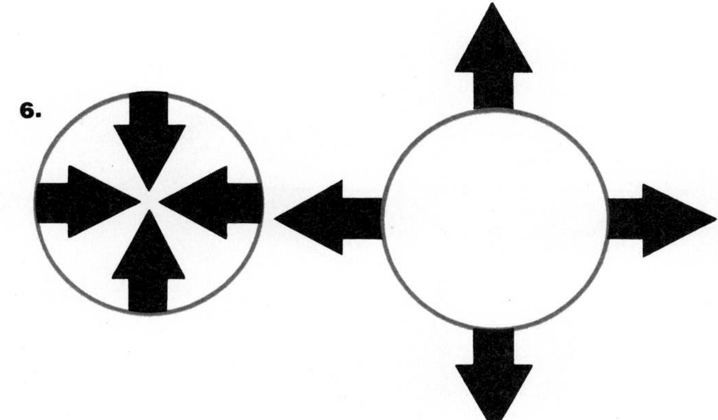

Finding Lines of Symmetry

If you fold a figure on a line and the two parts of the figure fit exactly over each other, then the line is a ***line of symmetry***.

A. This figure has one line of symmetry.

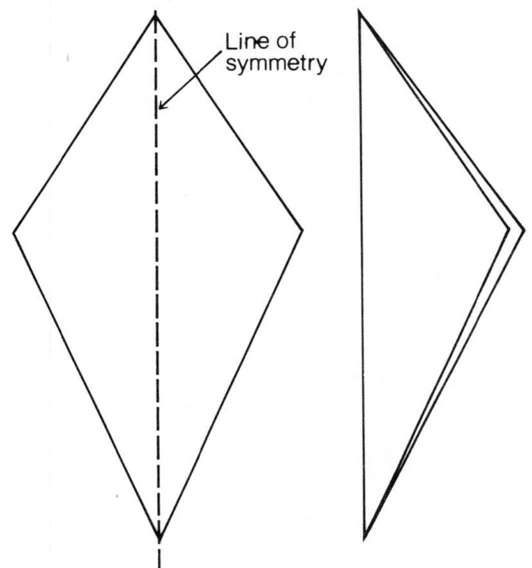

B. This figure has four lines of symmetry.

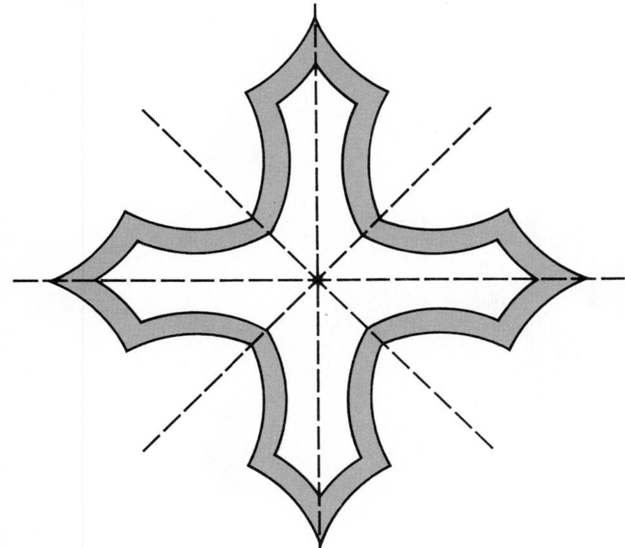

Copy each figure in exercises 1 through 9. Show all lines of symmetry. If there are none, write "no lines of symmetry."

1.

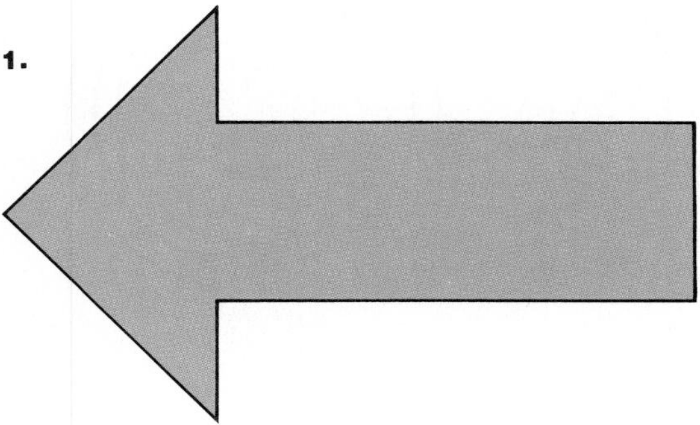

2.

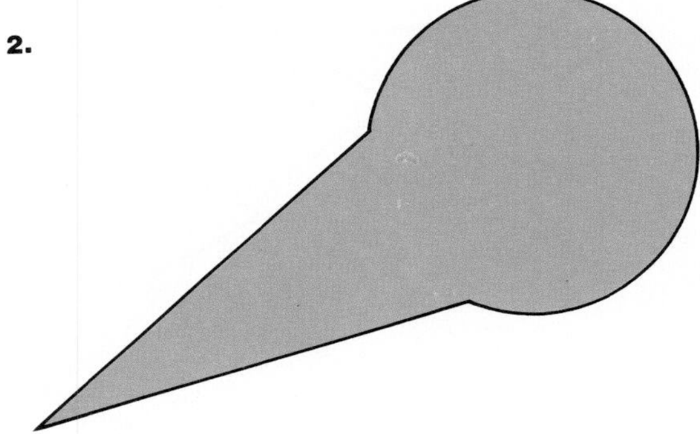

3.

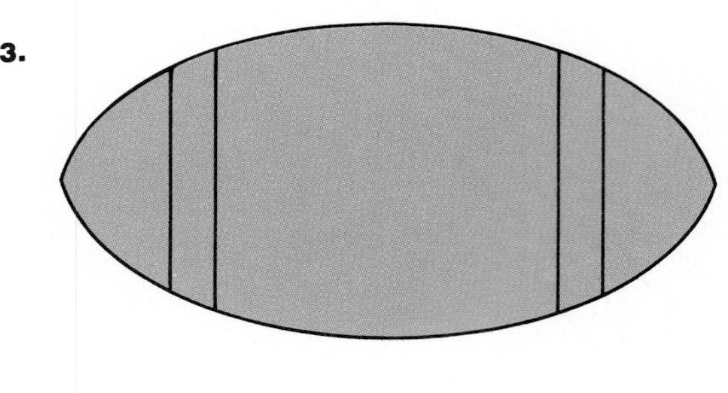

4.

7.

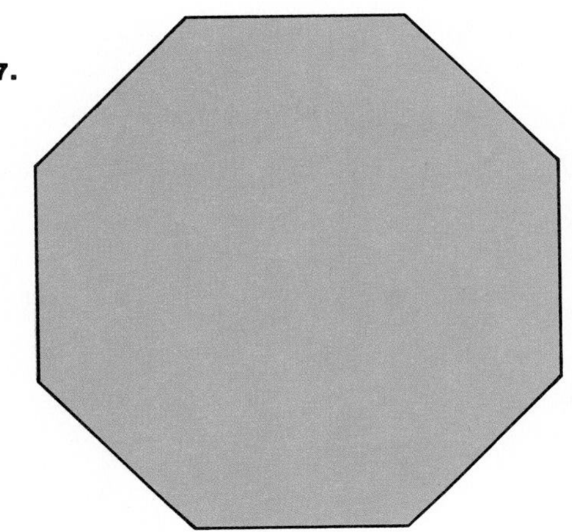

5.

8.

6.

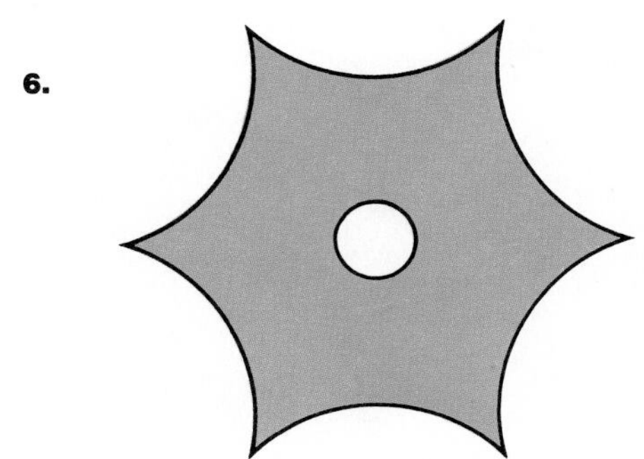

9.

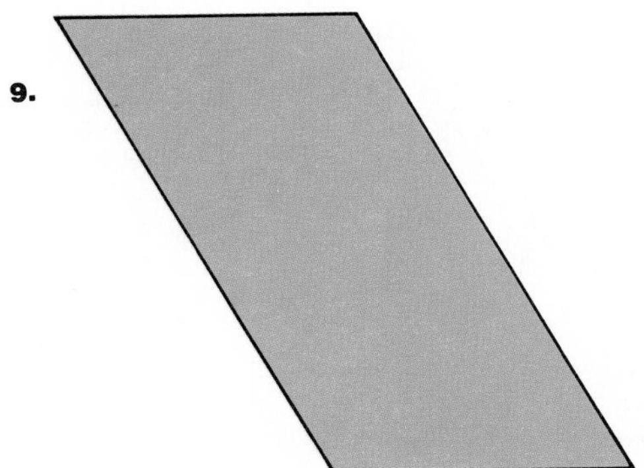

Explore

Use a mirror to help you find lines of symmetry.

Stand the mirror straight up with its edge on the dotted line. Do you see the same figure with and without the mirror? If you do, the line is a line of symmetry for the figure.

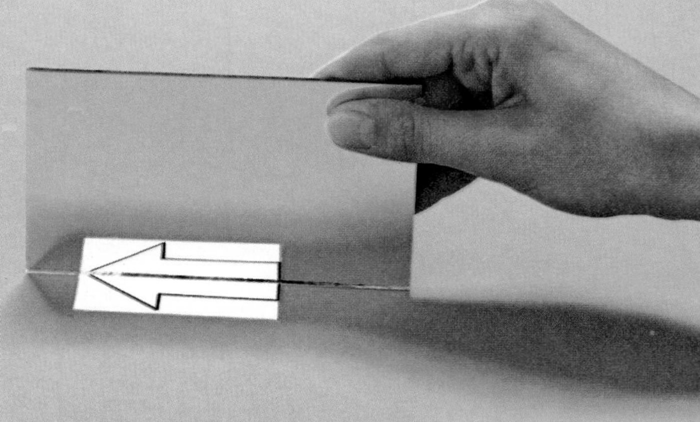

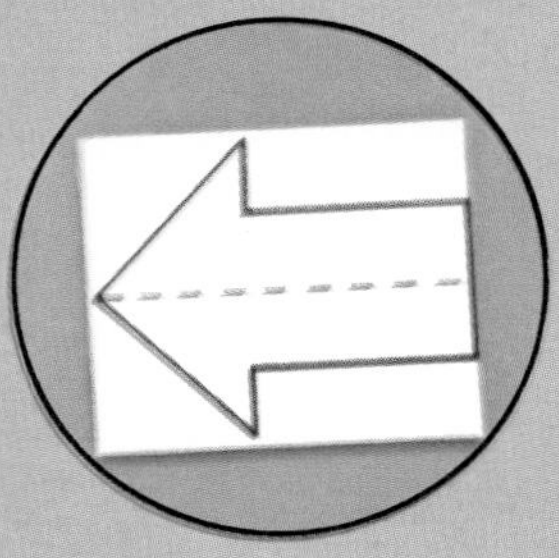

1. Use a mirror to see if the lines in these figures are lines of symmetry.

2. Use a mirror to find lines of symmetry in this figure.

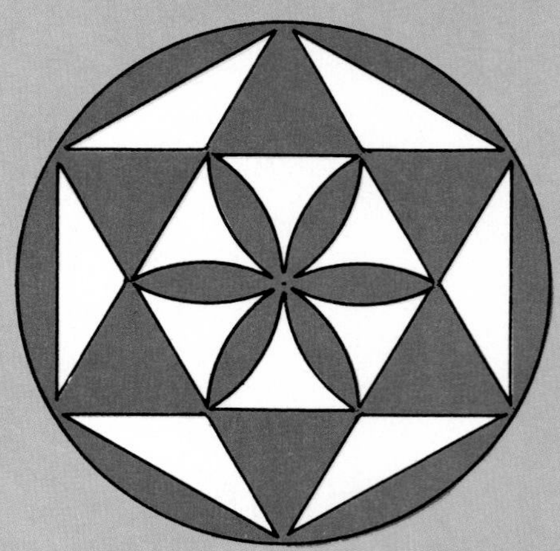

3. Carefully print some capital letters. Use a mirror to find lines of symmetry for the letters.

Using Mathematics: At the Movies

PREVIEW THEATER

TICKETS	CONCESSIONS	
Evening Show	Popcorn	Candy
Adult — $2.50	Small — $.25	Crunch Bar — $.15
Child — 1.25	Large — .40	Jolly Good Bar — .20
		Mini Munch Bar — .10
Matinee	Soda	Junior Jelly Bar — .25
Adult — 2.00	Small — .30	
Child — .75	Large — .40	

1. Tell how much each family paid for an evening movie.

a. The Ziolkowskis
2 adults
6 children

b. The Bowdens
3 adults
3 children

2. Mr. Nordberg and his two children went to a matinee. How much did they save by going to the matinee?

3. Mr. and Mrs. Fitch and their three children bought tickets for an evening movie. How much change did they receive from $10?

4. How much would matinee tickets cost for

a. a class of 34 children?

b. a class of 29 children?

5. Tell how much each family spent on concessions.

a. The Sullivans
3 Junior Jelly Bars
2 small popcorns
4 large sodas

b. The Mays
2 Mini Munch Bars
6 small sodas
3 Crunch Bars

6. The movie about Stuart Little lasted $1\frac{3}{4}$ hours. How many minutes was the movie?

7. The Preview Theater has 1000 seats. At a matinee, $\frac{3}{8}$ of the seats were filled. How many people attended the matinee?

8. The balcony of the theater has 360 seats. There are 24 seats in each row. How many rows are there?

Keeping Skillful

Add.

1. $\frac{5}{6} + \frac{1}{2}$

2. $\frac{2}{3} + \frac{3}{4}$

3. $1\frac{1}{4} + \frac{5}{6}$

4. $4\frac{1}{2} + \frac{7}{8}$

5. $3\frac{1}{3} + 7\frac{11}{12}$

6. $2\frac{4}{5} + 8\frac{1}{2}$

7. $4\frac{3}{4} + 10\frac{1}{2}$

8. $6\frac{1}{5} + 2\frac{3}{10}$

Subtract.

9. $\frac{11}{12} - \frac{7}{12}$

10. $\frac{7}{8} - \frac{3}{4}$

11. $\frac{5}{6} - \frac{2}{3}$

12. $4\frac{1}{2} - 2\frac{2}{3}$

13. $6\frac{3}{5} - 5\frac{1}{4}$

14. $3\frac{5}{8} - 1\frac{5}{6}$

15. $8\frac{1}{6} - 7\frac{3}{4}$

16. $5\frac{1}{2} - 3\frac{3}{5}$

Finding Similar Figures

Figures that are the same shape are ***similar***.
Similar figures are not necessarily the same size.
These four figures are similar.

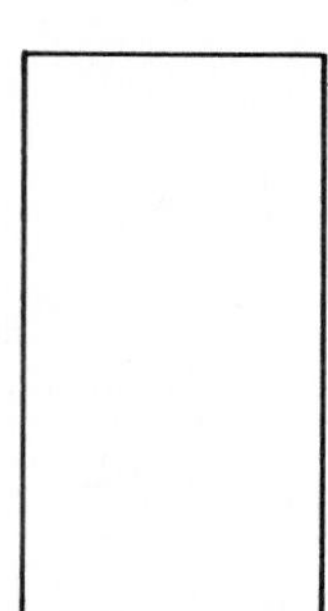
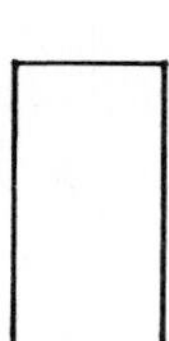

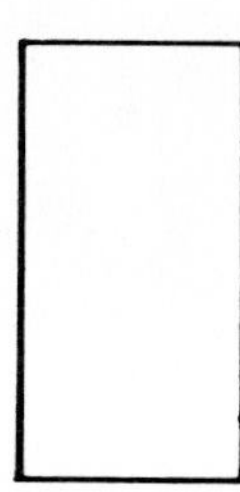

In exercises 1 through 6, find the figure that is not similar to the others.

1. a. 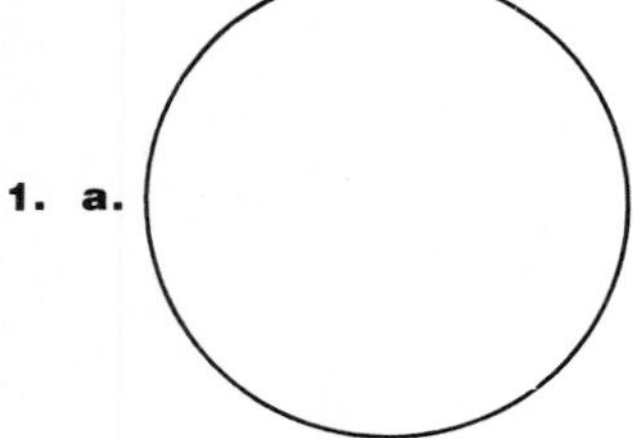 **b.**  **c.** 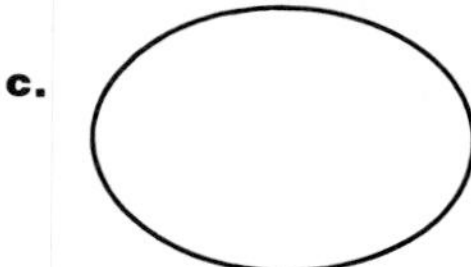 **d.** 

2. a.  **b.** 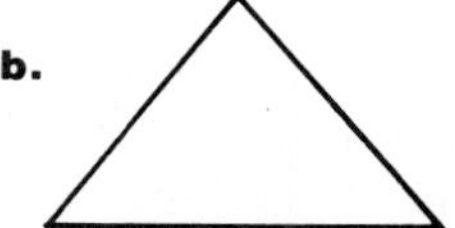 **c.** 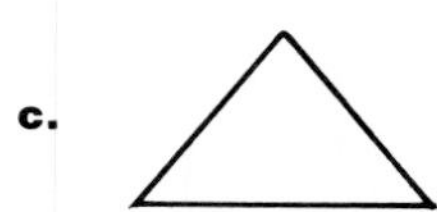 **d.** 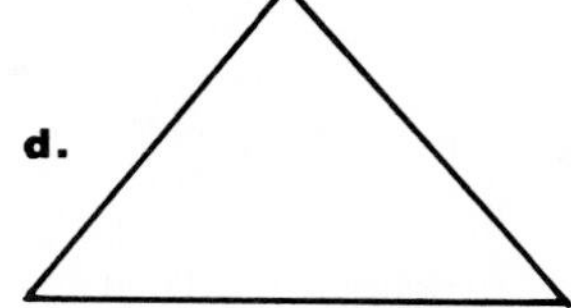

3. a. 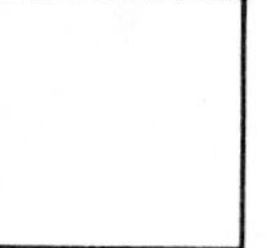 **b.** 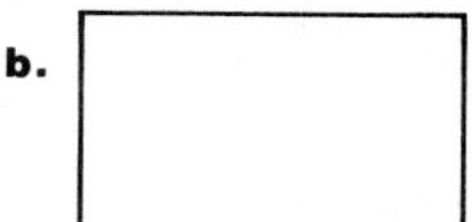 **c.**  **d.** 

4. a.

b.

c.

d.

5. a.

b.

c.

d.

6. a.

b.

c.

d.

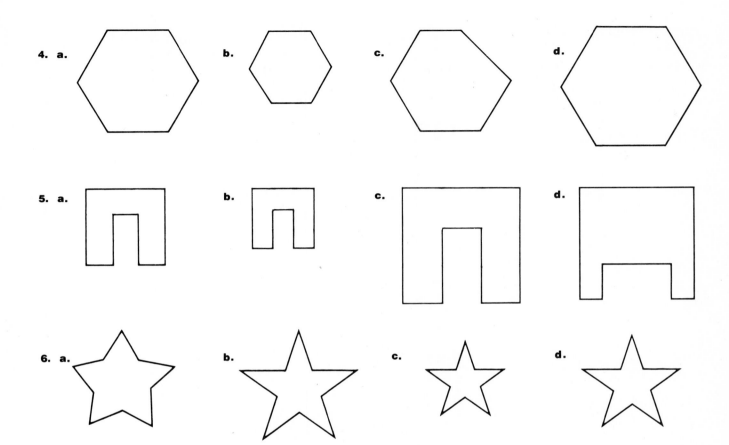

★ **7.** Are the squares similar?

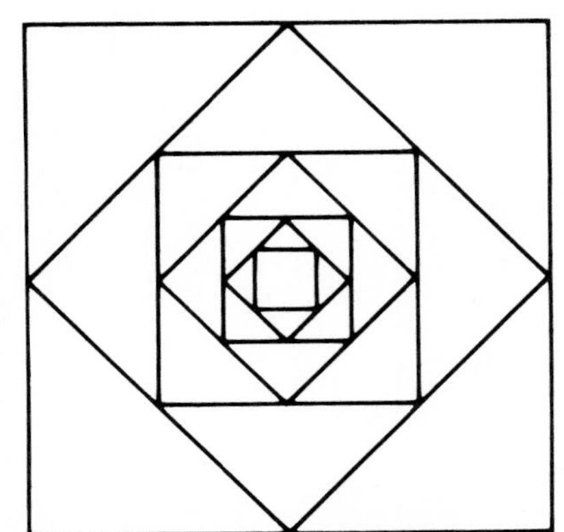

★ **8.** Are the circles similar?

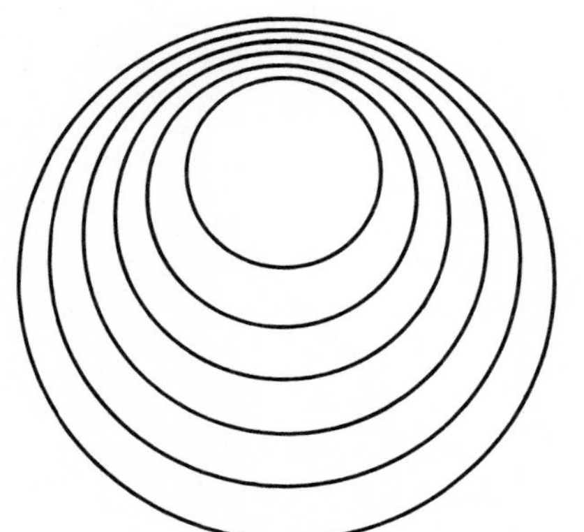

Finding Similar Figures on a Grid

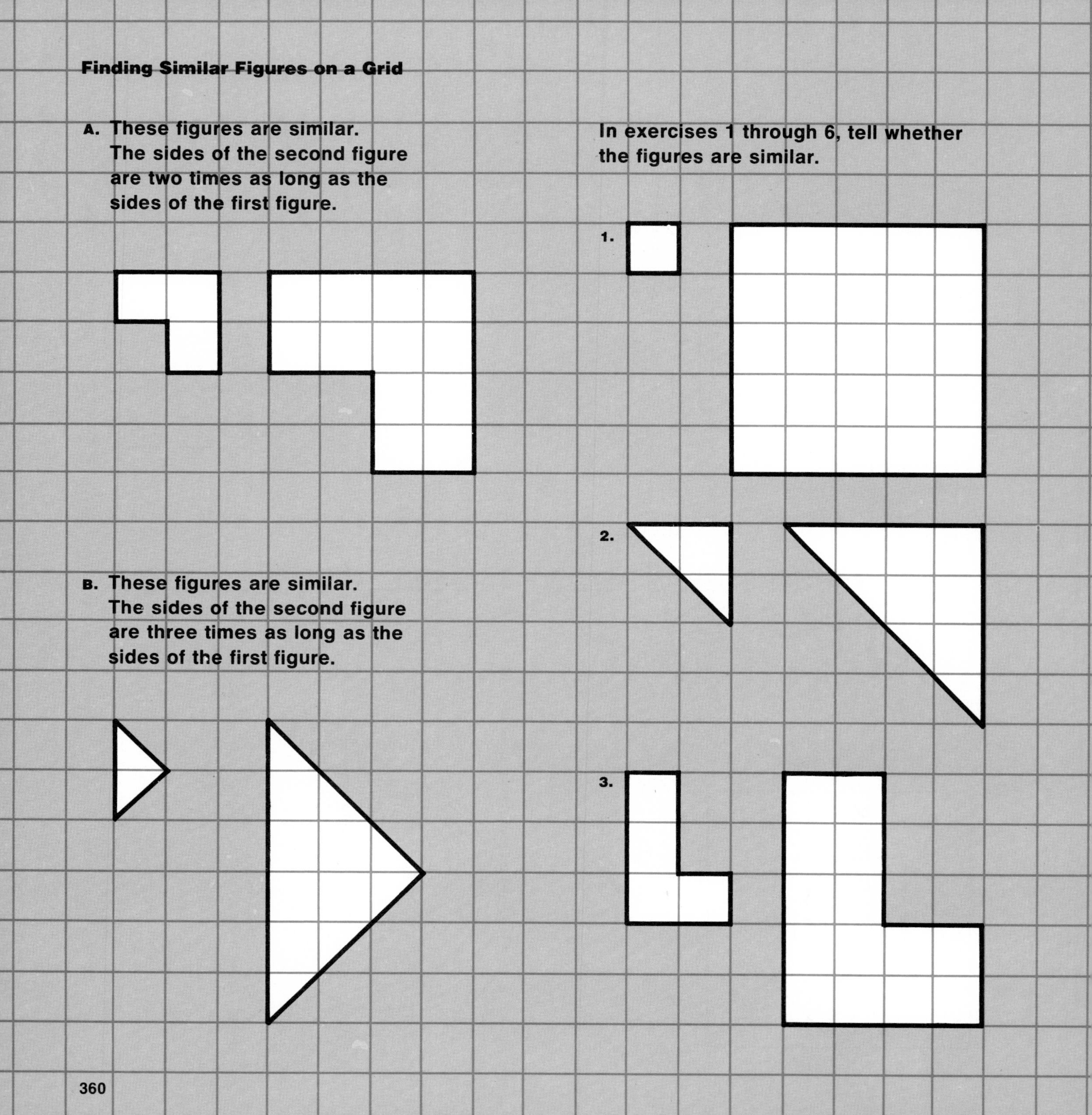

A. These figures are similar. The sides of the second figure are two times as long as the sides of the first figure.

B. These figures are similar. The sides of the second figure are three times as long as the sides of the first figure.

In exercises 1 through 6, tell whether the figures are similar.

1.

2.

3.

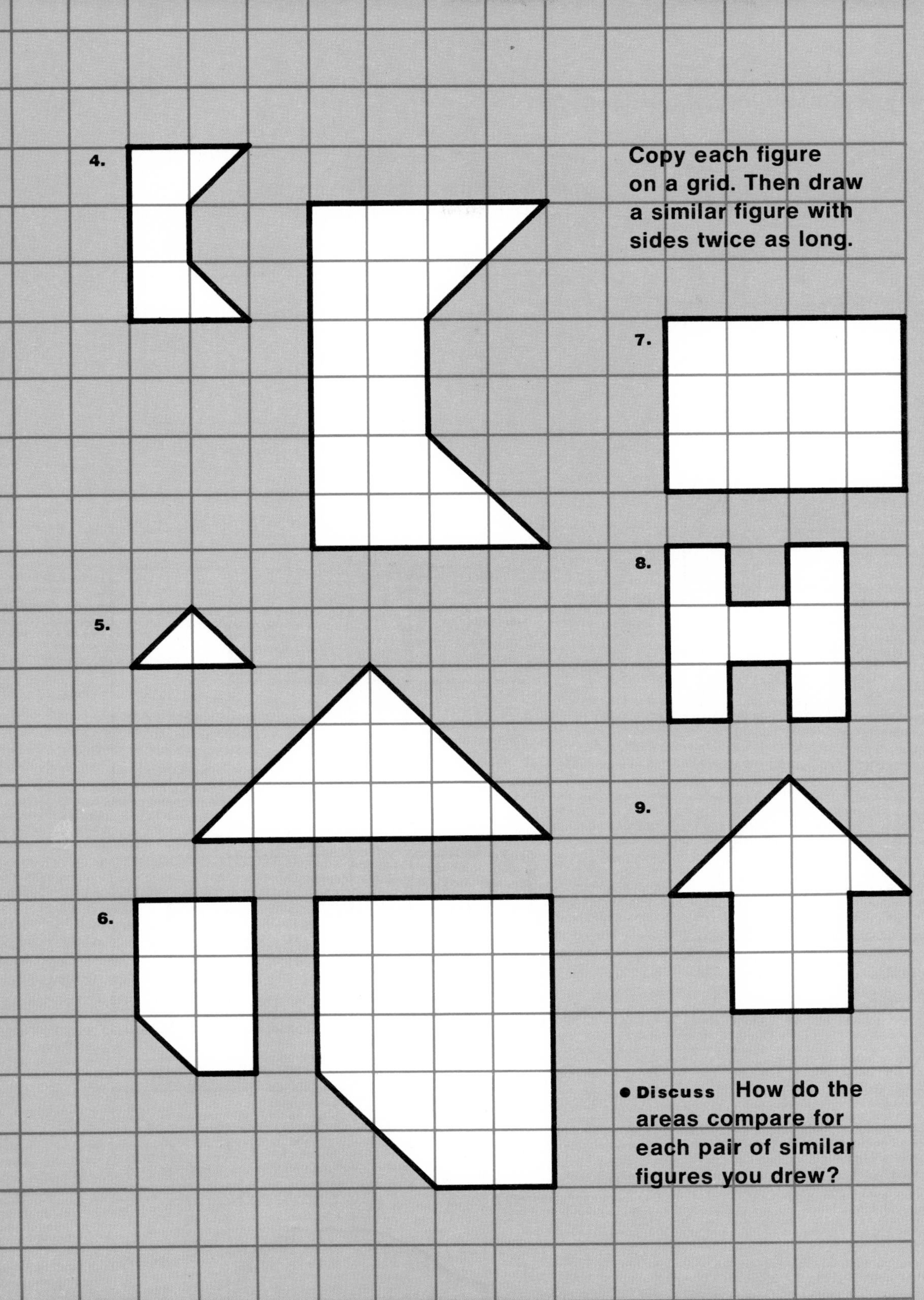

Copy each figure on a grid. Then draw a similar figure with sides twice as long.

● **Discuss** **How do the areas compare for each pair of similar figures you drew?**

Keeping Skillful

Multiply.

1. $\frac{5}{6} \times \frac{1}{2}$
2. $\frac{2}{3} \times \frac{3}{4}$
3. $1\frac{1}{4} \times \frac{5}{6}$
4. $4\frac{1}{2} \times \frac{7}{9}$
5. $6 \times 5\frac{1}{3}$
6. $4\frac{3}{10} \times 3\frac{1}{3}$
7. $5\frac{5}{6} \times 3\frac{3}{7}$

Multiply.

8. $.6 \times .4$
9. $.7 \times .6$
10. $.9 \times .1$
11. $.5 \times .49$
12. $.3 \times 1.6$
13. $.6 \times .03$
14. $.12 \times .12$
15. $9.6 \times .08$
16. $.63 \times .36$
17. $.05 \times .05$
18. $.48 \times .85$
19. $.29 \times .45$
20. $.02 \times .51$

Check Yourself
Congruence, Symmetry, and Similarity, Pages 348–361

Congruence, pages 348–352

Tell whether the two figures are congruent.

1.

2.

3.

Tell whether the figure is divided into congruent parts.

4. 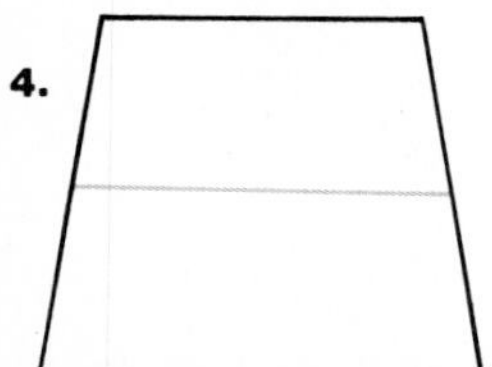

5. 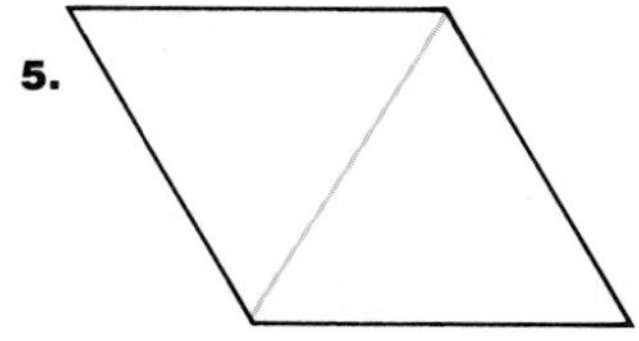

Symmetry, pages 354–355

How many lines of symmetry does each figure have?

6. 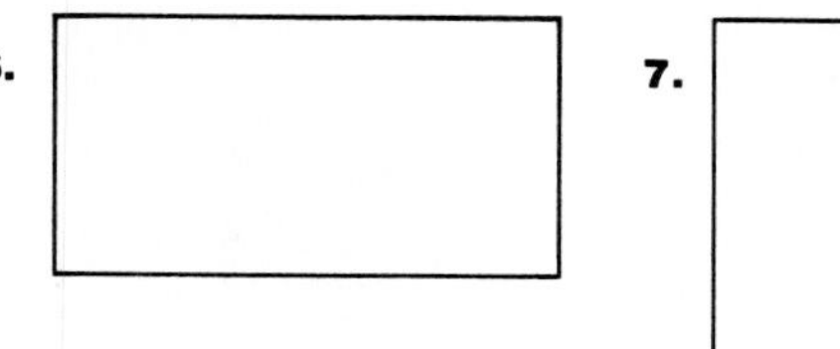

7.

Similarity, pages 358–361

Are the two figures in each exercise similar?

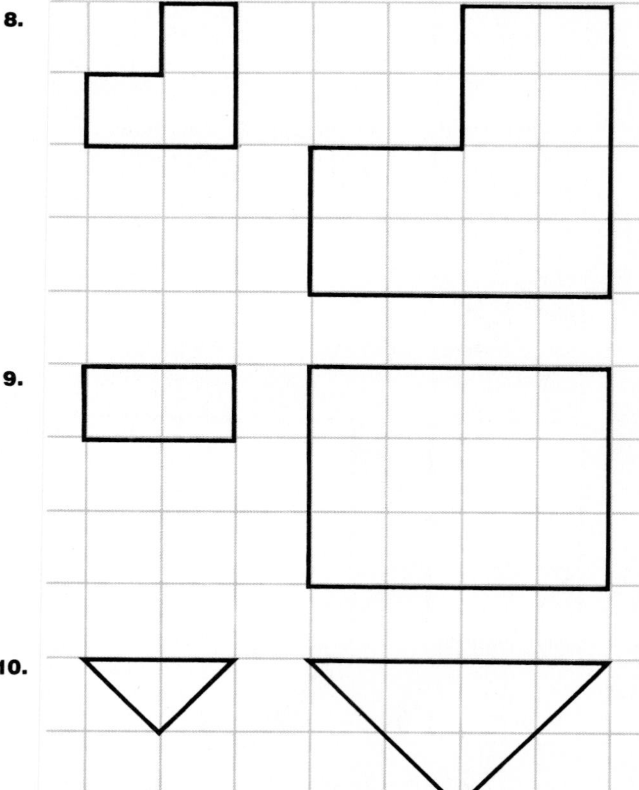

8.

9.

10.

Check Yourself: Level 30

Multiplying fractions and mixed numbers, pages 306–326

Find each product. Give your answers in lowest terms.

1. $\frac{1}{3} \times \frac{7}{8}$

2. $\frac{3}{4} \times \frac{4}{5}$

3. $\frac{5}{6} \times 12$

4. $3\frac{1}{2} \times \frac{4}{7}$

5. $1\frac{2}{3} \times 4$

6. $2\frac{1}{3} \times 1\frac{1}{2}$

7. 1 yard = 36 inches
A ribbon is $\frac{3}{4}$ yard long.
How many inches long is the ribbon?

Multiplying decimals, pages 328–346

Find each product.

8. $.9 \times 3$

9. $6.6 \times .7$

10. $9.38 \times .04$

11. $.79 \times 51$

12. .4 × .2

13. .03 × .012

14. 100 × .08

15. 1000 × 6.3

16. Dana saves $.25 each week.
How much will Dana save in 8 weeks?

17. A dictionary is 0.045 meter thick.
How tall is a stack of 100 dictionaries?

Congruence, symmetry, and similarity, pages 348–361

18. Tell whether the two figures are congruent.

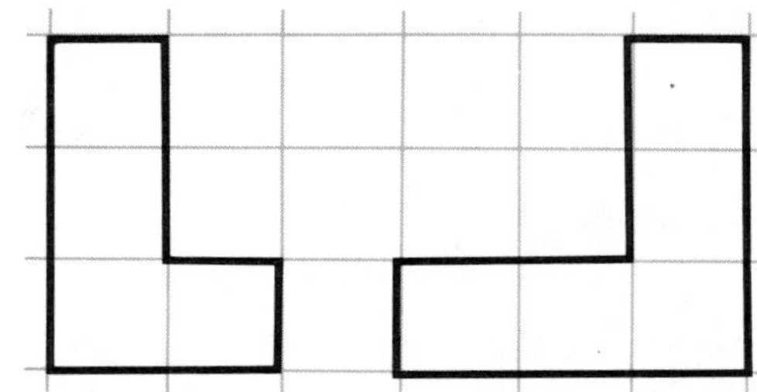

19. How many lines of symmetry does this figure have?

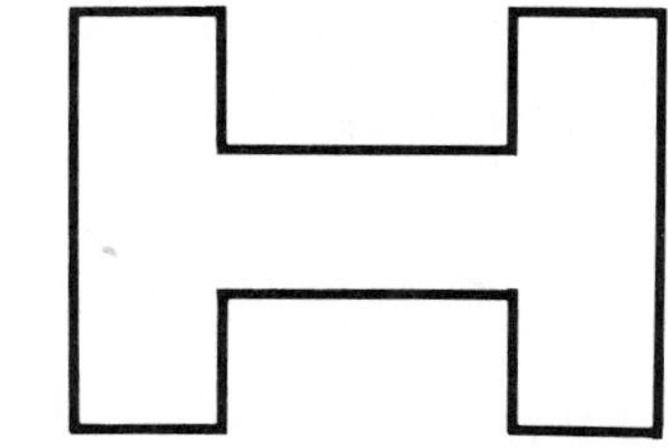

20. Are the two triangles similar?

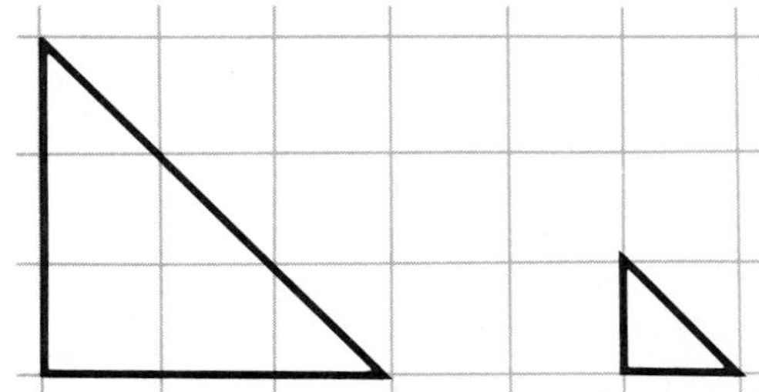

Evaluation: Levels 25–30
Part A

Adding whole numbers, pages 8–15, 22–24

Add.

1. $28 + 47$ **2.** $765 + 309$ **3.** $184 + 57$

4. $35 + 78 + 256$

5. Find the perimeter.

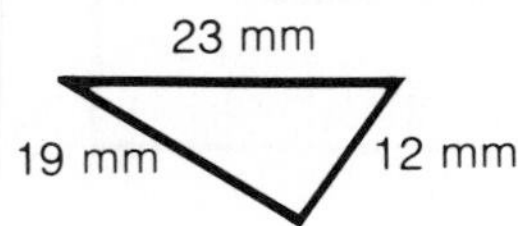

Subtracting whole numbers, pages 16–24

Subtract.

6. $45 - 39$ **7.** $716 - 308$ **8.** $1534 - 765$

9. $1006 - 378$

10. The home team is leading by how many points?

Home: 53 points
Visitors: 39 points

Multiplying whole numbers, pages 32–49

Multiply.

11. 93×8 **12.** 76×29 **13.** 425×87

14. 275×569

15. There are 12 eggs in a carton. How many eggs are in 59 cartons?

Dividing whole numbers, pages 68–91

Divide.

16. $7\overline{)540}$ **17.** $41\overline{)376}$

18. $49\overline{)5782}$ **19.** $27\overline{)8586}$

20. 56 students went on a field trip. 4 students were assigned to each car. How many cars were needed?

Ratio, pages 94–107

Find *n*.

21. $\frac{3}{5} = \frac{15}{n}$ **22.** $\frac{10}{6} = \frac{n}{39}$

23. A newborn baby's heart beats 35 times in 15 seconds. At this rate, how many times will it beat in 42 seconds?

Volume, pages 114–122

24. Find the volume.

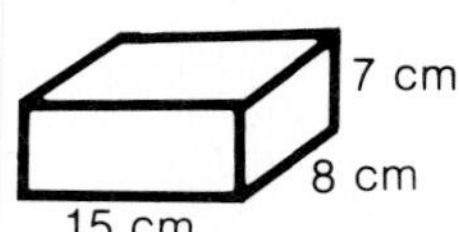

Metric measures, pages 144–151

Choose the best measure.

25. Width of your math book

23 mm 23 cm 23 m

26. Length of a baseball bat

1 mm 1 cm 1 m

Evaluation: Levels 25-30
Part B

Adding decimals, pages 154-157

Add.

1. $\begin{array}{r} 6.3 \\ +\ .5 \\ \hline \end{array}$ **2.** $\begin{array}{r} 7.28 \\ +\ 4.95 \\ \hline \end{array}$ **3.** $\begin{array}{r} .395 \\ +\ .708 \\ \hline \end{array}$

4. 7.085 + .952 + 1.028

5. Alan paid $1.75 for a book and $.59 for drawing paper. How much did he spend?

Subtracting decimals, pages 158-163

Subtract.

6. $\begin{array}{r} 17.4 \\ -\ 1.6 \\ \hline \end{array}$ **7.** $\begin{array}{r} 4.32 \\ -\ 3.18 \\ \hline \end{array}$ **8.** $\begin{array}{r} .841 \\ -\ .652 \\ \hline \end{array}$

9. 4.52 − .36

10. Martha had $4.05. She bought a concert ticket for $1.25. How much money did she have left?

Adding fractions, pages 204, 206-209, 212, 214

Add.

11. $\begin{array}{r} \frac{1}{5} \\ +\ \frac{3}{5} \\ \hline \end{array}$ **12.** $\begin{array}{r} \frac{2}{3} \\ +\ \frac{1}{6} \\ \hline \end{array}$ **13.** $\begin{array}{r} \frac{1}{4} \\ +\ \frac{2}{3} \\ \hline \end{array}$

14. $\frac{1}{2} + \frac{2}{3} + \frac{1}{4}$

15. Marian walked $\frac{1}{10}$ mile to Nancy's house. Then she walked $\frac{1}{5}$ mile to school. How far did she walk?

Subtracting fractions, pages 205, 210, 213-217

Subtract.

16. $\begin{array}{r} \frac{9}{10} \\ -\ \frac{6}{10} \\ \hline \end{array}$ **17.** $\begin{array}{r} \frac{5}{6} \\ -\ \frac{1}{2} \\ \hline \end{array}$ **18.** $\begin{array}{r} \frac{3}{4} \\ -\ \frac{2}{3} \\ \hline \end{array}$

19. $\frac{5}{8} - \frac{1}{4}$

20. The white eraser is $\frac{7}{8}$ inch long. The pink eraser is $\frac{1}{2}$ inch long. How much longer is the white eraser?

Graphing, pages 222-235

This graph shows the number of kilometers this car can travel for each liter of gas.

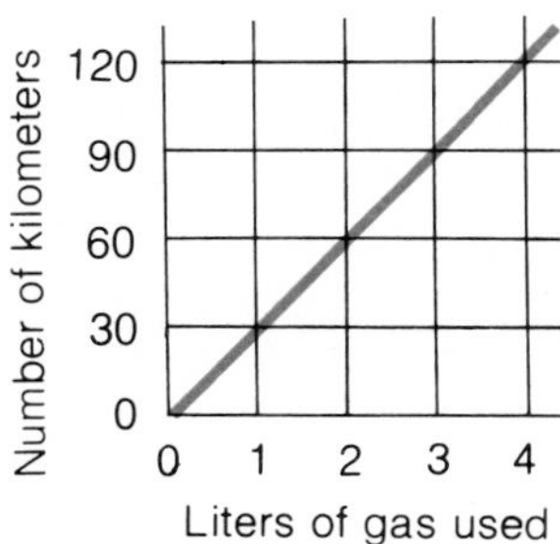

21. How far can this car travel on 4 liters of gas?

22. How many liters of gas were used after traveling 60 kilometers?

Evaluation: Levels 25–30
Part C

Adding mixed numbers, pages 258–267

Add.

1. $5\frac{1}{6} + 3\frac{4}{6}$

2. $16\frac{3}{8} + 5$

3. $9\frac{1}{10} + 3\frac{2}{5}$

4. $8\frac{3}{4} + 5\frac{3}{8}$

5. $9\frac{1}{3} + 7\frac{1}{2}$

6. $2\frac{2}{3} + 5\frac{3}{4}$

7. $1\frac{1}{2} + 2\frac{3}{4} + 1\frac{2}{3}$

8. Ms. Bryan made cookies. She used $1\frac{1}{2}$ cups of brown sugar and $1\frac{1}{3}$ cups of white sugar. How many cups of sugar did she use?

Subtracting mixed numbers, pages 268–279

Subtract.

9. $8\frac{4}{5} - 6\frac{2}{5}$

10. $4\frac{3}{10} - 2$

11. $6 - 2\frac{1}{2}$

12. $5\frac{1}{6} - 3\frac{5}{6}$

13. $6\frac{1}{8} - 3\frac{3}{4}$

14. $9\frac{2}{5} - 4\frac{1}{2}$

15. Marlene walked $3\frac{2}{5}$ miles. Jack walked $2\frac{3}{10}$ miles. How much farther did Marlene walk than Jack?

Multiplying fractions and mixed numbers, pages 306–326

Multiply.

16. $\frac{3}{4} \times \frac{5}{8}$

17. $\frac{2}{3} \times \frac{2}{5}$

18. $\frac{1}{8} \times 7$

19. $1\frac{1}{3} \times 6$

20. $3\frac{1}{2} \times 1\frac{2}{3}$

21. $1\frac{2}{5} \times 1\frac{1}{4}$

22. The average life span of a human being is 70 years. A grizzly bear lives $\frac{4}{7}$ as long as a human being. What is the life span of a grizzly bear?

Multiplying decimals, pages 328–346

Multiply.

23. $.8 \times 6$

24. $4.7 \times .8$

25. $3.9 \times .04$

26. $.27 \times .38$

27. $.04 \times .612$

28. The Markhams bought 5 hot-turkey sandwiches at $1.85 each. What was the total cost?

More Practice

Set A

1. $\frac{1}{2} \times \frac{1}{3}$
2. $\frac{3}{4} \times \frac{1}{5}$
3. $\frac{2}{3} \times \frac{4}{5}$
4. $\frac{3}{7} \times \frac{1}{8}$
5. $\frac{2}{3} \times \frac{9}{10}$
6. $\frac{4}{5} \times \frac{5}{7}$
7. $\frac{1}{2} \times \frac{3}{4}$
8. $\frac{5}{6} \times \frac{1}{5}$
9. $\frac{3}{8} \times \frac{4}{5}$
10. $\frac{1}{4} \times \frac{2}{5}$
11. $\frac{2}{7} \times \frac{3}{5}$
12. $\frac{5}{9} \times \frac{7}{10}$
13. $\frac{1}{6} \times \frac{3}{4}$
14. $\frac{2}{3} \times \frac{2}{5}$
15. $\frac{5}{8} \times \frac{3}{10}$
16. $\frac{3}{4} \times \frac{2}{3}$
17. $\frac{3}{5} \times \frac{7}{9}$
18. $\frac{5}{6} \times \frac{3}{5}$

Set B

1. $\frac{3}{4} \times 8$
2. $\frac{1}{3} \times 12$
3. $6 \times \frac{2}{5}$
4. $14 \times \frac{7}{10}$
5. $\frac{2}{5} \times 25$
6. $\frac{1}{6} \times 45$
7. $\frac{2}{3} \times 15$
8. $\frac{1}{2} \times 9$
9. $18 \times \frac{4}{5}$
10. $48 \times \frac{1}{4}$
11. $\frac{5}{6} \times 30$
12. $72 \times \frac{1}{8}$
13. $\frac{1}{2} \times 37$
14. $\frac{4}{7} \times 21$
15. $40 \times \frac{3}{10}$
16. $15 \times \frac{3}{4}$
17. $\frac{2}{5} \times 65$
18. $\frac{2}{3} \times 75$

Set C

Write each mixed number as an improper fraction.

1. $2\frac{1}{5}$
2. $1\frac{2}{3}$
3. $5\frac{1}{4}$
4. $6\frac{1}{2}$
5. $4\frac{2}{3}$
6. $7\frac{1}{4}$
7. $8\frac{3}{5}$
8. $3\frac{5}{6}$
9. $9\frac{3}{4}$
10. $5\frac{1}{3}$
11. $6\frac{9}{10}$
12. $7\frac{5}{8}$
13. $10\frac{5}{9}$
14. $24\frac{1}{6}$
15. $18\frac{7}{8}$

Set D

1. $1\frac{1}{3} \times 3\frac{1}{2}$
2. $2\frac{1}{4} \times 2\frac{1}{3}$
3. $1\frac{3}{5} \times 3\frac{1}{3}$
4. $2\frac{1}{6} \times 4\frac{1}{3}$
5. $3\frac{1}{6} \times 3$
6. $1\frac{7}{8} \times 1\frac{1}{2}$
7. $5 \times 2\frac{3}{5}$
8. $2\frac{3}{4} \times 3\frac{1}{2}$
9. $4\frac{4}{5} \times 1\frac{3}{8}$
10. $3\frac{5}{6} \times 4$
11. $2\frac{1}{3} \times 1\frac{3}{4}$
12. $6 \times 2\frac{2}{3}$
13. $1\frac{2}{5} \times 2\frac{1}{7}$
14. $1\frac{1}{4} \times 6\frac{1}{3}$
15. $6\frac{1}{2} \times 5$
16. $2\frac{7}{10} \times 1\frac{1}{3}$
17. $1\frac{5}{6} \times 12$
18. $80 \times 1\frac{3}{4}$

Set E

1. $\begin{array}{r} 91.2 \\ \times \quad .04 \\ \hline \end{array}$
2. $\begin{array}{r} 3.97 \\ \times \quad 2.5 \\ \hline \end{array}$
3. $.018 \times 3.2$
4. $.605 \times .016$
5. $.72 \times .035$
6. $.435 \times 2.4$
7. $.063 \times 9.5$
8. $.005 \times .119$

Set F

1. $.0048 \times 10$
2. $.083 \times 100$
3. 100×7.5
4. 6.16×1000
5. $100 \times .0096$
6. $10 \times .12$
7. $.4054 \times 1000$
8. $10 \times .055$
9. $1000 \times .7575$
10. 13.12×100

Check Yourself Answers: Level 30

Check Yourself, page 327

1. $\frac{2}{5}$
2. $\frac{5}{8}$
3. $\frac{4}{21}$
4. 6
5. $2\frac{1}{8}$
6. 8
7. $1\frac{7}{8}$
8. $1\frac{6}{25}$
9. 10
10. $17\frac{1}{2}$
11. 3
12. $5\frac{5}{6}$
13. $\frac{1}{3}$
14. 77 lb.
15. About 122 times
16. About 305 times
17. $2\frac{2}{3}$ cups
18. 10 years
19. 8 hours
20. $2\frac{1}{4}$ cm^2

Check Yourself, page 347

1. 3.2
2. 2.58
3. .217
4. 1.14
5. .1557
6. .672
7. 460.2
8. .0425
9. 57.372
10. .048
11. .000075
12. .0168
13. 7
14. 4270
15. 8.605
16. $13.25
17. $18.00
18. 40 m
19. 174 m
20. 41.6 m

Check Yourself, page 362

1. Yes
2. Yes
3. No
4. No
5. Yes
6. Two
7. Four
8. Yes
9. No
10. Yes

Check Yourself: Level 30, page 363

1. $\frac{7}{24}$
2. $\frac{3}{5}$
3. 10
4. 2
5. $6\frac{2}{3}$
6. $3\frac{1}{2}$
7. 27 in.
8. 2.7
9. 4.62
10. .3752
11. 40.29
12. .08
13. .00036
14. 8
15. 6300
16. $2.00
17. 4.5 m
18. No
19. Two
20. Yes

Tables

Metric System

Length

10 millimeters (mm) = 1 centimeter (cm)
10 centimeters, 100 millimeters = 1 decimeter (dm)
10 decimeters, 100 centimeters = 1 meter (m)
1000 meters = 1 kilometer (km)

Area

100 square millimeters (mm^2) = 1 square centimeter (cm^2)
10,000 square centimeters = 1 square meter (m^2)
100 square meters = 1 are (a)
10,000 square meters = 1 hectare (ha)

Volume

1000 cubic millimeters (mm^3) = 1 cubic centimeter (cm^3)
1000 cubic centimeters = 1 cubic decimeter (dm^3)
1,000,000 cubic centimeters = 1 cubic meter (m^3)

Mass

1000 milligrams (mg) = 1 gram (g)
1000 grams = 1 kilogram (kg)
1000 kilograms = 1 metric ton (t)

Capacity

1000 milliliters (ml) = 1 liter (ℓ)
1000 liters = 1 kiloliter (kl)

Customary System

Length

12 inches (in.) = 1 foot (ft.)
3 feet, 36 inches = 1 yard (yd.)
1760 yards, 5280 feet = 1 mile (mi.)
6076 feet = 1 nautical mile

Area

144 square inches (sq. in.) = 1 square foot (sq. ft.)
9 square feet = 1 square yard (sq. yd.)
4840 square yards = 1 acre (A.)

Volume

1728 cubic inches (cu. in.) = 1 cubic foot (cu. ft.)
27 cubic feet = 1 cubic yard (cu. yd.)

Weight

16 ounces (oz.) = 1 pound (lb.)
2000 pounds = 1 ton (T.)

Capacity

8 fluid ounces (fl. oz.) = 1 cup (c.)
2 cups = 1 pint (pt.)
2 pints = 1 quart (qt.)
4 quarts = 1 gallon (gal.)

Addition-subtraction table

+	0	1	2	3	4	5	6	7	8	9
0	0	1	2	3	4	5	6	7	8	9
1	1	2	3	4	5	6	7	8	9	10
2	2	3	4	5	6	7	8	9	10	11
3	3	4	5	6	7	8	9	10	11	12
4	4	5	6	7	8	9	10	11	12	13
5	5	6	7	8	9	10	11	12	13	14
6	6	7	8	9	10	11	12	13	14	15
7	7	8	9	10	11	12	13	14	15	16
8	8	9	10	11	12	13	14	15	16	17
9	9	10	11	12	13	14	15	16	17	18

Multiplication-division table

×	1	2	3	4	5	6	7	8	9
1	1	2	3	4	5	6	7	8	9
2	2	4	6	8	10	12	14	16	18
3	3	6	9	12	15	18	21	24	27
4	4	8	12	16	20	24	28	32	36
5	5	10	15	20	25	30	35	40	45
6	6	12	18	24	30	36	42	48	54
7	7	14	21	28	35	42	49	56	63
8	8	16	24	32	40	48	56	64	72
9	9	18	27	36	45	54	63	72	81

Time

60 seconds (sec.) = 1 minute (min.)
60 minutes = 1 hour (hr.)
24 hours = 1 day (da.)
7 days = 1 week (wk.)
365 days, 52 weeks, 12 months (mo.) = 1 year (yr.)
366 days = 1 leap year

Glossary

Acute angle
An angle whose measure is less than 90°.

Addend
A number used in addition. In the equation $5 + 7 = 12$, 5 and 7 are addends.

Angle
Two rays with the same endpoint.

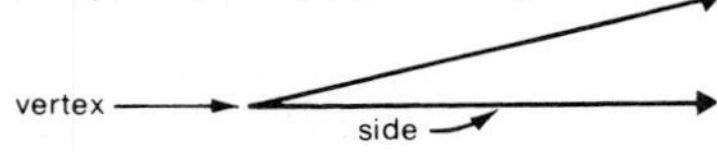

Area
A number indicating amount of space inside a plane figure. The area of this figure is 8 square units.

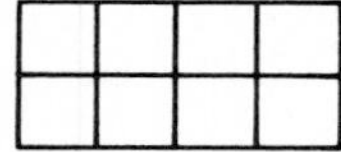

Array
A rectangular arrangement of objects in rows and columns.

Associative property
See Grouping property of addition *and* Grouping property of multiplication.

Average
The quotient obtained by dividing the sum of a set of numbers by the number of addends.

Celsius temperature (° C)
A temperature scale in which 0° C represents the freezing point of water and 100° C represents the boiling point.

Central angle
An angle whose vertex is the center of a circle.

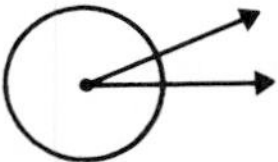

Circle
A closed curve in a plane, all of whose points are the same distance from a given point called the center.

Circumference
The distance around a circle.

Common denominator
A common multiple of two or more denominators. 12 is a common denominator for $\frac{2}{3}$ and $\frac{1}{4}$.

Common factor
A number that is a factor of two or more numbers. 3 is a common factor of 6 and 12.

Common multiple
A number that is a multiple of two or more numbers. 12 is a common multiple of 4 and 6.

Commutative property
See Order property of addition *and* Order property of multiplication.

Composite number
A whole number greater than zero that has more than two factors. 12, 20, and 35 are composite numbers.

Cone
A space figure shaped like this.

Congruent
Having the same size and shape.

Cross-products
For two ratios, the products of the first number of one ratio and the second number of the other ratio. For $\frac{3}{4}$ and $\frac{9}{12}$, the cross-products are 3×12 and 9×4.

Cube
A rectangular prism with all square faces.

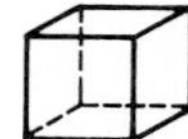

Cylinder
A space figure shaped like this.

Decimal
The numerals 3.84, .076, and 90.0 are decimals. Place value and a decimal point are used to write decimals.

Degree (of an angle)
A unit for measuring angles.

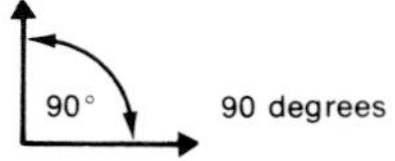

Denominator
In the fraction $\frac{5}{6}$, the denominator is 6.

Diagonal
In a polygon, a segment that connects one vertex to another and is not a side of the polygon.

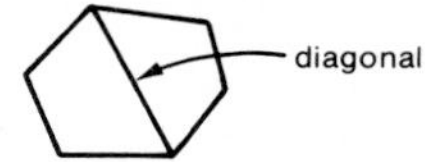

Diameter
In a circle, a segment having its endpoints on the circle and passing through the center.

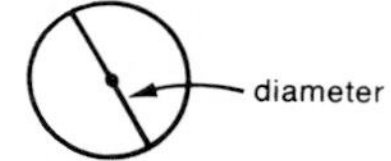

Difference
The result of a subtraction. In the subtraction $95 - 68$, the difference is 27.

Digit
Any of the individual symbols used to write numerals. In the base-ten system, the digits are 0, 1, 2, 3, 4, 5, 6, 7, 8, 9.

Distributive property of multiplication over addition
A property that relates multiplication and addition as follows:

$$4 \times (7 + 3) = (4 \times 7) + (4 \times 3)$$

Dividend
In $45 \div 6$, 45 is the dividend.
$6\overline{)45} \longleftarrow$ dividend

Divisor
In $45 \div 6$, 6 is the divisor.
divisor $\longrightarrow 6\overline{)45}$

Edge
In a space figure, a segment where two faces meet.

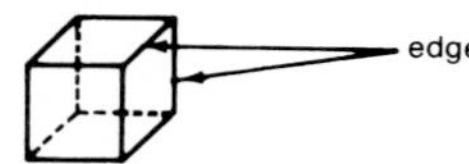

Endpoint
A point at the end of a line segment or ray.

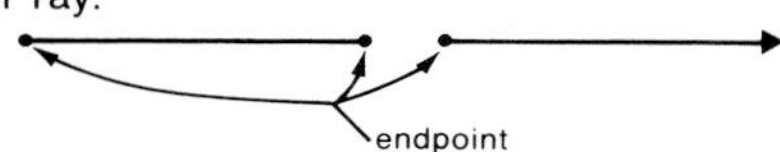

Equal fractions
Fractions that name the same number.
$\frac{2}{3}$ and $\frac{8}{12}$ are equal fractions.

Equal ratios
Ratios that indicate the same rate or comparison. The cross-products of equal ratios are equal.
$\frac{3}{4} = \frac{9}{12}$ because $3 \times 12 = 9 \times 4$.

Equation
A mathematical sentence that uses the symbol $=$.
$7 + 5 = 12$

Equilateral triangle
A triangle whose three sides are congruent.

Even number
A whole number with a factor of 2.

Expanded numeral
An expanded numeral for 5176 is shown.
$5000 + 100 + 70 + 6$

Exponent
In 4^3, 3 is the exponent. It tells that 4 is to be used as a factor three times.
$4^3 = 4 \times 4 \times 4 = 64$

Face
A plane region of a space figure.

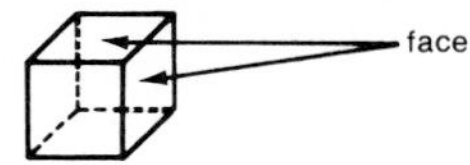

Factor
A number used in multiplication.
In $3 \times 8 = 24$, 3 and 8 are factors.

Fahrenheit temperature (° F)
A temperature scale in which 32° F represents the freezing point of water and 212° F the boiling point of water.

Fraction
A number such as $\frac{1}{3}$, $\frac{5}{5}$, $\frac{7}{2}$, and $\frac{0}{4}$.

Graph
(1) A picture used to show data. The data may be shown by a bar graph, a circle graph, a line graph, or a pictograph.
(2) Points on a grid matched with given ordered pairs.

Greater than (>)
An inequality relation between two numbers.
$8 > 5 \quad 9 > 1.4 \quad \frac{1}{3} > \frac{1}{4}$

Grouping property of addition
The way in which addends are grouped does not affect the sum. Also called the associative property of addition.
$(7 + 2) + 5 = 7 + (2 + 5)$

Grouping property of multiplication
The way in which factors are grouped does not affect the product. Also called the associative property of multiplication.
$(7 \times 2) \times 5 = 7 \times (2 \times 5)$

Hexagon
A six-sided polygon.

Improper fraction
A fraction whose numerator is equal to or greater than its denominator. Examples of improper fractions are $\frac{4}{4}$, $\frac{15}{2}$, and $\frac{8}{1}$.

Inequality
A mathematical sentence that uses $>$ or $<$ or $\neq$.
$6 > 2 \quad 7 < 15 \quad 3 + 2 \neq 6$

Integer
Numbers such as -1856, -45, 0, $+320$, and $+17{,}056$ are integers.

Intersecting lines
Two lines with exactly one point in common.

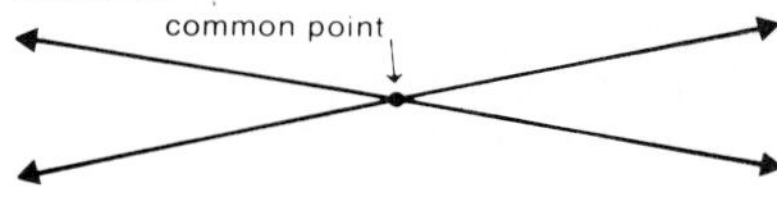

Isosceles triangle
A triangle with two congruent sides.

Least common multiple
The smallest number that is a common multiple of two given numbers. For the numbers 6 and 8, the least common multiple is 24.

Less than (<)
An inequality relation between two numbers.
$5 < 8 \quad 1.4 < 9 \quad \frac{1}{4} < \frac{1}{3}$

Line of symmetry
If folding a figure along a line makes one part match the other part, then that line is a line of symmetry.

Lowest terms
A fraction is in lowest terms if the only common factor of the numerator and the denominator is 1.

Metric system
A system of measurement that uses the meter, the kilogram, and the second as basic units.

Mixed number
A number such as $7\frac{1}{4}$, $5\frac{3}{10}$, or $6\frac{7}{8}$.

Multiple
A multiple of a number is a product of that number and a whole number. 3, 6, 9, 12, and so on, are multiples of 3.

Negative integer
An integer less than zero, such as -1, -2, -5, or -10.

Number sentence
An equation or an inequality.
$3 + 5 = 8$ $\quad 4 < 7 \quad$ $9 > 6$

Numeral
A symbol for a number.

Numerator
In the fraction $\frac{5}{6}$, the numerator is 5.

Obtuse angle
An angle whose measure is greater than 90°.

Octagon
An eight-sided polygon.

Odd number
A whole number that does not have 2 as a factor.

Opposites
Two numbers whose sum is zero. 5 and -5 are opposites since $5 + -5 = 0$.

Order property of addition
The order in which numbers are added does not change the sum. Also called the commutative property of addition.
$4 + 6 = 6 + 4$

Order property of multiplication
The order in which numbers are multiplied does not change the product. Also called the commutative property of multiplication.
$4 \times 6 = 6 \times 4$

Ordered pair
A number pair, such as (3, 5), where 3 is the first component and 5 is the second component.

Parallel lines
Lines in the same plane that do not intersect.

Parallelogram
A quadrilateral whose opposite sides are parallel.

Pentagon
A five-sided polygon.

Percent
A fraction whose denominator is 100. Percent means "hundredths" or "out of 100." For example, $\frac{45}{100} = 45\%$.

Perimeter
The distance around a closed figure.

Perpendicular lines
Two lines which intersect to form right angles.

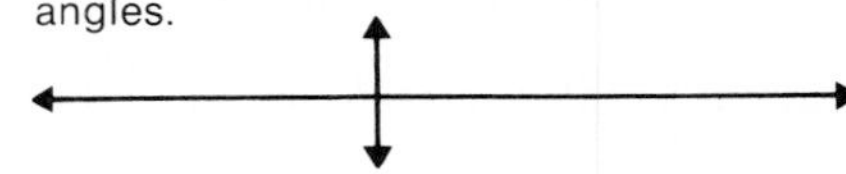

Place value
The value given to the place in which a digit appears in a numeral. In 683, 6 is in the hundreds place, 8 is in the tens place, and 3 is in the ones place.

Polygon
A closed figure made up of segments.

Polyhedron
A space figure with faces that are all polygons.

Positive integer
An integer greater than zero, such as $+1$, $+2$, $+10$, or $+35$.

Power
2^3 is read "2 to the third power."
$2^3 = 2 \times 2 \times 2 = 8$. The third power of 2 is 8. *See also* Exponent.

Prime factor
A factor that is a prime number. 2 and 5 are prime factors of 10.

Prime number
A whole number, such as 17, that has exactly two factors—itself and 1.

Prism
A space figure with two parallel faces, called bases, that are congruent polygonal regions.

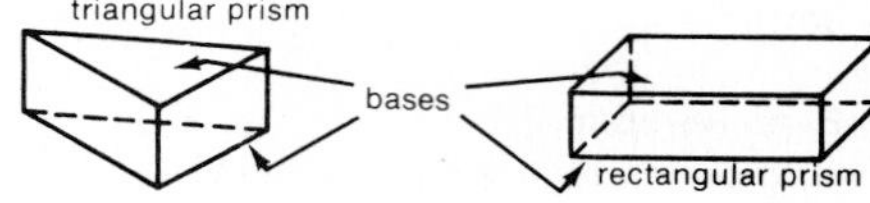

Probability
A number that tells how likely it is that a certain event will happen.

Product
The result of a multiplication.
21 is the product in this multiplication:
$3 \times 7 = 21$

Pyramid
A space figure having a base that is a polygon and faces that are triangles.

triangular pyramid

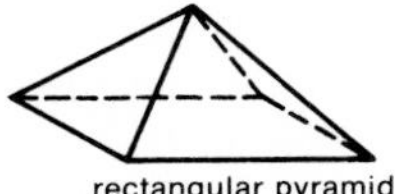
rectangular pyramid

Quadrant
One of the four parts into which a plane is divided by two perpendicular lines.

Quadrilateral
A polygon with four sides.

Quotient
The result of a division.
7 is the quotient in this division.
$42 \div 6 = 7$

Radius
A segment whose endpoints are the center of a circle and a point on the circle.

Ratio
A pair of numbers that expresses a rate or a comparison.

Ray
Part of a line that has one endpoint and goes on and on in one direction.

Reciprocals
Two numbers whose product is 1.
$\frac{3}{4}$ and $\frac{4}{3}$ are reciprocals.

Rectangle
A parallelogram with four right angles.

Regular polygon
A polygon that has all sides congruent and all angles congruent.

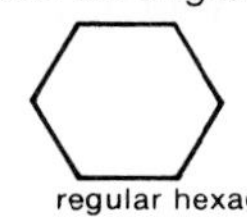
regular hexagon

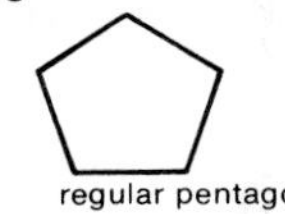
regular pentagon

Remainder
When 20 is divided by 6, the remainder is 2.

Right angle
An angle whose measure is 90°

Right triangle
A triangle that has one right angle.

Rounded number
A number expressed to the nearest 10, 100, 1000, and so on. To round 352 to the nearest 10, you would write 350.

Scale drawing
A drawing that shows the correct shape of an object but differs in size. A scale drawing of an object and the object are similar.

Scalene triangle
A triangle in which no two sides are congruent.

Segment
Part of a line, including two endpoints.

Similar figures
Similar figures have the same shape but not necessarily the same size.

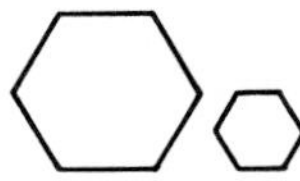

Square
A rectangle with all four sides congruent.

Square number
The product of a number and itself.
Since $4 = 2 \times 2$ and $9 = 3 \times 3$, 4 and 9 are square numbers.

Standard numeral
5176 is the standard numeral for 5 thousands 1 hundred 7 tens 6 ones.

Sum
The result of an addition. When 5 is added to 16, the sum is 21.

Surface area
The sum of the areas of all the different faces of a space figure.

Triangle
A polygon with three sides.

Vertex
(1) The common endpoint of two rays that form an angle.
(2) The point of intersection of two sides of a polygon.
(3) The point of intersection of the edges of a space figure.

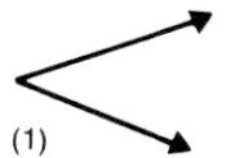

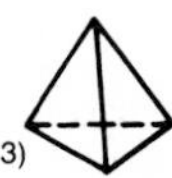

Volume
A number indicating amount of space inside a space figure. The volume of this figure is 12 cubic units.

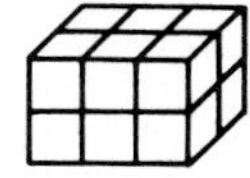

Whole number
One of the numbers in the set 0, 1, 2, 3, and so on.

Index